MOON

NDBOOKS

BELIZE

LEBAWIT LILY GIRMA

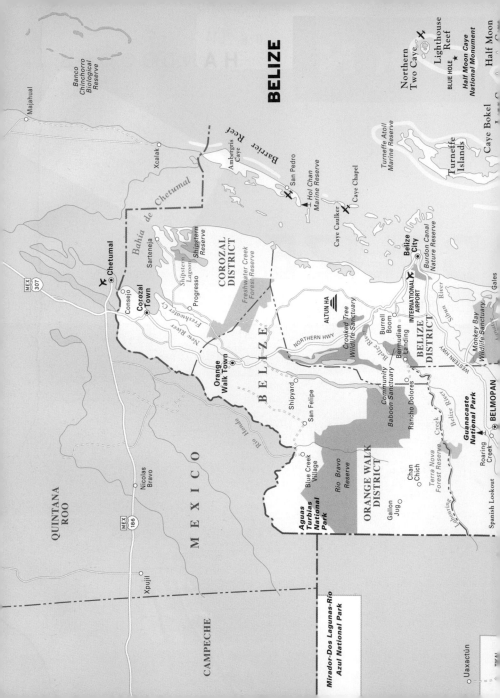

Contents

DISCOVER
Belize

Belize has a mind-boggling diversity in both natural and cultural offerings.

"The Jewel," as Belizeans affectionately call their home, has a spectacular reef—the second-largest in the world—with premier diving and snorkeling. A handful of its 200 offshore islands offer the kind of seclusion and dreamlike surroundings that continue to attract both luxury and romance.

For those willing to explore deeper, the rewards are even richer. Virgin rainforests with more than 30 percent of protected land. The largest cave system and the tallest waterfall in Central America. Riverbanks home to hundreds of singing birds, giant iguanas, and roaming jaguars. Miles of turquoise Caribbean water and golden sand, all a mere one-to-two-hour hop from the interior. A dazzling array of marine life—from whale sharks to the rare seahorse.

Beyond its natural wonders, Belize is a cultural and sensory feast. This is a Caribbean country at heart, with splashes of ancient Mayan, African, and European influences. That mélange underpins every aspect of life, from a cuisine of coconut rice and beans and fish stew with mashed plantains to annual celebrations of both Caribbean and Latin Carnivals.

In Belize, no two days are ever the same. Canoe down to the farmers market to sample fresh *pupusas*. Scour ancient Mayan ceremonial caves and cool off under waterfalls. Drink cashew wine from a Kriol vendor and hike through jungles filled with medicinal trees to the roar of howler monkeys. Or laze around a beachfront village all day and dance barefoot to Garífuna drums at night.

Even all this barely scratches Belize's surface. It will continue to surprise and teach you. And that's the Jewel you'll take home with you.

Planning Your Trip

Where To Go

Belize City

This stretch of coastline, islands, and swampy lowlands includes former capital Belize City, still the hub of Belizean city life and the heart of its colonial past. A few historic sights and events, such as Carnival, make it worth a quick visit, even for a day. Whether or not you appreciate the city's unique grit and Caribbean texture, don't miss nearby attractions like The Belize Zoo, The Community Baboon Sanctuary and surrounding Creole villages, Crooked Tree Wildlife Sanctuary, and Altun Ha.

The Northern Cayes

This group of islands is the most visited part of Belize. Ambergris Caye lures with swanky beach resorts, endless bars, and plentiful restaurants. Caye Caulker, just down the reef, offers a less dizzying pace with an authentic, Caribbean vibe and opportunities for snorkeling at The Split or viewing manatees at

IF YOU ARE...

- **A CULTURE BUFF:** Visit Belize City, Dangriga or Hopkins, and Punta Gorda.
- **DIVING AND SNORKELING:** Visit the Northern Cayes and the Southern Coast.
- **HONEYMOONING:** Visit San Pedro in the Northern Cayes, book a jungle lodge in Cayo, or escape to Glover's Reef Atoll on the Southern Coast.
- **ON A BUDGET:** Visit Caye Caulker, Cayo, or Hopkins.
- **TRAVELING WITH KIDS:** Visit Caye Caulker and Cayo.
- **WILDLIFE-WATCHING:** Visit Crooked Tree near Belize City, Cayo, and Punta Gorda.

Swallow Caye Wildlife Sanctuary. The northern atolls of Turneffe Islands and Lighthouse Reef Atoll offer spectacular wall diving, beautiful beaches and bird life, and Jacques Cousteau's old favorite, the great Blue Hole.

Belmopan and Cayo

Once the heart of the Mayan civilization, Belize's western interior offers a remarkable selection of outdoor activities. Explore the Mayan archaeological sites of Xunantunich, near San Ignacio, or Caracol, further south. Wander the Belize Botanic Gardens, spelunk through Actun Tunichil Muknal—one of the world's most amazing caves—or overnight in a jungle lodge on the Macal River or in the Mountain Pine Ridge. While the capital of Belmopan can be largely skipped, don't miss the surrounding countryside along the beautiful Hummingbird Highway, snaking south through the district to some of the most beautiful parks, including St. Herman's Blue Hole National Park.

Southern Coast

Dangriga is the center of Belize's Garífuna population, with an Afro-Caribbean beat, cultural and outdoor activities, and a strategic location close to Billy Barquedier National Park. Just down the coast, lazy Hopkins has long stretches of beach, and plenty of dining and accommodation options, as well as a strong Garífuna vibe. Further south, the Placencia Peninsula, is the home of "barefoot perfect," 16-mile beaches and the low-key but touristy village of Placencia. The surrounding Stann Creek District offers some of the best hiking in Belize, including Mayflower Bocawina National Park in the Maya Mountains, and the world's only jaguar preserve at Cockscomb Basin Sanctuary. Off the coast of Dangriga, the southern cayes of Tobacco Caye and Glover's Reef Atoll offer spectacular diving and snorkeling, while Laughingbird Caye

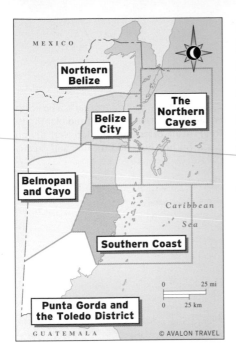

National Park, off the coast near Placencia, is a World Heritage Site.

Punta Gorda and the Toledo District

Forest and reef, river and ruins, caves and ridges—all await the small handful of visitors who get off the beaten path into the "deep south" of Belize. Whether you follow the cacao trail through Punta Gorda or take a private drumming lesson at one of the Garífuna drum schools, don't miss the opportunity to sign up with a homestay program in the Maya villages, where you can immerse yourself in everyday life. The archaeological site of Lubaantun begs exploring, as do the beautiful waterfalls at Río Blanco National Park and Blue Creek Cave. Further off the coast, Sapodilla Cayes offers top-notch snorkeling and diving.

Northern Belize

Northern Belize is often skipped by travelers—unless they've heard about Chan Chich Lodge, a unique rainforest eco-lodge at the Gallon Jug Estate, or the gorgeous accommodations at Lamanai Outpost Lodge, set amid the remote, vast Maya ruins of Lamanai Archaeological Site. Both are set deep in the bush and are as popular with birders and naturalists as they are with archaeologists and biologists. Aside from these draws are the hubs of Orange Walk Town and Corozal. Corozal is a great launching pad to nearby picturesque Sarteneja, home of Belize's traditional wooden sailboat building.

When to Go

High season is mid-December through May, a period many travel agents will tell you is the "dry season," in a vain effort to neatly contain Belize's weather patterns. In many years this is true, with sunny skies and green vegetation throughout the country during the North American winter. However, November can be dry and sunny, while December, January, and even February can play host to wet cold fronts that either blow right through or sit around for days. The weather has become more unpredictable each year, like most places in the world.

June, July, and August technically form the rainy season—which may mean just a quick afternoon shower or rain for days. This also means significantly discounted accommodations. August is most popular with European backpackers, while December and February are dominated by North Americans. Some tourism businesses shut down completely during the month of September and part of October, the peak of hurricane season.

Your best bet? Be prepared for clouds or sun at any time of year. A week of stormy weather may ruin a vacation planned solely

a lovely stretch of beach near Hopkins

around snorkeling, but it could also provide the perfect setting for exploring the rainforests or enjoying a hot tub and fireplace in the Mountain Pine Ridge.

Before You Go

Passports and Visas

You must have a passport that is valid for the duration of your stay in Belize. You may be asked at the border (or airport immigration) to show a return ticket or ample money to leave the country. You do *not* need a visa if you are a British Commonwealth subject or a citizen of Belgium, Denmark, Finland, Greece, Iceland, Italy, Liechtenstein, Luxembourg, Mexico, Spain, Switzerland, Tunisia, Turkey, the United States, or Uruguay. Visitors for purposes other than tourism must obtain a visa.

Vaccinations

Technically, a certificate of vaccination against yellow fever is required for travelers aged older than one year arriving from an affected area, though immigration officials rarely, if ever, ask to see one.

In general, your routine vaccinations—tetanus, diphtheria, measles, mumps, rubella, and polio—should be up to date. Hepatitis A vaccine is recommended for all travelers over age two and should be given at least two weeks (preferably four weeks or more) before departure. Hepatitis B vaccine is recommended for travelers who will have intimate contact with local residents or potentially need blood transfusions or injections while abroad, especially if visiting for more than six months. It is also recommended for all health care personnel and volunteers. Typhoid and rabies vaccines are recommended for those headed for rural areas.

Transportation

The vast majority of travelers arrive in Belize by air at Philip Goldson International Airport, nine miles outside Belize City. From the airport, short domestic connections are available

Garífuna *jankanu* dances are a December tradition in Dangriga and other Garífuna areas.

around the country. A few travelers fly into Cancún as a cheaper back door to Belize; once there, they board a bus or rent a car and head south through the Yucatán Peninsula to reach Belize, or catch a bus and a boat over to the northern cayes.

Belize is small and extremely manageable, especially if you fly a domestic airline from tiny airstrip to tiny airstrip. You can also get around by rental car, taxi, or bus, which is most affordable. Another option is to let your resort or lodge arrange your airport transfer and all tours.

Water taxis are another way to get around in Belize, especially to and from Ambergris Caye and Caye Caulker and the mainland; there are regular daily routes between Belize City and these islands.

The Best of Belize

A week and a half provides just enough time to see a few of Belize's major destinations and get a taste for just how much more there is to discover. This trip includes plenty of self-guided activities, as well as some guided tours. One thing is certain: you won't run out of things to do and see!

Day 1

Arrive in Belize City. After dropping off your bags at the hotel, head out for lunch at Deep Sea Marlin's Restaurant & Bar. Walk off your meal by exploring the city on foot: cross the Swing Bridge and stop at the Image Factory before making your way to the historic Fort George area. Stop for coffee at Le Petit Café, then walk up to the Fort George Lighthouse for some photo ops. In the evening, catch a taxi to Bird's Isle Restaurant to dine alfresco.

Day 2

Stash your bags at the San Pedro Belize Express water taxi terminal and buy an open ticket to the Caribbean fishing village on Caye Caulker. Spend the morning at the Museum of Belize, then hop on the water taxi, arriving in Caye Caulker in time for a swim. Schedule a dive or snorkel trip for the next day, then watch the sunset at The Split. Grab a fresh seafood dinner at Rose's Grill and Bar.

Day 3

Today you'll dive 135 feet into the Blue Hole on Lighthouse Reef, formerly explored by Jacques Cousteau. Or head instead to San Pedro for a snorkel trip at Hol Chan Marine Reserve, Belize's most popular snorkel and dive site. Spend the rest of the day exploring San Pedro, with plenty of opportunities to shop, eat, swim, bar hop, and be merry.

Day 4

Catch the first water taxi to Belize City, then head to the Cayo District by bus, shuttle, or car. At you travel along the Western Highway, visit the Belize Zoo or stop for a hike at

The laid-back island of Caye Caulker is just 40 minutes from Belize City by water taxi.

FLIP-FLOP ZONES

The Southern Cayes have some of the nicest beaches in Belize.

With a coastline along the Caribbean Sea and more than a dozen offshore sandy islands, Belize has enough variety on and off the mainland to satisfy the most avid beachcomber. The best stretches of beach are along Belize's east and south coasts and on the southern cayes. Following are the best sandy spots.

- **Half Moon Caye Wall:** Located on the southeast corner of Lighthouse Reef Atoll, crescent-shaped Half Moon Caye has a stunning beach dotted with palm trees and endless views of the Caribbean (page 128).

- **Hopkins :** Located on the eastern coast of Belize, this long stretch of beach is perfect for morning walks and jogs (page 222).

- **South Water Caye Marine Reserve:** Easily reached from the coasts of Dangriga or Hopkins, this mile-long island is one of the few spots in Belize where you can actually swim from beach to reef. The best stretch belongs to **Pelican Beach Resort** (page 214).

- **Placencia Village, Maya Beach, and Seine Bight:** The 16-mile-long Placencia Peninsula in southern Belize has been dubbed "barefoot perfect," with thick, golden sand and clear water (page 237).

- **Laughingbird Caye National Park and Silk Caye Marine Reserve:** These protected marine reserves are ideal for sunning and swimming in glorious Caribbean turquoise waters. Both are also popular snorkeling and dive spots (pages 256-257).

- **Sapodilla Cayes:** Sapodilla Cayes' **Lime Caye** and **Hunting Caye** have beautiful turtle-nesting beaches (Oct.-Apr.). You'll likely be the only one burying your toes beneath the fine white sand (page 277).

- **Sarteneja:** In northern Belize, this sleepy fishing village with gorgeous turquoise water and a narrow stretch of beachfront is as off the beaten path as it gets (page 314).

Guanacaste National Park, near Belmopan. Arrive in downtown San Ignacio and settle into your guesthouse or stay in Cahal Pech Village, with stunning views and access to nearby ruins. For more solitude, opt for Black Rock Lodge, one of the areas' charming jungle lodges. Spend the evening strolling the mellow town, then grab food at Flayva's or Mr. Greedy's on cobblestoned Burns Avenue.

Days 5-6

Rise early and visit the Mayan ruins of Xunantunich or El Pilar, either on foot, mountain bike, or horseback. Or opt instead for a canoe trip up the Macal River. Depending on the water level, you might make it to duPlooy's Jungle Lodge, where you can tour the Belize Botanic Gardens. Fill the remaining day with an exhilarating cave trip to Actun Tunichil Muknal in the Tapir Mountain Nature Reserve.

The next day, enjoy a ride along the Mountain Pine Ridge to the Mayan ruins of Caracol. Along the way, take a dip at Río on Pools. Stop at Calico Jack's for a unique zip line experience or for a photo op at Thousand Foot Falls, one of the highest waterfalls in Central America.

Day 7

Catch the morning bus down the Hummingbird Highway to Dangriga. Get off at St. Herman's Blue Hole National Park for a delightful swim. Settle in at Dangriga, then take an afternoon trip to Cockscomb Basin Wildlife Sanctuary, where you can hike through the jungle past fresh jaguar tracks and chill in waterfalls under a green canopy. End the night with a fancy dinner back in Dangriga at Pelican Beach Resort.

Days 8-9

Catch a water taxi to Tobacco Caye or South Water Caye for diving and snorkeling along the pristine southern Barrier Reef. These islands are oh-so-stunning and romantic! Back in Dangriga, spend the next morning at the Gulisi Garífuna Museum, tour the Marie Sharp Store and Factory, then ride south to Hopkins for a Garífuna drumming lesson at Lebeha Drumming Center.

Day 10

Return to Dangriga, then take two quick Tropic Air puddle jumper flights back to Belize City.

Maya-themed cabanas at Cahal Pech Village offer stunning views of San Ignacio and the surrounding area.

Adventure Junkies

With pristine coral reefs, epic mountains, and teeming jungles, Belize is the ideal destination for outdoor adventure. Get your heart racing by exploring the largest cave system in Central America, more than 11 national parks, and numerous forest and marine reserves and wildlife sanctuaries.

Bag a Peak

Arrangement a summit hike of Victoria Peak, the second-highest point in Belize at 3,675 feet. The steep three-to-four day trek (30 miles round-trip, Feb.-May only) starts from Cockscomb Basin Wildlife Sanctuary, near Maya Centre. You'll be one of the few to reach the summit, where you can celebrate with a panoramic view of Belize's coastline.

Climb a Waterfall

Thrill seekers will love rappelling their way down Mayflower Bocawina National Park's five stunning waterfalls of varying heights— from the "smaller" Bocawina Falls, at a height of 125 feet, to the 1,000-foot Big Drop Falls.

In the Toledo District, take a refreshing swim in the gorgeous waterfall pool at the Río Blanco National Park—after cliff diving from the top of the waterfall.

Dive the Barrier Reef

Belize's claim to fame is the second-largest barrier reef in the world, home to some of the top dive sites. The great Blue Hole is the holy grail of diving. This circular sinkhole, with depths of more than 400 feet, is not for novices. Prepare to roam through caverns and around stalactites and, if you're lucky, hang out with nine-foot grey Caribbean reef sharks.

Go Underground

Spelunking in ancient Mayan caves is a must in Belize. Actun Tunichil Muknal tops the list, but there are numerous caves worth exploring. The Waterfall Cave, in the Cayo District, won't disappoint. Located at Ian Anderson's Caves Branch Adventure Company and Jungle Lodge, it's a long hike through a dry cave with low ceilings. The reward is a waterfall that topples over the rocks; the brave can climb up the rocks and jump down into the refreshing pool. While you're there, go for your next thrill: Ian Anderson's Black Hole Drop, an unforgettable full-day experience of rigorous hiking followed by rappelling 400-feet into the rainforest, landing at the entrance of a cave.

Cave tubing is as adventurous as it gets. This popular activity involves floating on a river in a large rubber inner tube as you pass through cavernous chambers and jungle, dodging stalactites and rocks as a helmet lamp lights your way. The most exciting cave tubing experience is on the Caves Branch River, in the Cayo District.

Hike the Rainforest at Night

The thrill of a night rainforest hike is unlike any other. You haven't experienced the jungle until you see it come alive in the dark of night, guided only by your flashlight. Ian Anderson's Caves Branch Adventure Company and Jungle Lodge and Pook's Hill Lodge offer nighttime hikes and tours, such as night canoeing on a lake or river—talk about an adrenaline rush!

Swing Through the Jungle

In Cayo's Mountain Pine Ridge, the folks at Calico Jacks challenge you to go for *el columpio,* the jungle swing. Grab hold of a rope from the top of a re-created Maya pyramid and swing 200 feet up in the air into rainforest oblivion.

UNDERWATER BLISS

Sea horses are among the many species thriving along Belize's reef system.

Diving is still Belize's initial claim to tourism fame. Many visitors are avid divers and snorkeling enthusiasts, all eager to explore the wonders of the second largest coral reef in the world.

- **Belize Barrier Reef:** Stretching approximately 155 miles north to south, the barrier reef is its own underwater ecosystem, home to three atolls and nine protected marine reserves.

- **Lighthouse Reef:** Lighthouse Reef Atoll is among Belize's favorite diving destinations, home to the great **Blue Hole** (page 126), **Half Moon Caye Wall** (page 128), and **Long Caye Aquarium** (page 129).

- **Turneffe Atoll:** This popular snorkel and dive destination is a declared protected marine reserve with two don't-miss dive sites: **The Elbow** (page 125) and **Gales Point** (page 125).

- **Hol Chan Marine Reserve:** Belize's most-visited marine site is worth a visit when staying on the Northern Cayes. Highlights include **Shark Ray Alley** (page 69) and the **Coral Gardens** (page 103).

- **Glovers Reef Atoll:** Belize's southern-most atoll spans nearly 80 square miles and is home to fantastic marine life (page 219).

- **South Water Marine Reserve:** Whether off **Tobacco Caye** (page 215) or **South Water Caye** (page 217), there is plenty of marine life to explore.

- **Gladden Spit Marine Reserve:** Come for that elusive, once-a-year (Mar.-June) whale shark experience (page 256).

- **Sapodilla Cayes Marine Reserve:** Sapodillas Cayes is as remote and exclusive as it gets. Top spots include **Lime Caye Wall** and **Ragged Caye** (page 278) and *The Shipwreck* (page 277), a massive sunken ship, surrounded with abundant marine life.

nurse sharks at Shark Ray Alley, Hol Chan Marine Reserve

Río On Pools in the Mountain Pine Ridge

children playing by the Macal River in the Cayo District

Local Culture

Belize is a cultural melting pot, where descendants of ancient civilizations and unique ethnic groups peacefully coexist. Immerse yourself in Belize's diverse population—which includes Kriol, Garífuna, Maya, Mestizo, Mennonite, East Indian, Chinese, and even Lebanese—to get the most of local culture. Listen to *Kriol,* dance to African drums, sample Mayan corn tortillas, tour a Garífuna temple, or attend one of many carnival festivals.

Day 1

Arrive in Belize City and sample your first plate of stew chicken with rice n' beans at Deep Sea Marlin's Restaurant and Bar. Gaze over Haulover Creek as you listen to daily Creole chatter drowning out the reggae music. Take a leisurely afternoon stroll to the Government House and House of Culture to soak in the colonial history, then cross the street to admire St. John's Anglican Cathedral. Catch a taxi to enjoy a quiet early evening al fresco at Bird's Isle Restaurant for fresh seafood.

Day 2

Rise early and head to Dit's to sample a Creole breakfast of fry jacks and eggs, then order some fresh-baked strawberry jam tarts for your trip to Burrell Boom. Catch a bus to The Community Baboon Sanctuary in nearby Bermudian Landing, where you'll hike, learn about Kriol culture, and explore local villages. Grab some fresh cashew wine from a roadside vendor (but save the drinking for later). To overnight in Burrell Boom, pitch a tent at The Community Baboon Sanctuary, arrange a homestay with a local family, or check into Black Orchid Resort, a riverside lodge where you can listen to the monkeys howling above the Belize River.

Day 3

Travel south to Dangriga on the southern coast. Dangriga is the "culture capital of Belize," where a mere walk in town is a cultural experience. Stop at renowned Austin Rodriguez's Drum Workshop at Y-Not Island,

hiking toward the rainforest near Caves Branch, Cayo District

where you can watch him carve a Garífuna drum from scratch. Stroll the Y-Not Island beach, then head to Wadani Recreation Centre (known as "Wadani Shed") to throw back a Guinness and watch the locals play dominoes. Better yet, stay late to catch some live drumming. Before the day ends, plan a trip to Sabal Farm, the only cassava-making farm in the country.

Day 4

Start your morning at the Gulisi Garífuna Museum and take in some history on this Afro-Caribbean culture. Afterward, tour the Marie Sharpe Store and Factory and learn why her hot sauce bottles are on every table top and in every restaurant in Belize. Don't forget to sample her jams, too. Save the afternoon for your pre-arranged trip to nearby Sabal Farm.

Days 5-6

Catch a bus south and hop off at the village of Maya Centre. Julio Saqui can give you a guided tour of the Maya Centre Maya Museum, where you'll learn about Maya culture through displays and live presentations.

Walk or get a ride to Nu'uk Che'il Cottages and Hmen Herbal Center, run by Aurora Garcia Saqui, niece of the late illustrious Maya healer, Don Eligio Panti. Tour the four-acre botanical garden and medicine trail, then overnight on-site or ask about a village homestay.

The next day, book a healing session or massage, attend a seminar on Maya herbal medicine, or explore the nearby Cockscomb Basin Wildlife Sanctuary.

Day 7

Hop on a bus north to sleepy Hopkins and take a well-deserved beach break. Hopkins' beaches are some of the best in the country—pick a spot along the thick, golden stretch and gaze out at the calm sea. When hungry, find Laruni Hati Beyabu Diner and sample Marva's plate of *hudut,* a signature Garífuna dish. Claim your hammock or treehouse at Hamanasi Adventure and Resort for a relaxing overnight stay.

Day 8

Enjoy breakfast at Tina's Kitchen; ask for a

WILDLIFE ENCOUNTERS

Tikatoo lives at Banana Bank Lodge in the Cayo District.

Filled with national parks and wildlife reserves, Belize is home to an estimated 145 species of mammal, 139 species of reptile, and at least 500 species of birds.

- **Belize Audubon Society:** In addition to managing Belize's protected areas and wildlife reserves, they can also arrange tours to top birding hotspots like **Crooked Tree Wildlife Sanctuary** (page 58) and **Half Moon Caye National Monument** (page 128).

- **The Belize Zoo:** Located outside Belize City, this delightful zoo is home to the native animals of Belize (page 60).

- **Blue Morpho Butterfly Breeding Center:** Naturalist guides explain the various butterfly stages in a wonderful flight room at The Lodge at Chaa Creek (page 155).

- **Chan Chich Lodge:** Located on the Gallon Jug Estate, lodge guests list their numerous wildlife sightings on a community chalk board (page 304).

- **Community Baboon Sanctuary:** Spot howler monkeys, birds, iguanas, and armadillos at this sanctuary in Bermuda Landing, less than an hour's drive from Belize City (page 54).

- **Cockscomb Basin Wildlife Sanctuary:** Increase your chance of an encounter with the jaguar, puma, ocelot and margay, or the tapir, with a hike or overnight stay (page 234).

- **Fallen Stones Butterfly Farm:** An exclusive visit here is for guests only of Hickatee Cottages (page 269).

- **Green Hills Butterfly Ranch and Botanical Collections:** In the Cayo District, this butterfly breeding, education, and research center sits on Mountain Pine Ridge Road (page 177).

- **Río Blanco National Park:** Beautiful butterflies flutter away in Punta Gorda's pristine park (page 286).

- **Tropical Wings Nature Center:** Located near San José Succotz, this center has one of the highest numbers of butterfly species (page 171).

RHYTHMS OF BELIZE

The marimba instrument is played during Mayan celebrations.

Belize's annual bashes are the perfect way to glimpse Belizeans' celebratory spirit and get a taste of the music—more than six genres, each unique to a particular region and culture.

- **Summer Fiestas:** (July) Towns celebrate their patron saints with giant fairs, games, concerts, and plenty of outdoor grills all set up inside the town stadium. Visit **Benque Viejo del Carmen**'s *Benque Fiesta,* **Orange Walk**'s *Fiestarama,* and **Ambergris Caye**'s *Día de San Pedro.*

- **Deer Dance Festival:** (Aug.) **San Antonio Village** showcases all things Mayan. The highlight is a deer dance costume performance (an ancient ritual reenacting the hunting of a deer) to traditional Mayan harps.

- **Pan Yaad:** (Sept.) This lively seaside, steel-pan concert is a treat, with up to five bands from around Belize performing at **Belize City**'s House of Culture.

- **Belize City Carnival:** (mid-Sept.) **Belize City** hosts a colorful Caribbean Carnival. **Orange Walk Town**'s Mestizo-themed Orange Walk Carnival is held on September 21, Belize's Independence Day. **San Pedro** celebrates its carnival in February.

- **Garífuna Settlement Day:** (Nov. 18)

Dangriga turns into a massive street party on the eve of Garífuna Settlement Day. Don't miss the drumming and *punta* dancing under the Wadani Shed.

- Mr. Peters' **Brokdong Bram:** (Dec.) A traditional *brokdong bram* celebration takes place in the village of **Gales Point** at Christmastime. *Brokdong* is a festive Creole genre blending various instruments, including drums, maracas, banjo, and even the jawbone of an ass (a donkey)!

A marching band performs in the streets of Orange Walk as part of *Fiestarama.*

tortilla making in a Mayan village

plate of *tahara,* a Garífuna specialty (her fry jacks are also some of the best in Belize). Spend the day beachcombing or kayaking before your afternoon drumming lesson with Jabbar at the award-winning Lebeha Drumming Center. At night drink shots of bitters with the locals at King Cassava's, or take in some live Garífuna drumming at Driftwood Beach Bar and Pizza Shack.

Day 9
Catch a morning bus back to Dangriga for your flight to Punta Gorda in the Toledo District, the most diverse district in Belize. Visit the Maya vendors on Punta Gorda's Market Days, stroll around The Waterfront, or take a drumming lesson with Raymond

"Ray" McDonald at the Warasa Drum School.

Day 10
The Toledo District has the highest number of Mayan villages in Belize. Arrange a village homestay with the Toledo Ecotourism Association (TEA) and live a day in the life of a Mayan household. Travel by bus to a rural Mayan village and help make corn tortillas, wash in the river, and dance to the marimba.

If you're short on time, but still want a taste of Mayan life, book a guided tour to Eladio Pop's Cacao Trail in the village of San Pedro Columbia. Watch and learn how the Maya turned cacao beans into hot chocolate, then sample the delicious concoction yourself.

THE MUNDO MAYA

Lamanai

It's estimated that at the height of the Classic Period, the area known as Belize was home to at least one million Maya. Today, Belize is home to 11 partly or fully excavated, protected Maya archeological sites. Each had an intricate role in Maya history and architecture. The **Belize Institute of Archaeology** (NICH, www.nich-belize.org) manages all archaeological sites.

- **Altun Ha:** This ancient trading center, surrounded by jungle and vine, is where the largest jade head carving in the Maya world was discovered (page 51).

- **Caracol:** Belize's largest and most impressive Maya site sits deep in the Chiquibul Forest Reserve, with several pyramids including the tallest countrywide, *Canaa*, at 136 feet above the plaza floor. It is believed that Caracol toppled neighboring Tikal and shut it down for more than a century (page 183).

- **Lamanai:** Besides the impressive temples engraved with jaguar heads, the boat ride on New River to Lamanai and the surrounding rainforest are ideal for birding and wildlife-watching (page 299).

- **Lubaantun:** The infamous site of the mysterious crystal skull also has the most unique construction design, with round-edged temples and stones cut to fit perfectly together (page 283).

- **Marco Gonzalez:** Ongoing excavations at this site on Ambergris Caye turn up exciting discoveries each year (page 73).

- **Xunantunich:** Located in the Cayo District, Xunantunich is easily one of the most scenic sites in Belize. This ancient ceremonial center has the second-tallest temple, El Castillo, at 135-feet high (page 171). Stop by the smaller **Cahal Pech,** a 10-minute walk from downtown San Ignacio (page 148).

BELIZE CITY

Belize City is often the first introduction to the country, and while the views you get when exiting Goldson International Airport may not match those of an exotic destination, it isn't long before the landscape of Belize District starts to live up to expectations. The nation's most populated district packs a lot in its punch: the hustle and bustle of Belize City, the bird-watching paradise of

© LEBAWIT GIRMA

HIGHLIGHTS

LOOK FOR ◖ TO FIND RECOMMENDED SIGHTS, ACTIVITIES, DINING, AND LODGING.

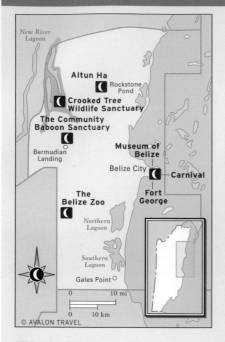

New River Lagoon

Altun Ha ◖
Rockstone Pond
◖ Crooked Tree Wildlife Sanctuary
The Community Baboon Sanctuary
◖
Bermudian Landing
Museum of Belize ◖
Belize City
◖ Carnival
The Belize Zoo ◖
Fort George
Northern Lagoon
Southern Lagoon
Gales Point

0   10 mi
0   10 km
© AVALON TRAVEL

shackle colonial homes, old hotels, restaurants, and cafés (page 30).

◖ **Museum of Belize:** Housed in the old prison, this museum has rotating exhibitions, an incredible stamp collection, and displays of Mayan history that make it worth a visit (page 32).

◖ **Carnival:** Belize City is at its most festive in September, when Belizeans celebrate their independence from Great Britain. The highlight is Belize City's Carnival, a full on Caribbean float parade held in mid-September (page 37).

◖ **Altun Ha:** Head north to this ancient Mayan trading center, the most extensively excavated—and the most visited—ruins in Belize (page 51).

◖ **The Community Baboon Sanctuary:** This community-managed ecotourism sanctuary offers an adventurous menu of wildlife hikes, nighttime canoe trips, and Creole culture (page 54).

◖ **Crooked Tree Wildlife Sanctuary:** One hour north of Belize City is this wondrous habitat for hundreds of resident and migratory birds (page 58).

◖ **Fort George:** Take a stroll through this breezy seaside neighborhood with its ram-

◖ **The Belize Zoo:** See animals native to Belize housed in natural environments and learn efforts to preserve Belize's jaguars (page 60).

Crooked Tree Wildlife Sanctuary, the black howler monkeys of Burrell Boom, the Mayan archeological site of Altun Ha, and the cashew wines of Kriol villages.

Although it hasn't been the capital since 1961, Belize City remains central to the life of Belizeans. At the heart of the country's British colonial past, it's the center of Creole culture and commerce, offering museums, art, markets, and authentic eateries. It's the rice and beans shacks, boisterous fish markets, men playing dominoes in the park, roadside drink stalls, and slow-paced surrounding

villages that give this district a distinctly Caribbean feel.

Thanks to the city's central coastal location, nowhere is too far, making Belize City a hub for exploring the country. In addition to Creole cultural experiences, a visit here means proximity to inland hiking and wildlife-watching—from crocs to howler monkeys or maybe even a jaguar—or escaping to nearby Burrell Boom, just 45 minutes outside the city, for a calm and picturesque river lodge. Activities abound on the nearby cayes for those who want to escape for the day. Transportation options

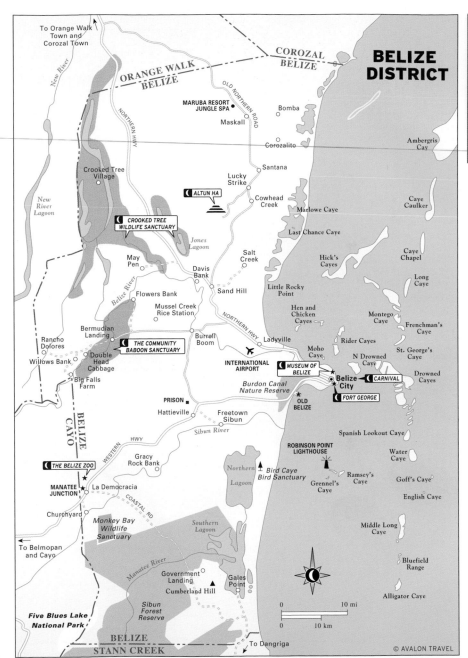

© AVALON TRAVEL

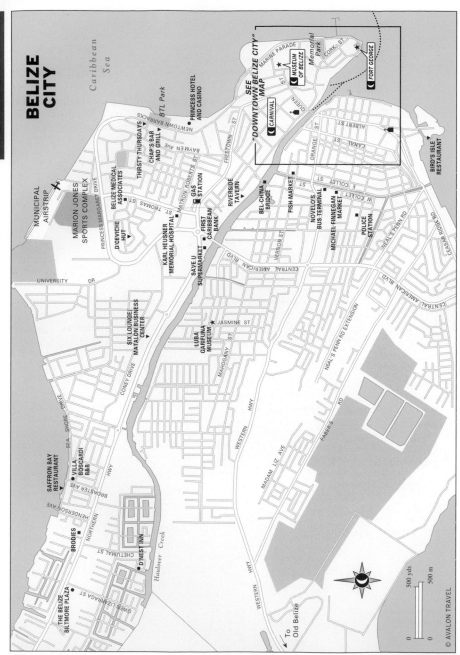

BELIZE CITY

Caribbean Sea

MUNICIPAL
AIRSTRIP

MARION JONES
SPORTS COMPLEX

PRINCESS MARGARET DRIVE

BTL Park

NEWTOWN BARRACKS

PRINCESS HOTEL
AND CASINO

BAYMEN AVE

THIRSTY THURSDAYS

CHAP'S BAR
AND GRILL

BELIZE MEDICAL
ASSOCIATES

D'CEVICHE
HUT

ST. THOMAS ST

MATRON ROBERTS ST

GAS
STATION

FREETOWN RD

MARINE PARADE

SEE
"DOWNTOWN BELIZE CITY"
MAP

CARNIVAL

MUSEUM
OF BELIZE

QUEEN ST

CORK ST

Memorial
Park

FORT GEORGE

ALBERT ST

CANAL ST

ORANGE ST

E COLLET ST

W COLLET ST

BIRD'S ISLE
RESTAURANT

CEASAR RIDGE RD

KARL HEUSNER
MEMORIAL HOSPITAL

FIRST
CARIBBEAN
BANK

RIVERSIDE
TAVERN

BEL-CHINA
BRIDGE

FISH MARKET

NOVELO'S
BUS TERMINAL

MICHAEL-FINNEGAN
MARKET

POLICE
STATION

NEAL'S PENN RD

SAVE U
SUPERMARKET

CENTRAL AMERICAN BLVD

VERNON ST

SIX LOUNGE/
MATALON BUSINESS
CENTER

UNIVERSITY   DR

CONEY DRIVE

JASMINE ST

LUBA
GARIFUNA
MUSEUM

MAHOGANY ST

NEAL'S PENN RD EXTENSION

CENTRAL AMERICAN BLVD

FABER'S RD

WESTERN HWY

SEA SHORE DRIVE

SAFFRON BAY
RESTAURANT

VILLA
BOSCARDI
B&B

BROASTER AVE

HENDERSON AVE

HWY

MADAM LIZ AVE

WESTERN HWY

BRODIES

D'NEST INN

NORTHERN

CHETUMAL ST

Haulover Creek

THE BELIZE
BILTMORE PLAZA

GWEN LIZARRAGA ST

To
Old Belize

WESTERN HWY

500 yds

500 m

0

0

© AVALON TRAVEL

are plentiful—from water taxis to the cayes to buses and flights within the country.

While it may lack beaches and the pretty ocean views of the cayes, Belize City has plenty to offer and offers a more complete view of Belize's historical background.

PLANNING YOUR TIME

Some may be tempted to skip this area to save time, but Belize City deserves a minimum half day's exploration. A self-guided daytime walking tour of Belize City is a must for anyone interested in a bigger picture of the country—even if you have only a few hours between bus and boat connections. You can see all the sights in one rushed day (or two relaxed ones) and get a sense of the true Caribbean, or "Kriol," spirit of this town. Favorite stops include the **Belize Museum,** the **House of Culture,** the busy Swing Bridge area leading to downtown **Albert Street** (with its gorgeous views of sailboats), and the seaside **BTL Park.** Although Belize City lacks the evolved dining scene of more touristed parts of the country, there are enough decent restaurants and authentic local eateries to get by, including the country's best Creole cuisine.

If you have a couple of days, spend one morning exploring Belize City on foot and the afternoon at **The Belize Zoo** or **The Community Baboon Sanctuary,** both a mere hour away by car and easily reached by bus. The following day can be saved for a drive to the Mayan site of **Altun Ha.**

Just outside the city is plenty of nature, wildlife, and history to explore. Stay outside of the hustle and bustle at one of the area's tranquil river lodges in nearby Burrell Boom. Take an afternoon ride down the Old Belize River from Burrell Boom to spot birds, crocodiles, and mangroves. Or head farther north to explore authentic Creole villages, such as the picturesque seaside **Bomba Village** or **Maskall.** Birders shouldn't miss **Crooked Tree Village,** the site of one of the world's top birding areas and sanctuaries. Just 1.5 hours by bus from

Belize City, this quiet lagoon-front village is filled with traditional homes, Creole farmers, horses roaming around freely, and, of course, birds.

ORIENTATION

The old **Swing Bridge** spans Haulover Creek, connecting Belize City's Northside to its Southside, and it is the most distinct landmark in the city. North of the creek, **Queen Street** and **Front Street** are the crucial thoroughfares. On this side of the bridge, you'll find the **Caye Caulker Water Taxi Terminal,** an important transportation and information hub. On Front Street, across from the water taxi, are the post office and the library, with a quiet sitting room and Internet access. Walking east on Front Street, toward the sea, you'll find several art galleries and shops before you come to the second water taxi terminal to the north cayes, the San Pedro Belize Express, and to the **Tourism Village,** the hopeful, Disneyesque name for the cruise-ship passenger arrival area. The mini malls and decorations that garnish this area of docks and shops are contrived and overpriced, and they are owned in part by the cruise-ship companies. The rest of the adjoining Fort George historic area is, in contrast, genuine and interesting to see. Some of the higher-end restaurants and best cafés are also here.

On the Swing Bridge's south end, **Regent Street** and **Albert Street** make a V-shaped split and are the core of the city's banking and shopping activity. There are a few old government buildings here too, as well as Battlefield (Central) Park—where you'll see men playing cards and women selling food—and a couple of guesthouses. Southside has a seedier reputation than Northside (aside from downtown, don't go south), which is monitored more closely by the police. For a walking map of the city, stop by the Belize Tourism Board office (tel. 501/227-2420, www.travelbelize.org) on Regent Street; the map includes a great walking tour of the city's main sights.

CRIME AND THE CITY

Like many Central American countries, Belize has its share of problems with drugs, gangs, and violent street crime. However, due to its extremely small population–70,000 inhabitants, compared to millions in most Central American capitals–Belize City's problems are nowhere near as severe as those of El Salvador, Honduras, and Guatemala's cities. Still, violent crime has increased in Belize City, mostly in the form of petty theft and shootings. Much of this violent gang culture is imported from the United States by deported Belizean youths.

Most–but not all–violent crime occurs in the Southside part of Belize City, many blocks away from the traditional walking paths of visitors, but occasional incidents have occurred throughout the city and in broad daylight. The government has taken steps to battle crime, including stiffer enforcement of the law and deployment of a force of tourist police, recognizable by their khaki shirts and green pants.

For the most part, you'll be fine sticking to the sights and general city center, where there's lots of pedestrian traffic and daytime activity. Most locals are friendly and helpful with directions or other questions. To be safe, use the same common sense you would in any city in the world:

- Before you venture out, have a clear idea of how to get where you're going and ask a local Belizean, like your hotel desk clerk or a restaurant waiter, whether your plan is reasonable.

- Don't walk around at night if you are at all unsure of where you're going or if the neighborhood is safe.

- Taxis are plentiful and inexpensive–use them. Generally, only those with green license plates should be considered. But most Belizeans have a personal taxi driver whom they know and trust; ask if they would be willing to call one for you at the local price.

- Don't flash money, jewelry, or other temptations; if threatened with robbery, hand them over. Report all crimes to the local police and to your country's embassy.

Sights

An early morning stroll through the weathered buildings of Belize City, starting in the Fort George Lighthouse area and walking toward the Swing Bridge, gives you a feel for this seaside population center. This is when people are rushing off to work, kids are spiffed up on their way to school, and folks are out doing their daily shopping. The streets are crammed with small shops, a stream of pedestrians, and lots of traffic. One thing Belize City isn't is boring.

◖ FORT GEORGE

The **Fort George** area, a peninsula ringed by Marine Parade Boulevard and Fort Street, is one of the most pleasant in Belize City. Meander in the neighborhood and you'll pass some impressive homes and buildings, including a few charming old guesthouses. The Baron Bliss Memorial and Fort George Lighthouse stand guard over it all.

The sea breeze can be pleasant here, and you can glimpse cayes and ships offshore. Once you round the point, the road becomes Marine Parade and runs past the modern Radisson Fort George Hotel and **Memorial Park,** a grassy salute to the 40 Belizeans who lost their lives in World War I.

From the Radisson Fort George marina, you'll get a good view of the harbor. Originally this was Fort George Island; the strait separating the island from the mainland (the site of today's Memorial Park) was filled in during the early 1920s. The entire area is undergoing a road facelift but remains easy to navigate on foot.

© LEBAWIT GIRMA

Belize City is a small but active Caribbean town.

Baron Bliss Memorial

Henry Edward Ernest Victor Bliss, also known as the "Fourth Baron Bliss of the Former Kingdom of Portugal," was born in the county of Buckingham in England. He first sailed into the harbor of Belize in 1926, although he was too ill to go ashore because of food poisoning he had contracted while visiting Trinidad. Bliss spent several months aboard his yacht, the *Sea King,* in the harbor, fishing in Belizean waters. Although he never got well enough to go ashore, Bliss learned to love the country from the sea, and its habitués—people on fishing boats and officials in the harbor—all treated him with great respect and friendliness. On the days that he was only able to languish on deck, he made every effort to learn about the small country. He was apparently so impressed with what he learned and the people he met that before his death, he drew up a will that established a trust of nearly US$2 million for projects to benefit the people of Belize.

More than US$1 million in interest from the trust has been used for the erection of the Bliss Institute, the Bliss School of Nursing, and Bliss Promenade as well as contributions to the Belize City water supply, the Corozal Town Board and Health Clinic, and land purchase for the building of Belmopan.

An avid yachtsman, Bliss stipulated that money be set aside for a regatta to be held in Belizean waters, now a focal point of the gala Baron Bliss Day celebrations each March, an important holiday that is now called National Heroes and Benefactors Day. The baron's white granite tomb is at the point of Fort George in Belize City, guarded by the Fort George Lighthouse and the occasional pair of late-night Belizean lovers.

Fort George Lighthouse

Towering over the coastline and facing the Belize Harbor, the **Fort George Lighthouse** was built as part of the memorial for Baron Bliss, Belize's greatest benefactor. In fulfillment of his dying wish and financed with the generous proceeds he left the country, the tall structure was erected next to his tomb and

© LEBAWIT GIRMA

The Museum of Belize is within walking distance from the city center.

memorial. While the public cannot enter the lighthouse, it remains an important, historic landmark in Belize City and is easy to spot while touring the Fort George area. The views from there also make for a nice photo op.

◖ MUSEUM OF BELIZE

Housed in the old city jail (Her Majesty's Prison was built in 1857 and served as the nation's only prison until the 1990s), the small but worthwhile **Museum of Belize** (8 Gabourel Lane, tel. 501/223-4524, www.museumofbelize.org, 9am-4:30pm Tues.-Fri., 9am-4pm Sat., US$5) includes historical artifacts, indigenous relics, and rotating displays on topics such as *Insects of Belize, Maya Jade,* and *Pirates of Belize.* Philatelists and bottle collectors will love the 150 years of stamps and bottles on display.

IMAGE FACTORY

A few doors up from the Swing Bridge, the **Image Factory Art Foundation** (91 N. Front St., tel. 501/223-4093, chokscatter@yahoo.com, www.imagefactorybelize.com, 9am-5pm Mon.-Fri., 9am-noon Sat.) is the official pulse of the Belizean art and literary scene. In addition to offering the best book selection in the country (both local authors and some foreign titles), there is gallery space for semi-regular art events, usually held on Friday evenings at happy hour. There's also a separate arts and crafts shop at the back filled with gorgeous Belizean paintings, sculptures, and other unique creations.

ST. JOHN'S ANGLICAN CATHEDRAL

The lovely old **St. John's Anglican Cathedral** (S. Albert St. at Regent St., 7am-6pm daily), across from the House of Culture, is one of the few typically British structures in the city. It is also the oldest Anglican church in Central America. In 1812, slaves helped erect this graceful piece of architecture, using bricks brought as ballast on sailing ships from Europe. Several Mosquito Coast kings from Nicaragua and Honduras were crowned in this cathedral with ultimate pomp and grandeur; the last was in

1815. The church is surrounded by well-kept green lawns and sits next to a lively schoolyard. It's usually okay to walk right in and quietly admire the impressive interior with its stained-glass windows, mahogany pews, and the antique organ. You can leave a little something in the donation box on your way out.

One block from the cathedral is the **Yarborough Cemetery,** the city's first burial ground, with the graves of Belizean citizens dating back to the 18th century, some of whom died during World War II.

GOVERNMENT HOUSE AND HOUSE OF CULTURE

Opposite St. John's Cathedral, at the southern end of Regent Street and facing the Southern Foreshore, is the **House of Culture** museum in the old **Government House** (tel. 501/227-3050, www.nichbelize.org, 8:30am-5pm Mon.-Thurs., 8:30am-4:30pm Fri., US$5), which, before 1961's Hurricane Hattie and the ensuing construction of Belmopan, was the home and office of the governor-general, the official representative of Queen Elizabeth. (Today's governor-general can be found in Belmopan, at Belize House.) For a long time these grounds were used as a guesthouse for visiting VIPs and a venue for social functions. Queen Elizabeth and Prince Philip stayed here in 1994. The elegant wooden buildings (built 1812-1814) are said to be based on designs by acclaimed English architect Christopher Wren. Sprawling lawns and wind-brushed palms facing the sea surround Government House, making it ideal for the year-round outdoor functions, art events, and concerts that are still held here.

Wander through the wood structure and enjoy the period furniture, silverware, and glassware collections—plus a selection of paintings and sculptures by modern Belizean artists. Stroll the grounds, on the water's edge, and enjoy the solitude. Also on-site is the headquarters of the National Kriol Council, with some Kriol language phrasebooks for sale, although its doors have remained closed in the months before press time.

LUBA GARÍFUNA MUSEUM

Founded in 1999, even before the Museum of Belize, the **Luba Garífuna Museum** (4202 Fern Lane, tel. 501/202-4331, Luba_Garifuna@yahoo.com, 8am-5pm daily and by appointment, US$5) is the first Garífuna museum in the country. Tucked off the beaten path in a residential area, the museum showcases Garífuna culture and history. You'll be surprised at the collection of arts and crafts, cooking utensils, photographs, and traditional clothing. Items have been gathered over a period of 30 years and are clearly displayed, showcasing key rituals and ceremonies. If you're lucky, you'll meet Sebastian Cayetano, founder of the museum and cofounder of the National Garífuna Council, a well-respected teacher and resource on the Garinagu people of Belize.

The museum is located off Jasmine Street, which is off Mahogany Street in the St. Martin's area. A guided tour (US$10) is also available, and the museum offers a cultural package (on request, US$200 for 10 people) for large groups, which includes a tour of the museum, food sampling, and a dance and drumming show.

OLD BELIZE

In addition to Cucumber Beach, a swimming lagoon, a zip line, a waterslide, and other water sports, **Old Belize** (Mile 5, Western Hwy., tel. 501/222-4129, www.oldbelize.com, museum tour US$2.50, zip line US$20) also features the **Cultural and Historical Center** (10am-8:30pm daily), a 45-minute tour through 1,000 years of Belizean history—probably the only thing even slightly worth seeing if you venture here. It's kind of like a walk-through museum, but with various relics and simulations. Some of the displays from the former Maritime Museum are now housed here and include models of boats used in Belize as well as photos and bios of local anglers and boat builders. On cruise-ship days (usually Tues. and Thurs.), a Belizean cabaret showcases the dances and songs of Belize's cultural groups. There's also a boat marina, a helipad, and an average restaurant (tel. 501/222-5588, 11am-10pm daily) that is mysteriously popular with well-off locals, perhaps due to the waterfront setting. It's five miles out of the city on the Western Highway and, to be honest, not worth the trip if you're pressed for time.

Sports and Recreation

Belize City is the hub of the country. Thanks to its eastern coastal location coupled with more transportation options from here than most of the country, many sites and key activities are easily reached in a short time.

PARKS

A simple, enjoyable way to spend an afternoon or watch the sun go down in Belize City is to hang out "seaside" (as the locals call it) in one of the city parks. **BTL Park**, within walking distance of the Princess Hotel, is a favorite; grab a drink and some fresh tacos from the park vendors and sit back on the benches while the breeze blows all along the seaside. There are also swings and other distractions for kids. You're likely to spot lovers as well as families, who come here in the early evenings to stroll, wind down, jog, or just chat. Going seaside is popular on Sunday, with lots of families taking a breather from their long week. Another popular seaside spot is across from Memorial Park and along the Marine Parade promenade.

Located on the south side, **Battlefield Central Park** sits at the mouth of the city's main shopping area and downtown businesses along Albert and Regent Streets. This tiny yet bustling park attracts mostly card-playing locals, taco vendors, and market stalls with fruits, coconut water, and other goods. The park has a few benches and is safe to enjoy during the day, but steer clear at night. Across from the park on the Regent Street side, is the Supreme Court building, decorated with a long veranda overlooking the park and square. An antiquated town clock is perched atop the white clapboard building.

DIVING AND SNORKELING

The Belize Barrier Reef is less than 30 minutes away and offers excellent wall dives and idyllic snorkeling. Turneffe Islands Atoll and Lighthouse Atoll are one and two hours away, respectively, by boat. These sites are perfect for anyone in the city on business or for travelers staying in Belize City. There are also manatee-encounter trips available as well as outings to Swallow Caye Marine Reserve.

Belize City has two dive shops: **Sea Sports Belize** (83 N. Front St., tel. 501/223-5505, www.seasportsbelize.com, US$160 for a 2-tank dive, US$95 for a snorkel tour, lunch included) is across from the post office, two buildings east of the Swing Bridge. Sea Sports has been in business 15 years and is a PADI 5-Star Instructor Development Center, offering equipment sales, scuba instruction, daily dives and snorkeling at Hol Chan and Shark Ray Alley, fishing, and manatee-encounter trips. They use small boats and take groups of no more than eight people per guide. They can also arrange overnight packages with lodging at St. George's Caye, Belize's first capital.

Hugh Parkey's Dive Connection (tel. 501/223-4526 or cell 501/670-6025, www.belizediving.com, www.belizeadventurelodge.com, barrier reef dive US$105 pp, minimum 4 people; US$150 pp 2-tank dive at Turneffe, minimum 4 people, lunch and equipment included) is based at the Radisson Fort George Marina and offers all manner of trips and certification courses. Hugh Parkey's has the biggest day-trip boat fleet around and provides diving services for the cruise ships that call on Belize; they can arrange accommodations at nearby Spanish Lookout Caye.

BOATING AND SAILING

Explore the waterways, marshlands, and mangroves of the Almond Hill Lagoon and Indian Creek from a 450-hp airboat via **Chukka Caribbean Adventures** (Mile 9, Western Hwy., tel. 501/635-1318, U.S. tel. 877/424-8552, www.chukkacaribbean.com, US$55 pp). This is a great way to glimpse some of Belize's birds and wildlife in just an hour; if you're lucky, you'll spot 15-foot crocs. Chukka's enthusiastic and knowledgeable guides make it a fun experience with a few speedy twists and turns. Chukka also offers adventure tours out of Jaguar Paw that get rave reviews, with cave tubing, rappelling, and more.

Ask at any of the tour companies, marinas, or dive shops to see what's available; there should be a decent range of charter opportunities, plus day trips and sunset cruises. Sailing and snorkeling trips to Caye Caulker (US$65) are offered, as well as sunset cruises to Ambergris Caye (US$35).

FISHING

Fantastic river, reef, flats, and deep-sea fishing is available from Belize City. You can fish for tarpon in the morning and bonefish in the afternoon. Deep-sea opportunities include mackerel, wahoo, kingfish, and billfish. Most lodges in the area can set up fishing trips; contact the **Belize River Lodge** (tel. 501/225-2002, www.belizeriverlodge.com, US$1,400 for a 3-night package) to start. You can also try **Sea Sports Belize** (83 N. Front St., tel. 501/223-5505, river fishing US$500 per stop, reef fishing US$600 per stop for up to 4 people), which runs professional custom sportfishing trips on rivers and to stunning sights offshore; prices include equipment, a guide, and lunch.

SPECTATOR SPORTS

The basketball court on Bird Isle used to be packed to the gills during local championship games. Ask around to see if any games are coming up. Catch a soccer game (called "football"

© LEBAWIT GIRMA

Exploring the Old Belize River via Chukka Caribbean Adventures is a great way to see the area's rich flora and fauna.

here) at the stadium at 3:30pm Sunday through mid-December or so. There's loud, booming pregame music and lots of security. The stadium is across the street from the Princess Hotel on Barrack Road.

MASSAGE AND BODYWORK

The Radisson Fort George Hotel offers spa services at the **Nim Li Punit Spa** (2 Marine Parade, tel. 501/223-3333, sam.rah@radisson.com). Or put yourself in the hands of **Harold Zuniga** (85 Amara Ave., tel. 501/604-5679, haroldzuniga@yahoo.com), a U.S.-trained physical therapist, masseur, and acupuncturist. If you're up for relaxation coupled with a day trip, tucked in the village of Maskall just 1.5 hours' drive from the city is the unique **Maruba Resort Jungle Spa** (U.S. tel. 713/799-2031, Mile 40½ Old Northern Hwy., www.maruba-spa.com, US$50-100). The offerings are numerous, but don't miss getting the Mood Mud Massage; you'll not only leave with baby-soft skin but also a memorable photo of your body covered in nothing but mud and…a hibiscus flower. You can also get manicures, pedicures, and facials.

Entertainment and Shopping

Belize City is even more alive during the September Celebrations, a month packed with events, music, dancing, and a full-blown carnival parade along Central American Boulevard. It's quite possibly one of the most interesting towns in the Caribbean, one you must dig into to appreciate. Just don't listen when they tell you to skip it.

Bliss Promenade skirts the waterfront and brings you to the towering **Bliss Center for Performing Arts** (Southern Foreshore, tel. 501/227-2110, www.nichbelize.org), which hosts social functions, seminars, arts festivals, and drama series throughout the year. It is also the location of a theater, a museum, and a library as well as the Institute of Creative Arts. Step in to grab a calendar of events.

NIGHTLIFE

Thursday is the biggest night for dancing in Belize City, followed by Friday, especially those that fall on a payday. Nightclubs come and go like hurricanes; keep your wits about you and ask where the latest safe place to party is. At the moment, one of the best nightspots for dancing is **Club Next** (Princess Hotel, Newton Barracks, tel. 501/223-2670, 10pm-4am Thurs.-Sat.), offering bottle service and international DJs. For a notch up, the trendy **Six Lounge** (Matalon Business Center, Coney Dr.,

6th Fl., tel. 501/637-4722 or 501/223-2821, 8pm-2am Thurs.-Sat.) is where you'll rub elbows with Belize's elite. This rooftop nightclub serves expensive cocktails in a roomy, disco-lit interior or outside on the Vegas-like open-air terrace lounge, complete with red lounge sofas, tables, a bar, and a nice city view. Serious dancing usually doesn't get started until after 11pm, and the crowd gets younger or rowdier as the hours pass.

For a quiet, relaxing evening away from the crowds, try **Tinto & Blanco Wine Bar** (13 Cork St., tel. 501/223-5700, tintoandblanco@gmail.com, 4pm-midnight Tues.-Sun.), tucked inside the Great House building. Its dim, cozy interior is perfect to enjoy wine by the glass or bottle without music drowning out your conversation, and before turning in for the night.

Ask around to find out where the best happy hours are held—they often feature live music and free *bocas* (deep-fried something, probably). The bars at the **Radisson Fort George Hotel** (2 Marine Parade, tel. 501/223-3333), the **Biltmore** (Mile 3, Northern Hwy., tel. 501/223-2302), and **Princess Hotel** (Barrack Rd., tel. 501/223-2670) are popular and provide safe, contained venues—and some of the highest drink prices in the city. **Bird's Isle** (90 Albert St., past the House of Culture, tel. 501/207-6500), or "Island" as locals call it, is popular for karaoke on Thursday (5pm-1am). **Riverside Tavern** (2 Mapp St., tel. 501/223-5640), or just "Tavern," has plenty of bar fare and cocktails on Friday as well as other weekday happy hours.

FESTIVALS AND EVENTS

September is Belize's golden month. For three weeks—from September 1 all the way through September 21 (Independence Day)—the city hops on one long party train to celebrate the country's freedom from Great Britain in 1981. Along the highways, you'll spot massive billboards listing events in districts countrywide leading up to Independence Day. The streets, lights, and bridges in Belize City are decked in the national colors—red, blue, and white—and everyone is on a celebration high. It's quite the time to visit Belize City, particularly if you're a culture and history buff (not to mention the prices in low season are oh-so-right).

St. George's Caye Day (Sept. 10) commemorates the 1798 Battle of St. George's, when British forces repelled a Spanish invasion of Belize. The day begins around 10am with a ceremony full of pomp and circumstance at Memorial Park on Marine Parade Boulevard, just a few steps from the Radisson, where you'll glimpse the Prime Minister along with other important figures. A colorful citizens' parade follows around noon, with plenty of music and dancing, from the park all the way to Albert Street.

Sir Barry's Belikin Bash (Sept.) is held at Memorial Park with live performances from the country's top artists. Launched in 2011, this free, two-day outdoor concert commemorates the life of Sir Barry Bowen, the popular Belizean business magnate who created Belize's beer brewing empire and passed away tragically in 2010. There's plenty of dancing, food tents, and beer keg contests from 9pm until the wee hours of the morning. This is where you'll get acquainted with Belizean music and party spirit; watching the men and women competing in exaggerated "hip shaking" just to win free beer is highly entertaining.

Catch the **Independence Day Parade** (Sept. 21) celebrating Belize's Independence from Great Britain. Similar to the St. George's Caye Day, Belize City holds its own with uniform parades, marching bands, floats, and children and adults all wearing the blue-red-white national colors and waving flags. The celebrations usually begin at Memorial Park around late morning, and continue on throughout the afternoon and evening. Check with your hotel or the local newspapers for accurate timing.

The **Baron Bliss Day Parade and Annual Boat Regatta** (Mar. 9) is a national holiday that both celebrates and commemorates the nation's largest benefactor, Sir Baron Bliss. Festivities are centered around an annual boat regatta and are usually followed by parties. The events and times can vary; consult your host or local papers for details on location and times.

The **National Arts Festival** (usually in Feb.), organized by the National Institute of Culture and Heritage, was launched in 2012 to showcase local artistic talent in Belize—from painters to sculptors, tattoo artists, jewelers and more. Booths and displays are located downtown along Albert Street, and there is a parade and live music stages at Central Park. It's one big celebration of creativity. Contact the Institute of Creative Arts at the Bliss Center for Performing Arts (Southern Foreshore, tel. 501/227-2110, www.nichbelize.org) for a schedule of events.

Carnival

Belize's Caribbean spirit is on full display during a Caribbean-flavored Carnival (mid-Sept.). You'll see colorful floats, men and women in sexy, extravagant costumes, trucks and massive speakers blasting either *punta* or soca music as the crowd and revelers hop and dance all along Central American Boulevard. The parade often starts on the south side of town around 2pm; be sure to arrange a taxi ride to and from the event and arrive about an hour early if you want to save a spot. After Carnival, the celebrations continue at the BTL Memorial Park with an all-night outdoor concert, food and drink vendors, and plenty of seaside dancing.

SHOPPING

Gift shops, craft stalls, and street vendors line Front Street near Tourism Village as well as just south of the Swing Bridge. In the Fort George area, check out the **Belize Handicraft Market Place** (Memorial Park, 8am-5pm Mon.-Fri., 8am-4pm Sat.), near the Radisson. Across from Memorial Park, look for the **National Handicrafts Center** (8am-5pm Mon.-Fri., 8am-4pm Sat.), an official Chamber of Commerce-sponsored shop with fine crafts purchased directly from artisans around the country.

There is a **flea market** (at the Catholic Church, N. Front St.) at 7am on Saturday. Also seek out the **Mennonite Furniture Market** (47 N. Front St., daylight hours Fri.-Sat.), next to Smokin' Balam Guest House, for nice handmade wooden furniture at reasonable prices (but they don't do shipping).

Wine is increasingly sought out in Belize. Once difficult to find, it's now fairly well stocked at the super-size **Brodie's** (Mile 2½, Northern Hwy., tel. 501/223-5587, 8am-9pm Mon.-Sat., 8am-2pm Sun.) and at the Belize City retail location of **Wine de Vine** (Northern Hwy., tel. 501/223-2444, www.

winedevine.com), where you can even find Dom Pérignon.

At the **Traveller's Liquors Heritage Center** (Mile 2½, Northern Hwy., tel. 501/223-2855, www.onebarrelrum.com, 10am-6pm Mon.-Fri., bar until midnight Fri.-Sat.), Belize's premier rum producer offers a fun stop on your way in or out of town. The Heritage Center consists of a historical display, a selection of their many products at bargain prices, an open-air bar and restaurant, and most importantly, a tasting bar where you can sample all 27 varieties of Traveller's Liquors rum. Ask about the "vintage edition rum" to bring home some premium spirits.

A few stores have small but pertinent book selections featuring several shelves of Belizean and about-Belize books. The **Image Factory** (91 N. Front St., tel. 501/223-4093, www.imagefactorybelize.com, 9am-5pm Mon.-Fri., 9am-noon Sat.) has the best collection. **Angelus Press** (10 Queen St., tel. 501/223-5777, 7:30am-5:30pm Mon.-Fri., reduced hours Sat.-Sun.), right around the corner from the Image Factory on Queen Street, has a complete corner of books and maps behind all the office supplies and services.

Accommodations

All room rates are for double occupancy in the high season and may or may not include the 9 percent hotel tax. If you're traveling alone or from May to November, expect discounts at some, but not all, of the following hotels.

UNDER US$25

The **Seaside Guest House** (3 Prince St., tel. 501/605-3786 or 501/632-7660, www.seasideguesthouse.org, US$20-45) is popular among backpackers. The guesthouse is down a narrow, quiet alley off Regent Street, near the Belize Tourism Board. The couple of guest rooms are tiny, barely bigger than the beds, but the common spaces both upstairs and downstairs are good for meeting travelers from all over

the world. Choose from shared bunk space or private guest rooms. There is hot water in the community bathroom, a breeze on the ocean-facing porch, and a friendly family-run atmosphere in this former Quaker house. Three cheap meals a day (US$3-5 each) are available, though there are plenty of outside eateries in this central area. If you know you're coming to town, make a reservation—the Seaside can sometimes fill up fast.

On North Front Street, a short walk from the Swing Bridge, is the quiet family-run **⟨ Smokin' Balam Guest House** (59 N. Front St., tel. 501/628-2003, smokinbalam2@yahoo.com, US$15 s, US$30 d) with four cozy and clean rooms, all airy with fans, two with private baths; all have access to a caged balcony over Haulover Creek at the back (with a small dock for sunning, if you choose) and a nice upper-floor balcony with street views as well as a nice downstairs café (meals from US$2). There's a gift shop, a pay phone, and Internet access on the ground floor. The guesthouse also offers weekly and monthly rates, bag storage (US$2 per bag per day), and a friendly atmosphere.

Across the street is **North Front Street Guest House** (124 N. Front St., tel. 501/663-7368, US$13-20), offering seven Spartan guest rooms with a shared dark basement bath. It is decrepit and has a seedy atmosphere, but it

might be doable if you're utterly desperate and the other places are booked up; the guest rooms have foam mattresses and fans.

US$25-50

The **(Belcove Hotel** (9 Regent St. W., tel. 501/227-3054, www.belcove.com, US$33-52), centrally located on the south bank of Haulover Creek, just west of the Swing Bridge, is well taken care of, clean and bright, and easy to recommend. There are 13 guest rooms on three floors; options include shared or private baths with fan or the works (a/c and TV). The porch over the creek is fun to watch boats from, and

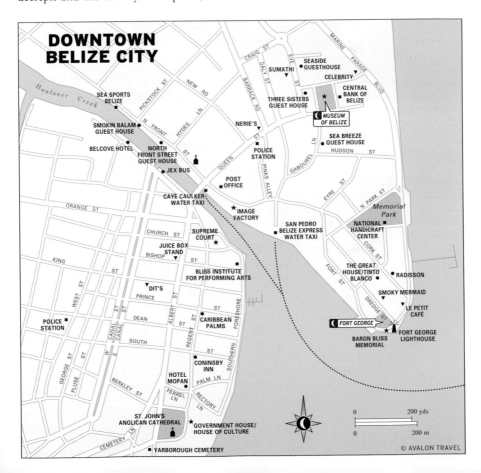

© LEBAWIT GIRMA

Smokin' Balam Guest House is one of the few decent budget hotels in the city.

cheap lively eats are right next door at Deep Sea Marlin's Restaurant & Bar. It's a great base for a walking tour of the city, and tour packages can keep you busy on the reef or at inland sights. The only downside is the slightly seedy two blocks on Regent Street between the hotel and the Swing Bridge; take a cab to and from the hotel door at night.

Three Sisters Guest House (36 Queen St., tel. 501/203-5729, US$32) has three big, clean guest rooms with private baths and fans plus a massive cavernous common space, all on the second floor of an old building on Queen Street. There's even one guest room with three or four beds. It's good for groups looking simply for a place to rest, and it's friendly, clean, and has a small secure front gate. Ask about the additional guest rooms for rent at the Isabel Guest House on Albert Street, by the Swing Bridge.

On the Northside, a short walk away from the Belize Museum, **Sea Breeze Guest House** (18 Gabourel Lane, tel. 501/203-0043 or 501/621-9651, http://seabreeze-belize.com,

US$30-40) has nine small guest rooms with stained sheets, fans, and TV; some have shared baths, others have private baths and air-conditioning, and all are in a rickety building with a common space and wireless Internet access.

US$50-100

Built in 1973, the ◖**Hotel Mopan** (55 Regent St., tel. 501/227-7351, www.hotelmopan.com, US$50-65) is an old standby with a very pleasant rooftop lounge area. There are 12 guest rooms, some with ocean views, all with tile floors, private baths, TV, free wireless Internet, mini fridges, and air-conditioning. Balcony rooms are worth the extra couple of dollars. On the same street, **Coningsby Inn** (76 Regent St., tel. 501/227-1566, www.coningsbyinn.com, US$50-60) has 10 rooms with TV, private baths, air-conditioning, wireless Internet, and minibars. There's a second-story bar and restaurant with a front balcony; breakfast is US$6. Common-area carpets are run down, but guest rooms are clean and the staff is friendly. Both Hotel Mopan and Coningsby

Inn are in Southside, steps from the House of Culture and the Tourism Board.

A few doors up, even closer to the center of town, is **The Caribbean Palms Inn** (26 Regent St., tel. 501/227-0472, cpalms@hotmail.com, US$50-70), with more guest rooms and space than meets the eye. There are basic but clean and spacious double beds; solo travelers should ask for the top floor corner room with a queen bed. All have wireless Internet, air-conditioning, fans, and dedicated or attached private baths. There's a living room upstairs to relax, and a unique three-bunk bedroom (US$18 pp for 4 or more) on the ground floor with a bath attached, ideal for a group of backpacking friends.

Next to the Fort George Radisson, the **Chateau Caribbean** (6 Marine Parade, tel. 501/223-0800, www.chateaucaribbean.com, US$89) resides in an 84-year-old wooden building with wide porches, ocean breezes, and plenty of character, although overall it is in need of some TLC. The 19 guest rooms are a bit worn but have clean beds and private baths, cable TV, fridges, wireless Internet, and air-conditioning. The lounge areas, restaurant, and bar have big east-facing bay windows; definitely ask for an upstairs room. The restaurant, serving a range that includes Chinese, international, and Belizean dishes, is popular with locals, and the food is actually quite good.

On the Northside, toward "the Flags" traffic circle, the **Bakadeer Inn** (74 Cleghorn St., tel. 501/223-0659, www.bakadeerinn.com, US$55, includes breakfast) has 12 clean, well-kept guest rooms with comfy beds, private baths, ceiling fans, TV, and optional air-conditioning in any of the rooms (singles, doubles, triples, and quads available), as well as laundry service, a dining area, high-speed Internet access, and a cozy common space. Another functional place, run by a second-generation Belizean-Chinese family, is the **Royal Orchid Hotel** (153 New Rd. at Douglas Jones St., tel. 501/223-2783, US$50), a four-story hotel across the street from a pizza shop; the 21 guest rooms have hot and cold water, private baths, air-conditioning, and TV.

Just a few minutes farther north, located in Buttonwood Bay, an upscale residential area just three miles north of downtown and seven miles south of the international airport, **Villa Boscardi Bed & Breakfast** (6043 Manatee Dr., tel. 501/223-1691, www.villa-boscardi.com, US$75 plus tax, includes breakfast) is an excellent value and wonderful retreat from city noise. It's just a block away from the sea and from the prime minister's home, and a 10-minute drive into the city. Owner Françoise, an interior decorator by training, takes pride in her villa, ensuring the spotless guest rooms convey the cozy at-home atmosphere of a bed-and-breakfast but with a notch up. Guest rooms and suites are located inside the house or at the back of the property with garden views. A honeymoon suite is also available. Hot breakfast is included and served fresh daily, courtesy of the friendly housekeeper, Anna. There's free Internet access and a common desktop and kitchen, and taxis are easy to come by as the guesthouse keeps a list of drivers handy. It's an ideal place to return to after a long day of activities. Shopping and several restaurants are within walking distance, including the delicious Saffron Bay Restaurant just a street behind on Seashore Drive.

In the same area as Villa Boscardi, but a few blocks on the other side of the highway in the Belama neighborhood, **D'Nest Inn** (475 Cedar St., tel. 501/223-5416, www.dnestinn.com, US$82-92) is a two-story Caribbean-style bed-and-breakfast surrounded by an English garden. Gaby and Oty offer five comfortable guest rooms decorated with Belizean antiques, all equipped with private baths, air-conditioning, TV, and wireless Internet. Multicourse breakfasts feature lots of fresh fruit and conversation with your hosts.

US$100-150

The six-floor **Princess Hotel and Casino** (Barrack Rd., tel. 501/223-2670, U.S. tel. 888/790-5264, www.princessbelize.com, US$120) has 170 concrete guest rooms, some recently updated and with new bedding but still slightly worn baths, and all with the same

© LEBAWIT GIRMA

Villa Boscardi is an excellent bed-and-breakfast just 15 minutes from the city center.

air-conditioning, cable TV, and breakfast. Overall, you'll find much better value elsewhere, particularly at the B&Bs mentioned above. But if you're looking for lots of on-site entertainment, the Princess houses Belize City's only cinema and bowling alley; there's also a pretty but shallow pool, a gift shop, a beauty salon, a conference room, bars, restaurants (the one over the dock has lovely views), and a tour desk. The on-site marina has docking facilities and water sports, and the popular casino and disco are open midnight-4am.

After World War II, visiting dignitaries from England came to Belize with plans for various agricultural projects, but they couldn't find a place to stay. As a result, the **Radisson Fort George Hotel** (2 Marine Parade Blvd., tel. 501/223-3333, U.S. tel. 800/333-3333, www.radisson.com/belizecitybz, US$139-174 plus tax) was built, and it remains the premier lodging in town. The Radisson's 102 nicely appointed full-service guest rooms sport all the amenities you'd expect, including outrageously priced minibars. This resort-style hotel has two

swimming pools (for guests only), a poolside bar, the Stone Grill (with delicious burgers), and fine dining and a massive breakfast buffet in St. George's Dining Room. All the restaurants host special events and happy hours. Full catering facilities and banquet rooms are available. All kinds of tours, such as diving, caving, and golfing, are organized right out of the hotel. The Villa Wing across the street includes restrooms, a new business center, a gym, and an expansion of Le Petit Café, connecting it to the Villa Lobby with expanded seating and wireless Internet (for guests only).

The Belize Biltmore Plaza (Mile 3, Northern Hwy., tel. 501/223-2302, U.S. tel. 800/528-1234, www.belizebiltmore.com, US$140) is the local Best Western branch, three miles north of the city center (seven miles south of the international airport) on the Northern Highway. The Biltmore is popular with business travelers; its 75 midsize guest rooms surround a garden, a pool, and a bar and have cable TV, phones, and modern baths. There's also Internet service, an excellent gift shop, an overpriced dining room (US$12-20) with mediocre international food, and a lounge. The hotel may be convenient for flights, but the Biltmore is walking distance to nothing, so you may feel a bit trapped.

OVER US$150

◀The Great House (13 Cork St., tel. 501/223-3400, www.greathousebelize.com, US$150) is a charming colonial-style boutique hotel, built in 1927 and recently renovated to show off its 16 unique, spacious, and colorful guest rooms (there are no elevators, just stairs). Both tiled and hardwood floors offset the pastel walls and modern furniture; the guest rooms in back have more charm than the rest. Internet access is included in the room rates, as is a light continental breakfast at the best café in town, Le Petit, next door. Downstairs, you'll find a high-end real estate company, a business service center, a delightful wine bar, and the Smoky Mermaid restaurant, with a new sushi bar extension.

Food

Belize City's upscale restaurant scene has yet to explode, but in its place you'll find a host of tasty, reasonably priced, and authentic Belizean food. Residents often grab a boxed meal on the way to work, home, or the next errand. Lunch is big, often consisting of stewed meat and rice and beans, seafood, soup, and other Creole and Latin specialties. Pastries and desserts are popular as well, and you'll find plenty of street vendors selling fast foods, snacks, fresh fruit juices, and more.

CAFÉS

European in flavor is **Le Petit Café** (2 Marine Parade, tel. 501/223-33336, ext. 750, 6am-8pm daily), attached to the Radisson Hotel in the Fort George area. It offers delicious twice-daily baked Belizean and European pastries and cakes, ham-and-cheese croissants, and possibly the best cup of freshly brewed coffee in town. They also make excellent johnnycakes, plain or stuffed.

The **Smokin' Balam** (59 N. Front St., tel. 501/601-4510, 7am-5pm daily) is a casual local café, gift shop, guesthouse, and Internet hub. They have a comfortable little space with a back porch and dock over Haulover Creek, ideal for sunning or people-watching. There are also local dishes available for lunch. Up on Marine Parade, **Pandora Café** (lunch and dinner daily, US$4-10) is a favorite, with all sorts of delicious frozen and gourmet coffee drinks, smoothies, teas, ice cream, and Chinese and Belizean plates in a cozy upstairs seating area. There is also an espresso bar in the Caye Caulker Water Taxi Terminal while you wait for your boat.

Over on Bishop Street is the **Juice Box Stand** (Bishop St. and Albert St., across from Scotiabank), with a host of cheap yet freshly squeezed and chilled fruit and vegetable juices by the bottle—even beet and spinach (US$0.75-1.50). It's a great stop on a hot day. You can also refresh yourself across the street by getting fresh "coconut wata" from **Devon** (US$1), who slices and dices coconuts and bottles the juice all afternoon at Battlefield Park along the sidewalk market.

The Taiwanese-owned **Milky Way Café** (29 Baymen Ave., tel. 501/223-5185, 10:30am-9:30pm daily) is a favorite with locals, from adults to schoolchildren. They offer frozen cappuccinos, mochas, bubble milk tea (originally a Taiwanese specialty), and other coffee concoctions as well as delicious smoothies and Chinese food. There's a second, smaller location (29 Albert St., tel. 501/669-0551, 10am-8pm Mon.-Sat.) on Albert Street, ideal for those in town and on the go.

Dessert and ice cream junkies can find their joy at **Zero Degrees** (18 St. Thomas Place, tel. 501/223-5132, zerodegreesicecream@yahoo.com, 9am-8pm Mon.-Thurs., 10am-9pm Fri.-Sat., 2pm-9pm Sun.), also serving ice cream cakes.

BELIZEAN

The city is packed with traditional Creole eateries. An excellent long-standing local option is (**Dit's** (50 King St., tel. 501/227-3330, 8am-6pm Mon.-Sat., 8am-3pm Sun., US$4-6), a fifth generation family-run Creole institution, serving amazing freshly baked pastries—you must try the jam rolls—as well as pies and other traditional Creole desserts along with the wide menu of local specialties. It's always packed with Belizeans—a good sign. **Nerie's** (Queen St. and Daly St., tel. 501/223-4028, 7:30am-10pm daily, US$5-9) was featured on the Travel Channel in a program about traditional Belizean fare; order stew chicken, fish fillets, soups, and daily specials, including oxtail, jerk, and Garífuna *serre*.

A couple of streets from the swing bridge are the infamous meat pies at **Dario's** (33 Hyde's Ln., US$0.75), delicious hot, flaky pastries filled with meat or chicken. Go early if you want them fresh. **Pou's Meat Pies** (New Rd.) is also nearby; try both and decide who rules the city's meat pie district.

Over on Regent Street, close to the Belize Tourism Board, is the tiny shack and window service of **Caribbean Palm Fast Food** (11:30am-2pm Mon.-Fri., US$3-5), where Shawna and her mother dish out savory, super cheap Creole lunches every day. Get here early—it's popular.

Deep Sea Marlin's Restaurant & Bar (Regent St. W., tel. 501/227-6995, 7am-9pm Mon.-Sat., US$4) is on Haulover Creek, next to the Belcove Hotel. It's a cheap and sometimes raucous fishing joint, with tasty Belizean and American staples and simple seating with breezy waterside views. The breakfast fry jacks are said to be out of this world. **Tropicolada Cocktail Hut** (7 Fort St., tel. 501/223-1066, 11am-10pm Tues.-Sat., US$6-10), near Tourism Village, serves some of the best ceviche in Belize City as well as a wide range of Belizean and Central American dishes and pretty cocktails. Tropicolada closes earlier on Tuesday and later on karaoke Friday.

(**Bird's Isle Restaurant** (tel. 501/207-2179, 10am-midnight Mon.-Sat., US$5-13), or *Island* as the locals call it, has a long-standing reputation and an excellent waterfront location on a small islet to the south of downtown Belize City. Any taxi driver will know it, or just walk south past the Anglican Church on Albert Street until you can't walk any more. This is a casual affair in a gorgeous outdoor setting, with a spacious yard as well as indoor seating and a waterfront deck where you can watch the fish and birds glide by. Expect large portions of local comfort dishes, including stew beans, hamburgers, and sandwiches.

A nice neighborhood experience is a trip to the **D'Ceviche Hut** (5672 Vasquez Ave., tel. 501/223-6426, 11:30am-10pm Thurs.-Sat., US$11). The proprietor, Don Enrique, works for the fishing cooperative, and he doesn't mess around about freshness. There's no menu, just ceviche. As you take your seat, shout out "shrimp," "conch," or "mixed" (also lobster in season) and you'll get a large plate that feeds 3-4 people. It's fun, friendly, and very popular with locals. Arrange a taxi there and back so you don't have to negotiate the confusing streets in this neighborhood.

A couple of blocks past the Princess Hotel, **Thirsty Thursdays** (164 New Town Barracks, tel. 501/223-1677, thirstythursdaysbz@gmail.com, 10am-10pm Mon.-Thurs., 10am-midnight Fri.-Sat., US$8-15) is a popular pre-party joint with a savory menu and breezy patio overlooking the ocean.

In Buttonwood Bay, three miles north of central Belize City, the dockside (**Saffron Bay Restaurant** (5865 Seashore Dr., one street behind Villa Boscardi, tel. 501/203-1400, saffronbaybz@gmail.com, 11:30am-3:30pm Mon.-Fri., 7am-9am and 11:30am-5pm Sat., US$4-5) has an excellent, casual waterfront location and friendly service. More importantly, the local dishes are delicious with (I dare say) the best rice and beans in the district. Mother and daughter team Estelae and Daisy Ramclam cook lunches that vary from stewed chicken to Garífuna *serre* or East Indian *tarkari;* there's no set menu, but choices always include one seafood dish.

CHINESE

There are more authentic Chinese restaurants in Belize City than you can imagine. They all

WAH BELLY FULL: KRIOL EATS

© LEBAWIT GIRMA

Stew beef and stew chicken served with coconut rice and beans are typical Kriol dishes.

The most authentic Belizean Kriol food you'll find is right here in Belize City and area, the heart of the Kriol or Caribbean culture. There's no way you could starve here, between the coconut-based dishes, the meats, the multitude of baked treats, and the very affordable meals. Here's what you shouldn't miss.

- **Boil up:** This isn't served as frequently, but when available, you should jump at the chance to taste this uniquely Caribbean stew mix of pig tail, fish, hard-boiled eggs, yams, plantains, sweet potato, cassava and yam–all *biled up* in a sauce of tomatoes, onions, and peppers.

- **Meat pies** are serious business–so much so that there's a constant debate on who makes the best: **Dario's** (33 Hyde's Ln.) or **Pou's Meat Pies** (New Rd.)? Join the club and be the judge.

- **Pastries and sweets** are a part of Kriol life. You'll find children selling their mothers' Creole bread, buns, and johnnycakes, often baked with coconut oil. Stop by **Dit's** (50 King St., tel. 501/227-3330, 8am-6pm Mon.-Sat., closes earlier Sun.) to sample traditional jam rolls, hot off the oven by noon. While you're at it, sample their bread pudding, coconut pie, or some "plastic" pudding, made with cassava.

- **Soup:** Of the more than a dozen Kriol soups you could sample, the best-known is beef soup (head to Bird's Isle on Tuesday for the best) and cow foot soup.

- **Stew chicken** is the unofficial national dish of Belize. Often served family style on Sunday, it's also sold throughout the week at various eateries. Along those same lines, you'll find stew beef on the menu and some sort of fry fish or fry chicken. These dishes are almost always served with a heap of coconut rice and beans (not to be confused with beans and rice, which is white rice and stewed beans served separately) or plantains and coleslaw. For some of the best, head to **Deep Sea Marlin's** (Regent St. W., tel. 501/227-6995, 7am-9pm Mon.-Sat.), by the Swing Bridge, or **Nerie's** (Queen St. and Daly St., tel. 501/223-4028, 7:30am-10pm daily).

- **Wine.** Fermenting fruits, plants, and herbs is a tradition in the Belize River Valley. Locally made and potent (6-12 percent alcohol) but delicious wines are worth sampling, particularly the blackberry, cashew, or rice wines. These can be found in villages across the district, including Burrell Boom, on the roads to Altun Ha and Maskall Village, and in Crooked Tree.

© LEBAWIT GIRMA

Bird's Isle Restaurant's setting and food make it a popular stop for lunch or dinner.

make decent greasy dishes, but a few stand out, such as **Chon Saan Palace** (1 Kelly St., tel. 501/223-3008, 11am-11:30pm Mon.-Sat., 11am-2:30pm and 5-11:30pm Sun., US$4-7). In addition to Chinese standards, there are many seafood and steak options.

Mama Chen's (7 Eve St., tel. 501/223-4568 or 501/620-4257, 10am-6pm Mon.-Sat., US$4-6), on the corner of Eve and Queen Streets and close to the Belize Museum, is a good choice for vegetarians. Choose from veggie chow mein, spicy beef dumplings, crispy spring rolls, sushi, and bubble tea (the "bubbles" are sweet seaweed balls that are slurped up through a thick straw).

ITALIAN
Pepper's Pizza (4 St. Thomas St., tel. 501/223-5000, 10am-10pm daily, US$17) offers free delivery within city limits.

MEXICAN
Across from the BTL Park, **(Chap's Bar and Grill** (160 Newtown Barracks Rd., tel. 501/223-1299, 11am-10pm Tues.-Sat., noon-6pm Sun.,

US$7-11) is a welcome addition. This Mexican restaurant specializes in savory *arrachera* as well as many other Central American dishes, sandwiches, and bar eats. There's a nice outdoor poolside terrace with partial views of the seaside park. The pool is run by a membership club along with the tennis courts next door, but you're welcome to bring your bathing suit and cool off for US$7.50 pp.

MIDDLE EASTERN AND INDIAN
Belize City's small Lebanese community ensures that there are a few authentic Lebanese restaurants in town. You can't go wrong with **Sahara Grill** (Mile 3½, Northern Hwy., Vista Plaza, tel. 501/203-3031 or 501/605-3785, 10am-3pm and 5pm-10pm Mon.-Sat., 5pm-10pm Sun., US$4-15), right across the Northern Highway from the Best Western Biltmore Hotel. They have a long menu of kebabs, hummus, and falafel, plus addictive *shawarma* wraps and gyros as well as *sheesha* water pipes. There's also **Manatee Landing**

(tel. 501/225-3461 or 501/205-2391, noon-midnight Tues.-Sat., earlier close Sun.-Mon., US$6), near the entrance to the international airport and about 15 minutes north of the city. Watch dolphins swim by in the Belize River while you enjoy your hummus, kebabs, burgers, or wings.

For East Indian curries and dal, **◖ Sumathi** (31 Eve St., tel. 501/223-1172, 11am-3pm and 6pm-11pm Tues.-Sun.) is a solid choice. They've got a great weekly lunch buffet (US$5), plus air-conditioning and a large Indian menu with plenty of vegetarian options. They also offer takeout and delivery anywhere in the city. The food is so good that expats from as far away as San Pedro or Punta Gorda order takeout via plane. There's a second location (19 Baymen Ave.) in the works.

FINE DINING

Belize's Belikin brewing family runs the **◖ Riverside Tavern** (2 Mapp St., tel. 501/223-5640, 11am-10pm Mon.-Thurs., open later Fri.-Sat., US$15-35), an upscale sports bar whose massive "gourmet burger" (10-ounce patty US$9, super-size 16-ounce patty US$12.50), made of Belizean beef from the Bowens' Gallon Jug Estate, is one of the best in the country. The Cuban burger is also delicious, but the King Kong just sounds scary. Or try the coconut-crusted shrimp, other rich bar foods, pastas, and seafood options. There's beer on tap, and the very convivial atmosphere is popular at happy hour or for Thursday karaoke; it's a meeting place for Belize's who's who crowd. There's just one downside to this place: Table service can be very slow.

Celebrity Restaurant and Bar (Volta Bldg., Marine Parade Blvd., tel. 501/223-2826 or 501/223-7272, www.celebritybelize.com, 11am-10pm daily, US$9-20) is near the water, next to the national bank and museum. You enter through a dark, swanky lounge emerging into a bright restaurant with a huge variety of seafood, pasta, steaks, and salads. The best deal is Celebrity's takeout menu (US$5) and the giant plate of fish and chips. They're also open for hearty breakfasts on Saturday and Sunday (8am-3pm). Folks rightfully rave about their quesadillas and Budapest Chicken.

The **Smoky Mermaid** (13 Cork St., opposite the Radisson, tel. 501/223-4759, www.smokymermaid.com, 7am-10pm, US$12-20) specializes in smoked fish, meats, and assorted fresh breads. Breakfast, lunch, and dinner feature Belizean cuisine and freshly baked Creole bread served on a lovely dining patio under thatched roofs surrounding a porcelain mermaid. Inside the Smoky Mermaid, but also with a separate street-side entrance, is a delightful sushi bar. The **Nautical Fusion** (tel. 501/672-4759, 11am-2pm and 5pm-10pm daily, US$7-10) serves classic and tasty sushi offerings as well as noodle bowls, teriyaki dishes, a dessert or two, and wines (even local cashew wine) by the glass or bottle. It's a great date night choice, with soothing music and colorful seating.

The **St. George's Restaurant** (Radisson Fort George Hotel, 2 Marine Parade, tel. 501/223-3333, 6:30am-10am, 11:30am-2pm, and 6:30pm-10pm daily, US$20) serves a grand buffet and has a standard menu of international fare and seafood. Outside around the bar, the **Stonegrill Restaurant** (10am-10pm daily, US$15-20) offers a fun, meat-sizzlin' meal inside or on the heavily vegetated outdoor patio. The burgers are surprisingly good.

GROCERIES

Brodie's (Albert St. and Regent St., tel. 501/227-7070, 8am-6pm Mon.-Fri., closes earlier Sat.-Sun.) is a department store, supermarket, deli, drugstore, and more—a Belizean institution. You can also stock up on your way into or out of the north edge of town at **Save-U Supermarket** (San Cas Plaza, tel. 501/223-1291, 8am-9pm Mon.-Sat., 8am-2pm Sun.). This modern air-conditioned market sells everything any supermarket in the United States would carry, and it's reasonably priced, though not necessarily less than Brodie's. There's also a gorgeous massive Brodie's on the Northern Highway, just before you reach the Biltmore Hotel and next to a Scotiabank branch.

Located in the Smoky Mermaid, Nautical Fusion is the city's new sushi bar.

Information and Services

TOURIST INFORMATION

The central office of the **Belize Tourism Board** (BTB, 64 Regent St., tel. 501/227-2420, U.S. tel. 800/624-0686, info@travelbelize.org, www.travelbelize.org) is in the Southside, near the Mopan Hotel and the House of Culture. They have an excellent free first-timer's map with a suggested walking tour of the city. The **Belize Tourism Industry Association** (10 N. Park St., tel. 501/227-1144, 8am-5pm Mon.-Thurs., shorter hours Fri., www.btia.org) can also answer many of your questions and provide lodging suggestions. **The Belize Hotel Association** (BHA, 13 Cork St., tel. 501/223-0669, www.belizehotels.org) is a nonprofit industry group representing some of the country's most respected resorts and lodges; they can help you decide where to stay.

BANKS

Most of the city's banking is clustered in one strip along Albert Street, just south of the Swing Bridge. This includes **Atlantic Bank** (tel. 501/227-1225), **Scotiabank** (tel. 501/227-7027), **First Caribbean International Bank** (tel. 501/227-7211), and **Belize Bank** (tel. 501/227-7132). Most banks have ATMs and keep the same hours (8am-1pm Mon.-Thurs., 8am-1pm and 3pm-6pm Fri.).

HEALTH AND EMERGENCIES

For **police, fire,** or **ambulance,** dial 90 or 911. Another ambulance service is **B.E.R.T.** (tel. 501/223-3292). **Belize Medical Associates** (5791 St. Thomas St., tel. 501/223-0302, bzmedasso@btl.net, www.belizemedical.com) is the main private hospital in Belize City. The fairly modern 25-bed facility provides

24-hour assistance and a wide range of specialties. Or try **Karl Heusner Memorial Hospital** (Princess Margaret Dr., tel. 501/223-1548, www.khmh.bz).

MEDIA AND COMMUNICATIONS

The main **post office** (150 N. Front St., tel. 501/227-2201, www.belizepostalservice.gov. bz, 8am-5pm Mon.-Thurs., 8am-4:30pm Fri.) is across from the Caye Caulker Water Taxi Terminal. A second post office is at Queens Square on the Southside (corner of Dolphin St. and Racoon St., tel. 501/227-1155, 8am-5pm Mon.-Fri.).

As elsewhere in the country, an increasing number of hotels and guesthouses offer at least a single computer for guests or even wireless Internet for your laptop. There are a few broadband Internet cafés in Belize City, though not as many as in San Ignacio or San Pedro.

The **Turton Library's Computer Center** (9am-7pm Mon.-Fri., 9am-1pm Sat.), tucked away in a narrow air-conditioned room above the library, has five speedy computers; they are the cheapest in town at US$1.25 per hour. On the Southside, try **KGS Internet** (29 King St., tel. 501/207-7130, 8am-7pm Mon.-Fri., reduced hours Sat., US$1.50 per hour), a few steps from Dit's Restaurant. It's a clean, organized space with quite a few desktops and fast cable connections. **Angelus Press** (10 Queen St., tel. 501/223-5777, 7:30am-5:30pm Mon.-Fri., reduced hours Sat.-Sun.) has a few machines available for US$1.75 per hour. More expensive options are available in Tourism Village and in the business centers of fancier hotels.

Getting There and Around

Most sights are relatively close together in Belize City, and you can walk from the Southside's House of Culture to the National Museum in about 30 leisurely minutes. This route is generally safe during the day, even more so if you are traveling in a group; I have walked it solo several times.

Check with the travel agencies in the main Caye Caulker Water Taxi Terminal; they may be able to hold your backpacks for the day or arrange for longer storage (US$1 per hour, US$5 per day). The nearby **Smokin' Balam Guest House** (N. Front St., US$2 per bag) offers storage for the day if you're passing through. Ask your guesthouse if you can leave a bag there as well.

BY AIR

The **Municipal Airport** (TZA), called "Muni," is on the waterfront behind the Marion Jones Sports Complex, one mile from the city center. Belizean commuter planes provide steady service in and out of Belize City to outlying airports all over the country. It's cheaper to fly to local destinations from here.

From **Goldson International Airport** (BZE, 10 miles west of town, 501/225-2045, www. pgiabelize.com), it's a 20-minute taxi ride to downtown Belize City (US$25), less in the opposite direction. There are no other transportation alternatives unless a friend is picking you up.

BY BUS

Domestic bus service is handled almost entirely out of **Novelo's Terminal,** on West Canal Street at the western terminus of King Street. If you arrive by bus, it's about 10 blocks to walk downtown to the Swing Bridge. From Novelo's, cross the canal and stay on King Street until you reach Albert Street, then make a left. Continue three blocks to the Swing Bridge and Water Taxi Terminal. You can also cross the street and take a right on Orange Street just one block up, then stay on Orange Street all the way to town; it's always busy with foot traffic. This walk is usually safe during the day, but should not be attempted at night. When in doubt, take a taxi, and have one referred if possible; a good rule of thumb is not to walk any streets that appear deserted. International bus service to Guatemala and Mexico and ferry service to Honduras is offered by a handful of companies with offices in the **Caye Caulker Water Taxi Terminal** (north end of the Swing Bridge).

BY BOAT

It's a crime to stay in Belize City and not hop over to one of Belize's beautiful northern cayes for the day, even for lunch. The country's two water taxi companies have their terminals here, with an all-day schedule of departures and returns. The islands are very close; Caye Caulker is a mere 45-minute ride, and St. George's Caye is about 25 minutes away. Travelers passing through will find it well worth the time.

Three water taxi companies offer regular service to San Pedro and Caye Caulker. The **Caye Caulker Water Taxi Terminal** (San Pedro tel. 501/226-4646, Caye Caulker tel. 501/226-0992, Belize City tel. 501/223-5752, www.cayecaulkerwatertaxi.com) is at the north end of the Swing Bridge, with boats leaving between 8am and 5pm.

San Pedro Belize Express (tel. 501/223-2225, www.belizewatertaxi.com) departs just a few blocks farther down, near the Tourism Village, between 7:45am and 5:30pm daily.

Water Jets Express (tel. 501/207-1000, www.sanpedrowatertaxi.com) leaves between 8am and 5pm daily from Bird's Isle Water Taxi and Marina.

Verify first and last departures, as those tend to change seasonally. Boat transit to Caye Caulker takes about 45 minutes, then it's another half hour to Ambergris Caye. The trip to Caulker costs about US$10 one-way; to San Pedro costs US$15 one-way. The trip is pleasant on calm sunny days when the boat isn't full, but otherwise be prepared to squeeze on, and it can be a cold and wet ride if the sky to the east is dark. A few of the boats are covered; others will pass out plastic tarps if it's really raining hard.

BY TAXI

To hail a taxi, look for the green license plates, but better yet, ask your hotel or guesthouse to call you one, and keep the numbers or make arrangements with the driver for the duration of your stay. From the international airport to Belize City, the flat fare is US$25; from the municipal airstrip, expect to pay US$5 or less. The fare for one passenger carried between any two points within Belize City or any other district town is US$3-5. If you plan to make several stops, tell the cabbie in advance and ask what the total will be; this eliminates lots of misunderstandings, as taxis often charge by the stop. They can also be hired by the hour (about US$16-25). For long trips out of town; try Kenneth Bennett of **KB Taxi Service** (501/634-2865).

TOURS

If you prefer to delegate the logistics of your trip, local travel agencies can book local and international transportation, tours, and accommodations across the country. **S & L Travel and Tours** (91 N. Front St., tel. 501/227-7593 or 501/227-5145, www.sltravelbelize.com) is easy to find, next door to the Image Factory. Belizean owners Sarita and Lascelle Tillet run a first-class and very personable operation; they've been in business for more than 30 years. They can get as creative as you like, whether you want a custom vacation, a photo safari, a bird-watching adventure, or anything else you can imagine.

Got extra cash? Splurge on a helicopter tour over the Belize Barrier Reef and the magnificent Blue Hole with **Astrum Helicopters** (Mile 3½, Western Hwy., tel. 501/222-5100, U.S. tel. 888/278-7864, US$1,200 for 4 people). Astrum also offers airport helicopter transfers to 22 of Belize's five-star resorts.

Along the Northern Highway

After escaping the Belize City's traffic and passing the international airport, you'll cruise up the Northern Highway to Mayan sites, monkeys, and Creole villages.

◖ ALTUN HA

Altun Ha (9am-5pm daily, US$5), a Mayan trading center as well as a religious ceremonial site, is believed to have accommodated about 10,000 people. Archaeologists, working amid a Mayan community that has been living here for several centuries, have dated construction to about 1,500-2,000 years ago. It wasn't until the archaeologists arrived in 1964 that the old name, Rockstone Pond, was translated into the Mayan words "Altun Ha."

A team led by Dr. David Pendergast of the Royal Ontario Museum began work in 1965 on the central part of the ancient city, where upward of 250 structures have been found in an area of about 1,000 square yards. So far, this is the most extensively excavated of all the Maya sites in Belize. For a trading center, Altun Ha was strategically located—a few miles from Little Rocky Point on the Caribbean and a few miles from Moho Caye at the mouth of the Belize River, both believed to have been major centers for the large trading canoes that worked up and down the coasts of Guatemala, Honduras, Belize, Mexico's Yucatán, and all the way to Panama.

Altun Ha spans an area of about 25 square miles, most of which is covered by trees, vines, and rainforest. It was rebuilt several times during the Pre-Classic, Classic, and Post-Classic Periods. The desecration of the structures leads scientists to believe that the site may have been abandoned because of violence.

© LEBAWIT GIRMA

Because of its proximity to Belize City, Altun Ha is Belize's most visited Maya site.

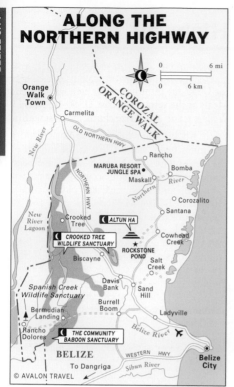

ALONG THE NORTHERN HIGHWAY

Archaeologists say that an insignificant little stream ran through the rainforest for centuries. No doubt it had been a source of fresh water for the Maya—but maybe not enough. They diverted the creek and then began a major engineering project, digging and enlarging a deep, round hole that was then plastered with limestone cement. Once the cement dried and hardened, the stream was rerouted to its original course, and the newly built reservoir filled and overflowed at the east end, allowing the stream to continue on its age-old track. This made the area livable. Was all of this done before or after the temple structures were built? Is the completion of this reservoir what made the Mayan elite choose to locate themselves in this area? We may never know for sure.

Today, Rockstone Pond is surrounded by thick brush, and the pond is alive with rainforest creatures, including tarpon, small fish, turtles, and other reptiles.

Sun God Temple

The concentration of structures includes palaces and temples surrounding two main plazas. The tallest building is the **Sun God Temple,** rising 59 feet above the plaza floor. At Altun Ha, the bases of the structures are oval and terraced. The small temples on top have typical small rooms built with the Mayan trademark—the corbel arch.

Temple of the Green Tomb

Pendergast's team uncovered many valuable finds, such as unusual green obsidian blades, pearls, and more than 300 jade pieces—beads, earrings, and rings. Seven funeral chambers were discovered, including the **Temple of the Green Tomb,** rich with human remains and traditional funerary treasures. Mayan scholars believe the first man buried was someone of great importance; he was draped with jade beads, pearls, and shells.

Next to his right hand, the most exciting find was located—a solid jade head now referred to as **Kinich Ahau** ("The Sun God"). Kinich Ahau is, to date, the largest jade carving found at any Mayan site. The head weighs nine

Altun Ha is located 34 miles north of Belize City and has become one of the more popular day trips for groups and individuals venturing from Belize City, Ambergris Caye, and Caye Caulker; it is the most visited archeological site in Belize. A gift shop and restroom facilities are at the entrance. Local tour guides (US$10 per group per half hour) are available at the entrance. If you're coming to Altun Ha as part of a package, consider insisting that your tour provider use a local guide; this ensures that local communities benefit from the site.

Rockstone Pond

Located near Plaza B, the Reservoir, also known as **Rockstone Pond,** is fed by springs and rain runoff. It demonstrates the advanced knowledge of the Maya in just one of their many fields of expertise: engineering.

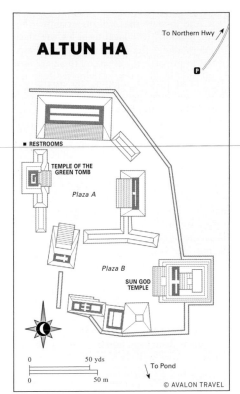

ALTUN HA

To Northern Hwy

P

■ RESTROOMS

TEMPLE OF THE
GREEN TOMB

Plaza A

Plaza B

SUN GOD
TEMPLE

0   50 yds

0   50 m

To Pond

© AVALON TRAVEL

casita for rent at the **Mayan Wells Restaurant** (tel. 501/205-5641 or 501/225-5505, www.mayanwells.com, US$40); it has a kitchenette, a screened porch, and hammocks. You can also camp out for US$5 pp and have internet access for US$2 for 30 minutes, or free with lunch. Meals at the restaurant cost US$6-10. Mayan Wells is set on a nice-size chunk of forest within walking distance from the Altun Ha ruins and offers meals, tours, and free admission to their butterfly house.

Getting There

To reach Altun Ha from the Northern Highway, continue past the Burrell Boom turn-off (to the Baboon Sanctuary) and continue to about Mile 19, where the road forks; the right fork is the Old Northern Highway, which leads to Altun Ha and Maskall Village. The entrance is 10.5 miles from the intersection. The road is in horrible condition and is not getting any better with the increased traffic.

Altun Ha is close enough to Belize City that a taxi ride is your best bet (US$100 round-trip). Kenneth Bennett of **KB Taxi Service** (tel. 501/634-2865) is an excellent driver who will wait for up to 2.5 hours while you tour the site. You can also opt for a tour operator that specializes in these trips, such as Mr. Lascelle of **S & L Travel and Tours** (91 N. Front St., tel. 501/227-7593 or 501/227-5145, www.sltravel-belize.com).

Note that Altun Ha is a popular destination for cruise-ship passengers (usually Tues. and Thurs.), so if you don't want to share your experience with busloads of tourists, check with the park before coming. In general, it's easy to avoid the crowds if you get here when the park first opens.

pounds and measures nearly six inches from base to crown. It is reportedly now housed far away in a museum in Canada. The two men who discovered the jade head some 40 years ago, Winston Herbert and William Leslie, still reside in Rockstone Pond and Lucky Strike villages. On November 29, 2006, they were honored by the National Institute of Culture and History for their discovery.

Accommodations and Food

There are several budget-oriented lodgings in the area around Lucky Strike and Rockstone Pond villages, but few travelers choose to stay here, probably because there's not much offered in the area apart from a short hike through the nearby ruins and the tranquil sounds of the rainforest. The best option is only about a mile from the entrance to the ruins. There's a small

MARUBA RESORT JUNGLE SPA

By any standard, **Maruba Resort Jungle Spa** (Mile 40½, Old Northern Hwy., Maskall Village, U.S. tel. 713/799-2031 or 800/627-8227, www.maruba-spa.com, US$200-700) is an interesting sight in the middle of the forest, located about a mile out of Maskall Village.

Many visitors come just for the day; it's a popular stopover for Altun Ha explorers who decide to enjoy lunch and a mud mask (pick the Mood Mud Massage if you have time) before heading back to San Pedro, Belize City, or other nearby destinations. The resort's verdant landscaping is enhanced by intriguing focal points spread around the grounds: a tiny glass-decorated chapel, a *palapa*-covered stone chess table, and a pool that seems to spring from the rainforest, complete with waterfalls. The uniquely named guest rooms—Moon, Fertility, Mayan Loft, and Bondage, to name a few—continue the eclectic motif with carved masks, mosaic-tile floors, standing candles, concrete fountains, tiled tubs, screened windows, and fresh flowers on the massive feather beds and in the bathrooms.

The **restaurant** often offers decent international fusion fare, and at the bar you will find viper rum ("for real men only"), an insanely strong shot of liquor infused with snake venom. Instructions on how to properly down a shot will be given by owner-bartender, Nicky. Massages, mud wraps, manicures, and pedicures are available, as well as a free-weight gym. Packages are available with tours to the reefs, ruins, and inland destinations.

BURRELL BOOM

This village of about 1,200 people is named after the Scottish logger who built a boom across the river to catch his logs. Today, Burrell Boom is inhabited by subsistence farmers, anglers, cashew growers, and fruit-wine vintners. It is the gateway to the Community Baboon Sanctuary, but also conveniently close to the international airport and a good way to avoid staying in Belize City if you don't want to, thanks to a few wonderful river lodges.

◖ The Community Baboon Sanctuary

The Community Baboon Sanctuary (CBS, tel. 501/245-2009 or 501/245-2007, 8am-5pm daily, US$7) is a nonprofit organization consisting of 220 members in seven local communities who have voluntarily agreed to manage their land in ways that will preserve their beloved "baboon" (the local term for the black howler monkey). Because of community-based efforts to preserve the creature, there are now 3,000 individual monkeys living freely in the forests and buffer zones between people's farms. Since 1998 the CBS Women's Conservation Group has overseen the organization and its members, with a female representative from each of the seven villages. More recently, the CBS member landowners received US$15,000 in microgrants to improve their small businesses and communities. CBS feels remote but is less than an hour's drive from Belize City, making it both a popular day trip and a destination for anyone who'd rather wake up to the throaty roars of Belizean howler monkeys than the bustle of Belize City.

There are enough trails, rivers, and guided tours to keep you busy here for a couple of days. All activities are arranged through the **CBS Visitors Center** (tel. 501/245-2009 or cell tel. 501/622-9624, www.howlermonkeys.org, 8am-5pm daily) in Bermudian Landing; group trips and guides from local hotels are also available. A basic nature walk is included with the entrance fee to the visitors center and museum (feel free to tip your guide), which is small but has very informative displays on a range of topics—from the history of CBS to the local Kriol culture and Belize's wildlife.

There are 1.5-hour and 3-hour **canoe tours** and a two-hour **driving tour** of some of the different sanctuary villages. Those staying overnight should definitely take advantage of the nighttime trips, such as the 3.5-hour crocodile canoe trip up Mussell Creek and the two-hour night hike into the surrounding forest. If you'd like to experience the local culture, request a **Kriol cultural package** (groups of 12 or more, US$15 pp), with food and dance performances.

If you're lucky, between February and August you might catch a village softball game or cricket match.

Accommodations and Food

The ◖ **Black Orchid Resort** (tel. 501/225-9158, www.blackorchidresort.com,

HISTORY OF THE COMMUNITY BABOON SANCTUARY

© LEBAWIT GIRMA

a howler monkey at The Community Baboon Sanctuary

One of the six species of howler monkeys in the world, the black howlers, *Alouatta caraya,* are the largest monkeys in the Americas. Robert Horwich of the University of Wisconsin-Milwaukee was the first zoologist to spend extended time in the howler's range, which covered southern Mexico, northeast Guatemala, and Belize. The results of his study were disturbing. In Mexico the monkeys were being hunted for food, and their habitat was fast disappearing. Conditions in Guatemala were only slightly better. Here, too, the monkeys were hunted by locals in the forests around Tikal, and as the forest habitat shrank, so too did the number of howler monkeys.

In the Belizean village of Bermudian Landing, however, the communities of monkeys were strong and healthy, the forest was intact, and the locals seemed genuinely fond of the noisy

creatures. This was definitely the place to start talking about a wildlife reserve. Horwich, with the help of Jon Lyon, a botanist from the State University of New York, began a survey of the village in 1984. After many meetings with the town leaders, excitement grew about the idea of saving the "baboon." Homeowners agreed to leave the monkey's food trees—hog plums and sapodillas—and small strips of forest between cleared fields as aerial pathways for the primates, as well as 60 feet of forest along both sides of waterways.

An application was made to World Wildlife Fund USA in 1985 for funds to set up the reserve. Local landowners signed a voluntary management agreement set forth by Horwich and Lyon—and a sanctuary was born.

According to sanctuary manager Fallett Young, who died in 2009, there have been successful relocations of some of the thriving monkey troops around the country, including to the Cockscomb Basin Wildlife Sanctuary, where howlers hadn't been heard since they were decimated by yellow fever decades ago.

In the case of the Community Baboon Sanctuary, educating people about conservation and encouraging their fondness for nature was more successful than stringent hunting laws. The managers of the sanctuary are villagers who understand their neighbors; much of their time is spent with schoolchildren and adults in the villages concerned. Part of their education includes basic farming and sustained land use techniques that eliminate the constant need to cut forest for new milpas (cornfields).

Another result is the unhindered growth of 100 species of trees, vines, and epiphytes. The animal life is thriving—anteaters, armadillos, iguanas, hickatee turtles, deer, coatis, amphibians, reptiles, and about 200 species of birds all live here.

A lively debate continues among traditional conservationists about allowing people to live within a wildlife preserve. However, Belize's grassroots conservation is proving that it can succeed.

US$120-140) is a relaxed riverside resort within striking distance of a number of area attractions. Locals and guests rave about this place, which is a mere 11 miles from the international airport, but feels as remote as other upcountry jungle lodges. Black Orchid's owner, Doug Thompson, is a native Belizean who lived in the United States for 36 years and is currently the president of the Belize Hotel Association. He also runs a tour company to whisk you around the region (and a free airport shuttle); or stay on the grounds and enjoy the swimming pool, popular among locals on the weekends, or the shaded picnic tables, kayaks, and canoes. Sixteen spacious guest rooms are comfortable and have all the basic amenities, and there is an on-site restaurant and bar. Ask about the Jaguar Eco-house and three-bedroom villa for longer-term rental or for families.

Another excellent choice for anglers or ecotour seekers is the **Belize River Lodge** (tel. 501/225-2002, U.S. tel. 888/275-4843, www.belizeriverlodge.com, 3-night package US$1,400), offering package stays only. A fishing lodge par excellence, it's run by a welcoming couple, Mike Heusner and Marguerite Miles, both of whom know their country inside out and have plenty of tales to share. There are eight cozy guest rooms with screened porches and gorgeous river views. Meals are shared family style and often consist of delicious Belizean specialties. Mike sits on the board of the Audubon Society and is a great source of information on the country's wildlife and conservation efforts. You really don't have to be an angler to stay here, and the lodge is accessed via a short two-minute boat ride from Burrell Boom's banks. The lodge now also operates a sister resort on Long Caye, near Caye Chapel.

A popular choice for adventurous travelers is the homestay program—you'll stay with a local family in primitive conditions, bathing with a bucket and talking with your host family in the evening. The **Women's Bed-and-Breakfast Group** (US$42 pp, includes breakfast and dinner) has established a network of accommodations throughout the seven sanctuary villages, offering visitors a traditional Creole-style stay.

Arrange your stay in one of these "bed-and-breakfasts" at least 24 hours in advance through the CBS Visitors Center (tel. 501/245-2009 or cell tel. 501/622-9624, www.howlermonkeys. org, 8am-5pm daily) at Bermudian Landing.

Campers can pitch a tent (US$5 pp) on the visitors center grounds or arrange for a meal (US$5) with a local family. There are privies and cold showers available. Next door, the **Howler Monkey Resort** (tel. 501/607-1571, www.howlermonkeyresort.bz, US$99-138) has a selection of cabins, a screened restaurant, and a path to the river.

Getting There

Bermudian Landing is only 26 miles from Belize City, or about a 45-minute drive, and 22 miles from the Orange Walk District. From Belize City, drive north on the Northern Highway for 13 miles, then turn left toward Burrell Boom (notice a sign to turn left for the Black Orchid Resort). Follow signs to the Community Baboon Sanctuary Museum and Visitors Center, located across a soccer field. Try not to get confused by the distracting private tour guide signs posted en masse just prior to the museum, and ignore any gestures for you to stop. This is not the official CBS site, and you won't be supporting the community by skipping CBS, who have very competent guides, know the history of the sanctuary, and work with the villages. Look for the CBS logo.

Two bus companies travel between Bermuda Landing and Belize City. In Belize City, McFadzean buses depart from the corner of Cemetery Road and Amara Avenue, and Russell leaves from Euphrates Street and Cairo Street. Seven buses depart Belize City between noon and 9pm Monday-Friday; there's a shorter schedule on Saturday. There are no buses in either direction on Sunday. The bus takes about an hour. Four early-morning buses leave Bermudian Landing 5:30am-7am, and there are two in the afternoon at 3:30pm and 4pm Monday-Saturday.

The sanctuary is close enough to the city or the international airport that you can consider a taxi or an escorted tour for a day trip. Negotiate taxi prices ahead of time. The Community Baboon Sanctuary can arrange airport transfers for reasonable prices.

SPANISH CREEK WILDLIFE SANCTUARY

Spanish Creek Wildlife Sanctuary is a protected area rich in wildlife but short on infrastructure. It's located near Rancho Dolores, due west along the Burrell Boom Road, beyond the Community Baboon Sanctuary, and it is accessible by bus from Belize City. For more information and to visit, contact the **Rancho Dolores Environmental and Development Group** (tel. 501/625-2837, www.belizeability.com).

CROOKED TREE

Crooked Tree is only a 33-mile drive from Belize City, or a little over an hour by bus. The island village and the wildlife sanctuary are primary destinations for serious bird-watchers. Other visitors will enjoy paddling in the water, hiking numerous trails, or reveling at the annual cashew festival. Most visitors to the area can also enjoy the simple pleasure of mingling with the islanders, the majority of whom are of Kriol descent and were born and raised here. Walking through the village will reveal the simple farming and fishing community lifestyle they lead. Most villagers are related by blood or marriage, making it "one big family" in every sense of the phrase.

The Crooked Tree area itself is a network of inland lagoons, swamps, and waterways. The sanctuary also encompasses the freshwater lagoon that surrounds the area. The Crooked Tree Lagoon is up to a mile wide and more than 20 miles long. Along its banks lies the village of Crooked Tree, settled in the 1750s during the early days of the logwood era. This island, surrounded by fresh water, was once accessible only by boats traveling up the Belize River and Black Creek; the waterways were used to float the logs out to the sea. It wasn't until 1981 that the three-mile-long causeway leading into the village was built, bringing cars, buses, and other modern conveniences to the village.

Crooked Tree Village

The village is divided into three neighborhoods: **Crooked Tree, Pine Ridge,** and **Stain,** with a total population of about 1,000. Villagers

ANNUAL CROOKED TREE CASHEW FESTIVAL

The namesake of this relaxed inland island village is the cashew tree, which grows prolifically throughout the area. The unique nut has always contributed to the community's economy, especially for its women, who have been able to secure additional income for their households by selling cashew products. The situation is even better today, as the products are more often sold directly to local consumers and travelers than to distributors in Belize City, as they were in the past.

To celebrate the bent branches and their heavy fruit, the people of Crooked Tree Village throw a big cashew harvest festival the second weekend in May. It's a fun hometown fair with regional arts, music, folklore, dance, and crafts. And, of course, it's a chance to sample delicious cashew wine, cashew jellies, stewed cashews ... you get the picture.

Seek out the demonstrations showing how the cashew nut is processed—it's interesting stuff. The fruit, or the cashew "apple," is either red or yellow, with the seed hanging from the bottom of the apple. The meat of the apple can be stewed or made into jam or wine, while the seedpod is roasted in an open fire on the ground. Roasting the cashew stabilizes the highly acidic oil and at the same time makes the pod brittle enough to crack. The nut is partially cooked during this step in the processing. The seeds are then raked so they cool evenly and quickly.

The cashews are then cracked by hand, one at a time. Those who handle the nuts wear gloves, as the shell contains a highly irritating poison that for most people causes blisters and inflammation. Processing removes all the poison.

operate farms, raise livestock, and have a small fishery. Visitors will find the village spread out on the island, with more cattle trails, half roads, and fence line than roads. There are a few well-grazed athletic fields, five churches, a couple of eateries, a nurse-staffed clinic, and scores of stilted wooden houses, each with its own tank to catch rainwater. It's a tranquil community with children playing football and softball, biking around, racing horses, or whacking a ball around the cricket pitch.

◑ Crooked Tree Wildlife Sanctuary

At the **Crooked Tree Wildlife Sanctuary,** 16,400 acres of waterways, logwood swamps, and lagoon provide habitat for a diverse array of hundreds of resident and migratory birds all year long.

The sanctuary was established by the Belize Audubon Society to protect its most famous inhabitant, the jabiru stork—the largest flying bird in the western hemisphere, with a wingspan of up to eight feet. Multitudes of other birds (285 species, at last count) find the sanctuary a safe resting spot during the dry season, with enormous food resources along the shorelines and in the trees. (During my visit, I saw beautiful vermillion fly catchers and a white ibis, among many others.) After a rain, thousands of minuscule frogs, no more than an inch long, seem to drop from the sky; they're fair game for the agami heron, snowy egret, and great egret, quick hunters with long beaks. A fairly large bird, the snail kite uses its particular beak to hook meat out of the apple snails.

Two varieties of ducks—the black-bellied whistling duck and the Muscovy—nest in trees along the swamp. All five species of kingfishers live in the sanctuary, and you can see ospreys and black-collared hawks diving for their morning catch.

Black Creek, with its forests of large trees, provides homes to monkeys, Morelet's crocodiles, coatimundis, turtles, and iguanas. A profusion of wild ocher pokes up from the water, covered with millions of pale pink snail eggs. Grazing Brahma cattle wade into the shallows

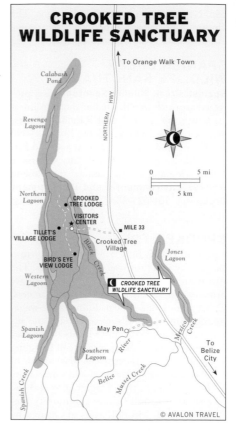

of the lagoon to munch on the *tum tum* (water lilies), a delicacy that keeps them fat and fit when the grasses turn brown in the dry season.

Although several organizations had a financial hand in founding the park, the **Belize Audubon Society** (tel. 501/223-5004, www.belizeaudubon.org) runs the show, with the continued help of devoted volunteers. Sign in at the small **visitors center** (a green building on the right just as you enter the village, 8am-4:30pm daily, US$5 per person) at the end of the causeway. You will always find a knowledgeable curator willing to answer questions about the flora and fauna of the sanctuary. It's possible to explore the area in a rented canoe or kayak, motor through on a guided tour, or hike the system of boardwalks through lowland savanna and logwood forests; observation towers provide wide views across the lagoons.

Hunting and fishing are not permitted.

Crooked Tree Lagoon

The best way to experience **Crooked Tree Lagoon** is by boat, and there are all kinds available at each hotel. The **Belize Audubon Society** (tel. 501/223-5004, www.belize-audubon.org) will be happy to have a guide and boat waiting for you when you arrive at Crooked Tree; the best days to find a full staff are Wednesday-Friday. All accommodations in the village can arrange birding and village tours. Birding is possible year-round, but peak times are February-April.

Chau Hiix Ruins

The **Chau Hiix** archaeological site is being studied nearby. Archaeologists have made some startling discoveries, including a ball court and ball-court marker, along with small artifacts. Preliminary studies indicate the site was occupied from 1200 BC to AD 1500. Chau Hiix is located south of Crooked Tree on **Sapodilla Lagoon** and is accessible by canoe.

Accommodations and Food

There are several options in low-key Crooked Tree as the area continues to gain popularity, starting with **Tillet's Village Lodge** (tel. 501/671-7100, www.tilletvillage.com, US$40-80). The famous Sam Tillet—renowned as one of the premier Belizean naturalists—died in 2007, but his family is carrying on the tradition. The lodge is located in the middle of the village, not on the water, and the guest rooms are small and plain but clean and with private baths and tiled floors. Nature walks are US$15, and you can also go horseback riding or do a "jungle survival" trip.

As you approach the island on the causeway (on the shoreline off to your left), you'll see Crooked Tree's most upscale property: **Bird's Eye View Lodge** (tel. 501/225-7027 or 501/203-2040, www.birdseyeviewbelize.com, US$80-120 d). This hotel stands above the rest

in modernity and service, and that is reflected in its higher rates. The 20 guest rooms all have private baths and various comforts, including air-conditioning. Camping (US$10) is also available. The rooftop bar and patio is a nice spot to take in the breeze and bird-watch, even after your four-hour daybreak bird-watching boat cruise on the lagoon. Meals are US$12 for breakfast and lunch; dinner is US$15. Boat rentals, tours, and airport pickups can be arranged. Boat tours for up to three people cost about US$125; ask about village tours and cashew-making tours in season (Mar.-June).

Not far off is **Da Hibiscus Cabanas** (tel. 501/661-7034 or 501/668-7491, www.dahibiscuscabanas.com, US$80), with four small but clean guest rooms set in a long stand-alone wooden cabana to the back of a well-kept yard. Guest rooms include a full-size bed, a small bathroom, a fan, a TV, air-conditioning and a porch. Friendly owner Rose Kelly recently retired from her life in Nevada and moved back to her native village.

On the shore of the lagoon north of the causeway, **Crooked Tree Lodge** (tel. 501/626-3820, www.crookedtreelodgebelize.com, US$40-60) is a small, well-landscaped, and quiet retreat of 11.5 acres with six stilted en suite wooden cabanas, including a bigger one for families (sleeps up to 7, US$120). Camping (US$10) is possible, and pets and children are welcome. Three daily meals are available at additional cost. Wide-ranging boat and birding tours are available with local guides. There is wireless Internet, a restaurant, and a small bar, all on the lagoon's edge.

The lagoon-front **Jacana Inn** (tel. 501/604-8025 or 501/620-9472, jacanainn@yahoo.com, US$50 d) has 13 ground-floor guest rooms with queen beds, mini fridges, private baths with cold showers, fans, and Internet access. The building isn't much to look at, thanks to a second-floor extension left under construction, but being steps from the lagoon at this price is a highlight. There are bikes and canoes for rent as well as in-room meals on request.

In the village, dine at **Triple J's** or **Carrie's Kitchen** (10am-9pm Mon.-Thurs., 10am-11pm

Fri.-Sat., US$4-5), a cute little spot with plenty of seating and local Kriol dishes. Both restaurants are found by walking into Crooked Tree Village, although the latter may require a drive or bike ride.

Getting There

To reach Crooked Tree by car, drive north on the Northern Highway to Mile 33 and turn left. Continue until the dirt road turns into the three-mile-long earthen causeway that leads into Crooked Tree. You can also catch the **Jex Bus** (34 Regent St. W., tel. 501/663-3301 or 501/663-2740, US$5) in downtown Belize City to Crooked Tree. The bus leaves promptly at 10:55am Monday-Friday, arriving in Crooked Tree at 12:30pm; it is parked an hour prior to departure. You can also hop on any of the buses heading north from the main Novelo bus station to Corozal; starting early in the morning, request a stop at the Crooked Tree junction and then get a ride from there into the village.

From Crooked Tree back into Belize City, the Jex buses depart mornings only at 5am, 6am, and 6:45am Monday-Friday, and 6:45am only on Saturday; verify the times before departure. Other options include catching an hourly bus back toward Belize City from the Crooked Tree junction on the highway, which is an easy option, or hire a taxi or local tour operator. Check with the Belize Audubon Society (tel. 501/223-5004, www.belizeaudubon.org) for additional transportation information, rates, and an updated schedule.

Along the Western Highway

Driving west from Belize City, the Western Highway passes from wetlands to pine savanna, with the Maya Mountains draped across the horizon through your windshield. Most of this region is drained by the Sibun and Caves Branch Rivers, which empty out into a large lowland wetland before arriving at the sea. This central chunk of Belize is mostly wild, dotted by a handful of small villages, rainforest lodges, natural attractions, and parks. The most popular of these is the Belize Zoo.

The milepost markers between Belize City and San Ignacio will help you find your way around the countryside. If you're driving, you can match the markers as you go by setting your odometer to zero as you turn onto Cemetery Road at the western edge of Belize City.

The Western Highway eventually leads to Belmopan, the smallest and most unassuming national capital in Central America.

FREETOWN SIBUN

Three miles south of Hattieville, as you make a left turn by the Hattieville Police Station (a yellow building), this small village (community tel. 501/209-6006) has a population of less than 100, if that. Runaway slaves founded the village back in the day, and its population used to peak around 2,000 during big logging runs. Today, you can find campsites, canoe rentals, and hiking trails. Taxis to the village are plentiful from the traffic circle in Hattieville.

◖ THE BELIZE ZOO

Established in 1983, **The Belize Zoo** (Mile 29, Western Hwy., tel. 501/822-8000, www.belizezoo.org, 8:30am-4:30pm daily, US$15) is set on 29 acres of tropical savanna and exhibits more than 125 animals, all native to Belize.

Zoo director Sharon Matola's accidental career began when, as a former lion tamer, she agreed to manage a backyard collection of local animals for a nature-film company next door. After only five months' work on the project, funds were severely reduced, and it became evident that the group of animal "film stars" would have to be disbanded. Sharon says that not only had these wild cats, birds, anteaters, and snakes become her friends and companions but that semi-tame animals, dependent on people for care, could not just be released back

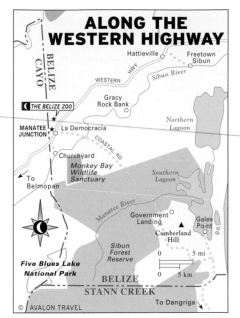

ALONG THE WESTERN HIGHWAY

BELIZE CAYO

Hattieville
Freetown
Sibun

WESTERN HWY
Sibun River

THE BELIZE ZOO

Gracy
Rock Bank

Northern
Lagoon

MANATEE JUNCTION
La Democracia

COASTAL RD

Churchyard

Monkey Bay
Wildlife
Sanctuary

Southern
Lagoon

To
Belmopan

Manatee River

Government
Landing

Gales
Point

Cumberland
Hill

Sibun
Forest
Reserve

0   5 mi

0   5 km

Five Blues Lake
National Park

BELIZE

STANN CREEK

To Dangriga

© AVALON TRAVEL

In collaboration with the Panthera organization, the government of Belize, and the U.S. Fish and Wildlife Service, the Belize Zoo also runs the only problem **jaguar rehabilitation** program and in situ jaguar research program in the world. Problem jaguars, which prey on livestock and domestic animals, are trapped and brought to the zoo for behavior modification training—instead of a bullet. In difficult cases, the animals are transferred to zoos in the United States; the Milwaukee and Philadelphia zoos have received problem cats from Belize.

In 2010, Hurricane Richard tore through the zoo, destroying many of the cages and structures. With superhuman efforts, the zoo staff and an army of volunteers participated in immediate reconstruction. And it was literally an army—in addition to Belizean volunteers, tour operators, students, ambassadors, and Belize Zoo fans from abroad, U.S. Special Forces and British Forces Belize took part. The zoo was up and running again in only six weeks, but it still has a lot of work to do. The zoo continues to do amazing work with Belizean wildlife, but needs all the help—and visitors—it can get.

The Belize Tropical Education Center

The Belize Tropical Education Center (tel. 501/832-2004, tec@belizezoo.org), located across the street from the zoo, was created to promote environmental education and scientific research. Meetings are held here for zoological news, reports, and educational seminars attended and given by people involved in zoology from around the world. The center is equipped with a classroom, a library, a kitchen and dining area, and dormitories that can accommodate as many as 30 people (US$30 pp, includes breakfast and dinner). Great nature trails weave through the 84-acre site, and birdwatchers can avail themselves of a bird-viewing deck. Also available are canoe trips, nocturnal zoo tours (a real treat), and natural history lectures. Cafeteria-style meals cooked for the zoo staff are available for purchase.

into the wild. As an alternative, she thought, "This country has never had a zoo. Perhaps if I offered the chance for Belizeans to see these unique animals, their existence here could be permanently established."

A zoo was born. From the very beginning, the amount of local interest in the zoo was incredible. The majority of the people in Belize live in urban areas, and their knowledge of the local fauna is minimal. The Belize Zoo offers Belizeans and visitors alike the opportunity to see the country's native animals. Today, the Belize Zoo receives over 10,000 Belizean schoolchildren every year as part of its progressive education programs.

The zoo keeps only orphaned animals, those injured and rehabilitated, those born in the zoo, and those received as gifts from other zoos. The environment is as natural as possible, with thick native vegetation, and each animal lives in its own wildlife compound. Displays include Tapir Town; ask about Lucky Boy, a beautiful black jaguar the zoo helped rescue and rehabilitate.

Getting There

The zoo is at Mile 29 on the Western Highway. It is included in many day tours from Belize City and often as a stop during airport transfer to or from your lodge in the western or southern parts of Belize. Independent travelers can easily jump off the bus from Belize City or Cayo; bus fare from Belize City is US$1-2.

MANATEE JUNCTION

Driving west, note the junction with **Manatee Road** to the left at about Mile 29. Look for a service station and motel of sorts on the southeast corner of the junction; its Petrofuel sign makes an especially good landmark at night, when the sign glows with bright colors. This improved dirt road or "Coastal Highway" is the shortcut to Gales Point, Dangriga, and the Southern Highway. It's always a good idea to top off your tank, stock up on cold drinks, and ask for current road conditions here. Heavy rains can cause washouts on a lot of these "highways." This is a drive best done in daylight because of the picturesque views of rainforest, Mayan villages, and the Maya Mountains in the distance. Your best bet, however, is to drive the Hummingbird Highway to Dangriga and the south to avoid roughing up your car.

GALES POINT

This tiny, unique Creole settlement occupies a thin two-mile-long peninsula jutting north into the Southern Lagoon. Gales Point is 15 miles north of Dangriga or 25 miles southwest of Belize City, but getting here makes it feel farther. Depending on which accounts you read, the 400 or so modern inhabitants are descended from either logwood cutters or escaped slaves known as "maroons" who settled here in the 1700s. Gales Point is a traditional Creole cultural stronghold. If you're lucky, your visit to Gales Point will coincide with the full moon, when the entire village often participates in a roaming call-and-response drumming and dance circle. In the weeks before Christmas, the frequency of *sambai* drumming events increases, reaching a crescendo on Christmas Day and December 26 with a unique village-wide

celebration called *bram*. Gales Point is also known for its homemade cashew wine.

The **Southern Lagoon**, which surrounds Gales Point on three sides, is part of an extensive estuary bordered by thick mangroves. Their tangled roots provide the perfect breeding grounds for sport fish, crabs, shrimp, lobsters, and a host of other marinelife. Rich beds of sea grass line the bottom of the lagoon and support a population of manatees. These gentle mammals are often seen basking on the surface of the water or coming up for air, which they must do about every four minutes. This is a popular spot to observe the manatees, often spotted close to a warm spring-fed hole in the lagoon. Tours to see manatees can be arranged through any of the Gales Point accommodations; trips are also available to see birds and caves in the region and to go fishing.

In July 2008 Gales Point experienced the most devastating floods in its history, as the entire lagoon rose and covered much of the peninsula, a phenomenon that did not occur even during massive Hurricane Hattie in 1961. It has since recovered and remains just as remote as ever.

Accommodations

There are some loose homestay programs and places to camp in the village; ask around the village for the latest information. **Gentle's Cool Spot** (tel. 501/668-0102 or 501/666-9847) is one local service that provides traditional *fiyah haat* (fire hearth) cooking plus a few stuffy clapboard guest rooms (US$18-28). Gentle's veranda is a favorite gathering place for locals, and Gentle also provides tours.

Manatee Lodge (tel. 501/532-2400 or 501/662-2154, U.S. tel. 877/462-6283, www.manateelodge.com, US$85) is at the very northern tip of the peninsula and caters to birders, sportfishers, and independent nature-loving travelers and families. The eight guest rooms have nice wood furnishings, private baths, 24-hour electricity, and a veranda with views of the surrounding lagoon and sunsets behind the Maya Mountains; rooms sleep up to four. The lodge offers access to a wildlife habitat completely different from the rest of Belize, living in the shallow brackish water and mangroves of the Southern Lagoon. The number of shorebirds and waterfowl is impressive, and to encourage guests to see local wildlife, the lodge provides each room with a canoe. Binoculars and bug repellent are a must. Children under age six stay free, and children ages 6-12 are half price. Moderately priced and delicious home-cooked Creole and continental meals are available; so are transfers and multi-day packages.

Getting There

To get to Gales Point by car, either choose the Manatee Highway, a.k.a. the Coastal Road, and expect rough muddy roads if it's raining, or take the Hummingbird Highway, which is about 25 miles longer but smoother (for most of the way, anyway). The most enjoyable—and expensive—way to reach Gales Point is the 90-minute boat ride from Belize City, which winds through bird-filled canals, rivers, and lagoons, and you may spot crocodiles, manatees, or dolphins. Manatee Lodge can arrange a boat transfer, but it is very expensive; it's worth it if you have a group. There used to be several weekly buses from Belize City, but they were not running regularly at last check; call Manatee Lodge for current schedules or possible rides. You could also reach out to Dangriga-based and Gales Point native Brother David of **CD's Transfer** (1163 3rd St., tel. 501/502-3489 or cell 501/602-3077, breddadavid@gmail.com) to negotiate a simple ride to and from Gales Point.

MONKEY BAY WILDLIFE SANCTUARY

Monkey Bay Wildlife Sanctuary (tel. 501/822-8032, www.belizestudyabroad.net) comprises tropical forest and riparian and savanna habitats stretching from the Western Highway down to the Sibun River, which flows from the Maya Mountains through the coastal savanna on its path to the Caribbean Sea. The 3,300-acre wildlands of Monkey Bay include the natural habitat of nearly all the animals represented at the Belize Zoo, just east on the Western Highway.

This is a fantastic retreat—for student groups, families, naturalists, and paddlers alike (though most of the sanctuary's business is with study-abroad and service groups). The sanctuary maintains field stations in the Mountain Pine Ridge and Tobacco Caye. The main campus is home to exotic mammal species, including tapirs, pumas, and jaguars, as well as Morelet's crocodiles. More than 250 species of birds have been recorded. The sanctuary borders the Sibun River biological corridor and contains documented remains of ancient Maya settlements and ceremonial caves. A trail system carries you through it all; you can hike, rent a canoe, or hire a caving guide—this is serious spelunking country as well. One option is a three-night camping expedition, where you'll hike to Five Blues Lake National Park. Another is a canoe trip on the Sibun River (US$35 pp), which you can combine with a caving expedition (US$50 pp).

You'll find two miles of trails and good swimming at nearby Sibun River. With the government's 1992 declaration of the 2,250-acre Monkey Bay Nature Reserve across the river, there now exists a wildlands corridor between the sanctuary and the Manatee Forest Reserve to the south.

Accommodations

Some travelers find themselves intrigued enough by the goings-on at this environmental education center and tropical watershed research station that they opt to stay in one of Monkey Bay's primitively rustic guest rooms longer than they had planned. The accommodations share the grounds with a screened-in dining area and a shared barnlike library and study space (more than 500 titles are available for reference, with lots of local information).

Choose from a campground in a grove of pine trees with sturdy wooden tent platforms (US$8 pp) or dormitories (US$19 pp); they all share common composting toilets and solar showers. You can also stay in one of the primitive wooden field station rooms in the central building (US$27). Including all the bunks in the dormitory, there are 50 beds here. Freshly prepared meals are available, as are a range of learning and adventure activities throughout Belize. There's a lovely backyard peppered with hammocks and a path leading to the river.

Monkey Bay offers various cultural learning programs that include homestays with Maya and Creole communities at Maya Centre or Crooked Tree Village; it also has a curriculum of tropical watershed ecology field courses. Groups and individuals are welcome for internships and volunteer programs as well.

Food

There are a few notable restaurants clustered around Mile 31, right around where you first see the sleeping Mayan giant in the hills to the south (the hill formations in this area look like a person laying on their back). You'll first come

to the popular **Cheers** (Mile 31¼, Western Hwy., tel. 501/822-8014, www.cheersrestaurant.bz, 6am-8:30pm Mon.-Sat., 7am-7:15pm Sun.), with its interesting collection of orchids, license plates, and T-shirts. Oh, and the food is excellent. Ask about their cabana accommodations.

A bit farther, just past the turnoff for Monkey Bay, is **Amigo's** (Mile 31 2/3 Western Hwy., tel. 501/802-8000, adellalockwood@ yahoo.com, 8am-9pm daily, US$5-9), another friendly, screened-in bar and restaurant with Belizean and continental food, from salads to burgers and more.

Getting There

Monkey Bay Wildlife Sanctuary is located at Mile 31 on the Western Highway; look for the entrance sign on the left side of the highway. The entrance is a stone's throw from Cheers Restaurant.

THE NORTHERN CAYES

Once the favorite hideout and playground of pirates, the Northern Cayes are Belize's greatest tourism draw, and with good reason: postcard-perfect islands, quick access to the Barrier Reef and Hol Chan Marine Reserve, a dizzying array of outdoor activities, and enough lodging, restaurants, and entertainment options to fit celebrity and backpacker budgets alike.

© LEBAWIT GIRMA

HIGHLIGHTS

LOOK FOR 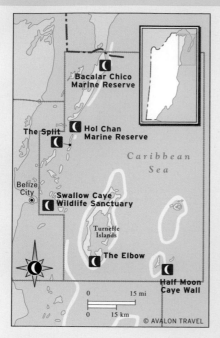 TO FIND RECOMMENDED SIGHTS, ACTIVITIES, DINING, AND LODGING.

NORTHERN CAYES

largest barrier reef in the world is less than a mile offshore from both Ambergris Caye and Caye Caulker. Spending a day here is akin to swimming in a giant aquarium (page 69).

Bacalar Chico Marine Reserve: This UNESCO World Heritage Site, located at the northern tip of Ambergris Caye, boasts spectacular snorkeling and diving (page 69).

The Split: Caye Caulker's best swimming beach is a unique scene where visitors and locals alike sun themselves on concrete slabs, snorkel, or dance at the on-site bar (page 101).

Swallow Caye Wildlife Sanctuary: This protected area is home to the endangered West Indian manatee and is one of several worthwhile excursions offered from the Northern Cayes (page 103).

The Elbow: Advanced divers visit this steep drop-off where swift currents collide hoping to spot deep-water predatory fish as well as a wall of interesting sponges (page 125).

Half Moon Caye Wall: A birder's paradise, this beautiful crescent-shaped island is home to more than 4,000 red-footed boobies and 120 other species. It's also one of the best diving spots in Belize (page 128).

Hol Chan Marine Reserve: The second-

Located close to Belize City, the Northern Cayes are ideal for adventurers short on getaway time. This cluster of islands includes the iconic Great Blue Hole and two of Belize's three atolls—Turneffe and Lighthouse Reef—for world-class diving, snorkeling, and fishing. And that's not all: as the most tourist-ready region in all of Belize, the Northern Cayes host an estimated 70 percent of visitors for their first Belizean experience. This fusion of local culture with a constant stream of international visitors makes for one lively scene.

Avid divers tend to stay on one of the atolls to minimize travel time to top dive sites; otherwise, it's a two-hour boat ride each way from Ambergris Caye or Caye Caulker. Ambergris, generally referred to as San Pedro, attracts those seeking constant activity—there is incessant hustle and bustle, not to mention pretty hotels and pools, chic lounges, fine dining, and plenty of bars and nightlife. Smaller Caye Caulker attracts the laid-back, off-the-beaten-path traveler, those who seek immersion in local island life, exploring sand-only streets on foot or bicycle (there are no cars here!), and lesser-known sights. There's an amusing sibling rivalry between the two cayes—larger Ambergris Caye considers Caye Caulker slow

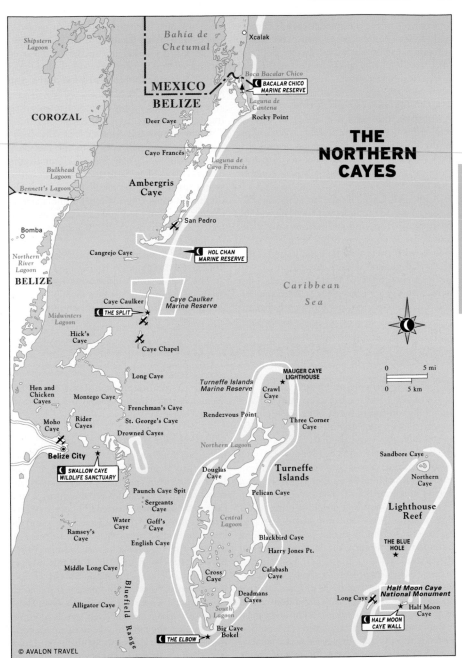

Shipstern
Lagoon

*Bahía de
Chetumal*

Xcalak

Boca Bacalar Chico

🌙 **BACALAR CHICO
MARINE RESERVE**

MEXICO

BELIZE

COROZAL

Deer Caye

*Laguna de
Cantena*

Rocky Point

Cayo Francés

*Laguna de
Cayo Francés*

Bulkhead
Lagoon

Bennett's Lagoon

**Ambergris
Caye**

San Pedro

Bomba

Northern
River
Lagoon

Cangrejo Caye

🌙 **HOL CHAN
MARINE RESERVE**

BELIZE

Caribbean

Sea

**THE
NORTHERN
CAYES**

*Caye Caulker
Marine Reserve*

Midwinters
Lagoon

Caye Caulker

🌙 **THE SPLIT**

Hick's
Caye

Caye Chapel

Long Caye

*Turneffe Islands
Marine Reserve*

**MAUGER CAYE
LIGHTHOUSE**

Crawl
Caye

0   5 mi

0   5 km

Hen and
Chicken
Cayes

Montego Caye

Frenchman's Caye

St. George's Caye

Drowned Cayes

Moho
Caye

Rider
Cayes

Rendezvous Point

Three Corner
Caye

Sandbore Caye

Belize City

🌙 **SWALLOW CAYE
WILDLIFE SANCTUARY**

Northern Lagoon

Douglas
Caye

Pelican Caye

**Turneffe
Islands**

Northern
Caye

**Lighthouse
Reef**

Paunch Caye Spit

Sergeants
Caye

Goff's
Caye

Water
Caye

Ramsey's
Caye

English Caye

*Central
Lagoon*

Blackbird Caye

Harry Jones Pt.

**THE BLUE
HOLE**
★

Middle Long Caye

Cross
Caye

Calabash
Caye

Deadmans
Cayes

Long Caye

*Half Moon Caye
National Monument*

★ Half Moon
Caye

Alligator Caye

*Bluefield
Range*

*South
Lagoon*

Big Caye
Bokel

🌙 **THE ELBOW**

🌙 **HALF MOON
CAYE WALL**

© AVALON TRAVEL

and boring, while the smaller caye is content with the lack of noise, paved roads, and crowds. In reality, each has a varied slice of Belize to offer, excellent water sports, and island fun, and neither is a wasted visit.

PLANNING YOUR TIME

A common dilemma is whether to stay on Ambergris Caye or Caye Caulker, each unique in rhythm and scenery. The good news is that they are a mere 30-minute water-taxi hop away from each other, with tours available from either base.

Ambergris Caye's foodie treasures and luxury accommodations attract travelers seeking both excellent diving and nonstop nightlife. San Pedro is considered the "trendy" part of Belize, with more resorts, bars, lounges, eateries, and general day-to-day activities than most of the country. There's a steady buzz here, and events take place year-round, attracting not only visitors but also Belizeans

from the city seeking a quick, fun getaway. **Hol Chan Marine Reserve** is the most popular dive and snorkel site in Belize. Located on and around the northern tip of Ambergris Caye, **Bacalar Chico National Park and Marine Reserve** hosts an incredibly diverse array of wildlife and offers excellent snorkeling and diving.

Caye Caulker's slower yet rhythmic Caribbean vibe will appeal to the laid-back visitor while still offering excellent diving opportunities. **The Split** is the favorite go-to swimming and sunset rendezvous spot on the island. **Swallow Caye Wildlife Sanctuary**, at the north end of the Drowned Cayes, is a protected area with nearly 9,000 acres of sea and mangroves to explore.

Outside these two cayes are the upscale **Turneffe Islands,** with diving opportunities at **The Elbow** and **Lighthouse Reef Atoll,** home to the some of the best dive spots in the world—**Half Moon Caye** and **Long Caye.**

San Pedro and Ambergris Caye

Ambergris Caye is Belize's largest island, just south of the Mexican Yucatán mainland and stretching southward for 24 miles into Belizean waters. Ambergris ("AM-bur-giss") is 35 miles east of Belize City and about 0.75 miles west of the Belize Barrier Reef. The island was formed by an accumulation of coral fragments and silt from the Río Hondo as it emptied from what is now northern Belize. The caye is made up of mangrove swamps, a dozen lagoons, a plateau, and a series of low sand ridges. The largest lagoon, fed by 15 creeks, is 2.5-mile-long **Laguna de San Pedro,** on the western side of the village.

San Pedro Town sits on a sand ridge at the southern end of the island, the only actual town on the island and the most-visited destination in Belize. It is chock-full of accommodations, restaurants, bars, golf carts, and services. San Pedro is also the most expensive part of Belize, with prices for some basic goods and foods

double the mainland prices and sometimes even more than similar services and restaurants in the United States.

ORIENTATION

Whether arriving by air or sea, your trip to Ambergris begins in San Pedro Town—the heart of the island's activity, where most of the restaurants, bars, nightlife, shopping, and a range of hotels are clustered. There are three streets running north-south and paralleling the beach on the island's east side. Residents still refer to them by their historic names: **Front Street** (Barrier Reef Drive), **Middle Street** (Pescador Drive), and **Back Street** (Angel Coral Street). Another landmark is at the north end of town, where the San Pedro River flows through a navigable cut. This spot is often referred to as **"the cut"** or "the bridge," referring to the toll bridge that replaced the hand-drawn ferry. Past the bridge are some exclusive resorts,

SAN PEDRO AND AMBERGRIS CAYE

MEXICO
BELIZE

Boca Bacalar Chico

BACALAR CHICO MARINE RESERVE

Laguna de Cantena

Rocky Point

Deer Caye

Basil Jones

Punta Azul

Cayo Pajaros

Laguna de Cayo Francés

Palermo Point

Blackadore Caye

Ambergris Caye

MEXICO ROCKS

CATALAN ROCKS

Inner Channel

Punta Arena

Buena Vista Point

Laguna de San Pedro

San Pedro

Caribbean Sea

ENTRANCE THROUGH THE REEF

Congrejo Caye

HOL CHAN MARINE RESERVE

0   5 mi

0   5 km

© AVALON TRAVEL

hotels, and lounges. You'll also hear the term "south of town," referring to the continually developing area south of the airstrip and south of San Pedro Town, accessed by Coconut Drive and starting past Ramon's Village, where more posh retreats can be found, along with some casual and lively outdoor bars.

SIGHTS
Hol Chan Marine Reserve

Once a traditional fishing ground, back when San Pedro was a sleepy village of a few hundred people, **Hol Chan Marine Reserve** (www.hol-chanbelize.org, US$12.50 pp) is the most popular dive and snorkel site in Belize, with tens of thousands of visitors each year. The site is four miles south of San Pedro and makes for an affordable morning or afternoon trip. In town is a small visitors center on Caribeña Street with

information on the reserve. Nearly all tour operators on Ambergris and Caye Caulker offer trips to the Hol Chan cut.

Once you visit, you'll quickly understand the popularity of the reserve—and why it is important to help preserve it. Established as a marine park in 1987, when fishing was banned, Hol Chan boasts an amazing diversity of species. The reserve focuses on creating a sustainable link between tourism and conservation, protecting the coral reef while allowing visitors to experience and learn about the marinelife living here.

Along with a stop at Hol Chan is one at **Shark Ray Alley**—a nearby zone of the reserve where stingrays and six-foot-long nurse sharks have gathered over the years thanks to anglers who often cleaned their catch in this area. Used to getting their scraps of fish, the nurse sharks anticipate the boats and are used to humans—although it is best to keep a safe distance. The thrill of jumping in waters surrounded by these creatures is something to experience at least once.

While you may see a guide or two pose with stingrays or stroke a nurse shark, note that officially it is illegal to feed or touch the fish. Even if your guide tells you differently, and even if you see other groups caressing the nurse sharks and rays, this is against the reserve rules and regulations and against all normal protocol for interacting with wildlife, as it should be. That said, San Pedro anglers and tour guides have been feeding the animals in this spot every day for over 15 years, so some argue that an exception should be made, or that there is some educational benefit to interacting with the animals. Best to leave only bubbles, I say.

Bacalar Chico Marine Reserve

Located on and around the northern tip of Ambergris Caye, **Bacalar Chico National Park and Marine Reserve** hosts an incredibly diverse array of wildlife, offers excellent snorkeling and diving, and is rich with history. The Bacalar Chico Canal is reputed to have been dug by Mayan traders between AD 700 and 900, creating Ambergris Caye by separating it from

© LEBAWIT GIRMA

the toll bridge connecting San Pedro with north Ambergris Caye

the Yucatán Peninsula. The reserve has a wide range of wildlife habitat; 194 species of birds have been sighted there. The landscape consists in part of sinkholes and cenotes created by the effects of weathering on the limestone bedrock of Ambergris Caye. On the eastern side of the reserve is **Rocky Point,** the only location in the Belize Barrier Reef Reserve System where the reef touches the shore. This is one of Belize's most important and prolific sea turtle nesting sites, home to at least 10 threatened species. In 1997, Bacalar Chico—along with the Belize Barrier Reef Reserve System—was designated a World Heritage Site by UNESCO.

Bacalar Chico also contains at least nine archaeological sites: Mayan trading, fishing, and agricultural settlements that were inhabited from at least AD 300 to 900. A 10th site just outside the reserve boundary is regarded as especially important for its remaining wall network throughout the settlement and its potential to provide missing information about the transition from the classic Mayan period to modern times. The reserve also contains

evidence of Spanish and English habitation during the colonial period, including several Spanish-period shipwrecks offshore.

There is a ranger station in the northwest area of the park with a **visitors center** (tel. 501/226-2833, http://bacalarchico.org) and displays of area history, including old glass bottles and Mayan relics found within the reserve. There is a picnic area with a barbecue and a grill.

ACCOMMODATIONS AND FOOD

The two places to stay nearest Bacalar are on a beautiful hard-packed white-sand beach 12 miles north of San Pedro. The boat ride from town takes anywhere from 30 to 40 minutes, well past the last stop on the water taxi. These options are for folks who want to feel like they are on another island, not for people who want to drive golf carts, party, and be "in the mix" (though all the standard tours are still available, probably with a little extra transportation cost).

Tranquility Bay Resort (U.S. tel. 800/843-2293, www.tranquilitybayresort.com, from

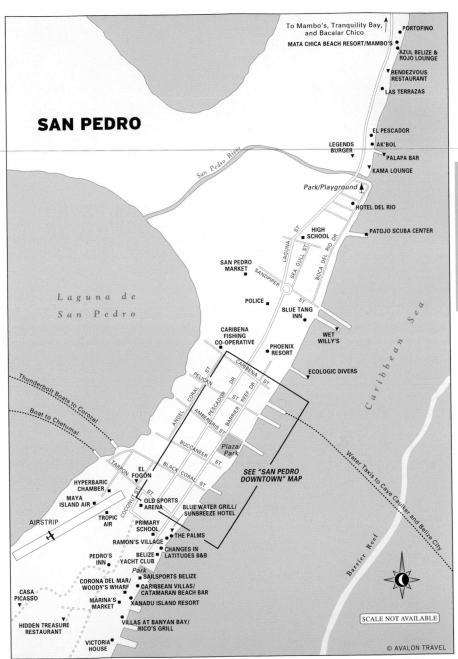

SAN PEDRO

To Mambo's, Tranquility Bay, and Bacalar Chico

PORTOFINO

MATA CHICA BEACH RESORT/MAMBO'S

AZUL BELIZE & ROJO LOUNGE

RENDEZVOUS RESTAURANT

LAS TERRAZAS

EL PESCADOR

AK'BOL

LEGENDS BURGER

PALAPA BAR

KAMA LOUNGE

San Pedro River

Park/Playground

HOTEL DEL RIO

PATOJO SCUBA CENTER

HIGH SCHOOL

LAGUNA ST

SEA GULL ST

BOCA DEL RIO DR

SAN PEDRO MARKET

SANDPIPER

POLICE

BLUE TANG INN

Laguna de San Pedro

CARIBENA FISHING CO-OPERATIVE

PHOENIX RESORT

WET WILLY'S

CARIBENA ST

PELICAN ST

CORAL ST

ANGEL ST

PESCADOR DR

AMBERGRIS ST

BARRIER REEF DR

ECOLOGIC DIVERS

Thunderbolt Boats to Corozal

Boat to Chetumal

BUCCANEER ST

Plaza/Park

SEE "SAN PEDRO DOWNTOWN" MAP

TARPON ST

EL FOGÓN

BLACK CORAL ST

COCONUT DR

HYPERBARIC CHAMBER

MAYA ISLAND AIR

OLD SPORTS ARENA

BLUE WATER GRILL/ SUNBREEZE HOTEL

AIRSTRIP

TROPIC AIR

PRIMARY SCHOOL

RAMON'S VILLAGE

THE PALMS

CHANGES IN LATITUDES B&B

PEDRO'S INN

BELIZE YACHT CLUB

Park

SAILSPORTS BELIZE

CASA PICASSO

CORONA DEL MAR/ WOODY'S WHARF

CARIBBEAN VILLAS/ CATAMARAN BEACH BAR

MARINA'S MARKET

XANADU ISLAND RESORT

HIDDEN TREASURE RESTAURANT

VILLAS AT BANYAN BAY/ RICO'S GRILL

VICTORIA HOUSE

Caribbean Sea

Water Taxis to Caye Caulker and Belize City

Barrier Reef

NORTHERN CAYES

SCALE NOT AVAILABLE

© AVALON TRAVEL

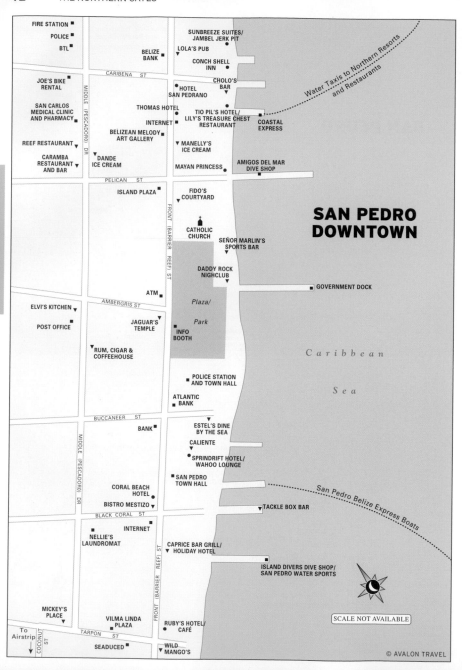

NORTHERN CAYES

FIRE STATION
POLICE
BTL
BELIZE
BANK
SUNBREEZE SUITES/
JAMBEL JERK PIT
LOLA'S PUB
CONCH SHELL
INN
CARIBENA ST
JOE'S BIKE
RENTAL
CHOLO'S
BAR
HOTEL
SAN PEDRANO
SAN CARLOS
MEDICAL CLINIC
AND PHARMACY
THOMAS HOTEL
INTERNET
TIO PIL'S HOTEL/
LILY'S TREASURE CHEST
RESTAURANT
COASTAL
EXPRESS
BELIZEAN MELODY
ART GALLERY
MANELLY'S
ICE CREAM
REEF RESTAURANT
CARAMBA
RESTAURANT
AND BAR
DANDE
ICE CREAM
MAYAN PRINCESS
AMIGOS DEL MAR
DIVE SHOP
PELICAN ST
ISLAND PLAZA
FIDO'S
COURTYARD

MIDDLE (PESCADORO) DR
FRONT (BARRIER REEF) ST

CATHOLIC
CHURCH
SEÑOR MARLIN'S
SPORTS BAR

**SAN PEDRO
DOWNTOWN**

DADDY ROCK
NIGHCLUB
ATM
AMBERGRIS ST
Plaza/
GOVERNMENT DOCK
ELVI'S KITCHEN
POST OFFICE
JAGUAR'S
TEMPLE
Park
INFO
BOOTH
RUM, CIGAR &
COFFEEHOUSE

C a r i b b e a n

POLICE STATION
AND TOWN HALL
ATLANTIC
BANK

S e a

BUCCANEER ST
BANK
ESTEL'S DINE
BY THE SEA
CALIENTE
SPRINDRIFT HOTEL/
WAHOO LOUNGE
SAN PEDRO
TOWN HALL
CORAL BEACH
HOTEL
BISTRO MESTIZO
BLACK CORAL ST
INTERNET
TACKLE BOX BAR
NELLIE'S
LAUNDROMAT

MIDDLE (PESCADORO) DR
FRONT (BARRIER REEF) ST

CAPRICE BAR GRILL/
HOLIDAY HOTEL
ISLAND DIVERS DIVE SHOP/
SAN PEDRO WATER SPORTS
MICKEY'S
PLACE
VILMA LINDA
PLAZA
RUBY'S HOTEL/
CAFÉ
To
Airstrip
COCONUT ST
TARPON ST
SEADUCED
WILD
MANGO'S

Water Taxis to Northern Resorts
and Restaurants

San Pedro Belize Express Boats

SCALE NOT AVAILABLE

© AVALON TRAVEL

THE MARCO GONZALEZ MAYAN SITE

© LEBAWIT GIRMA

Bone fragments discovered at the site are still being studied.

Those looking for a little Mayan history right on the island can find it at the Marco Gonzalez Maya Site (contact Jan Brown for a tour, 501/662-2725, www.marcogonzalezmayasite.com, US$10 site, US$8 transportation), just a 30-minute golf-cart ride from San Pedro to the south end of Ambergris Caye. Of an estimated 18 Mayan sites on the island, Marco Gonzalez was the first site to receive archeological reserve status in 2011. History and adventure buffs will enjoy private guided tours of this virgin site, currently under study, which was inhabited by the Maya for 1,600 years. Head here with Jan Brown, a passionate expat and the reserve's chairperson, as your guide.

While the site continues to be preserved, cleaned, and examined for its history of the coastal Maya, it is literally a museum in the wild.

A tour is an eco-adventure in itself, requiring careful navigation to avoid stepping on pieces of Mayan ceramics, with rainforest wildlife encounters along the way. Over the past few years, students have helped excavate parts of the site, revealing plaza structures and tombs. Human bones have been found, including skull fragments and skeletons as well as cutting tools made out of volcanic rock, thought to have been imported from Honduras and used for Mayan bloodletting rituals.

This may be the only place in the world where you can visit an ancient Maya trading city on an island and spot pieces on the site that date back to 100 BC. On the way back to San Pedro, stop along the way to enjoy the scenic views from the south side, some of the most beautiful on Ambergris Caye.

US$139) is the only resort on the island where you can snorkel directly from the beach to the reef. Every evening, tarpon, barracuda, and eagle rays swim under the lights of the dockside restaurant, appropriately named The Aquarium. They have a budget room just off the beach, along with seven brightly painted two-bedroom cabanas and three one-bedrooms with lofts, lining one of the nicest white-sand beaches on the island. Bedrooms are air-conditioned, and each cabana is equipped with a refrigerator and a microwave. The cabins have Belizean hardwoods, Mexican tiles, and spectacular ocean views. They offer free use of kayaks, which can cover a lot of ground at this site, and there is an on-site dive shop and a handful of fishing, snorkeling, scuba, and sailing trips.

The Turtleman's House (tel. 501/664-9661, http://turtlemanshouse.com) is a stilted shack above the water built out of salvaged material, much of it pieces of destroyed docks that wash ashore after hurricanes, by Greg "Turtleman" Smith, a resident of this beach for three decades and the man who is partly responsible for the creation of the reserve and protection of its wildlife. At first glance, US$80 a night with a three-night minimum seems overpriced, but you're paying for the location and the unique, albeit rustic, experience of being completely away from it all, with the Barrier Reef at your doorstep. Plus the meals are cheap, and you'll have the sunrise all to yourself. Guests sleep in the primitive room with a solar bag shower and sea grass compost bucket toilet, then join Greg, his wife, Rosemary, and their children in their home on the island, 50 feet away, for delicious home-cooked meals and cinnamon buns. Guests can also take advantage of Tranquility Bay's restaurant and dive shop, a stone's throw down the beach.

GETTING THERE

Most Ambergris dive shops and a few tour companies that do dive and snorkel trips to Bacalar Chico are based in San Pedro. Start with **Seaduced by Belize** (tel. 501/226-2254, www.seaducedbybelize.com, US$105 pp) and **Searious Adventures** (tel. 501/226-4202, www.seariousadventures.com, US$90), or arrange a trip with **Tranquility Bay Resort** (U.S. tel. 800/843-2293, www.tranquilitybayresort.com) or **The Turtleman's House** (tel. 501/664-9661, http://turtlemanshouse.com).

SPORTS AND RECREATION
Beaches

It is often said that you shouldn't expect the wide-open uninterrupted beaches seen in neighboring Mexico and other Caribbean destinations. The comparison is one between apples and oranges: Belize is unique in having a barrier reef, and one that's a short distance from the coastline, stopping any wave action from reaching the shores and leading to the buildup of sea grass in the shallow waters along the beach. This is a small sacrifice for a nearby natural wonder. To say there is no beach whatsoever is a stretch. It does require a little trekking away from San Pedro Town to find the better ones; the town's beachfront is nothing more than a long sandy pedestrian sidewalk, although you can still feel sand beneath your toes, and the ocean views are as beautiful as ever.

The best swimming and sunning section in San Pedro Town is directly in front of Ramon's Village Resort. This is where most head for a swim and a snorkel. Numerous docks also give access where swimming might otherwise be difficult.

Beach enthusiasts have more choices just a short 15 to 30 minutes from town. A few of the hotels and bars on Ambergris Caye's north and south ends have wider, softer white-sand areas and better swimming entry points, although patches of sea grass are ever present.

One option is to head north of the bridge (by water taxi, bike, or cart, depending on how far you are going), and park yourself at one of the several beachfront bars or resorts—Palapa Bar is a great spot, as is Portofino Resort, well worth the lengthier 30-minute boat ride with its boutique yet laid-back atmosphere, infinity pool, and calming views. Grab a meal or a cocktail and you can use the docks and dip your toes in that sand and clear water. One

This sandy stretch by Ramon's Village is the best swimming beach in town.

of the best natural swimming and snorkeling beaches is also 12 miles north of San Pedro at Tranquility Bay Resort.

Going south, lovely stretches shaded by dozens of palm trees are by Victoria House, one of the most gorgeous resorts on the island, or by Catamaran Beach Bar at Caribbean Villas. Start at any of these and hop your way along the beach.

Diving and Snorkeling

Almost every hotel on Ambergris either employs local dive shops or has its own on-site shop and dive masters. They offer similar services: resort courses, PADI or NAUI certification classes, day trips, and snorkel trips to Hol Chan Marine Reserve, Bacalar Chico, and others. Some also offer night dives, and a few have nitrox capabilities. Ultimately, what makes the difference is the experience of the instructor or dive master, the quality of the equipment, the specialty in dive sites, the size of the boat, and the size of the groups (an important factor if you want to avoid "cattle boats"). Prices are

pretty standard around the island: local two-tank dives are about US$75, plus rental fees and tax; resort courses are US$160; open-water certification runs US$450-470; advanced certification is US$380; three-tank dives to the Blue Hole are US$250-325 and to Turneffe US$235.

Beginners and experienced divers or snorkelers alike have several solid choices. **Amigos del Mar** (at the Mayan Princess Hotel beachfront dock, tel. 501/226-2706, www.amigosdivebelize.com), based on the pier across Cholo's Bar, is a bustling place with top-notch gear and a solid reputation for safety. Many clients return year after year to dive with the same long-term and friendly staff. Amigos runs frequent trips to the Blue Hole in their 56- and 60-foot boats (important for the long journey to and from the famous site). Other extremely reputable dive shops are **Hugh Parkey's Diving** (at the SunBreeze Hotel beachfront in central San Pedro, tel. 501/226-4526 or 501/670-5239, www.belizediving.com), specializing in local dives only; **Ecologic Divers** (tel. 501/226-4118, www.ecologicdivers.com), with the

© LEBAWIT GIRMA

one of the main dive shops on Ambergris Caye

best-looking dock in town and offering regular Blue Hole and atoll journeys in the comfort of their new covered dive boat—taking no more than 12 divers at a time—as well as night dives; and **Patojo's Scuba Center** (tel. 501/206-2283, patojos99@yahoo.com), all with proven reputations for safety and service.

Snorkeling gear can be rented from **Ramon's Village Resort** (Ramon's Dive Shop pier, half-day US$5, full-day US$10), and there is decent marinelife just at the end of their dock, specially created for those seeking to snorkel in town. If you decide to explore from another dock, beware of boat activity at all times, as there have been serious accidents in the past.

Snuba and Sea Trek

To change it up a bit from regular snorkeling or for those who want to avoid diving, try snuba or sea trek. Snuba lets you explore the Barrier Reef at depths of up to 20 feet without getting scuba certified and without a heavy tank strapped to your back: breathing is through a regulator, receiving air through a long 20-foot

line attached to a support raft that floats safely at the surface. Training is provided in 15 minutes, and anyone over age eight can participate as long as they can swim.

Sea trek consists of hiking the sea floor, literally: plop on a cool helmet that receives almost three times the amount of air needed through a hose. Both allow for an underwater experience and a chance for fun photo ops and videos without fretting about a tank or equalizing. So far, the only certified outfitter to offer this new way of experiencing Hol Chan is **Discovery Expeditions** (tel. 501/671-2882 or 501/671-0748, www.discovery-belize.com, US$68-74, including hotel transfers but not the US$10 Hol Chan park fee) out of San Pedro. If you're staying on Caye Caulker, you may be able to arrange the tour through your hotel and catch the water taxi over to San Pedro for a day. Another option offered is to "power snorkel"—snorkeling with a hand-held power scooter.

Boating and Sailing

Explore the Caribbean the way it was meant to be traveled: by sea. Old standby boats include

SNORKELING AND DIVING OFF AMBERGRIS CAYE

Choose from a casual snorkel in town or a half- or a full-day snorkel or dive tour by boat. The first option is for days when you want to stay close to shore; the second is for exploring marinelife and coral, a must when in Belize. Be sure to remember and observe snorkel and reef etiquette at all times.

· **Ramon's Village Resort** (Ramon's Dive Shop pier, tel. 501/226-2071, U.S. tel. 800/624-4215, www.ramons.com) has an artificial reef that is home to a wide variety of small reef fish. Snorkel trips to the Barrier Reef are available.

· **Hol Chan Marine Reserve** (reserve office on Caribeña St., www.holchanbelize.org) is the crown jewel of snorkeling, located four miles southeast of San Pedro Town.

· **Shark Ray Alley** is usually included on a trip to Hol Chan Marine Reserve. Snorkel alongside large southern stingrays and nurse sharks, spectacular coral formations, or dive the *Amigos Del Mar* tugboat wreck.

· **Mexico Rocks,** on the reef north of town, is the place to see a huge diversity of coral formations.

· **Bacalar Chico Marine Reserve,** near the northern tip of Ambergris Caye, is an incredible site with a stunning diversity of wildlife and coral—at least 187 species of fish and several important spawning aggregation sites, plus loggerhead, green, and hawksbill sea turtles.

the "old-school sailing trip" aboard the refurbished *Rum Punch II* (parked north of Cholo's Bar, tel. 501/610-3240), operated by longtime resident and captain George Eiley, offering glass-bottom-boat snorkel tours, beach barbecues, and sunset charters.

The newest sailboat in town is the *Sirena Azul,* a 40-foot Belizean hardwood beauty operated out of the Blue Tang Inn. Built by a boat-building family in the northern village of Sarteneja, and with an added diesel onboard engine and restroom, it's an experience worth the extra cost. Sunset sails (US$50 pp, drinks included; private charter US$350 for 1-6 people) are popular, although the boat also goes on snorkeling day trips.

Another popular and fancy cat for private rent or for sunset sails is *Seaduction,* operated by **Seaduced by Belize** (tel. 501/226-2254, www.seaducedbybelize.com). Ecological divers now offer sailing charters aboard their two 50-foot catamarans as well as sunset dinner cruises by the reef.

For a more rustic and laid-back sail, spend the day with the Rubio brothers snorkeling, fishing, drinking aboard *No Rush,* a quaint 36-foot

catamaran that can be booked through **Unity Tours** (tel. 501/600-5022, www.ambergriscaye.com/unitytours, full-day snorkel US$75 pp, half-day US$50 pp). **Reef Runners** (tel. 501/602-5055 or 501/610-1061, www.ambergriscaye.com/reefrunner, full-day snorkel US$45 adults) has 24-foot-long glass-bottom boats for snorkel tours and fishing trips, and they know these waters well. You can't miss their bright-yellow boats docked beside the San Pedro Belize water taxi terminal. **Searious Adventures** (tel. 501/226-4202, www.seariousadventures.com) offers sailing and snorkeling activities.

A notch up is **Belize Sailing Vacations** (tel. 501/621-0417 or 501/664-5300, U.S. tel. 800/640-2182, www.belizesailingvacations.com, from US$1,295), providing luxury sailing charters with "the amenities of an all-inclusive luxury resort aboard your own private catamaran, tailored to your own personalized itinerary." This dream itinerary goes from island-hopping to snorkeling and diving on the way or just relaxing on board. A popular choice is *Doris,* a 50-foot catamaran with four air-conditioned cabins, four baths, lounge areas, plasma TVs, and your very own chef on board.

BELIZE'S BIG THREE: THE GRAND SLAM

Chasing tail in Belizean waters is on the dream list of anglers worldwide and has been for decades. Many also head here for a chance to achieve the grand slam: catching a tarpon, permit, and bonefish in one day. Doing so is no small feat—some spend as much as a week of daily excursions and even years attempting it. Those who succeed automatically gain a spot in a de facto exclusive group of top-rated anglers.

While visitors can conduct their own grand slam fly-fishing mission year-round in Belize, Ambergris Caye holds an annual catch-and-release sportfishing tournament and event known as the **Tres Pescado Slam Tournament** (www.tres-pescado-tournament.org). It's the fly-fishing competition of all fishing competitions, with teams descending on San Pedro from other countries and parts of Belize to compete in catching the big three in just three days. Teams consist of one or two fly-fishers and a Belize Tourism Board licensed guide. Now in its fifth year, the competition is more intense than ever to win prestigious titles, including Top Guide—won every year thus far by Anglers Abroad guides out of Caye Caulker—as well as Top Female Angler, Best Men's and Women's Casting, and generous cash prizes.

The money raised by the tournament supports a worthwhile cause. Up to 15 teams participated in 2012, donating US$7,000 to the Bonefish Tarpon Trust Project in Belize, benefiting bonefish, permit, and tarpon fisheries.

Nonfishing family members can have fun too, as the three-day event includes weekend long games and activities, usually held at the Central Park in San Pedro.

Fishing

The area within the reef is a favorite for tarpon and bonefish. Outside the reef, the choice of big game is endless. Most hotels and dive shops will make arrangements for fishing, including a boat and a guide. Ask around the docks (and your hotel) for the best guides. Serious anglers should consider Abner Marin at **Go Fish Belize** (beachfront at Boca del Rio Dr., tel. 501/226-3121, www.gofishbelize.com), one of the most qualified and reputable guides around. Or try **Fishing San Pedro** (Front St., above Manelly's, tel. 501/607-9967, www.fishingsanpedro.com), another sure bet where half- or full-day chartered fishing trips are relatively affordable at US$325 for a full day for two people, including tackle, bait, soft drinks, and water; a fish or lobster barbecue costs a bit extra.

Kayaking

Little wave action and regular trade winds make kayaking a great option off Belize's cayes. Ideal spots to navigate are on the south side of the island near Xanadu Resort or Caribbean Villas, with wider open space and less boat activity. The north end also offers quieter options for rowing in safety. Many hotels offer complimentary use of kayaks. If not, check with **San Pedro Water Sports** (beachfront dock near Holiday Hotel, tel. 501/226-2888, www.sanpedrowatersports.com, single kayak US$15 per hour) or with **Ramon's Village** (dockside, US$15 per hour, US$35 per day).

Wind Sports

The latest wind sports are all the rage. It's not surprising, given the often ideal weather conditions. There's that "constant breeze in Belize" that locals love to brag about—the result of Caribbean trade winds that hit the islands from November to July. Combine it with a nearby reef that creates flat waters, and voilà!

Sailsports Belize (beachfront by Caribbean Villas Hotel, tel. 501/226-4488 or 501/610-0773, www.sailsportsbelize.com) is a solid and affordable choice for windsurfing, kite surfing, and sailing. Their location is on a calm stretch of beach with plenty of open water. Lessons and courses are offered with licensed instructors (introduction to windsurfing and two-hour rental US$99; beginner kite surfing five-hour course US$303) and hotel delivery is available for rentals (windsurfing US$22 per hour, sailing US$49 per hour).

San Pedro Water Sports (dock across from Holiday Hotel, tel. 501/226-2888, www.sanpedrowatersports.com) has a variety of equipment for rent, including paddleboards (US$15 per hour) and windsurfing boards. Adrian is happy to give you pointers on paddleboarding if it's your first time.

Ramon's Village Resort's dive shop has windsurfing or Hobie Cat catamaran lessons (US$45-70 for 2 hours) and equipment rentals (windsurfing US$20 per hour, Hobie Cat US$30 per hour).

KiteXplorer (beachfront, tel. 501/635-4967, http://kitexplorer.com/kitex, 9am-6pm daily) shares a dock with Patojo's Dive Center and has two licensed instructors offering kite surfing or paddle surfing lessons (kite surfing intro US$90, stand-up paddle surfing US$45 for 1.5 hours). Rentals are also available for paddle surfing and kite surfing (US$20-120 per hour). The ideal months for these weather-influenced sports are November to July, with March to July offering the strongest winds. KiteXplorer also operates out of Caye Caulker.

A great way to relax and catch spectacular views of the island and reef, weather permitting, is to parasail with **Funtasea** (Fido's dock, tel. 501/226-3866, www.funtasea.net, US$77 pp, US$145 double). Funtasea also offers other boat and ecotours of the island.

Birding and Wildlife-Watching

Although many people come here for the reef, Ambergris also offers birding and nature tour opportunities.

Take a boat ride along the north of the island, where wildlife can be spotted along the beach but also in the lagoon on the back side, a peaceful, rarely visited part of Ambergris. Sightings may include egrets and great herons, and if you're lucky, crocodiles. For customized tours and other island nature tours, check with any of the beachfront operators or with **Seaduced by Belize** (tel. 501/226-2254, www.seaducedbybelize.com). Ask about half-day trips to two bird sanctuaries, Cayo Rosario

and Little Guana Caye, where you can spot more species.

Another popular bird-watching spot near town is the unique **"People Perch"** at **Caribbean Villas Hotel** (tel. 501/226-2715, www.caribbeanvillas.com, 6am-6pm daily), located south of San Pedro. It's a tall viewing tower built by the owners, Will and Susan Lala, who are avid bird-watchers. The tower is reached after hiking the nature trail on the property, and once at the top, there are 360-degree views over a canopy of trees and flowers, and to the east, the Caribbean Sea. Look for signs to this private sanctuary or contact the hotel for more information. Numerous species of birds can be spotted from here, but you must arrive by sunrise to spot them. Otherwise, you can glimpse and hear them in the small forest. Next door, **Xanadu Island Resort** also has a lush marked nature trail at the back of the property; stop in at the front desk for directions.

Massage and Bodywork

If your hotel lacks a proper gym and you'd rather pump iron than dive, the **Train Station** (tel. 501/226-4222, www.trainstationfitness.com) is 2.5 blocks south of the bridge. In San Pedro, you'll find both scheduled yoga classes (drop-in US$15) and private sessions at **Sol Spa** (Phoenix Hotel, tel. 501/226-2410, www.belizesolspa.com, 9am-5pm daily), a small but cozy retreat offering a range of treatments and massages like Honeymoon Bliss, Solar Therapy, and Maya Abdominal Massage.

The **Asian Garden Day Spa** (Coconut Dr., across from Ramon's Village, tel. 501/226-4072, www.asiangardenspasalon.com) is a family-run spa in a lovely courtyard, specializing in Thai massage, hot stone therapy, reflexology, facials, scrubs, and specials like sunset or starlight couples massage.

Jordana's Touch of Art Massage Studio (Beachfront San Pedro, tel. 501/226-3357, www.artoftouchspa.com) is in the entrance to the Sunbreeze Hotel. The spa offers massages, reflexology, aromatherapy, manicures and pedicures, and even hair-braiding services for that extra tropical look (full head US$40).

A block away from Front Street is **Black Orchid Spa** (Tarpon St., Vilma Linda Plaza, 2nd Fl., tel. 501/226-3939, www.blackorchid-spa.com, 9am-8pm Mon.-Sat., 10am-5pm Sun.), with good reviews but set in the hustle and bustle of San Pedro, which might snap you back into reality too quickly as you leave the oasis.

A short distance before reaching the bridge going north, for a more casual option and an authentic Caribbean setting, look for Shirlene Santino's **Just Relax Massage** and her seaside massage chair and hut (near Wayo's Beach Bar, tel. 501/666-3536, deep tissue US$40 per hour, house calls US$55). Shirlene has special oils for any ailment ranging from sunburn to back aches. Call ahead for an appointment.

Farther up north is **Serenity Spa and Wellness Center** at Las Terrazas Resort (U.S. tel. 800/557-1553, www.lasterrazasresort.com), with the "Unbelizeable Facial" and other treatments.

Ak'Bol Yoga Retreat (tel. 501/226-2073, www.akbol.com) is one of the few places in Belize offering daily yoga classes (usually at 9am), popular among residents.

ENTERTAINMENT AND EVENTS

San Pedro boasts the best nightlife in the country, whether your idea of fun is dancing up a storm, barhopping, dining to live music, or betting on chicken poop—it's all here. San Pedranos have a weeklong calendar of places to be. Wednesday and Saturday are the biggest nights out, and water taxis actually change their schedules to accommodate revelers. But other nights are popular as well, including Monday for live *punta* music, and Thursday because of the Chicken Drop. In general, the hot spots don't get going until 11pm or midnight, with lots of warming up in various bars before the bumpin' and grindin' begins.

Nightlife
BARS AND LOUNGES

Diving or touring by day and partying by night is the standard San Pedro scene—although some really do barhop all day long. There are enough watering holes on the island for serious drinkers. Lately, more upscale lounges have found their way to the north and south of the island.

Starting in the center of town, the beachfront **Cholo's Sport Bar** (tel. 501/226-2406, 10am-midnight daily) is a modest but perfect local hangout and the heart of San Pedro's social scene. You'll find the cheapest drinks in town (US$1.50 for a rum and Coke) and plenty of people-watching from the outdoor tables as it's close to the water taxis and dive shops. Ceviche is the only bar snack. Expect to see only men on the inside, sitting at the bar or playing pool.

A few stumbling steps from Cholo's on the roadside is **Lola's Pub** (Front St., tel. 501/206-2120, 11am-midnight daily), one of my favorites and a popular after-work or weekend hang out, not to mention a great pre-party warm-up spot. Beautifully lit shelves house top-shelf liquor and the bistro-like atmosphere is casual and friendly, with a couple of flat-screen TVs and music. If you're lucky, your bartender will be Trevor, whom I'm convinced is one of the top three in town (try his Cadillac Margarita).

Farther down the beach is **Fido's Courtyard** (10am-midnight Mon.-Fri., 10am-2am Sat.-Sun.), the largest bar-restaurant complex in town, catering mostly to travelers with a live rock band almost every night in the high season and an all-day full menu that ranges from bar foods to dinner.

Place your bets at the weekly **Chicken Drop** at 6pm Thursday in front of **Wahoo's Lounge and Bar** (beachside in the Spindrift Hotel, tel. 501/226-2002) and **Caliente Restaurant** (tel. 501/226-2170, 11am-9:30pm Tues.-Sun.). A chicken is let loose on a numbered grid after revelers place bets on which number the chicken will choose to soil. The winner takes a cash prize, but not before cleaning up the poop. Warm up at Wahoo's Bar—with two-for-one rum punches and a DJ playing calypso and upbeat local sounds on the beach; or just next door with Caliente Restaurant's two-for-one happy hour (4pm-6pm daily) and delicious nachos.

The newest hot spot in town at press time is the beachfront outdoor **Señor Marlin's Sports Bar** (tel. 501/672-0212, 11am-midnight daily), named after the massive marlin caught and brought back in the owner's canoe. Just a few steps from the Central Park, the bright green exterior and the interior *palapa* decor are complemented with stiff drinks and an excellent DJ playing reggae, dancehall, and house tunes. Umbrella-covered seating is available directly on the beach.

The newly renovated and slightly more upscale **Caprice Bar Grill**, with interior and beachfront dock seating, is a decent choice for its popular half-price weekday happy hour (3pm-6pm Mon.-Fri.).

BC's (on the beach, just east of the airstrip, tel. 501/226-3289, 9am-close daily) is popular among expats and has live music on Sunday as well as great nachos and burritos all day. Opposite BC's is **Hurricane's Ceviche Bar and Grill** (tel. 501/226-4124, 10am-10pm Wed.-Mon.), set on a dock over the water and serving a variety of—you guessed it, ceviche. It has very friendly barkeep and a narrow hidden top deck for views of the water and the beach. The **Rehab Bar** (Front St., open daily), a small patio bar next to the Jaguar's Temple disco, is a favorite for people-watching.

South of San Pedro, **Crazy Canuck's Beach Bar** (S. Coconut Dr.) has live music and dancing on Monday, Thursday, and Sunday afternoon. You'll find happy customers and meet interesting characters playing cards, horseshoes, dominoes, and other games. Also on Coconut Drive directly across from Canuck's, look for the **Roadkill Bar** (S. Coconut Dr., 3:30pm-midnight daily), another popular open-air hangout with joke Monday, karaoke on Wednesday, and a free beer with a shot of tequila for US$5 until 9pm. Their Panty Rippers are delicious.

Continuing south, you'll find a neighborhood gem in **Average Joe's Bar** (Blake St., tel. 501/602-7564, 4pm-midnight Mon., 11am-midnight Tues.-Sun.), a casual bar with the most comfortable bar stools I've sat on, live music on Wednesday and Friday, karaoke Saturday night, and special drinks (try the frozen raspberry lemon margarita). The finger licking good "dawgs" and wings menu will soak up the alcohol nicely.

A short distance before the north bridge is the lively **Wayo's Beachside Beernet** (Boca del Rio, tel. 501/661-8271, 10am-midnight daily), a casual, colorful outdoor hangout ideal for drinks, a bite, and a swim all day long, or for nighttime fun with the occasional karaoke night. Across from the bar are a *palapa* and a hammock set even closer to the water. Owner "Wayo from Cayo" will even pick you up at night and give you a ride back if needed, ideal for solo female travelers. A stone's throw away is the **Sand Bar** (across from Wet Willy's dock, tel. 501/630-1241, 11am-midnight daily), serving cheap local drinks as well as tasty bar food and pizza.

North of San Pedro, the legendary **Palapa Bar** (tel. 501/226-3111, 10am-about 9pm daily) is an absolute must-stop while on Ambergris, whether for lunch, sunset, or a lazy evening of appetizers (US$4-6), barbecue, beer, and cocktails. For the full Palapa experience, bring a bathing suit so you can swim and float in an anchored inner tube and have the bartender lower you down a bucket of beer and take up your empty ones. It's a short golf cart ride north of the bridge, or US$3.50 by water taxi from the Coastal Express dock in San Pedro.

Kama Lounge (set in from the north-side road, tel. 501/610-3775 or 501/226-3709, kamalounge@yahoo.com, noon-10pm daily), raises it up a whole notch and is quite possibly the sexiest lounge and bar in Belize. This waterfront escape is a sight to be seen, with lilac voile curtains flowing over a maze of red cushy beds, a small plunge pool in the center, hookahs standing tall on every table, a full bar, and a delicious menu of kebabs, ceviche, pasta, and paninis. The evening red mood lighting is impossible to miss from the water, not to mention lounge beats that make you sink farther into the *camas*. There are regular Tuesday hookah nights, live music or a DJ on weekends,

© LEBAWIT GIRMA

Wayo's Beachside Beernet is one of several fun outdoor bars on Ambergris Caye.

occasional movie nights on a 15-foot screen, full moon parties, and more.

Farther up north is **Rojo Lounge** (at Azul Resort, next to Matachica Resort, tel. 501/226-4012, info@azulbelize.com, noon-close Tues.-Sat.), a trendy waterfront spot with beds and fancy cocktails.

If a quieter, pre-dinner glass of wine is more your beat, try the Friday-night wine social at **Wine D'vine** (Coconut Dr., tel. 501/226-3430, www.winedevine.com, 4pm-7pm Fri.).

DANCING

Monday is "happening" at **Crazy Canucks** (S. Coconut Dr.) with a live *punta* band. Get ready to throw back the cocktails, meet locals, and shake your hips Garífuna-style. The band begins around 9pm.

Wednesday is ladies' night at **Wet Willy's** (beachfront, tel. 501/226-4136), a cool thatched-roof waterfront pier nightclub, and Saturday gets going when the bars close at midnight and everyone wanders across the street to **Jaguar's Temple** (tel. 501/226-4077, www.

jaguarstempleclub.com, from 9:30pm Thurs.-Sat.), the most popular and decent nightclub in Belize. The two-story interior is complete with a large dance floor, two bars with spacious standing room, air-conditioning, and just the right amount of snazzy disco lighting. After Jaguar's, the insatiable night owls often stumble over to **Daddy Rocks Nightclub** (10am-4am Thurs.-Sat., 11am-4am Sun.), just across the street in the park. It has a can't-miss-it flamboyant exterior (you'll have to see it to believe it) and stays open until 7am. The music is more the reggae and dancehall type, while Jaguar plays a mix of all genres, from house to reggae and Latin, and attracts more of a 'cool' crowd, though as a visitor you'll dance at either one. The fun gets started around 11pm-midnight and can go until 4am and later.

Festivals and Events

San Pedro's events are a year-round affair. These celebrations bring even more crowds, but experiencing them is a chance to witness the San Pedrano joie de vivre.

LIVE MUSIC IN SAN PEDRO

Music aficionados will find their fix in San Pedro. It's the most frequent, steady, weeklong schedule of musicians and bands you'll find anywhere in Belize, although other parts of the country tend to have more local sounds and less in Western genres. Overall, San Pedro's offerings reflect a mix that keeps visitors and locals happy on a year-round basis—from soothing Latin melodies over dinner to light rock, jazz, and blues bands catering to travelers and expats, and local *punta* rock sounds for a taste of the Afro-influenced Garífuna side of Belize. And there's no extra cover charge! Up for it? Here's your weeklong itinerary.

Monday, start out at **Crazy Canucks Beach Bar** (beachfront, tel. 501/670-8001, 7:30pm-11pm Mon.) with the local and popular Punta Boys Band. Grab a few drinks before the live Garífuna drums, turtle shells, and hip-shaking fun start around 9:30pm. The crowd is a mix of visitors, expats, and locals.

Tuesday gives you a chance to get behind the mic at popular **Legends Burger House's** (north of the bridge, tel. 501/226-2113, noon-midnight Tues.) Jam Night. Ask about the other live-music nights, including Saturday. To continue the night, head to the waterfront pier bar **Tackle Box** (beachfront, tel. 501/226-4313, www.tackleboxbarandgrill.com, 9pm-close Tues.) for a mix of late-night Belizean sounds.

Wednesday, start out mellow with Cuban music and tapas at **Red Ginger** (Phoenix Resort, tel. 501/226-4623, www.redgingerbelize.com, 6pm-9pm Wed.), a more intimate option. If you're up for post-dinner fun, head to the island's biggest dance night at the infamous **Wet Willy's** (Beachfront, tel. 501/226-4136), which gets going around 11pm.

Thursday, it's **Fido's** (Front St., tel. 501/226-2056, www.fidosbelize.com, 6pm-close Thurs., 9pm-close Fri.) for a beachfront setting. A regular lineup of light rock or jazz bands fills this large indoor and outdoor space. While there isn't much "local" about Fido's, it's there if you need an option. Not to be missed, however, is the local Belizean music at the Chicken Drop event just down from Fido's at **Wahoo's Lounge** (Front St., 501/634-6008, www.wahoosloungebelize.com, 6pm-midnight Thurs.), playing a mix of calypso, reggae, *punta*, and more. It's possibly the closest you'll come to dancing barefoot to local music on San Pedro's "beach."

Friday nights are also popular at Fido's; Saturday, you can rock and roll at Wahoo's.

Sunday is "Funday" in Belize. Everything but the bars and restaurants shut down and everyone relaxes, swims on the beach, drinks Belikins, listens to music, and breaks out the barbeque grills. Try Crazy Canucks (noon-close Sun.) or **Caribbean Villas** (Seagrape Dr., tel. 501/226-2715, www.caribbeanvillashotel.com, 7:30am-9pm Sun.). Wherever you end up, don't forget your swimming gear to take advantage of the docks or swimming pools.

Copious amounts of colorful paint splattered on the crowd, egg throwing, men dressed like women, and all-around Mardi Gras-type of debauchery takes place at the **San Pedro Carnival** (mid-Feb.). The highlights of three days of partying include cultural dance performances on opening night as well as *comparsas,* or street dance groups competing for prizes.

Now in its ninth year, the two-day **Lagoon Reef Eco-Challenge Kayak Race** (tel. 501/226-2247, www.ecochallengebelize.com, June, registration US$200-500) attracts professional, amateur, and junior kayakers (over age 15) from around the world to compete in a 60-mile race around the entire island. The race begins south of Ambergris, passes by the lagoon side and through mangrove cayes on day one, and reaches the northern tip at Bacalar Chico for the night before continuing back down the island along the reef on the second day. The funds raised go toward promoting the connection between the island's lagoons and the reef—both an integral part of the island's ecosystem and vital to the livelihood of its inhabitants.

San Pedro holds the **Día de San Pedro** (first weekend in July), a three-day festival in honor of St. Peter, the island's patron saint. There are traditional dances, pageants, food vendors, and music showcasing the island's mixed Belizean, Mexican, and Mayan heritage. If you can only attend one day, come opening night.

The **Costa Maya Festival** (first weekend in Aug.) is considered Belize's biggest festival—perhaps in size, because it attracts guests and participants from the neighboring Maya Mundo in one big celebration of heritage. It's worth checking out to sample all the fantastic food vendors.

The island celebrates Independence Day (Sept. 21) with the **Independence Day Parade.** San Pedro's parade rivals even the capital's, with carnival floats, costumes, marching bands, free rum and beer, beach after-parties, and children and adults dancing in the streets. It's an ideal time to visit, not least for the festivities and off-season prices.

One of San Pedro's biggest and most unique year-end festivities is the **San Pedro Holiday Boat Light Parade** (http://sanpedroboatparade.com, 7pm first weekend in Dec.). Watch as a spectacular display of illuminated boats cruises along San Pedro's shores from Boca del Rio all the way to Caribbean Villas. Children singing carols, marching bands, dancing, and loud cheers and music from the beachfront watering holes add to the holiday spirit. At the end of the course, judges pick the prize-winning boats, from most artistic to most religious.

SHOPPING

Gift shops abound in San Pedro, especially on Front and Middle Streets; they've got your postcards, beach apparel, towels, hats, T-shirts, hot sauces, and the usual knickknacks.

Arts and Crafts

Belizean Arts (Fido's Courtyard, tel. 501/226-2056, www.belizeanarts.com, 11am-7pm daily) sells art, jewelry, ceramics, and carvings by Central American and Belizean artists. The well-established shop has the largest selection of original paintings in Belize.

Paradise Gallery (Vilma Linda Plaza, tel. 501/226-4437, belizeframeshop@gmail.com, 10am-6pm Mon.-Sat.) has a small collection of local paintings and crafts and offers framing services.

Get your rocks at **Ambergris Maya Jade and History Museum** (across from town hall, 9am-6pm daily). Also a retail jade shop, it's designed "to give visitors an overview of 3,000 years of Mesoamerican jade and its importance to the cultures in the region." When you're finished, check out **The Emerald Mine,** a few doors down.

Belizean Melody Art Gallery (Front St., 501/226-2787, www.belizemelodyart.com, 9am-6pm Mon.-Sat.) has carefully selected paintings, crafts, and unique handmade souvenirs, all guaranteed to be made in Belize. Transforming her great grandmother's house into a gallery, San Pedro native, owner, and artist Melody Sanchez Wolfe—currently the visual and expressive arts director for the island's cultural committee—is passionate about providing an outlet for the success of fellow Belizean talents, some as young as 18. Hand-painted shell magnets are just an example of some unique made-in-Belize souvenir items, and the gorgeous paintings aren't to be found anywhere else.

Books

A decent book selection is available at **San Pedro Books** (in Vilma Linda Plaza, Tarpon St., tel. 501/226-4797, 9am-5pm Mon.-Sat.).

Clothing and Jewelry

Located in Fido's Courtyard (10am-5pm) is **Bambar,** offering handcrafted jewelry made with resin ambers, Maya jade, shells, and silver. **Mambo Chill** imports expensive women's clothing.

Gourmet Goodies

Chocolate lovers should look two new chocolate stores in town, both of which source their cacao from Punta Gorda's Cacao Growers Association. The **Chocolate Boutique** (Front St., next to Wild Mango's, tel. 501/610-4828 or cell 501/634-9878, www.belizechocolate-company.com, 10am-6:30pm Mon.-Sat.) has chocolate bars, truffles, and "kakaw" powder as well as chocochino and other delicious chocolate drinks. The cacao body oil and bars make great gifts. A few steps down Front Street, right beside the water taxi alley, is **Moho Chocolate** (cell 501/633-6595, www.mohocholate.com, 9am-6pm daily), also selling chocolate bars and chocolate-anything gifts; get some free samples and then get a bottle of the Maya Cocoa Kahlua mix to make your own Belizean chocolate-based Kahlua. The owners of Moho also run the Cotton Tree Lodge in Punta Gorda, famous for their chocolate-making workshops. Moho works with several independent cacao growers in the Toledo District. The original Moho Chocolate store is located in Belize City's Tourism Village.

For unique decadent gifts, the **Cigar and Rum Shop** (Middle St., a block from Elvi's Kitchen, tel. 501/226-2020, 9am-9pm daily) has a walk-in humidor with Cuban and Belizean cigars as well as their own San Pedro-made Jankunu rum cream creations (which are very tasty, I might add) and delicious freshly roasted Guatemalan Arabica coffee in the morning—for sale and sampling (US$1 per cup), with a couple of tables should you decide to savor it on-site.

Wine de Vine (Coconut Dr., tel. 501/226-3430, www.winedevine.com) has the finest selection of imported wines in all of Belize and a worldwide selection of cheeses and meats. They offer free wine tastings and also sell it by the glass. **Premium Wines** (tel. 501/226-3700, gisellekv@gmail.com, 9am-6pm Mon.-Sat.) on Front Street has a selection from seven countries and offers wholesale pricing: Buy 12 bottles and get a 17 percent discount. Prices range from US$17 for a California wine to US$14 for a white French table wine.

ACCOMMODATIONS

In addition to hotels and luxury lodges, there are many apartment and house rentals available around the island. To start, check the classifieds from the *San Pedro Sun* (www.

sanpedrosun.net) and the *San Pedro Daily* (sanpedrodaily.com). Other sources for vacation homes are **M&M Rentals** (U.S. tel. 949/258-5268, www.mandmrentalsbelize.com) and **Caye Management** (tel. 501/226-3077, www.cayemanagement.com), which has an office that's open daily on the north edge of town at Casa Coral.

Under US$25

San Pedro has slim pickings in this category. The hands-down best is (**Ruby's Hotel** (tel. 501/226-2063, rubys@btl.net, US$20-40), with 23 basic, clean guest rooms in a well-maintained building right on the water in the heart of the village. Ruby's Café and pastry shop downstairs is excellent and a San Pedrano institution, and you can sit on your room's balcony or the common deck space with some fresh morning johnnycakes and watch the beach traffic below. Guest rooms have either shared or private bath with fan or air-conditioning.

The only youth hostel option is **Pedro's Inn** (Seagrape Dr., off Coconut Dr., tel. 501/226-3825, www.backpackersbelize.com, US$12.50 s, US$22.50 d), with two rows of 14 wooden stalls, each with a bed, a ceiling fan, a locker, and access to shared bath facilities. The rooms are right above Pedro's Sports Bar and poker room, so you've got an on-site nightly social scene with a lively cast of characters and pizza available for delivery. Pedro's has a small pool with lounge chairs, a deck, and a shaded picnic area. It's back by the airstrip (you'll wake up to the morning's flights taking off overhead), a 10-minute walk from the town center or US$3.50 by taxi. Across the street, Pedro's has 30 functional hotel rooms (US$50-65) with air-conditioning, TVs, private baths, and fans.

US$25-50

Right in town, the family-run (**Hotel San Pedrano** (Front St., tel. 501/226-2054, sanpedrano@btl.net, US$35 with fan, US$45 with a/c) has six guest rooms, from single to triple, that make up the island's self-proclaimed "top of the low end." From the breezy upstairs

CHOOSING A HOTEL ON AMBERGRIS CAYE

At last count, Ambergris had about 154 licensed hotels, mostly mid-range and upscale lodging. The few places geared toward backpackers and extreme budget travelers are located either right in San Pedro Town or on the outskirts by the airstrip. Otherwise, here are a few things to keep in mind when deciding on a hotel.

First off, in downtown San Pedro, the word *beachfront* refers to the very narrow strip of sand that is used more as a pathway for pedestrians and boats than for lounging on sand. The views are still pretty and you can still find plenty of space to sun yourself, but as you move farther from town, either to the north or south along the island, the beaches fronting the resorts become wider, softer, and more exclusive.

Of course, what you give up in beach quality, you get back in location: "in town" means being in the middle of the buzz of cafés, bars, boutiques, dive shops, dancing, and dining. If you're more into privacy, all this action is easily accessible from any resort on the island by boat, taxi, or golf cart. And those in town can easily escape north or south for the day as well for more exclusive restaurants and scenery.

Keep in mind that rates across the board are subject to seasonal fluctuations, service charges, and government taxes. Always verify and ask about discounts before booking. Remember that rates are for double occupancy during the high season.

---

veranda it's easy to eat a bite, read a book, or watch the street below. Each guest room has hot and cold water, a private bath, a ceiling fan, and optional air-conditioning. The amenities are basic, but the hotel is a stone's throw from all the action in town and steps from the water taxi pier.

Thomas Hotel (Front St., tel. 501/226-2061, US$35-43) has six cheap and barebones but clean guest rooms with private baths, fans or air-conditioning, and aged refrigerators, all 100 feet from the beach; this humble *hotelito* is 40 years old.

The only budget option north of the bridge is the **Ak'Bol** retreat center (a.k.a. the "yoga barracks") on the lagoon side, which has 30 guest rooms (US$35 s, US$50 d) in a long wooden building with a massive shared restroom-shower-locker room. The resort is on a narrow beach strip and has a yoga deck and an average restaurant on-site.

US$50-100

Right in the center of town and on the street side, the **Coral Beach Hotel** (Front St., tel. 501/266-2013, US$55 with fan, US$67 for a/c) offers 16 small clean guest rooms, each with a

private bath, hot and cold water, and air-conditioning or a fan. The guest rooms are basic and dated for the price, but perhaps location is what you're paying for. There's a large veranda with a nice view of the hustle and bustle of Front Street.

Across the street and a few steps away is the brighter, well-kept **Spindrift Hotel** (Front St., tel. 501/226-2174, U.S. tel. 888/705-9978, www.ambergriscaye.com/spindrift, US$54-85), a three-story building offering clean, spacious guest rooms with all the amenities, including Wi-Fi and balconies. There's a wonderful massive veranda overlooking the beach, and the hotel is sandwiched between Wahoo's Lounge, home of the Chicken Drop, and Caliente Restaurant. This is where I stayed my first time in San Pedro, and it was ideal.

Nearby **Tio Pil's Hotel** (Front St., tel. 501/206-2059, U.S. tel. 800/345-9786, www.tiopilshotel.com, US$55-70), formerly Lily's Hotel, has six good-value guest rooms with private baths, air-conditioning, and a large shared veranda overlooking the beach at the heart of San Pedro; there are a few apartments too. Lily's Treasure Chest family-run restaurant still lives on downstairs, with a new patio and

Centrally located beachfront hotels abound in San Pedro.

additional seating. It has been known for years for offering delicious ceviche, breakfasts, and local food in plentiful family-style servings.

A few steps away is the cute pink-and-white beachfront ◖ **Conch Shell Inn** (tel. 501/226-2062, conchshellinn@gmail.com, US$74-94), beside Sunbreeze Suites. It was the third hotel to open in the early days of tourism. Renovated in 2008 and well maintained, the five upstairs single and double guest rooms have great views, tiled floors, and kitchenettes with all the amenities; the cheaper downstairs rooms are steps from the sea. All guest rooms are beachfront, and there are portable air-conditioning units (US$10) available if needed. Daily maid service and a lovely private front courtyard with hammocks and beach chairs make this a great beach vacation spot in town.

South of San Pedro, a quaint and homey option is **Changes in Latitudes Bed and Breakfast** (36 Coconut Dr., next to Belize Yacht Club, tel. 501/226-2986, U.S. tel. 800/631-9834, www.ambergriscaye.com/

latitudes, US$95-115), with six small and cozy guest rooms with air-conditioning, ceiling fans, private baths, and pool privileges at Exotic Caye Beach Resort, a few doors down. They're serious about the breakfast, made fresh daily and served in the outdoor common room, and there's a board updated daily with suggested activities and nightlife. The location is ideal, just a few steps from Ramon's Village, the best swimming stretch in town. Use of bicycles is complimentary, as are outdoor lockers for drying wet clothes, and there's on-site security at night.

On the north end of town, toward the bridge, **Hotel del Rio** (tel. 501/226-2286, www.hoteldelriobelize.com, US$65-145) is a quiet hotel on the beach that offers great value. Accommodations range from basic economy rooms with shared baths and cold water to bigger colorful casitas built of pimento palm, some with a king or two queen beds. There is also a larger villa (US$1,200 per month) in the back. There are hammocks to enjoy in the private beachfront courtyard.

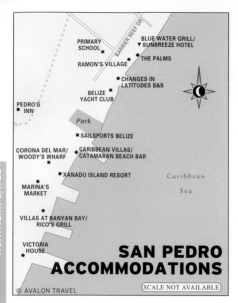

PRIMARY SCHOOL
BARRIER REEF DR.
BLUE WATER GRILL/ SUNBREEZE HOTEL
THE PALMS
RAMON'S VILLAGE
CHANGES IN LATITUDES B&B
BELIZE YACHT CLUB
PEDRO'S INN
Park
SAILSPORTS BELIZE
CORONA DEL MAR/ WOODY'S WHARF
CARIBBEAN VILLAS/ CATAMARAN BEACH BAR
XANADU ISLAND RESORT
Caribbean Sea
MARINA'S MARKET
VILLAS AT BANYAN BAY/ RICO'S GRILL
VICTORIA HOUSE
SAN PEDRO ACCOMMODATIONS
© AVALON TRAVEL   SCALE NOT AVAILABLE

US$100-150

The central and cheerful **San Pedro Holiday Hotel** (Front. St., tel. 501/226-2103, U.S. tel. 713/893-3825, www.sanpedroholiday.com, US$110-125), the island's first hotel and still under the original family's management, keeps getting better. The 17 clean, spacious guest rooms have air-conditioning and fans, private baths, and beachfront verandas. Lots of water sports and boats are available.

Inside an elegant three-story building of tropical colonial design, on the corner of Sandpiper Street and the sea, is the **Blue Tang Inn** (tel. 501/226-2326, U.S. tel. 866/881-1020, www.bluetanginn.com, US$120-225). The 14 tasteful guest rooms sport lots of warm, rich wood paneling and have kitchens, private baths, ceiling fans, and air-conditioning; third-floor guest rooms have whirlpool tubs. The grounds are well kept, and the rooftop balcony is breezy and pleasant.

Popular with birders, **◖ Caribbean Villas** (Seagrape Dr., tel. 501/226-2715, U.S. tel. 866/290-6341, www.caribbeanvillashotel.com, US$105-225) has a fantastic spot on the beach just south of town, offering a range of economy

rooms, including a garden studio (US$99), and luxury suites. The loft suites—such as Hawk's Roost—are gorgeous, with immaculately clean and colorful beach decor, sea-facing balconies, kitchenettes, and large closets. The property's small bird sanctuary is one of the few remaining areas of original littoral forest on the island and has a "people perch." In addition, the guest rooms are designed to catch the cooling trade winds to reduce the need for air-conditioning.

One of Belize's only dedicated yoga resorts, **Ak'Bol** (1 mile north of the bridge, www.akbol.com, US$145-165) has seven cabanas on the beach in a naturally landscaped garden, a small pool, and a shaded yoga garden within earshot of the sea. The cabanas have raised beds, local decor, a loft for the kids, unique conch-shell sinks, and private outdoor rainforest showers. There's an on-site beach bar, although the food is hit or miss and service can be slow. There are also daily yoga classes, which are popular with residents, and retreat packages.

US$150-200

The **SunBreeze Hotel** (tel. 501/226-2191, U.S. tel. 800/688-0191, www.sunbreeze.net, US$179-236) is a full-service beachfront hotel with 43 guest rooms built around an open sand area and pool. Guest rooms have two queen beds, air-conditioning, tile floors, local artwork, private baths, and direct-dial phones; Front Street starts next door, and the entrance is yards from the airstrip. There's an on-site dive shop, a top-notch restaurant (Blue Water Grill), and many other services. The SunBreeze has some of the few fully disabled-accessible guest rooms in the country. They also rent suites at the other end of Front Street; on the beach across from the Belize Bank, at **SunBreeze Suites** (tel. 501/226-4675, U.S. tel. 800/820-1631, www.sunbreezesuites.com, US$165-205), which offers one-bedroom suites with full kitchens, guest queen sofa beds, and air-conditioning. The suites can sleep up to four adults per room; families and children are welcome. They have less of a standard hotel feel and are more akin to self-catering condos and cozier for it. There is a wonderful small

Jamaican restaurant on-site called **Jambel Jerk Pit**.

A full-service resort with 71 guest rooms, **Ramon's Village** (tel. 501/226-2071, U.S. tel. 800/624-4215, www.ramons.com) has standard guest rooms from US$155 and a presidential suite for US$450; the guest rooms are nice, although the "kitchenettes" are not much more than a sink and a microwave. The property's 500-foot beach is practically in San Pedro Town and has decent walk-in snorkeling; there is a restaurant, a bar, and a pool as well as on-site dive shops, guides, and an inland tour operator. You can rent windsurfing boards, snorkel gear, and golf carts.

C **Xanadu Island Resort** (tel. 501/226-2814, U.S. tel. 866/351-4752, www.xanaduislandresort.com, from US$170) is one of my favorite accommodations in San Pedro. The resort is a cluster of luxury monolithic domes with thatched overlay roofs nestled in lush landscaping. There is a beachfront pool as well as a private nature walk and bird sanctuary. Nineteen suites are available with fully equipped kitchens, and there is a choice of studios and one-, two-, and three-bedroom units. The beachfront lofts are stunning, and the service is top-notch. There's a restaurant-bar next door at Caribbean Villas' **Catamaran Beach Bar** if you need coffee first thing in the morning and don't care to brew your own.

Farther south is **Mata Rocks Resort** (tel. 501/226-2336, U.S. tel. 888/628-2757, www.matarocks.com, US$145-220), a small hotel tucked on the south end of Ambergris with six suites and 11 ocean-view guest rooms centered around a pool; the guest rooms, while not huge, have plenty of basic amenities, such as air-conditioning, cable, wireless Internet, bikes, transfers, and continental breakfast at the tiny on-site bar. The architecture is unusual—all white, clean, and Mediterranean. Don't forget your sunglasses if you stay here.

US$200-300

One of the island's top class acts, C **Victoria House** (tel. 501/226-2067, U.S. tel. 800/247-5159, www.victoria-house.com, US$195-1,235)

has a luxurious selection of suites and several multifamily mansion-like villas set along one of the nicest stretches of beach in town. Expect grand colonial elegance on a well-manicured tranquil piece of property about two miles south of San Pedro. The stucco and thatched casitas with tile floors are placed around several sleek infinity pools; you also get a full-service dive shop with private guides, the Admiral Nelson Bar, and one of the top-rated restaurants in the country (Restaurant Palmilla).

The Villas at Banyan Bay (tel. 501/226-3739, U.S. tel. 866/352-1163, www.banyanbay.com, from US$275) is a luxury family resort with all the amenities in its 32 suites, including a whirlpool tubs. Lots of activities and lessons for children are available; full dive trips and inland trips can be arranged. There's also an on-site dock restaurant, Rico's, and a wedding chapel at the tip of the dock. It's close to San Pedro Town, yet away from the noise and on a nice section of the beach.

Less than three miles north of San Pedro, the family-run C **El Pescador** (tel. 501/226-2398, U.S. tel. 800/242-2017, www.elpescador.com, from US$200) was constructed in 1974 as one of the world's premier sportfishing lodges, and it has evolved into an modern upscale eco-lodge resort. There are 12 seafront double rooms in the original mahogany lodge—cozy and with touches of Mayan decor—and private one-, two-, and three-bedroom villa accommodations, all of which are centered around three stunning saltwater and freshwater swimming pools and gorgeous palms. The villas can be locked off into smaller sections, and each is outfitted with a spacious seafront deck, a full kitchen with sit-up bar, baths with gorgeous tiling, and Belizean-made hardwood floors. The resort offers more than fly-fishing trips, including smaller customized ecotours and diving with resident licensed dive master Alonzo Flota. Guests mingle over communal meals on the lovely large outdoor patio and at the on-site lounge, complete with a bar and a pool table, at the end of the day's activities. You'll find that anglers and their nonfishing families (there are spa services available, yoga classes nearby,

© LEBAWIT GIRMA

the beach at the stunning Mata Chica Beach Resort

cycling, and more) are repeat visitors, and many know each other from past years.

Las Terrazas (U.S. tel. 800/447-1553, www. lasterrazasresort.com, US$225) is a slick affair of 39 fully equipped "residential townhomes" around a pool area and restaurant serving "Southwestern cuisine with Caribbean flair." This is a full-service luxury resort with many activities and packages.

A little more than four miles north of San Pedro, you'll fall in love with the über-stylish yet unpretentious 【 **Mata Chica Beach Resort** (tel. 501/220-5010, www.matachica. com, from US$256), with 24 spacious casitas, suites, and luxury villas clustered along a beautiful stretch of white sand, front and back. The casitas are named after fruits (mine was Cherry); each bears its own color and matching porch hammock and is styled with local art and a blend of African and Oriental-tinged decor. The resort offers a full range of amenities, a spa, an infinity pool with a jetted tub, plus a vast lounge that connects to the Mambo restaurant. There are no flat-screen TVs or

phones, nor will you miss them—Mata Chica is all about Zen. Proximity to the reef, which is visible from the white sandy shores, makes it ideal for water sports, from paddleboarding to kayaking; all are complimentary, as are the private daily boat shuttles to town. The resort is ideal for an intimate wedding, a honeymoon (even with yourself), or a secluded couple getaway. The six-person beach mansion goes for a cool US$1,015 per night plus taxes. The view of the Barrier Reef from the beach is stunning.

【 **Portofino** (tel. 501/678-5096, www. portofinobelize.com, US$250-335) is another long-standing luxury lodge right on the beach, but with a deep swimming pool, an excellent on-site restaurant (meal plan available), and friendly staff. They have 15 units, including two treetop suites, and a honeymoon-VIP villa with full amenities. You can use the lodge's sporting equipment to play around all day— it's only a 15-minute kayak paddle to excellent snorkeling at Mexico Rocks.

Luxurious in a shaded compounded in town are the beautiful oceanfront suites at

◖ The Palms (tel. 501/226-3322, www.belizepalms.com, US$204-292), a boutique condominium resort on the beach next to Ramon's Village Resort. Secluded yet centrally located, there's a beautiful small freshwater pool in a well-kept garden and a variety of 12 one- and two-bedroom ocean-view suites, executive suites, and a poolside casita. Amenities aren't spared, and the furnishings are wonderful. The Palms feel like your own luxurious vacation home.

Over US$300

The **Phoenix Resort** (U.S. tel. 877/822-5512, tel. 501/226-2083, www.thephoenixbelize.com, US$465-795) raises luxury up a couple of notches in San Pedro. This large condo resort has 28 of the largest furnished suites on the island, with every amenity you can imagine both in and out of your room, including king beds, granite countertop kitchens, and even iPads. It has a pool, a restaurant, a gym, and a spa, all in a big walled compound toward the north of town on the beach side, and there is full concierge service for activities on and off the island. It's *très* contemporary chic.

Located next door to Mata Chica Beach Resort, go for the full rock-star treatment in one of two 3,000-square-foot villas at **Azul Belize** (tel. 501/226-4012, www.azulbelize.com, from US$1,000, all-inclusive); watch the horizon from your private rooftop jetted tub with one of Azul's famous frozen mojitos in hand. Your enormous three-floor crib boasts a full Viking kitchen, lady-wood beams, wraparound balconies, flat-screen TV, and wireless Internet throughout the property. Or, unplug at the infinity pool or adjoining Rojo Lounge, where world-class chef Jeff Spiegel prepares some of the island's best cuisine. In 2011 Azul expanded to include several high-luxury options, including a massive 14,400-square-foot villa with its own pool, patio, swim-up bar, and beer on tap.

FOOD

Dining out can be expensive in San Pedro, but there are cheap meals and snacks at many bakeries as well as the fast-food carts in the central park.

Bakeries and Cafés

Breakfast is serious business in San Pedro. You can smell the freshly baked bread and johnny-cakes as you walk down Front Street early in the morning, starting with ◖**Ruby's Café** and **Celi's,** which for decades have been bustling every morning with workers, visitors, and party animals eating breakfast at dawn and stocking up for day trips.

Head to the **Rum, Cigar and Coffee House** (Middle St., tel. 501/226-2020, 9am-9pm daily) which, believe it or not, sells and serves some of the best coffee in town—fresh-roasted Guatemalan beans daily. There's interior seating to enjoy, although it's limited. You might as well try their Belizean-made rum cream while you're here.

Mesa Café (tel. 501/226-3444, 8am-4pm Mon.-Fri.) serves delicious and affordable breakfasts (the coconut french toast is heaven), quiche, salads, delicious sandwiches, burgers, pies, and even homemade gelato in several flavors, although it does have a slight an ice cream texture (try the coconut or eggnog flavors). It's at the entrance to the Vilma Linda Plaza, a peaceful oasis in the bustle of downtown; the tiled courtyard is filled with lush plants and a small fishpond.

Barbecue

Besides the informal street barbecues, which offer the best-value food around, a rotating schedule ensures a beach cook-up nearly every night of the week, starting with **BC's** (on the beach, just east of the airstrip, tel. 501/226-3289, 11am-3pm Sun.). Your choice of chicken, ribs, or fish runs US$5-10. Also on Sunday, a host of beachfront eateries offer a special barbecue menu, coupled with live music; it's a sort of tradition on San Pedro.

On Friday, you'll see a steaming grill outside the **Lions Club** building (Front St., across from Manelly's) for the weekly fund-raising barbecue. Starting at 2pm, anyone is welcome to buy a plate or "boxed lunch" of grilled chicken with

BELIZEAN SUNDAY BEACH BARBECUE

© LEBAWIT GIRMA

Grilling starts at dawn at Estel's for their famous Sunday beachfront barbecue.

Sunday is "Funday," as they say in San Pedro and in the rest of Belize. Businesses close, families lunch together after church, kids swim off the docks, and adults relax in the shade beside barbeque grills. Heaps of perfectly smoked chicken, lobster, and other meats come off the grill and are washed down with Belikins. The rest of the afternoon is spent fishing, competing in horseshoe tournaments, dancing to live music, or napping beside a palm tree. It's the cure for a week's hard work (or a Saturday-night hangover).

Belizeans are masters of the barbecue, and this skill manifests itself most on the weekend. Unless you're invited to a local's outdoor food fest, there are a few options where visitors can get a taste of this Belizean tradition. Several beachfront establishments in San Pedro Town offer a Sunday barbecue special, complete with beachside seating, pools or docks, and live music. Some also throw in games for all-around good cheer.

You can't go wrong at **Estel's Dine by the Sea** (tel. 501/226-2019, 6am-close Sun., US$12.50), a family-run gem serving succulent barbecue ribs with your choice of pork, chicken, jerk wings, sausage, and generous sides. You'll see owner Charles Worthington outside at 6:30am, perfecting the meat on a massive grill. Get your outdoor patio table early (by noon) and sip a cold beverage while you listen to a soothing acoustic band play light rock tunes.

Just a bit farther down the beach, local and expat favorite **BC's Beach Bar** (on the beach just east of the airstrip, tel. 501/226-3289, 11am-3pm Sun., US$10) has a feast of ribs, chicken, fish, sausage, and sides, all of which you can savor while seated at tables directly on the beach or perched under the thatched-hut bar.

Catamaran Beach Bar (at Caribbean Villas, Seagrape Dr., tel. 501/226-2715, US$6-15) offers a similar barbecue lunch starting at noon–from chicken to pork ribs, delicious shrimp kebabs, or lobster. A small band usually performs. Side note: the Bloody Marys are fantastic.

Sunday Funday at **Crazy Canucks** (beachfront, tel. 501/670-8001, US$5-10) is somewhat of an expat institution. The place attracts the largest crowd of all on Sunday afternoons and starts later than most at 3pm. They also have a live blues band, or try your hand at their horseshoe tournament.

To escape the Sunday action in town, the ever-wonderful **Palapa Bar and Grill** (tel. 501/226-3111, 10am-about 9pm Sun., US$4-6), north of the bridge, is perfect almost any day, not just Sunday.

Another option is to head out on a special day's sail to a nearby caye for an island beach barbecue getaway Belizean-style. For more information, check with the **Rubio Brothers** (tel. 501/600-5022).

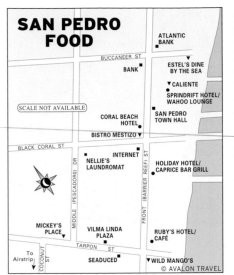

SAN PEDRO FOOD

ATLANTIC BANK
BUCCANEER ST
BANK
ESTEL'S DINE BY THE SEA
CALIENTE
SPRINDRIFT HOTEL/ WAHOO LOUNGE
SCALE NOT AVAILABLE
CORAL BEACH HOTEL
SAN PEDRO TOWN HALL
BISTRO MESTIZO
BLACK CORAL ST
INTERNET
NELLIE'S LAUNDROMAT
HOLIDAY HOTEL/ CAPRICE BAR GRILL
MIDDLE (PESCADORO) DR
FRONT (BARRIER REEF) ST
MICKEY'S PLACE
VILMA LINDA PLAZA
RUBY'S HOTEL/ CAFÉ
TARPON ST
To Airstrip
COCONUT ST
SEADUCED
WILD MANGO'S
© AVALON TRAVEL

NORTHERN CAYES

few local eateries offering the cheapest stew chicken, rice and beans, or burrito dishes on the island. The popular **El Fogón** (Trigger Fish St., tel. 501/206-2121, 11:30am-3pm and 6:30pm-9pm Mon.-Sat., US$4-6) is an authentic family-style eatery with flavorful Creole and mestizo dishes home-cooked on an open-fire hearth and served in a small, shaded, sand-floored space. Tucked toward the back of the island, just north of the airstrip, it will not let you down. The restaurant recently started serving dinner (US$16-30), with plenty of grilled seafood choices and kebabs along with either rice or pasta and sides.

Exactly one street back and parallel to El Fogón is **Neri's Taco Place** (Chicken St., 5:30am-11:30am and 5:30pm-9pm Mon.-Sat., 5:30am-noon Sun.), dishing out some of the best tacos (US$0.50 for 3) and cheap, delicious eats that you order at a small window. There are a couple of picnic tables outside, and it gets very crowded with locals on Sunday. It's off the beaten path but well worth finding.

On the beach side, **Estel's Dine by the Sea** (on the beach behind Atlantic Bank, tel. 501/226-2019, 6am-4:30pm Wed.-Mon., US$12.50) is a relaxed, ideal breakfast spot. Besides the morning treats, Estel's is great on Sunday with barbeque lunch and live music.

Ruby's (Front. St., 4:45am-6pm Mon.-Sat.) has the absolute best local pastries in town, from stuffed massive fry jacks to soft and crunchy johnnycakes and more, not to mention coffee early in the morning—in short, you cannot visit San Pedro and not stop in at Ruby's. Other reputable spots are **Ambergris Delights** (Middle St., tel. 501/226-2135) and **Celi's Deli** (Front St., tel. 501/226-0346, 6am-6pm daily), second only to Ruby's and popular for its plain or stuffed johnnycakes and sought-after meat pies.

Also on Front Street is the small family-style restaurant, **Bistro Mestizo** (below Coral Beach Hotel, tel. 501/226-4465, 10am-10pm daily, US$3-10), serving Central American specialties infused with a touch of Caribbean, and where I enjoyed the largest, most delicious fish tacos I've had anywhere. The new Belizean-run

generous side servings (US$4.50). There's also a bar on-site. All the money made is pooled to help members who are in need or suffer a disaster. In case you were curious, Friday night is also bingo night, so popular among the locals that many negotiate their weekly work shifts around it.

The island's only falafel joint, **Alibaba's** (across Coconut Dr. from the Tropic Air terminal and Moncho's Golf Carts, tel. 501/226-3337, 10am-10pm daily, US$5-12), is run by two cousins from Jordan and is best known for its takeout rotisserie chicken, served Lebanese style with generous portions of hummus and tabbouleh; there are also kebabs, veggie plates, and sometimes hookahs to smoke.

It's often difficult to find authentic Jamaican jerk outside Jamaica, but **Jambel Jerk Pit** (Front St., beachside at Sunbreeze Suites, tel. 501/226-3515, 7am-9pm daily, US$8-20) rises to the challenge, and its weekly Wednesday all-you-can-eat buffet with live music is a great value (6pm-9pm Wed., US$20 pp). The new location, on a poolside and beachfront deck with umbrellas, is wonderful.

Belizean and Central American
On the back side of the island, you'll find a

NORTHERN CAYES

© LEBAWIT GIRMA

El Fogón is famous for serving authentic Belizean food in a casual setting.

establishment has live *cumbia* music nights (Thurs. and Sun.) to add to the cultural experience and a popular daily *hora feliz* (happy hour, 6pm-8pm), a nice change from the otherwise rock and blues offerings in town.

Mickey's Place (Tarpon St., tel. 501/226-2223, breakfast, lunch, and dinner daily, US$5.50) is the home of the huge Wednesday burrito. Mickey's has an ample menu of local fare, especially seafood and conch fritters, fresh juices, and cinnamon rolls, and offers a bit more ambience than the other Belizean places, even if it doesn't have outdoor seating.

For top-notch Latin Caribbean cuisine, ◖ **Wild Mango's** (sandwiched between Ruby's Hotel and the library on the beach, tel. 501/226-2859, noon-3pm and 6pm-9pm Mon.-Sat., US$12-20) serves amazing versions of local favorites (ceviche, fish tacos, quesadillas, burritos) prepared by one of Belize's most distinguished chefs, Amy Knox; you cannot go wrong here, with Mango's Mongo Burrito, seafood specials, Amy's Chef Salad, and rum-glazed bacon shrimp.

For fun beach-like ambiance with sandy floors, picnic tables, and Latin music, **Elvi's Kitchen** (Pescador Dr., 501/226-2404, 11am-10pm Mon.-Sat., US$10-40) is a great San Pedrano experience. Doña Elvi's family-run restaurant serves the ultimate Belizean version of soul food—home cooked, authentic cuisine with a kick. Don't miss the cheese-stuffed jalapeños, the Mayan fish, or the to-die-for coconut shrimp curry, among many other options. There's also a popular Mayan buffet on Friday nights with live Mayan music (and if you must know, they make some of the best margaritas in town).

Not far off from Elvi's is **Waruguma** (Middle St., tel. 501/651-7961, 11am-9:30pm daily, US$8-18), rightly famous for its savory *pupusas,* available for lunch but grilled outdoors on the patio in the evenings starting at 5pm, and their megasize burritos as well as other Salvadoran treats, all at a great price. So gigantic are the burritos that there's a wall of fame dedicated to those who have managed to finish one by themselves.

If you're searching for the absolute best conch fritters on the island along with fresh seafood in all sorts of combinations—grilled, blackened, steamed, Mexican, Creole, breaded, fried, you name it—don't miss a stop at **Caramba Restaurant and Bar** (Pescador Dr., tel. 501/226-4321, 11am-10pm Thurs.-Tues., US$5-15) with its new, lively, and colorful indoor and outdoor bar and patio. Seriously, the seafood here is tasty and plentiful, as is the meat—look out for the Bacon Macho Burger. Prepare your stomach, and make reservations for dinner as the place gets packed.

Slightly higher-end yet still casual, **Caliente** (in the Spindrift Hotel, Front St., tel. 501/226-2170, 11am-9:30pm Tues.-Sun.) offers Mexican cuisine and seafood on an open porch or in a waterfront dining room. It is famous for the lime soup (only US$4.50) at lunch (good for hangovers) and generous lobster dinners and other entrées (US$12-22). Caliente also has the best nachos in town—a perfect snack on Thursday before the Chicken Drop event next door at Wahoo's Lounge.

The old Celi's Restaurant (not to be confused with Celi's Deli) inside the San Pedro Holiday Hotel has metamorphosed into the swankier beachfront **Caprice Bar Grill** (Front St., tel. 501/226-2014, 9am-midnight Mon.-Sat., 11am-9pm Sun., US$15-32), delivering Caribbean and Latin cuisine. The quesadillas are to die for and the portions are large. The outdoor covered deck is ideal to the popular happy hour (3pm-6pm), with half-price mojitos, margaritas, and rum punch as well as US$2 beer specials.

Keep walking south and you'll run into **Hurricane's Ceviche Bar & Grill** (tel. 501/226-4124, 10am-10pm Wed.-Mon., US$8-18), set on a pier and specializing in all kinds of ceviche—including horse conch, octopus, lobster, and other seafood. The sea views and the friendly barkeep make it stand out.

Another longtime popular ceviche venue in town is the casual **Lily's Treasure Chest Restaurant** (beachside on Front St., across from Amigos Del Mar, tel. 501/226-2650,

7am-9pm daily, US$9-17) serving ceviche through the day and with a spacious outdoor patio.

For a nice Ambergris evening away from town, take a golf cart or water taxi to one of the restaurants north of the bridge. The cheapest and most casual places are Palapa Bar and Ak'Bol. Easily accessible and a notch up in style is the chic **Kama Lounge** (tel. 501/610-3775 or 501/226-3709, kamalounge@yahoo.com, noon-10pm daily, US$10-35), offering a nice variety of affordable "kama eats" that include bar food, salads, pastas, kebabs, paninis, and more, served under the stars in a beautiful setting of couches, hookahs, and dim red lighting. I can't imagine a more relaxing evening spot.

You can get a decent burger at many restaurants in San Pedro, but only **Legends Burger Bar** (tel. 501/226-2113, noon-9pm Mon.-Sat., US$10), 0.5 miles or so north of the bridge, specializes totally in beef and chicken patties. The atmosphere is tropical frat house, with live music till midnight on weekends and a popular Tuesday-night live jam. The menu is entertaining, with each burger dedicated to the owner's various heroes. The most Belizean is the Sir Barry Burger, a tribute to local legend Barry Bowen, a widely admired businessman who was tragically killed in a plane crash in 2010; it's a beef patty topped with Belikin beer-battered shrimp, representing three of the commodities Bowen produced and sold.

Italian

Pizza is available for delivery or dining in at dozens of places on the island. **Pepperoni's Pizza** (Coconut Dr., tel. 501/226-4515, 5pm-10pm Tues.-Sun.) is the most popular for both quality and price—a large 16-inch specialty pie goes for US$20 and is served deep-dish style. **Pirates** (Middle St., tel. 501/226-4663, US$4-25) is also good and does slices in the evenings.

Mexican

Mexican food lovers will enjoy the **Lone Star Grill & Cantina** (tel. 501/226-4666, noon-9pm Wed.-Mon., US$10-18) a very far trek south but well worth it both for the ambiance and the tasty belly-filling dishes that include chimichangas, El Jefe burritos, chalupas, enchiladas, and more Mexican favorites. There are also "gringo favorites" of the burger-and-fries variety.

Fine Dining

San Pedro is blessed with an ever-evolving selection of trendy restaurants offering international fare and flair; if you don't pay for such indulgence with an expanded waistline, you'll surely pay for it in cash. If you're *really* dining out—an appetizer, a couple of drinks, an entrée, and a dessert—expect to pay as much as you would in a U.S. city: US$40-80 pp, more if you like your wine. Remember that many upscale restaurants add tax and a service charge, and a fee for using a credit card, so bring enough cash. Reservations are recommended at all of the following restaurants, especially in the high season.

Of the finer restaurants, **◖Blue Water Grill** (on the beach, behind the SunBreeze Hotel, tel. 501/226-3347, 7am-9:30pm daily, entrées from US$19) is known to offer some of the best values and biggest portions. The menu has hints of Hawaiian and Southeast Asian cuisine; try the coconut shrimp stick with black-bean sweet-and-sour sauce. Sushi is offered on Tuesday and Thursday; there are dishes like snook with banana curry along with comfort plates like lasagna.

Red Ginger (tel. 501/226-4623, 7:30am-10:30am, 11:30am-2:30pm, and 6pm-9:30pm daily, US$9-37), in the Phoenix Resort toward the north part of San Pedro, has an indoor air-conditioned dining room and trellised outdoor patio. The food here is absolutely divine. They specialize in local cuisine with an international twist—grouper ceviche with mango, empanadas with pork, and plantains with buffalo mozzarella and sautéed basil. There are homemade bagel sandwiches for breakfast, Indian chicken curry and Cajun gumbo for lunch, and a variety of appetizers, salads, pastas, seafood, and steaks, plus a delicious and filling five-course tasting menu (US$45) for dinner; there's a big

wine list, half-price wine on Monday, and tapas on Wednesday and Sunday.

◖ Casa Picasso (Sting Ray St., tel. 501/226-4443, www.casapicassobelize.com, 5:30pm-10pm Tues.-Sun., US$10-30) is one of the best fine-dining experiences in San Pedro. The restaurant, a cozy dining-room setting with art, drapes, and mood lighting, serves tapas (think lobster sliders, potato ricotta gnocchi, or pork belly in oyster sauce, yum!), salads, steaks, seafood, and unique entrées (the lobster risotto is otherworldly). Desserts aren't to be missed either, including the banana wontons. Enjoy a free pick up and return with your reservation.

Hidden Treasure Restaurant (4088 Sarstoon St., tel. 501/226-4111, www.hiddentreasurebelize.com, 5:30pm-9:30pm daily, US$15-22) is an intimate open-air restaurant, beautifully lit under a *palapa* roof. They have a long list of appetizers, lunches, dinner items, and desserts, from seafood bisque to Mayan-accented snapper and spare *buhurie* (Garífuna-spiced ribs).

The chef at Victoria House's **Restaurant Palmilla** (at Victoria House, 2 miles south of San Pedro, tel. 501/226-2067, 6:30am-2:30pm and 6pm-9pm daily, US$24-50) was born in Mexico City, trained in the United States, and comes from a family of renowned chefs. His unique style is "Mayan bistro," which combines the chili peppers of Mexico with fresh local produce, seafood, and meats. Start with crispy snapper cakes with chipotle beurre blanc, black beans, and roasted corn succotash; follow with black-bean or *chilapachole* (corn) soup; then savor main dishes like cashew-crusted grouper.

Glen and Colleen at the **Rendezvous Restaurant and Winery** (tel. 501/226-3426, wwww.ambergriscaye.com/rendezvous, lunch and dinner daily) offer free wine tasting to anyone wandering by. They blend, ferment, and bottle their own wine in recycled bottles. The restaurant has a stellar 12-year reputation for its blend of Thai and French cuisine. Start with escargot with lemon-garlic butter sauce for an appetizer (US$10), and then have grilled shrimp (US$22) or chicken with coconut red curry sauce (US$15).

A few more miles up the coast, **☾Mambo's** (Matachica Beach Resort, tel. 501/220-5010, www.matachica.com, lunch and dinner daily) is pure indulgence, serving rich and artful heaps of snappers, scallops, shrimp, lobsters, and calamari—you can try them all in the amazing Deep Blue entrée (US$34). Appetizers, such as soy-glazed snapper carpaccio, are US$10-16; save room for the chocolate mousse.

Rojo Lounge (at Azul Belize, www.azul-belize.com, tel. 501/226-4012, lunch and dinner Tues.-Sat., entrées from US$27) has a succulent, sophisticated menu that will leave you grasping for adjectives. Or maybe you'll just reach for your peppered cocktail in stunned silence after each bite of shrimp-stuffed grouper or conch pizza; it's spendy but worth every savory cent. The self-made chef, Jeff Spiegel, is a former punk record producer from California.

Portofino Restaurant and Green Parrot Beach Bar (tel. 501/226-5096, lunch and dinner daily, dinner entrées US$18-35) is six miles north of San Pedro, and they'll give you a complimentary boat ride to join them for dinner, although from no farther south than Fido's dock; expect local cuisine with European flair, including spider crab-laced snapper and other creative seafood specials. Lunch is also excellent with delicious chicken finger baskets and an enormous vegetarian selection (US$6-14), and they'll set up a romantic table on the end of their pier if you like.

Dessert

Go to **Manelly's** (Front St.) for homemade ice cream—they are known for their "coconut creation." Or sample the frozen custard at **DandE's Ice Cream** (Pescador St.), where a couple from Pennsylvania dairy country turn out fresh flavors every day, including soursop, from a local fruit that makes for a tart Belizean treat.

Groceries

There are several medium-size supermarkets around San Pedro; one of the cheapest is the locally owned **Marina's Market** (next to Xanadu Island Resort, Coconut Dr., tel. 501/226-3647). The best selection is at **Island Supermarket** (Coconut Dr., tel. 501/226-2972), which is large and modern and offers free delivery. **The Greenhouse** (Pescador Dr., next to St. Francis Xavier Credit Union, tel. 501/226-2084) boasts the most fresh produce and seafood, including cold cuts and unique grocery selections. **Caye Mart Supermarket** (north of Castillo's Hardware Store, tel. 501/667-4243, samirbelize@gmail.com) has wine selections as well as imported Carib beer.

INFORMATION AND SERVICES
Banks

There are plenty of banks in town. Belize, Scotiabank, Atlantic, and First Caribbean have international ATMs. There's also an ATM in the big supermarket just south of Ramon's Village. **Milo's Money Exchange** (Middle St., tel. 501/226-2196) is another option. It exchanges Belizean, U.S., Guatemalan, Mexican, Canadian, and British currencies, and it's also a Western Union branch.

Health and Emergencies

Prescriptions and other medicines can be found at **R&L Pharmacy** (tel. 501/226-2890, open daily), by the airstrip, and there are plenty of smaller pharmacies around town. If you need medical attention, all hotels and resorts keep a list of doctors and transportation options to call in the middle of the night, including a helicopter to take you to the hospital in Belize City in the event of a major emergency. For other medical concerns, go to the **San Pedro PolyClinic II** (tel. 501/226-2536, 8am-noon and 2pm-5pm Mon.-Sat.), located behind Wine de Vine and the Island Supermarket, facing the airstrip.

Dr. Daniel Gonzalez's **Ambergris Hope Clinic** (tel. 501/226-2660), located next to Castillo's hardware store, is another option. For diving emergencies, the island has one hyperbaric chamber (tel. 501/226-2851 or

501/226-3195), or call Dr. Antonia Guerrero (tel. 501/628-3828).

The **police department** (for emergencies tel. 911, south substation tel. 501/206-2022 or 501/610-4911) and **fire department** (tel. 501/226-2372) are both located in San Pedro Town near the big BTL antennae on Middle Street.

Media and Communications

Things change quickly in San Pedro, especially prices. Before your trip, always take a good look at **www.ambergriscaye.com,** by far the best portal for all things Ambergris, including a lively message board filled with opinionated characters. You'll find links to hundreds of island businesses as well as Ambergris's two weekly papers, the **San Pedro Sun** (tel. 501/226-2070, www.sanpedrosun.net) and the online **Ambergris Today** (Middle St., tel. 501/226-3462, www.ambergristoday.com), both wonderful resources. *Ambergris Today,* a favorite of mine, includes comprehensive reviews of the latest and best establishments in town, including resorts, restaurants, and more. Also check the **San Pedro Daily** (http://sanpedrodaily.com).

The **post office** (Middle St., 8am-4pm Mon.-Thurs., 8am-3:30pm Fri.) is next to Elvi's Kitchen Restaurant.

There are several Internet cafés in town, some with Wi-Fi and others with desktops. **Caribbean Connection** (Front St., tel. 501/226-4664, 7am-10pm Mon.-Sat., 8am-10pm Sun., US$5 per hour) is directly across from the water taxi alley, with a speedy DSL line, wireless Internet access, coffee drinks, and air-conditioning.

GETTING THERE
By Air

The 2,600-foot-long runway of San Pedro Airport (SPR) is located practically in downtown San Pedro. Belize's two airlines, **Maya Island Air** (tel. 501/223-1140 or 501/223-1362, www.mayaislandair.com) and **Tropic Air** (tel. 501/226-2012, U.S. tel. 800/422-3435, www.tropicair.com) fly more than a dozen daily flights between San Pedro, Caye Caulker, and

Belize City—and another five to and from Corozal. Tropic Air has a computerized system and offers more reliable service; there are flights from San Pedro to Belmopan, offering quicker access to the Cayo District. Maya Island Air is good too and sometimes gives 50 percent discounts on cash purchases; be sure to ask if a discount is available. The flight from Belize City's international airport to San Pedro takes about 15 minutes and costs US$120 round-trip. Flying in and out of Belize City's Municipal Airport is much cheaper (US$35 each way, not much more expensive than the water taxi), although you'll need to catch a taxi from the international airport to get there.

By Boat

Two companies providing scheduled water taxi service between Belize City and the islands: **Caye Caulker Water Taxi Association** (San Pedro tel. 501/226-2194, Caye Caulker tel. 501/226-0992, Belize City tel. 501/223-5752, www.cayecaulkerwatertaxi.com) and the **San Pedro Water Taxi Express** alternate schedules, each offering four daily trips between Belize City and Ambergris Caye, a 75-minute ride that costs US$15 one-way.

In Belize City, the Caye Caulker Water Taxi Terminal is at the north end of the Swing Bridge, with boats leaving between 8am and 4:30pm daily. The San Pedro Water Taxi Express departs from the Tourism Village in Belize City. Boats depart San Pedro from Wet Willy's Pier 8am-3:30pm daily. Always check the schedule before making plans; usually there are extra boats on weekends and holidays.

Thunderbolt Travels (tel. 501/422-0026, http://ambergriscaye.com/thunderbolt) runs a once-daily trip to Corozal (3pm, US$22.50 one-way, US$42.50 round-trip), leaving Corozal at 7am. The trip takes two hours in each direction. The departure pier in San Pedro is by the old football field; ask anyone to direct you to Thunderbolt.

GETTING AROUND

Walking is feasible within the town of San Pedro; it's about a 20-minute stroll from the airstrip to the split. Once you start traveling between resorts to the south or north, however, you may want to go by bicycle, golf cart, taxi, or boat. At one time, cars were a rarity, but together with golf carts they are taking over the town streets and even the north side of Ambergris. Most of the electric golf carts have been replaced by gas-powered ones, and hundreds ply San Pedro's rutted roads. Cobbled streets mean less dust and fewer potholes downtown.

The toll bridge connecting San Pedro Town with Ambergris's north side is free for pedestrians. From 6am to 10pm, bicycles pay US$1 to cross, and golf carts pay US$5 round-trip.

By Boat

Usually the smoothest and quickest way to travel up and down Ambergris Caye, water taxi service is available from **Coastal Express** (tel. 501/226-2007, or 501/226-3007, www.coastalxpress.com). Boats share a dock with Amigos del Mar Dive Shop, in front of Cholo's Sports Bar, departing for points north and south 5:30am-11:30pm daily, with special late-night schedules on big party nights (Wed.-Sat.). Daily scheduled runs are posted online. The fare, usually US$5-25 each way, depends on how far you are going, all the way up to El Secreto, the newest and farthest resort at press time. Most restaurants will radio the ferry to arrange your ride back to San Pedro Town. Coastal Express also offers private charters starting at a minimum of three people.

By Taxi

Minivan taxis (with green license plates) run north and south along the island at most hours; just wave one down and climb in. Expect to pay about US$4-7 to travel between town and points south. Within town, you'll pay around US$4. There are several drivers that you (or your accommodation's front desk) can call as well, including **Island Taxi** (tel. 501/226-3125) and **Herman Wade** (tel. 501/624-4912, 6am-9pm daily).

By Bicycle

Many resorts have bicycles that their guests can use for free, and others have them for rent, as do a handful of outside shops. Rentals are available by the hour (about US$5), day (US$10), and week (US$25). Many resorts refer guests to **Joe's Bikes** (tel. 501/226-4371), so check with your hotel for referrals.

Tours

Travel & Tour Belize (just north of the airstrip, tel. 501/226-2137 or 501/226-2031, www.traveltourbelize.com, 8am-5pm Mon.-Fri., 8am-noon Sat.) is the oldest and only full-service travel agent in San Pedro; they'll handle all your bookings, both local and international, and can help with weddings and events too.

Segway of Belize (Coconut Dr., Fairdale Plaza, tel. 501/620-9345, www.segwayofbelize.com, 8am-5pm daily) offers a guided two-hour Discover San Pedro Segway tour twice a week (Wed. and Fri., US$60 pp). A second tour option is to Segway to the Marco Gonzales Archeological Reserve (US$75 pp). Rentals are also available and include up to 30 minutes of safety training (US$35 per hour).

NORTHERN CAYES

THE GOLF CARTS OF SAN PEDRO

© LEBAWIT GIRMA

Golf carts are one of the main modes of transportation on Ambergris Caye.

It's the most common dilemma when planning a stay on Ambergris: Do I really need a golf cart to get around? It can take a chunk out of your travel budget, so decide beforehand whether to stay in San Pedro Town or not. Carts are most useful for those staying at one of the many resorts south of San Pedro, especially if you plan on coming into town often to shop, eat, and explore, day or night. The road to the north end of Ambergris, however, gets pretty bumpy and worse in the rainy season, requires a toll fee (US$5 per day) to cross the north bridge, and most companies won't allow you to drive farther north than the Palapa Bar or Grand Caribe Resort, 1.5 miles north of town. To explore past that point, you either have to hike or take the Coastal Express water taxi. If you're staying right in San Pedro, everything is pretty walkable, although a golf cart could be fun for a day's exploration.

Ambergris's carts all used to be electric, but now most companies have gas-powered carts. It'll set you back as much as renting an automobile on the mainland, but if you're staying south of town and have multiple passengers (a family, for example), it's probably worth it. Expect to pay more than US$75 for 24 hours and at least US$310 for a week. Drivers must be age 17 and have a valid driver's license. You will likely be required to leave a security deposit in the form of your credit card imprint or cash.

In the high season, reserve a cart in advance. Most companies will deliver to your hotel or pick you up at the airstrip. Your choices begin with **Moncho's** (Coconut Dr., tel. 501/226-4490, www.sanpedrogolfcartrental.com) and **Carts Belize** (south, next to Xanadu Resort, tel. 501/226-4090, www.cartsbelize.com), both close to the airstrip with relatively large fleets. Toward the north end of town, **Cholo's** (Jewfish St., in town, tel. 501/226-2406, www.choloscartrental.com) is reliable and has a small fleet of carts, and **Island Adventures Golf Cart Rentals** (Coconut Dr., near Tropic Air, tel. 501/226-4343, islandadventure@btl.net) has weekly deals and will deliver your cart. Another option is **La Isla Bonita** (north of town, tel. 501/226-3446), an extension of the Caye Mart supermarket; it's a family-run business offering reasonable cart prices. Be sure to check these companies' websites and social media pages for specials throughout the year.

When driving your cart, carry your valid driver's license and follow all normal traffic laws, including one-way street rules. Note that Front Street closes to all but pedestrian traffic on Friday, Saturday, and Sunday evenings. Make sure you park on the correct side of the street (it alternates every few weeks; just do what the locals are doing). Be sure to pay attention to the map you are given, don't speed or terrorize pedestrians into a corner, beware of unexpected bicycle riders, and watch for schoolchildren and one-way streets.

Caye Caulker

About 1,300 Hicaqueños (hee-ka-KEN-yos; derived from the island's Spanish name, Cayo Hicaco) reside on this island 21 miles northeast of Belize City, just south of Ambergris Caye and a mile west of the reef. Five miles long from north to south, the developed and inhabited part is only a mile long, from the split to the airstrip.

It's true that there have been changes in recent years, including the arrival of boutique luxury condominium resorts as the island realizes its unique spot in Belize's growing tourism economy. Yet the authenticity of life on a small Caribbean fishing village remains—original clapboard houses dot the coastline and side streets, and the only rumble you'll hear is from the sound of the few golf carts and bicycles crushing the sand-only roads, or the daily street chatter among residents. There's a happy, familial coexistence on Caye Caulker among expats and locals, and are all determined to conserve the island's history and surroundings through community education and involvement. In the end, Caye Caulker remains more affordable than Ambergris, and it's as laid-back as its "Go Slow" motto indicates, but no less entertaining.

ORIENTATION

The best landmark to start with is Caye Caulker's "Split"—also the most popular swimming and snorkeling spot. The Split cuts Caye Caulker into two areas: the southern inhabited part of the island, or "the Village," and the northern mangrove swamps.

Walking south from the Split, the main path lining the shore is **Front Street,** where you'll find seafront hotels, eateries, and the water taxi terminal. The other two main streets that shoot off parallel to Front Street are the simply named **Middle Street** and **Back Street.** Each leads to sandy roads with more accommodations, restaurants, and residents' homes. The entire island can be quickly explored in a couple of hours yet is big enough that it can take weeks to delve into each corner.

There's a fuel pump on the western pier. Sailors exploring nearby cayes can anchor in the shallow protected waters offshore; the water here is open ocean but is still often referred to as a "lagoon."

Front Street's south end comes to a dead-end by the **cemetery,** and you have three choices: Follow the narrow beach path along the water on foot or bicycle, or turn right and then left, where you'll find another sandy avenue that leads to the airstrip to the back of the island.

Bordering the airstrip is a rapidly developing neighborhood called Bahia Puesta del Sol, which has a small grocery store and a new high school. The land opposite the airstrip, called South Point, consists of mangrove swamps, with a narrow path cleared for golf cart or bicycle passage, for a coastal ride through an area rich in nature—trees, birds, and crocodiles—and lined with off-the-grid solar powered homes and docks.

SIGHTS
◖ The Split

Popular long before it appeared on the TV show *The Bachelor,* Caye Caulker's infamous "Split," or "cut," as it's still called by residents, is the favorite go-to swimming and sunset rendezvous spot on the island. It resembles a perfect island movie-set—not least for having the most decent stretch of sand, although it's narrow and flat. The story most people like to tell is that The Split came to be when Hurricane Hattie widened the channel in 1961 and "cut" the island in two, north and south. Boat captains and long-time residents will tell you that in fact the hurricane created only a tiny water passage that was later dug wider by anglers and politicians who wanted larger boats to pass. Eventually, daily sweeping tides made it as large as it is today. Either way, travelers and locals can be found here at all hours of

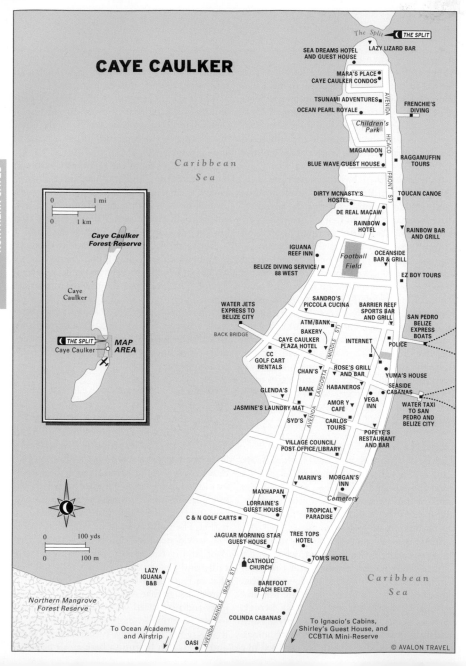

CAYE CAULKER

The Split

THE SPLIT

LAZY LIZARD BAR

SEA DREAMS HOTEL
AND GUEST HOUSE

MARA'S PLACE
CAYE CAULKER CONDOS

TSUNAMI ADVENTURES

OCEAN PEARL ROYALE

FRENCHIE'S
DIVING

AVENIDA HICACO (FRONT ST.)

Children's
Park

MAGANDON

RAGGAMUFFIN
TOURS

BLUE WAVE GUEST HOUSE

DIRTY MCNASTY'S
HOSTEL

TOUCAN CANOE

DE REAL MACAW

RAINBOW
HOTEL

RAINBOW BAR
AND GRILL

IGUANA
REEF INN

Football
Field

OCEANSIDE
BAR & GRILL

BELIZE DIVING SERVICE/
88 WEST

EZ BOY TOURS

SANDRO'S
PICCOLA CUCINA

BARRIER REEF
SPORTS BAR
AND GRILL

WATER JETS
EXPRESS TO
BELIZE CITY

ATM/BANK

BAKERY

INTERNET

SAN PEDRO
BELIZE
EXPRESS
BOATS

BACK BRIDGE

CAYE CAULKER
PLAZA HOTEL

MIDDLE ST.

POLICE

CC
GOLF CART
RENTALS

CHAN'S

ROSE'S GRILL
AND BAR

YUMA'S HOUSE

LANGOSTA

SEASIDE
CABANAS

GLENDA'S

BANK

HABANEROS

VEGA
INN

WATER TAXI
TO SAN
PEDRO AND
BELIZE CITY

JASMINE'S LAUNDRY MAT

AMOR Y
CAFÉ

AVENIDA

SYD'S

CARLOS
TOURS

POPEYE'S
RESTAURANT
AND BAR

VILLAGE COUNCIL/
POST OFFICE/LIBRARY

MARIN'S

MORGAN'S
INN

MAXHAPAN

Cemetery

LORRAINE'S
GUEST HOUSE

TROPICAL
PARADISE

C & N GOLF CARTS

JAGUAR MORNING STAR
GUEST HOUSE

TREE TOPS
HOTEL

AVENIDA MANGLE (BACK ST.)

CATHOLIC
CHURCH

TOM'S HOTEL

LAZY
IGUANA
B&B

BAREFOOT
BEACH BELIZE

Caribbean
Sea

Northern Mangrove
Forest Reserve

COLINDA CABANAS

To Ignacio's Cabins,
Shirley's Guest House, and
CCBTIA Mini-Reserve

To Ocean Academy
and Airstrip

OASI

Caribbean
Sea

Caribbean
Sea

0   100 yds
0   100 m

Inset map

0   1 mi
0   1 km

**Caye Caulker
Forest Reserve**

Caye
Caulker

THE SPLIT

Caye Caulker

MAP
AREA

© AVALON TRAVEL

© LEBAWIT GIRMA

The beach at The Split is the best on the island.

the day swimming, snorkeling, sunbathing on concrete slabs, sharing finger foods on picnic tables anchored in shallow water, or drowning in rum punch and reggae from the on-site **Lazy Lizard Bar.** Others partake in "split jumping" fun into the sea, feeding magnificent frigate birds hovering over the area, or showing off their water-sports skills offshore. Those who seek peace and quiet should venture to the Split in the morning for a glorious peaceful swim.

Caye Caulker Marine Reserve

The island's very own "local channel" off the reef, where you can snorkel surrounded by dozens or more stingrays and nurse sharks as well as explore beautiful coral at the "coral gardens," is 0.5 mile from shore and just under 10 minutes by boat. It's an area often overlooked by those who head to Hol Chan—but if you prefer a similar but less crowded experience, this is a great choice. Note that you must have a tour guide present, as these are protected waters. The tour can also be combined with other snorkel stops for a small additional fee. Let **EZ Boy**

Tours (Front St., tel. 501/226-0349 or 501/610-2759) take you there; both guides were raised on the island and they know these waters like the backs of their hands.

On the north end of this reserve is a channel that attracts manatees during their mating season (May-Sept.). Two or three manatees, sometimes more, can be spotted at the surface at any time. It's a spectacular sight; just remember to respect the reserve rules and not touch or swim with the marine animals. Any of the tour companies will bring you here.

◖ Swallow Caye Wildlife Sanctuary

The protected area comprises nearly 9,000 acres of sea and mangrove at the north end of the Drowned Cayes, just a few miles east of Belize City. The sanctuary is co-managed by **Friends of Swallow Caye** and the **Belize Forest Department.** Check out www.swallowcayemanatees.org for more information, including membership, tours, and manatee facts.

Many tour operators will take you to Swallow

Caye, usually for US$60 pp. Chocolate's Manatee Tours was the premiere operator for Swallow Caye; unfortunately, Mr. Chocolate (a local legend on the island and in the ecotourism trade) passed away in April 2013. Mr. Chocolate was instrumental in the sanctuary's creation in July 2002. He earned environmental and tourism awards for providing quality trips to hundreds of tourists per season. Other guides are sure to uphold his legacy.

From Belize City this trip is combined with snorkeling on the barrier reef and looking for Atlantic bottlenose dolphins. Park fees are US$5 pp.

Northern Mangrove Forest Reserve

Just before the airstrip is a northern mangrove forest reserve area of about 100 acres that has been protected since 1998. Three kinds of mangroves—red, white, and black—and other trees provide an ideal habitat for crocodiles, turtles, fish, and water birds. Bird-watching is ideal here, with some 130 species, including the rufous-necked rail, the black catbird, and others that have not been spotted elsewhere in Belize. Tours can be arranged through the Caye Caulker branch of the **Belize Tourism and Industry Association** (tel. 501/623-9810).

South Point

Located directly opposite the airstrip, away from town and tucked behind the abandoned Belize Odyssey Resort, is a narrow sandy path that leads to a little-visited side of the island. The trail winds through a maze of glorious landscape—mangroves, almond trees, coconut palms, and saltwater palmettos—with pockets of sea views on the left and off-the-grid solar- and wind-powered homes on the other. Keep straight on the path and follow its twists and turns until you reach a dead end, noting the last house on the right. After dousing yourself generously with mosquito repellent, hike through a small littoral forest to reach the last dock. There lies a breathtaking scene of open water, blue skies, and sailing birds at the southernmost point of the island. This is South Point, the raw

inhabited Caye Caulker, where electric poles are nonexistent and where selling seafront lots has yet to completely change the nature that fills this area.

Don't venture here in the rainy summer months without a golf cart—not least because the occasional crocodile could very well be crossing your path as you pass. The ground could also prove particularly muddy and treacherous during rains. Golf-cart taxis can also bring you here; just ask around for a reliable driver.

SPORTS AND RECREATION

There's enough to do on this five-mile island to keep you occupied for days if you so choose—with ideal calm waters and fewer crowds than San Pedro, pick from an exciting list of water activities above or below the sea, including turf action such as biking, yoga, or indulging in healing spas.

Beaches

Beaches on most of Caye Caulker are of the thin, hard variety—don't expect to find a thick, soft, endless stretch of sand. Still, there's sand to feel under your toes, and the ratio of crowds versus beach space is favorable, such that finding your own sandy plot of the island is an easy feat. And if you can get past the first few inches of harmless sea grass and don't mind the lack of wave action due to the mile-distant Barrier Reef, you'll find the water is just as soothing and in the same jade color of Belize—all in all, a happy compromise.

The beachfront is a public area, and if you prefer to jump deeper into the sea to avoid the sea grass, docks are also a dime a dozen, unless marked "private." Just be mindful of boat activity and stay alert while snorkeling or swimming underwater.

The island is relatively small, so finding the beach merely requires going to the front or back areas of Caye Caulker. The best stretch for your towel is the Split area on the north end of the island. Other options for those looking to read quietly is the stretch of beach going along the front side—formerly known as Playa

CONSERVATION EFFORTS ON CAYE CAULKER

The **Forest and Marine Reserves Association of Caye Caulker** (FAMRACC, www.famracc.org) is a nongovernmental organization comprising representatives from different island organizations and service groups, including tour guides, schools, and the police. FAMRACC comanages the Caye Caulker Marine Reserves with the Fisheries and Forests Departments and works on projects like mangrove restoration, reef rapid assessments, community reef-technician training, and environmental education field trips for local children.

FAMRACC sometimes accepts volunteers to work with the mangrove and littoral forest restoration projects in the Forest Reserve as well as maintenance of reef mooring lines and buoys in the Marine Reserve. Guest researchers and scientists are also welcome.

The Caye Caulker Branch of the Belize Tourism Industry Association (CCBTIA) manages a 1.5-acre private **Forest Reserve** (www.gocayecaulker.com/forest.html), which is just before the airstrip. This tiny but lush littoral forest reserve has a nice walking trail that winds to the mangroves on the beach, and flora and fauna along the way are identified with hand-painted signs. CCBTIA has published a trail guide to the reserve as well as two books about the plants and birds of Caye Caulker; these are for sale at Cayeboard Connection or from CCBTIA. There is no charge to walk the trails. Guided tours are also available, and there is a small interpretive center.

FAMRACC can help you plan a tour in the Forest Reserve. Birding tours (3 hours, US$32) leave very early, and natural history tours of the project sites can be booked, followed by snorkeling in the North Channel (US$50-70, depending on duration). Contact marine biologist and guide Ellen McRae (tel. 501/226-0178) to arrange details.

Asuncion—from the arrival dock but going south (turning left). Along the back of the island are smaller stretches of beach, and swimming may be best off a dock, but the views are still lovely. Grab a cocktail at Sea Dreams Resort's upstairs Banyan Tree Bar or at Iguana Reef and sit by their beach to watch sunset.

Diving and Snorkeling

The reef you see from Caulker's eastern shore provides fantastic snorkeling and diving opportunities right in your front yard. Snorkeling can be as simple and cheap as renting masks and fins for US$5 per day from one of the tour operators (or bringing your own) and using them off almost any dock. If renting, you may be required to leave your ID behind for the day as security. Note that several tour operators are hesitant to pass out equipment so as not to encourage snorkeling beyond the docks in the protected marine reserves without a guide.

You could snorkel at the island's most popular swimming spot: the Split. It can be crowded with sunbathers and onlookers; avoid the heavily trafficked part and beware, as swimming here can be dangerous because of the pull of the current, which is strong enough to overpower children or weak swimmers. Your best bet is to go around the bend, only a few yards out of the Split, to avoid the dangerous boat traffic. Be mindful where you step or dive at the Split, as old construction materials have been dumped here for fill.

To snorkel the reef itself—just a mile away, leaving no excuse not to before leaving the island—boat tours are necessary and plenty are offered for both beginner or advanced snorkelers and divers. Trips can go for half a day or a full day, depending on the excursion, and there are enough to fit all budget ranges.

The most popular snorkel and dive sites are Hol Chan Marine Reserve and Shark Ray Alley, Caye Chapel Canyons, and the reefs around St. George's Caye, Long Caye Wall, and Sergeant's Caye. A common snorkeling tour package is to Hol Chan with stops at Shark Ray Alley and the Coral Gardens; lunch, not included, in San Pedro; and ending with a visit to the Sea Horse Sanctuary behind the Split.

For snorkeling tours, you can rely on the cheerful, capable guides at **Raggamuffin Tours** (Front St., tel. 501/226-0348, www.raggamuffintours.com), who will take you out on *RaggaGal, Ragga Prince, RaggaQueen,* or *RaggaKing*—beautiful Belizean-built boats designed especially to access shallow snorkeling spots. Raggamuffin regularly sails to Hol Chan (full-day trip, US$50, includes lunch and rum punch on board). When there's enough demand, a snorkel trip is also offered via motorboat to Turneffe Atoll (full-day trip, US$75, includes lunch).

Belizean guide and dive master Shedrack Ash offers friendly, professional snorkeling, manatee watching, fishing trips, and night dives through his company **French Angel Expeditions** (tel. 501/206-0037 or 501/670-7506, www.frenchangelexp.com), which gets rave reviews from past clients. Walk straight down the street from the water taxi on Calle del Sol.

For a reggae vibe, join **Ras Creek** on his boat *Heritage Cruze,* docked at the Lazy Lizard Bar when not plying the reef with happy reggae-crazy customers; this is one of the best ways to tour the Caye Caulker Marine Reserve (US$30). Ras Creek was the first to guide visitors to the Sea Horse Sanctuary behind the split.

Climb aboard the *Gypsy* with **Carlos Tours** (tel. 501/600-1654, carlosaya@gmail.com), which has an excellent reputation for personal attention and a focus on safety. Carlos is the only shop to offer a full-day snorkel tour to Hol Chan combined with a lunch stopover in San Pedro, where you get to eat and explore Ambergris Caye for 1.5 hours on your own (US$50 pp). Carlos loves underwater photography and will share and sell photo CDs immediately after a trip (US$15). His office is on Front Street next to Amor y Café.

Two local brothers run **Anwar Tours** (tel. 501/226-0327, www.anwartours.page.tl), and with 15 years of experience, they get positive reviews for both snorkel trips and inland tours. **Tsunami Adventures** (tel. 501/226-0462, www.tsunamiadventures.com) is located near the Split and books snorkel and inland trips and rents underwater cameras (US$8 per day). **EZ Boy Tours** (tel. 501/226-0349, ezboytours-bze@yahoo.com) offers all the standard snorkel tours as well as overnight camping trips and night snorkeling.

Many visitors are willing to brave four hours (two hours each way) on a boat in mostly open ocean to dive the Blue Hole and Turneffe Islands or other atoll sites. There is no "best" dive site, as every diver is looking for something different; just be sure to discuss the options before booking the trip, and make sure you're comfortable with the boat, guides, group size, and gear. Consider whether gear is included in the price or not, and don't quickly jump on the cheapest package.

Caye Caulker has two main dive shops offering similar tours, albeit with slightly varying prices and packages. The main offerings include Hol Chan (US$110-125 for 2 tanks); Blue Hole, Half Moon Caye, and Lighthouse (US$190-255 for 3 tanks); Turneffe day trips (US$125 north, US$150 south); certification courses (US$325-375 open water, US$275-300 advanced); as well as a variety of snorkeling excursions and other trips.

Dive master couple Chip and Danielle Petersen run **Belize Diving Services** (Chapoose St., across from the soccer field, tel. 501/226-0143, www.belizedivingservices.com), with an excellent reputation and an operation that is all computerized and offers both recreational and technical dives at Miner's Gold and Treasure Hunt dive sites. They also offer weekly dives at the Blue Hole and the atolls thanks to their 46-foot custom Newton dive boat, equipped with showers, ideal for the long ride. Certification courses are available. **Big Fish Dive Center** (tel. 501/226-0450, info@bigfishdivecenter.com, www.bigfishdivecenter.com) is a Belizean-owned dive shop with knowledgeable dive masters and a 45-foot dive boat with a small onboard restroom for farther destinations, such as the Blue Hole. My three dives to the Blue Hole and Lighthouse Reef with them were wonderful and safe. Note that as of 2012 the shop is no longer PADI certified, thus courses aren't available.

Snuba and Sea Trek

The new way of exploring Hol Chan is to snuba or sea trek with **Discovery Expeditions** (tel. 501/671-2881 or 501/671-2882, www.discoverybelize.com, US$68-74, includes hotel transfers but not the US$10 Hol Chan park fee) out of San Pedro. Catch the 8am water taxi over to San Pedro, where you will get picked up for your tour. The experience includes orientation before experiencing depths of 20-30 feet, enjoying marinelife and corals without needing a tank or worrying about being dive certified. Both activities are safe for anyone in good physical condition and older than age eight.

Boating and Sailing

Who doesn't love a great sail? **Raggamuffin Tours** (tel. 501/226-0348, www.raggamuffintours.com) offers sunset cruises and day sails. The best adventure has to be their unique overnight sailing trip on the 50-foot Stonington Ketch *RaggaQueen* sailboat south to Placencia (Tues. and Fri. departures), where you'll be dropped off at Tobacco Caye to continue your travels; with three days of sun and sea and two nights camping out in style on idyllic cayes. The trip costs US$350 pp, includes all gear, food, snorkeling, and fishing; expect a higher holiday rate (US$400) during the last week of December.

Stuart Trent Adventures (on the beach, in front of Sand Box Restaurant, tel. 501/631-9134, trenteesh@yahoo.com) offers instruction (US$25 per hour) and charters on traditional sailboats.

Fishing

Try to catch your dinner off one of the island's many piers. You can buy bait and rent fishing rods at the Badillos' house near the soccer field (look for a small porch sign). Or fish like a local with a hook, line, and weight. Or take a walk toward the back of the island, where you'll find fishers cleaning their fish, working on lobster traps, or mending their nets in the morning. Many will be willing to take you out for a reasonable fee. The main trophies are groupers, barracuda, snappers, and amberjacks—all good eating. Small boats are available for rent by the hour.

For professional fishing tours, go to **Anglers Abroad** (tel. 501/226-0602, www.anglersabroad.com, half-day US$220, full-day US$330, includes lunch) near the Split. Owner Haywood Curry sells and rents a complete selection of fly and spin gear (US$20-30 per day), and he is happy to give advice for the novice or expert fisher. He offers lessons (US$100 for 4 hours) and DIY instruction by canoe or on foot and sets up half-day, full-day, and overnight adventure trips. Group tours, as well as private lessons, are available. The shop works with well-known, award-winning, and experienced reefs and flats fishing guides, including Parnel and Kenan Coc—2011 and 2012 Top Guide title winners in the prestigious annual Tres Pescado Slam Tournament—as well as Rafael Alamilla, and Eloy Badillo. Anglers Abroad now also teaches a fly-fishing high school class at Ocean Academy.

Shadrack Ash, owner of **French Angel Expeditions** (tel. 501/670-7506 or 501/670-9155, www.frenchangelexp.com, half- or full-day US$200-350), can take you catch-and-release fly-fishing, spin casting with an option to grill your catch for you, and lobster fishing (June 15-Feb. 15).

Kayaking

Toucan Canoe and Kayaks (Palapa Gardens, Front St., across from Real Macaw, tel. 501/625-8024, toucancanoe@yahoo.com) has the most comprehensive canoe and kayak tours and rentals on the island (single US$5 per hour, double US$10 per hour). Private and group lessons are offered by Canadian-Belizean owner Allie Johnstone, who is a top-placing international canoe racer and licensed tour guide and naturalist. All two-hour tours are US$25. Ask Allie about beach stargazing options,

NORTHERN CAYES

© LEBAWIT GIRMA

Sea kayak rentals are an affordable way to explore the island.

mangrove tours, and her herbal walk to learn about the various medicinal plants and other flora on the island. **Tsunami Adventures** (tel. 501/226-0462, www.tsunamiadventures.com) also offers kayak and canoe rentals (US$7.50 per hour).

Wind Sports

Nondivers can rest assured: Caye Caulker is on the cutting edge of water sports, including the latest trend of stand-up paddleboarding, in part thanks to great bump and jump conditions— shallow crystal-clear waters protected by a nearby reef and the Caribbean trade winds.

For fun in the water and the wind, find **KiteXplorer** (Front St., toward the Split, tel. 501/635-4967, www.kitexplorer.com, 9am-6pm daily), offering beginner to advanced kite surfing, stand-up paddle surfing, and wind-surfing lessons (introduction to kite surfing US$90, or US$50 pp for 1.5 hours) with three licensed instructors, or equipment rentals (stand-up paddleboard US$20 per hour, windsurfing board US$15 per hour). Note that

these sports are seasonal and best from October through March.

Reef Watersports (Ave. Hicaco/Front St., just before the Split, tel. 501/635-7219, www. reefwatersports.com) offers Jet Ski rentals (US$75 for 30 minutes) as well as wakeboarding, waterskiing, and boat tubing (all US$100 per hour for 2 people).

The best place to practice paddleboarding solo on the island is on the "lee side" of the island, as Hicaqueños call it—the calm, flat side starting behind the Split.

An exciting newcomer is **Contour Ocean Adventures** (Front St., tel. 501/635-8757, henry@countourbelize.com, 9am-noon and 1pm-5pm daily), a right turn after the arrival dock, offering 7-10-foot-long paddleboards for rent (US$25 per hour, US$67 per day, includes 15-minute lesson, full damage insurance optional). Passionate water-sports couple Henry (born on the island) and Stefi Lopez, trained dive masters and surf enthusiasts, offer workout sessions and yoga on paddleboards. Surfboard rentals are also available.

Biking

An ideal way to explore the island and get a workout is by renting a bicycle (US$5-6 per day, US$25 per week) and exploring its nooks and crannies at your leisure. Most locals here are on bikes, even with their little ones in tow. The better spots to rent are **M&N Mel's Bike Rentals** (Chapoose St., off Front St., tel. 501/226-0229, US$2 per hour, US$7 per day, US$25 per week) or at the Friendship Convenience Store on Front Street. Many hotels also throw in complimentary bicycle use, so be sure to check beforehand.

Birding

More than 190 species of resident and migratory birds have been identified on Caye Caulker, some of which are rarely seen elsewhere. The white-crowned pigeon, rufous-necked wood-rail, and black catbird are commonly seen here. The northernmost part of the island, part of a protected forest and marine reserve system since 1998, is ideal for birding and is made up of miles of reef, grass flats, lagoons, and mangroves. Guided ecotours can be arranged through the **BTIA Resource Center** (cayecaulkerbtia@gmail.com). Caye Caulker's South Point has plenty of birdlife; rent a golf cart and explore at your leisure.

Massage and Bodywork

You'll feel rejuvenated and have new friends after a treatment at **Purple Passion Beauty Studio** (Calle del Sol, cell 501/666-8845 or 501/633-4525, 9am-noon and 1pm-6pm Mon.-Sat., purplepassionbze@hotmail.com), just a few steps from Rose's Grill. There's more to this green-and-purple cabin than meets the eye. Talented Belizean sisters Stacy and Gina Badillo, with more than a decade in the industry, run a tight beauty ship, offering full salon services that later expanded into spa services, including body scrubs, facials, and hot-stone massages in a cozy treatment oasis of a room in the back. The spa has a contemporary boho-chic feel, and it's a welcome respite from the outside rush of bicycles and pedestrians. Don't miss Gina's magical hands (US$50 per hour,

hot stone US$65 per hour) or Stacy's skillful nail art (get a Belizean flag on those tips). You might even pick up a couple of Creole phrases while there.

Eva McFarlane's cozy, fragrant **Healing Touch Day Spa** (tel. 501/206-0380 or 501/601-9731, www.healingtouchbelize.com) on Front Street offers everything from deep tissue and Swedish massage to Reiki, reflexology, aura cleansing, waxing, manicures, and facials. All treatments are US$60 for an hour, US$85 for 90 minutes.

Great Island Yoga (207/729-7883, www.greatislandyoga.com) offers classes from Christmas to Easter at a beautiful oceanfront location. Drop-in classes are US$7.50, if space is available, and organized groups are also welcome. **RandOM Yoga** (tel. 501/664-9444, www.randomyoga.com) is a donation-based seasonal outdoor yoga studio; for schedules, look for their sign on Front Street by Anwar Tours.

For those feeling more energetic, there is **Miss Louise's step aerobics** (Ave. Langosta, tel. 501/226-0118, 5pm-6pm Mon.-Thurs.); you can register or just drop in (US$2).

ENTERTAINMENT AND EVENTS

For a small island, Caye Caulker offers just enough "liming" (socializing over food and drink) options, from watering holes to late night dancing.

Nightlife

For drinks over sunset, head to the lively **Lazy Lizard Bar** at the Split and opt for two-for-one rum punches (Tues.-Sun., US$5) or, if you're feeling brave, the "lizard juice" cocktail, a thick, potent neon-green concoction. Lazy Lizard also serves good bar munchies, including chicken fingers and lobster burritos. The top deck has a second bar, additional seating, and a great view.

For live music, bar fare, burgers, and trivia-game nights (7:30pm Wed., Fri., and Sun.) that remind you of North America, head to the **Barrier Reef Sports Bar and Grill** (Front St., tel. 501/226-0077), directly on the beach and a few steps from the water taxi docks. The Friday guitar jam (3pm-7pm) attracts a lively crowd of visitors and residents; feel free to get up there and sing your heart out or dance. Service can be very slow at the busy bar, so go early. Tuesday nights are for free movies and popcorn, with matinees and evening screenings.

Those looking to extend sunset romance can go for an after-dinner outdoor movie under the stars at **Paradiso Lot 84 Outdoor Cinema** (Front St., next to Amor y Café, 6:30pm and 8:30pm Mon., Wed., and Fri., US$5). Recently relocated from its beachfront location, it's no less appealing thanks to a giant screen, surround sound, and gated modern lounge vibe. Pick a chair and dig your toes in the sand while sipping on a fancy cocktail—mojitos to martinis—from the neon-lit bar. Movies are new and old, with the schedule announced on a chalkboard outside the venue.

Do not dare leave the island without a drink and a glimpse of the three-story **I&I Reggae Bar** (Traveler's Palm St., 4pm-1am daily), one of the best in the Caribbean with its eye-catching interior decor of all things Rastafarian, swing bar chairs, and late night ambiance of reggae and dance beats. For more of a lounge vibe, head upstairs and people-watch on the deck. A small but nicely lit VIP room with its own bar adds a special touch, although the real party is still in the main room, where tipsy sun-kissed travelers and locals on the prowl converge on a disco-lit floor until closing.

Late-night revelers continue on to **Oceanside Nightclub** (Front St.), a local dive where nothing takes off until midnight and lasts till 3am, offering *punta* beats and occasional live bands on its large floor.

Of course, your night could be just as memorable buying drinks from a store and laying back on your hotel's seaside dock for stargazing. Whatever you choose to do, common sense rules: keep your wits about you and don't walk solo late at night.

Festivals and Events

With a claim to being the original host and creator of **Lobsterfest** in 1995, now held here annually in late June, in neighboring San Pedro, and in the southern beach town of Placencia, Caye Caulker's lobster season launch celebration remains as authentic as it was decades ago and attracts visitors from across Belize. The three-day weekend event is filled with Belizean-style recreation, including a Miss Lobsterfest beauty pageant, dozens of food booths to sample the crustacean in all its forms—grilled, stewed, or in ceviche—and beach parties with live music and games. The fun continues on at the Split for one big late outdoor party.

SHOPPING

All shops on the island are open daily. You'll find **Toucan,** the largest souvenir store, and a sprinkling of small gift shops on and around Front Street selling T-shirts, hot sauce, hammocks, art, sarongs, beachwear, postcards, photo albums, and other Belizean souvenirs. Caye Caulker's sandy streets have several skilled artisanal vendors. On Front Street is a collection of numbered stalls called **Palapa Gardens.** Here you can find hand-carved ziricote and rosewood, hand-painted T-shirts, Guatemalan textiles and handicrafts, beautiful model sailboats complete with rigging, jewelry, and music CDs. Look out for **Jacob & Stevens,** a modest art and jewelry stall just before Palapa Gardens, with longtime island resident Jacob Cabral's colorful and unusual fish-motif paintings.

Jewelry is a popular craft on the island and often sold from tables set up in the street. **Calvin** sells his cool handmade island necklaces, anklets, and earrings at his table set up Habaneros and Rose's Grill; he started 30 years ago, well before souvenir stores opened on the island. **Celi's Music** (Front St.) is where Mr. August can be found at a small table beside the shop, cutting and polishing conch shell pieces. There's a good selection of popular Belizean music and videos.

Cooper's Art Gallery (tel. 501/226-0330, www.debbiecooperart.com, 11am-5pm Mon.-Tues., 10am-8pm Wed.-Sun., US$10-220) on Front Street sells colorful Caribbean primitive art and posters, many in funky frames, big and small, hand-painted by artist Debbie Cooper and other local Belizean artists; they make great gifts. Lee Vanderwalker's colorful zen living room turned gallery, **Caribbean Colors Art Gallery and Café** (Front St., tel. 501/668-7205, www.caribbean-colors.com, 6:30am-9pm Fri.-Wed., US$6-10) is upstairs beside the police station and serves excellent coffee as well as breakfast burritos and omelets, brownies, and other baked treats. The porch is ideal for watching Front Street foot traffic and catching the breeze, when you're not eyeing the gorgeous local paintings for sale inside. The **Go Slow Art Gallery,** in Palapa Gardens stalls 6 and 7, encourages the Belizean art community and sells paintings of different styles, including acrylic on canvas, realism, and primitive. Seek out pieces by well-known local artists Nelson Young and Marcos Manzanero, and beautifully crafted mini drums for sale, handmade by Garífuna artist **Mark Welch** (tel. 501/620-1020, www.mccaribbeandrums.com, US$50).

Hair braiders along Front Street create "head art" with their lightning-fast fingers, adding colorful beads and extensions.

For clothing, **Chocolate's Gift Shop** (Front St.), run by Annie Seashore, sells high-quality Balinese sarongs, bags, and Guatemalan textiles. Several small shops sell a limited selection of imported women's clothing.

ACCOMMODATIONS

Prices given are for high-season double occupancy, but you can often get discounts year-round, especially if you're staying for five or more days. Be sure to check directly with the hotel or take note of social media pages for the latest specials. Reservations are recommended during the high season (late Dec.-Apr.), as rooms tend to fill quickly, particularly during national holidays such as Easter. The rest of the year, rooms are easy to find on the spot, and choices will be plentiful (except in October, when a few properties close for renovation).

Staying at a seafront property or by the hustle and bustle of Front Street is always lovely, but since everything is a short walk away, staying off the main drag and in the center or back of town won't hurt your vacation—particularly with the sandy streets all around. Be warned that you'll be spoiled for choice of affordable, cozy places to stay. Plenty of delightful hotels, condos, and B&B options are spread around the island with great sea views or relaxing gardens.

When arriving off the boat or plane, ignore any pushy taxi drivers or local "guides" who attempt to help with your bags and pressure you into staying at specific properties; often these individuals obtain commissions, or worse, you may end up at a hotel with low security, hence the aggressive tactics. Like anywhere else, smile and head to your first choice of accommodations, or ask around for advice on the way to the island. Both airline and water taxi terminals often carry pamphlets and maps for visitors. My best advice, if you're completely unsure and traveling solo, is to head to Caye Caulker Plaza Hotel (Calle del Sol, across from Chan's Supermarket), which has 24-hour friendly front-desk staff.

Under US$25

There are many budget guest rooms along Front Street, or even Middle Street, that are easy to find. The best deal in town is **◖Dirty McNasty's Hostel** (Crocodile St., off Front St. past Red Macaw, US$10-30), located down a quiet side street just a stone's throw from all the action. This is the place for "world travelers." The hard-to-miss red building offers upper-floor coed dorm rooms (with bunk beds and private indoor bath) and spacious private rooms with double beds. The balcony, outfitted with hammocks, enjoys a nice breeze and a nifty view of the sea and reef. A second building houses a communal kitchen with a coffee maker, fridge, and microwave, and a game room with pool tables and a dartboard. Free Wi-Fi is included and a swimming pool is in the works.

Yuma's House (tel. 501/206-0019, yuma-housebelize@gmail.com) is a small, waterfront hostel located to your right as you walk off the town arrival dock. It offers dorm-style rooms

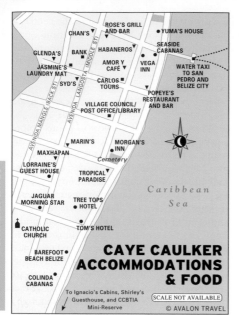

CAYE CAULKER
ACCOMMODATIONS
& FOOD

To Ignacio's Cabins, Shirley's
Guesthouse, and CCBTIA
Mini-Reserve

SCALE NOT AVAILABLE
© AVALON TRAVEL

communal outdoor cooking area as well. Across the lane is **M & N Apartments** (tel. 501/226-0229, US$15-30), which has eight basic and clean guest rooms with shared baths.

A bit farther south along the beach, you'll find **Tom's Hotel** (tel. 501/226-0102, toms@btl.net, US$21-33), popular with budget travelers. There are many options among the 24 guest rooms, including a few simple bungalows. Tom's is well kept and clean, with hot and cold water, fans, louvered windows, tile floors, wireless Internet, and a sea view. Avoid walking to and from Tom's after dark, however; opt for golf cart taxi (US$2.50) instead.

If you're packing a tent, the only place to camp is on the beach at **Vega Inn and Gardens** (tel. 501/226-0142, www.vegabelize.com, US$12 pp). The family-run site provides communal hot and cold showers, flush toilets, luggage storage, and security. They also have comfortable hotel rooms, furnished apartments, and rental homes with all the amenities.

US$25-50

For a dose of "old Caye Caulker," check in to one of the funky beachfront cabins at **Morgan's Inn** (tucked away in a cluster of palms near the old cemetery, tel. 501/226-0178, siwaban@gmail.com, US$28-45); cabins are spacious and rustic. Kayaks and windsurfing are available. Owner Ellen McRae is a marine biologist and birder who can guide interested groups.

The colorful building on your right as you get off of the water taxi is **Trends Beachfront Hotel** (tel. 501/226-0094, www.trendsbze.com, US$35-40), with seven basic guest rooms, comfortable queen beds, refrigerators, fans but no air-conditioning, and private baths. Despite a need for renovations, it's a decent choice for a one-night stopover.

Set in a private villa, **Ocean Pearl Royale** (tel. 501/226-0074, oceanpearl@btl.net, US$27.50-45) is on a side street before the Split. There are 10 guest rooms with a choice of fan or air-conditioning, single or double beds, and wireless Internet around a large communal living area and kitchen with a fridge, a microwave, and a coffeemaker. In the pretty garden is a

(US$13) plus a few private rooms (US$29-30) with shared bath and kitchen. There's a dock peppered with hammocks, or you can chill in the garden while looking out at the sea. Just beware of the owner's strict rules: non-guests are not allowed past the front gate and no outside chatter permitted after nightfall.

Edith's Hotel (tel. 501/206-0069, edithsguesthouse@gmail.com, US$15-20), with small, no-frills guest rooms on ground level, is a landmark on the central street of the island. Guest rooms come with hot and cold water, ceiling fans, a communal kitchen area, and shared or private baths. Upstairs are three spacious, newly converted apartment units, one with a full kitchen, for US$400 per month.

In the heart of the village, by the soccer field, are two great options for reasonable rooms and cabanas. Set in a private fenced yard is **Sandy Lane** (tel. 501/226-0117, www.belizeexplorer.com), offering nine guest rooms (US$12.50 with shared outdoor bath, US$17 with private bath) and four basic cabanas with kitchenettes, TVs, and hard beds (US$25). There is a delightful studio-size cabana with a full kitchen and a porch, for rent by the week (US$250) or month (US$500), without air-conditioning.

The **《 Blue Wave Guest House** (Front. St., tel. 501/669-0114 or 501/206-0114, www.blue-waveguesthouse.com, US$25-33) has clean, basic guest rooms with shared baths, TV, an outdoor communal kitchen, wireless Internet, and a private dock. There are also private guest rooms (US$71), one of which is seafront, cozy, and clean, with a flat-screen TV; it's ideal for one or for a couple. It's a great deal for the location, just a few steps from the Split. There are also options for guest rooms with private baths.

A short walk down the end of Middle Street and past Edith's is **《 Lorraine's Guest House** (tel. 501/206-0002, US$30), off the beaten path but close to town and a good deal for short budget stays. There are three clean and spacious stand-alone cabins with double beds, screened porches with street views, three fans, a coffee-maker, a full bath, and Internet access. Owners Orlando and Martha are a nice couple who live on property and are very welcoming.

US$50-100

A few steps down from the Rainbow Hotel, **De Real Macaw** (Front St., tel. 501/226-0459, www.derealmacaw.biz, US$50-70) is a small and rustic pet-friendly thatched-roof property whose 10 units have private baths, mini kitchens, TVs, wireless Internet, and spacious private verandas with hammocks. A condo-apartment and a two-bedroom beach house (both US$130) are also available.

Closer to the Split are the seven wood cabin rooms at **Mara's Place** (just before the Split, tel. 501/600-0080, maras_place@hotmail.com, from US$85-93). There's a communal kitchen, and the guest rooms have private baths but are basic and small for the high rates—you decide if it's worth being just a couple of steps away from the Split. The best feature may be the private dock with lounge chairs for guests only.

Before **《 Caye Caulker Plaza Hotel** (Calle del Sol/Middle St., tel. 501/226-0780, www.cayecaulkerplazahotel.com, US$90-100) came along, traveling groups had difficulty staying under one roof as the smaller hotels on the island lacked capacity. Located in the heart of the island, the two-year-old three-story building, with 32 guest rooms, some with street-view balconies, is family-run. Past the outside concrete look, it offers great value in the heart of the action, with guest rooms that include air-conditioning, free Internet access, in-room safes, fresh coffee every morning from 6am, a top-floor terrace overlooking the island, and an invaluable 24-hour front-desk presence. Add to that friendly young Belizean staffers who are in the know, as well as easy scheduling of numerous tour options. If you don't have a reservation coming off the boat, this is a great first stop.

The **Jaguar Morning Star Guest House** (tel. 501/626-4538, www.jaguarmorningstar.com, US$85) is a big white building with a rainforest mural, across from the Catholic church and primary school, just a short walk from the center of town. Set in a private home, it offers a newly converted top-floor one-bedroom apartment-slash-condo with a private bath, a full kitchen, air-conditioning, a coffee-maker, cable TV, Internet access, and a massive front patio with a great ocean view and breeze as well as a back patio for privacy. The apartment comes with the use of two bicycles. In the beautiful tropical garden there is also a private stand-alone cabin with full amenities.

The southernmost beachfront option on Caye Caulker consists of the five cabins at **Shirley's Guest House** (south end of the beach, tel. 501/600-0069, www.shirleysguesthouse.com, adults only, US$50-75), built with beautiful tropical woods. They are clean, quiet, and comfortable, with a range of amenities, including free Internet access.

You'll find bright and spotless accommodations at **Barefoot Beach Resort Belize** (southern end of Front St., tel. 501/226-0205, www.barefootcariberesort.com, US$69-89), all clustered on the beach; a few bigger suites are the size of a small apartment and go for US$129-145, depending on length of stay, each with outdoor patios. The small, cheerful guest rooms each have comfortable queen or king beds, ceiling fans, small refrigerators, private baths with hot showers, air-conditioning, plus their own deck or patio with seating and access to a dock. Complimentary use of one bike is provided per room, although walking to town is entirely feasible.

Just a few steps south is a quiet, postcard-perfect boutique property, secluded yet close to town, at **Colinda Cabanas** (tel. 501/226-0383, www.colindacabanas.com, US$49-139). The resort offers eight cabana rooms and a few more on the way. Standard guest rooms have fans, and the upstairs beachfront suites are spacious and tastefully decorated with Belizean paintings, with full kitchens and air-conditioning, and an amazing deck view of the Barrier Reef. A lovely *palapa* sunning and swimming dock is available, and all rooms have their own coffee-maker, porch, hammock, and wireless Internet access.

Quite possibly the most charming B&B on the island, **◖ Tree Tops Hotel** (tel. 501/226-0240, www.treetopsbelize.com, US$56-110) is tucked down a private side alley off the beach near Tom's Hotel. It's a luxurious little gem in a tall white building. Austria native Doris has created a wonderful ambience with her colorful ceramics and thematically decorated guest rooms—including two sea-facing suites, the African Room and the Malaysian Room, that have private balconies, TVs, fridges, full baths, and memorable decor. Two cheaper guest rooms share a bath and each has a TV, a fan, and a fridge. The two-level rooftop has 180-degree views of the island and hammocks to enjoy them.

Maxhapan Cabañas (close to the primary school, tel. 501/226-0118, maxhapan04@hotmail.com, US$65) is another hidden gem. Belizean owner Louise Aguilar is passionate about the three self-catering cabanas she offers, originally built for her children, who ended up living abroad. Nestled to the back of a lush yard maintained by her husband, both upper and lower-level rooms are immaculately clean and have their own verandas and hammocks, full-size beds, small fridges, coffeemakers,

© LEBAWIT GIRMA

Colinda Cabanas is one of a few secluded and affordable beachfront resorts on the south side of Front Street.

air-conditioning, cable TV, Wi-Fi, and full baths with hot and cold water. Bicycles are provided for each room. There is a common recreation area set in the middle of the yard with lots of seating options and shade under a gigantic breadfruit tree (*maxhapan* in Mayan).

◖ Oasi (tel. 501/226-0384, www.oasiholidaysbelize.com, US$75-95), outside the main buzz of town toward the airstrip, gets rave reviews from its previous guests. It's no surprise—there are four quiet, self-contained, beautifully kept and decorated apartments with patios, air-conditioning, and ceiling fans, hot and cold rainwater showers, equipped kitchens, TVs, and wireless Internet. The top-floor apartment in particular is simply lovely (I could live there). The entrance is a large tropical garden with a fountain, and there are two dogs on the property. There's a recreation area in the garden with a grill for guest use. Your warm host, Luciana Essenziale, will help plan your days; complimentary use of bikes makes the five-minute ride to town easy.

US$100-150

In recent years, a host of boutique and "higher end" accommodations have sprouted on the island—offering more luxurious surroundings but still at a reasonable price compared to neighboring San Pedro.

The bright, centrally located, and long-time family-run **◖ Rainbow Hotel** (Front St., tel. 501/226-0123, www.rainbowhotel-cayecaulker.com, US$115) completed major guest room upgrades in December 2011, giving them upscale decor throughout, with quality bedding, spacious baths with glass shower doors, flat-screen TVs with premium cable, wet bars with mini fridges, coffeemakers, and microwaves. The popular waterfront Rainbow Bar and Grill is across the street.

Ideally tucked along the last side street before the Split, **◖ Sea Dreams Hotel and Guest Houses** (Hattie St., tel. 501/226-0602, www.seadreamsbelize.com, US$105-175) offers a private thatched-roof one-bedroom cabana with a partial sea view, as well as five single "court-yard" or ground-floor guest rooms and three beautiful two-bedroom apartments with full kitchens. Air-conditioning, wireless Internet, complimentary use of bicycles and snorkel gear, and a daily hot breakfast on the second floor at outdoor table seating are included. The private dock and *palapa* for impromptu swims or sunset viewing (even better than at the Split) and a rooftop deck peppered with hammocks for yoga, naps, or massages (US$65 per hour), and cocktails from the Banyan Tree Bar, make it as ideal a spot for lovers—a few have left here engaged—as it is for solo travelers. Owners Heidi and Haywood Curry and their friendly staff have transformed Sea Dreams into a perfect home away from home.

Located at the foot of the town dock, **Seaside Cabanas** (Calle del Sol, tel. 501/226-0498, www.seasidecabanas.com, US$115-130) is a brightly painted 16-room mini resort. The smart guest rooms and cabanas are equipped with air-conditioning, cable TV, wireless Internet access, and cheerful decor surrounding a fine swimming pool and sporting lots of rooftop space. The **Uno Mas** bar is open daily until 10pm, and upstairs seating has ocean views.

Island Magic Beach Resort (beachfront, Ave. Hicaco, tel. 501/226-0505, www.island-magicbelize.com, US$110-135) offers 11 beachfront and island guest rooms along with two fourth-floor penthouses with great views of the sea and Barrier Reef in the distance. All guest rooms, with kitchenettes and baths, are spacious, although the overall decor leaves a bit to be desired. There's a lovely decent-size on-site swimming pool with a kiddie section, ideal for families, as well as a bar and a private dock.

Just up from the main dock, you'll see **Sailwinds Beach Suites** (tel. 501/226-0286, www.staycayecaulker.com, US$129-149), which has colorful upscale beachfront suites with full amenities. A cluster of other colorful guest rooms and apartment units are next to it, all family-run, including **Kokomo Beach Suites** (tel. 501/226-0777) and **Diana's Beach House** (tel. 501/604-1256).

The Lazy Iguana B&B (Alamina Dr., tel. 501/226-0350, www.lazyiguana.net, US$95-130) is a secluded three-story home toward the back side of the island. The four spacious and clean guest rooms have private baths, hot water, air-conditioning, and wireless Internet. The residential setting is safe but isolated. The top floor is a deck for lounging with a 360-degree view of the island. Rates include a breakfast spread in the owners' kitchen. It's as far back as it gets from the village center but still an easy bike or cart ride away. There are rainwater showers; bikes are available.

The **Iguana Reef Inn** (tel. 501/226-0213, www.iguanareefinn.com, US$190) was one of the first to raise the bar with its 13 upscale rooms built around a well-kept complex on the west side of the island, behind the soccer field. Its rooms are spacious, standard in looks, and all have comfortable touches like mini fridges, porches, bathtubs, hot and cold water, and other modern conveniences. Continental breakfast is included. The bar, swimming pool, and clean beach area face the sunset and are more private and quiet than those on the island's windward side.

Apartment-style accommodations are found at **Caye Caulker Condos** (tel. 501/226-0072, www.cayecaulkercondos.com, US$99-139), near the north end of the village by the Split; eight fully furnished suites, each facing the sea, have all the amenities, including a small pool. The balconies and rooftop hangout have nice views.

Over US$150

Caye Reef (Front St., US$200-235) has the most upscale boutique accommodations on the island: six spacious luxury apartments, and although the decor isn't mind-blowing, they have all the bells and whistles. Fully furnished sea-facing units have full kitchens and two bedrooms with en-suite baths; a penthouse is on the third floor. There's a swimming pool with an infinity-like view from the apartments' top-floor balconies.

Vacation Homes

Caye Caulker Rentals (tel. 501/226-0029 or 501/630-1008, www.cayecaulkerrentals.com) rents over 20 holiday houses, cabanas, and cottages. The website sorts homes by price, location, and size and provides photos. Nightly rental rates range US$60-379, with one luxury villa that sleeps six going for US$379. A minimum number of nights is required, and monthly rentals are available.

Caye Caulker Accommodations (tel. 501/226-0381 or 501/610-0240, www.cayecaulkeraccommodations.com) manages nine vacation properties and books suites for two upscale hotels. You can see photos and make reservations through the website.

FOOD
Bakeries and Cafés

Hicaqueños love their baked goods, street food, and mobile vendors—who wouldn't want grab-and-go pieces of home-cooked goodness at super-cheap prices?

It all begins on Back Street—you simply cannot leave the island without sampling the morning and afternoon delights at **Glenda's** (tel. 501/226-0148, 7am-10am and 11:30am-1pm Mon.-Sat.), literally set up inside someone's home and offering inexpensive, ridiculously delicious Belizean breakfast and lunch options. Getting up early for her homemade cinnamon roll and a large glass of fresh-squeezed orange juice (all for US$2) is well worth it; go early before she sells out. For lunch, try the *garnaches* or burritos—you won't regret it. The chalkboard menu is updated daily, and the choices will have you drooling.

No breakfast in Belize is complete without sampling fry jacks—delicious fried dough that resembles a flat beignet, best accompanied by jam or as a side to your beans and eggs. Several eateries serve them, but the best I've tried are at **Marin's Restaurant** (Traveler's Palm St., tel. 501/226-0104, 8am-2pm and 6pm-10pm daily, fry jacks with eggs US$1.50), also serving lunch and dinner on the upstairs porch, and at **Tropical Paradise** (end of Front St., tel. 501/226-0124, 7:30am-9pm Mon.-Sat.).

Two blocks south of the dock, **Amor y Café** (6am-noon daily, US$4-6) is a laid-back spot for a morning coffee (no refills) and breakfast, with seating choice between an upper deck or

© LEBAWIT GIRMA

Glenda's restaurant is an institution.

street-level sandy-floored patio for early bird people-watching. Omelets, waffles, grilled sandwiches, and other options are served in regular portions. It's a tad pricey for the island, but the yogurt-granola option is welcome when you tire of starch and eggs.

Happy Lobster (Front St., tel. 501/226-0064, 6am-9:30pm Wed.-Mon.) has a solid breakfast menu, with morning coffee and refills as long as you're eating; it's always good and reasonably priced.

The Internet coffee shop **La Perla Del Mar** (Middle St., beside Atlantic Bank, 7am-9pm daily) serves Cuban coffee (and it is nice and strong) with a new espresso machine for gourmet drinks, served hot or cold. Seating is available on an outdoor porch or in the air-conditioned space, although seating is limited with all the computer cubicles. Wi-Fi is free, and five desktops are available for use at US$4.50 per hour.

Paradiso Sandwich Shop (Front St., tel. 501/226-0511, 6:30am-close daily, US$6-9) has deluxe baguette deli sandwiches as well as salads, smoothies, wine, and breakfast. There's a cute shaded seating area, ideal for a sea view while using the free Wi-Fi and people-watching along Front Street.

Barbecue

Award-winning ◖**Rose's Grill and Bar** (Front St., beside Habaneros, tel. 501/226-0407, www.rosesgrillandbar.com, 11am-3:30pm and 5pm-10pm daily, US$10) is everyone's favorite and always has a nice crowd; it's not surprising given its popular, affordable outdoor dinner barbecue, with fresh catch-of-the-day beautifully laid out for your pick and subsequently grilled as you wait, from black snapper to lobster (other entrées are available); orders come with side choices of the day, and the ceviche is one of the best.

The barbecue dishes from **Meldy's** (Middle St., across from the bakery, tel. 501/600-9481, 7am-10pm Sun.-Fri., US$4.50) are divine, served with delicious spiced baked beans, slaw, and a warm tortilla. Wash it down with fresh fruit juice (try the soursop if it's in season).

NORTHERN CAYES

© LEBAWIT GIRMA

catch of the day on display outside Rose's Grill and Bar

Belizean

For fresh johnnycakes (also known as journey cakes), plain or stuffed with cheese, chicken, or beef, find the taco woman running **Rico's Tacos** (Front St., across from Sand Box), an unassuming stand that opens in the wee hours of the morning every day. The most popular orders are stuffed tortillas, and a small crowd of children and adults often forms, so be vocal about your order lest you be skipped over by other hungry souls.

Those in search of a cheap lunch snack should listen for (and will hear) the calls of the gregarious **Dukunu Man** (Mark Fitzgibbon) as he starts his rounds from the beachfront water taxi arrival dock area at 8:30am and continues along Back, Middle, and Front Streets all the way to the Split until he sells out of his US$0.50 delicious vegetarian or US$1.25 chicken-filled hot *dukunu*—a Creole version of the *tamalito,* made of corn and wrapped in a banana leaf. At the very least, you should meet him!

Syd's (Middle St. at Ave. Langosta, tel. 501/206-0294) is famous for its fry chicken,

one of the best I've ever tasted anywhere in Belize, with a crispy, perfectly seasoned flavor, served with two large sides for just US$4.50. Orders can take about 20 minutes for the fry chicken and sell out quickly, so go by noon if you can. The stew chicken is also quite good. Those with time can enjoy the lovely garden patio seating in the back.

Directly across from EZ Boy Tours is **Martinez Fast Food** (off Front St., US$2.50-3.50), a popular local boxed-lunch spot, selling a half- or full-size lunch of rice and beans with stew chicken or the day's entrée. Even if you don't eat, you must get a cup of the refreshing, delicious homemade ginger ale juice (US$1.50). Not far from Martinez, starting at noon on "good weather" days, you will spot **Pastorina** (Front St., US$4) and her cart parked and serving fresh lunch out of her steel pots and into boxes for hungry locals. Her Creole dishes include chicken stew or beef and other offerings, with two sides.

Chan's Fast Food (Calle del Sol, tel. 501/226-0478, 7am-9pm Fri.-Wed., 7am-3pm

Thurs., US$3.50-6), also known as Auntie's, comes to the rescue when you crave a quick, plentiful boxed lunch in the mid-afternoon to assuage post-snorkeling hunger pains. The window-service establishment dishes out everything from delicious chicken fingers to stew chicken or beef and daily local Central American specialties, such as *escabeche,* conch soup, or barracuda, along with rice and beans or slaw. Don't judge the place by its appearance; you'll be surprised. There's a reason locals constantly flock to this window.

A little farther south off Back Street and up two flights of steep stairs is **Little Kitchen** (501/667-2178, 11am-3pm and 5pm-10pm daily, US$5-10), where you can get excellent appetizers such as *salbutes, garnaches,* and *panades* (3 for US$1), one of the best ceviches in the village, burritos, and home-cooked seafood dishes, all for very cheap. Seating is casual at outdoor picnic tables, with reggae music and a nice breeze. Back in the kitchen, the cook is the friendly owner, Ms. Elba.

Italian

Sandro's Piccola Cucina (Pasero St., tel. 501/622-0604, US$8-12) is in an off-the-beaten-path location around the corner from Atlantic Bank, serving consistently authentic Italian pasta specialties, which even locals rave about, in a charming, open-air, dimly lit, and incredibly romantic picnic-table setting. Sandro is from Bologna, so you'll be getting the real thing.

Casual Dining

Right at the end of the water taxi dock is **Sand Box** (tel. 501/226-0200, www.trendsbze.com/sandbox.html, 7:30am-10pm daily), with sandy interior floors and a laid-back atmosphere, including an outdoor picnic-table seating option, delightful on a breezy night. The breakfast offerings are hearty, and seafood is served all day: fish with curry rice, conch ceviche, and salads (meals US$3-16). Some days tend to be hit-or-miss, but it's decent for those on a budget.

The beachfront **Barrier Reef Sports Bar and Grill** (9am-midnight daily, US$2-9) serves breakfast, lunch, dinner, and bar food. With options such as steaks, seafood, and pasta entrées for US$12-25 and satellite television screens showing sports, it's an easy choice for those picky eaters seeking a taste of home.

Happy Lobster (Front St., tel. 501/226-0064, 6am-9:30pm Wed.-Mon., US$4-15) is an easy choice for lunch or dinner, with a choice of outdoor seating and free wireless Internet. Service can be slow at times, but prices are reasonable. It's also one of the few eateries open on Sunday.

Craving savory chicken wings and tacos? Head to **88 West** (Chapoose St., beside Belize Diving Services, tel. 501/226-0643, 8am-8pm Tues.-Fri., 8am-6pm Sat.-Sun., US$2-10) close to happy hour; these two menu options won't disappoint, and other offerings include salads, a rarity on the island. Go early to avoid a long wait.

Another great choice for a casual meal throughout the day, **◖ Tropical Paradise** (Front St., tel. 501/226-0124, 7:30am-9pm Mon.-Sat., $US4-15) has a solid menu of dishes that include Belizean, seafood, burgers, and nachos, not to mention a full bar for cocktails. The appetizers are on point—the ceviche in particular—and there are plenty of entrées. (Ask for the seafood or chicken kebab options, listed on a hidden wall menu!) The service is friendly, and the wait on orders is surprisingly short despite crowds in the busy season.

Fine Dining

Magandon (Front St., close to Raggamuffin Tours, tel. 501/226-0025, 5pm-9pm Mon.-Sat., US$10-22) has an upscale, dim, cozy interior, with just average Italian dishes and choices that include gnocchi, pizza, pastas, seafood, and specialty Italian desserts.

◖Habaneros (Front St., tel. 501/626-4911, 6pm-9pm daily, US$6-25) is the priciest restaurant and lounge by the island's standards, but its Central American cuisine is a notch above the others, with unique and absolutely delicious seafood options—from the seafood curry to coconut-encrusted snapper—and several other vegetarian and meat specialties. The raised porch is ideal to enjoy the lavishly pre-sented meals and live music, and the indoor bar is tiny but has chic ambiance. Make sure to try the frozen mojito, and the Creole voodoo cakes are to die for (watch out for the habanero pepper sauce). Reservations are highly recom-mended; this popular restaurant only seats 36 and gets booked as early as 7pm!

The **Rainbow Bar and Grill** (off Front. St., tel. 501/226-0281, 10:30am-9pm Tues.-Sun., US$10-25) offers diners a lovely seaside am-bience and view—the covered outdoor deck stretches over the water—and solid local food options. Lunch is very popular with day-trip-pers to the island because of its ideal location a short walk from both the water taxi and the Split.

Dessert

Got a sweet tooth or craving dessert? **Andrew** (Front St., 6pm-close daily, US$2) starts with a sweet evening aroma as he rolls his bicycle cart filled with delicious daily homemade cakes and pies, in addition to dinners. Try his coconut pies or banana bread, so fresh they are warm to the touch.

Groceries

Chan's Mini Mart (Middle St., across from Caye Caulker Plaza Hotel, tel. 501/226-0165, 7am-9pm daily) is pretty much the heart of "downtown" Caulker—check the bulle-tin board for ads and events or go inside for a full-size supermarket minus a deli coun-ter. **Chinatown Grocery** (Ave. Langosta and Estrella St., tel. 501/226-0338, 7am-11pm daily) also has a good selection. There are a few great fruit, vegetable, and juice stalls around town; look near the bakery and Atlantic Bank. A favorite is **Julia's Juice** (Front St., US$2.50), where she sells watermelon, orange, lime, soursop, and mixed-fruit juice in recycled plastic bottles—you can mix and match your fruit juices. Another great stand is the newer **Seachoice Island Produce** (Pasero St., oppo-site Atlantic Bank, 6:30am-5pm Mon.-Thurs., 8am-noon Sun.). Rony serves freshly made fruit smoothies and mixes of your choice at **Coro's**

Juice Stand (Front St.), right beside the art booths of Palapa Gardens. For fresh fish or lobsters, go to the **Lobstermen's Co-op Dock** (Calle del Sol), on the back side of the island; ask what time the fishing boats come in with their catch.

INFORMATION AND SERVICES

There is plenty of online research you can do while planning your trip to the Northern Cayes. Check the official website of the **Caye Caulker Belize Tourism Industry Association** (CCBTIA, www.gocayecaulker.com). The best-run and most active website is probably **www.ambergriscaye.com.** The forum also has a Caye Caulker section that is easily searched and where you'll find a large community of knowledgeable folks who are generally quick to answer. There is no tourist information booth on the island; just walk off the dock and ask around.

Tsunami Adventures (tel. 501/226-0462, www.tsunamiadventures.com), up toward the Split, acts as a local travel agency. **Seaside Cabanas** (Calle del Sol, tel. 501/226-0498, www.seasidecabanas.com) also has reliable travel agents.

Banks

Atlantic Bank (Middle St., 8am-3pm Mon.-Fri., 8:30am-noon Sat.) is the only bank on the island. Atlantic's ATM accepts international cards. A Western Union office is located in the bank, and another is down the street inside Syd's. Be warned that the ATM tends to run out of cash by noon, but it is replenished again in the afternoon. Be sure and get enough cash if you're on the island just before a weekend.

Health and Emergencies

The free **health clinic** (south end of Front St., tel. 501/226-0190, 8am-7pm) will help you with meds, if they have the supplies; it is staffed by a Cuban doctor and a Belizean nurse. For any serious emergency, your best bet is an emer-gency flight to the mainland; all hotels keep a list of emergency boat captains and pilots.

CAYE CAULKER OCEAN ACADEMY

© LEBAWIT GIRMA

the Ocean Academy when it was first built

The story behind the 2008 opening of Caye Caulker's first high school, Ocean Academy (near the airstrip, tel. 501/226-0321, www. cayecaulkerschool.com), speaks to the island's strong community spirit. In 2007, Hicaqueños had no option but to send their children to the mainland once they completed primary school. Only the privileged few could afford daily or even weekly commute costs to Belize City, much less the school fees and uniforms. As a result, many children on the island stopped attending school at age 12, falling behind in the most basic of skills.

Enter Heidi Curry, an American expat who left the rat race to make a new life for herself and her family in Belize. While tutoring primary schoolchildren in her free time, she learned of the alarming gap in learning opportunities. It wasn't long before her passion for the island's children led her to the idea of opening a high school. After an initial phone inquiry to the Ministry of Education (as simple, she says, as asking "How does one open a high school?") the community rallied behind her—including cofounder Joni Miller, parents, business owners, volunteers, and resident Dane Dingerson, who donated land and funded construction. Within eight months, a nonprofit high school was born. The first high school graduation ceremony took place in 2011.

In addition to core academic classes, subjects taught include marine biology, graphic design, tour guiding, and scuba certification. Environmental education has a big place here, with projects such as mangrove restoration and composting. Students are offered annual apprenticeship placements on the island, giving them a role in Caye Caulker's growing tourism industry.

Travelers have many opportunities to get involved. The school hosts service-learning groups, volunteer teachers, and mentors year-round; needed volunteer skills and school supplies are listed online. Cash donations are welcome and can help sponsor the school year-round, particularly supporting the construction of a much-needed second floor of classrooms. Guided tours of the school campus (US$5 pp) are available.

Media and Communications

At the south end of Front Street is the Village Council office (upstairs in the community center) and community library, health clinic, and **post office** (8am-noon and 1pm-5pm Mon.-Thurs., 1pm-4:30pm Fri.). The mail goes out every morning. **FedEx** services are available at the **Tropic Air** cargo office at the airstrip.

The **BTL Office** (Back St., 8am-noon and 1pm-5pm Mon.-Fri.) sells Digicell SIM cards for those with an unlocked phone; getting a local number requires an ID for registration purposes (passport or driver's license) for registration purposes.

Cayeboard Connection (Front St., tel. 501/629-3680, 8am-9pm daily, US$6 per hour) is a cozy Internet café and bookstore with an extensive collection of used guidebooks and novels, and will burn CDs and print photos; printing, scanning and copying services are also offered. **Island Link** (Front St., tel. 501/226-0592, theislandlink@hotmail.com, 8am-9pm daily, US$6 per hour), near the Split, combines access and office copy services with a small ice-cream parlor.

GETTING THERE
By Air

Tropic Air (tel. 501/226-2012, U.S. tel. 800/422-3435, www.tropicair.com) and **Maya Island Air** (tel. 501/223-1140 or 501/223-1362, www.mayaislandair.com) make daily flights to Caye Caulker from Belize City's municipal and international airports as part of their San Pedro run. The airstrip on Caye Caulker and most others throughout Belize is simple—you arrive just 15 minutes early and wait outside or on the veranda of the small building that serves all flights. Fares on Tropic Air, slightly lower than Maya Island Air, are US$41.50 one-way to Belize City's municipal airport (about 10 minutes) and US$72 one-way to the international airport (8 minutes). Tropic Air also flies between the Belize International Airport and Cancún, Mexico, with connections to Caye Caulker and San Pedro—yet another option of flying into Belize.

By Boat

The short water taxi ride between Caye Caulker and either Belize City or San Pedro is the most common and affordable way to get to the island. The Belize City-Caye Caulker trip costs US$10 one-way. Many boats are partially open-air, with benches for seats, although San Pedro Belize Express has a fleet of forward-facing three- and four-seat rows and covered interiors, but with less leg room. A light cardigan or rain jacket is always handy for windy trips. The boats are often packed to the point of being overloaded and sometimes depart late, although some companies are guiltier of these offenses than others. The safest bet is often the San Pedro Belize Express.

Three competing water taxi companies have alternative schedules and similar fares. Tickets for the **San Pedro Belize Express** (San Pedro tel. 501/226-3535, Caye Caulker tel. 501/226-0225, Belize City tel. 501/223-2225, www.belizewatertaxi.com) can be purchased from the ticket office on Caye Caulker's Front Street. Boats depart from the dock across the police station. Express departures to Belize City run 7am-5pm daily, to San Pedro 7am-6:15pm daily. San Pedro Belize Express Water Taxi also offers daily service to the Muelle Fiscal in Chetumal, Mexico. The boat departs from Caye Caulker at 7am or San Pedro at 7:30am and returns from Chetumal at 3:30pm. Caye Caulker connections are available. The 2.5-hour one-way trip costs US$40.

Caye Caulker Water Taxi (San Pedro tel. 501/226-2194, Caye Caulker tel. 501/226-0992, Belize City tel. 501/223-5752, www.cayecaulkerwatertaxi.com) boats depart Caye Caulker from the main pier on the east side of the island; buy tickets at the office right on the dock before boarding the boat. Departures to Belize City run 6:30am-4pm daily, to San Pedro 8:45am-5:45pm daily.

Water Jets Express (San Pedro tel. 501/226-2194, Caye Caulker tel. 501/206-0234, Belize City tel. 501/207-1000, www.sanpedrowatertaxi.com) boats depart from the lagoon on the back side of the island to Belize

City 6:30am-4pm daily, to San Pedro 8:45am-5:45pm daily. Water Jets Express also offers daily service to Chetumal in Mexico (US$45 one-way) that departs Caye Caulker at 7am or San Pedro at 8am and returns at 3pm. They also have a daily boat that leaves San Pedro at 3pm for Corozal and Sarteneja, which returns at 7am.

GETTING AROUND

The navigable part of town—from the airstrip north to the split—is one mile long and easily explored on foot. Still, a bicycle will make things easier, particularly on hot days and if you're staying in one of the more southern accommodations. Ask if your hotel provides one, or rent at **Friendship Center** on Front Street. **M&N Mel's Bike Rentals** is also a safe bet (Chapoose St., just off Front St., tel. 501/226-0229, US$2 per hour, US$25 per week).

If you're staying far south of the village, you might consider renting a golf cart from the centrally located **Caye Caulker Golf Cart Rentals** (Ave. Mangle, across Caye Caulker Plaza Hotel, tel. 501/226-0237, US$13 per hour, US$63 per day for more than 5 hours with return by nightfall, or US$85 per 24 hours), a local family-run business with friendly owners. The other alternative is the pricier **C&N, Island Boy Rental** (Traveler's Palm St., tel. 501/226-0252 or 501/610-5236, US$88 per day).

A golf cart taxi ride is cheap and worth it when moving around the island with heavy luggage. Taxi guy **Luis** (tel. 501/624-8578, US$2.50) is responsive, friendly, and sends colleagues right away if he's busy; taxis also operate from the **Rainbow Hotel** front desk (Rainbow Taxi, tel. 501/226-0123) and several remain parked outside the water taxi terminals awaiting arrivals.

NORTHERN CAYES

Diving the Northern Atolls

Belize's atolls are a sight to behold—some of the clearest turquoise waters and abundant marinelife is found on these easterly islands. No trip here is ever wasted, whether to snorkel, dive, or swim, taking in Belize's breathtaking waters, not to mention some of the most beautiful beaches.

TURNEFFE ISLANDS

A renowned diving and fishing destination about 30 miles east of Belize City, most of the Turneffe islands are small dots of sand, mangrove clusters, and swamp, home only to seabirds and wading birds, ospreys, manatees, and crocodiles. Only **Blackbird Caye** and **Douglas Caye** are of habitable size, supporting small populations of fishers and shellfish divers. In November 2012, Turneffe Atoll was officially declared a protected marine reserve.

If you're looking to hook a bonefish or a permit, miles of crystal flats are alive with both hard-fighting species. Tarpon are abundant late March-June within the protected creeks and channels throughout the islands. Those who seek larger trophies will find a grand choice of marlin, sailfish, wahoo, groupers, blackfin tuna, and many more.

Most visitors to Turneffe are day-tripping divers based in Ambergris Caye or Caye Caulker; a select few choose to book an island vacation package. There are a couple of upscale resorts and one research facility where visitors can stay.

Rendezvous Point

This is a popular first dive for overnighters out of Ambergris Caye. It provides a great opportunity for divers who haven't been under in a while. The depth is about 40-50 feet and affords sufficient bottom time for you to get a good look at a wide variety of reef life. Angelfish, butterfly fish, parrot fish, yellowtails, and morays are well represented. This will whet appetites for the outstanding diving to come at the Elbow.

TURNEFFE ISLANDS

Mauger Caye

Crawl Caye

Three Corner Caye

Rendezvous Point

Northern Lagoon

Turneffe Islands

Freshwater Creek

Douglas Caye

● **TURNEFFE FLATS**

Snake Pt

BLACKBIRD CAYE RESORT ●

Pelican Caye

Cross Caye

Blackbird Caye

Central

Lagoon

Soldier Caye

Harry Jones Pt

Shag Caye

Calabash Cayes

Joe's Hole

BLUE CREEK

Pelican Caye

TRIPLE ANCHORS

Deadman's Cayes

HOLLYWOOD

PERMIT PARADISE

South Lagoon

WRECK OF SAYONARA

DEADMAN CAYE III

FRONT PORCH

GALES POINT

TURNEFFE ISLAND LODGE ●

MAJESTIC POINT

Big Caye Bokel

LEFTY'S LEDGE

◀ *THE ELBOW*

BLACK BEAUTY

MYRTLE'S TURTLE

Caribbean Sea

0   5 mi

0   5 km

© AVALON TRAVEL

The Elbow

Most divers have heard of the Elbow (just 10 minutes from Turneffe Island Lodge), a point of coral that juts out into the ocean. This now-famous dive site offers a steep sloping drop-off covered with tube sponges and deep-water gorgonians, along with shoals of snappers (sometimes numbering in the hundreds) and other pelagic creatures. Predators such as bar jacks, wahoo, and permits cruise the reef, and the drop-off is impressive. Currents sweep the face of the wall most of the time, and they typically run from the north. However, occasionally they reverse or cease all together.

Lefty's Ledge

A short distance farther up the eastern side of the atoll from the Elbow is another dive to excite even those with a lot of bottom time under their weight belts. Lefty's Ledge features dramatic spur-and-groove formations that create a wealth of habitats. Correspondingly, divers will see a head-turning display of undersea life in both reef and pelagic species. Jacks, mackerels, permits, and groupers are present in impressive numbers. Wrasses, rays, parrot fish, and butterfly fish are evident around the sandy canyons. Cleaning stations are also evident, where you'll see large predators allowing themselves to be groomed by small cleaner shrimp or fish. The dive begins at about 50 feet and the bottom slopes to about 100 feet before dropping off into the blue.

Gales Point

Gales Point is a "don't-miss" dive located a short distance up the eastern side of the atoll from Lefty's Ledge. Here the reef juts out into the current at a depth of about 45 feet, sloping to about 100 feet before the drop-off. Along the wall and the slope just above it are numerous ledges and cave-like formations. Rays and groupers are especially common here—some say this may be a grouper breeding area. Corals and sponges are everywhere in numerous varieties.

Sayonara

On the leeward, or western, side of the atoll, the wreck of the *Sayonara,* a tender sunk by Dave Bennett of Turneffe Island Lodge, lies in about 30 feet of water. Close by is a sloping ledge with interesting tunnels and spur-and-groove formations. Healthy numbers of reef fish play among the coral, and some barracuda tag along. Divers' bubbles often draw down large schools of permits.

Hollywood

A bit farther up the atoll from the *Sayonara,* Hollywood offers divers a relatively shallow dive (30-40 feet) with moderate visibility, unless the currents have reversed. Here you'll find lots of basket and tube sponges and lush coral growth. Many angelfish, parrot fish, grunts, and snappers swim here. Although not as dramatic as an eastern side dive, Hollywood has plenty to see.

Accommodations

Turneffe Island Resort (tel. 501/532-2990, U.S. tel. 800/874-0118, www.turnefferesort.com, US$1,590-2,790 3-night package) is on Little Caye Bokel, 12 acres of beautiful palm-lined beachfront and mangroves. Book a seven-night dive or fishing package and stay in one of eight ground-floor deluxe guest rooms, four second-floor superior rooms, and eight stand-alone cabanas. It's a popular location for divers, anglers, and those who just want a hammock under the palms. At the southern tip of the atoll, the lodge is a short distance north of its larger relative, Big Caye Bokel. This strategic location offers enthusiasts a wide range of underwater experiences—it's within minutes of nearly 200 dive sites. Shallow areas are perfect for photography or snorkeling; you can see nurse sharks, rays, reef fish, and dolphins in the flats a few hundred yards from the dock. All the dives mentioned earlier and many more are within 15 minutes by boat. The dive operation is first-rate, and advanced instruction and equipment rentals are available. Anglers have a choice of fishing for snappers, permits, jacks, mackerel, and billfish from the drop-offs. They can stalk the near-record numbers of snook, bonefish, and tarpon in the flats and mangroves. The lodge's fishing guide has an uncanny way of knowing where the fish will be.

On the eastern side of the Turneffe Islands, **Blackbird Caye Resort** (tel. 501/223-2772, U.S. tel. 888/271-3483, www.blackbird-resort.com) encompasses 166 acres of beach and jungle. It can accommodate 36 guests (double occupancy) with hot-water showers, private baths, and double and queen beds, as well as a duplex and a triplex featuring private guest rooms and air-conditioning. Snorkeling, fishing, and diving packages are offered for about US$2,000-3,000 per week, depending on activities and accommodations, and can include three dives a day, all meals, lodging, and airport transfers.

Turneffe Flats (tel. 501/232-9022, U.S. tel. 800/512-8812, www.tflats.com, US$2,000 packages) is famous among international saltwater fly fishers who know the value of being able to sight fish in wadable flats for permits, bonefish, and tarpon. Or go for barracuda, snappers, jacks, or snook and eat it up at night. Guided fishing is in the lodge's 16-foot Super Skiff flats boats. Divers are welcome and will enjoy daily forays to scores of sites throughout Turneffe Atoll and Lighthouse Reef. Varied beach accommodations are comfortable and well appointed, and meals are eaten family style.

LIGHTHOUSE REEF

The most easterly of Belize's three atolls, Lighthouse Reef lies 50 miles southeast of Belize City. The 30-mile-long, 8-mile-wide lagoon is the location of the Blue Hole, a dive spot that was made famous by Jacques Cousteau and a favorite destination of dive boats from Belize City, Ambergris Caye, and Caye Caulker. The best dive spots, however, are along the walls of Half Moon Caye and Long Caye, where the diving rivals that of any in the world.

Think of the atoll as a large spatula with a short handle and a long blade. At the northern tip of the spatula blade, **Sandbore Caye** is home to a rusty lighthouse and a few fishing shacks. It is also the favorite anchorage

of several of the dive boats that do overnight stops, including *Reef Roamer II.*

Big Northern Caye, across a narrow strait, has a landing strip that used to serve the now-closed resort here. There are long stretches of beach to walk, beautiful vistas, mangroves, and lagoons, home to snowy egrets and crocodiles.

Halfway down the spatula-shaped atoll, about where the blade meets the handle, lies the magnificent **Blue Hole,** a formation best appreciated from the air, but also impressive from the bridge of a boat.

At the elbow of the handle is **Half Moon Caye,** a historical natural monument and protected area with its lighthouse, bird sanctuary, shipwrecks, and incredible diving offshore. Finally, on the handle, is **Long Caye,** a lonely outpost with a small dock, large palms, and glassy water.

Blue Hole

This circular underwater formation, with its magnificent blue-to-black hues surrounded by neon water, is emblematic of Belize itself. The submerged shaft is a karst-eroded sinkhole with depths exceeding 400 feet. In the early 1970s, Jacques Cousteau and his crew explored the tunnels, caverns, and stalactites here, angled by past earthquakes.

Most dive groups descend to a depth of about 135 feet. Technically, this is not a dive for novices or even intermediate divers, though many intermediate divers do it with a guide. It requires a rapid descent, a very short period at depth, and a careful ascent, requiring excellent buoyancy control. For a group of 10 or more, at least three dive masters should be present. The Blue Hole is everything it is hyped up to be; my own personal experience there was extraordinary, and I gasped at the sight of the gigantic formations, the infinite depth, and the Caribbean reef sharks that circled nearby. It's akin to an out-of-body experience. The lip of the crater down to about 60-80 feet has the most life: fat midnight parrot fish, stingrays, angelfish, butterfly fish, and other small reef fish cluster around coral heads and outcroppings.

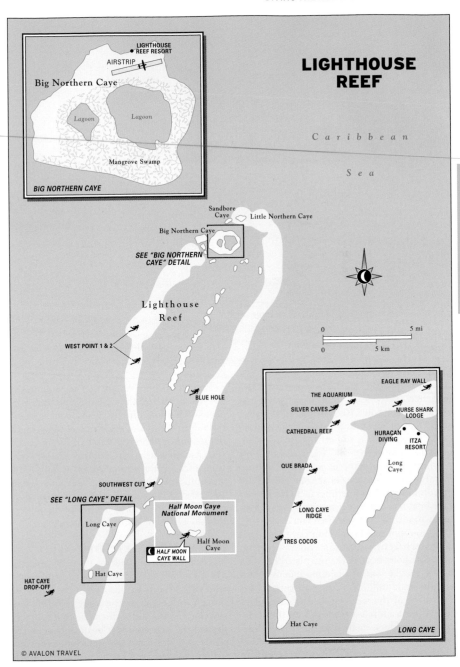

LIGHTHOUSE REEF

BIG NORTHERN CAYE

LIGHTHOUSE REEF RESORT
AIRSTRIP
Big Northern Caye
Lagoon
Lagoon
Mangrove Swamp

C a r i b b e a n

S e a

Sandbore Caye
Little Northern Caye
Big Northern Caye

SEE "BIG NORTHERN CAYE" DETAIL

Lighthouse Reef

WEST POINT 1 & 2

BLUE HOLE

0   5 mi
0   5 km

EAGLE RAY WALL
THE AQUARIUM
SILVER CAVES
NURSE SHARK LODGE
CATHEDRAL REEF
HURACAN DIVING
ITZA RESORT
QUE BRADA
Long Caye

SOUTHWEST CUT

SEE "LONG CAYE" DETAIL

Half Moon Caye National Monument

Long Caye

LONG CAYE RIDGE

HALF MOON CAYE WALL
Half Moon Caye

TRES COCOS

Hat Caye

HAT CAYE DROP-OFF

Hat Caye

LONG CAYE

© AVALON TRAVEL

© LEBAWIT GIRMA

beach on Half Moon Caye, Lighthouse Reef Atoll

HALF MOON CAYE NATIONAL MONUMENT

Dedicated as a monument in 1982, this crescent-shaped island was the first protected area in Belize. Half Moon Caye, at the southeast corner of Lighthouse Reef, measures 45 square acres, half of which is a thriving but endangered littoral forest; the other half is a stunning palm-dotted beach. This is also the only red-footed booby sanctuary in the Western Hemisphere besides the Galápagos. The US$40 pp admission fee is sometimes included in your dive boat fee, but sometimes you'll pay it directly to the park ranger when you disembark.

As you approach Half Moon Caye, you'll believe you have arrived at some South Sea paradise. Offshore, boaters use the rusted hull of a wreck, the *Elksund*, as a landmark in these waters. Its dark hulk looms over the surreal blue and black of the reef world. The caye, eight feet above sea level, was formed by the accretion of coral bits, shells, and calcareous algae. It's divided into two ecosystems: The section on the western side has dense vegetation with rich fertile soil, while the eastern section primarily supports coconut palms and little other vegetation.

Besides offshore waters that are among the clearest in Belize, the caye's beaches are gorgeous. You must climb the eight-foot-high central ridge that divides the island and gaze south before you see the striking half-moon beach with its unrelenting surf erupting against limestone rocks. Half Moon Caye's first lighthouse was built in 1820, modernized and enlarged in 1931, decommissioned in 1997, then felled by the elements in 2010. A newer lighthouse was built in 1998 and is still functioning.

(Half Moon Caye Wall

Here on the eastern side of the atoll, the reef has a shallow shelf in about 15 feet of water where garden eels are plentiful. The sandy area broken with corals extends downward till you run into the reef wall, which rises some 20 feet toward the surface. Most boats anchor in the sandy area above the reef wall. Numerous fissures in the reef crest form canyons or tunnels leading out to the vertical face. In this area, sandy shelves and valleys frequently harbor nurse sharks and gigantic stingrays. Divers here are sure to return with a wealth of wonderful pictures.

Long Caye Aquarium

Minutes from Half Moon Caye Wall, often combined with a Blue Hole trip, is a spectacular dive site ideal for photos and with the most marinelife spotting, even more than at Half Moon Caye Wall. The electrifying deep-blue waters will stun you, as will the schools of bright colorful fish and the large eagle rays, sea turtles, stingrays, and nurse sharks.

Silver Caves

The shoals of silversides (small gleaming minnows) that gave this western atoll site its name are gone, but Silver Caves is still impressive and enjoyable. The coral formations are riddled with large crevices and caves that cut clear through the reef. As you enter the water above the sandy slope where most boats anchor, you'll be in about 30 feet of water and surrounded by friendly yellowtail snappers. Once again you'll see the downwardly sloping bottom, the rising reef crest, and the stomach-flipping drop into the blue.

Tres Cocos

On the western wall, "Three Coconuts" refers to trees on nearby Long Caye. The sandy bottom slopes from about 30 feet to about 40 feet deep before it plunges downward. Overhangs are common features here, and sponges and soft corals adorn the walls. Another fish lover's paradise, Tres Cocos does not have the outstanding coral formations you'll see at several other dives in the area, but who cares? There's a rainbow of marinelife all about. Turtles, morays, jacks, coral, shrimp, cowfish, rays, and angelfish are among the actors on this colorful stage.

West Point

Farther north and about even with the Blue Hole, West Point is well worth a dive. Visibility may be a bit more limited than down south, but it's still very acceptable. The reef face here is stepped. The first drop plunges from about 30 feet to well over 100 feet deep. Another coral and sand slope at that depth extends a short distance before dropping vertically into very deep water. The first shallow wall has pronounced overhangs and lush coral and sponge growth.

The Tower

Everyone should go to the observation tower, built by the Audubon Society in the ziricote forest; climb above the forest canopy for an unbelievable 180-degree view. Every tree is covered with perched booby birds in some stage of growth or mating. In March, you'll have a close-up view of nests where feathered parents tend their hatchlings. The air is filled with boobies coming and going, attempting to make their usually clumsy landings (those webbed feet weren't designed for landing in trees). Visitors also have a wonderful opportunity to see the other myriad inhabitants of the caye. Magnificent thieving frigates (the symbol of the Belize Audubon Society) swoop in to steal eggs, and iguanas crawl around in the branches, also looking for a snack.

Accommodations

The only place to stay overnight on Lighthouse Reef Atoll is on Long Caye, with **Huracan Diving** (U.S. tel. 518/253-7705, ruth@huracan-diving.com, www.huracandiving.com), where you can choose from either a four- or seven-night all-inclusive dive packages (US$990-1,490). The four guest rooms at Huracan's lodge have private baths, king beds, ceiling fans, and screened windows. Pickup and transfer from Belize City is included in your package. A second option is the **Itza Resort** (U.S. tel. 305/600-2585, or tel. 501/223-3228, www.itzaresort.com, R&R package US$995-1,650 for 3 nights, US$1,395-2,795 for 7 nights, rates vary), a 20-room oceanfront resort offering diving, fishing, water sports (kite surfing) and "R&R" packages.

Getting There

It's 52 miles from the mainland to Half Moon

Caye, a long boat trip over open ocean. Most visitors make the trip through one of the bigger dive shops, like Amigo's on Ambergris Caye. Otherwise, only chartered or privately owned boats and seaplanes travel to Half Moon Caye. Check with the Belize Audubon Society in Belize City for other suggestions.

ST. GEORGE'S CAYE

The most historically significant caye—a national landmark and the first capital of the British Settlement (1650-1784)—is a little-known getaway. Nine miles or a 20-minute water taxi hop from Belize City, this small caye is home to St. George's Caye Mangrove Reserve, established in 2005 and covering 12.5 acres on the southernmost point of the island, and one luxury resort with a full-service dive shop that also offers other water sports. Check **St. George's Caye Resort** (tel. 800/813-8498 or 501/220-4444, www.gooddiving.com, US$168 pp includes meals). The rest of the island is lined with private villas and docks owned by affluent Belizeans who escape here on the weekends. St. George's Caye Day is celebrated nationwide on September 10 to honor a 1798 British battle that took place here and prevented Spanish invasion. Today, the small cemetery gives evidence of St. George's heroic past and is Belize's smallest archaeology reserve.

The St. George's Caye Research Station and Field School, founded by ECOMAR in 2009, hosts a group of Texas State University professors and students who spend a month on the island to conduct research digs. They also conduct coral reef research and educational trips based here.

DROWNED CAYES

Spanish Lookout Caye is a 187-acre mangrove island, located at the southern tip of the Drowned Cayes, only 10 miles east of Belize City. There are many day-trip possibilities to Spanish Lookout Caye, including the country's first and only "dolphin encounter" program, a beach, kayaks, and snorkeling.

If you're not researching manatees or mangroves with Earthwatch Institute, you're most likely coming to meet the dolphins or stay at **Belize Adventure Lodge** (tel. 501/220-4024, U.S. reservations 888/223-5403, www.belizeadventurelodge.com, US$100), a full-service island facility offering 12 quasi-colonial cabanas over the water, two student dormitories, classrooms, a restaurant, a bar, a gift shop, and a dive center. Five colorful cabanas with 10 guest rooms, hot showers, and private baths are connected to the island by a dock. The resort offers popular four-night packages (US$799 per person for two) that include all meals and transfers to the island.

Diving is one of the favorite activities here, and guests can participate in educational and research programs. Manatees and dolphins are regularly seen foraging near the island. Juvenile reef fish, seahorses, lobsters, and mollusks live among the red mangrove roots and sea grass beds. Tarpon and barracuda often come into the bay to feed on the abundant silversides. The resort is only one mile west of the main barrier reef and about eight miles west of central Turneffe Island.

THE BLUEFIELD RANGE

Scattered along the coast is a constellation of small cayes, some accessible by travelers, others only by drug traffickers. The Bluefield Range is one such group of cayes, a short distance south of Belize City. Accommodations are no longer available here, unfortunately, thanks to Hurricane Richard, which destroyed the range in 2010.

GOFF'S CAYE

Near English Caye, Goff's Caye is a favorite little island stop for picnics and day trips out of Caye Caulker and Belize City, thanks to a beautiful sandy beach and promising snorkeling areas. Sailboats often stop overnight; camping can be arranged from Caye Caulker by talking with any reputable guide. Bring your own tent and supplies. Goff's is a protected caye, so note the rules posted by the pier. Goff's has seen major impact from the cruise ship industry, which sometimes sends thousands of people per week to snorkel around and party on the tiny piece of sand, and a few reports have said this is destroying the coral.

ENGLISH CAYE

Although this is just a small collection of palm trees, sand, and coral, an important lighthouse sits here at the entrance to the Belize City harbor from the Caribbean Sea. Large ships stop at English Caye to pick up one of the two pilots who navigate the 10 miles in and out of the busy harbor. Overnights are not allowed here, but it's a pleasant day-trip location.

BELMOPAN AND CAYO

Tucked in the foothills of the Maya Mountains, the Cayo district is Belize's largest and most visited area after the Northern Cayes. This westernmost district begins where the Western Highway leaves the outskirts of Belize City toward Belmopan, the nation's quiet and landlocked capital. From there, it spills onto part of the aptly named Hummingbird Highway and

© LEBAWIT GIRMA

HIGHLIGHTS

LOOK FOR ◖ TO FIND RECOMMENDED SIGHTS, ACTIVITIES, DINING, AND LODGING.

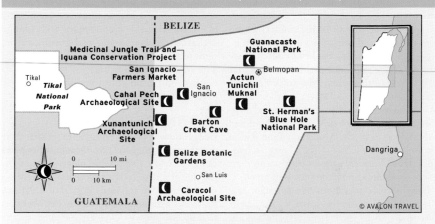

© AVALON TRAVEL

◖ **Guanacaste National Park:** An easy stop along the Western Highway, this 50-acre patch of forest has flat, well-maintained hiking trails through massive trees and ferns (page 143).

◖ **St. Herman's Blue Hole National Park:** Get out the hiking boots, binoculars, flashlight, and a bathing suit for a visit to this park, halfway down the Hummingbird Highway. St. Herman's Cave offers fun for novice spelunkers, and a swim in the Blue Hole should not be missed (page 146).

◖ **Cahal Pech Archaeological Site:** The site is unique for both its archaeological intrigue and its location within the city limits of San Ignacio. The walk up the hill to Cahal Pech Village Resort offers spectacular views (page 148).

◖ **San Ignacio Farmers Market:** Head to the most colorful and enjoyable farmers market in Belize, where Cayo's diverse community gathers on Saturday morning for their weekly shopping and socializing (page 149).

◖ **Medicinal Jungle Trail and Iguana Conservation Project:** Explore this successful iguana breeding and release project via a pleasant and informative guided tour (page 149).

◖ **Belize Botanic Gardens:** This unique low-key attraction features beautiful grounds with hiking trails through a variety of habitats; the Native Plant House is magical (page 151).

◖ **Actun Tunichil Muknal:** The "Cave of the Crystal Maiden" is the wettest, dirtiest, most adventurous spelunking trip available (page 167).

◖ **Xunantunich Archaeological Site:** This ancient city is easily one of the most gorgeous Mayan sites in Belize (page 171).

◖ **Barton Creek Cave:** This cathedral-like cave is filled with giant stalactites, ancient Mayan ceramics, and plenty of mystery. After exploring by canoe, bring a bathing suit to end the day in the emerald pool by the cave entrance (page 175).

◖ **Caracol Archaeological Site:** One of the most difficult major ruins to access in Belize, Caracol is rife with discovery and beauty. Enjoy long, peaceful views of the wild countryside from atop its excavated temples (page 183).

stretches west all the way to Guatemala, leading toward rivers, rainforests, swimming holes, national parks, Maya temples, caves, Thousand Foot Falls—the largest waterfall in Central America—and Mennonite villages, all in the space of two hours.

Cayo is home to four of the country's nine protected areas and offers a world of eco-adventures, solo and guided, low-key or adrenaline-inducing. Hike rainforest paths and medicinal trails that lead to ancient Mayan ceremonial caves. Canoe the Macal River on the way to the farmers market or ride a hand-cranked ferry across the Mopan Rover. Climb the boulders of the Río Frio in the Mountain Pine Ridge Reserve. Trek to the top of the Mayan archeological site of Caracol, where scarlet macaws can be seen swooping across the valleys of green.

The district's true hub, San Ignacio, is a hilly, pedestrian-friendly town with a Latin pulse that's all its own. It's a favorite among Belizeans and expats, with outdoor cafés, authentic eateries, and arguably one of the best farmers markets in the country. Staying in town is an option, with several budget favorites, but a short drive away are the country's best jungle lodges, offering a variety of experiences—campsites, riverside cabins, and luxury tree houses. Recent developments have given San Ignacio a more modern look, with a cobblestoned main street (Burns Ave.) and a new Welcome Center, but it's still a lovely place to visit. For those seeking seclusion, the Mountain Pine Ridge, one of the most remote areas in the country, offers more accommodations options and plenty of outdoor exploration.

Once the heartland of the indigenous Maya, the Cayo District's countryside stretches to San José de Succotz and the border town of Benque Viejo del Carmen, revealing a diverse mix of mostly Creole, Mayan, and Mennonite rural villages alongside a mixed population of gringo expats, Lebanese, and Chinese. Green pastures with mahogany and sapodilla trees—reminders of a colonial past—are peppered with orange orchards, chicken coops, and grazing cattle, signs of Cayo's main industry besides tourism. The region produces most of the livestock, poultry, and grain consumed in the country, earning it the name "breadbasket of Belize."

PLANNING YOUR TIME

Budget travelers will be pleased to see that their dollar goes farther in Cayo than in other parts of Belize. Most visitors find plenty to do, signing up for a new activity every day, but there's no rush, and you can easily bop around the area for weeks without getting weary. The beauty is that no two stays in Cayo are the same.

Belmopan is worth an overnight stop for its surrounding natural parks and attractions. Save half an hour for a hike in **Guanacaste National Park,** explore **Monkey Bay Wildlife Sanctuary,** and take a dip in **Blue Hole Natural Park**'s sinkhole. The world-famous **Ian Anderson's Caves Branch** offers easy accommodations near each.

Even if you've only got a day or two, **San Ignacio** is close enough to the coast and worth a trip; the forest runs right up to the city limits, where you'll find several trails and a fascinating archaeological site. San Ignacio also provides an excellent base for tours to **Actun Tunichil Muknal** or into **Tikal,** Guatemala. Jungle lodges line the Macal River and into the **Mountain Pine Ridge.**

Belmopan

After Hurricane Hattie destroyed government buildings and records in Belize City in 1961, the new capital, Belmopan, was built far away from the coast to keep it safe from storm damage, with the expectation that large numbers of the population of Belize City would move with the government center. They didn't. Industry stayed behind, and so did most jobs. Today, while there is some growth in Belmopan, the masses are still in Belize City, which remains the cultural and commercial hub of the country. Some capital employees live in Belize City and commute 50 miles back and forth each day. Belmopan, however, was designed for growth and has continued to expand, with a population of around 20,000, plus a surge of several thousand commuters during weekdays. Today, Belmopan still isn't a destination for travelers; but it has several services, including a bus station and hub for going to other parts of the country, an excellent coffee shop nearby, and a couple of decent restaurants. You'll also find most foreign embassies and international organizations here as well as most important Belizean government services, including immigration. Other than that, it's a city—and the feel inside the city grid (within Ring Road), with rows of small cement homes and chain-link fencing, has been compared to a lower-middle-class Los Angeles suburb.

The majority of travelers, however, see only Belmopan's bus terminal and, if they have time, the small open-air market right next door. Some jog across the market to take a peek at the government buildings (only a few hundred yards away)—an incredibly gray, squat, postapocalyptic bit of architecture. Their intentionally Maya-influenced arrangement—built around a central plaza—gives the scene just enough strange irony to make it worth the visit. Just beyond Belmopan, the Hummingbird Highway is one of the most beautiful roads in the region, snaking through densely forested hills that are riddled with trails, rivers, cenotes, and caves.

ORIENTATION

Belmopan is just east of the Hummingbird Highway and just south of the Western Highway; it is usually accessed by Constitution Drive, which leads straight into the center from a traffic circle. Banks, buses, the market, and government buildings are tightly clustered within easy walking distance of one another. Turning right on Bliss Parade from Constitution Drive, you'll find the dilapidated Belmopan Hotel on your right and Novelo's bus station and the market on your left. Bliss Parade joins Ring Road, which loops around the central town district. Ring Road passes various government buildings and embassies on the left before meeting back up with Constitution Drive.

SIGHTS
George Price Centre for Peace and Development

This homage to the founding father of Belize, George Price, is an impressive and modern air-conditioned museum, library, and center for conflict resolution and peace. The **George Price Centre** (Price Centre Rd., tel. 501/822-1054, www.gpcbelize.com, 8am-6pm Mon.-Fri., 9am-noon Sun., free) is just off the eastern part of the Loop Road, near the Catholic Church. Set aside at least 30 minutes to tour the display, which now includes a setup of Price's modest living quarters while he was alive, and watch a worthwhile 23-minute documentary, *Man of Purpose and Vision*, in the media center, or admire the original flag that flew at Belize's independence ceremony in 1981. The website features a list of events and some fascinating information on George Price's legacy and Belizean history.

Born in 1919, Price died at the age of 92 on September 19, 2011, just two days before the country's 30th anniversary of independence from Great Britain. I happened to be in Belize at the time of his passing and attended the state

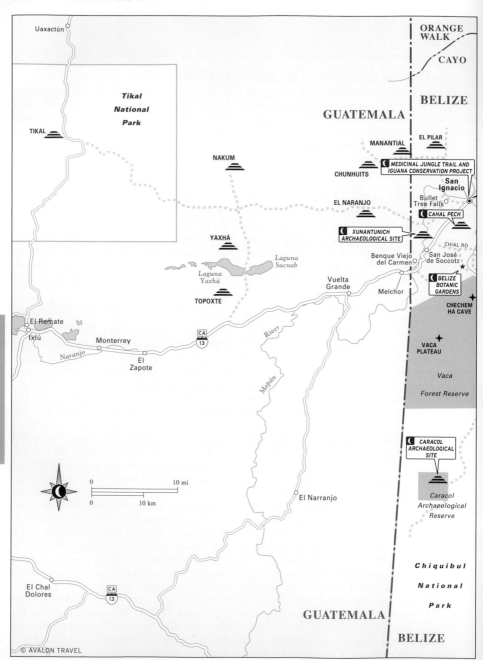

© AVALON TRAVEL

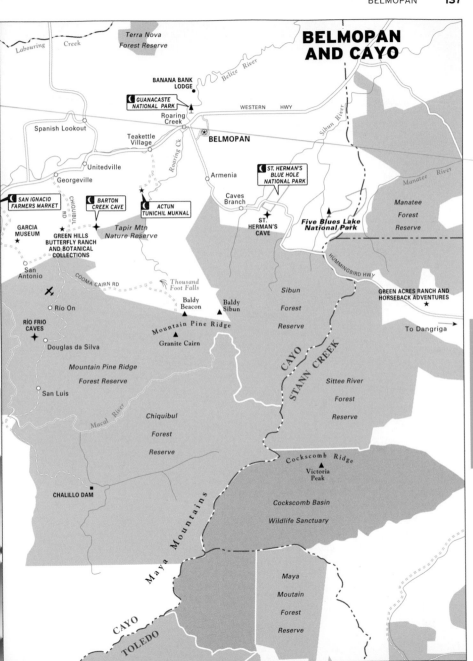

BELMOPAN AND CAYO

Terra Nova Forest Reserve

Labouring Creek

Belize River

BANANA BANK LODGE

GUANACASTE NATIONAL PARK

Roaring Creek

WESTERN HWY

Spanish Lookout

Teakettle Village

Roaring Ck.

BELMOPAN

Sibun River

Unitedville

Georgeville

Armenia

ST. HERMAN'S BLUE HOLE NATIONAL PARK

Manatee River

SAN IGNACIO FARMERS MARKET

BARTON CREEK CAVE

ACTUN TUNICHIL MUKNAL

Caves Branch

CHIQUIBUL RD

GARCIA MUSEUM

GREEN HILLS BUTTERFLY RANCH AND BOTANICAL COLLECTIONS

Tapir Mtn Nature Reserve

ST. HERMAN'S CAVE

Five Blues Lake National Park

Manatee Forest Reserve

San Antonio

COOMA CAIRN RD

Thousand Foot Falls

Baldy Beacon

Baldy Sibun

Sibun Forest Reserve

HUMMINGBIRD HWY

GREEN ACRES RANCH AND HORSEBACK ADVENTURES

Río On

RÍO FRIO CAVES

Mountain Pine Ridge

Granite Cairn

CAYO

STANN CREEK

To Dangriga

Douglas da Silva

Mountain Pine Ridge Forest Reserve

Sittee River Forest Reserve

San Luis

Macal River

Chiquibul Forest Reserve

Cockscomb Ridge

Victoria Peak

CHALILLO DAM

Cockscomb Basin Wildlife Sanctuary

Maya Mountains

Maya Moutain Forest Reserve

CAYO

TOLEDO

BELMOPAN AND CAYO

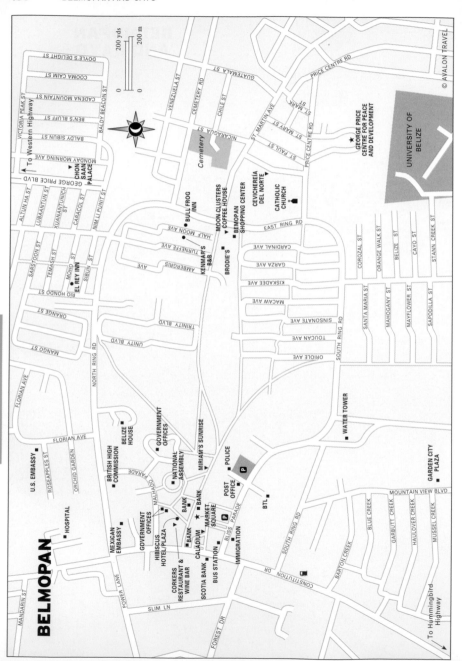

BELMOPAN AND CAYO

BELMOPAN

© AVALON TRAVEL

UNIVERSITY OF BELIZE

GEORGE PRICE CENTRE FOR PEACE AND DEVELOPMENT

CATHOLIC CHURCH

CEVICHEREIA DEL NORTE

BEMOPAN SHOPPING CENTER

MOON CLUSTERS COFFEE HOUSE

BULL FROG INN

BRODIE'S

KENMAR'S B&B

EL REY INN

CHON SAAN PALACE

To Western Highway

WATER TOWER

GARDEN CITY PLAZA

HOSPITAL

U.S. EMBASSY

BRITISH HIGH COMMISSION

BELIZE HOUSE

GOVERNMENT OFFICES

NATIONAL ASSEMBLY

MIRIAM'S SUNRISE

POLICE

POST OFFICE

BTL

BANK

BANK

MARKET SQUARE

BANK

MEXICAN EMBASSY

GOVERNMENT OFFICES

HIBISCUS HOTEL/PLAZA

CALADIUM

BUS STATION

SCOTIA BANK

CORKERS RESTAURANT & WINE BAR

IMMIGRATION

To Hummingbird Highway

200 yds
200 m

DOYLE'S DELIGHT ST
COOMA CAIM ST
CADENA MOUNTAIN ST
VICTORIA PEAK ST
BEN'S BLUFF ST
BALDY BEACON ST
MONDAY MORNING AVE
BALDY SIBUN ST
GEORGE PRICE BLVD
ALTUN HA ST
LUBANTUN ST
XUANANTUNICH ST
CARACOL ST
NIM LI PUNIT ST
SARSTOON ST
TEMASH ST
MOHO ST
SIBUN ST
RIO HONDO ST
ORANGE ST
MANGO ST
FLORIAN AVE
FLORIAN AVE
ROSEAPPLES ST
ORCHID GARDEN
MANDARIN ST
POWER LANE
SLIM LN
FOREST DR
CONSTITUTION DR
BARTON CREEK
HAULOVER CREEK
GARBUTT CREEK
BLUE CREEK
MUSSEL CREEK
MOUNTAIN VIEW BLVD
SOUTH RING RD
BLISS PARADE
UNITY BLVD
TRINITY BLVD
MAHOGANY ST
PARADE
NORTH RING RD
AMBERGRIS AVE
TURNEFFE AVE
HALF MOON AVE
EAST RING RD
CARDINAL AVE
GARZA AVE
KISKADEE AVE
MACAW AVE
SINSONATE AVE
TOUCAN AVE
ORIOLE AVE
SOUTH RING RD
COROZAL ST
ORANGE WALK ST
BELIZE ST
CAYO ST
STANN CREEK ST
SANTA MARIA ST
MAHOGANY ST
MAYFLOWER ST
SAPODILLA ST
VENEZUELA ST
CEMETERY RD
CHILE ST
GUATEMALA ST
NICARAGUA ST
ST MARK ST
ST MARTIN AVE
ST MARY'S ST
ST PAUL ST
PRICE CENTRE RD
PRICE CENTRE RD

Cemetery

© LEBAWIT GIRMA

The Hummingbird Highway is one of Belize's most beautiful drives.

funeral ceremony, the country's very first, in Belmopan. It was one of the most moving days I've experienced in Belize, watching the crowds standing for almost eight hours in the sun, from the procession along the Western Highway in Belmopan—aptly renamed the George Price Highway in 2012—to the burial in Belize City, saying good-bye to their hero. He was dearly loved by Belizeans.

Market Square

This is where the action is for local shoppers. Starting at the crack of dawn, the lines of stalls are alive with the commerce and gossip of the area. Hang out here for a little while and you are sure to see a parade of local farmers, government workers chowing down on tacos or stew beef for breakfast, and colorful characters going about their business. The coffee may be instant, but the food is freshly made—try some fry jacks, a tasty tamale, or a plate of *garnaches* (crispy tortillas topped with tomato, cabbage, cheese, and hot sauce) for next to nothing. Bananas, oranges, mangoes, tomatoes, chilies,

and carrots are cheap too; stock up before heading deeper into Belize.

ENTERTAINMENT AND EVENTS

Despite Belmopan's reputation for being a "dead" town, weeknights and Saturday can be quite alive in the capital city, although you shouldn't expect a big party scene. Monday-Wednesday are fairly quiet; in fact, most nightspots only open midweek. Thursday starts with karaoke at the **Bull Frog Inn's Restaurant & Bar** (25 Half Moon Ave., tel. 501/822-2111, www.bullfroginn.com) but turn into a rockin' dance party around 11pm, when the place gets packed. The rest of the weekend is ruled by **Twilight Lounge,** located on the northeast corner of the traffic circle on the Hummingbird Highway. The new Wing Stop's **Puccini Lounge** (Nim Li Punit St., tel. 501/636-0048) turns into a dance spot on Thursday and Friday, with a DJ. Nightspot **La Cabaña** (tel. 501/822-1577, www.aguallos.com/lacabana, 6pm-2am), in the western part of town on a hill above Hummingbird Highway by Las Flores, attracts partygoers from around the district and sells drinks and cheap bar food, but there have been occasional violent brawls there as recently as November 2012, so be sure and ask around on the latest before heading out.

Barrio Fino Night Club (off Constitution Dr., opposite the gas station, 5pm-3am Thurs.-Sat.) is a local cool spot, dance club, and bar, with popular pool tables.

On September 21, Belmopan celebrates **Independence Day** along with the rest of the country. The day begins with a morning official ceremony at the Court House Plaza (you may glimpse the prime minister of Belize from a distance making an address) and includes military parades. After the speeches comes the fun part of the day, with food and music all around the Market area and town, and a citizens parade along Bliss Parade, complete with colorful floats and costumes. Line up around the Bliss Parade area or Constitution Drive near the Market to catch the start of all the fanfare, and follow the crowds.

SHOPPING

Besides Market Square, you'll find a few handy stores in Belmopan. It the market area you'll find plenty of pharmacies, shops, and Internet spots. **Angelus Press** (Constitution Dr., 7:30am-5:30pm Mon.-Fri., 8am-noon Sat.) has a good office supply store and bookstore in the building right across from the bus station. **The Art Box** (Mile 46, Western Hwy., tel. 501/623-6129, www.artboxbz.com, 8am-6pm Mon.-Sat.) is on the Western Highway and has an excellent selection of woodworking materials, watercolors, and picture frames in addition to standard gift shop fare (as well as Christian books and CDs). But the best part is the collection of originals by acclaimed artist and Belize resident Carolyn Carr.

ACCOMMODATIONS
Under US$50

If you're staying in downtown Belmopan, you're either a businessperson, a diplomat, a development worker—or just lost. The most

reasonably priced beds are found at the newly refurbished **❰ El Rey Inn** (23 Moho St., tel. 501/822-3438 or cell 501/620-4808, www. elreyhotel.com, US$30-90 plus key deposit), with 10 tidy, decent guest rooms, from simple fan-only budget guest rooms to cozier, roomy junior suites with private baths, hot and cold water, Internet access, air-conditioning, flat-screen TVs, and coffeemakers. On a side residential street, this small hotel is an easy walk to the center of town, and its on-site **Bystro Mia** serves tasty home-cooked meals and desserts.

The **Hibiscus Hotel** (Hibiscus Plaza, Melhado Parade, below Corkers Restaurant, tel. 501/822-0400 or cell 501/610-0400, www.hibiscusbelize.com, US$50) offers six decent-size guest rooms with king beds, flat-screen TVs, air-conditioning, Internet access, and simple baths. The location is convenient for those arriving by bus, just one street over from the hustle and bustle of the bus terminal and Market Square. Half of the profits go to the Parrot Rescue and Rehabilitation Centre of Belize (www.belizebirdrescue.com), a non-profit created and run by Hibiscus owners and British expats Jerry Larder and Nikki Buxton.

US$50-100

❰ KenMar's Bed & Breakfast (on the side street behind the Bull Frog Inn, 22-24 Halfmoon Ave., tel. 501/822-0118, www. kenmar.bz, US$80-138) is an adorable, spotless guesthouse, with 10 air-conditioned guest rooms in a large house, each with an en suite bath and plenty of amenities, cable TV, mini fridges, coffeemakers and more; there's a luxury suite for US$140. Owner Marion Fuller (call her "Miss Mar") has thought of everything, including irons, shower gel bottles, purified water in the guest rooms, and free continental breakfast (if you're lucky, it will include her homemade cinnamon rolls), and she's a gem of a host. There is a very nice common living area, a small pool at the back, full Internet access, and sometimes the smell of fresh baking from the kitchen.

The **Bull Frog Inn** (25 Half Moon Ave., tel. 501/822-2111, www.bullfroginn.com, US$85 plus tax) has 28 guest rooms that could be mistaken for those of any basic roadside hotel in the United States. The inn reports that 80 percent of its guests are businesspeople doing work for the government or private businesses. The on-site restaurant is solid, and the bar turns into an all-night disco on Thursday.

Over US$100

There are rave reviews for **Twin Palms Bed and Breakfast** (Mile 54, Hummingbird Hwy., tel. 501/822-0231 or cell 501/610-2831, tasmithbz@yahoo.com, US$115-125), a six-room inn tucked away from Pan city noise yet a close ride to town; it has nicely landscaped grounds and a lovely swimming pool. The guest rooms, equipped with queen or double beds, are nicely furnished and include all the necessary amenities, including air-conditioning, mini fridges, coffeemakers, irons, cable TV, and Wi-Fi. The home-cooked breakfasts and ample garden seating areas are the icing at this authentic B&B.

Jungle Lodges

When they first arrived in Belize more than 30 years ago, Montana cowboy John Carr and his wife, Carolyn, ran ◖**Banana Bank Lodge and Jungle Equestrian Adventure** (tel. 501/832-2020, www.bananabank.com, US$77-225) as a working cattle ranch. Today, most pastures have been converted to fields for growing corn and beans, and the ranch now hosts a lodge. Half of the 4,000-acre ranch is covered in rainforest, and within its borders guests will discover not only a wide variety of wildlife but a small Mayan ruin.

There are five guest rooms in the main house (three share a bath) to accommodate guests, and five cabanas that sleep up to six people each. There's an old-school elegance to the guest rooms, suites, cabanas, dorm rooms, and chalets—no two are alike, and most have beautifully funky bathtubs. Food is delicious and served family style; breakfast is included in the room rate (lunch US$10, dinner US$15).

With 85 saddle horses in its stables and 25 miles of horse trails, Banana Bank is passionate about guests experiencing horseback riding. John Carr is known for using the horse-whisperer method, and horses are carefully matched to their riders. Ask about moonlight rides, often followed by a riverside bonfire.

Banana Bank is also a place to bird-watch, fish, hike, or take a boat trip down the Belize River, with plenty of time left for a cooling swim in the river or in a gorgeous swimming pool. Look for Tikatoo, a beautiful jaguar the Carrs rescued as a cub and have cared for ever since (they are the only people in the country, besides the Belize Zoo, to have a license to do so). You can take a closer look at Tikatoo in her fenced-off jaguar enclosure right on the lodge grounds. Take photos—she's used to it.

The Carrs are wonderful hosts who will make you feel right at home. Artist and owner Carolyn Carr is considered one of the country's premier artists; be sure to seek out her paintings in the House of Culture in Belize City, or view her originals at the Art Box.

Next door to Banana Bank Lodge, the **Belize Jungle Dome Hotel Resort** (tel. 501/822-2124, www.belizejungledome.com, US$105-200) has five guest rooms in a unique geodesic dome setting. The guest rooms are fully equipped with queen beds, air-conditioning, private baths, and wireless Internet, and there is a lovely pool and a separate four-bedroom villa. The Jungle Dome serves three meals daily and caters to all dietary requirements. The resort is a licensed tour operator and runs a full range of tours as well as airport transfers. The owner, Andy Hunt, is a retired British Premier League soccer player.

Banana Bank is located across the Belize River, about 10-15 minutes by car from the Western Highway. Turn into Roaring Creek by taking the turn next to the big Westar gas station and hotel on the right. You'll come across the Calendar Hamilton Trust Bridge; continue straight to head to the entrance, and two miles in is the actual lodge.

FOOD

Even if you're not staying in Belmopan, it is a common lunch stop for anyone traveling to or from Belize City. The cheapest meals, which are quite good, I might add, are at the market stalls and small restaurants that surround the bus terminal. Don't be surprised to see folks eating full meals at eight in the morning, including stew beef and rice.

Get your coffee fix at 【 **Moon Clusters Coffee House** (E. Ring Rd., behind Brodies, tel. 501/602-1644, 11am-7pm Mon.-Sat.), the second of two Belizean-owned Moon Clusters in the country (the other is in Belize City), serving the most delicious frozen espresso drink I've had in a while: the Choli—a double shot of espresso topped with ice cream, and cinnamon. It's to die for. There's a nice seating area and plenty of other hot and cold beverage options, including hot chocolate and smoothies. Owner Amilcar Aguilar takes pride in his coffeehouse, a place to "have a nice drink and good conversation," with no Internet to distract: Now, there's a refreshing concept.

【 **Miriam's Sunrise** (across from First Caribbean Bank and Court House Plaza, 6am-3pm daily, US$2-5) is a delightful spot for breakfast and a good alternative to Market Square, serving up excellent, inexpensive local dishes—stews, soups, burgers, tacos, and more—from breakfast through lunch, as well as fresh squeezed local fruit juices (try the *horchata,* very refreshing on a hot Belmopan day). Seating is casual on picnic tables and is often shared, ideal for meeting locals or expats and asking about the town.

【 **Caladium Restaurant** (across from Market Square, tel. 501/822-2754, caladium@btl.net, 7:30am-8pm Mon.-Fri., closes earlier Sat., US$5-14) is a favorite among locals and expats, serving up solid local breakfasts, rice and bean dishes, and stews for lunch—ask for the day's special (the relleno looked amazing)—and an international menu of seafood, salads, steaks, burgers, and a lot more. The tiled dining room is cozy and air-conditioned, with a full bar. **Cevichería del Norte** (11am-11pm Wed.-Sun.) is on the east side of town, with fresh ceviche (US$3-10), nachos, tacos, and beer. What else could you need? It's in a purple house on a residential street just north of the George Price Centre.

Pepper's Pizza (St. Martin Ave., across from Bull Frog Inn, tel. 501/822-0666, US$5-16) delivers free anywhere in town. **Pasquale's Pizzeria** (corner of Forest Dr. and Slim Lane, delivery tel. 501/822-4663, 11am-9pm Mon.-Sat., noon-9pm Sun., US$8-15) is quite popular with those who can afford U.S. prices, and offers large hand-tossed New York-style pizzas, pastas, wings, and burgers. To be honest, a better bet would be **Bystro Mia** (El Rey Inn, 23 Moho St., tel. 501/822-3438, 6:30am-9pm daily, US$3-8), in a residential area but worth finding, with a small but savory menu offering local breakfasts with gourmet coffee if you choose as well as pizzas, quesadillas, burgers, and pasta (the Bolognese sauce was delicious). Also worthwhile is **Wing Stop** (Nim Li Punit St., tel. 501/636-0048, 11am-11:45pm daily, US$5-14) where you can get, you guessed it, wings—from a six-piece to a bucket of twenty-four or more.

The open-air restaurant and bar at the **Bull Frog Inn** (25 Half Moon Ave., tel. 501/822-2111, www.bullfroginn.com, 7am-10pm daily, US$10-40) has a long-standing reputation among the elite of Belmopan, and this is one of the most popular spots in town to dine. The fish fillet, chicken, and burgers are all good and moderately priced, and there's a daily local special. For an international menu prepared by a chef from England, and the prices to go with it, **Corkers Restaurant & Wine Bar** (top floor of Hibiscus Plaza, tel. 501/822-0400, www.corkersbelize.com, lunch and dinner Thurs.-Tues., US$7-25) caters to the expat crowd and has salads like tuna niçoise as well as wraps, burgers, steaks, and pastas. There are trivia nights on Monday, and happy hours with half-price cocktails (4pm-10pm Thurs.-Sat.).

Among the many Chinese restaurants, **Chon Saan Palace** (7069 George Price Blvd., tel. 501/822-3388, US$5-10) is the best.

INFORMATION AND SERVICES

For well-stocked supermarkets and drugstores, head to the Belmopan branch of **Brodies** (tel. 501/822-2010 or 501/822-3078, brodiesbmp@

btl.net, 8am-7pm Mon.-Sat., 9am-1pm Sun.) or try the newer **The Mall** (Hummingbird Hwy., tel. 501/822-3399, 8am-9pm daily) selling everything from groceries to hair extensions.

Some students and scientists come to Belmopan to do research in the **Belize Archives Department** (26-28 Unity Blvd., tel. 501/822-2097, archives@btl.net, 8am-5pm Mon.-Thurs., closes earlier Fri.), a closed-stacks library popular with both local students and foreign researchers.

Garden City Plaza (Mountain View Blvd., about US$2.50 by taxi from the city center) has a few shops, including **Antonini's Restaurant** (tel. 501/802-0263), offering decent fast food and sandwiches, an Internet café, a health food store, and an Atlantic Bank branch.

GETTING THERE AND AROUND

If you are traveling Belize by bus, it's nearly impossible *not* to visit Belmopan, as all buses traveling between Belize City and points west and south—even express buses—pull into the main Belmopan terminal for 5-30 minutes as they rustle up new passengers (and the driver takes a lunch or smoke break). If you need a local taxi driver while in Belmopan, contact **Tirzo Briceño** (cell 501/602-5265); he's usually parked by Market Square, outside the bus terminal, when not on runs.

Buses leave Belize City to Belmopan (US$2) every 15 minutes 4am-8:30pm daily. Buses from Belmopan to Benque at the Guatemalan border leave every 15 or 30 minutes 6:30am-7pm daily. Buses from Belmopan to points south such as Dangriga and Punta Gorda leave hourly 6:30am-7:30pm daily.

VICINITY OF BELMOPAN

The Hummingbird Highway stretches south from Belmopan to St. Margaret's and farther on to Dangriga. The road was paved only recently and boasts some of the most scenic driving in Central America (in my humble opinion). The drive from Belmopan southeast toward Dangriga is an awesome reminder of just how green and wild Belize really is. Some

of the canopy took a hit during Hurricane Richard's strange inland rampage in 2010, but the forest grows quickly in these parts, and it is still most impressive.

The highway passes through towering karst hills and long views of broadleaf rainforest as you cross the Caves Branch Bridge and enter the Valley of Caves. It climbs into the Maya Mountains and then descends toward the sea. The junction with the Southern Highway is 20 miles east of "Over the Top" pass, and Dangriga is another five miles from there.

Guanacaste National Park

Located at the T-junction on the Western Highway where the Hummingbird Highway begins, the 50-acre **Guanacaste National Park** (on-site guide Alfonso, cell. 501/635-0787, 8am-4:30pm daily, US$2.50 pp) is probably one of the most overlooked small attractions in Belize. Co-managed by the **Belize Audubon Society** (tel. 501/223-4987 or 501/223-5004) and the government, this park gets its name from a massive 360-year-old *guanacaste,* or *tubroos,* tree on the property. The original tree is no longer living (they had to cut the limbs off for safety), but the park is still filled with ceibas, cohune palms, mammee apple, mahogany, quamwood, and other trees as well as wildlife like agoutis, armadillos, coatis, deer, iguanas, jaguarundis, kinkajous, and more than 100 species of birds. Among the rare finds here are resident blue-crowned motmots. The *amate* fig also grows profusely on the water's edge and provides an important part of the howler monkeys' diet.

This is a perfect place for a picnic and a dip on your way to or from Belize City. There are three easy trail loops. Or bring a swimsuit and take a dip at the quiet spot in the Roaring River just before it enters the Belize River.

Roaring River Golf Course

The only functioning golf course in all of Belize is the **Roaring River Golf Course** (Mile 50½, Western Hwy., tel. 501/664-5441, www.belizegolfcourses.com), an unpretentious executive-type nine-holer (3,892 yards, par 64, slope

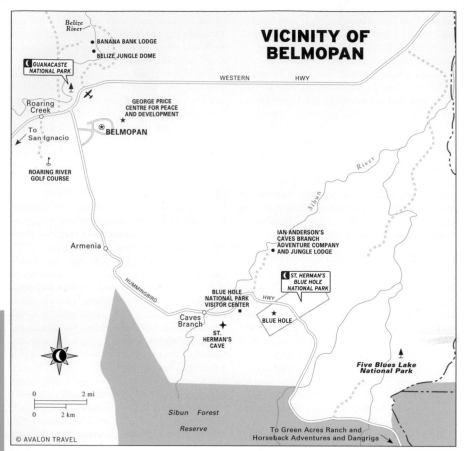

VICINITY OF BELMOPAN

Belize River
Banana Bank Lodge
Belize Jungle Dome
GUANACASTE NATIONAL PARK
WESTERN HWY
Roaring Creek
GEORGE PRICE CENTRE FOR PEACE AND DEVELOPMENT
BELMOPAN
To San Ignacio
ROARING RIVER GOLF COURSE
Sibun River
Armenia
IAN ANDERSON'S CAVES BRANCH ADVENTURE COMPANY AND JUNGLE LODGE
ST. HERMAN'S BLUE HOLE NATIONAL PARK
HUMMINGBIRD
BLUE HOLE NATIONAL PARK VISITOR CENTER
HWY
BLUE HOLE
Caves Branch
ST. HERMAN'S CAVE
Five Blues Lake National Park
0   2 mi
0   2 km
Sibun Forest Reserve
To Green Acres Ranch and Horseback Adventures and Dangriga
© AVALON TRAVEL

rating 116). It's a short drive from Belmopan and a worthy activity for anyone staying in an area lodge or resort, whether you're a seasoned slugger or just golf curious (free lessons are offered for beginners). The feel of the course, clubhouse, and restaurant is tranquil, the staff is friendly, and the greens fees are reasonable (US$18 per round or US$25 all-you-can-play).

This is a unique rainforest-golf opportunity by any measure. More than 120 bird species have been identified on and around the property, there are crocodiles in the water hazards, and you'll hear the sound of the nearby river, which flows from Thousand Foot Falls in the Mountain Pine Ridge. After sweating out a

round, take a dip in one of the cool, clean, shady pools of the river.

Roaring River Golf Course is well maintained with a level layout and interesting landscaping dividing the fairways; greens boast Bermuda grass, grown from seed. Paul, the South African owner, notes that his course uses chemicals very sparingly, almost not at all—"just a bit of spraying for the ants," he says. The property uses water from a natural spring flowing from within the mountain.

Plant your nongolfing family members in the river for the day while you hit those links. The "Meating Place" restaurant has earned several "best steak in Belize" comments from

GUANACASTE NATIONAL PARK

Living Cycle Trail

GUANACASTE NATIONAL PARK

LIMESTONE ★ AREA

Belize River

SWIMMING ★ DECK

Guanacaste Trail

Riverview Trail

GUANACASTE TREE

PARK ENTRANCE AND VISITOR ■ CENTER

★ BIRDING DECK

Roaring Creek

To San Ignacio

WESTERN HWY

HUMMINGBIRD HWY

To Belmopan

To Belize City

0   200 yds
0   200 m

© AVALON TRAVEL

reviewers (Paul's wife, Jennie, who hails from South Carolina, cures and ages the meat herself); their top filet goes for US$18.

Guests can stay in one of four well-furnished villas with air-conditioning, Internet access, TVs, queen beds, fridges, coffeemakers, work counters, lounge suites, and stunning back porches over the river. Staying here is a perfect option for someone who really wants to get some early rounds in, or for anyone trapped by an assignment in Belmopan, which is only 10-15 minutes away.

Armenia

Bed-and-breakfast homestay options are sometimes available in several villages up and down the Hummingbird Highway, notably Armenia. This is a quiet settlement, eight miles south of Belmopan, with a Mayan and Latino population offering **Rock of Excellence Homestays** (call Maria "Betty" Gonzalez, tel. 501/630-7033, 501/625-0088, or community tel. 501/660-1881, sreynosa18@yahoo.com). There are about seven participating families, with a wide range of accommodations, though all are simple, rustic, and usually within the home of your hosts (US$30 for a night's lodging and three meals); it's best to call a day ahead. They can also arrange tours for the day, at extra cost.

◖ St. Herman's Blue Hole National Park

Covering 575 acres, the St. Herman's Blue Hole National Park (Belize Audubon Society, tel. 501/223-5004, www.belizeaudubon.org, 8am-4:30pm Mon.-Fri., US$4) encompasses a water-filled sink hole, St. Herman's Cave, and the surrounding rainforest. Rich in wildlife, the park harbors jaguars, ocelots, tapirs, peccaries, tamanduas, boa constrictors, fer-de-lance, toucans, crested guans, blue-crowned motmots, and red-legged honeycreepers.

The pool of the **Blue Hole** is an oblong collapsed karst sinkhole, 300 feet across in some places and about 25 feet deep. Water destined for the nearby Sibun River surfaces briefly here only to disappear once more beneath the ground. Steps lead down to the swimming area, a pool 25 feet deep or so. It is a 45-minute hike from the visitors center, or you can cheat and park closer a little farther down the highway. You can also go tubing and caving here.

St. Herman's Cave requires a hike of a little more than a 1.5 miles across rugged ground. A flashlight and sturdy, rubber-soled shoes are necessities (you can rent flashlights), and a light windbreaker or sweater is a wise choice in the winter. The trail begins near the changing room. The nearest cave entrance is actually a huge sinkhole measuring nearly 200 feet across, funneling down to about 65 feet at the cave's lip. Concrete steps (laid over the Mayan originals) aid descending explorers. The cave doesn't offer the advanced spelunker a real challenge, but neophytes can safely explore it to a distance of about one mile. Pottery, spears, and the remains of torches have been found in many caves in the area. The pottery was used to collect the clear water of cave drippings, called *zuh uy ha* (sacred water) by the Maya. For a guided trip (recommended, US$40), call **Job Lopez** (tel. 501/633-7008), who is on-site at the park. If you're interested in bird-watching, park director Israel Manzanero is considered one of the most knowledgeable birders in Belize.

Blue Hole National Park is located 12 miles southeast of Belmopan on the right side of Hummingbird Highway. It's wise to visit most caves with a guide, and don't visit the park unless the wardens are there. Amenities include a parking area and a changing room. Blue Hole is a perfect daytime stop on your drive to either Belmopan, San Ignacio, or Dangriga.

Five Blues Lake National Park

Located at Mile 32 on the Hummingbird Highway, Five Blues Lake National Park is home to several Mayan sites accessible to visitors. Within the **Duende Caves,** ceremonial pottery can still be found. While some of the more significant sites are heavily regulated by the Belizean Institute of Archaeology, Five Blues Lake provides ample opportunity for visitors to see Maya writings and pottery. In 2006 a mysterious draining of some of the lakes occurred as the earth sucked some of the famous blue water back into the limestone. In 2010 the water returned. Spooky. There are many birds and other wildlife species here, including coatimundis, collared peccaries, and agoutis.

Entrance fees (US$5 pp) support the park and can be paid to the ranger on duty. At the park entrance, a visitors center has maps of the trails available, along with picnic tables and restroom facilities. From the visitors center, you can take any of the park's trails or go directly to the lake.

St. Margaret's (Mile 32) is the entrance to Five Blues Lake National Park and may have some of the same homestay services as Armenia.

Blues Lake National Park can be reached by taking a local bus from the terminal in Belmopan to St. Margaret's Village. From the deserted park office in the village, a rutted 2.5-mile road leads to the park. This road can be hiked, or local park rangers may be willing to provide transportation.

Green Acres Ranch and Horseback Adventures

The Green Acres Ranch and Horseback Adventures (Mile 36, Hummingbird Hwy., tel. 501/670-5698, www.upclosebelize.com/greenacres.html) offers a variety of riding and nonriding opportunities run by the tour company UpClose Belize. A quick drive through the orange orchard, across the brook, and up the hill, and you'll find well-built healthy quarter horses waiting to take you into the countryside. Green Acres welcomes inexperienced riders, including children, and offers a high level of personalized attention from their guides. Rides range one to two hours depending on rider experience. Hourly rides, day rides, and even overnight camping rides are available. A US$85 pp fee includes round-trip transfer from Belize City (or an equivalent distance), two to three hours of on-site riding, and a farm-fresh lunch served under the thatched *palapa,* including grilled meats, homemade tortillas, salads, and drinks.

Ian Anderson's Caves Branch Adventure Company and Jungle Lodge

One of the premier adventure lodges in Belize, Ian Anderson's Caves Branch Adventure Company and Jungle Lodge (Mile 41½, Hummingbird Hwy., U.S. tel. 866/357-2698,

a tree house at Ian Anderson's Caves Branch Adventure Company and Jungle Lodge

© LEBAWIT GIRMA

tel. 501/610-3451, www.cavesbranch.com) offers expeditions that can be strenuous and exciting; it is also a hub for social active travelers. As Ian said a few years ago, "We're certainly not for everyone—thank God!" On the 58,000 acres of this private estate are 68 known caves, and Ian has discovered and explored them all, developing a variety of trips around many of them. The longest and deepest of these Mayan ceremonial caves extends seven miles. Pristine dry caves glisten with crystal formations. Some caves still have pottery shards, skeletal remains, and footprints coated with an icing of rock crystals. Ian offers expeditions ranging 1-7 days, including tubing trips through river caves. All expedition guides have received intensive training in cave and wilderness rescue, evacuation, and first aid; they are, in my mind, some of the best guides in the country, in every sense of the term. Popular excursions include the Black Hole Drop—an amazing 400-foot rainforest rappelling experience—waterfall trips, river caves, and the best tubing in the district. Their honeymoon packages are particularly creative and adventurous.

The lodge offers their brand of "rustic luxury" in their 25 units, which include rainforest cabanas and suites (US$169-294), all the way up to spectacular 800-square-foot luxury tree house suites (US$426-591) with views to write home about. The screened accommodations are open to the sights and sounds of the surrounding wildness. Lighting is still by the glow of kerosene lamps and the moon, but flush toilets and hot and cold water are available throughout (actually, the warm "jungle shower" is the highlight of many a guest's stay). The guest rooms have electricity for lights and wicker fans, but there are no outlets or appliances. New additions include a spa, wedding facilities, and a helipad. The on-site Botanical Gardens' orchid collection, a must-see, has over 400 species of rescued specimens, less than one-quarter of which have yet bloomed. Guests dine together in the main open-air lodge, where they discuss the day's stories and the next day's plans over family-style meals (breakfast US$8, lunch US$12, dinner US$16, plus taxes).

Access to Ian Anderson's Caves Branch is on the Hummingbird Highway between the Blue Hole National Park visitors center and the parking lot for the Blue Hole; turn left (if you're headed south) and continue to the end of the mile-long dirt road. If you're traveling by bus, you'll have to hike in from here if you haven't arranged to be picked up by lodge staff.

San Ignacio

The region from San Ignacio and beyond is referred to as "Cayo" by the locals. Most visitors choose to stay in this area rather than Belmopan, mostly because of the allure of bustling San Ignacio. San Ignacio is a charming town located in the heart of Belize's much-visited green and hilly western Cayo District—home of Mayan sites and caves amid a lush interior of mountains, rivers, pine forests, waterfalls, and citrus plants. One of Belize's crown jewels of tourism, San Ignacio is popular with locals and visitors alike for its hip, laid-back village feel, its picturesque landscape, a Latin vibe, cheap and authentic eateries, a wide variety of accommodations options—from camping to some of the most upscale jungle lodges in the country—and outdoor activities. The area around San Ignacio is ideal for travelers seeking an outdoors type of getaway and organized activities in Belize's lush rainforest interior. There is plenty to do here, from the mild to the extreme, canoeing the rivers, spelunking, rappelling, exploring archeological sites and botanical gardens, or sampling authentic Belizean cuisine. Together with the neighboring "sister town" of Santa Elena, the population here is mostly mestizo—a mix of Mayan and Spanish—and there are sizeable Mennonite and U.S. as well as Chinese expat communities. Spanish is spoken more frequently than Creole, in addition to English.

ORIENTATION

Driving to San Ignacio from Belize City, you'll first pass through its sister town of Santa Elena, turning right at the Social Security building and continuing across the **Wooden Bridge** to the San Ignacio side of the Macal River, close to the open market grounds. From there, turning left will take you directly into "downtown" San Ignacio, marked by a five-road intersection that is nearly always abuzz with activity. **Burns Avenue** crosses here and is the main drag for locals and travelers alike. Within two or three blocks in any direction of that intersection, you'll find most of San Ignacio's budget accommodations, restaurants, Internet cafés, and tour operators.

The town's three banks are on the block of Burns Avenue that runs east toward the river from the big intersection, and at the end of that block you'll find a tiny traffic circle in front of the police station, which guards the western abutment of the **Hawksworth Bridge.** Built in 1949, the Hawksworth is the only suspension bridge in Belize; it is also the starting line of the big canoe race in March. Normally, only eastbound traffic is allowed on the one-lane bridge from Santa Elena to San Ignacio, except when the lower bridge floods and traffic is diverted, as it was several times in 2008 during the highest recorded river levels since 1961. Any of the roads that lead uphill from downtown San Ignacio will eventually place you back on the Western Highway heading toward Benque and the Guatemalan border.

SIGHTS
◀ Cahal Pech Archaeological Site

A 10-minute walk uphill from downtown San Ignacio, **Cahal Pech** is a great tree-shaded destination where your imagination can run wild with all that once occurred here. The ruins of Cahal Pech (Place of the Ticks) features an excavated series of plazas and royal residences. The site was discovered in the early 1950s, but research did not begin until 1988, when a team from San Diego State University's

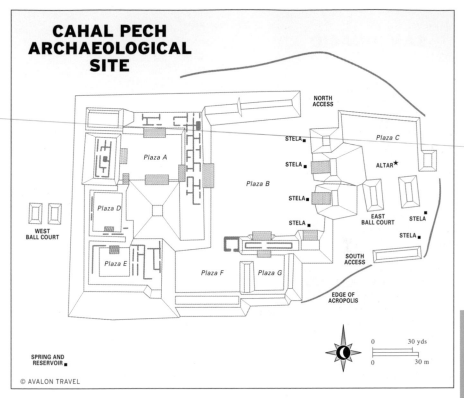

CAHAL PECH
ARCHAEOLOGICAL
SITE

NORTH
ACCESS

STELA ■

Plaza C

STELA ■

ALTAR ★

Plaza A

Plaza B

STELA ■

Plaza D

STELA ■

EAST
BALL COURT

STELA ■

WEST
BALL COURT

STELA ■

Plaza E

SOUTH
ACCESS

Plaza F   Plaza G

EDGE OF
ACROPOLIS

0   30 yds

0   30 m

SPRING AND
RESERVOIR ■

© AVALON TRAVEL

anthropology department began work with local archaeology guru Jaime Awe. Thirty-four structures were built in a three-acre area. Excavation is ongoing and visitors are welcome. It is well worth your trip and admission fee (US$10), paid at the Cahal Pech visitors center (tel. 501/824-4236, 6am-6pm daily). The visitors center also houses a small museum of artifacts found at the site, along with a skeleton from Xunantunich.

Nearby **Tipu** was a Christian Mayan town during the early years of colonization. Tipu was as far as the Spanish were able to penetrate in the 16th century.

◖ San Ignacio Farmers Market and Macal River Park

Every Saturday morning, from dawn through the afternoon, vendors from all corners of

Cayo's villages descend on San Ignacio's market to sell everything from locally grown fruits and vegetables, dairy, Guatemalan spices, and meats to clothing and more. Fresh mestizo food is cooked and sold on-site as well, and everyone comes out to shop and sit and enjoy a brunch of *pupusas,* tacos, empanadas, or tamales. They sit in families around long picnic tables and enjoy the live music. Others relax in the shade by the Macal River, just beside the market, or riffle through tents looking for a new dress. It's San Ignacio's one big social event of the week.

◖ Medicinal Jungle Trail and Iguana Conservation Project

When the local iguana population was in a noticeable downward cycle, the folks at the San Ignacio Resort Hotel created this successful

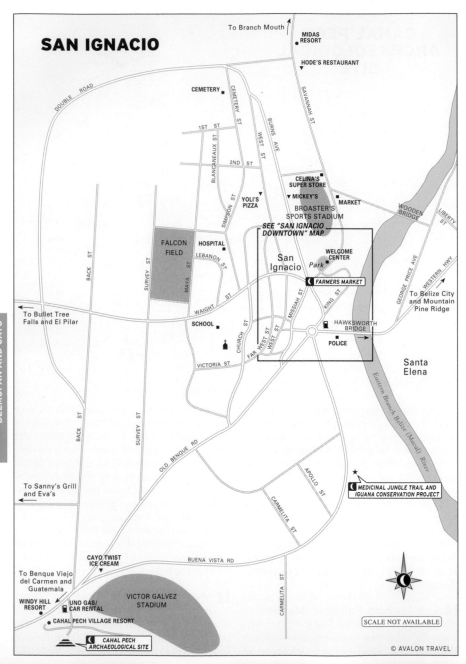

SAN IGNACIO

To Branch Mouth

MIDAS RESORT

HODE'S RESTAURANT

DOUBLE ROAD

CEMETERY

CEMETERY ST

SAVANNAH ST

BURNS AVE

WEST ST

1ST ST

2ND ST

BLANCANEAUX ST

SIMPSON ST

YOLI'S PIZZA

CELINA'S SUPER STORE

MICKEY'S

MARKET

BROASTER'S SPORTS STADIUM

WOODEN BRIDGE

LIBERTY ST

BACK ST

SURVEY ST

FALCON FIELD

HOSPITAL

MAYA ST

LEBANON ST

SEE "SAN IGNACIO DOWNTOWN" MAP

San Ignacio

WELCOME CENTER

Park

FARMERS MARKET

GEORGE PRICE AVE

WESTERN HWY

To Belize City and Mountain Pine Ridge

To Bullet Tree Falls and El Pilar

WAIGHT ST

SCHOOL

CHURCH ST

FAR WEST ST

WEST ST

MISSIAH ST

KING ST

HAWKSWORTH BRIDGE

POLICE

Santa Elena

VICTORIA ST

Eastern Branch Belize (Macal) River

BACK ST

SURVEY ST

OLD BENQUE RD

APOLLO ST

CARMELITA ST

To Sanny's Grill and Eva's

★ MEDICINAL JUNGLE TRAIL AND IGUANA CONSERVATION PROJECT

CAYO TWIST ICE CREAM

BUENA VISTA RD

CARMELITA ST

To Benque Viejo del Carmen and Guatemala

WINDY HILL RESORT

UNO GAS/ CAR RENTAL

CAHAL PECH VILLAGE RESORT

VICTOR GALVEZ STADIUM

CAHAL PECH ARCHAEOLOGICAL SITE

SCALE NOT AVAILABLE

© AVALON TRAVEL

© LEBAWIT GIRMA

the Native Plant House at the Belize Botanic Gardens, located at duPlooy's Jungle Lodge Resort

breeding and release project to bring the animals back and protect the riverside from further development. Groups go on hunts for eggs, capture the females, and hijack the eggs, which they raise in a predator-free, food-rich environment before releasing the iguanas back into the wild. The program has also trained former iguana hunters to become iguana guides, a far more profitable and sustainable endeavor, and hosts many school groups, featuring their Adopt an Iguana program.

The Green Iguana Conservation Project and interpretive herb trail is accessed through the **San Ignacio Resort Hotel** (perched above the Macal River, a short downhill walk from the town center, tel. 501/824-2034, 501/824-2125, or 800/822-3274, www.sanignaciobelize.com). To date, 175 species of birds have been observed here, including a rare family pair of black hawk eagles, plus a number of mammals. Tours of the herb trail or the iguana project (30 minutes for either, US$7 pp) are offered on the hour 7am-4pm daily.

C Belize Botanic Gardens

Visiting the country's only botanical garden (tel. 501/824-3101, www.belizebotanic. org, entrance US$7.50, includes self-guided booklet, or guided walk US$15) makes a wonderful half or full-day activity, no matter where in the area you are staying. Walk through 45 acres of fruit trees, palms, tropical flowers, and native plants of Belize as you learn about the medicinal and ritual plants of the Maya and experience the Native Plant House, with more than 100 species of orchids. Botanists' work here has resulted in 20 new orchid records for Belize and one species new to science: *Pleurothallis duplooyii* (named after Ken duPlooy), which has a bloom about the size of a flea. There is also a rainforest trail, a pine forest habitat complete with a 30-foot fire tower, plenty of bird-watching, a special guidebook for children, and a sustainably built visitors center for meetings, yoga, and other activities. There are picnic tables too, and you can easily spend a fun afternoon here,

LAND OF ORCHIDS

© LEBAWIT GIRMA

The black orchid is Belize's national flower.

Flower lovers are in for a treat: Belize has well over 300 native species of orchids, hence its national flower, the year-round blooming black orchid or *Prosthechea cochleata*. While you're likely to spot a few in the wild while hiking, you can enjoy them in their full glory by visiting the two top orchid and native plant gardens in Belize, right here in Cayo.

The **Orchid Garden at Ian Anderson's Caves Branch** (tel. 501/610-3451, www.cavesbranch.com, 9am-4pm, free) is a lovely retreat on the lodge's property; it is now home to one of the largest collections in Belize of orchids native to Belize and Central America. Ella Anderson, who oversees the garden, received several of the plants from the older women in the nearby city of Belmopan who were no longer able to care for them. Once a month, these women come by the resort to enjoy the pool and visit

the botanical garden to check on their favorite orchids. If you go during spring, you will get to examine the hundreds of blooming flowers here, all carefully labeled for an easy self-guided tour; grab a bench and enjoy the fragrant air. Guides are also available to show you around; stop by the lodge's front desk for more information.

Another favorite is the original **Native Plant House** at the **Belize Botanical Gardens** (tel. 501/834-4800, www.belizebotanic.org, 7am-3pm daily, US$7.50 entrance fee, US$15 guided tour), located at duPlooy's Jungle Lodge Resort (take a shuttle or taxi from San Ignacio), with only Belizean orchids. Look out for the vanilla orchid—native to Belize—the original source of the famous flavor enjoyed worldwide. Make it a full day by grabbing lunch at the restaurant, swimming in the river, and relaxing in the gardens.

with an on-site restaurant and the river below for a freshwater swim. Call to find out about a shuttle from San Ignacio, or get a taxi ride. The gardens' office is in the reception area of duPlooy's Jungle Lodge Resort.

SPORTS AND RECREATION

Cayo District is home to a beautiful lattice of trails, from short nature walks and medicine trails to a range of hiking trips through the surrounding hills. Mountain biking the Cayo District is fun, beautiful, and a great way to burn off a few Belikins, but it can be dusty in the dry season. Equestrians will find horseback riding at a growing number of jungle lodge resorts and custom tour operators in and around San Ignacio.

Many Cayo resorts offer excellent guided cave trips of varying levels of difficulty, for everyone from the beginning spelunker to the professional speleologist; day and overnight trips are available. Ask about the varied experiences to be had in Actun Tunichil Muknal (worth every penny), Barton Creek Cave, Actun Chapat, Actun Halal (on private property), or Chechem Ha Cave, or any of the most recently discovered ones that are as yet unnamed.

Canoeing, kayaking, and tubing are absolute musts and popular ways to enjoy the Macal and Mopan Rivers. Actually, one popular trip is to paddle up the Macal River from downtown San Ignacio, making your way to the Ix Chel Rainforest Medicine Trail or Belize Botanic Gardens.

Canoeing and Kayaking

Canoe five miles up the Macal River to Chaa Creek and the Botanic Gardens at duPlooy's (or vice versa); rent a boat and guide from **Tony's Guided Tours** (tel. 501/824-3292, US$20 pp). Another excellent canoeing guide is the vivacious **Andy Tut** (tel. 501/834-4016 or cell 501/634-5441, US$40 pp, includes pickup from San Ignacio), stationed at the Crystal Paradise Resort and offering trips along the

© LEBAWIT GIRMA

Cave tubing on a river is one of the most enjoyable activities in Cayo.

BELMOPAN AND CAYO

CAYO GUIDES AND TOUR OPERATORS

Cayo is famous for both the quantity and quality of its guides, naturalists, and tour operators. Signing up for a tour is as easy as contacting your hotel's front desk or walking up Burns Avenue, where most of Cayo's tour operator offices are located. It's often the same price to book a trip through your hotel as it is directly with the tour company, but if you'd like to handle it on your own, here are a few recommendations.

- **Pacz Tours** (tel. 501/604-6921 or 501/824-0536, www.pacztours.net, cave trip US$110 pp, Tikal US$150) are the number one tour operator in town, offering the Actun Tunichil Muknal cave trip as well as overnight camping options with some combination of river running, a waterfall, ruins, caves, and rappelling. They are also the only licensed guide to camp overnight at Caracol. Walk-in prices are a little less than online, but you risk not getting your preferred tour dates as Pacz sells out fast.

- **Cayo Adventure Tours** (tel. 501/824-3246, www.cayoadventure.com) offers all kinds of day trips in the area, including horseback riding and mountain biking (both US$75).

- **Belizean Sun Tours** (San José de Succotz, tel. 501/601-2630, www.belizeansun.com, US$95) is passionate about preserving Cayo's history and giving visitors an off-the-beaten track experience. Operator Kenneth Dart is an excellent guide whose Actun Chapat and Actun Halal Caving Adventure begin with a rugged eight-mile Land Rover ride through the rainforest (quite the adventure!), then a hike to several sites, including Actun Chapat, a cave with 60-foot ceilings and huge formations. The Maya used this cave extensively for rituals and left behind altars, terraces, carved faces, and artifacts. These two caves are among the most unique in Belize. Since it's on private property, this is an exclusive trip and you will be the only people there.

- **Hun Chi'ik Tours** (tel. 501/670-0746 or 501/600-9192, www.hunchiik.com, US$85-90) has experienced guides and a creative range of trips. They are conscious about the importance of "oral tradition and local knowledge" to enhance the educational value of their tours.

- **David's Adventure Tours** (tel. 501/804-3674 or cell 501/628-2837, www.davidsadventuretours.net, davidstoursbz@gmail.com, canoe trips US$15-50 pp, birding US$30 pp, overnight rainforest tour US$75 pp, includes food and gear) is one of the old standbys, offering volumes of local knowledge and the full range of tours.

- **River Rat** (tel. 501/628-6033, www.riverratbelize.com) specializes in Actun Tunichil Muknal, kayak expeditions, and overnight float trips.

- **Tony's Guided Tours** (tel. 501/824-3292, US$17.50 pp) is probably the most economical independent trip on the river. For the more adventurous, Tony also offers a five-day all-inclusive canoe and camping trip to Belize City (US$65 pp per day).

- **Yute Expeditions** (Burns Ave., opposite Hotel Casa Blanca, tel. 501/824-4321, yute-exp@btl.net, www.inlandbelize.com, cave trip for two US$90 pp for, includes equipment, entrance fees, and lunch; half-day Xunantunich trip US$45 pp) is run by a very experienced Cayo family. They're especially good for families and groups, and have a top-notch fleet of air-conditioned vehicles.

Macal River as well as river birding; he'll pick you up from San Ignacio.

Cave Tubing

Plop yourself in a tube and float along the stream passing through deep caves (weather and water levels permitting), while admiring the stunning scenery of limestone, pottery shards, and rainforest canopy; your best option is the seven-mile float across the Caves Branch river and cave system. **Ian Anderson's Caves Branch Adventure Company and Jungle Lodge** (Mile 41½ Hummingbird Hwy., tel. 501/610-3451, U.S tel. 866/357-2698, www.cavesbranch.com, offered Mon., Wed., and Fri., US$95 pp, minimum of 4 people) is the original creator of this signature Belize adventure activity. Cave tubing inside the cave system at Jaguar Paw also gets great reviews—contact any of the Cayo tour operators to arrange or compare pricing.

Hiking

Right in town is San Ignacio Resort's self-guided **medicinal trail,** easily explored in 30 minutes or for as long as you'd like to examine all the "bush medicine" surrounding you.

Just outside of town, visitors can head over to The Lodge at Chaa Creek (tel. 501/824-2037, entrance US$10 pp), for a short riverside hike, highlighting the medicinal plants of the Maya and their uses. The site also boasts the **Blue Morpho Butterfly Breeding Center,** and the **Chaa Creek Natural History Museum,** with exhibit areas that examine ecosystems, geology, and Mayan culture in the Cayo area.

Love exploring on foot? A nice walk is from San Ignacio town to the Hawksworth Bridge and crossing over into **Santa Elena,** with lovely views of the Macal River and everyday life as you go along.

Horseback Riding

Book your horseback riding trip with **Andy Tut** (tel. 501/634-5441, half-day US$45 pp for 2 people, US$50 pp)—a reliable local guide to have whether you're a novice or advanced rider; his energy and laughter are contagious. He'll pick you up from San Ignacio and you'll ride through the Cristo Rey Village, stopping at a waterfall to cool off.

Off the Chiquibul Road, **Mountain Equestrian Trails** (Mile 8, Mountain Pine Ridge Rd., tel. 501/669-1124, www.metbelize.com, half-day and full-day rides US$61-90) is the area's premier riding center, with one of the biggest trail systems in the Pine Ridge.

Swimming

Who doesn't love a cool dip in fresh water, along with a picnic on a sunny afternoon? On the weekends in particular, you'll spot local families and children splashing about along the banks of the Macal River. Some swing from a tree branch, and others sit on the grass to contemplate their beautiful district. Another wonderful river, safe and even cleaner to swim in, is the Mopan.

Birding

The Cayo District has an abundance of birdlife, and it's almost impossible to go wrong wherever you choose to roam—over 300 species have been spotted within 10 miles of San Ignacio. But the best way to increase your sighting odds is to explore with the best guides in the area. Contact the Tut brothers at **Crystal Paradise** (tel. 501/834-4016 or cell 501/610-5593, www.birdinginbelize.com), who offer multiple bird-watching tours in the area for all levels of birders; ask them about birding at Aguacate Lagoon. You can also do it solo and head to one of the jungle lodges—try duPlooy's with its Botanic Gardens, rainforest trails, and expert on-site birding guides for advice.

Massage and Bodywork

Eva's Massage Therapy (16 Collins Blvd., tel. 501/824-3423, ebuhler@btl.net) offers an hour-long full-body massage at her studio for US$35, or a 30-40 minute "back and neck therapy session" for only US$20. Right in San Ignacio, you can find reasonably priced massages (US$40 per hour), pedicures, manicures, facials, and body waxing at **Gretel's Salon and Spa** (7 Far West St., tel. 501/604-1126 or 501/666-4576, 8:30am-7pm Mon.-Sat., later close on weekends, 1-hour massage US$37.50, wash and blow dry US$17.50), a locally owned and oriented beauty salon.

Of course, there are full spa services at some of the upscale resorts in the area, notably **Hilltop Spa** at The Lodge at Chaa Creek (US$85-105); combine a visit here with a trip to the nearby botanic gardens or a paddle on the river. **Ka'ana Resort and Spa** (Mile 69¼, Western Hwy., U.S. tel. 305/735-2553, tel. 501/824-3350, www.kaanabelize.com, US$80-150) offers massages, facials, and body scrubs with homegrown brown sugar, cacao, and coffee; they also offer energy work with a Mayan healer.

BUSH MEDICINAL TRAILS

© LEBAWIT GIRMA

The "hot lips" plant helps women to expel the placenta after giving birth.

Belize's rainforests are home to hundreds of trees, plants, fruits, and vines that have traditionally been used for medicinal purposes. "Bush medicine" in Belize dates back to the days of the Maya, thousands of years ago, when they relied on nature both to survive and to cure their ailments. Sadly, the number of living bush doctors and practitioners has declined, particularly since the 1996 death of Cayo's great Don Elijio Panti, Belize's most respected Mayan healer.

Medicinal plants are everywhere today—in the rainforests and in gardens, even while driving along the highway—though less abundant. Today, Belizeans continue to use the same plants for medicinal purposes, as many were raised learning of the benefits as well as the dangers of the rainforest. There are plants for ailments ranging from sunburn, cough, and toothache to male impotency.

As a traveler, exploring the various medicinal trails in Cayo will teach you quite a lot about the rainforest and the various plant and tree uses. Knowing what's in your backyard can come in very handy when there's no pharmacy nearby. You'll also hear fascinating stories from your local guides and even children about their own healing experiences, passed on from their parents and grandparents, and some of the amusing names given to these plants.

- **Calico Jack's** (Mountain Pine Ridge, tel. 501/832-2478, www.calicojacksvillage.com) has a guided walk of their "Ancient Jungle Garden Trail," one of the most informative and entertaining tours around. Learn about

the "tourist plant," or red gumbo-limbo (*Bursera simaruba*), whose tree bark looks just like peeling red skin and is used to treat sunburn.

- **Rainforest Medicine Trail at Chaa Creek** (8am-4pm daily, guided tour US$10 pp, self-guided US$5) features many of the medicinal plants Don Elijio Panti used in his practice and offers a historical background on his achievements. Guided hour-long tours run every hour on the hour, or you can walk the trail on a self-guided tour.

- **San Ignacio Resort Hotel** (above the Macal River, downhill from the town center, tel. 501/824-2034, www.sanignaciobelize.com, uS$5) offers another great medicinal trail, where you can take a 30-minute guided tour (9am, noon, 1pm, and 4pm).

- **Hmen Herbal Center** (Maya Centre, near Cockscomb, tel. 501/533-7043 or cell 501/665-1313, nuukcheil@yahoo.com, entrance US$2.50) is about a two-hour drive from Belmopan. Owned and operated by Aurora Garcia Saqui, niece of the late Don Pant, it features a four-acre botanical garden, a medicinal trail, herbs for sale, and seminars on herbal medicine.

To learn more about bush medicine, pick up a copy of *Sastun: My Apprenticeship with a Maya Healer* by Rosita Arvigo, about her decade-long apprenticeship with Don Elijio Panti, or *Rainforest Remedies: 100 Healing Herbs of Belize* by Dr. Rosita Arvigo and Dr. Michael Balick.

ENTERTAINMENT AND EVENTS
Nightlife

San Ignacio's nightlife has grown by leaps and bounds over the past couple of years—not to the level of San Pedro, but still with quite a few more bar, dancing, and happy-hour options than other spots in the country. There's always somewhere to go for a drink after a long day exploring the countryside. It's a small town, so finding the party is not difficult; just follow the masses as they trek between bars, or ask around for the latest. Thursday through Saturday are the most happening nights. Start your evening with the popular happy hour at **Mr. Greedy's** (34 Burns Ave., tel. 501/804-4688, 6am-midnight daily), especially on "ladies night" when women get happy hour prices all night (we're talking US$2 cocktails and occasional live music), or one of the copycat happy hours at other restaurants on Burns Avenue. For a more upscale bar scene, check the **Stork Club** bar at San Ignacio Resort Hotel (above the Macal River, downhill from the town center, tel. 501/824-2034, www.sanignaciobelize.com).

Meluchi's (Joseph Andrews Dr., across from the cemetery, tel. 501/668-2920, 10am-2pm and 5pm-10pm daily) is another good bet for happy hour and delicious tacos, among other options, as well as karaoke on Thursday. On weekends, tables are cleared and it turns into a dance club. I'm not sure there's anywhere else in the world where you can dance while looking onto a cemetery on one side and a playground on the other. **Mi Cocina** (across from Victor Galvez Stadium, on the left side of the climb up to Cahal Pech) is a clean bar with reasonably priced drinks. On weekends, the **Cahal Pech Village** bar is buzzing with locals and travelers hanging out poolside, with lovely views of the Cayo hills at night and a boom box playing all the latest tunes. Ask for bartender Oscar's signature Belizean Snow cocktail; he won the 2009 Best Bartender title at the annual Taste of Belize event. You can play pool and have drinks at **BB's Camp 6,** a sports bar just across from the Macal River park.

For dancing, you can try the only decent nightclub in San Ignacio, **Club Next** (inside the Princess Casino, 9pm-2am Thurs.-Sat.). Across the street is the popular outdoor **Club Rehab at Piache's** (2pm-midnight Tues.-Wed., 2pm-3am Thurs.-Sat.), set back in a lush garden under a *palapa* with a large disco-lit dance floor, a seating area, a full bar, and a yard with mini-*palapas* and stools for those seeking a little quiet conversation. Folks start here before continuing across the street at Club Next. Also downtown is **Blue Angel's** (Post Office Rd., 10pm-2am), which gets a bit dicey late at night.

Festivals and Events

Belize's Super Bowl is **La Ruta Maya Belize River Challenge** (www.larutamayabelize.com), an exciting and convivial canoe race held during the first week of March and timed to coincide with National Heroes and Benefactors Day (formerly Baron Bliss Day) celebrations. If you are in San Ignacio for the start of the race, you'll watch 100 teams of paddlers mass together in the Macal River, then bolt downstream—racing five days down the 173-mile length of the Belize River all the way to Belize City. Crowds gather all around the river, and it makes for one lively event. Increasingly popular since its inception in 1998, La Ruta Maya has many divisions to compete in, including women's, mixed gender, amateur, dory, and pleasure craft, and it offers more than US$15,000 in prize money. The race is part athletic event, part tourism draw, and several parts fiesta.

Organized by the Belize Cycling Association (www.belizecycling.com), Belize's **Annual Holy Saturday Cross-Country Cycling Classic** takes place every year on the Saturday before Easter Sunday. Teams race from Belize City all the way to the hills of Cayo, passing through the twin towns of San Ignacio and Santa Elena, and back.

SHOPPING

There are small gift and supply shops along Burns Avenue in San Ignacio, but the best shopping in the area (some would say in all of Belize) is a few miles east of San Ignacio at **Orange Gifts & Gallery** (Mile 60, Western

Hwy., tel. 501/824-2341, www.orangegifts. com, 7:30am-5:30pm Mon.-Fri.). Orange Gifts (there's also a shop in San Pedro) has an enormous collection of original and imported arts and crafts, including the custom hardwood furniture and art of proprietor Julian Sherrard. You'll also find jewelry, paintings, textiles, and practical items for travelers like laminated maps, books, postcards, and Gallon Jug Coffee. Orange has an excellent restaurant and bar.

Nearly across the highway from Orange, **Hot Mama's Belize** (Mile 60, Western Hwy., tel. 501/824-0444, www.hotmamasbelize.com) makes some fine and spicy condiments. Gift packages and other sundries, as well as tours, are available.

To sample Belizean music and take some home, **Venus Records** (6 Hudson St., across from the post office, tel. 501/824-2101, 8am-6pm Mon.-Sat., closed for lunch Mon.-Fri.) has an excellent selection.

ACCOMMODATIONS

Choices abound for such a small town; there are many cheap, clean, converted family homes, most within a few blocks of one another. Cayo can get hot at times, but remember that it's generally cooler than the rest of the country, so air-conditioning may not be a big priority, especially from October to February. Also, note that most (but not all) accommodations in Cayo quote prices with tax and service charges included; most also offer deep discounts in low season and for multiple nights. The rates quoted in this chapter, as in the rest of the book, are high-season double-occupancy rates only.

Under US$25
The **Hi-Et Guest House** (West St., tel. 501/824-2828, thehiet@yahoo.com, US$12.50-25) is an excellent option built right into the owner's large home. The five guest rooms with shared baths and cold water are clean and comfortable and have hardwood floors. The five guest rooms with private baths in the next building are a big step up in quality and not

much in price—they're well-kept and have tiled floors and balconies but no air-conditioning. There's a common area with a fridge and seating, and Wi-Fi access is included.

The **Tropicool Hotel** (30A Burns Ave., tel. 501/804-3052, US$17.50-38) has seven simple, clean guest rooms with shared baths and four nicely kept and furnished cabins around a peaceful garden, each with a private bath, a TV, and a fan.

Find quiet, friendly lodging at **J & R's Guest House** (20 Far West St., tel. 501/626-3604, jr-guesthouse@yahoo.com, US$10-23); there are four guest rooms, two with private baths, and breakfast is included, for now. It may be a bit tricky to find, but once you do, it's amazing how close it is to town, just a couple of minutes' walk downhill.

US$25-50
One of the best-value mid-range hotels is the **Casa Blanca Guest House** (Burns Ave., tel. 501/824-2080, www.casablancaguesthouse. com, US$30-50, with a/c US$50-70), where Ms. Betty keeps eight immaculate, cozy guest rooms with private baths, hot and cold water, and TVs as well as access to a beautiful common living room, kitchen, balcony, and rooftop deck. It's on Burns Avenue near the banks and across from Hannah's restaurant.

Rosa's Hotel (65 Hudson St., tel. 501/804-2265, rosashotel@yahoo.com, US$28-38, breakfast included) has a selection of guest rooms with private baths and fans or air-conditioning; guest rooms range from small and stuffy to high and airy—check out a few before deciding, and check the door locks: Some show wear and tear. A longtime standard is **Venus Hotel** (Burns Ave., tel. 501/824-3203, www. venushotelbelize.com, US$34-47), right in the middle of town with 32 decent guest rooms with private baths; take your pick of those overlooking the park or the street.

US$50-100
Martha's Guesthouse (10 West St., tel. 501/804-3647, www.marthasbelize.com, US$70-95) continues to offer a tasteful

SAN IGNACIO
DOWNTOWN

BROASTER'S
SPORTS
STADIUM

BURNS AVE

CHURCH

VENUS
HOTEL

MR. GREEDY'S

GRETEL'S SALON
AND SPA

SERENDIB

NEW
FRENCH BAKERY

OPEN
MARKET

SAN IGNACIO
FARMERS MARKET

TROPICOOL
HOTEL

JNC MALL

PACZ TOURS

TOURIST INFO/
TAXI CO-OP

BUS TERMINAL/
BENQUE TAXIS

WOODEN BRIDGE

FLAYVA'S

Coronation
Park

ERVA'S

WELCOME
CENTER

HI-ET GUEST
HOUSE

GUESTHOUSE

WAIGHT'S   AVE

NEW
BELMORAL
HOTEL

MARTHA'S
GUESTHOUSE

MARTHA'S KITCHEN

5-Way
Intersection

MAXIM'S
CHINESE
RESTAURANT

BULLET TREE
TAXIS

POST
OFFICE

Macal River

POP'S

TRADEWINDS
INTERNET

KING ST

YUTE
EXPEDITIONS

BLUE
ANGEL'S

MOSSIAH ST

CASA BLANCA
GUEST HOUSE

KO-OX-
HAN-NAH

ROSA'S
HOTEL

SCOTIABANK

Santa
Elena

COMMUNITY
COMPUTER CENTER

ATLANTIC
BANK

FAR WEST ST

WEST ST

TOWN
HALL

SHELL
STATION

WESTERN   HWY

HAWKSWORTH BRIDGE

POLICE

J & R'S GUEST
HOUSE

OLD BENQUE RD

SAN IGNACIO
RESORT HOTEL

0   100 yds

0   100 m

© AVALON TRAVEL

atmosphere in the center of San Ignacio town, with an abundance of common lounging areas for guests to mingle in if they so desire. The 16 guest rooms have hardwood floors and furniture, private baths, fans, hot water, wireless Internet access, and cable TV. Laundry services are available. There's a decent restaurant downstairs that has outdoor patio seating, and the front desk can arrange tours. Martha's just expanded into a six-room annex, about a three-minute walk up Burns Avenue, with beautiful apartment-style options, several with

kitchenettes and porches (US$50-65, weekly rates available).

Talk about a vista! **Cahal Pech Village** (tel. 501/824-3740, www.cahalpech.com, US$79-119) offers a variety of guest rooms and cabanas spread out on a spacious hillside with stunning views of San Ignacio and the valley below. The 21 guest rooms have private baths and air-conditioning, or choose a thatch-and-wood cabana, overlooking the hills, with a private bath, hot and cold water, and a screened porch with a hammock. There are new third-level suites, from which the already amazing views of Cayo are now jaw-dropping, with a 180-degree wrap-around balcony—you can see San Ignacio, Santa Elena, and even Spanish Lookout in the distance. Cahal Pech is ideal for groups, families, and retreats. A restaurant, a lively bar, and a creative swimming pool round out the resort, in addition to its quick access to the Cahal Pech ruins down the hill. The road leading up to Cahal Pech is just a little rough, but it's well worth it. The resort also sells water taxi tickets to the Cayes and has an on-site tour-operating company as well as an on-call masseuse, Flor (1-hour Swedish US$55).

☾**Clarissa Falls Resort** (tel. 501/833-3116 or cell 501/661-6689, www.clarissafalls.com) is at the end of a mile-long dirt road, accessed on the right at Mile 70½ on the Western Highway. I fell in love with the grounds when I first visited. This is an intimate, laid-back, and affordable lodge. Whether you can hang out by the outdoor dining area or swing in a hammock in the yard by your cabana, you can listen to and enjoy the view of the cascading water below. You can walk down just a few steps from there to the waterfall and the Mopan River for a swim, or tube down the stream. Guests either camp in their own tents (US$7.50 pp) or stay in a cottage with private bath (US$75 d). The shared toilet and shower building has hot and cold water and is cement-basic. Don't miss the nature trails and a hike (or horseback ride) to Xunantunich, the highest pyramid visible from the cottages. The dining room serves tasty food, including a few specialties such as black mole soup and great cheap Mexican-style tacos or stuffed squash (US$6-9). You'll get much bang for your buck at Clarissa Falls.

Over US$100

The **San Ignacio Resort Hotel** (tel. 501/824-2034, U.S. tel. 855/488-2624, www.sanignaciobelize.com, US$182-350) is proud of having hosted Queen Elizabeth in 1994 and has never stopped improving the property toward the luxury side of things. From the grand marble

The views of San Ignacio from Cahal Pech Village just keep getting better.

lobby and reception hall to the lap pool and range of services, this is definitely an excellent upscale option that is both in town and a tad remote-feeling. The hotel is perched above the Macal River and is a short downhill walk from the town center (it feels longer walking back uphill). There are 24 deluxe air-conditioned guest rooms, some with their own secluded balconies; the guest rooms have private tiled baths, TVs, comfy furniture, and telephones. There is also a honeymoon suite on the second floor. The hotel hosts the Stork Club Bar & Grill, Running W Steakhouse & Restaurant, a rainforest-view patio deck ideal for bird-watching, a tennis court, a disco, a casino, and convention and wedding facilities. Bird-watching tours are available with the on-site guide, who can also show you the Green Iguana Conservation Project and Medicinal Jungle Trail on the hotel's grounds (tours on the hour).

Only a two-minute drive from San Ignacio, **Windy Hill Resort** (Western Hwy., tel. 501/824-2017, www.windyhillresort.com, US$230-266, includes meals) sits on its own lovely rise, just above the Western Highway. You'll find 25 well-appointed, clean, air-conditioned deluxe cottages and standard guest rooms with private baths, hot and cold water, ceiling fans, private verandas with hammocks, an infinity swimming pool, a fitness center, and a recreation room complete with a TV, a bar, table tennis, and darts. Windy Hill specializes in tours and multiday packages with meal plans. Guests enjoy canoeing, caving, horseback riding, nature tours, and hiking trails. Meals are served in the casual thatched-roof Black Orchid Restaurant.

Ka'ana Boutique Hotel & Spa (Mile 69¼, Western Hwy., tel. 501/824-3350, www.kaanabelize.com, US$275-450) opened in 2007, a few miles west of San Ignacio. Ka'ana is a small, full-service boutique resort with 15 guest rooms and 10 fully equipped casitas around a pool, spa, and lounge. Newly built are luxurious one- and two-bedroom private-pool villas. The restaurant and bar offer an elite departure from the standard fare in San Ignacio (7am-9pm daily, dinner entrées US$12-33); at the

bar, try the sweet corn colada (cocktails US$5-12). There are tastings held at 7pm each evening in the well-stocked, climate-controlled wine cellar.

Camping

Smith's Family Farm (13 Branch Mouth Rd., tel. 501/604-2227) is a peaceful 25-acre retreat up Branch Mouth Road with a shaded campground (US$7.50 pp) and a collection of cabins (US$25), all with private baths, hot and cold water, and simple furniture. Weekly rates are available, and the owner, Roy, sometimes lets you trade labor on his organic farm for a stay at the place. On the same road, **Cosmos Camping** (15 Branch Mouth Rd., tel. 501/824-2116, cosmoscamping@btl.net, US$5 pp) is a 15-minute walk from town and has pretty grounds, many big trees, and mowed lawns where you can pitch your tent. It's on the Mopan River and has shared baths and showers, but it's kind of isolated, as the office is back up the road toward town. It's near the Midas Resort, and the old sign still reads "River Park Inn," so don't get confused and pass it.

A couple of miles outside San Ignacio on the Western Highway, **Inglewood** (tel. 501/824-3555, www.inglewoodcampinggrounds.com, US$15; electricity metered at US$0.40 per kWh; tent camping US$7.50-10) offers full hookups for RVs. Following the same road, you'll find campgrounds at the lovely **Clarissa Falls Resort** (tel. 501/833-3116, www.clarissafalls.com, US$7.50 pp).

Jungle Lodges

Set on 90 lush acres of rolling countryside on the banks of the Macal River is **duPlooy's Jungle Lodge** (tel. 501/824-3101, www.duplooys.com, US$195-315). Guests have a number of choices, including Jungle Lodge rooms (US$195) and comfy bungalows (US$250, includes breakfast, canoes, and Botanic Gardens admission) with king beds, bathtubs, full kitchens, and private decks; you'll get to your room via wooden catwalk, which gives you your own canopy tour on the steep riverbank. Other options include La Casita (sleeps up to 8,

US$310). Meals, packed lunches, and a dining room provide top-notch, cow-free sustenance—vegetarians welcome. DuPlooy's offers a sandy river beach with swimming, walks in the garden, horse trails, hiking, orchids, and bird-watching tours. In addition to composting, waste reduction, and recycling, they also use zero chemicals on their vast landscaping—no small feat in the rainforest. In 2010 they went fully solar (with a backup generator).

The Lodge at Chaa Creek (tel. 501/824-2037, www.chaacreek.com, from US$380, includes breakfast) is one of the top-rated jungle lodges in Central America. Chaa Creek's 365 acres on the Macal River host the ever-evolving vision of owners Mick and Lucy Fleming, an American-British couple who came to Belize in the late 1970s, fell in love with the land, and stayed. The 23 *palapa*-roofed cottages have electricity and private verandas for viewing wildlife and are furnished with fine fabrics and works of art from around the world; two "treetop" suites with jetted tubs perch on the riverbank, their wide porches boasting views of iguanas basking in the branches. Chaa Creek guests choose among on-site activities, included in the rates, such as daily birding walks, canoeing and swimming in the Macal River, a butterfly farm tour, and a medicinal trail walk. There is full concierge service and meals prepared with many local ingredients (packed lunch US$15, dinner US$36).

One of the best deals in the region is Chaa Creek's (**Macal River Camp** (US$55 pp), a 10-minute walk from the main lodge. Accommodations are in a screened lantern-lit casita with a porch and access to all the main Chaa Creek facilities and activities. Dinner and breakfast are included. There are 10 units centered around a fire pit and eating area, all with access to a shared restroom and shower house. Homemade meals are excellent and are eaten communally under a thatched roof, with a bar available as well.

Upstream on the Macal River, **Ek' Tun** (tel. 501/820-3002, www.ektunbelize.com, US$190 per night, 3-night minimum, breakfast and dinner US$32) is one of the remotest and most romantic lodgings in Belize. Accommodations consist of two quaint, tastefully appointed cottages in the middle of a vast green chunk of the upper Macal River Valley. The cascade-fed mineral-water swimming pool is surrounded by beautiful landscaping and meditation platforms. Excellent meals include Mexican specialties, fresh fruit, spicy local dishes, and desserts. The cottages are rustically elegant and comfortable; there is no electricity. Ek' Tun's intimate atmosphere makes this a favorite for honeymooners, and it's for couples only, no children.

Another couple of river bends later is (**Black Rock Lodge** (tel. 501/834-4038, www.blackrocklodge.com, US$105-210, meals and taxes extra), easy to recommend for the sheer beauty of its location. The seven-mile drive to the lodge takes in grazing cattle, citrus orchards, coconut trees, and river views, and there's an incredible vista from the open-air dining pavilion. Guests stay in one of 14 units that include gorgeous River Suites, a stone's throw from the river below the main lodge, with marble floors, wooden decks, and French windows. Communal meals are served at long tables, and the menu includes four-course dinners (US$22) as well as breakfast and lunch (US$12 each). There are numerous hikes on the 242-acre property, 30 species of trees in a fruit orchard, a small organic garden, unique bird habitats, and plenty of wildlife in the area, as the lodge is located is across the river from Elijio Panti National Park. Yoga practitioners will enjoy the yoga *palapa;* inquire about occasional yoga retreats. Black Rock is off the grid and is powered by a combination of solar and hydro technology, including solar hot-water heating.

FOOD
Barbecue

The best barbecue cooks set up in Santa Elena, just over the Hawksworth Bridge, and they cater especially to weekend party crowds, offering grilled mounds of meat, rice, and beans used by many customers to soak up all that beer sloshing around in their stomachs. Some swear

© LEBAWIT GIRMA

Black Rock Lodge, located high above the Macal River, is surrounded by stunning scenery and offers excellent birding and outdoor activities.

by the chicken at **Boiton's Bar-B-Q and House of Pastries** (23 Western Hwy., Santa Elena, tel. 501/804-0403, 10:30am-9pm Tues. and Thurs.-Sat., 5pm-close Wed. and Sun., US$8), just after the bridge entrance, and others are loyal to **Rodriguez** (US$2.50), just a couple of blocks farther up—a more casual experience where your crispy chicken is served on a piece of foil and bench tables are shared.

Belizean

Some say **Erva's** (4 Far West St., tel. 501/824-2821, 8am-10pm Mon.-Sat., US$3-10) dishes out reasonably priced Belizean food. It is a quality family-run restaurant that often caters to groups. Dine inside or out on the patio and choose from breakfast, stew chicken, rice and beans, burritos, and a full menu of comfort dinners, including chicken cordon bleu. Prepare to wait, as everything is prepared from scratch.

◖ **Pop's** (tel. 501/824-3266, 6:30am-2:30pm daily, US$3-6) may be the closest Belize comes to a small-town American-style diner, with booths, bottomless cups of coffee, and customers watching CNN and talking religion and politics—except Pop's is owned by a 100 percent Belizean Hemingway look-alike; the delicious breakfast is the best in Cayo. It's just around the corner from the five-way intersection, to the south; ask anyone nearby for directions.

Chinese

Maxim's Chinese Restaurant (23 Far West St., lunch and dinner daily, US$10) is a family-run café with a good reputation among the locals. Prices are moderate; you won't pay much for the best meal in the house and a beer.

International

◖ **Ko-Ox-Han-Nah** (5 Burns Ave., tel. 501/824-3014, 6am-9pm daily, entrées US$5-16), which means "let's go eat," offers Belizean fare plus a large cosmopolitan menu that includes Asian, Indian, and vegetarian dishes

© LEBAWIT GIRMA

Saturday street barbecue in neighboring Santa Elena

(and an ample wine list), all prepared with organic ingredients and meat raised by the owner himself. Though portions have gotten smaller over the past couple of years, and prices are a tad high for its location near other fast food joints, the food remains excellent.

Serendib Restaurant (27 Burns Ave., tel. 501/824-2302, 6am-3pm and 6pm-10pm Mon.-Sat., US$12) serves curries and dal, along with reliable hamburgers, steaks, and chow mein. There's outdoor sidewalk seating and friendly service. (**Mr. Greedy's** (34 Burns Ave., tel. 501/804-4688, 6am-midnight daily) understands the importance of a superhot oven in the production of succulent pizza crust (large cheese pie US$14). They also do a kick-ass breakfast, burger platter, wings, and sandwiches and have a long cocktail menu. The environment is very casual, and wireless Internet is available.

Martha's Kitchen (10 West St., tel. 501/804-3647, 7am-midnight daily, US$4-8) has some good pizza in Cayo, plus a full menu that includes stir-fried vegetables, T-bone steak with

gravy and fries, and a simple club sandwich. Visitors give high praise to **Yoli's Pizza** (West St., next to Plaza del Rio Mall, tel. 501/804-4187. 9am-9pm Mon.-Sat., 5pm-9pm Sun., US$2-20), which also delivers.

(**Flayva's** (22 Burns Ave., tel. 501/804-2267 or cell 501/662-4853, www.flayvasbarandgrill.com, 6:30am-10:30pm Wed.-Mon. US$5-12) is the place for hearty breakfasts and, later in the day, creative comfort dishes like stew sheep, mango shrimp, nachos, sandwiches, and curries. Check out the patio through the back door; there's Internet access and you can book tomorrow's tour while you wait.

For ambience, you'll want to try **Sanny's Grill** (E. 23rd St., tel. 501/824-2988, 6pm-11pm daily, US$6-10), which is a bit out of the way (toward the western exit to Benque, just down from the UNO station) but well worth it for the fine menu and nice lighting and music.

In addition to steaks, pork chops, and seafood entrées (from US$10), the **Running W Steakhouse** (in the San Ignacio Resort Hotel, tel. 501/824-2125, 7am-10pm daily) also serves up an open-air dining patio above the Macal River. Belizean classic plates start at US$5 and feature meat from the restaurant's own ranch. The indoor sports bar, The Stork, is a good choice for a rainy day with decent bar food.

Mestizo

San Ignacio has a higher-than-average number of cheap mestizo fast-food places—a mix of Mayan and Spanish dishes—and a few *pupuserías* serving El Salvadoran *pupusas:* fried tortillas stuffed with beans, cheese, and meat for good measure. Check out the stalls in the basement of the Burns Avenue Mall or across from the Belize Bank. Saturday morning at the market, very early, is the best bet for cheap eats, as organic farmers, local cooks, and produce vendors congregate at the outdoor market. This is the best place to chow down before catching a bus to other regions or even before your next activity. Fresh *pupusas,* tacos, barbecued meats, and more are made on-site, and locals come here to eat all day long on shared picnic tables.

The **New French Bakery** (tel. 501/804-0054 or 501/620-0841, 6:30am-6pm Mon.-Sat.), near the Cayo Welcome Center directly across from the Market, serves delicious fresh-baked breads and pastries and has a small interior seating area and open doors.

Mickey's (Burns Ave.), a small joint next door to Hannah's Restaurant, serves up excellent Creole dishes, made fresh and served quickly. The rice and beans are delicious, and there's always a daily special. It gets crowded with locals at lunchtime, all the validation you need. Right next to Mickey's is a similar "fast food" shack, **Mincho's** (Burns Ave.), serving mestizo grub from *garnaches* to tacos and *panades* (3 for US$0.50) and the best fresh-squeezed juice (US$0.50) you'll find anywhere in town—choose among papaya, lime, watermelon, coconut water, and more.

Dessert

For ice cream, go to **Cayo Twist** (near the western exit to town, nearly across from the UNO station, tel. 501/667-7717, 6pm-9:30pm Thurs.-Sun.), which has delicious soy ice cream. Get your gelato fix at Fabio's **Amor e Mio** (11am-7pm Mon.-Sat., later on Fri.-Sat.), a small outdoor stand right on Burns Avenue's cobblestones, with flavors like soursop, mango, and more.

Groceries

Across from the Belize Tourism Industry Association, **Celina's Super Store** (43 Burns Ave., tel. 501/824-2247 or cell 501/669-1222, celinasbz@yahoo.com, 8am-noon and 1pm-6pm Mon.-Sat.) is the largest, best-equipped supermarket in town, but there are many other Chinese shops scattered around as well.

INFORMATION AND SERVICES
Tourist Information

There is an official tourist information post at the **Cahal Pech Visitors Center** (8am-5pm daily). The **Belize Tourism Industry Association** has a stand near the Savannah Taxi Co-op downtown (tel. 501/824-2155), offering brochures for local resorts, taxi charters, and a town map. However, you'll find out much more by reading the posters and advertisements at the various restaurants around town. The most regularly updated website on Cayo's businesses and attractions is **www. bestofcayo.com.**

For travel arrangements, **Exodus International** (2 Burns Ave., tel. 501/824-4400 or 501/824-4401, exodusbze@yahoo.com) is at the beginning of Burns Avenue, near the bridge.

Banks

Atlantic Bank, Scotiabank, and **Belize Bank** are all on Burns Avenue, just past the Hawksworth Bridge as you come into town; all have 24-hour ATMs.

Media and Communications

The **post office** (Hudson St., 8am-4pm Mon.-Fri.) is in the center of town. **Tradewinds Internet** (Hudson St., next to the post office, tel. 501/824-2396, 7am-10pm Mon.-Sat., 10am-10pm Sun.) has fast machines, scanners, and printers. **Venus Photos and Records** (6 Hudson St., tel. 501/824-2101, 8am-6pm Mon.-Sat.), across from the post office, sells camera batteries, memory cards, and some camera equipment.

GETTING THERE AND AROUND

Downtown San Ignacio is tiny and entirely walkable, although there are a few steep hills, including the trek to Cahal Pech and the walk to San Ignacio Resort.

By Air

All resorts can arrange for a transfer (US$125) from **Goldson International Airport** (BZE, 10 miles west of Belize City, 501/225-2045, www.pgiabelize.com); as of December 2012, visitors can fly direct from the Belize City international airport to Cayo on **Tropic Air** (www.tropicair.com, US$94.50 pp one-way), landing at the Maya Flats airstrip, located near Chaa Creek. **Belize San Ignacio Shuttle & Transfer** (tel. 501/620-3055, belizeshuttle@ yahoo.com, US$95 for two people) can arrange rides anywhere, including both airports; the owner, William Hoffman, is accommodating and flexible.

By Bus

Westbound buses from Belize City and Belmopan run through the middle of town, stopping at the lot beside the market as part of the daily runs to Benque. The street next to the main park is the de facto bus station. Expect limited service on Sunday. Express buses take about two hours between Belize City and San Ignacio, including the quick stop in Belmopan. Regular buses leave every hour, and there are a handful of expresses 7am-7pm daily. Check the express departure times the day before your journey, as the bus schedules are constantly changing as companies battle it out over routes and turf.

In addition to the main buses running back and forth on the Western Highway, village buses come into Market Square from most surrounding towns, returning to the hills in the

afternoon. To the south, buses only run as far as the village of San Antonio—perhaps someone will think to start public transportation to Caracol once the road is improved.

By Taxi

Taxis anywhere within the city limits cost US$2.50-4 pp. Cheap *colectivo* taxis run from San Ignacio in all directions throughout the day, making it easy to get to towns and destinations in the immediate vicinity (including Bullet Tree, Succotz, and Benque). If you want your own driver, a safe bet is Mr. William from **William's Taxi Service** (tel. 501/625-4365, williams_taxiservice@yahoo.com); he'll take you pretty much anywhere you want to go, whether around town or to sites and other parts of Belize.

Car Rentals

Anyone wishing to travel independently to the Mountain Pine Ridge, Caracol, Hydro Road, or El Pilar might consider renting a car—either in Belize City or at one of the few places in San Ignacio and Santa Elena. Renting in Cayo (as low as US$60 per day) is cheaper than in Belize City, and it's a good way to go if you really want to explore this area.

At the top of the Old Benque Road at the western edge of San Ignacio, by the UNO gas station, you'll find **Cayo Rentals** (tel. 501/824-2222 or cell 501/610-4779, www.cayoautorentals.com), with a handful of newish vehicles for rent in the UNO parking lot; US$45-75 for 24 hours *includes* insurance, which is cheaper than any place in Belize City. There's also **Matus Car Rentals** (tel. 501/663-4702 or 501/824-2089, www.matuscarrental.com, US$58-68 per day, US$315-367 per week), on the hill up from the town center, which offers decent weekly rates.

VICINITY OF SAN IGNACIO

On the Western Highway toward San Ignacio, after passing the Hummingbird Highway junction, you are greeted with a jarring series of speed bumps at the roadside village of Teakettle. Turning left at the Pook's Hill sign carries you past cornfields grown atop ancient Mayan residential mounds.

C Actun Tunichil Muknal

This is the acclaimed "Cave of the Crystal Maiden," one of the most spectacular natural and archaeological attractions in Central America, and recently named the number one-cave by *National Geographic*. The trip to ATM, as the cave is also known, is for fit and active people who do not mind getting wet and muddy—and who are able to tread lightly around ancient artifacts.

Tours start in San Ignacio with a ride to Teakettle. After the initial 45-minute hike to the entrance (fording three rivers on foot) and a swim into the cave's innards, you will be asked to remove your shoes on climbing up the limestone into the main cathedral-like chambers. The rooms are littered with delicate Mayan pottery and the crystallized remains of 14 humans. There are no pathways, fences, glass, or other partitions separating the visitor from the artifacts, nor are there any installed lights. The only infrastructure is a rickety ladder that, toward the end of the journey, will lead you up to the chamber of the Crystal Maiden herself, a full female skeleton that sparkles with calcite under your headlamp's glare, more so during the drier months.

Be careful—the fact that visitors are allowed to walk here at all is as astonishing as the sights themselves. At the time of this writing, somebody had already trod on and broken one of the skulls, and just a year ago in 2012, a visitor dropped a camera on a second ancient skull, prompting the current strict no-camera rule.

Only a few tour companies are licensed to take guests here: **Pacz Tours** (San Ignacio, tel. 501/604-6921 or 501/824-0536, www.pacz-tours.net, US$110) is the most popular provider. The Actun Tunichil Muknal cave is neither for the out of shape—you need to be agile and in good health—nor recommended for small children or claustrophobics. In fact, children under the age of 8 (or 12, depending on whom you ask) are not permitted inside. Entrance to the site is US$25 pp.

POOK'S HILL LODGE

Arriving at the remote clearing that is **Pook's Hill Lodge** (tel. 501/832-2017, www.pook-shillbelize.com, accommodations US$198), you'll have a hard time believing that you are only 12 miles from Belmopan and 21 miles from San Ignacio, so dense and peaceful is the forest around you. Towering hardwoods, flowering bromeliads, and exotic birds hem in the accommodations, which are built around a small Mayan residential ruin. Pook's Hill is a 300-acre private nature reserve, bordered by the Tapir Mountain Nature Reserve and the Roaring River and offering active travelers 10 thatched-roof cabanas from which to base their Cayo explorations. The cottages have private baths, electricity, and comfortable furnishings. The lounge-bar area overlooks a grassy knoll that gently slopes toward the creek. The dining room is downstairs from the lounge, and good filling meals are shared on lantern-lit dining tables, communal style. Vegetarian or other food preferences can be accommodated with advance notice. There are plenty of guided walks, birding, tubing, and night walks, all included in the lodging rates for guests. Pook's Hill is the only lodge within walking distance of Actun Tunichil Muknal and offers early morning private tours before the crowds arrive.

To get there, look for the hand-painted sign at Teakettle Village (around Mile 52.5, Western Hwy.); turn left and follow the signs to Pook's Hill for 5.5 miles (there are a couple of turns). The road can be rough, and four-wheel drive is recommended, as is calling ahead so they know to expect you.

TAPIR MOUNTAIN NATURE RESERVE

Covering 6,741 acres, the **Tapir Mountain Nature Reserve** (www.belizeaudubon.org, no public access) is one of the jewels in the country's crown of natural treasures. The deep, steamy rainforest is ripe with an abundance of plantlife. Every wild thing native to the region roams its forests, from toucans to tapirs, coatis to kinkajous. At present, the reserve is off-limits to all but scientific expeditions, but you can

EXTREME ADVENTURES

© LEBAWIT GIRMA

Extreme adventures—like spelunking through ancient Maya caves—are plentiful in Belize.

There's more adventure in Cayo than you can possibly experience in one trip, even if you stayed for a whole month. Below is a cheat sheet of must-see activities for adrenaline junkies who like to be on the go and make the most of each day (though I recommend a day's rest after intense hiking).

- **Spelunking:** The Actun Tunichil Muknal Cave is popular for all the right reasons—there's no hype to it. Or experience the unique caves of Actun Halal and Chapat, located on private property in nearby San José de Succotz, not for the faint of heart. Be sure to pick the right tour guide: **Pacz** (tel. 501/604-6921 or 501/824-0536, www.pacztours.net) or **Belizean Sun Tours** (San José de Succotz, tel. 501/601-2630, www.belizeansun.com).

- **Rappelling:** There's no better place to rappel than in Cayo's dense rainforests. The most intense experience is the Black Hole Drop, offered by **Ian Anderson's Caves Branch Adventure Company and Jungle Lodge** (Mile 41½, Hummingbird Hwy., tel. 501/610-3451, U.S tel. 866/357-2698, www.cavesbranch.com). A grueling

1.5-hour hike is followed by rappelling 400 feet into the rainforest and landing at the entrance of an enormous cave.

- **Hiking waterfalls:** Climb over boulders and swim in the pools among them; the scenery at **Río on Pools,** in the Mountain Pine Ridge, is spectacular and worth the journey alone. If you're feeling intrepid, arrange a hike over to **Thousand Foot Falls,** the highest waterfall in Central America.

- **Zip-lining:** Head to **Calico Jack's Village** (tel. 501/832-2478, www.calicojacksvillage.com), in the rainforests of the Mountain Pine Ridge, and swing like Tarzan or Jane from a rope off a 50-foot-high pyramid. Then make your way across 2,700 feet of zip line over and through the rainforest, complete with a cable walk and rappel.

- **Rainforest night hike:** You haven't experienced the rainforest until you're surrounded by it at night. During a night hike at **Pook's Hill Lodge** (tel. 501/832-2017, www.pookshillbelize.com), prepare to see all sorts of creepy crawlies—including the occasional snake—and listen as the rainforest comes alive.

see a piece of it by going on an Actun Tunichil Muknal trip.

Spanish Lookout

Turn off the Western Highway at the Spanish Lookout sign and watch the landscape change from ragged forest to neat, rolling green countryside with green lawns and men riding John Deere lawnmowers. Spanish Lookout is one of Belize's largest Mennonite communities, with about 3,000 farmers and builders who supply a large part of the furniture, dairy, and poultry products for the country. Many Mennonites here have embraced organic living, and if you drive around you'll find produce and items that cannot be found anywhere else in Belize. The recent discovery of oil in the area has added a modern twist to this unique scene (you'll pass a few pumps and the refinery on your way in).

Spanish Lookout has no accommodations, but it has a few excellent places to eat as well as shopping and services (Scotiabank has an ATM here, and there are three gas stations). Folks from all over Belize come to shop at places like Farmer's Trading Centre, Reimer's Feeds, the Computer Ranch, and Westrac (the best place for car parts, period). There's an average restaurant, **The Golden Corral** (tel. 501/823-0421, www.spanishlookout.bz/goldencorral.htm, 10:30am-2:30pm Mon.-Wed., Sat., 10:30am-2:30pm and 5pm-8:30pm Thurs.-Sat.); it's about US$7.50 for the all-you-can-eat buffet and all-you-can-drink homemade iced tea. There are amazing meat pies and other goodies at **Midway Convenience.**

Bullet Tree Falls

This lazy old village of a few thousand people is less than three miles north of San Ignacio on the road to El Pilar. Bullet Tree's ultra-mellow riverbank mood, combined with cheap and easy access to the relative bustle of San Ignacio, makes it a pleasant mid-range alternative to the usual Cayo fare of fancy jungle lodges and backpacker camps. On my first visit to Belize, I stayed in this village and still had access to the full range of Cayo-area activities, and San Ignacio was easily reached by *colectivo*

taxi (US$2 pp) or private cab (US$5). Most people like to just sit by the river or float it in a tube. You can also arrange a hike with Don Beto Cocom, a Mayan shaman who offers medicinal-plant trail walks for donations; ask at any local hotel. Hotels can also arrange horseback expeditions to El Pilar and other sites.

ACCOMMODATIONS AND FOOD

Rolling into town, you'll pass the soccer field on your right and then come to a fork in the road; this is the bus stop. Fork left to cross the bridge and reach the turnoff for El Pilar, or right to reach **Parrot Nest Lodge** (tel. 501/669-6068 or 501/660-6336, www.parrot-nest.com, US$49-65), which is a rustic hideaway with immediate river access (and free inner tubes). The tropical gardens have remarkable on-site birding. There are seven simple, cozy cabins, including two tree houses on stilts under the limbs of a gigantic *guanacaste* tree. Each cabin has 24-hour electricity, a fan, linoleum flooring, and a simple single or double bed; four have private baths, and others share a bath. Meals are reasonably priced (breakfast US$4-6, dinner US$12).

A mile or so upstream (turn left before the bridge when you enter Bullet Tree Falls), **Mahogany Hall** (Paslow Falls Rd., tel. 501/664-7747, www.mahoganyhallbelize.com, US$150-600) has a spectacular castle-door entrance to a striking view of the Mopan River. In this three-story building, there are six luxurious and stately guest rooms with heavy wooden furniture, high ceilings, large windows, and French doors, all cradling a pool and restaurant practically on top of the river; it's a good choice for folks who want their air-conditioning and TV but want a unique setting.

El Pilar Archaeological Site

Seven miles north of Bullet Tree Falls, these rainforest-choked Mayan ruins are visited by only a handful of curious travelers each day; the rough approach road plus the lack of attention paid to the site by most tour operators helps make El Pilar the excellent uncrowded day trip that it is. Entrance is US$10. Two groupings

MENNONITE LIFE IN BELIZE

© LEBAWIT GIRMA

a Mennonite horse and buggy parked in Barton Creek

Cayo is a cultural melting pot, home to at least five different cultural groups. Of these, you will no doubt notice the tall, blond, blue-eyed Mennonites, who also reside in various parts of the country, notably the west and the north.

The German-speaking Mennonites started emigrating to Belize in 1958, after a long nomadic journey that took them from Switzerland to the Netherlands, Russia, and Canada in the 1800s, and Mexico after World War I. They decided to remain in Belize after finding the land ideal for farming. The government agreed not to subject them to either property tax or military service and gave them freedom to practice their own religion, schools, and banking. In turn, they have brought valuable farming knowledge and enough capital to invest in the country, although they do not vote.

You'll notice Mennonites as you head to the Saturday market in San Ignacio, selling cheese, fruits, and desserts. The men grow long beards and often wear overalls and straw hats, while the women wear long plain dresses and head caps. Mennonites travel for trade within Cayo, but choose to live in their own communities,

notably Barton Creek (traditional Mennonites)—where a traditional sawmill is powered by horses—and Spanish Lookout (progressive Mennonites).

Traditional Mennonites tend to stand out—they do not use any modern machinery or conveniences, traveling instead by horse and buggy. Most traditional Mennonite men work hard at farming, cutting wood, or selling produce at the markets or on the roadside; women tend to the home and children. Mennonite villages run their own churches and schools (most education consists of home schooling) and, on Sunday, go to church and rest.

Visiting a traditional Mennonite community is a worthwhile experience, although you cannot disturb them on Sunday. Most Mennonites are friendly and will welcome your questions; be courteous and don't take photos without asking, even from a distance. Mennonite markets supply most of the country with poultry, dairy and vegetables (plus they sell the sweetest tasting watermelon I've ever had). Look for Mennonite supermarkets and market stands in and around San Ignacio, and for stands on the highway.

of temple mounds, courtyards, and ball courts overlook a forested valley. Aqueducts and a causeway lead toward Guatemala, just 500 yards away. There have been some minor excavations here, including those by illegal looters, but the site is very overgrown, so the ruins retain an intriguing air of mystery. Many trees shade the site: allspice, gumbo-limbo, ramon, cohune palm, and locust. It's a beautiful hiking area and wildlife experience as well.

Even if you book your El Pilar trip in San Ignacio, be sure to start your quest with a visit to the **Amigos de El Pilar Visitors Center** (9am-5pm daily) and **Be Pukte Cultural Center** in Bullet Tree Falls. Here you'll find a scale model of the ruins, some helpful booklets and maps, and guide and taxi arrangements (it's about US$25 for a taxi to drive a group out and wait a few hours before bringing you back).

San José de Succotz

About 6.5 miles from San Ignacio, you'll find this hillside village on your left, above the Mopan River, right where the ferry to Xunantunich is located. In Succotz, the first language is Spanish, and the most colorful time to visit is during one of their fiestas: March 19 (feast day of St. Joseph) and May 3 (feast day of the Holy Cross).

A stroll through the rough village streets is enjoyable if you're into observing village life. **Magana's Art Center** (Western Hwy., across from the Xunantunich ferry) is the workshop of David Magana, who works with the youth of the area, encouraging them to continue the arts and crafts of their ancestors. You'll find the results inside in the form of local wood carvings, baskets, jewelry, and stone (slate) carvings unique to Belize. There are a few taco stands in town, including the popular local eatery **Benny's Kitchen** (Western Hwy., across from the Xunantunich ferry, tel. 501/823-2541, 7am-9pm Mon.-Fri., closes later Sat.-Sun.), where you can get a substantial breakfast and other tasty items for low prices. Cold draft Belikin is served in frosty mugs, a nice touch. There's also a new coffee shop directly across Xunantunich, **Clay Mountain Café.**

Foreign doctors who donate free medical assistance visit the Good Shepherd Clinic in Succotz every year.

ACCOMMODATIONS AND FOOD

Just before entering the roadside village of San José de Succotz, look on your left for the **⟨ Trek Stop** (Mile 71½, Western Hwy., tel. 501/823-2265, www.thetrekstop.com, US$24-38), a backpacker classic offering 10 cabins set in lush gardens on 22 acres of second-growth tropical forest. You can hear the highway, but you can also hear howler monkeys, birds, and the inspired conversation of your hosts and fellow travelers. There are camping facilities (US$5 pp) with access to composting toilets and solar showers, a patio restaurant with inexpensive Belizean dishes, and walking access to the Xunantunich ruins. Simple wood cabins have twin or double beds, electricity, porches, and a shared bath; a larger, more private cabin with a private bath is available. Even if you're not spending the night here, come visit the **Tropical Wings Nature Center** (9am-5pm, daily, US$3 adult, US$1.50 children under 12), one of the best and most diverse butterfly ranches in the country. Be sure to leave time for a round on Belize's only disc golf course, a nine-basket Frisbee golf game through the rainforest; discs are available (US$3 pp). The course is a par 31 with narrow and challenging fairways that leave little room for error (wear long pants and closed footwear to retrieve those errant drives). There is a nice view and sometimes a breeze from the Mayan ruins atop hole 6.

⟨ Xunantunich Archaeological Site

One of Belize's most impressive Mayan ceremonial centers, **Xunantunich** rests atop a natural limestone ridge with a grand view of the entire Cayo District and Guatemalan countryside. The local name for the site, Xunantunich (shoo-NAHN-ta-nitch), or "Stone Lady," continues to be used, even after the ancients' own name for the site, Ka-at Witz, or "Supernatural Mountain," was recently discovered, carved into a chunk of stone.

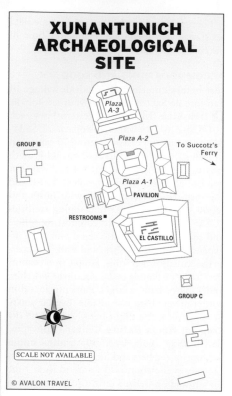

XUNANTUNICH ARCHAEOLOGICAL SITE

Plaza A-3

GROUP B

Plaza A-2

To Succotz's Ferry

Plaza A-1

PAVILION

RESTROOMS

EL CASTILLO

GROUP C

SCALE NOT AVAILABLE

© AVALON TRAVEL

the Guatemala border in Tikal, built a facility in Xunantunich for more study. In 1954 visitors were invited to explore the site after a road was opened and a small ferry built. In 1959 archaeologist Evan Mackie made news in the Mayan world when he discovered evidence that part of Xunantunich had been destroyed by an earthquake in the Late Classic Period. Some believe it was then that the people began to lose faith in their leaders—they saw the earthquake as a sign from the gods. But for whatever reason, Xunantunich ceased to be a religious center long before the end of the Classic Period.

Located eight miles west of San Ignacio, the site is accessed by crossing the Mopan River on the Succotz ferry, easily found at the end of a line of craft vendors. The hand-cranked ferry shuttles you (and your vehicle, if you have one) across the river, after which you'll have about a mile's hike (or drive) up a hill to the site. The ferry, which operates 8am-3pm daily, is free, but tipping the operator is a kind and much-appreciated gesture. Don't miss the 4pm return ferry with the park rangers, or you'll be swimming. Be forewarned that during rainy season the Mopan River can rise, run fast, and flood, canceling this service until conditions improve.

Entrance to the site is US$10 pp; guides are available for US$20 per group and are recommended—both to learn about what you're seeing and to support sustainable tourism, as all guides are local and very knowledgeable.

Xunantunich is believed to have been built sometime around 400 BC and deserted around AD 1000; at its peak, some 7,000-10,000 Maya lived here. Though certainly not the biggest of Mayan structures, at 135 feet high **El Castillo** is the second-tallest pyramid in Belize, missing first place by just one foot. The eastern side of the structure displays an unusual stucco frieze (a reproduction), and you can see three carved stelae (stone monuments) in the plaza. Xunantunich contains three ceremonial plazas surrounded by house mounds. It was rediscovered in 1894 but not studied until 1938, by archaeologist Sir J. Eric Thompson. As the first Maya ruin to be opened in the country, it has attracted the attention and exploration of many other archaeologists over the years.

In 1950, the University of Pennsylvania, noted for its years of outstanding work across

BENQUE VIEJO DEL CARMEN

Benque Viejo del Carmen (www.benqueviejotown.com) is the last town in Belize (the Guatemalan border is about one mile farther), approximately eight miles west of San Ignacio. Located on the Mopan River, Benque Viejo has been greatly influenced by the Spanish, both from its historical past when Spain ruled Guatemala and later when Spanish-speaking *chicleros* and loggers worked the forest. At one time, Benque Viejo ("Old Bank"; riverside logging camps were referred to as "banks") was a logging camp. This was the gathering place for chicle workers, and logs were floated down the river from here for shipment to England.

After this industry waned in the 1940s, many deserted the town, and the area never quite recovered from this decline.

Today, Benque remains a quiet village between the road and the river, with a handful of shops and Chinese restaurants, but it is slowly coming out of its lull: Efforts are under way to revive the community and use the area's historical and cultural significance to attract more visitors. Renovations have taken place, including George Street and the main drag; parks are being cleaned up; and a couple of banks have opened, including Belize Bank.

Sights

On one side of town, behind the central **Centennial Park,** a Mayan mound was discovered and the National Institute of Culture and History's Archeology Department is considering ways to excavate it in the future. Don't miss seeing the beautiful **Catholic church,** built in 1907, and make sure you stop by the **Benque House of Culture** (64 St. Joseph St.,

tel. 501/823-2697, benquehoc@nichbelize.org, 9am-5pm Mon.-Fri.), established in 2001 and now one of the most active in the country, for museum displays on mestizo culture, the latest exhibits, and more information on the town itself.

Besides cultural experiences, it's only right that folks should pass through this charming town, if only to get a slice of the old Cayo. Music aficionados will want to arrange a visit of the country's famous recording studio, **Stonetree Records** (35 Elizabeth St., tel. 501/823-2241, www.stonetreerecords.com). The country's sole and excellent publisher, **Cubola Books** (Elizabeth St.), is also based in Benque.

Festivals and Events

Easter remains Benque's most vibrant and meaningful time of the year, when the village celebrates Holy Week or Semana Santa—complete with a reenactment of the Passion of Christ and beautiful *alfombras* or

This Catholic church is the spiritual center of Benque Viejo del Carmen.

© LEBAWIT GIRMA

BELMOPAN AND CAYO

colorful carpets of dyed sawdust all over the village streets; this spiritual experience is a sight to behold. **Christmas** is the culmination of the celebration called **Las Posadas.** Benque Viejo del Carmen remains the only area of Belize to celebrate this Latin tradition, a nine-day (Dec. 16-24) reenactment of Joseph and Mary's biblical journey from Nazareth to Bethlehem in search of an inn. I experienced the first *posada* night in December 2012, and it was a unique experience worth the short night drive from San Ignacio. Summer sees Benque's second-liveliest celebration of the year, and one of the most popular ones in the Cayo District: The **Benque Fiesta** celebrates the village's patron saint, Nuestra Señora de Monte Carmelo, with live marimba bands, food, drink, amusement park rides, and, of course, plenty of dancing late into the night.

Getting There and Around

Buses from Belize City to Benque and the Guatemalan border run daily, starting at ungodly morning hours on both ends. Most bus service to and from San Ignacio also serves Benque and the border. The most efficient way to travel to the border from San Ignacio is by *colectivo* taxi, which run in a constant and steady flow roughly 6am-7pm daily; the ride should cost approximately US$2, but you take the chance of sharing your cab with as many people as your driver can fit. By private taxi, expect to pay about US$10 for the same trip.

THE HYDRO ROAD

Look for the left-hand turn in the middle of Benque Viejo, at the top of the hill. The Hydro Road leads south to a few unique attractions and accommodations, all well off the beaten path. The road is equipped with mile markers on small white posts. A few miles in, a right turn leads to the border village of Arenal, where a few *milpero* (corn farmer) families scrape a life from the soils of the Mopan River Valley. The road continues south for 11 miles, where it dead-ends at the Mollejon Dam.

Poustinia Land Art Park

This 60-acre reclaimed cattle ranch is now devoted to the nurturing of art and nature, where foreign and Belizean artists can stay and contribute to the ongoing project and visitors can come take a look and soak it all in. If you're looking for an out-of-the-ordinary sight, this would be it. The lush grounds are part of a 270-acre second-growth forest. Visiting the unique **Poustinia Land Art Park** (www.poustiniaonline.org, admission US$10) is by appointment only and can be arranged at the **Benque Viejo House of Culture** (tel. 501/823-2697). If you are an artist, ask **Luis Alberto** (tel. 501/822-3532) how you may be able to contribute.

Chechem Ha Cave and the Vaca Plateau

At Mile 8, you'll find a turnoff to the left for **Chechem Ha Farm** (tel. 501/660-4714), a mile or so down a rutted road; it belongs to the Morales family. The place is designed to give nature-loving travelers the chance to enjoy the Chechem Ha Spring, Chechem Ha Falls (a 175-foot cascade with a treacherous trail down to its misty bottom), and Chechem Ha Cave, a dry cave except for the dripping water that has created all the formations over the years. The pottery inside is estimated to be as old as 2,000 years. You can climb and explore various ledges and passageways, but the highlight is a deep ceremonial chamber in the heart of the hill. In some places, you need a rope to help you get around. While those of average physical abilities can enjoy Chechem Ha Cave, take care when moving amid the pottery.

Stay at the farm in one of several simple **cabins** made of clay, rock, wood, and thatch; they are well constructed and comfy looking. For US$41 pp, you get a night's stay and three meals. There's no electricity, and the toilets are outhouses. **Camping** is US$5 pp; bring your own tent. Individual meals are available (US$5-10), as is an inexpensive transfer from Benque.

Martz Farm

Less than a mile beyond the Chechem Ha road,

another left turn will take you to **Martz Farm** (Mile 8½, Hydro Rd., tel. 501/834-4646, http://martz.kitsol.de, US$40-65), a unique and relaxed homestead built and maintained by the hardworking Martinez family. Two good-natured and burly brothers, Joe and Lazaro, hacked this place out of raw bush, and they continue improving their primitive homestead. They've constructed a handful of tree houses and natural cabins (one has a private bath and hot water), each seemingly sprung from wild childhood fantasies. All are open to the forest air (mosquito nets provided), and one is even built over a private dip pool in the passing creek. Joe's German wife, Miriam, cooks family-style meals over a traditional fire hearth in a quaint kitchen, and farm animals wander the grounds with the guests. Home-cooked meal plans and free transfers from San Ignacio or Benque are available. The facilities are slowly improving, with a few new flush toilets and hot water and showers.

The Mountain Pine Ridge

Some of Belize's most breathtaking natural and archaeological treasures are found within this vast crinkle of mountains and wildlands, as are a few of the country's remotest and most charming accommodations. Despite bark beetle damage to vast tracts of pine trees in the Mountain Pine Ridge (MPR) Forest Reserve, the forests are rebounding, and MPR's waterfalls, swimming holes, and vistas are well worth enduring the rutted roads. My first drive through this area left me speechless, and it reminds me why I fell in love with Belize.

CHIQUIBUL (PINE RIDGE) ROAD

The Chiquibul Road begins at **Georgeville** (Mile 63, Western Hwy.) and heads south over the Mountain Pine Ridge, terminating 30-some miles later at Caracol. You'll pass through tropical foothills, citrus farms, and cattle ranches before the terrain rises, gradually changing to sand, rocky soil, red clay, and finally groves of sweet-smelling pines. The road is notorious for becoming a slushy mud bed when it rains and a dusty back-breaker when it's dry. Once you start driving, there are few services besides those offered at the resorts, but if you need a drink, beer, a meal, supplies, or emergency gasoline, look for the **Junction Store,** a wooden building right where the San Antonio Road meets the Chiquibul Road.

◖ Barton Creek Cave

This unique cathedral-like wet cave was once used for ceremonial purposes and human sacrifices by the Maya. A pair of Peace Corps volunteers stumbled on the cave in 1970 and found that it had been looted but still contained an enormous amount of pottery and artifacts. Archaeologists didn't study the cave until 1998; they found large ceramics on high ledges, plus evidence of 20 human remains, including a necklace made of finger bones.

The tall, cavernous, and low ceilings **Barton Creek Cave** are fascinating, and in my opinion it is one of the top two must-see caves in Belize. The experience is impressive and available to anybody physically able enough to step into a canoe—but a heads up: The ceiling is so low through many parts of the cave that you'll occasionally have to lean all way back in the canoe to save your skull. Still, it's well worth the experience of gliding across, contemplating the quiet as your guide slowly paddles you deeper into the earth, the watery sound of his paddle echoing on the limestone. The cave is at least seven miles deep, but tours only go in about a mile or so before turning around.

Barton Creek is protected and managed by government archaeologists and is accessed by turning off the Chiquibul Road around Mile 4, then driving 20-30 minutes on a bumpy road through orange groves and a beautiful small Mennonite settlement. You'll need to

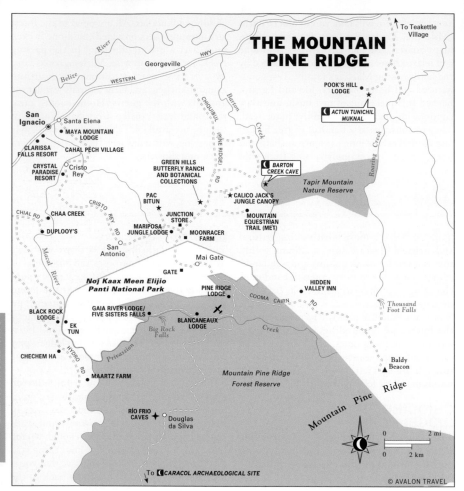

THE MOUNTAIN PINE RIDGE

To Teakettle Village

POOK'S HILL LODGE

ACTUN TUNICHIL MUKNAL

Georgeville

BARTON CREEK CAVE

San Ignacio

Santa Elena

MAYA MOUNTAIN LODGE

CLARISSA FALLS RESORT

CAHAL PECH VILLAGE

CRYSTAL PARADISE RESORT

Cristo Rey

GREEN HILLS BUTTERFLY RANCH AND BOTANICAL COLLECTIONS

Tapir Mountain Nature Reserve

PAC BITUN

CALICO JACK'S JUNGLE CANOPY

CHIAL RD

CHAA CREEK

JUNCTION STORE

MOUNTAIN EQUESTRIAN TRAIL (MET)

DUPLOOY'S

MARIPOSA JUNGLE LODGE

MOONRACER FARM

San Antonio

Mai Gate

GATE

HIDDEN VALLEY INN

Noj Kaax Meen Elijio Panti National Park

PINE RIDGE LODGE

COOMA CAIRN RD

Thousand Foot Falls

BLACK ROCK LODGE

GAIA RIVER LODGE/ FIVE SISTERS FALLS

BLANCANEAUX LODGE

EK TUN

Big Rock Falls

Creek

Baldy Beacon

CHECHEM HA

Priveassion

MAARTZ FARM

Mountain Pine Ridge Forest Reserve

Mountain Pine Ridge

RÍO FRIO CAVES

Douglas da Silva

0   2 mi
0   2 km

To CARACOL ARCHAEOLOGICAL SITE

© AVALON TRAVEL

have someone with you who knows the way, as there are many roads and no signs. The visitors center charges US$10 pp, then you'll have to rent canoes (US$7.50), lights, and a guide, all available at **Mike's Place** (tel. 501/670-0441, www.bartoncreekcave.com), right at the cave's entrance. If you come as part of a prepaid tour, you won't need to worry about such details.

Calico Jack's Village
Located on 365 acres in El Progreso (Mile 7), **Calico Jack's Village** (just off Chiquibul Rd.,

El Progreso, tel. 501/832-2478, www.calico-jacksvillage.com, US$110-170) is its own small, customized, and authentic adventure resort. Calico Jack's top offerings include an excellent medicinal hiking trail, caving in two unique caves, and a fantastic (and safe) zip line, one of the longest in Belize. Climb and zip among 15 platforms high in the trees and travel through the rainforest in an impressive hydraulic lift, designed by owner Chester Williams, a former engineer (he also helped design the zip line at Bocawina Falls). Tours range from a 20-minute "express" experience to the full two-hour "ex-tremo" exploration (US$40-85). Or try the massive "columpio," a one-of-a-kind rainforest swing, which will send you 200 feet in the air after you are hoisted above the top of a recreated Mayan pyramid.

The two Jungle Villas have one- and two-bedroom units, built in Mayan temple style, with kitchenettes, living rooms, and air-conditioning; all have access to a bar, restaurant, and pool.

Green Hills Butterfly Ranch and Botanical Collections

This beautiful butterfly breeding, education, and interpretive center is run by Dutch biologists Jan Meerman and Tineke Boomsma. **Green Hills** (Mile 8, Chiquibul Rd., tel. 501/834-4017, meerman@btl.net, www.greenhills.net, 7am-4pm daily, last tour 3:30pm, US$10 pp). The standard tour of the center takes about an hour. There's also a walk into the forest to see Maya artifacts and the impressive mahogany reforestation project. Your entrance fee (family discounts available) grants you access to the 3,000-square-foot butterfly house, blue morpho breeding facilities, botanical garden (with over 100 labeled species), hummingbird observation spot, and a display on the life cycle of a butterfly (egg-caterpillar-pupa-butterfly). Between 25 and 30 different species are raised at the center, including the tiny glass-winged butterfly, the banana owl (the largest butterfly in Belize), and of course the magnificent blue morpho. Arrive early enough in the morning to watch a butterfly emerge from a pupa right before your eyes. Or time your visit with "*Caligo* hour"—a unique event that begins one hour before sunset (in December around 4:45pm; in summer about 5:45pm) when the owl butterflies become very active and synchronize their flight; owl butterflies can have wing spans of up to seven inches, so it's quite impressive. Jan literally wrote the book on Belizean butterflies (*Lepidoptera of Belize,* Gainesville, FL: ATL Books, 2000), and both he and Tineke can be available to give lectures to student groups. Green Hills is a worthwhile stop for anyone traveling to and from other sites on the Chiquibul Road, not least for the hummingbird garden, where you can watch an amazingly active assortment of hummers buzz in and out all day long. Picnic facilities are available.

Slate Creek Preserve

A group of local landowners and lodge operators have set aside 3,000 acres as the private **Slate Creek Preserve** (closed to the public). The purpose of the preserve is to protect the watershed, plants, and animals of a valley called the Vega, one of several valleys in the area. The unique limestone karst ecosystem, which borders the Mountain Pine Ridge Forest Reserve, teems with life. Mahogany, Santa Maria, ceiba, cedar, and cohune palms tower above. Orchids, ferns, and bromeliads are common. Birds such as the aracari, emerald toucanet, keel-billed toucan, keel-billed motmot, king vulture, and various parrots and hummingbirds are to be found here. Pumas, ocelots, coatis, pacas, and anteaters roam the forests.

Mountain Equestrian Trails

At **Mountain Equestrian Trails** (Mile 8, Chiquibul Rd., tel. 501/669-1124, U.S. tel. 800/838-3918, www.metbelize.com), the Bevis family keeps 27 sturdy steeds with Endurance saddles. Visitors have a choice of gentle or spirited horses to carry them over 60 miles of trails to waterfalls, swimming holes, Mayan caves, and other sites. Beginners and experienced riders are welcome—children at least 10 years old with previous riding experience are welcome. Riders are required to sign a liability waiver.

Accommodations and Food

Accommodations at ⟨ **Mountain Equestrian Trails** (MET, Mile 8, Chiquibul Rd., tel. 501/669-1124, U.S. tel. 800/838-3918, www.metbelize.com, US$132) range from 10 "safari-style" cabanas of thatch and stucco with exotic wood interiors and private baths with hot and cold water (no electricity—yet). Meals are served in the cozy cantina-restaurant, which offers excellent food (breakfast US$8, lunch

US$11, dinner US$20, plus tax). Even though MET's small cantina is a 20-minute drive from San Ignacio, it still attracts visitors and locals from all around for drinks, dinner, and good conversation. All-inclusive, multiday packages are available; riding fees are extra.

CRISTO REY ROAD

Heading south from the Western Highway at Santa Elena, this road winds through the villages of Cristo Rey and San Antonio before joining the Chiquibul Road and the Mountain Pine Ridge. It is usually better maintained than the alternative route along the Chiquibul Road, and there are a handful of interesting stops along the way. Village buses that travel the road leave the center of San Ignacio daily, and shared taxis should be available for reasonable rates as well. Most tour operators who travel this road will stop at any of the following places, depending on group size and desires.

Slate Carving Art Galleries

About six miles south on Cristo Rey Road, look for the **Sak Tunich Art Gallery** (9am-6pm daily), home of the Magana brothers, Jose and Javier. This indoor-outdoor display is built into the hillside on your left and is worth a look for anyone interested in Mayan crafts. These industrious guys are recreating a Mayan temple and cave by carving them into the limestone for the steep hillside next to the road and their home.

A couple of miles farther, you'll find more art at **The Garcia Sisters** (tel. 501/820-4023, artistmai1981@btl.net, www.awrem.com/tanah). These six siblings made a nationwide name for themselves in 1981, when they turned to their Mayan heritage and began recreating slate carvings reminiscent of those done by their ancestors at Caracol. Their Mayan art gallery, shop, and museum are called the **Tanah Mayan Art Museum and Community Collection** (tel. 501/669-4023, 8am-6pm daily), located on the Cristo Rey Road just north of San Antonio. The Tanah Museum is an echoey one-room affair with long shelves full of fascinating artifacts. The sisters, nieces of the famed healer

Don Eligio Panti, are charming and determined ambassadors of San Antonio village. They're also clever artists who make Belizean dolls, native jewelry, and hand-drawn art cards. Ask about the Itzamna Society, a community-based NGO of which Maria is the chairperson, which works to protect the forest and community. They also sometimes offer language lessons in the Yucatec Maya language or cooking classes and can perform blessings, healings, and other ceremonies. The Garcias were instrumental in organizing a big December 21, 2012, Hawk Fire Ceremony, held at Caracol with elders from the various Mayan groups in Belize.

San Antonio Village

With a population of 3,500 descendants of the Maya, mostly milpa farmers and, increasingly, youth and employees of nearby lodges, San Antonio is approximately 10 miles from San Ignacio on the way to the Mountain Pine Ridge Reserve. It has the potential to serve as a low-key gateway to the surrounding wilderness, but as of yet, there are few visitor services in town (there is a gas station—better fill up before the drive to Caracol). There are horse and hiking trails nearby, as well as several caves, waterfalls, and ruins. You'll also notice plenty of farmland and men harvesting as you drive through, as San Antonio Village is one of the main sources of vegetables for all of Belize, producing carrots, sweet peppers, potatoes, peanuts, pumpkin seeds, corn, red beans, and more.

A women's group has a *palapa*-roofed shop (tel. 501/669-4023, mayanspirit7@yahoo.com) just off the main road with some nice ceramics for sale. On the way out of town is a little-visited Maya site called **Pac Bitun,** at the end of an unmarked side road, a mile or so before the T-junction.

Noj Kaax Meen Elijio Panti National Park

This 13,000-acre reserve (www.epnp.org) of mountains surrounding the village of San Antonio is filled with trails, waterfalls, and peaks, but there is not much access or tourism development. Ask at the Tanah Museum (tel.

© LEBAWIT GIRMA

farmers harvesting carrots in San Antonio Village

501/669-4023, 8am-6pm daily) or the women's center (tel. 501/669-4023, mayanspirit7@yahoo.com) if there are any licensed guides taking people into the park.

Accommodations and Food

Only one mile south of the Western Highway, **Maya Mountain Lodge** (Mile ¾, Cristo Rey Rd., tel. 501/824-2164, www.mayamountain.com, US$79-119) feels remote enough to warrant a listing outside of town; it's a US$5 taxi ride from San Ignacio. This is one of the most moderately priced rainforest hideaways, operated for the last three decades by Suzi and Bart Mickler, whose knowledge and passion for the area are contagious. The property is 108 acres and it's about a 20-minute walk to the river's edge. A meandering trail through the gardens has signs identifying plants, trees, and birds; there's a nice pool for after your hike. Accommodations range from six simple guest rooms in a raised wooden building to family cottages and a two-bedroom suite with tiled floors, air-conditioning, and extra bunks and

wood furniture. The restaurant features theme nights, homemade bread, and buckets of freshly squeezed orange juice (their Baha'i faith prevents them from selling liquor for profit, but you are welcome to bring your own). Breakfast costs US$6-10, and dinner is US$20. Ask about workshops on biodiversity and multiculturalism. This is a great place for families, with discounted or free lodging and tours for children and teens.

Before the advent of tourism, the Tut family (Victor and Teresa and their 10 children) grew fruit and vegetables and then transported them by canoe to the town market in San Ignacio. Today, they are the proud owners and operators of ◖ **Crystal Paradise Resort** (tel. 501/834-4016, www.crystalparadise.com, US$75-125, breakfast US$10 pp, dinner US$15 pp), a low-key lodge that attracts many satisfied repeat customers. The 21-acre property near Cristo Rey village is a few hundred yards away from the river, and it's an easy walk to a canoe. The Tuts' sons, who are avid bird-watchers and nature lovers, maintain the beautiful grounds and serve as your guides on a variety of tours, including hiking, biking, horseback riding, kayaking, and bird-watching. Find them at **Paradise Expeditions** (tel. 501/610-5593 or 501/834-4016, cell 501/610-5593, www.birdinginbelize.com), which is based at the resort. Teresa and her daughters keep the guest rooms clean and comfortable and also cook up the best in traditional Belizean and international cuisine. Near the property's wide, open dining *palapa,* the accommodations come in several styles; there are 17 units in all, including simple thatched cabanas with cement walls, tiled floors, hot and cold showers, and shaded verandas with hammocks for relaxing. Other units are clean and comfortable but more of a clapboard style; all offer ceiling fans and electricity. Additions include a pool and four canopy-level luxury guest rooms. The Tuts also offer bird-watching (ask about the birding platform), nature walks, and tours. There's an on-site medicinal trail.

Table Rock Jungle Lodge (tel. 501/834-4040, www.tablerockbelize.com, US$145-215, riverside camping US$30) is an eco-friendly touch of class on a 100-acre preserve. Five gorgeous cabanas (four-poster king and queen beds, private baths with hot water, ceiling fans, and private porches) are designed to stay cool the natural way, using adobe construction. There is a beautiful trail leading down a series of stone steps to the Macal River, where guests can go birding, canoeing, swimming, or tubing, all included in the room rates for guests. You can also tour the onsite fruit farm, growing all sorts of goodies from star fruit to craboo. The food is excellent, with unexpected dishes like pan-seared jack with chipotle papaya coconut sauce, cooked in cohune palm oil and served with couscous and okra. The palm-lined entrance through an orange grove is at Mile 5 on Cristo Rey Road.

At **Mystic River Resort** (tel. 501/834-4100, www.mysticriverbelize.com, all-inclusive packages US$1,300-2,030 and up, includes transfers and tours), "it's all about the river," say proprietors Tom and Nadege Thomas in their open-air restaurant on a point above the

Macal. Guests like to hike or ride upstream, then float back to the lodge in a canoe or on a tube. The six units (so far) are spacious and well furnished, with local tile floors, nice verandas, and fireplaces for cool December nights. The place is a model of sustainable living. They have an on-site stable and an organic garden, and they raise their own chickens; plans are underway to make cheese on-site as well. Tom is still cutting trails and discovering archaeological sites on his property, which you can explore—either by foot or on Tom's ATV. The lodge now has its very own **BushDog Adventures** tour company, offering off-the-beaten-track adventures in the area and accommodations packages tailored to your activity of preference, although room-only bookings are considered on request (US$250-275). Be sure to make it to Dancing Tree Lookout for sunset views of Guatemala. At the campsite atop this housing mound, you'll admire the same view that Mayan families saw 1,000 years ago. By car, Mystic River Resort is accessed at Mile 6 on the Cristo Rey Road.

Macaw Bank Jungle Lodge (tel. 501/665-7241, www.macawbankjunglelodge.com, US$145-175) occupies an isolated, peaceful clearing in the forest. There are five miles of nature trails on the 50-acre property, many birds and other wildlife, and you can go swimming at a sandy bend on the Macal River, a 5-10-minute walk away. The five comfortable units have wooden bunks and furniture, private baths, hot and cold water, some solar power, and kerosene lanterns. There is a nice restaurant *palapa* with wireless Internet. Campers (US$12.50 pp) are welcome.

Moonracer Farm (Mile 9, Mountain Pine Ridge Rd., www.moonracerfarm.com, US$75-140) gets rave reviews, providing a pair of comfortable wooden cabins in the forest in one of the best deals in the Mountain Pine Ridge. The cabins are fairly large, with private screened porches. Meals are available for US$30 per day and include the fresh home-made cooking of owners Marge and Tom. This property used to be the home of a feline rescue center, and the new owners have creatively repurposed some of the hardware. Hiking trails explore their 50 acres and connect to the Mountain Pine Ridge Forest Reserve and Elijio Panti National Park.

THE MOUNTAIN PINE RIDGE FOREST RESERVE

Prepare for a treat, this is one of Belize's most beautiful landscapes. After you steadily ascend along the Chiquibul (Pine Ridge) Road for 21 miles, a gate across the road marks your entrance to Belize's largest and oldest protected area, established in 1944. The 300-square-mile (126,825-acre) area features Caribbean pine and bracken ferns instead of the typical tropical vegetation found in the rest of Belize. It also features a massive granite uplifting; the exposed rocks are some of the oldest formations in the Americas, and they make for amazing swimming holes and waterfalls. In fact, some geologists think that the Mountain Pine Ridge, whose highest point is 3,336 feet above sea level at Baldy Beacon, was one of the few exposed islands when the rest of Central America was underwater.

Most San Ignacio tour operators offer day trips to the Pine Ridge's attractions, often combined with a trip to Caracol ruins. There are way more sights than can fit into a day, but a number of lodges can put you right in the thick of it all.

Thousand Foot Falls

Occasionally referred to as Hidden Valley Falls, this torrent of Roaring Creek is probably a good deal taller than 1,000 feet and is considered the highest waterfall in all of Central America. The turnoff to a viewpoint of the falls is a couple of miles beyond the forest reserve gate and is well signed. It's quite a little drive to get all the way there, and though the view is magical, you don't get the reward of being able to jump in. From the turnoff, the road continues down for about four miles and brings you to the falls (US$2 pp) and a picnic area. View the falls from across the gorge and through breaks in the mist. A small store (7am-5pm daily) and picnic tables can be found at the viewpoint.

Big Rock Falls

A hand-painted sign on the dirt road to Gaia Lodge is the only indicator to the trailhead for Big Rock. You can park and hike down a fairly steep trail (clinging to a rope at one point) to a series of spectacular pools below the site's namesake. Big Rock Falls is big, loud, impressive, and worth the stop.

Río On Pools and Río Frio Cave

Most Caracol packages try to squeeze in an afternoon stopover at these lovely sites. Heading south on Chiquibul Road toward Augustine, you will cross the Río On Pools. It's well worth the climb over an assortment of worn boulders and rocks to waterfalls and several warm-water pools. There's a parking area just off the road. Turn right at Douglas de Silva ranger station (the western division of the Forestry Department) and continue for about five miles to reach Río Frio Cave. Follow the signs to the

THE SOUTHERN PINE BARK BEETLE

Shortly after the creation of the Mountain Pine Ridge Reserve, the Pine Ridge experienced a huge forest fire; combined with the cycles of logging, the forest was left with an unnaturally uniform population of trees, making it more susceptible to disease and insects. In the 1990s, a three-year drought helped establish a disastrous infestation of the southern pine bark beetle (*Dendroctonus frontalis*), which has wreaked havoc throughout Central and North America.

Today, the forest is coming back wonderfully—thanks both to naturally rich seed sets and to a massive replanting campaign (24 million seedlings are required for reforestation of 70,000 acres over four years). It will be another 10-15 years before the new generation of pines fully matures, however. Check out www.reforestbelize.com for an update and to find out how you can help.

© LEBAWIT GIRMA

view of Río On Pools, in the Mountain Pine Ridge

parking lot. From here, visitors have a choice of exploring nature trails and two small caves on the road or continuing to Río Frio Cave, with an enormous arched entryway into the 0.5-mile-long cave. Filtered light highlights ferns, mosses, stalactites, and geometric patterns of striations on rocks. Watch for sinkholes. At times, a military escort is necessary to Río Frio. Ask at the Douglas de Silva ranger station on Chiquibul Road.

Accommodations and Food

Situated on 7,200 acres of private property in the heart of the Mountain Pine Ridge Forest Reserve, **Hidden Valley Inn** (4 Cooma Cairn Rd., tel. 501/822-3320, U.S. tel. 866/443-3364, www.hiddenvalleyinn.com, about US$275-375 plus taxes, meals not included) is a quiet paradise for hikers and bird-watchers, who have a blast exploring the resort's 90-plus miles of walking trails and old logging roads. Later, after dining under the stars, they cozy up in front of their cottage's fireplace. The property encompasses lush broadleaf forest

and pine tree habitat, and two diverse ecosystems are divided by a geological fault line that marks the edge of a towering 1,000-foot escarpment. Birders, be prepared to check off orange-breasted falcons, king vultures, stygian owls, azure-crowned hummingbirds, green jays, and golden-hooded tanagers. Picnic lunches are provided for the myriad day trips available. The main house, built of local hardwoods, feels more like a ski lodge than a tropical resort, with several spacious common rooms, including a fireside lounge, a card room, a bar, a library, and the restaurant. The cottages have Saltillo tile floors, vaulted ceilings, cypress-paneled walls, fireplaces, ceiling fans, screened louvered windows, comfy beds, and private baths with hot and cold water, some with waterfall orchid showers in a private outdoor bath. Hidden Valley Inn is three miles in from the Mile 14 turnoff onto Cooma Cairn Road—just follow the signs.

Francis Ford Coppola first came to Belize just after the country gained independence in 1981; he tried and failed to persuade the new government to apply for a satellite license in order to become a hub of world communications. He did, however, succeed in finding an abandoned lodge on a pine-carpeted bluff overlooking the rocks and falls of Privassion Creek. It served as a private retreat for the film producer until 1993, when he "tricked it open" by flying a group of family and friends down for his 54th birthday. Today, **Blancaneaux Lodge** (tel. 501/824-3878, www.blancaneaux. com, from US$250) remains one of Central America's premier resorts, featuring the design of Mexican architect Manolo Mestre. Splashes of color, dark hardwoods, Central American lines, and soaring thatched ceilings mark Blancaneaux's 20 guest rooms, consisting of luxurious cabanas and villas. There is a U-shaped hot pool above the river and a spa built in an Indonesian rice house with Thai massage therapists.

Blancaneaux's **Ristorante Montagna** offers an Italian-centric menu with a range of salads, pastas (US$14), seafood, sandwiches, pizzas (US$18), and, of course, a selection of wines from Coppola's Napa Valley vineyards—smooth and costly. Two honeymoon cabanas with their own private infinity pools and choice of two views (US$420) and the Enchanted Cottage kick things up a notch in luxury. The Enchanted Cottage is also available for a small group of friends looking to celebrate a special event who can afford US$1,470 per night. An on-site hydroelectric dam powers the entire operation, and a 3.5-acre organic herb and vegetable garden supplies many of the restaurant's needs (and those of Turtle Inn). They have a stable with 29 healthy horses and a number of guided trail trips. The lodge is at Mile 14½ and has its own airstrip, which many guests prefer to the 2.5-hour drive from Belize City.

Originally built in 1991, **Gaia River Lodge** (formerly Five Sisters Lodge, tel. 501/834-4024, www.gaiariverlodge.com, US$175-375) sits high atop the inviting Privassion Creek in the Pine Ridge, above the famous Five Sisters Falls. Guest rooms and suites are located on the top of the steep canyon; they include beautifully thatched, garden, mountain view, or

waterfall view cabanas—16 in all—as well as an exclusive riverside villa. The waterfall view suite is ideal for honeymooners, with two levels, a living room with an open deck, mosquito netting, and complete privacy. Various activity packages are offered. Even if you don't stay here, come by, have a beer on the multiple-level outdoor restaurant deck, and enjoy the commanding view above the river. The hardy can walk the 300 steps down to the river; if you're too tired after splashing around, not to worry—the hydro-powered rainforest tram will carry you back up the hill, at least between 8am and 4pm.

◖ CARACOL ARCHAEOLOGICAL SITE

Archaeologists Diane and Arlen Chase believe that **Caracol** (www.caracol.org), one of the largest sites in Belize, is the Maya city-state that toppled mighty Tikal, just to the northwest, effectively shutting it down for 130 years. Located within the Chiquibul Forest Reserve, Caracol is *out there,* offering both natural wonders and Mayan mystery. To date, only a small percentage of the 177 square kilometers that make up the site has even been mapped, identifying only 5,000 of the estimated 36,000 structures lying beneath the forest canopy.

The centerpiece is no doubt the pyramid of **Canaa,** rising 136 feet above the plaza floor (about a foot taller than El Castillo at Xunantunich), one of the tallest structures—ancient or modern—in Belize. Canaa was only completely cleared of vegetation in 2005 by the Tourism Development Project (TDP), whose work has unveiled most of the structures you see. The vistas from the top of Canaa are extensive and memorable.

In addition to the aforementioned superlatives, Caracol, a Classic Period site, is noted for its large masks and giant date glyphs on circular stone altars. There is also a fine display of the Maya's engineering skills, with extensive reservoirs, agricultural terraces, and several mysterious ramps. Caracol has been studied for more than 20 years by the Chases and their assistants, student interns from Tulane University

BELMOPAN AND CAYO

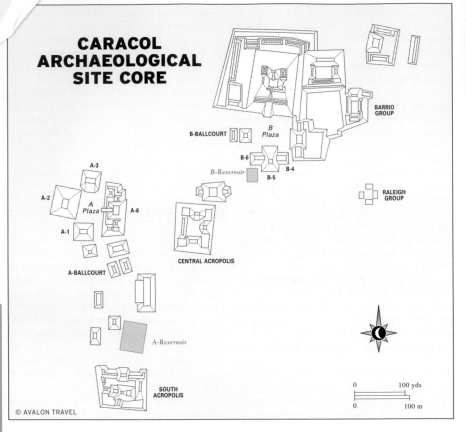

CARACOL
ARCHAEOLOGICAL
SITE CORE

BARRIO GROUP

B-BALLCOURT

B
Plaza

B-6

B-Reservoir

B-4

B-5

A-3

RALEIGH GROUP

A-2

A
Plaza

A-6

A-1

CENTRAL ACROPOLIS

A-BALLCOURT

A-Reservoir

SOUTH
ACROPOLIS

0   100 yds

0   100 m

© AVALON TRAVEL

in New Orleans and the University of Central Florida. According to John Morris, an archaeologist with Belize's Institute of Archaeology, a lifetime of exploration remains to be done for 6-9 miles in every direction of the excavated part of Caracol. It's proving to have been a powerful site that controlled a very large area, possibly once home to over 100,000 inhabitants. The rainforest you see now would have been totally absent in those days, as the wood was cleared to provide fuel and agricultural land to support so many people.

Many carvings are dated AD 500-800, and ceramic evidence indicates that Caracol was settled around AD 300 and continued to flourish when other Maya sites were in decline.

Carvings at the site also indicate that Caracol and Tikal engaged in ongoing conflicts, each defeating the other on various occasions. After the war in AD 562, Caracol flourished for more than a century in the mountains and valleys surrounding the site. A former archaeological commissioner named the site Caracol ("snail" in Spanish) because of the winding logging road to reach it, although some contend it was because of all the snail shells found during initial excavations.

Visiting the Site

Entrance to Caracol is US$15. The small visitors center presents a scale model and interesting information based mostly on the work of the Chases over the last two decades. A planned **Monument Museum** will allow visitors to view a range of artifacts and stelae from the site and will be based on the work of the Tourism Development Project. There are no official guides on-site, as most groups arrive with their own. However, the caretakers know Caracol well and will be glad to walk you through and explain the site for a few dollars. Most tours start with the Raleigh Group, move by the enormous ceiba trees, then circle through the archaeologists' camp, and end with a bang by climbing Canaa.

Getting There

Most tour operators offer Caracol day trips, often involving stops at various caves and swimming holes on the way back through the Mountain Pine Ridge. The ride should take 2-3 hours, depending on both the weather and the progress made by road improvement crews, who hopefully will not run out of money before you read this. If you're driving, a 4WD vehicle is a must; gas is not available along the 50-mile road, so carry ample fuel. Camping is not allowed in the area without permission from the Institute of Archaeology in Belmopan. The closest accommodations are those along the Pine Ridge Road.

At times, a military escort is necessary to visit Caracol. Be sure to ask at your lodge. Tour operators know to show up at 9:30am at the Augustine (Douglas de Silva) gate to convoy to the ruins.

Into Guatemala

The western *frontera* into Guatemala is only 11 miles from San Ignacio. Be prepared to pay a US$19 pp exit fee on the Belizean side, which includes the PACT fee (they will ask for exact change); the rest of the money goes to the private Border Management company, a point of contention for local tour providers and would-be Guatemalan day-trippers. Expect the usual throng of moneychangers to greet you on both sides of the border—they're fine to use as long as you know what rate you should be getting—or you can use the official Casas de Cambio on either side.

By Bus and Taxi

The trip from San Ignacio can be made for around US$3 pp in a *colectivo* taxi, less in a passing bus bound for Benque Viejo. A private taxi from San Ignacio should cost about US$15 total.

By Car

If you're driving your own car, make sure you have all the necessary papers of ownership and attendant photocopies of all your documents, including your driver's license and passport,

which they *will* want to see. You are required by law to have your tires fumigated when entering/exiting Belize and Guatemala, which costs a dollar or two. If driving a private or rental vehicle into Guatemala, you will have to pay a toll to cross the bridge going over the Mopan into Melchor. If your car has Belizean tags, the fee can be as low as 5 quetzales (US$0.65). If your tags are from far away, like Canada or the United States, be prepared to pay 50 quetzales (US$6.50) and not one peso more. Save the receipt if you are returning to Belize, as it is good for a two-way crossing. In addition, based on some reports, travelers have to ensure that they have received a proper exit stamp when leaving Belize for both themselves and their vehicle. Double-check your passport before continuing on to Guatemala.

Melchor

After clearing Guatemalan immigration and shaking off the sometimes aggressive *taxistas,* you'll find yourself on the edge of the Mopan River, across which begins the town of Melchor de Mencos. Before crossing the bridge, you'll find the **Río Mopan Lodge** (tel.

502/7926-5196, www.tikaltravel.com, US$20) on your left, a nice riverside hotel and restaurant whose proprietors (a Swiss-Spanish couple) are a wealth of information on remote ruins in the area. There are other places in Melchor if you get stranded in town for some reason or are embarking on your own rainforest expedition to unexplored ruins. Otherwise, head on toward the most popular place to visit in Guatemala from the western border of Belize: Tikal National Park.

TIKAL NATIONAL PARK

Guatemala's most-visited attraction opened to the public in 1955 and was declared a UNESCO World Heritage site in 1979. One of the most magnificent of all Mayan sites, the 222-square-mile **Tikal National Park** is located in northern Guatemala, in the heart of El Petén, Guatemala's largest department. The park also belongs to the 21,000-square mile Reserva de Biosfera Maya (Mayan Biosphere Reserve), considered the most biodiverse region in the country, with the largest area of tropical rainforest in Central America. Much of the reserve still consists of dense forests with more than 300 species of commercially useful trees, such as cedar, mahogany, and chicle, as well as abundant wildlife.

Amid El Petén's stunning canopy of green sit several Mayan archeological sites, including Uaxactún and El Mirador. But the most unique of all is Tikal. No visitor forgets that first glance at Tikal's gigantic pyramids dominating the park's green skyline. Temple I and Temple IV, at commanding heights of over 100 to 200-plus feet, are sheer masterpieces. Visitors can climb up some of these temples, while others are considered too steep and remain closed.

Even more mind-boggling is that only about 15 percent of Tikal has been uncovered thus far. Under the auspices of the University of Pennsylvania, the site was excavated and studied over a period of 13 years from 1956-1969. An estimated 4,000 structures were located, including temples, palaces, ball courts, a marketplace, and residential compounds. Restored areas include the Great Plaza, the North Acropolis, the Lost World, the Twin Pyramid complexes, and Temples I, II, IV, and V. Stelae, burials, ceramics, and other offerings were discovered during this time, and causeways connecting the various areas of Tikal were restored. Thousands more structures continue to lie buried under thick rainforest, covered up for the past thousands of years since the ancient Maya deserted this city around AD 900 for reasons that remain unknown.

Coupled with its natural and historical significance, and a host of affordable accommodations options in the nearby charming lakeside village of El Remate, or the neighboring island town of Flores, capital of El Petén, Tikal is a must-see if you have a day to spare during your stay in western Belize.

History

Tikal, commonly translated from Maya as "City of Spiritual Voices," was first inhabited in 600 BC, although its first structures weren't erected until at least 100 years later, around 500 BC. The Pre-Classic Period saw the erection of several structures, including the North Acropolis' ceremonial buildings and the Pyramid at El Mundo Perdido.

By the Early Classic Period, circa AD 250, the Great Plaza began to emerge as Tikal became a key city, with its growing commerce, population, and culture. Its first ruler was King Yax Ehb' Xook, who established the Tikal lineage; Tikal's history and the evolution of its architecture is closely tied to its rulers—33 of them presided over 800 years, and the most important of them all was Ruler 26, Hasaw Chan K'aawil, from the Late Classic Period (682-734).

There are signs that Tikal's history was linked to Teotihuacán, a non-Mayan city 630 miles away, northeast of Mexico City, which reached its peak AD 150-650. One example is that the designs at the Lost World Complex and other designs found on ceramics seem to replicate signs of the Teotihuacán, including its god Tlaloc. Moreover, in the fourth century AD, the Mexican city sent over one of its warriors to aid Tikal in a war against neighboring Uaxactún, and helped elevate Tikal to where it dominated the Petén region for centuries to come.

Five hundred years later, as Teotihuacán's influence waned, Tikal faced the threat of regional dominance by the powerful city of Calakmul, in northern Guatemala and present-day Mexico. Unfortunately for Tikal, Calakmul forged an alliance with Caracol, currently Belize's largest Mayan site. A preemptive strike on Caracol eventually backfired: Archeologists believe that during one counterattack against Tikal in AD 562, Caracol toppled Tikal, shutting down the city for 130 years, during which time no monuments were erected or inscribed and many of Tikal's stelae were desecrated; although it was discovered recently that Temple V was built during this period.

HEIGHT AND DECLINE

Eventually rebounding, in AD 682 Tikal entered a golden period when Ruler Ah-Cacao (Hasaw Chan K'awil, or Lord Chocolate) took over and began the construction of Tikal's most impressive structures, erecting them at a dizzying pace. Other significant achievements of his reign, which lasted until 723, were his two successive and successful attacks against Calakmul, capturing and executing its two kings, first Jaguar Paw (Ich'ak K'ak) and, a year later, Split Earth, thus weakening any further alliance against Tikal and reclaiming its position as the greatest city in Petén.

Hasaw Chan K'awil thereby reinstated a powerful dynasty at Tikal. During this Classic Period, AD 250-900, a time recognized as the peak in Mayan art, architecture, and intellectual achievements across the Mundo Maya, Tikal's five main temples were built. At the city's height, an estimated 100,000 Maya lived in Tikal, covering an area of about 12 square miles.

What caused the rapid decline of the Mayan civilization in the Late Classic Period, AD 800-900, remains a great mystery. At the start of the 10th century, Mayan sites were slowly deserted,

with the collapse of authority and the abandonment of cities. Similarly, by the late 10th century, Tikal was abandoned. Archeologists and scholars have suggested that a combination of climate change, overpopulation, deforestation, and disease may have led to the demise of this ancient civilization.

REDISCOVERY

In 1848 the Guatemalan government commissioned Ambrosio Tut and Modesto Méndez to explore the site, and Méndez produced a first official report on Tikal after a week's visit. Several other scientists passed through after viewing this report, including Dr. Gustav Bernoulli of Switzerland and British archeologist Alfred Maudslay in 1881, who was the first to draw a map of the area. He was also the first to obtain and take photographs of the site after the vegetation was removed after thousands of years of burial. It wasn't until an airstrip was built in the 1950s that the real study began, with the help of the University of Pennsylvania, which carried out excavations from 1956 to 1969.

The latest discoveries date to 1996, mainly including the inscriptions on Temple V that indicate that the site was built during the 130 years Tikal was previously believed to have shut down after a defeat by Caracol and Calakmul.

Visiting the Site

Tickets to Tikal National Park (www.tikalpark.com, 6am-6pm daily, US$20 per day) are sold at the main entrance gate, and you can also purchase an official site map (US$10). From the gate, there's a 15-20 minute drive to the parking lot and **visitors center.** Be sure to purchase your entrance ticket at the first gate and not at the second. Once on-site, there's a large parking lot, two museums, souvenir vendors, and a handful of restaurants and lodges.

Tickets are valid only for the day of purchase, regardless of what time you arrive. It is possible to stay past sunset (up to 9pm) or to watch the sunrise only if you are a guest of one of the park lodges *and* are accompanied by a certified tour guide. Tickets for sunset or

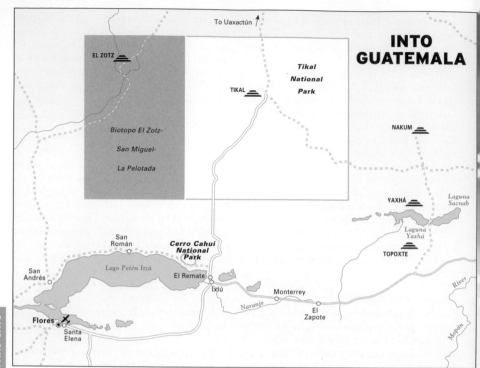

sunrise (additional US$10 fee) are not available at the main gate entrance but rather at the ticket booth by the parking lot after you reach the entrance site. Bring cash and small bills while visiting; credit cards are not accepted.

There' a lot to see and learn at Tikal. If you only have half a day, explore the Grand Plaza and climb up Temple IV. Don't forget to look for monkeys and coatimundis on the way.

CEIBA TREE
Start your tour by walking toward the entrance of the site from the parking lot. Soon you'll see a giant ceiba tree not far from which is a map indicating the various trails. The middle trail leads to Group F and the Great Plaza.

THE GREAT PLAZA
If you only have a couple of hours at Tikal, this is where you want to be. The central plaza

of Tikal is most impressive architecturally, with four temples towering over the gigantic plaza. The Great Plaza buildings—North Acropolis, Temple I, Temple II, and the Central Acropolis—took more than 1,000 years to construct. The sheer city-like size of this courtyard—as well as the 70 stelae carved with images and hieroglyphs—is sure to impress.

TEMPLE I
Temple I is one of three temples towering around the Great Plaza, the heart of what was once the great city of Tikal. Temple I, known as the Big Jaguar, was built by Hasaw Chan K'awil (Lord Chocolate) in AD 700. His tomb was later found under the 151-foot-high temple, his remains surrounded by jade, pearls, and other symbols of human sacrifice (you can see a replica of his tomb and his remains at the Museo Tikal).

© AVALON TRAVEL

is said to have been the site of palaces with interconnecting chambers and stairways centered around a courtyard.

TEMPLE III
Along the Tozzer Causeway is Temple III, or the Great Priest Temple, at 196 feet high. Temple III is unrestored and remains closed to the public. You can spot the temple's tip jutting out of the rainforest, while the remainder sits buried in jungle.

From Temple III, the Tozzer Causeway continues west to Complex N, the Bat Palace, and Temple IV. Another trail leads south to Mundo Perdido.

BAT PALACE
Located behind Temple III is a large palace complex, which includes the restored Bat Palace. Also known as the Palacio de las Venatas (Palace of Windows), thanks to the numerous openings at the back of the structure, the two-story building consists of several rows of rooms.

EL MUNDO PERDIDO
Another significant part of the site is El Mundo Perdido, or Lost World, named as such for having a varying architecture from the rest of the buildings at Tikal. Stand at the top of the Great Pyramid, at 105 ft. high, for stunning views of the Great Plaza and Temple IV in the distance.

TEMPLE IV
At the end of the Tozzer Causeway lies one of the site's most significant structures: Temple IV, the highest and most impressive of Tikal's temples. Temple IV was erected about AD 741 and stands at a dizzying height of 212 feet. This is the most popular temple to climb; look for parallel wooden staircases (one for those going up, another for returning). Take your time getting to the top, hold on to the railing, and take deep breaths. Once at the top, you'll be rewarded with a breathtaking canopy view: the rainforest extends endlessly in every direction, and you'll spot other temples in the distance. Find a spot on the steps and take it all in.

TEMPLE II
Temple II rises 125 feet directly opposite Temple I. This temple was also built by Hasaw Chan K'awil, to honor his wife. It was initially intended to be of identical height with Temple I.

Both Temple I and Temple II are roped off. This is in part due to insufficient climbing infrastructure, but also due to the death of two visitors in 1992 as they attempted to climb back down the steep steps. Use extreme care when exploring the temples.

NORTH AND CENTRAL ACROPOLIS
The North Acropolis lies along on the entire north side of the Great Plaza. This enormous, complex maze of structures includes a section housing smooth, engraved **stelae** that describe the history of Tikal's rulers as well as underground masks.

On the opposite side, the Central Acropolis

BELMOPAN AND CAYO

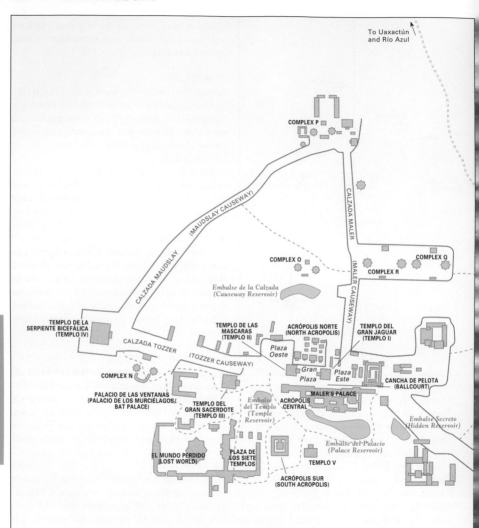

To Uaxactún
and Río Azul

COMPLEX P

CALZADA MALER

(MAUDSLAY CAUSEWAY)

CALZADA MAUDSLAY

COMPLEX O

COMPLEX Q

COMPLEX R

(MALER CAUSEWAY)

Embalse de la Calzada
(Causeway Reservoir)

TEMPLO DE LA
SERPIENTE BICEFÁLICA
(TEMPLO IV)

TEMPLO DE LAS
MASCARAS
(TEMPLO II)

ACRÓPOLIS NORTE
(NORTH ACROPOLIS)

TEMPLO DEL
GRAN JAGUAR
(TEMPLO I)

CALZADA TOZZER

Plaza
Oeste

(TOZZER CAUSEWAY)

COMPLEX N

Gran
Plaza

Plaza
Este

CANCHA DE PELOTA
(BALLCOURT)

PALACIO DE LAS VENTANAS
(PALACIO DE LOS MURCIÉLAGOS/
BAT PALACE)

TEMPLO DEL
GRAN SACERDOTE
(TEMPLO III)

Embalse
del Templo
(Temple
Reservoir)

MALER'S PALACE

ACRÓPOLIS
CENTRAL

Embalse Secreto
(Hidden Reservoir)

Embalse del Palacio
(Palace Reservoir)

EL MUNDO PERDIDO
(LOST WORLD)

PLAZA DE
LOS SIETE
TEMPLOS

TEMPLO V

ACRÓPOLIS SUR
(SOUTH ACROPOLIS)

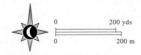

0   200 yds

0   200 m

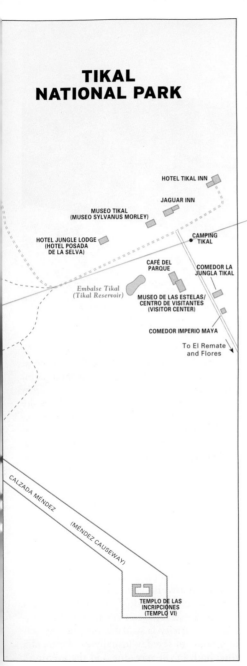

TIKAL
NATIONAL PARK

HOTEL TIKAL INN

JAGUAR INN

MUSEO TIKAL
(MUSEO SYLVANUS MORLEY)

HOTEL JUNGLE LODGE
(HOTEL POSADA
DE LA SELVA)

CAMPING
TIKAL

CAFÉ DEL
PARQUE

COMEDOR LA
JUNGLA TIKAL

Embalse Tikal
(Tikal Reservoir)

MUSEO DE LAS ESTELAS/
CENTRO DE VISITANTES
(VISITOR CENTER)

COMEDOR IMPERIO MAYA

To El Remate
and Flores

CALZADA MÉNDEZ

(MÉNDEZ CAUSEWAY)

TEMPLO DE LAS
INCRIPCIONES
(TEMPLO VI)

At Temple IV, the Maudslay Causeway leads north to Complex P, then curves back south, passing by Complex Q and R.

COMPLEX P

Complex P is believed to have been built by Yax Kin, son of the ruler Hasaw Chan K'awil, in celebration of the end of a *k'atun*. Jaguars and frogs, symbols of power and fertility, are carved on the structure.

COMPLEX Q AND R

Compex Q and R are sets of seven twin pyramids, found at Tikal and nearby Yaxhá. They were built to celebrate cyclical events, such as the end of a 20-year cycle, or *k'atun,* in the Mayan Long Count calendar. On the eastern side of Complex Q, facing one of the pyramids, are nine smooth steles and altars. On the south side is a building with nine doorways, believed to have been a ceremonial palace. Of note here is **Stela 22,** portraying Yax Ain II in his full costume; he took the throne in AD 768.

Museums

There are two museums at Tikal, located at opposite ends. The open-air **Museo Lítico** (9am-noon and 1pm-4:30pm Mon.-Fri., closes earlier Sat.-Sun., free) is located at the visitors center, set around a courtyard close to the entrance. Exhibits include a large-scale model of the site, showing the city as estimated around AD 800. There are also photographs of Tikal as it was first being excavated by a team from the University of Pennsylvania.

Save some time for a stop at the second museum, **Museo Tikal** (or Museo Sylvanus G. Morley, 9am-5pm Mon.-Fri., earlier close weekends, US$5), just past the Jaguar Inn. The museum houses a replica burial chamber with the remains of Hasaw Chan K'awil (Lord Chocolate), whose skeleton was found beneath Temple I. Also on display are ceramics, bloodletting instruments, and incense burners, all found in burial sites. Another exhibit showcases jade necklaces, amulets, and elaborate incense burners found beneath Temple V as well as stelae found buried under the North Acropolis.

© LEBAWIT GIRMA

The view from Temple IV at Tikal is spectacular.

To get the most out of these museums, ask a guide to explain the significance of these artifacts (there isn't much labeled).

Birding and Wildlife-Watching

Tikal's surrounding rainforest makes it an ideal wildlife-watching destination. More than 50 species of mammals and 400 species of birds have been spotted here. Look for toucans, oropendolas, spider and howler monkeys, coatimundis, deer, and more. Jaguars, whose symbolic faces were carved into the stelae at Tikal, still inhabit the park. There are also crocodiles and reptiles, including a resident alligator, and poisonous snakes, although these are known to be nocturnal.

Arrange for special bird-watching tours with **La Casa de Don David** (El Remate, tel. 502/7928-8469, www.lacasadedondavid.com), who have excellent English-speaking birding guides that are knowledgeable about the park. Another excellent tour company is outfitter **Cayaya Birding** (tel. 502/5308-5160, www.cayayabirding.com), based in Guatemala City.

Canopy Tour

Canopy Tikal Tours (tel. 502/5819-7766, www.canopytikal.com, gonregato@hotmail.com, 7am-5pm daily, US$30) offers a zip line across the park either before or after you tour the site (I recommend after). There are 11 platforms at heights of up to 80 feet above the forest canopy. A second, higher zip line is also available (if you dare). Pickups are free from within the park; you can also arrange to be picked up from Flores for an extra fee. Canopy Tikal Tours also offers horseback riding at Tikal.

Accommodations

There are three hotel options and a campground within Tikal National Park, all surrounded by lush tropical forest. Note that you're paying for the location and a unique experience at a World Heritage Site, and perhaps not so much for comfort or service. This is a protected reserve, so conservation is a high priority: Electricity is available only during certain hours of the day (usually 2-3 hours at a time both in the morning and the evening), and none of the hotels have air-conditioning (you might consider bringing a small battery-operated fan, but the temperature is usually bearable). For more "comfort" with less "creature," stay in nearby Flores and El Remate, although you won't get the spectacular rainforest surroundings.

Originally built to house archeologists working on Tikal, the guest rooms at **Jungle Lodge** (tel. 502/2477-0570, www.junglelodgetikal.com, US$40-80) are set around a lovely tropical garden and swimming pool. The hotel is located close to the park entrance and offers bungalows and junior suites, as well as cheaper guest rooms with shared baths. There's a restaurant on-site (US$5-10) serving three meals a day; tour groups are often brought here at lunchtime. There's also Wi-Fi, although it's spotty.

The **Jaguar Inn** (tel. 502/7926-0002, www.jaguartikal.com, US$80) is close to the Tikal Museum and just a couple minutes from the site entrance. They have 13 comfy bungalows with private baths, hot and cold water, fans, and 24-hour electricity. There's an on-site restaurant serving decent meals daily. Transfers or tours can be arranged. Although unadvertised, camping (US$3.50) is available, as well as hammocks with netting (US$5)—just bring your bug spray and a flashlight.

Next door, **Tikal Inn** (tel. 502/4216-3510, www.tikalinnsunrise.com, US$100-145, includes dinner and breakfast) gets rave reviews for service, location, and value. Choose among spacious standard hotel rooms, poolside bungalows, and junior suites. Electricity runs 6am-8am and 6pm-9pm. Both Jaguar and Tikal Inn are solid options if you plan to experience sunrise from the top of nearby Temple IV.

Looking to sleep even closer to nature? The Tikal **campground** area (US$4 pp) is opposite the visitors center and has shared shower and restroom facilities.

Food

All the hotels inside Tikal National Park have restaurants, the most popular of which is the one at the Jungle Lodge. However, there are also independent restaurants (*comedores*) clustered near the entrance, offering Central American fare as well as burgers for about US$5-10. These include: **Comedor Tikal** (the better one), **Restaurant Imperio Maya,** and **Restaurant Café Tikal.** All *comedores* open early for breakfast and serve food until 9pm daily.

For better menu options, don't hesitate to try the hotel restaurants. If you are a guest, your host may offer to-go lunch sandwiches for purchase.

Getting There and Around

If you're planning to visit Tikal on your own, have a strong dose of patience and be prepared. If traveling from the Belize border, bring your passport, exit tax (US$15), and the PACT conservation fee (US$3.75).

BY AIR

Tropic Air (tel. 501/226-2012, U.S. tel. 800/422-3435, www.tropicair.com) offers flights from Belize City's International Airport (Goldson International Airport, BZE, 10 miles west of Belize City, 501/225-2045, www.pgia-belize.com) to Flores (US$224 round-trip). Vehicles head to Tikal from the Flores airport, but be sure to reserve a reliable driver or tour operator ahead of time.

BY BUS

There are no direct buses to Tikal from Benque Viejo del Carmen on the Belize border. There are chicken buses that will pick up from the Guatemala side and head to Flores as well as taxis (US$20 pp, depending on the number of people). You'd then have to find your way to Tikal from Flores.

Another option is to catch the bus to Flores, get off at the crossroads in Ixlu, and then wait for another bus heading north to El Remate or all the way to Tikal. However, the wait could be long as the schedules are not published. It's also generally safer to arrange a ride with a recognized guide than going it alone.

It's possible to catch the bus all the way to the Cayo District, then all the way to Benque

Viejo del Carmen and the border, and then wing it once you make it past immigration. But if you're not fluent in Spanish, or would rather play it safe (recommended), there are several tour companies with buses heading directly to Flores and Tikal from Belize City's Water Taxi Terminal (by the Swing Bridge), as well as by the San Pedro Belize Express terminal, a couple of blocks farther down.

First try **S&L Travel Tours** (91 N. Front St., Belize City, tel. 501/227-7593, www.sltravelbelize.com), a very reliable company, or contact **Atlanta Tour Express Bus Service** (inside the San Pedro Belize Express Water Taxi Terminal, Belize City), with direct service to Tikal and Flores via the Guatemalan Línea Dorada buses (www.lineadorada.info). The journey to the border takes about 4.5 hours. If you're lucky, crossing the border will be smooth and painless, although lines can occasionally get long.

BY CAR

If you decide to rent a car, check out **Crystal Auto Rental** (Mile 5, Northern Hwy., Belize City, 501/223-1600, www.crystal-belize.com, from US$65 per day), one of the only companies that allow you to take a rental vehicle into Guatemala (be sure to inquire about insurance).

TOURS

Most tour guides in San Ignacio offer regular trips to Tikal, almost daily during the busy tourist season (Dec.-Apr.). If you opt for a tour, you won't have to worry about anything except bringing your passport, paying for the tour, and hopping in a van—the rest is taken care of, from border crossing to entrance fees. I highly recommend **Pacz Tours** (tel. 501/604-6921 or 501/824-0536, www.pacztours.net, full-day US$145, all-inclusive overnight US$400 with hotel, meals, guide, taxes, and fees), with its own resident Tikal expert.

EL REMATE

The lakeside village of El Remate is the closest town to Tikal National Park. Located just 22 miles away, it is 0.5 miles north of "El Cruce," the main traffic circle with signs to Tikal. El

Remate has become a favorite for overnight stays among travelers heading to the Mayan site who want to avoid the more distant Flores area and the expense of an overnight in the national park. There are plenty of transportation options in El Remate, making it easier to find shared rides with fellow travelers, and the lake is clean and safe to swim in. Hotels, restaurants, and recreation are also plentiful.

There's plenty to do in El Remate if Tikal isn't enough for you. Half- or full-day birding tours with local guides are available through **La Casa de Don David** (tel. 502/7928-8469, www.lacasadedondavid.com, US$40-75). La Casa de Don David can help arrange all kinds of other activities.

Kayaking is available at **Casa de Dona Tonita** (tel. 502/5701-7114, US$2 per hour), as is and mountain biking (US$5 per day). The best swimming is in front of the Biotopo Cerro Cahui Nature Reserve or at El Muelle Restaurant.

Accommodations and Food

UNDER US$25

A clean budget place that gets rave reviews is the **Sun Breeze Hotel** (Calle del Lago, tel. 502/7928-8044 or 502/5898-2665, US$10). The colorful double rooms have private baths, fans, porches, hammocks, and a working shower (the hot water is temperamental). For the price, you can't beat the quiet location within a minute's walk of the lake. The hotel can arrange for transportation to Tikal and even to Belize City.

US$25-50

Not far along on your route, ◖ **La Casa de Don David** (off the main road, tel. 502/7928-8469, www.lacasadedondavid.com, US$23-28, includes either breakfast of dinner) is the preferred choice of many. This is a cozy, simple, and safe place to stay with standard or premium guest rooms set in a lush garden, with private baths, balconies, fans or air-conditioning, and hot water. There's an on-site restaurant serving home cooked Guatemalan specialties as well as wireless Internet access. The hotel owners have a wealth of information on the area and can arrange for all kinds of tours.

The rustic and charming lakeside **(Posada del Cerro** (tel. 502/5376-8722 or 502/5305-1717, www.posadadelcerro.com, US$40-56) offers simple but charming accommodations, including cottages with a thatched roofs, a patio, and a serene environment. Posada del Cerro is located right next to the entrance of the Biotopo Cerro Cahui Reserve, hence the lovely lake views and freshwater swimming. There's an on-site restaurant and lounge area for guests to enjoy.

US$50-100

Located right on the main road, the Western-inspired **Palomino Ranch Hotel** (tel. 502/7928-8419, www.hotelpalominoranch.com, US$50) offers eight double rooms, each equipped with air-conditioning, a TV, and hot water, in a large villa with a swimming pool. The hotel also offers horseback riding trips and gets rave reviews for its service.

OVER US$100

Peten's ultimate in luxury is **(La Lancha** (tel. 502/7928-8331, U.S. tel. 800/746-3743, www.blancaneaux.com, US$160-240, breakfast included), Francis Ford Coppola's 10-room lodge in Guatemala. The lakeshore views may be its best feature, as its location in the village of Jobompiche is somewhat more remote than the other hotels. Choose from lake-view casitas or rainforest casitas, all tastefully decorated with Guatemalan fabrics, Balinese wood, and beautiful decks where you can laze in a hammock.

The on-site restaurant serves Guatemalan specialties (lunch and dinner US$20 pp) and there's a lovely pool below the restaurant.

FLORES

Flores is a small island town located in Lake Petén Itzá, with cobblestone streets and lakeside bistros. It is connected to its twin town on the mainland, Santa Elena (although they are often collectively referred to as Flores) by a causeway. Santa Elena itself is a noisy commercial center, and few visitors choose to stay here. Flores, once a popular stopover, is now slowly being replaced by the up-and-coming El Remate, mostly because the accommodations there offer better value, the lake is clean and safe to swim in, and its location is closer to both Tikal National Park and Belize.

Still, a couple of sights worth checking out in Flores include the **Yaxhá-Nakum-Naranjo Natural Monument** (8am-5pm daily, US$10), home to several Mayan sites, the most prominent of which is Yaxhá, made even more famous when the TV show *Survivor Guatemala* was filmed here in 2005.

Accommodations and Food

Eco Lodge El Sombrero (tel. 502/4147-6380 or 502/5320-7091, US$25-75) offers basic guest rooms in thatched-roof lakefront bungalows. While there's a dock, it isn't safe to swim here, unless you want to be chased by crocodiles. There's an on-site restaurant with decent food. The upside is the location, right next to the Yaxhá site and surrounded by rainforest, lakes, and the occasional visiting howler monkey.

SOUTHERN COAST

Just under two hours south of Belize City, the Southern Coast has an Afro-Caribbean soul. It also boasts a beautiful coastline, lush rainforests, waterfalls, the world's only jaguar preserve, the country's highest point, and the longest stretch of beach—from unmanicured Dangriga to the tourist-heavy Placencia Peninsula. The Stann Creek District is at the heart of the country's fascinating

© LEBAWIT GIRMA

HIGHLIGHTS

LOOK FOR  TO FIND RECOMMENDED SIGHTS, ACTIVITIES, DINING, AND LODGING.

Gulisi Garífuna Museum
Garífuna Settlement Day
Mayflower Bocawina National Park
Dangriga
Tobacco Caye
Hopkins
Glover's Reef Atoll
Cockscomb Basin Wildlife Sanctuary
Lebeha Drumming Center
South Water Caye Marine Reserve
Maya Beach and Seine Bight
Placencia
Caribbean Sea
Laughingbird Caye National Park
0   15 mi
0   15 km
© AVALON TRAVEL

❲ Gulisi Garífuna Museum: Located on the outskirts of Dangriga, this museum offers an interactive history lesson on the fascinating Garinagu and Garífuna culture (page 200).

❲ Garífuna Settlement Day: November 19 celebrates the arrival of the ancestral Garinagu people to Belize's shores. A colorful reenactment is followed by parades, processions, and a multitude of events in town, from outdoor concerts to all-night drumming (page 207).

❲ South Water Caye Marine Reserve: One of Belize's most beautiful offshore islands offers excellent snorkeling right off the beach and a magical landscape on its southern tip (page 214).

❲ Tobacco Caye: Sitting right atop Belize's barrier reef, Tobacco Caye can be a social gathering of world travelers or an isolated island experience, depending on the time of year (page 215).

❲ Glover's Reef Atoll: Glover's spectacular snorkeling and diving are a stone's throw from shore, and the waters are ideal for all kinds of water sports. The scenery above water, particularly on Southwest Caye, is just as gorgeous (page 219).

❲ Lebeha Drumming Center: Hopkins is home to the Lebeha Drumming Center, where hourly lessons provide a unique opportunity to learn about Garífuna music and dance (page 222).

❲ Mayflower Bocawina National Park: Rappel waterfalls, zip across 7,100 acres of forest canopy, and enjoy bird- and wildlife-watching at this unique park in Belize (page 233).

❲ Cockscomb Basin Wildlife Sanctuary: This extensive reserve is famous for its multitude of birds, jaguars, and other jungle critters (page 234).

❲ Maya Beach and Seine Bight: The Placencia Peninsula is home to two of the prettiest beaches in Belize. Maya Beach (page 237) is peppered with hotels, restaurants, and bars, while Seine Bight (page 239) offers low-key stretches of sand.

❲ Laughingbird Caye National Park: Palms, sand, and snorkeling are found at this national park, part of a 10,000-acre protected marine area (page 257).

Garífuna culture, declared endangered by the United Nations in 2001 yet still thriving thanks to a concerted effort to preserve tradition.

The seaside town of Dangriga, Garífuna hub and Belize's "culture capital," is home to a third of Stann Creek District's 36,000 inhabitants, and its economy is as varied as its culture and geography; tourism is as important as the orange, banana, and shrimp industries. Unassuming and untouristed, Dangriga is more than just a pit stop on the way to Placencia or the gateway to the southern Cayes; independent travelers can get off the beaten path here and explore African-inspired art galleries, make their own drums, and perhaps enjoy a meal at a Garífuna home. That's when you're not off trekking in the nearby Cockscomb Jaguar Reserve, waterfall rappelling at nearby Bocawina National Park, or cooling off in Billy Barquedier's emerald streams. It's astounding how many activities are within reach.

More traveler-friendly yet still authentic, the nearby fishing village of Hopkins has uncrowded wide-open beaches, a host of lodging options to fit all budgets, drumming lessons, and authentic Garífuna cuisine.

Beachcombers and dive enthusiasts looking to add pulsating nightlife to their trip will be happy to continue on to the Placencia Peninsula, one of the most rapidly developing tourist areas of Belize. With the longest (and nicest) stretch of beach on the mainland, a mixed Garífuna and Creole vibe, and the oft-photographed Silk Cayes and a UNESCO World Heritage Site just a quick boat ride away, Placencia offers plenty to love.

PLANNING YOUR TIME

There's a lot to see and do on the Southern Coast. Start with **Dangriga.** Walk along the North Stann Creek Bridge and Commerce Boulevard, and then head to Y-Not Island to watch Austin Rodriguez, a renowned Garífuna drum maker, at his seaside workshop. Squeeze in a visit to the **Gulisi Garífuna Museum** and Pen Cayetano's Gallery, where you'll learn all about this Afro-Caribbean Garífuna culture. With an extra day, you can tour the Marie Sharp Factory, where the most popular hot sauce in Belize is made and bottled.

Hopkins is just an hour away by bus from Dangriga. Stay right in the village at one of several budget beachfront guesthouses, bike around, sample Garífuna dishes, and take drumming lessons at **Lebeha Drumming Center.** The nearby Sittee River offers birding and wildlife watching.

From Hopkins, trek to a waterfall in **Mayflower Bocawina National Park** and spend the night in **Maya Centre.** Shop for crafts, converse with herbal healers, and arrange an expedition within the **Cockscomb Basin Wildlife Sanctuary.**

Placencia is the "barefoot perfect" beach of Belize. Journey along the gorgeous southern reef and dive to your heart's content. Rent a cheap cabana on **Maya Beach** and barhop the night away, or make a day-trip to **Laughingbird Caye.**

Dangriga

"Mabuiga!" shouts the sign in Garífuna, welcoming you to this cultural hub and district capital. Built on the Caribbean shoreline and straddling North Stann Creek (also called Gumagarugu River), Dangriga's primary boast is its status as the Garífuna people's original port of entry into Belize—and their modern-day cultural center. But although the majority of Dangriga's 12,500 or so inhabitants are Garífuna descendants of that much-celebrated 1823 landing, the remaining few are a typically rich mix of Chinese, Creoles, mestizos, and Maya, all of whom can be seen interacting on the town's main drag.

Aside from Dangriga's ideal location for accessing the surrounding mountains and

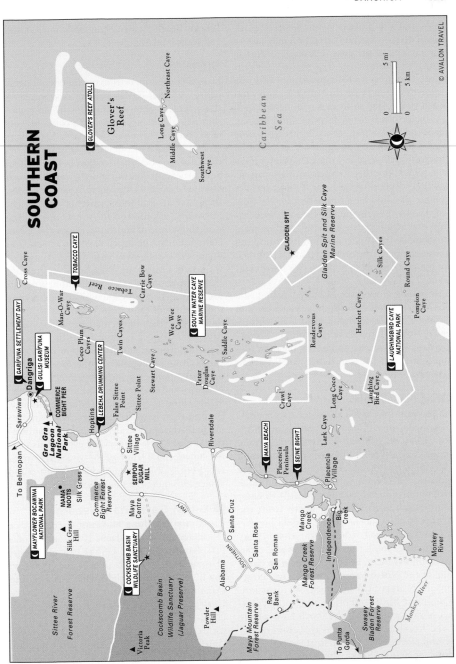

© AVALON TRAVEL

SOUTHERN COAST

Caribbean Sea

GLOVER'S REEF ATOLL

Glover's Reef

Northeast Cave

Long Cave

Middle Cave

Southwest Cave

GLADDEN SPIT

Gladden Spit and Silk Caye Marine Reserve

Silk Cayes

Round Caye

TOBACCO CAYE

Cross Caye

Man-O-War Caye

Tobacco Reef

Carrie Bow Caye

Coco Plum Cayes

Twin Cayes

Wee Wee Caye

SOUTH WATER CAYE MARINE RESERVE

Saddle Caye

Stewart Caye

Peter Douglas Caye

Crawl Caye

Rendezvous Caye

Hatchet Caye

Pompion Caye

LAUGHINGBIRD CAYE NATIONAL PARK

Laughing Bird Caye

Long Coco Caye

Lark Caye

GARIFUNA SETTLEMENT DAY

GULISI GARIFUNA MUSEUM

Dangriga

Sarawiwa

COMMERCE BIGHT PIER

LEBEHA DRUMMING CENTER

Gra Gra Lagoon National Park

Hopkins

False Sittee Point

Sittee Point

Sittee Village

Riversdale

MAYA BEACH

SEINE BIGHT

Placencia Peninsula

Placencia Village

To Belmopan

MAYFLOWER BOCAWINA NATIONAL PARK

Silk Grass

MAMA NOOTS

Silk Grass Hill

Commerce Bight Forest Reserve

Maya Centre

SERPON SUGAR MILL

COCKSCOMB BASIN WILDLIFE SANCTUARY

Sittee River Forest Reserve

Cockscomb Basin Wildlife Sanctuary (Jaguar Preserve)

Victoria Peak

Powder Hill

Santa Cruz

Santa Rosa

San Roman

Alabama

Red Bank

Maya Mountain Forest Reserve

Mango Creek Forest Reserve

Mango Creek

Independence

Big Creek

SOUTHERN HWY

Swasey Bladen Forest Reserve

To Punta Gorda

Monkey River

Monkey River

SOUTHERN COAST

seas—and the limited visitor services available to do so—its chief attraction may just be its total lack of pretense. Dangriga, formerly known as Stann Creek Town, does not outwardly cater to its foreign visitors the way Placencia or San Pedro do—there is simply too much else going on in this commercial center, including fishing, farming, and serving the influx of Stann Creek villagers who come weekly to stock up on supplies. Consequently, this area is still relatively undeveloped for tourism, which is either a shortcoming or an attraction, depending on what kind of traveler you are. It could be intimidating for the novice traveler, but the people here are welcoming. The area is slowly evolving, finding ways to showcase its wonders—from its drumming culture to its nearby national parks. Dangriga, by the way, means something like "sweet still waters" in Garífuna.

If poking around the casually bustling vibe of Dangriga sounds intriguing, you'd do well to stay a couple of nights. And if it's culture you're looking for, with the drumming "sheds," the daily local scenes, and one of the most picturesque seaside areas in Belize, you'll want to stay a bit longer.

ORIENTATION

As you pull into town, three massive ceremonial *dügü* drums of iron will greet you. This is the *Drums of Our Fathers* monument, erected in 2003 as a symbol of Garífuna pride—and as a call to war against the erosion of Garífuna culture. Turn right to reach the deep dock at Commerce Bight, or left (north) to enter Dangriga Town. Heading north from the drums on St. Vincent Street, the old bus terminal is on your left before the first bridge. Continuing, you'll find more shops and eateries, culminating in the center of town on either side of the North Stann Creek Bridge; crossing the bridge, St. Vincent Street turns into Commerce Street and offers an informal market often set up along the north bank of the river. Catch a boat to the cayes from one of several places here. The airstrip is a mile or so north of Stann Creek, where you'll also find

Pelican Beach Resort, Dangriga's fanciest digs and restaurant.

SIGHTS

Dangriga does not offer many traditional sights per se. A better term would be *experiences* because there is plenty going on—it's an explosion of culture, scenery, and people for any newcomer to this town. Moreover, Dangriga's central location—a detail often lost on travelers new to the area—makes it an excellent base for excursions around the region, much more so even than Placencia. You can browse the few crafts and music stores on St. Vincent Street and ask around for the drum-making workshops, one of which is set up at the Y-Not compound by the beach at Stann Creek. You might even walk away with an instrument of your own. Drums are often heard throughout the town to mark celebrations and funerals; sometimes it's simply a few people practicing the rhythms of their history. There's an abundance of artistic talent that can't be missed. Austin Rodriquez is known for his authentic Garífuna drums, which end up in musicians' hands around the country. Other local artists of national prominence include painter Benjamin Nicholas and craftswoman Mercy Sabal, who makes colorful dolls sold all over the country. Beyond this, however, what makes Dangriga unique is the opportunity to experience authentic culture. Those with a keen eye will also notice how scenic Dangriga is—you will want to take photos of its bridges, rivers, pelicans and anglers; it's quite the photographer's dream.

◖ Gulisi Garífuna Museum

The **Gulisi Garífuna Museum** (George Price Dr., ngcbelize@gmail.com, 10am-5pm Mon.-Fri., 8am-noon Sat., US$5) is a mile west of town on the south side of the highway; you'll see it on your right when driving into Dangriga, next to the thrusting Chuluhadiwa Garífuna Monument (taxi from downtown US$2-3). The small two-room display is packed with a wealth of fascinating information on the Garífuna people of Belize and a vast collection of artifacts, quotes, photos, and biographies of

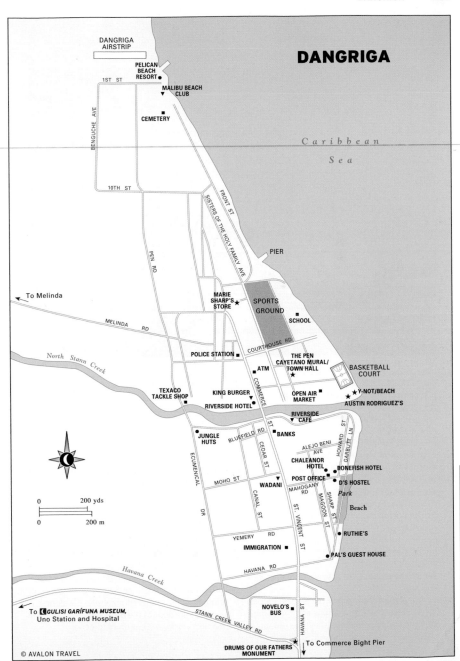

DANGRIGA

DANGRIGA
AIRSTRIP

PELICAN
BEACH
RESORT

1ST ST

MALIBU BEACH
CLUB

CEMETERY

BENGUCHE AVE

10TH ST

C a r i b b e a n

S e a

FRONT ST

SISTERS OF THE HOLY FAMILY AVE

PEN RD

PIER

To Melinda

MELINDA RD

MARIE
SHARP'S
STORE

SPORTS
GROUND

SCHOOL

COURTHOUSE RD

North Stann Creek

POLICE STATION

ATM

THE PEN
CAYETANO MURAL/
TOWN HALL

BASKETBALL
COURT

COMMERCE ST

TEXACO
TACKLE SHOP

KING BURGER

RIVERSIDE HOTEL

OPEN AIR
MARKET

Y-NOT/BEACH

AUSTIN RODRIGUEZ'S

RIVERSIDE
CAFE

ST

JUNGLE
HUTS

BLUEFIELD RD

BANKS

ALEJO BENI
AVE

HOWARD ST

GARBUTT LN

CEDAR ST

ECUMENICAL DR

CHALEANOR
HOTEL

BONEFISH HOTEL

MOHO ST

WADANI

POST OFFICE

D'S HOSTEL

MAHOGANY
RD

Park

CANAL ST

ST VINCENT ST

MAGOON ST

SHARP ST

Beach

0   200 yds

0   200 m

YEMERY RD

IMMIGRATION

RUTHIE'S

PAL'S GUEST HOUSE

Havana Creek

HAVANA RD

To **GULISI GARÍFUNA MUSEUM,**
Uno Station and Hospital

STANN CREEK VALLEY RD

NOVELO'S
BUS

HAVANA ST

To Commerce Bight Pier

DRUMS OF OUR FATHERS
MONUMENT

© AVALON TRAVEL

SOUTHERN COAST

DRUMS OF OUR FATHERS: FROM POEM TO MONUMENT

Drums of Our Fathers Monument at entrance of Dangriga

"In our culture, songs aren't composed, they just come from inspiration," explained Garífuna National Council cofounder, author, and educator Roy Cayetano. Cayetano's famous poem "Drums of Our Fathers" was turned into a monument erected in 2003. The structure consists of three large, equal-size Garífuna *dügü*, or ceremonial drums. It stands high at the entrance of Dangriga, greeting every newcomer to the Garífuna hub and cultural capital.

Roy Cayetano wrote "Drums of Our Fathers" in 15 minutes. It was "a call to war" and the need to act to preserve the endangered Garífuna culture, language, and heritage. At the time he dedicated the poem to his grandmother, his wife, and his child to be, each of whom represented the three spiritual symbols of past, present, and future.

When then-Dangriga Area Representative Sylvia Flores mentioned her desire to commission the construction of a Garífuna monument in Dangriga, one that represented the spiritual aspect of the culture, Cayetano knew just what to suggest. The placement of three ceremonial Garífuna drums of equal size would be symbolic: the top middle drum resting on the lower two would symbolize the Garinagu present resting on the past and the ancestors and yet looking to the future. The goal was to immortalize the culture's most significant symbol: the drum, the sound of a people that was never quieted by the colonial masters, a sound that must continue to be heard.

Artist Steve Okeke, of Nigerian origin and based in Belize City, completed the monument within two months after it was commissioned. The resulting artwork was so impressive that a more central place was given to *Drums of Our Fathers* at the entrance to town. A constant reminder that the Garífuna culture was never silenced, the beat of the drums goes on, and its people's voices will continue to echo.

SOUTHERN COAST

prominent Garífuna figures in Belize. The museum is named after the person thought to be the first Garífuna woman to arrive and settle in Dangriga. She had 13 sons, and many of Dangriga's modern residents believe they are descended from her. In 2008 the "language, dance, and music of the Garífuna" was inscribed on UNESCO's Representative List of the Intangible Cultural Heritage of Humanity, originally proclaimed in 2001.

Marie Sharp Store and Factory

Be sure to save time to stop by **Marie Sharp's Store** (north of Stann Creek Bridge, tel. 501/522-2370, 8am-5pm Mon.-Fri.) to stock up on the area's famous hot sauce and other products; you can purchase hot sauce here for a tiny fraction of the normal retail price. Better yet, make the trip to **Marie Sharp's Factory** (Melinda Rd., Stann Creek Valley, tel. 501/532-2087, www.mariesharps-bz.com, 9am-4pm), just a short ride from town, where you'll be offered a free tour of the farm and factory. The factory sits on a 400-acre estate. To reach it, drive west on the Hummingbird Highway from Dangriga about eight miles and turn right after you cross a bridge and see the White Swan on your left.

Austin Rodriguez's Drum Workshop

There's little doubt that Austin Rodriguez has a deep-rooted passion for his culture and his drums. He spends all day and evening here, across from the beach at Y-Not Island, carving new drums into existence beside the sea, as he has for the past 12 years. His purpose for setting up shop was to teach the children this dying Garífuna skill and keep the culture going. You can buy ready-made drums from him in different sizes, or with notice, watch him make one from scratch. There's no set cost for the latter, simply a donation of your choice. Be generous, because this is an invaluable experience: to witness the making of instruments that will end up being played across the country and even used during the annual spiritual Garífuna Settlement Day reenactment events.

Rodriguez doesn't play the drums himself; he simply listens and knows whether they sound right. His daughter is also a drum maker and works with her father at the workshop.

The Pen Cayetano Mural at Dangriga Town Hall

While in town, drop by the **Dangriga Town Hall** to view the impressive 2012 mural by Pen Cayetano, one of the country's foremost painters and musicians and creator of the popular Belizean music genre *punta* rock. The mural, *Hayawadina Wayúnagu* ("images of our ancestors"), depicts the Garífuna culture, including the landing of the Garinagu (plural of Garífuna) in Dangriga, and pays homage to those who have documented and perpetuated the culture. The mural also shows the interaction of other Belizean ethnic groups—the Maya, Kriol, mestizo, Chinese, and Caucasian—with the Garinagu, a glimpse of how multiethnic Belize has become. It's a "cultural mural," as he describes it, intended to further educate the young but also resist the potential disappearance of a rich history.

Mercy Sabal

Born and raised in Dangriga, with over 20 years of experience in her craft, **Mercy Sabal** (cell 501/604-6731, US$25-35) is a well-recognized name in town thanks to her striking, handmade Garífuna folklore dolls, each telling a story through art. Some have reversible outfits, holding firewood or other symbolic tools. They make for unique souvenirs; you might also spot Mercy's dolls on sale at the airport gift shops. And if you're into learning more about the Garífuna people, Mercy is your lady. You can ask to spend the day with her; she'll cook a Garífuna dish or two and share tales of Garífuna life.

Sabal Farm

Three miles outside Dangriga, you can visit the country's sole cassava-producing farm. Sabal Farm (group of 8 US$2.50 pp or US$20 pp), not to be confused with Mercy Sabal, has operated for the past 25 years. Those with an

SOUTHERN COAST

MARIE SHARP: THE SPICE LADY

© LEBAWIT GIRMA

the spice queen of Belize

She's a household name. Her bottles of hot sauce—ranging from Mild to Beware—are on almost every restaurant tabletop in the country and in every grocery store. Some Belizeans even carry her in their purse. You can't consume anything without an extra dash of Marie. It's the first thing to look for when served at a local eatery. And if it's not on the table or within immediate view, everyone asks "gat some Marie Sharp?"

You can visit her hot sauce factory—and if you're extremely fortunate, meet her in person—in Dangriga. It's a 10-minute ride outside town, down a gravel road and past some citrus orchards, to the 400-acre **Marie Sharp farm and factory** (Melinda Rd., Stann Creek Valley, tel. 501/532-2087, www.mariesharps-bz.com). This humble Belizean entrepreneur, mother, and grandmother is nothing short of a legend in her country, and her story is one of adversity and success.

Marie started experimenting in her kitchen with a batch of leftover peppers she didn't want to throw out. Using a carrot base that became a hit with friends, she sold her sauce out of that kitchen for three years under the name Me-

linda's. The real kicker? She partnered with a U.S.-based distributor who conned her out of her product's name and tied her into an exclusivity contract, attempting to force her to give up the recipe. Years of hard work and a legal battle later, Marie decided not to give up. Instead, she started over from scratch using her original recipe, which she never revealed. Marie gave the sauce her name, so no one could steal it, and her name is now known throughout the country and Central America. "I was the chief cook and bottle washer up to five years ago," she said, smiling and pointing at the small room in her factory where she started over.

Marie's factory, run with the help of her spouse, sons, and grandson, is on the verge of a major expansion, already producing nine different types of pepper sauce (the most popular is the Fiery Hot) and nine types of jams and jellies (my favorite is the guava). For all her fame, Marie Sharp doesn't want anyone to recognize her when they visit her factory. But she's proud of her success, as she should be—her products are a symbol of Belizean cultural pride. Rare is the visitor who leaves without a bottle or two in their suitcase.

© LEBAWIT GIRMA

cassava breadmaking at the Sabal Farm

interest in African culture and the Garinagu will be fascinated by this family-run operation, producing most of the cassava bread and other cassava-based products, sold all around the country. Cyril Sabal and his sister, Clotilda, run the impressive 30 acres, of which six are used for harvesting other crops, including citrus. Learn the process of making cassava, from peeling a cassava root—which takes up to eight women to produce 12 bags—all the way to baking and roasting it the old fashioned, organic way. Beyond the cassava, the farm is a symbol of cultural preservation at its finest.

Contact Brother David of **CD's Transfer** (1163 3rd St., tel. 501/502-3489 or cell 501/602-3077, breddadavid@gmail.com) to arrange a ride to and from the farm and to figure out the best day to visit.

Billy Barquedier National Park
Established as a protected area in 2001, **Billy Barquedier National Park** (Mile 16 1/2 Hummingbird Hwy., Steadfast, http://billy-barquediernp.webs.com, 9am-4:30pm, US$4) is an often overlooked and little-known attraction. The park is co-managed by the Steadfast Tourism and Conservation Association, a grassroots community organization, and the Forestry Department. The approximately 1,500 acres of untouched jungle are home to abundant wildlife, including howler monkeys, numerous bird species, and even the elusive tapir. The park has a separate entrance at Mile 17 ½ for quick access to the **Billy Barquedier Waterfall**, its principal attraction. A 20-minute hike along a marked (albeit a bit run down) trail and spelunking across some tricky rocks will lead you to a beautiful stream with a refreshing, emerald pool.

There are no accommodations in the park but primitive **camping** (US$10 pp) is available. Accommodations are a 10-minute ride away in Dangriga, easily accessible by bus along the Hummingbird Highway.

SPORTS AND RECREATION
Dangriga is ideally placed within a short drive of several of Belize's most stunning

© LEBAWIT GIRMA

Y-Not Island is Grigans' favorite beach for swimming and relaxing.

parks and wildlife reserves; it's just 20 miles from Cockscomb Basin and Maya Centre, 17 miles from both Billy Barquedier and Mayflower Bocawina National Park, and 40 miles from Blue Hole National Park. This puts an incredible amount of activity at your fingertips, particularly for day trips, from birding to jaguar-track spotting, waterfall swimming or rappelling, and hiking numerous nature trails.

For input on which areas to explore and for a wealth of local wisdom, contact award-winning **C & G Tours and Charters** (29 Oak St., tel. 501/501-3641, www.cgtourscharters.com). C & G is a local tour operator, and their guides speak many languages. Unfortunately, they now only cater to large groups.

For a simple transfer to and from numerous sites, contact David Obi, or "Brother David," of **CD's Transfer** (1163 3rd St., tel. 501/502-3489, cell 501/602-3077, breddadavid@gmail.com, 2-person Cockscomb tour US$140; Hopkins Village US$65 pp; 2-person Xunantunich tour US$190). Obi is an excellent

and accommodating local guide who will take good care of getting you to and from your chosen site.

Beaches

The locals' favorite beach in Dangriga is at **Y-Not Island,** just along the Y-Not basketball court. Although erosion tends to push the beach back, it's still a lovely, picturesque stretch to take a dip, and the views of the pelicans and the anglers are reminders of Dangriga's peacefulness and authenticity. There are often events held here as well as fruit and food vendors throughout the week. Another ideal swimming beach is at **Pelican Beach,** by the Pelican Beach Resort. If you're not staying there, treat yourself to lunch or drinks and bring your bathing suit to jump off the dock and enjoy the water.

Diving and Snorkeling

The most untouched parts of the Barrier Reef, along with some of the most beautiful cayes and one of Belize's three atolls, are a few miles offshore, along the **South Water**

Caye Marine Reserve and the Port Honduras Marine Reserve off the Punta Gorda coast. The Southern Coast is more than a mere gateway to these idyllic plots of land, and the islands have a lot more to offer than a day trip for those who love to fish, dive, or want a "castaway" experience.

ENTERTAINMENT AND EVENTS
Nightlife
There's no such thing as a dull evening in Dangriga. You won't find big shiny nightclubs, but there's plenty of entertainment, whether it's watching lively and intense dominoes tournaments at the sheds, dancing to in-club drumming and live *punta,* or barhopping across neighborhoods. "Griga" isn't as dead as they'll have you think.

Dangriga is home to the Warribaggabagga Dancers, the Punta Rebels, the Punta Boys, the Turtle Shell Band, and the Griga Boyz, among other nationally known party bands. The music and dancing features syncopated West African-style rhythms and interesting mixtures of various southern Belizean cultures. There is often live music or drumming on weekends; ask around for where the latest event is (taxi drivers are often the best source of information, or even your hosts).

Start with some drinks and people-watching at the local "sheds" in town, where you'll find men slamming dominoes and throwing back Guinness in a thatched-roof hut. Try the **Wadani Recreation Centre** (St Vincent St., 11:30am-midnight daily), known as "Wadani Shed," **Waruguma** (Ecumenical Dr. at Teddy Cas St., 6pm-midnight daily), or continue to **Illagulei Sports Bar** (George Price Dr., near the entrance to Dangriga, tel. 501/666-9184, 9pm-2am Thurs.-Sun.), where there will be lively dominoes tournaments and music. At "club" time, the lights are dimmed and the tables are cleared for when the venue transforms into a full-on nightclub, starting no earlier than midnight.

Equally popular among the locals is **Di Spot** (Teachers St.), which is someone's living room-turned-dance floor. It's pitch-black save for the lit-up bar and an excellent DJ on a raised platform playing reggae and other house tunes. The crowd is decent, and there's a large outdoor yard with seating. Be advised that Di Spot occasionally has karaoke nights, especially American country music, which is popular around these parts.

From Di Spot, hop over to **Mexicana Club** (Lemon St., tel. 501/664-6570, 8:30pm-2am Thurs.-Sat.), a spacious nightclub offering DJ music as well as live music. At last visit, the Punta Boys were playing and the sound of Garífuna drums inside the club had everyone moving.

Festivals and Events
The month of December is a festive time in Dangriga. The days leading up to Christmas are celebrated with *jankanu* dancing in the streets and dancers performing from house to house. The Institute of Creative Arts, a branch of the National Institute of Culture and Heritage (tel. 501/227-2110, www.nichbelize.org), sponsors the annual **Habinaha Wanaragua Jankanu Dance Contest** every December 26 (Boxing Day) at Y-Not Island. The beachfront basketball court becomes a makeshift dance floor where adult dance teams from the various Garífuna communities compete for the best *jankanu* dance team title. It's a fun, colorful event attended mostly by locals from around the country, which attests to the town's authentic vibe. The festivities usually start at 2pm; arrive early for a good seat and wear a hat to avoid the afternoon sun. Plenty of food and drinks are sold at the venue.

◖ GARÍFUNA SETTLEMENT DAY
Easily one of the most popular cultural events in Belize, Garífuna Settlement Day (Nov. 19) celebrates the arrival of the first Garinagu onto Belizean shores, and it's a national holiday. The biggest celebration in the country takes place in Dangriga, with a complete reenactment of the first Garinagu arrival on the shores of Belize in dugout canoes filled with cassava, plantains,

THE GARÍFUNA *JANKANU* DANCE

The centuries-old tradition of *jankanu*, a West African masquerade dance, dates back to the days of slavery. *Jankanu* was a celebration by the enslaved of their few days of freedom at Christmastime, during which they would dance and mock the European masters by wearing pink flesh-colored masks, white clothes, and suspenders.

In the Garífuna *jankanu* dance, the performer dictates the beat to the drummer with his movements: feet together, knees bent, arms raised, palms facing the drummers, and hips rocking quickly side to side. There are costumes that include special touches, including cowrie shells strapped above the knee and feathers shooting up from the masks.

In 2010 an annual *jankanu* dance contest was launched in Dangriga to improve the quality of the dance and pass it on to younger generations. The contest is held every December, usually the day after Christmas, at Y-Not Island in Dangriga, where the basketball court is transformed into a makeshift dance floor.

© LEBAWIT GIRMA

A *jankanu* dancer competes at an annual contest in Dangriga.

and other staple foods. The town comes alive the entire week of November 19, with concerts, art exhibits, drumming, and more; a schedule is printed that month, or you can inquire with your guesthouse or host. Almost every night leading up to Settlement Day, there is dancing and drumming under the "sheds" in town, such as Wadani Shed, from 8pm until the wee hours of the morning. On the morning of the 19th, the crowd heads over to the main bridge in town across the North Stann Creek River, lining up along the river starting at 7am, waiting for the boats to arrive and cheer them on. The merriment continues with a colorful, hair-raising procession to the church, and ends with an afternoon parade in town. Settlement Day in Dangriga is one of the best cultural experiences in all of Belize. Hotels book up months

in advance, so make sure you make arrangements well ahead.

SHOPPING

Mercy Sabal's Garífuna Dolls (tel. 501/604-6731, US$25-35) make for a unique gift; each is meticulously made by hand and depicts an aspect of the culture. Call ahead to view them at her home, which is currently being converted into a ground-floor shop. If you're lucky, she may treat you to a Garífuna immersion day.

Pen Cayetano Studio Gallery (3 Aranda Crescent, tel. 501/628-6807, www.cayetano. de, 9am-5pm Mon.-Fri.) is a must-see. The master painter, musician, artist, and ambassador of the Garífuna culture keeps his oil canvas collection here, along with wife and fellow artist Ingrid Cayetano's unique textile art.

Garinagu Craft & Arts Gallery

© LEBAWIT GIRMA

There's also a museum section to the gallery (US$2.50 entrance fee), as well as CDs, drums, and souvenirs.

Tucked along a side street just up from Riverside Café, you'll find a nice assortment of made-in-Stann Creek drums, turtle shells, paintings, carvings, and more at the **Garinagu Crafts & Art Gallery** (46 Oak St., tel. 501/522-2596, grigaservices@yahoo.com, 9am-6pm Mon.-Fri.). Don't miss peeking into the adjoining museum, a room displaying traditional Garífuna tools and instruments. You can get an interpretive tour from passionate owner Francis Swaso, who patiently built and collected items for this gallery for more than a decade.

ACCOMMODATIONS
Under US$25

Dangriga's main drag has a handful of low-budget options, including the **Riverside Hotel** (north end of the bridge on Commerce St., tel. 501/660-1041, US$15 pp). Pick one of the basic front guest rooms for a chance of a breeze; all have shared baths, wood floors, a thin sheet, and fans. A better budget bet is ◖**D's Hostel** (tel. 501/502-3324, valsbelize@yahoo.com, www.valsbackpackerhostel.com, US$12.50 pp), across from a pleasant park overlooking the ocean. Val is a cheerful and friendly host who loves meeting her guests from around the world and putting them up in one of her cement bunkrooms; each bed has a fan and a massive locker to stash your gear (even a suitcase). The communal lounge area has a chess table, a book exchange, and a movie library. Amenities include wireless Internet, bikes for rent (US$5 per day), and laundry service. Val can arrange a fishing trip, transfer to Tobacco Caye, a night wildlife tour, or language and cultural exchange opportunities.

US$25-50

◖**Pal's Guest House** (868 Magoon St., tel. 501/522-2095 or cell 501/660-1282, palbz@btl.net, US$43, US$60 with a/c), around the corner from the bus station, has upgraded its 16 clean, modest cement guest rooms at the corner of North Havana Road and Magoon Street.

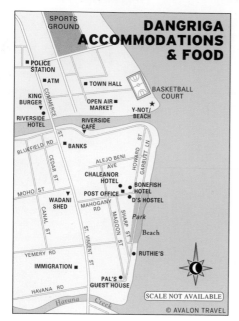

DANGRIGA ACCOMMODATIONS & FOOD

SCALE NOT AVAILABLE

© AVALON TRAVEL

Guest rooms all have private baths, cable TV, optional air-conditioning. Seaside guest rooms are better, with linoleum floors, ceiling fans, hot and cold private showers, TVs, and balconies at the ocean's edge; louvered windows on both ends of the rooms create good cross-ventilation. Wireless Internet is available for extra cost. In the high season, the Raati Grill has breakfast, lunch, and dinner options for guests.

At the towering **Chaleanor Hotel** (35 Magoon St., tel. 501/522-2587, chaleanor@ btl.net, US$23-75), friendly owners Chad and Eleanor offer a homey atmosphere in a residential neighborhood. Economy guest rooms (US$21.50) are equipped with a bed and a fan; the restroom and shower are shared. The well-used standard rooms have private baths with hot water, TVs, and fans (air-conditioning is optional at extra cost). Laundry service is available. There's a gift counter in the lobby, and you can help yourself to coffee and bananas all day long. Numerous tour operators book their guests in the Chaleanor, sometimes arranging a drumming or dance session on the roof.

If you'd rather hear the waves lapping below your window, try one of the four stilted wooden cabanas at **Ruthie's** (tel. 501/502-3184, ruthies@btl.net, US$28), an excellent value if you snag one of the seafront cabins. It's a 10-minute walk from the bus station; follow the sign from Magoon Street.

US$50-100

The **Bonefish Hotel** (15 Mahogany St., tel. 501/522-2243, www.bluemarlinlodge.com, US$95) is near the water with eight guest rooms, offering well-used private baths, airconditioning, Wi-Fi, complimentary coffee, and a second-floor lobby and bar. It caters to active travelers who want to fish and dive—most guests continue on to **Blue Marlin Lodge** on South Water Caye, which is allied with the Bonefish. Guest rooms are clean and carpeted, with private hot and cold water baths, cable TV, wireless Internet, and air-conditioning.

Jungle Huts Resort (4 Ecumenical Dr., tel. 501/522-0185, junglehutsresort@gmail. com, US$60-90) offers 13 guest rooms and three cabanas at its riverside location. All guest rooms have private baths, hot and cold water, cable TV, fans or air-conditioning, Internet access. Screened porches allow you to listen to the frogs in the evening without mosquitoes. The on-site Garden of Eatin' Restaurant serves breakfast, lunch, and dinner to guests (when it's open, that is).

Over US$100

Griga's high end is found at the north end of town at the end of Ecumenical Drive, right next to the airstrip: **❰ Pelican Beach Resort** (tel. 501/522-2044, www.pelicanbeachbelize. com, from US$135 plus taxes, includes breakfast) rests comfortably on the Caribbean. Its 17 guest rooms are open and well lit with wood and tile floors, bathtubs, and porches facing the ocean, with gorgeous views of the beach and dock. Various packages are available that include meal plans, excursions, and time spent at the Pelican's stunning sister resort on South Water Caye (easily the most beautiful caye in

© LEBAWIT GIRMA

Ruthie's budget beachfront cabanas

Belize, in this island-lover's opinion). Pelican is a full-service resort with many amenities and plenty of history behind its owners.

FOOD

Most of Dangriga's few eateries are open only during mealtimes, so expect some closed doors in the middle of the afternoon and on Sunday, when only the Chinese restaurants are open. Your best value is probably **King Burger** (tel. 501/522-2476, 7am-3pm and 6pm-10pm Mon.-Sat.), on the left as you cross the North Stann Creek bridge from the south. It offers excellent breakfast, fresh juices, sandwiches, shakes, and simple comfort dinners.

Another standby is the **(Riverside Café** (tel. 501/669-1473, 6:30am-9pm daily). It's popular with travelers (boats to the cayes leave from right outside) and is a gathering spot for local fishers. Grab a table or belly up to the bar and order a Guinness with your eggs and beans to fit in with the locals; it's US$4.50 for stew chicken, US$6 and up for fish and shrimp. For something different, try the cassava fries.

Dinner is also available with plenty of seafood options (US$9-13).

If you want cheaper food, walk back to the main drag and grab a fistful of street tacos for a few coins. There's also **Edith's** by the North Stann Creek bridge, selling burritos, *panades,* fry chicken, and more fast food under a Coca-Cola-branded shack. Street barbecues are another common sight, offering a plate of grilled chicken with flour tortillas, baked beans, and coleslaw for about US$2.50. There are a few other local shacks with solid dishes: try **Letty's Kitchen** (62 Commerce Dr., tel. 501/665-7412, 9am-5pm Mon.-Sat., US$3.50-4) serving Creole options, including your good ol' plate of chicken stew as well as fish. For delicious fire hearth-cooked meals, be sure to check out the yellow and black painted shack **Tugucina Nuguchu** (Ecumenical Dr., close to Waruguma Shed, tel. 501/664-2017 or 501/661-2472, 11am-9pm Mon.-Sat., US$3-12), offering Creole and Garífuna specialties—rice and beans, pigtail, boil up and fish stew in a delicious tomato sauce, conch fritters, and even

SOUTHERN COAST

salbutes, garnaches, and other Central American goodies. Be sure and ask owner Elizabeth about her okra punch (it's an aphrodisiac!).

A local favorite, **Sean's Barmouth Grill** (6pm-midnight Tues.-Sat.) is a modest *palapa* along the river with good vibes. They serve excellent home-cooked fajitas and burgers and, of course, cold beer and plenty of rum.

For Chinese, the best are **Starlight** (8am-11pm daily, closed in the afternoon, US$3-10), on the north end of Commerce Street, and **Sunlight** (8am-11pm, US$3-10), with good food and poor service on the south end of Commerce Street. There is "fry chicken to take" at any number of Chinese shops.

Dangriga's only proper restaurant is found at the **Pelican Beach Resort** (tel. 501/522-2044, www.pelicanbeachbelize.com, 7am-10pm daily, US$5-15) on the north end of town, where delicious food is prepared by Creole cooks and served in the dining room or in an open beachside eating area. There are occasional Garifuna dish specials offered, particularly on Sunday. Happy hour (5pm-9pm Thurs.-Fri.) is very popular, especially on the 15th and 30th of each month because they're paydays.

You can't miss the **Café Casita De Amor** ("Little House of Love," Mile 16½, Hummingbird Hwy., tel. 501/660-2879, 7:30am-5pm Tues.-Sun., US$4) on the Hummingbird Highway. This heart-shaped eatery serves both German and local dishes for breakfast and lunch—everything from milk shakes, coffee, and smoothies to burgers and sandwiches. Campers are welcome to pitch a tent, and the Billy Barquedier waterfall is just down the road.

Groceries

Pick your own liquor or wine from the impressive imported selection at **Family City** (Ecumenical Dr., 8am-9pm daily); the large supermarket also has a well-stocked perfume and beauty-products counter. Another well-stocked store is **Grigalizean Shopping Center** (Stann Creek Valley Rd., tel. 501/522-3668) on the highway—look for the misspelled "Gregalizean" sign.

INFORMATION AND SERVICES

Belize Bank (8am-3pm Mon.-Thurs., 8am-4:30pm Fri.) and **Scotiabank** (8am-2:30pm Mon.-Thurs., 8am-2:30pm Fri., 9am-11:30am every other Sat.) are on St. Vincent Street near the bridge; both have ATMs.

Southern Regional Hospital (tel. 501/522-3834) is just out of town and serves the entire population of Stann Creek District.

Mail your postcards at the **post office** (Mahogany Rd., across from D's Hostel, tel. 501/522-2035, 8am-11am and 1pm-5pm Mon.-Thurs., reduced hours Fri.).

Val's Laundry and Internet (tel. 501/502-3324, 7:30am-7pm Mon.-Sat., morning Sun., US$1 per pound) is on Sharp Street near the post office. Fast and friendly satellite Internet is available (US$2.50 per hour), as well as FedEx service, local information, and organic fresh-squeezed juices. You can also get online at the air-conditioned **DNK Internet Café** (15 St. Vincent St., across from Scotiabank, tel. 501/522-0383 or U.S. tel. 646/522-7939, dnkInternetcafe@gmail.com, US$2.50 per hour).

GETTING THERE AND AROUND

Dangriga is on the coast, only 36 miles south of Belize City as the crow (or local airline) flies. However, the land trip is much longer, roughly 75 miles along the Manatee Road or 100 miles via the Hummingbird Highway.

By Air

Maya Island Air (tel. 501/223-1140, U.S. tel. 800/225-6732, mayair@btl.net, www.mayaislandair.com) and **Tropic Air** (tel. 501/226-2012, U.S. tel. 800/422-3435, reservations@tropicair.com, www.tropicair.com) have a number of daily 20-minute flights between Belize City and Dangriga. It's also possible to fly from Dangriga to Placencia and Punta Gorda.

By Boat

You can arrange boat service from Belize City, but there is no scheduled service; they tried

A TASTE OF GARÍFUNA

© LEBAWIT GIRMA

a plate of *hudut*

Dangriga is so authentic that you'll be hard-pressed to find public Garífuna eateries–most residents prepare and eat their traditional dishes at home. If you're lucky, you might be invited to break bread at a Grigan home. Otherwise, you can sample some of these dishes at **Tugucina Nuguchu** ("my mother's kitchen," Ecumenical Dr., close to Waruguma Shed, tel. 501/664-2017 or 501/661-2472, 11am-9pm Mon.-Sat., US$3-12), a small shack serving *darasa* on Wednesday, *hudut* on Saturday. They are also able to prepare other dishes with a couple of days of advance notice (most take at least a day to gather ingredients and cook). The following are the specialties to sample when in the land of the Garinagu. All have cassava, fish, banana, and coconut as common ingredients.

· **Cassava:** You're likely to find a soothing bowl of cassava porridge in Dangriga. On Settlement Day morning, it's common to see folks warming up with a few spoonfuls of this cassava flour and coconut milk mixture while waiting on the reenactment canoes to come in. Cassava bread has the consistency of a crispy cracker or flat bread and is made in Dangriga at the only cassava-producing farm in the country, then sold in other districts. It's the Garífuna staple, a snack that

symbolizes the ancestors' survival on long boat journeys in search of freedom and preservation.

· **Darasa:** These banana tamales are a Garífuna snack, with the green banana steamed in coconut milk and wrapped in green banana leaves.

· **Hudut:** Pronounced "hoodoot," this is fish–usually snapper–simmered in a coconut milk sauce, then served with a mound of mashed plantain all in one bowl. Grab some of the mashed plantain with your fingers, pinch a bit of fish as well, dip it in the coconut sauce, and savor away. It takes almost three hours to prepare this dish from scratch, and it's the most labor-intensive of all Garífuna dishes, so when you find it, enjoy every bite.

· **Serre:** A favorite of mine, *serre* is fish (often snapper) stewed in a broth of green banana and coconut milk and spiced with garlic, black pepper, and thyme. Make sure there's a hammock nearby.

· **Tahara:** I first tasted this in Hopkins at Tina's Kitchen, where I learned that there is such a thing as a Garífuna breakfast. Chunks of mashed green bananas are wrapped inside heated banana leaves, left in the oven, and eventually unwrapped. The final crunchy roasted pieces are served with fried fish, sprinkled with a tomato and onion sauce.

SOUTHERN COAST

running a regularly scheduled shuttle, but it didn't make money. Ask around the docks by the gas station, at your hotel, or at the Belize Tourism Board. Expect to pay a fair amount for this trip (probably US$100 each way). Service to and from local cayes or other coastal villages is also dependent on how many people want to go. Only two passengers are required to make the trip to Tobacco Caye (US$35 pp); ask around the Riverside Café or the Tackle Stop. You can also check with Pelican Beach Resort as to whether you can catch a ride with them (for an additional fee) when they head to South Water Caye.

By Bus

Bus service between Belize City and Dangriga takes close to three hours, including a stop in Belmopan, and costs US$6 each way; buses run between 5:15am and 6:15pm daily. There are a few express buses during the day, but the schedule is changing all the time, so be sure to check at the station.

James Bus Line (tel. 501/702-2049) operates several daily southbound buses to Punta Gorda (from 7:30am until the day's only express at 5:30pm), a three-hour trip. Buses to Punta Gorda stop in Mango Creek; from there you can make a connection to Placencia on the water taxi. As of press time, there are four buses that go directly to Placencia (2.5 hours), thanks to **Ritchie's Bus Service** (tel. 501/634-8479): 11am daily, 2pm Mon.-Sat., 4:30pm daily, and

6pm daily. These buses used to stop in Hopkins and Sittee River, but that schedule is in question, so ask around the station. Buses leave from Dangriga to Hopkins at 10am daily; the first pickup is by the riverside, next to Ricky's Restaurant, where the bus will be parked starting at 9am.

By Car

From Belize City, take the Western Highway to either the Coastal (Manatee) Road or Hummingbird Highway, which you follow till it ends. Taking the Coastal Road may shave 20 minutes off the Hummingbird Highway route—but the rutted, red-dirt surface may also destroy your suspension and jar your fillings loose. The unpaved Coastal Road is flat and relatively straight and is occasionally graded into a passable highway, but you'd better have a sturdy ride. Be prepared for lots of dust in the dry season and boggy mud after a rain. Numerous tiny bridges with no railings cross creeks flowing out of the west, and the landscape of pine savanna and forested limestone bluffs has nary a sign of human beings (except for the crappy road, of course). About halfway to the junction with the Hummingbird Highway, you'll find a pleasant place to stop and take a dip at Soldier Creek; just look for the biggest bridge of your trip and pull over. Watch out for snakes in the bush, and once you reach your destination, try not to spend those hard-earned extra 20 minutes all in one place.

Islands near Dangriga

◖ SOUTH WATER CAYE MARINE RESERVE

Belize's largest protected marine area, included in the sweeping World Heritage Site designation of the Belize Barrier Reef System, the **South Water Caye Marine Reserve** (tel. 501/661-9568, www.swcmr.org, park fee US$5, US$15 per week) covers 117,878 acres and is 15 miles southeast of Dangriga's coast. Few will disagree that this marine zone

includes some of the healthiest and most abundant marine and coral life along the reef, hence some of the best snorkeling and diving. The reserve also consists of littoral forests, mangroves, and beds of sea grass. With depths going only to 20 feet, the area is an ideal spot for beginning snorkelers and divers, particularly right off the beach at Pelican Resort on South Water Caye, where the reef is within a swim's reach. The shallow waters off Carrie

Bow Caye, across South Water Caye, are another good option for beginners.

TOBACCO CAYE

If your tropical island dream includes sharing said island with a few dozen fellow travelers, snorkelers, divers, rum drinkers, and hammock sitters from around the world, then **Tobacco Caye** is your place. This tiny island, located within South Water Caye Marine Reserve, has long been a popular backpacker and Belizean tourism destination, especially for divers. Tobacco Caye is just north of Tobacco Cut (a "cut" is a break in the reef through which boats can navigate).

Accessed as part of a resort package, boats will whisk you each day to snorkeling and fishing trips or to Man-o-War Caye and Tobacco Range to look for manatees. Glover's Reef, Blue Hole, and Turneffe trips are available (US$150-200); whale shark tours are usually running March-July.

Tobacco Caye offers plenty of budget cabana options.

Accommodations

Tobacco Caye's "resorts" offer similar packages but for a range of budgets. All accommodations are Belizean-run family affairs, each a bit different according to the owner's vision, and are comfortably crowded together on the five acres of sand. Apart from some basic differences in room quality, the more you pay, the better the food you'll be eating—a pretty important thing when checking into a guest room that also locks you into a meal plan. Some of the accommodations prices are per person per night and include three meals; always ask to be sure.

Blue Dolphin Lodge (formerly Gaviota Coral Reef Resort, tel. 501/542-2032 or cell 501/665-9837, US$40 pp private bath, US$35 pp shared bath, meals included) welcomes you to one of their four basic guest rooms or five cabanas; there are three boats that can be used for visiting the reef and cayes. There is also a snack shop and a beach volleyball court.

Paradise Lodge (tel. 501/532-2101 or 501/621-1953) occupies the northern tip of the island with guest rooms (US$12.50 pp) and six clean, basic cabins with porches built right over the sea (US$40 pp, includes three meals) that will make you want to stay forever. **Lana's on the Reef** (tel. 501/532-2424, US$40, includes 3 meals) has four basic, clean guest rooms with private baths and screened windows.

Stepping things up a notch, find **Reef's End Lodge** (tel. 501/670-3919, www.reefsend-lodge.com) on the southern shore; guest rooms (US$40, meals not included) and cabanas (US$50) have fans and hot and cold water with private baths. The newest cabana (US$100) is clean, spacious, and has air-conditioning; take in the romantic sunset view from your seaside veranda. There is a bar and restaurant built over the water, and prepaid meal plans are available. Reef's End has the caye's only dive shop, which can be utilized by anyone on the island; this is an excellent location to begin a shore dive or snorkeling adventure. Dive master Eric can take you to his favorite local dive sites; two-tank dives range US$100-150.

Tobacco Caye Lodge (tel. 501/532-2033 or

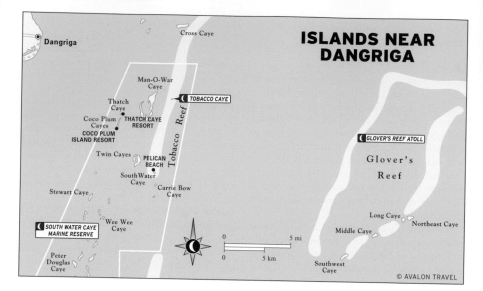

ISLANDS NEAR DANGRIGA

Dangriga

Cross Caye

Man-O-War Caye

Thatch Caye

TOBACCO CAYE

Coco Plum Cayes   THATCH CAYE RESORT

COCO PLUM ISLAND RESORT

Tobacco Reef

GLOVER'S REEF ATOLL

Glover's Reef

Twin Cayes   PELICAN BEACH

SouthWater Caye

Carrie Bow Caye

Stewart Caye

Long Caye   Northeast Caye

Middle Caye

Wee Wee Caye

SOUTH WATER CAYE MARINE RESERVE

Peter Douglas Caye

Southwest Caye

0   5 mi

0   5 km

© AVALON TRAVEL

501/223-6247, www.tclodgebelize.com, US$55 pp, includes 3 meals) occupies a middle strip of the island and offers six guest rooms in four colorful cabins facing the reef. You are summoned to meals by a dinner bell. There's a small on-site bar and snack shop as well as hammocks on the beach. A few steps away, the **Tobacco Marine Station** (tel. 501/620-9116, www.tcmsbelize.org) hosts visiting scientists, and you can ask to check out their reference materials on the area's habitats and species, use the Internet (US$5 per hour), rent snorkel gear (US$7.50 per day), or head out on a night snorkel (US$10 pp) with these experts.

Getting There

Water taxis to Tobacco Caye leave when the captain says there are enough passengers—usually around mid-afternoon from the Riverside Café or the Tackle Stop farther upstream. **Captain Buck** (tel. 501/669-0869) is one option, or try Fermin, a.k.a. **Compa** (tel. 501/666-8699). The trip costs US$15 one-way or US$35 round-trip, with a return trip usually made mid-morning. **Captain Doggie** (tel. 501/627-7443) is another charter option who will take 1-3 people for US$70; groups of 4-12

can expect to pay US$17.50 pp. Compa has the newest, largest, and most comfortable boats. All the captains usually hang out by Riverside Café, either outside or inside.

By calling ahead to Blue Dolphin, Reef's End Lodge, or Tobacco Caye Lodge, you can arrange a pickup any time from Dangriga and ensure a boat will still be there if you are arriving after midday. Be advised that if you need a boat after 3pm, you'll pay a lot more—seas get rough, and a private charter is necessary. Plan accordingly.

MAN-O-WAR CAYE

Man-o-War Caye (Bird Isle) is a raucously chirping bird-choked clump of protected mangroves that is a crucial nesting site for frigates and brown boobies—one of only 10 in the Caribbean—amid beautiful turquoise waters. It's quite a sight to be surrounded by the birds, and it makes for great photographs; ask for a quick boat stop as you travel along the south cayes.

Coco Plum Caye

Coco Plum Island Resort (U.S. tel. 800/763-7360, www.cocoplumcay.com, 4 nights

© LEBAWIT GIRMA

frigates hovering over the protected bird sanctuary of Man-o-War Caye

US$1,120-2,800) boasts 10 bright cabins on a 16-acre private island that is associated with the Belizean Dreams resort in Sittee; they specialize in exclusive romantic packages.

THATCH CAYE

Thatch Caye Resort (U.S. tel. 800/435-3145, tel. 501/532-2414, www.thatchcayebelize.com, 3-night cabana package US$979-1,053) is an island complex nine miles from Dangriga, within the South Water Marine Reserve. The "handmade eco-resort" consists of four casitas and seven cabanas (with en suite baths, king beds, ceiling fans, and plenty of lounging room), which were constructed without the use of heavy equipment. Instead, they're run by solar and wind power. There's also a family villa and a soaring thatched-roof dining *palapa*. Various all-inclusive snorkeling packages require a three-night minimum stay; that means all meals, three guided snorkeling trips, unlimited use of sea kayaks, and round-trip water transfer from Dangriga. **Camping** (US$15 pp) is allowed on the island; campers

must have their own equipment and are welcome to join other guests in the dining room for meals.

SOUTH WATER CAYE

South Water Caye is a privately owned postcard-perfect island 14 miles off the shore of Dangriga and 35 miles southeast of Belize City. The reef crests just a stone's throw offshore, sitting atop a 1,000-foot coral wall awash in wildlife. The island stretches 0.75 miles from north to south and 0.25 miles at its widest point. This southern caye is what dream getaways are made of—it's easily the most beautiful caye in southern Belize.

Accommodations and Food

Once a convent for the Sisters of Mercy, the ◖**Pelican Beach Resort** (tel. 501/522-2044, www.pelicanbeachbelize.com, US$258-292, includes three meals) is what every dream island resort should look like: charming yet unpretentious. It occupies the entire southern end of the island—the best end, by far—with five second-story guest rooms, three duplex cottages, and two single-unit casitas, all decently space from one another, and all of which are surrounded by dozens of coconut trees and fine, powdery white sand. The beach offers some of Belize's best and rare walk-in snorkeling sites—that's if you manage to get yourself out of the dozens of hammocks on the beach. Power is from the sun, and private composting toilets help protect the fragile island ecology.

The owners also have a strip of island toward the north end that is home to **Pelican's University,** which hosts student research groups throughout the year; there are plans to refurbish it, so inquire ahead. Plenty of unique day trips are available with Pelican's guides or with one of several area dive shops, and there are kayaks and snorkel gear available; they charge US$62 pp for the boat transfer to the island.

Lesley Cottages is the common name for **International Zoological Expeditions** (IZE, tel. 501/532-2404, U.S. tel. 508/655-1461, www.ize2belize.com, US$175 pp). Named for an old local fisherman, Dan Lesley, the compound here specializes primarily in student groups and "educational tourism" but also has some nice private cabins in addition to their own dive shop, dormitory, and classroom. Guest rooms are nestled to the back on the shoreline; three meals and transportation are included. It's a nice spot for couples (but check to see if you'll be sharing with student groups). There's an on-site bar and pool table, as well as complimentary glass-bottom kayaks, paddle boats, and other water sports equipment.

Blue Marlin Lodge (tel. 501/532-2104, U.S. tel. 800/798-1558, www.bluemarlinlodge.com, US$235), sister resort of the Bonefish Hotel in Dangriga, is on the northern tip of the island, offering a variety of 17 guest rooms, air-conditioned "igloos," and five cabanas just steps away from the sea. There's not much beach, and the sand is the hard, flat variety. The bar/dining room over the sea serves meals (3 meals roughly US$90 per day), snacks (included), and

drinks. The Blue Marlin specializes in fishing trips and has a full dive shop, cable TV, and Internet access. Many packages are available with a three-night minimum stay. It's an easy and short walk along a coastal foot trail to the other parts of the island.

Getting There

South Water Caye is a 40-minute boat ride from Dangriga in good weather. You can either arrange for a pickup from Pelican Beach Resort, since it's the sister resort (US$68 pp, minimum 4 people for nonguests, but pricing varies according to space availability) or inquire with your resort on the island ahead of time.

CARRIE BOW CAYE

Just a few minutes' ride from South Water Caye, this dot of sand and palms, close to both the reef and mangrove systems and named after the original owner's spouse, Carrie Bowman, is home to the **Smithsonian Museum of Natural History's Caribbean Coral Reef Ecosystems Program** (http://ccre.si.edu), which has produced more than 800 published papers since 1972. The caye houses up to six international scientists at a time.

The public is welcome to stop by, but it's best to call ahead or arrange a visit through your resort host. Be sure to stop by the library to read and flip through the guestbook, filled with fascinating observations and drawings from visitors over the years, most of whom are scientists and marine illustrators. On your way back, you can snorkel off the caye in very shallow waters.

WEE WEE CAYE

Wee Wee Caye, affiliated with the Possum Point Biological Station on the mainland near Sittee River, hosts a tropical field station, a marine lab, and an educational center, with a neat system of raised catwalks through the mangroves (it's beautiful, but there are lots of bugs). The caye also hosts a population of boa constrictors; contact **Paul and Mary Shave** (tel. 501/523-7021, www.marineecology.com) about bringing your students here.

◀ GLOVER'S REEF ATOLL

The southernmost of Belize's three atolls, **Glover's** (named for a pirate, of course—John Glover) is an 80-square-mile, nearly continuous ring of brilliant coral, flanked on its southeastern curve by five tiny islands. A UNESCO World Heritage Site along with the Belize Barrier Reef, the atoll is 18 miles long and 6 miles across at its widest point; to the east the ocean bottom drops sharply and keeps on dropping, eventually to depths of 15,000 feet at the western end of the Caiman Trench, one of the deepest in the world.

The southern section of the atoll around the cayes serves as a protected marine reserve, with the largest no-take zone in Belize; however, someone should remind the government Fishery Department rangers on Middle Caye of this fact, as they reportedly skip patrols and ignore illegal fishing activity (although they're very efficient at collecting tourist fees).

Diving and Snorkeling

Divers and snorkelers will find a fabulous wall surrounding the Glover's Reef Atoll, plus more than 700 shallow coral patches within the rainbow-colored lagoon. There are wreck dives and an abundance of marinelife, especially turtles, manta rays, and all types of sharks, including reefs, hammerheads, and whale sharks. The names of the dive sites speak for themselves: **Shark Point, Grouper Flats, Emerald Forest Reef, Octopus Alley, Manta Reef, Dolphin Dance,** and **Turtle Tavern.** Snorkeling is no less impressive, with amazing visibility and abundant marinelife—spotted stingrays; barracuda; queen, blue, and French angelfish; trunkfish; hogfish; butterfly fish; blue tangs; groupers; sergeant majors; and blue-headed wrasses, among a host of other species.

Anglers will have a chance at bonefish and permits as well as the big trophy species, including sailfish, marlins, wahoos, snappers, and groupers. There is also fantastic paddling, sailing, stand-up paddleboarding, and anything

© LEBAWIT GIRMA

Island Expeditions' adventure camp site is on Glovers' Reef Atoll.

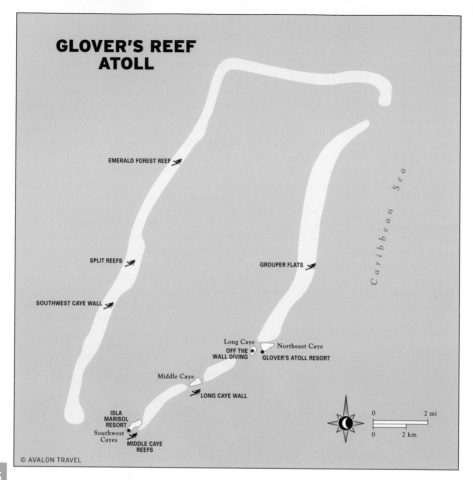

GLOVER'S REEF ATOLL

EMERALD FOREST REEF

SPLIT REEFS

SOUTHWEST CAYE WALL

GROUPER FLATS

Caribbean Sea

Long Caye
OFF THE
WALL DIVING
Northeast Caye
GLOVER'S ATOLL RESORT

Middle Caye

LONG CAYE WALL

ISLA
MARISOL
RESORT
Southwest
Cayes
MIDDLE CAYE
REEFS

0   2 mi
0   2 km

© AVALON TRAVEL

else you can dream up. Glover's is a special place indeed.

Accommodations
SOUTHWEST CAYE

The first bit of land you'll reach from the mainland is owned by the Usher clan, which runs the high-end full-service **Isla Marisol Resort** (tel. 501/520-2056, toll-free tel. 855/350-1569, www.islamarisolresort.com, 3-night all-inclusive scuba package US$1,290) for serious divers and sportfishers. There are comfortable, equipped cabanas with air-conditioning and

porches, soon to be outfitted with composting toilets; or stay in one of two reef houses, with spectacular deck views of the reef and ideal for either families or honeymooners. Many all-inclusive packages are available for a three-night minimum. There's a lovely dockside bar that is the center of nighttime activity, where guests get merry, fish, or play board games.

Island Expeditions (U.S. tel. 800/667-1630, www.islandexpeditions.com, US$60-275 pp) is an adventure-travel outfitter with a tent camp on the north tip of Southwest Caye; it's a well-run, professional operation with daily water-sports activities of all kinds—for the novice and expert alike—and a great option if you like meeting other travelers and bonding with them on a group trip. The sturdy tents have single or double beds and kerosene lamps, and they are well sheltered from the elements. This eco-friendly camp provides shared composting toilets, cold-water showers (with outdoor warm-water hoses when the weather cooperates), and evening generator use until 9:30pm. The communal meals are excellent, and guests are welcome to head over to the bar at Isla Marisol at night.

MIDDLE CAYE

There are no accommodations on Middle Caye, unless you're a Belize Fisheries Department ranger, a marine biologist with the Wildlife Conservation Society, or a PhD student with special permission. If staying on one of the surrounding cayes, ask your host about arranging a trip to see what's going on here.

LONG CAYE

The 13 acres of Long Caye form the gorgeous backdrop to the thatched-roof base camp of **Slickrock Adventures** (U.S. tel. 800/390-5715, www.slickrock.com, 5-night package US$1,450 pp); check out the website for a range of active Belizean adventures. Slickrock has a veritable armada of kayaks, windsurfing boards, and other water toys; conditions and equipment will cover beginners and experts alike. Guests stay in very private rustic beach cabins overlooking the reef and equipped with kerosene lamps, foam-pad mattresses, and great views. Outhouse toilets are of the plein air variety, surrounded by palm leaf "walls"—offering possibly the best views from a toilet in the entire country. Book a trip to the island, or link the trip with wild inland adventures as well (call for a catalog).

Off the Wall Dive Center (tel. 501/532-2929, www.offthewallbelize.com, US$1,395 per week all-inclusive) is a PADI 5-Star Resort. Stay on Long Caye in a rustic oceanfront cabana with access to a top-notch dive shop, gift shop, and yoga deck. The maximum capacity is 10 guests. Package prices include seven days' lodging, boat transportation, meals, diving, snorkeling, fishing, kayaking, and stand-up paddleboarding. Whale shark trips and PADI scuba certification courses are popular; yachties are welcome to come ashore and browse the gift shop.

NORTHEAST CAYE

This island is privately owned and run as **Glover's Atoll Resort and Island Lodge** (tel. 501/520-5016 or 501/614-7177, www.glovers.com.bz), a primitive island camp run by the Lomont family, which also runs Glover's Guest House in Sittee River. Their 68-foot catamaran takes you from Sittee River to Glover's remotest caye, where you can camp or shack up for the cheapest weekly rates on the atoll: US$99 per week of camping, US$149 to stay in the dorm, or US$249-299 for rustic thatched cabins perched over the water. Prices include transportation, a week of primitive lodging, use of the kitchen, and nothing else—not even water. Show up at the guesthouse in Sittee River at 7am Saturday and be prepared for the week. It's best to bring your own food, drinking water, and a few camping basics, or pay at least US$42 per day to be provided these amenities. A dive shop and kayak rentals are also available, and the snorkeling is out of this world.

Hopkins and Vicinity

Hopkins was built in 1942 after a hurricane washed away Newtown, just up the coast; it is a loose coastal fishing village that has steered more and more toward tourism in the past decade. More beachfront condominium developments and luxury private villas are going up on either end of the village's beautiful long stretch of beach, one of the nicest in Belize, but rest assured that nearly everything in between remains chill, spread out, and reasonably priced. There's really no place in Belize like Hopkins. Its 1,000 or so inhabitants are mostly Garífuna, making this one of the more exciting places to be to learn about the Garinagu. Traditional village life is ever-present here, and residents are holding on to it to make sure it isn't likely to disappear anytime soon. This is where you can experience culture on every corner simply by walking around or sitting on an outdoor patio. It's a much smaller area than Dangriga and is less intimidating for newcomers; those with an open mind and a thirst for cultural immersion, coupled with a love for beaches and the outdoors, will leave happy.

With the advent of new resorts and timeshare condos in Sittee, the continual trickle of backpackers that still show up in Hopkins village, and visitors seeking a mix of beach and culture, there are a few decent makeshift art galleries, craft shops, and cafés along the main drag. There's also drumming once or twice a week, and karaoke nights are big at one or two local bars. Other than that, the sights are really just those that make up everyday village life, rarely seen elsewhere in Belize, along with, of course, the beach. On a weeknight, this means drinking beer and bitters, playing drums and dominoes, and laughing away another hot, breezy day from a hammock. Of course, things pick up considerably on festival days, Christmas, and Easter Week; expect accommodations to be in high demand during these times.

SIGHTS

The road that carries you into Hopkins from Dangriga splits the village into **Northside** (or "Baila" as the locals call it—pronounced "BAY-la") and **Southside** (or "False Sittee"). Northside is a bit denser with local flavor, while Southside hosts most of the shops, restaurants, and accommodations.

◖ Lebeha Drumming Center

You can't leave Hopkins without a Garífuna drumming lesson. Drums are a key part of the Garífuna culture, a symbolic connection to their African ancestors and a sound that is considered a metaphor for the collective voice that colonial masters were unable to silence. At the award-winning **Lebeha Drumming Center** (tel. 501/665-9305, www.lebeha.com), way up on Northside (*lebeha* means "the end" in Garífuna), Garífuna drum master Jabbar Lambey offers both private (US$15 per hour) and group lessons (2 hours US$12.50 pp). He will ensure that you learn a couple of beats and have a grand time. You might even learn how to *punta* dance. Call or stop by to schedule a lesson. Once you're there, ask him about the Annual Battle of the Drums in Punta Gorda.

Serpon Sugar Mill

If you're a history buff, head to Belize's first protected historical reserve. Sitting on 114 acres of rainforest, the **Serpon Sugar Mill** (www.nichbelize.org, 8am-5pm) houses remnants of Belize's colonial history—a semi-mechanized sugar mill's machinery and tools, including a boiler, a locomotive, a steam engine, and more. Once considered a technological breakthrough, seeing these old life-size machines today is nothing short of surreal. The Serpon Sugar Mill was established in 1865 and operated until the early 20th century, when it was finally abandoned after sugar production became more profitable in the north of Belize. At

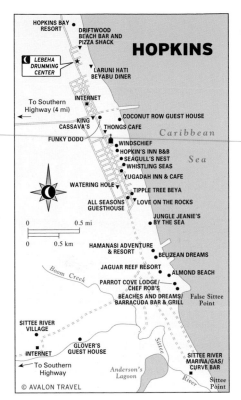

To Southern Highway (4 mi)

HOPKINS BAY RESORT
DRIFTWOOD BEACH BAR AND PIZZA SHACK
LEBEHA DRUMMING CENTER
LARUNI HATI BEYABU DINER
HOPKINS
INTERNET
KING CASSAVA'S
THONGS CAFE
COCONUT ROW GUEST HOUSE
FUNKY DODO
WINDSCHIEF
HOPKIN'S INN B&B
SEAGULL'S NEST
WHISTLING SEAS
YUGADAH INN & CAFE
WATERING HOLE
TIPPLE TREE BEYA
ALL SEASONS GUESTHOUSE
LOVE ON THE ROCKS
JUNGLE JEANIE'S BY THE SEA
HAMANASI ADVENTURE & RESORT
BELIZEAN DREAMS
JAGUAR REEF RESORT
ALMOND BEACH
PARROT COVE LODGE/ CHEF ROB'S
BEACHES AND DREAMS/ BARRACUDA BAR & GRILL
False Sittee Point
SITTEE RIVER VILLAGE
INTERNET
GLOVER'S GUEST HOUSE
To Southern Highway
Anderson's Lagoon
SITTEE RIVER MARINA/GAS/ CURVE BAR
Sittee Point
Caribbean Sea
Boom Creek
Sittee River
0   0.5 mi
0   0.5 km
© AVALON TRAVEL

its peak, it produced and shipped an estimated 1,700 pounds of sugar per month.

There's a small entrance fee to this National Institute of Culture and History–protected site (US$5) and a museum complete with interesting manufacturing details and a historical timeline. The Mill is located about a mile along the Sittee River Village access road, off the Southern Highway, and can be toured within an hour.

SPORTS AND RECREATION

There's plenty of inland exploration to keep you occupied near Hopkins, which is ideally located close to two of southern Belize's great parks, Cockscomb and Bocawina, offering plenty of hiking, rappelling, birding, and zip-lining.

For Mayflower Bocawina National Park, your best bet is **Bocawina Adventures &**

Eco-Tours (tel. 501/670-2622 or 501/670-8019, U.S. tel. 928/300-1969, www.bocawinaadventures.com, single waterfall US$50 pp, zip-lining and rappelling US$150 pp, lunch included), the only company to offer waterfall rappelling from the park's five stunning chutes, including 500-foot-high Antelope Falls, as well as birding and zooming across the canopy on the longest zip line in Belize.

Charlton Castillo (cell 501/661-8199 or 501/543-7799, charltoncastillo@yahoo.com) can guide you to the Cockscomb or to Mayflower Bocawina National Park. Charlton conducts night tours (6pm-11pm) in Cockscomb in case you want to try your luck with a jaguar encounter (US$60 pp for 2 people), daytime hiking and tubing on the South Stann Creek River (US$60 pp), and waterfall hikes at Bocawina (US$55 pp).

Beaches

Hopkins's beaches, all public, are some of the best in the country—I dare say even better than Placencia Village. Stretching nearly five miles Northside to Southside, they're wide, thick, never crowded, and have calmer waters. In the village you can take one very nice, very long beach walk, and you can lay your towel pretty much anywhere you please, except for chairs at private resorts.

If you're looking to mingle, a great spot to hang out is in the north on the wide stretch by **Driftwood Pizza Shack** (tel. 501/667-4872, 11am-10pm, Thurs.-Tues., US$8-23), where you can use Wi-Fi, eat, and hang out all day. On the south end, there's no shortage of space either, although it tends to be quieter, if that's what you seek. In False Sittee, **Hamanasi Resort** (tel. 501/533-7073, www.hamanasi.com) has a nice pool and beachfront, both of which you can use while having lunch at the restaurant.

Snorkeling and Diving

For diving, make plans with PADI dive shop **Hamanasi Adventure and Resort** (tel. 501/520-7073, U.S. tel. 877/522-3483, www.hamanasi.com, 3-tank dive at Turneffe

© LEBAWIT GIRMA

Award-winning drummers teach at the Lebeha Drumming Center.

US$185, 2-tank dive at Southern Barrier Reef US$115).

For snorkeling trips to the nearby cayes or fly-fishing, **Noel Nuñez** (tel. 501/523-7219, full-day snorkel trip US$175 for 2 people; half-day fishing US$238) is your man, located in his tour shack at the Watering Hole (his wife's restaurant). You can rent snorkel gear and even goggles with an integrated camera and video camera (US$20 per day) from Emma at **Motorbike Rentals** (main road, Hopkins Village, tel. 501/665-6292, www.alternateadventures.com, 8am-5pm daily).

Kayaking and Windsurfing

Most guesthouses in Hopkins rent kayaks and other small craft or provide them for guests to use. Hopkins waters are calmer than the windier Northern Cayes, so kayaking is a safe bet, from the sea to the lagoon at the north end of the village.

Windschief Windsurfing School and Rental (on the beach toward the south, tel. 501/523-7249 or 501/668-6087, www.windschief.com, 1pm-close Fri.-Wed., US$10 per hour, private lessons US$30 per hour, group lessons US$20 pp) has a selection of slightly used windsurfing boards of various sizes for rent and offers lessons for mostly beginner levels, as wind conditions aren't consistently ideal to offer advanced sessions.

Biking

Many guesthouses and hotels either provide complimentary bicycles or rent them at a reasonable rate. It's really the best way to navigate Hopkins's sandy, rocky roads and explore its nooks and crannies. Bike rental shops in the village include **Fred's** (6am-7pm daily, US$2.50 per hour, US$10 per day) just behind Tina's, on the main drag.

Birding

Birding in Hopkins is as easy as walking out your front door. There are over 200 species of birds in the north and south parts of the village alone. You'll see grackles crossing the street, trotting along the beach, or, especially

rappelling Bocawina Falls with Bocawina Adventures & Eco-Tours

© LEBAWIT GIRMA

ENTERTAINMENT AND EVENTS
Nightlife

King Cassava's (tel. 501/608-6188 or 501/503-7305, 7am-midnight daily with a 2-hour afternoon break) is at the intersection where the road from Dangriga meets the sea. Here you'll find a bar, a restaurant, taxi service, a pool hall, and the bus stop (when the buses are running, anyway). Lobster dinners go for US$10, shots of bitters are US$1, and they serve finger-lickin' barbecue. It's a great place to meet the parade of local characters.

The most local bar in town is the lively **Newtown Bar** (Back St.), a cool bamboo structure with sandy floors, drums hanging on the wall, dart boards at the back, and dimly lit Garífuna quotes, but where, to my own dismay, karaoke rules early in the evening Thursday-Saturday, followed by a DJ. The drinks are cheap and the locals do come in droves.

From Friday onward, you may find other music or entertainment around Hopkins. As far as beach bars go, **Driftwood Beach Bar and Pizza Shack** (tel. 501/667-4872 or 501/664-6611, www.driftwoodpizza.com, 11am-10pm Thurs.-Tues., US$8-23) has a nice little operation going, with daily half-price happy hours, Monday movie nights on the beach, plenty of travelers and expats, a few locals, and "jam night" on Tuesday, when anyone is welcome to pick up a guitar and a mic, followed by live, Garífuna drumming by the Lebeha lads for the rest of the night (the crowd picks up close to 9pm, so come earlier if you want to sit inside rather than out by the beachside picnic tables).

A popular choice among expats is **Windschief Bar** (on the beach toward the south, tel. 501/523-7249, www.windschief. com, 1pm-11pm Fri.-Wed., 6pm-11pm Sun., US$4-10), particularly on Friday, when the small beachfront bar gets packed with expats playing darts and table football and nibbling on the excellent small menu of the day.

Festivals and Events

Launched in 2011 and sponsored by the Belize Tourism Industry Association, the **Mango**

in November-December, mass-migrating across the village's trees at sunset. It's an incredible, intense sound I have yet to hear anywhere else. On the north end, beside Hopkins Bay Resort, you'll spot pelicans and dozens of other species at sunrise. Most of the tour companies offer birding tours to the nearby national parks, and while you can ask around for the best choice to fit your budget, first try the area's highly recommended birding expert, **Charlton Castillo** (cell 501/661-8199 or 501/543-7799, charltoncastillo@yahoo.com, US$50 pp). Charlton also goes birding along the nearby Sittee River.

North of the village, **Fresh Water Creek Lagoon** offers plenty of birding; start early to spot beautiful herons and egrets, and navigate along the lagoon's lush mangroves. You can rent a kayak and explore solo, or take along a guide for better wildlife spotting. Keep an eye out for the 35-foot lookout tower, then climb it and take in the views. For the more adventurous, ask about guided night canoeing along Boom Creek, near Sittee River.

SOUTHERN COAST

Festival (May) celebrates all things mango. There are more than 15 varieties of mango in Belize, and villagers—from Garífuna locals to expat residents—offer up all sorts of dishes, including mango ceviche, mango salads, and mango pies.

The last weekend of July celebrates the existence of the Garífuna village of Hopkins with a big annual festival, **Hopkins Day,** held since 2000. The fun begins on Friday evening with cultural shows and food at the village basketball court. There are games, drumming, and dancing on Saturday lasting late into the night. Sunday is for family beach time. Check local listings for a detailed schedule.

As one of the main Garífuna areas in the country, Hopkins celebrates the arrival of the Garinagu in Belize with **Garífuna Settlement Day** (Nov. 19). A reenactment of the day the Garinagu arrived in the 19th century starts in the late morning of November 19 and is smaller in scale than Dangriga's full day of celebrations, but no less intense. There is plenty of drumming, singing, and chanting on the beach. Plan for accommodations well in advance.

SHOPPING

Hopkins has its share of talented wood-carvers and drum makers. While strolling through the village, you'll find several small shops, including **David's Woodcarving** and **Kulcha Gift Shop**, with Garífuna drums made in Hopkins and Dangriga, Marie Sharp hot sauce, and plenty of local carvings. Both are located on the main road in Hopkins Village.

Save time for a bike ride just south of the village to pay a visit to **Sew Much Hemp** (11am-4pm Mon.-Sat.), where Barbara, a dreadlocked Oregonian, can teach you everything you need to know about the plant that can save the world. She sells excellent hemp products as well. If the sandflies are out, this is a great place to pick up some natural repellent.

ACCOMMODATIONS
Under US$25

On the Northside, next to Driftwood Pizza Shack, budget travelers love the **Lebeha**

Drumming Center (tel. 501/665-9305, www. lebeha.com), which has campsites (US$5) and a couple of shared-bath stilted wooden guest rooms (US$25) set within the courtyard area; they are very simple (a ceiling fan, no hot water, a mosquito net, and a teakettle). There is wireless Internet.

Right in the village and hard to miss is the bright, eccentric **Funky Dodo** (tel. 501/667-0558, www.thefunkydodo.com, US$8-19), a classic small backpacker hostel with a 14-bunk bed dormitory and shared baths as well as private three-person guest rooms with outdoor baths. Camping is also available (US$4). There's a sandy courtyard, Wi-Fi, and a thatched-roof bar on-site. **Yugadah Inn** (tel. 501/503-7089, yugadahinn@yahoo.com, US$15) is another budget option, with four guest rooms and a common area.

US$25-50

From the main junction, head south on the road (or along the beach) and you'll find a few decent, affordable clusters of beachside cabins, including **Seagull's Nest** (tel. 501/663-5976, jc-seagull@yahoo.com, US$33-88), with shared-bath doubles and a nice, albeit a bit rustic, common space with a full kitchen, a dining area, and a TV. There's also a two-bedroom stand-alone beachfront casita (a great deal at US$88) on a lovely shaded stretch of beach set between local homes. Guests can also rent bikes.

Continuing south along the beach, you'll come across two rustic, stilted seafront cabanas at **Windschief** (tel. 501/523-7249, www. windschief.com, US$25-40), right next to the Windschief bar and windsurfing school.

Another budget option is **Whistling Seas Vacation Inn** (tel. 501/664-3213, williams_marcello@yahoo.com, US$38), with three small cabana guest rooms with fans and very dated bath facilities—but it's on the beach side.

A notch up yet still casual, ◖ **Tipple Tree Beya** (tel. 501/533-7006, www.tippletree. com) is a longtime favorite. This well-maintained spot right on the beach offers basic guest rooms (from US$45 with private bath), en suite

© LEBAWIT GIRMA

Hopkins' accommodations offer some of the best bang for your buck in Belize.

two-bedrooms (US$75), or a private cabin with a kitchenette (US$55). There is a shared porch with a hammock and beach chairs, and an outdoor cold-water shower if you stay in the budget room (US$30). Half-day or full-day kayak (US$15-20) and bicycle (US$5-9) rentals are available. Ask about inland tours and snorkeling trips.

Lebeha Drumming Center (tel. 501/665-9305, www.hopkinscabanas.com, US$49-80 plus tax) also has three cozy furnished cabanas set directly on a nice stretch of beach with kitchenettes, hot showers, and porches.

US$50-100

The best in the mid-range rates is ☾ **Hopkins Inn Bed & Breakfast** (tel. 501/533-7283, www.hopkinsinn.com, US$69-89), with four fully furnished spacious cabanas with tiled floors, screened windows, fans, hot and cold water, a kitchenette, and a veranda; a continental breakfast of fruits and local pastries is served, and the owners are friendly. It's a deal for what you get, and it's right in the village. You'll also find good value at the **All Seasons Guesthouse** (tel. 501/523-7209, www.allseasonsbelize. com, US$49-75, includes tax and coffee). It's not right on the beach, but it's just a few steps from it, and the guest rooms in the main compound are comfortable and nicely decorated by owner Ingrid, a longtime Hopkins resident. Just next door are two fully furnished and delightful brand-new, stand-alone, two-bedroom apartments (US$98, US$600 per week), making it a more ideal spot than ever for group stays. For beachfront options, ask Ingrid about the cozy two-bedroom apartments (US$140) that she manages, just across the road and next to Tipple Tree Beya.

For those seeking a self-catering option roadside and in the village center, try **Latitude 17°** (tel. 501/651-1322, www.latitude17.com, US$79), offering two furnished apartments across from Thongs Café, each with one bedroom and a bath, a kitchen, a living room, air-conditioning, wireless Internet access, wood floors and a spacious outdoor deck great for people-watching.

A short distance after the pavement of Hopkins village runs out, down the long dirt road, look for the left turn to **Jungle Jeanie's by the Sea** (tel. 501/523-7047, www.junglebythesea.com, US$55-120). This is a nice stretch of beach for guests staying in Jeanie's eight spacious rustic cabanas, three of which are beachfront. The more secluded ones, located along a small network of rainforest trails, have kitchenettes, private baths, hot and cold showers, and verandas with a sea view; the Palmetto cabana, with three beds, is ideal for a family, and the tree house cabana overlooks cocoplum and sea grape trees. Camping (US$15 pp) is available, and in case you either fear or love dogs, there are three dutiful German shepherds on the property. The kitchen serves breakfast and dinner daily (and lunch on request), and there's a screened "jungle *palapa*" for thrice-weekly yoga sessions. Ask to see the beautiful marimba.

Over US$100

A welcome option right in the village is the colorful and immaculate ⟨ **Coconut Row Guest House** (tel. 501/670-3000, www.coconutrowbelize.com, US$100-145)—you can't miss the rainbow-colored beach chairs set on an idyllic stretch amid a lush garden of red hibiscus flowers and plants. There are three beachfront single guest rooms on one side, but the highlight is the two-bedroom apartments, fully furnished with a kitchenette, air-conditioning, and outdoor patios. A cute picnic area on the beach is available to guests, and the water is less than 10 steps away. There's an optional US$6 pp breakfast.

On the northern tip of town, beside the Lagoon, **Hopkins Bay Resort** (tel. 501/523-7320, U.S. tel. 877/467-2297, www.hopkinsbayresort.com, US$300-750) has 19 one- and two-bedroom luxury villas that can be locked off, depending on your needs. No amenities are lacking in the homes, and there are two pools on-site as well as a restaurant, daily housekeeping at the hour of your choosing, and complimentary use of kayaks and bikes. The resort also offers unique cultural tours, including a "cook your catch" day and a Garífuna

immersion experience, among the other usual dive, snorkel, and inland tour options.

Fit for an episode of MTV's *Cribs,* **Villa Verano** (tel. 501/533-7016, U.S. tel. 877/646-2317, www.villaveranobelize.com, US$300-2,750) will have you gasping at every other step past the front door. Past the stunning open-ceiling Mediterranean courtyard are three floors, the second of which is rented as one unit (US$1,950); the remaining parts of the villa can either be locked off into separate units or rented as a whole. Some include rooms with bunk beds (with the plushest bunk mattresses I've seen) for families. Local paintings, wood carvings, granite tiling, French doors with stunning sea views, regally spacious baths with jetted tubs, library rooms fitted with gigantic plasma TVs, 70-foot infinity pool, and top-floor terrace "game room," complete with a pool, lounge seating, and a hot tub overlooking the Mayan Mountains at the back—no luxurious detail has been spared. This is an ideal place for weddings, groups of friends looking for a treat, family retreats, or just a decadent getaway. Don't miss the view of the pool and the beach from the rooftop.

FOOD

There are enough restaurants in Hopkins; most are very low-key small eateries serving either traditional Garífuna dishes or local Creole options. A couple of Western-style cafés and international or "fine cuisine" choices have popped up in the village in the past couple of years. Keep in mind that eating in Hopkins in itself is a cultural experience unlike any other, and one you will create for yourself as you explore the village.

Cafés

Morning coffee isn't quite a Garífuna tradition, so early risers will need to stock up or wait until 8am for **Thongs Café** (tel. 501/662-0110, www.thongscafe.com, 8am-2pm Wed.-Sun., US$8-12), with an outdoor roadside patio and light world music buzzing in the background; it's nice for people-watching and that first or second cup of morning coffee. The breakfast offerings range from cold sandwiches to cinnamon rolls. Steps from the village entrance on the Northside is the yellow-and-blue **Frog's Point** (tel. 501/621-3296, Fri.-Wed., US$8), run by a German expat couple and offering coffee and breakfast on an outdoor veranda.

The best local breakfast is at the small, cozy **Tina's Kitchen** (along the south of the village, look for signs, tel. 501/668-3268, 7am-8pm Mon.-Sat., reduced hours Sun., US$3-7), where you will taste the best Belizean breakfast for very cheap; her fry jacks are to die for, possibly the best I've tasted in Belize. Tina is a native of Hopkins, and you can see her cook in her open kitchen as you wait to be served. Ask her for a Garífuna breakfast if you want an even more special treat.

Garífuna

Several eateries are run by native Hopkins residents, the best way to experience authentic Garífuna cuisine. Most are casually set, with picnic tables under a thatched roof, but the meals are excellent. They require at least an hour's notice to have time to prepare, as Garífuna food is anything but the "fast" kind. The planning and wait, however, are well worth it. These dishes are also more likely to be ready on demand closer to the weekend (Fri.-Sat.). Most of these eateries also offer Belizean specialties, including stew chicken with rice and beans, or burritos, quesadillas, and other Central American fast foods.

Right on the village road going south is good but slow food at **Innie's** (tel. 501/503-7333, 7am-9pm daily, US$8-17). Her *hudut* is delicious, although you may wait at your table for over an hour, and there are several other options for dinner, including *bundiga*, fish tea, and seafood dishes. Nearby, **Yugadah Café** (tel. 501/503-7089 or 501/503-7255, 6am-2pm and 5pm-10pm Thurs.-Tues.) requires a couple of hours' notice.

Just a tad farther, don't miss the turn into **Tina's Kitchen** (tel. 501/668-3268, 7am-8pm Mon.-Sat., reduced hours Sun., US$3-7) where

© LEBAWIT GIRMA

Beachfront Laruni Hati Beyabu Diner serves authentic Garífuna dishes.

you'll find at least one, if not two, Garífuna options on Friday and Saturday, from *hudut* to *darasa*. Tina's food is excellent, Garífuna or otherwise; ask her who taught her to cook. Farther down, Jude will serve you fresh seafood, chicken, and other local treats at her longtime roadside thatched-roof restaurant, **The Watering Hole** (tel. 501/614-8686, loose hours, check daily), next to her home and across from Tipple Tree.

Still my favorite of all is Marva's **◖ Laruni Hati Beyabu Diner** (Northside, tel. 501/661-5753, 10am-9pm daily), a Garífuna-owned eatery and a favorite among locals, serving the best of Belizean and Garífuna fare for just US$4-6 and in the most ideal of settings—under a thatched roof and directly on a long stretch of beach. As long as you visit during high season, you can sample *hudut,* the traditional Garífuna dish of fried fish in a coconut broth with mashed plantains. Practice eating with your fingers, breeze blowing and toes buried in the sand. Note that to date, Marva's is the only beachfront eatery run and owned by a Garífuna in Hopkins (*laru ni hati* means "clear blue sky," and *beyabu* means "seaside").

Casual Dining

You're likely to head back to the north end more than once when you discover the **◖ Driftwood Beach Bar and Pizza Shack** (tel. 501/667-4872 or 501/664-6611, www.driftwoodpizza.com, 11am-10pm Thurs.-Tues., US$8-23), where you can have amazing wood-fired pizza, play beach volleyball, or surf the Internet. The bar is one of the most social in the village, crowded with locals, expats, and travelers. On a similar social wavelength is the bar at **Windschief** (tel. 501/523-7249 or 501/668-6087, www.windschief.com, 1pm-midnight Mon.-Wed. and Fri.-Sat., 1pm-6pm Sun., US$5-7), with a daily casual dinner menu that includes delicious fish-and-chips on Friday and gyros or burgers (that you can burn off while playing darts or table football).

Fine Dining

A unique experience is at **Love on The Rocks**

Hot Rock Grill Restaurant (Main St., tel. 501/672-7272, 5pm-10pm daily, US$13-25), created by Chef Rob, where you can finish cooking your own entrée on 400-degree hot stones in the old way of the ancient Maya. His protégé, Chef Ricky, now runs the kitchen solo, along with an attentive staff, and delivers seafood, chicken, or steak entrées with two sides—all of which are delicious. Have fun flipping your food over on the stone to your liking or warming up your sides at will. Those who don't want to "get stoned" can opt for pastas and other menu choices.

Groceries

There are five groceries and a produce stand in Hopkins, making it easier to stock up on nibbles and booze without breaking the bank; the longtime-running **Dong Lee's Supermarket** (9am-midnight daily) has the largest selection of liquor. The Garífuna women's group sells johnnycakes, bread, and Creole buns; look out for the kids selling their mothers' baked goods too.

INFORMATION AND SERVICES

The **Windschief Internet café** and cocktail bar (on the beach toward the south, tel. 501/523-7249, www.windschief.com, 1pm-11pm Fri.-Wed., 6pm-11pm Sun., US$4-10) is where it's at, although many mid-range hotels in Hopkins also offer computers and wireless service. Bring plenty of cash, as there's only one ATM in Hopkins (at the village entrance); the nearest ATMs are in Dangriga.

GETTING THERE AND AROUND

If you have your own transportation, getting to Hopkins is easy: just follow the Southern Highway until you see the well-signed turnoff on your left; from there it's a four-mile straight stretch of dirt road (which can be under water during intense rains). Figure 30-40 minutes' total drive time from Dangriga.

Motorbike Rentals (main road, Hopkins Village, tel. 501/665-6292, www.

alternateadventures.com, 8am-5pm daily, US$59 per day, US$299 per week) offers up a dozen 200-cc dirt or cruiser style motorcycles for rent. A rental, good for two, includes helmets, a map, a local cell phone, and help with designing a self-guided course to Cockscomb, Mayflower Bocawina, and other points of interest.

There are a few daily buses from Hopkins to Dangriga (8am and 5:15pm Mon.-Sat., US$2.50); buses return to Dangriga at 7am, 7:30am, and 2pm. Placencia buses used to go through Hopkins, but currently there are no buses taking that route. A popular alternative is to get off the bus at the Hopkins junction and hitch a ride to the village, or call for a taxi (contact **Mr. Abraham**, tel. 501/668-6166, or **Mr. Mac**, tel. 501/665-0181). Otherwise it's an expensive hotel shuttle or local taxi—which can cost up to US$50 from Dangriga. Once in Hopkins, you can rent a dirt motorcycle at Motorbike Rentals; some people do this to get to the Mayflower reserve or other nearby hiking spots. Bicycle rentals are also easy to find and useful for exploring the village.

FALSE SITTEE POINT

A few minutes' bicycle ride south from Hopkins village will bring you to a small ocean-side strip of upscale resorts, restaurants, and condos. The water off the beach resorts at False Sittee can be muddy at times because of the proximity of emptying rivers and streams, and depending on the time of year, sandflies and mosquitoes can get fierce. Still, this is a popular spot to stay because of the quality of the lodges as well as the location's direct access to so many inland and offshore attractions and activities.

Accommodations and Food

The most low-key lodging option in this stretch of resorts along False Sittee Point is **(Beaches and Dreams Seafront Inn and Pub** (tel. 501/523-7259, www.beachesanddreams.com, US$129, includes breakfast), whose four ample guest rooms have tiled floors, porches, and private baths; ask about the tree house, which is great for families. Use of kayaks and bikes is complimentary, and there's a lovely *palapa* dock, ideal for relaxing and napping by the sea. Customized tours can be arranged, and you won't have to deal with the "minimum number of people" limit; the owners are flexible and will link you with local guides. The on-site restaurant, the **(Barracuda Bar and Grill** (4pm-9pm or 10pm Wed.-Mon.) features chef "Alaska Tony" Marisco's amazing menu, including jerk smoked pork, aged beef, lots of seafood, and some of the best pizza this side of the Sittee River (dinner US$15-25 pp, large lobster pizza US$25, cheese pizza US$12). Set on a waterfront deck, it's a romantic dinner spot; reservations are recommended, as the restaurant can fill up quickly. Don't forget to ask Chef Tony about his "Mediteribean" specials and sample the desserts made by his wife, Angie, particularly her coconut flan.

Another pleasant mid-range option is next door at **Parrot Cove Lodge** (tel. 501/523-7225, U.S. tel. 877/207-7139, http://parrotcovelodge. com, US$150-400), with a handful of standard rooms and suites plus a few homes and villas for rent. It's a smaller, more intimate resort; take a kayak out to sea or lounge by the pool. On-site are also a full PADI dive shop, and the celebrated **Chef Rob's Gourmet Café** (tel. 501/663-1529 or 501/663-1812, 5pm-9pm Mon.-Sat., 4-course meal US$28), where Rob Pronk serves up his delectable daily created four-course dining experience with choices like coconut soup, rib eye steak, Thai-style pork and shrimp, or Lobster Robert.

Awarded Hotel of the Year 2010 by the Belize Tourist Board, **Jaguar Reef Resort** (tel. 501/533-7040, U.S. tel. 800/289-5756, www. jaguarreef.com, US$190-275) is a full-service place with an ever-improving variety of spacious, comfortably furnished guest rooms and cottages. The Jaguar Reef end feels more like a large all-inclusive resort, but connecting next door, if you can afford it, its charming sister property, **Almond Beach** (U.S. tel. 866/624-1516, www.almondbeachbelize.com, US$200-325), offers a selection of more intimate, luxurious stand-alone beachfront casitas and luxury suites that fill up fairly quickly with couples. The cozy Tiki swim-up bar is one of the few in Belize and has an infinity view of the sea. The two properties share a large open dining space and several more pools (including one for kiddies) and bars, along with bikes, kayaks, sand volleyball, and many activity-based packages. The ultra-luxe "beachfront vista suite" on the Almond Beach side is an outrageously decadent five-bedroom penthouse (US$870) that includes a private chef. This is a popular spot for fancy weddings, especially with the addition of the **Butterflies Spa** (8am-7pm daily, tel. 501/523-7291), offering a full range of treatments and salon care at about the same rates as back home. **Butterflies Coffee** next to it has grinds from all over Central America, roasted fresh daily, and cute patio seating.

Belizean Dreams (tel. 501/523-7272, U.S. tel. 800/456-7150, www.belizeandreams.com, US$285-625) has nine beach villas with one- and two-bedroom suite options, along with a restaurant and spa services. Area tours are available.

 Hamanasi Adventure and Resort (tel. 501/533-7073, U.S. tel. 877/522-3483, www.hamanasi.com, US$275-595) is the area's premier diving operation. Sitting on 17 acres, including 400 feet of beautiful beachfront, Hamanasi offers eight beachfront guest rooms, four suites (including a honeymoon option), and five deluxe tree houses tucked away in the littoral forest, all with views and tiled baths, air-conditioning, fans, and porches. Restaurant meals include delicious pasta and, of course, fresh seafood; it's open to outside visitors as well (bring a towel). It's ideal if you just want to laze and aren't into diving or inland adventures. There's a gorgeous pool overlooking the beachfront as well as kayaks, bikes, and hammocks to use at your leisure. Hamanasi is very popular among locals as much as visitors and has a high occupancy rate; make reservations ahead of time.

Information and Services

Sittee River Marina (tel. 501/670-8525, www.sitteerivermarina.com, 6am-6pm daily) has oil, gas, diesel, snacks, restroom and shower facilities, and cold beer. They also deliver fuel at sea on request.

Getting There

Driving south on the road from Hopkins, you'll pass through False Sittee, a short drive east of the Southern Highway. There are usually two daily buses that pass through Sittee River and False Sittee Point, but the schedule varies; most accommodations will provide transfer from Dangriga.

SITTEE RIVER

Sittee River is a peaceful, riverine corner of the country with its own calm mood. Sittee River qualifies as a village only in the loosest sense, with a few houses, a couple of riverside places to stay, and more often than not, a few insects. Choose from the now few screened accommodations from which to soak up the thick, tropical tranquility. There are boats to whisk you out to the cayes, excellent fishing (snook, tarpon, peacock bass, sheepshead, and barracuda), and, only 12 miles by road to the west, the entrance to the Cockscomb Basin Wildlife Sanctuary. Sadly, businesses have become sparse in Sittee, and as of late it appears nearly abandoned, with a couple of resorts now gone, but its wildlife and natural setting remain; if you're not staying here, it's good for a drive through and perhaps a stop at a local riverside restaurant to soak in Belize's deepest and most beautiful river.

Sports and Recreation

Popular local Sittee River-born and raised guide **Horace Andrews** (tel. 501/675-8358 or 501/603-8358, www.belizebyhorace.com) does river tours on the Sittee River, snorkel trips to the cayes, fishing trips to the nearby cayes or lagoons, and inland tours such as Cockscomb, Mayflower, and Red Bank to see the scarlet macaws (in season, mid-Jan.-Mar.). He's full of life, having captained his own boats as far as Cuba and Mexico, and will help you see the best of this area; he can also take you out on fun sailing trips aboard his new catamaran.

On the road to False Sittee, past Jaguar Reef Resort, you'll find **Diversity Café and Tours** (tel. 501/661-7444), offering help with tour planning, including snorkeling, fishing, and inland trips, which they outsource to local guides. There are also golf carts for rent (US$20 for 2 hours, US$50 per day).

Accommodations and Food

Glover's Guest House (tel. 501/532-2916, www.glovers.com.bz) provides cheap, Spartan lodging for both walk-ins and guests of the Glover's Atoll Resort. Stay in a bunkhouse on stilts (US$9 pp), or in one of the private, stilted, screened-in riverside cabins (US$19); meals and a cooking area are available. Camping is US$5 (bring your own tent). You can use the guesthouse's canoes and kayaks to explore the river.

A slight notch up is also the only other option in Sittee at publication time, **River House Lodge** (tel. 501/543-7044, www.riverhouselodgebelize.com, US$65-75), offering six cabanas with double beds, screened porches, and kitchenettes, and set along the Sittee River with a small dock to gaze at the gorgeous view (but not to swim, crocodiles live in the river). There's an on-site bar and restaurant, complete with an indoor pool.

Have a sunset drink over the Sittee River under the thatched roof at the new **Curve Bar** (Sittee River Marina, tel. 501/670-8525) or grab some drinks from the convenience store at the Marina.

Getting There

The Sittee River area is about a 10-minute drive east of the Southern Highway through mostly orange orchards and riverside lots. There are usually two daily buses that run through Sittee River and False Sittee Point, but this schedule is always up in the air; your accommodations will provide some sort of transfer from Dangriga. Driving south on the road from Hopkins, you'll pass through False Sittee, followed by the village of Sittee River, occupying a few bends of the slow, flat river of the same name.

MAYFLOWER BOCAWINA NATIONAL PARK

Located 17 miles from Dangriga and 12 miles from Hopkins, **Mayflower Bocawina National Park** (entrance fee US$10 pp) comprises more than 7,100 acres of Maya Mountain wilderness set aside in 2001 to protect and showcase the area's five waterfalls and green-fringed Mayan ruins. A trail system offers excellent hiking and, it's an adventurous climb to Antelope Falls. A hike in Mayflower Bocawina can be combined with a day trip to Cockscomb (just to the south), or it can easily fill a whole day or more.

Guides and Tours

Ramon Guzman (tel. 501/533-7136) is a long-time park warden, and he may even greet you at the entrance. Doreen Guzman is an officer in the **Friends of Mayflower Bocawina National Park** (mayflowerbocawina@yahoo.com), an organization that comanages the park with the government.

In Dangriga, **C & G Tours and Charters** (29 Oak St., Dangriga, tel. 501/522-3641, www.cgtourscharters.com) can arrange a trip to Mayflower for large groups. The licensed guides at **Bocawina Adventures & Eco-Tours** (tel. 501/670-2622 or 501/670-8019, www.bocawinaadventures.com) will pick you up wherever you stay in the area. A day-long adventure (from US$50 pp, no minimum number of people) hiking to and rappelling from one or all five waterfalls inside the park—Antelope, Bocawina, Tears of the Jaguar, Peck Falls, and Big Drop—is well worth it. When I rappelled the smaller 125-foot-high Bocawina Falls, the drive was just a little over 30 minutes, followed by a short hike of moderate difficulty but with an impressive view. Wear adequate shoes.

Additional adventures include Belize's longest single zip line, at 2,300 feet, and bird-watching. You can overnight at the renovated **Mama Noots Eco Resort** (tel. 501/670-8019, www.mamanootsbelize.com, US$155-275, continental breakfast included), duplex cabanas set on beautifully landscaped grounds right in the park and with an on-site bar and restaurant. For birding, the best guide is **Charlton**

Castillo (tel. 501/661-8199, US$50 pp, minimum 2 people).

Getting There

The biggest challenge to enjoying Mayflower Bocawina is simply getting to the trailhead, which lies 4.5 miles west of the Southern Highway with no public transportation of any kind making the trip. (The turnoff is just north of Silk Grass Village.) Sign in at the park office and interpretive center (7am-4pm daily) and pay the US$5 pp entrance fee. There is a **campground** (US$5) at the park entrance; bring your own gear.

RED BANK

Tucked away on a red dirt road is the small Mayan village of Red Bank. Here, at the edge of the Maya Mountains, rare and impressive scarlet macaws gather to feed on the ripe fruits of pole-wood trees outside the village. This annual phenomenon was unknown to outsiders until 1997, when conservationists learned that 20 birds had been hunted for table fare; at that time it was thought Belize had a population of just 30 to 60 scarlet macaws. In response, Programme for Belize worked with the village council to form the Red Bank Scarlet Macaw Conservation Group, led by the village leader, Geronimo Sho.

The small community-based ecotourism industry offers visitors accommodations, meals, crafts, and guide services. A reserve has been established about a mile from the village, and visitors must pay a small conservation fee; ask around for Mr. Sho. The best time to visit is sometime from mid-January to March, when the annatto fruit are ripe. As many as 100 scarlet macaws have been observed in the morning when the birds are feeding. Contact the **Red Bank Bed and Breakfast** (tel. 501/660-6320, US$20) if you want to stay overnight.

The Cockscomb Basin

The land rises gradually from the coastal plains to the Maya Mountains; driving south on the Southern Highway, you'll see the highlands to the west and flatlands to the left, mostly covered by orange and banana groves. The highway passes through a few villages and soon delivers you to the area's prime attraction: Maya Centre village and Cockscomb Basin Wildlife Sanctuary. Heavy rain along the peaks of the Maya range, as much as 160 inches per year, runs off into lush rainforest thick with trees, orchids, palms, ferns, abundant birds, and exotic animals, including peccaries, anteaters, armadillos, tapirs, and jaguars.

◀ COCKSCOMB BASIN WILDLIFE SANCTUARY

Commonly called the "Jaguar Preserve," this is one of the most beautiful natural attractions in the country. A large tract of approximately 155 square miles of forest was declared a forest reserve in 1984, and in 1986 the government of Belize set the region aside as a preserve for the largest cat in the Americas, the jaguar. The area is alive with wildlife, including margays, ocelots, pumas, jaguarundis, tapirs, deer, pacas, iguanas, kinkajous, and armadillos, to name just a few, along with hundreds of bird species and even howler monkeys. The park is also home to the red-eyed tree frog and the critically endangered Morelet's tree frog. And though you probably won't spot large cats roaming during the day (they hunt at night), it's exciting to see their prints and other signs—and to know that even if you don't see one, you'll probably be seen by one.

The **Cockscomb Basin Wildlife Sanctuary** is managed by the **Belize Audubon Society** (www.belizeaudubon.org), which also conducts research and community outreach in support of conservation. The park is open 8am-4:30pm daily. Entrance is US$5 for non-Belizeans (pay at the Maya Centre Women's Group craft shop at the head of the access road, immediately off the Southern Highway). Just past the entrance gate into the park is a gift shop and office where you'll be asked to sign in. Visitor facilities include an interpretive center, a picnic area, and an outhouse.

Victoria Peak

The second-highest point in the country is the top of **Victoria Peak** (3,675 feet). Geologists believe the mountain is four million years old, the oldest geologic formation in Central America. Reportedly, area Mayan populations thought the peak was surrounded by a lake, unapproachable by people and occupied by a powerful spirit. The first known people (a party led by Roger T. Goldsworth, governor of then-British Honduras) to reach the summit did so in 1888. Today, it is a protected natural monument, managed by the Belize Audubon Society.

Summit trips can be arranged in the dry season only (Feb.-May) and must include a permit and a licensed guide. The 30-mile round-trip trek takes three or four days; the up-and-down terrain is steep, and there are no switchbacks. Contact the **Belize Audubon Society** (www. belizeaudubon.org) for trail and campsite details; entrance is US$5 pp plus camping fees.

The Belize Audubon Society does not have guides for hire, but they can provide a list of guides with contact information. There are a few reputable mountain guides in the surrounding villages, including **Marcos Cucul** (tel. 501/670-3116, www.mayaguide.bz) who can take you rock climbing or on a backcountry trip to the top of Victoria Peak (US$500 pp).

Hiking

There are more than 20 miles of maintained hiking trails, which range from an easy hour-long stroll along the river to a four-day Victoria Peak expedition. An early morning hike on the **Wari Loop** offers the best chance to see wildlife and to admire the large buttress roots of the swamp kaway (*Pterocarpus officinalis*) trees. At the end of the **Tiger Fern Trail,** a rigorous hike, you'll find an impressive double waterfall—the most beautiful waterfall in Belize, according to top Belizean landscape and

underwater photographer Tony Rath. There are more waterfalls, including a less difficult fall with a pool, within a 30-minute hike. Check the front of the visitors center building for a detailed map.

If you climb **Ben's Bluff,** you're not just looking out over a park where jaguars live—you're at the entrance of a forest that goes all the way into the Guatemalan Petén, part of the largest contiguous block of protected forest in Central America. The bluff was named after Ben Nottingham, who monitored radio-collared jaguars with radiotelemetry. From here you can see Outlier Peak, a moderate one-day hike (about 8.5 miles round-trip) and great place to camp.

Bring your swimsuit when visiting, as you'll find cool natural waterfalls and pools for a refreshing plunge. You can also rent an inner tube and float down South Stann Creek. All visitors are encouraged to bring sturdy shoes, a long-sleeved shirt, long pants, insect repellent, sunscreen, and plenty of water. If you would like to hire a guide, there are several renowned wilderness guides who grew up in these forests and who can be found up the road in Maya Centre.

Accommodations and Camping

Bring your own tent to stay at one of three well-maintained **campgrounds** (US$10 pp). The park's overnight accommodations (US$20) begin with zinc-topped buildings with bunk space for 32 people. Expect a bed in a shared "rustic cabin" or a bunk in the main dormitory, clean sheets, shared baths with cold showers, and solar power. There are also a few private cabins (6 beds and a kitchen US$54).

Be prepared with food and supplies if you plan to stay a few days; the only food for sale in the visitors center is chips, cookies, candy bars, and soft drinks. There are a couple of small shops in Maya Centre, so feel free to stock up there before catching a taxi into the park. You may also be able to arrange for meals to be cooked in Maya Centre and delivered to you. Otherwise, there is a communal kitchen with a refrigerator, gas stoves, and crockery and cooking utensils for rent. Again, visitors are required to bring their own food and water. A walled-off washing area has buckets, and a separate cooking area has a gas stove and a few pots.

Getting There

Cockscomb Basin is about six miles west of the Southern Highway and the village of Maya Centre; from Dangriga, it's a total of 20 miles. The road can be rough after it rains. For public transportation, catch any bus traveling between Dangriga and Punta Gorda and hop off at Maya Centre. From there, it's an extremely long—at least an hour—and hilly walk; I strongly recommend a US$15-20 taxi ride.

MAYA CENTRE

This small village is at the turnoff to the famous Cockscomb Basin Wildlife Sanctuary. Many of the 400 or so Mopan Maya who live here were relocated when their original home within the Cockscomb Basin was given protected status. Since then, they have had to change their lifestyle; instead of continuing to clear patches of rainforest for short-term agriculture, many men now work as guides and taxi drivers, while the women create and sell artwork. Still, the people of Maya Centre are struggling to support their town with tourism. Ever since they were prohibited from using the now-protected rainforest for subsistence farming and hunting, tourism has been their only hope, aside from working for slave wages at the nearby banana and citrus farms. The village has a few places to stay, eat, and experience village life, literally right down the road from the famous reserve.

At the very least, make sure that you—or the driver of your tour bus—stop at one of the three Maya crafts stores, all on the road into the park. At the turnoff from the Southern Highway, you'll find the **Maya Centre Women's Group** (7:30am-4:30pm daily), which sells local crafts and collects the entrance fee for Cockscomb. The **Nu'uk Che'il Gift Shop** is 0.25 miles farther toward the park, offering fine jewelry, slate carvings, baskets, herbs, and other crafts.

Julio Saqui runs the store next to the women's co-op and offers satellite Internet access (US$4 per hour) and taxi service as well as meals to any overnight guests in the area who need it (US$7 pp per meal, including delivery). Julio is a great guide and offers many services and tours, including to Victoria Peak; information is available on his website (www.cockscombmayatours.com).

Julio and his wife also run the **Maya Centre Maya Museum** (tel. 501/660-3903, US$7.50 pp), opened in 2010 and providing hands-on cultural activities; learn how to make corn tortillas or process coffee beans, and take home Mayan Coffee to share with friends while you tell of your adventures abroad. They also now sell their very own Che'il Mayan Chocolate bars, made from cacao beans farmed in Stann Creek.

Accommodations

There are two guesthouses in Maya Centre, owned by different families that each offer transportation in and out of the preserve, guides, meals, and other services.

◖**Nu'uk Che'il Cottages and Hmen Herbal Center** (tel. 501/533-7043 or 501/665-1313, nuukcheil@yahoo.com) offers tranquil accommodations more removed from the highway than the village's other guesthouse. Bunks with a shared bath are US$10 pp, and private guest rooms with hot showers available are US$30, tax not included. Camping is US$4 pp, Internet access US$2.50 per hour, and bike rental US$10 per day. The place is very well kept, with beautifully planted grounds; the guesthouse has experience hosting student groups and can arrange seminars on herbal medicine, cultural performances, and the like. Proprietress Aurora Garcia Saqui's husband, Ernesto, was director of the Cockscomb Basin Wildlife Sanctuary until 2005 and is extremely knowledgeable about the area. Her late uncle, Don Eligio Panti, was a famous healer; she took over his work when he died in 1996. Aurora offers Mayan spiritual blessings, prayer healings, acupuncture, and massage (each for under US$15). Aurora also has a four-acre botanical garden and medicine trail (entrance US$2.50), offers herbs for sale, and can arrange homestays in the village for US$25 pp, which includes a one-night stay with a local family, one dinner, and one breakfast.

Another decent option is right on the highway, about 100 yards north of the entrance to Cockscomb: **Tutzil Nah Cottages** (tel. 501/533-7045, www.mayacenter.com, US$18-22) is owned and operated by the Chun family (they helped Dr. Alan Rabinowitz in his original jaguar studies and appear in his book, *Jaguar*). There are four screened wooden guest rooms, two with private baths, two with a shared bath and shower; all have queen beds,

fans, ample space, nice furniture, and a raised deck. Meals (US$6-12) are available, as camping (US$6-12) is possible on the grounds or in a separate campground about 0.25 miles into the bush. Inventive trips are available as an alternative to the standard fare, including kayak floats and night hikes.

Getting There

Maya Centre is accessed by hopping off any bus passing between Dangriga and Punta Gorda. Taxis will take you from the village to the Cockscomb Basin Wildlife Sanctuary for about US$15-20 per carload.

The Placencia Peninsula

This ribbon of barrier beach and mangroves winds 16 miles southward from the coastal wetlands and shrimp farms near the village of Riverside all the way to Placencia Village, on the tip of the peninsula. The area used to be a forgotten cul-de-sac on the tourist trail, but no more. Traveling to nearby cayes and inland attractions like the Cockscomb Basin Wildlife Sanctuary, Mayan villages, and ruins of Toledo District is possible from anywhere on the peninsula, although it's farther than from Dangriga or Hopkins. The area offers the full range of accommodations—whether you prefer to mingle with backpackers in Placencia Village or rub elbows with fellow guests at any of a number of beach resorts, from mid-range to luxurious, each with its own personality. This is also the site of several enormous, ambitious, and controversial development projects, more of which are springing up all over the area every year. They are currently overshadowed, however, by the construction of a new Municipal Pier and Plaza by the marina, likely to be completed in 2013.

There are three main areas on the Placencia Peninsula: Maya Beach, Seine Bight, and Placencia Village, where most of the bars, restaurants, and shops are, along with the general

buzz. Maya Beach and Seine Bight share a quiet, secluded vibe, with long stretches of beach, plenty of resorts sprawled along the shore, and a few restaurants. They are a bit of a distance from Placencia Village, so you'll have to either bike, if you're up for it, during the day, or catch a taxi to go back and forth, which can be costly, so plan wisely. Staying in the village means being close to all the action, nightlife, general noise, and also being near the beach, even if it's not as fine and pretty as in the other areas.

◖ MAYA BEACH

About halfway down the peninsula, **Maya Beach** is nothing more than a loose strip of simple, small accommodations. They're actually quite nice, in a relaxed, isolated way, offering more value for your money than nearly anything else in the area. However, the **beach** here is more beautiful than many places in Belize, including the rest of Placencia. You just have to be content with the relative lack of services in Maya Beach, since getting to and from Placencia Village can be an expensive endeavor, even though it's only seven miles away.

Art and greenery lovers will like the retreat feel to **Spectarte** (Maya Beach, tel.

501/533-8019, spectarte@gmail.com, 9am-4pm Thurs.-Sun.), a coffee shop and "art and garden gallery" featuring 90 percent Belizean artwork: paintings, including works by Nelson Young, along with carvings and *jipijapa* baskets. Other items are imported works from neighboring Guatemala and Panama. There's delightful screened greenhouse-like seating area where you can enjoy the peaceful surroundings, cookies, pies, and a hot beverage. Locals flock here on the first Sunday of the month for the weekly flea market.

For all-American fun in the tropics, try bowling at **Jaguar Lanes and Jungle Bar** (tel. 501/664-2583, jaguarlanes@yahoo.com, 2pm-8pm Wed. and Sat.-Sun., hours vary Mon. and Thurs.-Fri., US$3 per game, shoe rental US$1.25). There are four Brunswick bowling lanes and a snack bar (US$1.50-5.50) serving hot dogs, onion rings, nachos, and pizza. Outside the air-conditioned alley there's cold beer and mixed drinks. The venue holds various theme parties, including a "cosmic" bowling night (bowling with disco lights), and Wednesday is popular among the local women bowlers of Placencia.

You can grab a drink at the **Maya Breeze Inn's** casual beachfront bar (tel. 501/666-5238 or cell 501/628-4215, 11am-midnight daily), offering a full bar with imported liquor, cocktails, and local favorites. Don't forget your swimsuit, and eat before you come here.

Accommodations

Maya Beach hotels are of the beach cabana variety, with a few furnished apartments, many with kitchenettes for cooking on your own. Most of these hotels also manage full houses and a few condos in the area; ask about weekly and monthly rates.

The first place you'll come to from the north is ◖ **Maya Beach Hotel** (tel. 501/533-8040, U.S. tel. 800/503-5124, www.mayabeachhotel.com, US$90-125), with five well-kept guest rooms, a few with waterfront decks, all with wireless Internet, private baths, hot showers, and a great stretch of sand—oh, and one of the best restaurants in Placencia, the Maya Beach

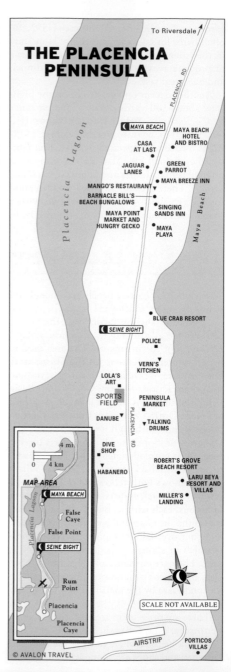

THE PLACENCIA PENINSULA

To Riversdale

PLACENCIA RD

Placencia Lagoon

MAYA BEACH
CASA AT LAST
MAYA BEACH HOTEL AND BISTRO
JAGUAR LANES
GREEN PARROT
MANGO'S RESTAURANT
MAYA BREEZE INN
BARNACLE BILL'S BEACH BUNGALOWS
MAYA POINT MARKET AND HUNGRY GECKO
SINGING SANDS INN
MAYA PLAYA
Maya Beach

BLUE CRAB RESORT
SEINE BIGHT
POLICE
VERN'S KITCHEN
LOLA'S ART
SPORTS FIELD
PENINSULA MARKET
DANUBE
TALKING DRUMS
PLACENCIA RD
DIVE SHOP
ROBERT'S GROVE BEACH RESORT
HABANERO
LARU BEYA RESORT AND VILLAS
MILLER'S LANDING

0   4 mi
0   4 km
MAP AREA
MAYA BEACH
Placencia Lagoon
False Caye
False Point
SEINE BIGHT
Rum Point
Placencia
Placencia Caye

SCALE NOT AVAILABLE

AIRSTRIP
PORTICOS VILLAS

© AVALON TRAVEL

Hotel Bistro. They have a small pool and one- and two-bedroom beach houses (US$100-180), all with fully equipped kitchens and amenities such as bicycles. A three-bedroom house (US$400), on a private beachfront parcel, has its own infinity pool.

On the lagoon side, **Casa At Last** (tel. 501/523-3630, www.casaatlast.com, US$125-200) is a couples-only resort with four nicely furnished thatched cabanas, a pool, and a restaurant. The restaurant serves breakfast, lunch, and dinner for resort guests only.

The Green Parrot Beach Houses (tel. 501/533-8188, www.greenparrot-belize.com, US$130-180 plus tax) feature cozy thatched-roof A-frame cabanas with decks and loft bedrooms facing the ocean. Each sleeps four people and includes multiple beds, couches, a kitchen, and hammocks on the decks. There's a restaurant on-site and it's on a lovely, quiet stretch of beach. Use of bikes and kayaks as well as continental breakfast are included.

Catering to relaxed couples and honeymooners, **Barnacle Bill's Beach Bungalows** (tel. 501/533-8110, www.barnaclebills-belize.com, US$110) are two secluded bungalows on the beach, with full kitchens, fans, and hot and cold water. Each sleeps three adults, and children under 12 are not allowed. Tours, free kayaks, and wireless Internet are available.

Lovers of orchids and boutique luxury will enjoy the small but cozy **Singing Sands Inn** (tel. 501/533-3022, U.S. tel. 888/201-6425, www.singingsands.com, US$110-275 plus tax). The six thatched-roof seafront cabanas have front porches and wood floors, and the two standard guest rooms offer sea and garden views. All units have private baths, ceiling fans, and constant ocean breezes. Portable air-conditioning is available if desired. Breakfast is served in the open-air restaurant next to the pool; fresh lunches and dinners are served as well at the Bonefish Grille. Drinks and light fare can be enjoyed at Chez Albert's bar on the pier, 220 feet out into the Caribbean. Use of bikes and snorkel gear is complimentary, and golf carts, clear-bottomed kayaks, and sailboats are available for rent.

Food

When you get tired of cooking in your cabana's kitchenette, visit the **Hungry Gecko** (8am-9pm Mon.-Sat.), which serves a cheap menu of Honduran and local goodies, fresh seafood, and smoothies. One of two stores in town, the **Maya Pointe Market** (Mon.-Sat.), is open most mornings and afternoons.

Mango's Beach Bar and Restaurant (tel. 501/533-8102 or 501/610-2494, fdasilva2@ yahoo.com, 4pm-midnight Wed.-Fri., noon-midnight Fri.-Sat., US$5-10) has a Belizean-Mexican menu and a breezy view to enjoy with your beer. Owner Frank da Silva was once chef at Robert's Grove. It's popular with the handful of locals, offering darts and occasional live bands at night.

The ◖ **Maya Beach Hotel Bistro** (tel. 501/533-8040, 7am-9pm daily, US$16-28) is a breath of fresh air on the Belize culinary scene. Just reading the appetizer and meal choices will make your mouth water—few restaurants in the country have a menu this savory and creative. Australian chef John prepares dinner entrées like Sassy Shrimp Pot, Cacao Pork, and Mojo Roasted Chicken (with a jerk and honey glaze), not to mention fresh bread, an inspired bar food menu (honey-coconut ribs and roasted pumpkin-coconut green chili soup), a wine cellar, and a lovely assortment of breakfasts (US$6-11), including homemade bagels and imported lox (smoked salmon).

At the **Bonefish Grille** (at the Singing Sands Inn, tel. 501/533-3022, www.singingsands. com, 7am-9:30pm daily, US$10-23), everything is made from scratch: homemade pasta, ricotta cheese, breads, and the salad dressings, and there's no MSG. The menu features Asian and Italian cuisine, prepared with fresh ingredients. This place was Restaurant of the Year runner-up at the 2010 National Tourism Awards.

◖ SEINE BIGHT

South of Maya Beach, a few more miles of dirt road will put you in the Garífuna village of **Seine Bight.** In this tiny town, most of the men are fishermen and the women tend family gardens. Some are attempting to clean up the town, with hopes it will become a low-key tourist destination, as foreign-owned resorts sprout like mushrooms up and down the coast around them. Seine Bight does have the nicest stretches of **beach** in the area, along with neighboring Maya Beach. There are a few casual eateries and bars. Venturing here on foot or by bicycle is where you'll get the best sense of local culture on the peninsula.

Lola's Art Gallery (behind the soccer field, follow the well-marked signs, tel. 501/523-3343 or cell 501/601-1913, lolasartgallery@yahoo.com, 7am-7pm daily) is a must-see. A renowned Creole artist, her inspired artwork includes paintings on canvas that depict scenes of village life as well as cards and gorgeous gourd masks, all in bright, primary colors. According to her parents, she started painting as a young girl, using her mother's lipstick on the walls. Lola also has a small on-site bar (10am-midnight daily) serving cold beer and soft drinks; ask her why she named it *The Fallen Angel.*

The owners of Blue Crab Resort also run a tiny chocolate factory in the house across the road. **Goss Chocolate** (north end of Seine Bight, tel. 501/523-3544, www.goss-chocolate.com, 9am-5pm Mon.-Fri., 10am-5pm Sat.) is made from 100 percent pure organic cacao and is available only in Belize; it costs US$1.50-2.50 for a bar.

Accommodations

Independent travelers may enjoy the laid-back feel of **Miller's Landing** (tel. 501/523-3010, www.millerslanding.net, US$85-150). The Millers like to keep things simple, and not much has changed since the couple opened their resort. The entrance is tucked in from the roadside, and there are three basic sea-view guest rooms and two private cabanas, all with coffeemakers and mini fridges, private baths, hot and cold water, and ceiling fans. This calm and quiet beach location is surrounded by native vegetation; watch birds and butterflies while having your complimentary breakfast. Lounge on the newly updated pool deck, or if you're feeling more active, take out a complimentary bike, kayak, or windsurfing board. It could be an ideal place to book a whole group of independent, well-traveled, and unfussy friends and family.

On a clean, shallow beach on the very northern end of Seine Bight is **Blue Crab Resort** (tel. 501/523-3544, www.bluecrabbeach.com, US$60-90). American-Belizean-owned, this humble hotel has four guest rooms with air-conditioning, fridges, coffeemakers, fans, and cable TV, plus two cabanas with high thatched roofs, louvered windows, private baths, and three fans. Blue Crab is on the primitive side, made mostly of wood and thatch, but its cabanas are more modern, and you're likely to see a few coatimundis foraging among the fruit trees.

The **Nautical Inn** (tel. 501/523-3595, U.S. tel. 678/528-7065, www.nauticalinnbelize.com, US$65-300 pp) offers various old-school but spacious beachfront accommodations surrounding a pool, and all guest rooms have air-conditioning, ceiling fans, and cable TV. Basic guest rooms have kitchenettes, and the two-bedroom suite has a full kitchen and a living room. Ask about special group rates.

One of the well-known resorts on the peninsula, **Robert's Grove Beach Resort** (just south of Seine Bight, tel. 501/523-3565, U.S. tel. 800/565-9757, www.robertsgrove.com, from US$215) is a classic grand resort. Its various structures are situated close together along a short stretch of decent beach, so it doesn't appear overwhelming. The various guest rooms, suites, and villas have high ceilings, king beds, and updated amenities. There are three pools, a tennis court, a spa, a gym, a trio of rooftop hot tubs, and an open-air restaurant. Robert's Grove has its own dive shop on the lagoon side across the street (next to its Mexican restaurant, Habanero) and offers all kinds of underwater, offshore, and inland trips and packages. Bikes, kayaks, and sailboats are available for your own explorations. The inn is popular with couples, families, and groups; ask about trips to their private islands.

If you're going luxury, you might as well

© LEBAWIT GIRMA

There are several upscale resorts in Seine Bight, including Laru Beya Resort and Villas.

stay right next door: **Laru Beya Resort and Villas** (tel. 501/523-3476, U.S. tel. 800/890-8010, www.larubeya.com, US$140-490) offers beautifully furnished beachfront accommodations and all the amenities (my favorite is the seafront balcony), with a touch of luxury yet unpretentious. The suites feel more like your own private condo than a resort. Penthouse suites have a ladder to a private rooftop jetted tub with a great view. It's a stone's throw from the beach, and you'll fall asleep to the sound of waves. The **Quarter Deck** restaurant and bar (7am-10pm) serves international cuisine and caters for destination weddings.

Food

Vern's Kitchen (main road, Placencia, 6am-2pm and 4pm-9pm Thurs.-Tues., US$2-5) serves up local dishes and often a Garífuna specialty. Besides Vern's, you'll have to wander up to Maya Beach, up the road, to get some cheap local food. But you can grab a couple of bottles of Guinness or other drinks at the Garífuna-flag colored **Talking Drums Bar** (3pm-midnight daily), which greets you a few minutes after you enter town from the north.

The menu at the **Danube Austrian Restaurant** (south end of Seine Bight, tel. 501/610-0132, www.danubebelize.com, 4:30pm-10:30pm Wed.-Mon., US$10-25) includes schnitzel, spaetzle, sweet dumplings, and strudels; call for reservations.

The **Seaside Restaurant** (just south of Seine Bight, tel. 501/523-3565, 7am-9pm daily, US$12-28) at Robert's Grove has an international menu: sandwiches, pizza, wings, and quesadillas for lunch; seafood appetizers and entrées, imported steaks, and à la carte options for dinner. The bar is open till midnight. **Habanero Mexican Café and Bar** (tel. 501/523-3565, noon-10pm daily Dec.-May, US$9-15) is an excellent lagoon-side Mexican restaurant across the road from Robert's Grove Marina.

If you need groceries, the **Peninsula** (main road Placencia to Seine Bight, 9am-10pm) has the widest selection.

SOUTHERN COAST

© LEBAWIT GIRMA

Splash Dive offers numerous diving and snorkeling trips to the reef and cayes.

PLACENCIA VILLAGE

A fishing village since the time of the Maya and periodically flattened by hurricanes (most recently by Iris in 2001), Placencia continues rebuilding and redefining itself, in large part to accommodate the influx of foreigners. Placencia Village is still worlds away from the condo-dominated landscape of San Pedro on Ambergris Caye, and most locals claim it will never go that way, but time will tell. There are plenty of bulldozers, swaths of cut mangroves, golf carts for rent, and a new marina under construction to welcome cruise ships late in 2013.

It's everyone's hope that despite area development, this town will remain the *tranquilo* ramshackle village it is today for years to come. Find a room, book some day tours, pencil in a massage before happy hour, and relax. Oh, yeah, and feel free to drink the tap water as you explore: Placencia's *agua* is piped in from an artesian well across the lagoon in Independence, reportedly the result of an unsuccessful attempt to drill for oil, and it's clean and pure.

Sights

There are few sights per se in this beach village. What you'll find, however, is plenty of sand, water sports, food, active bars and nightlife, and all the options you can think of to embody a perfect beach vacation.

The north-south Placencia Road runs the length of the peninsula, doglegs around the airstrip, continues along the lagoon, and then parallels the famous central sidewalk as it enters town. You'll see the soccer field on your right before the road curves slightly to the left, terminating at the Shell station and the main docks. If there is a "downtown" Placencia, it's probably here, in front of the gas station and dock. This is where buses come and go, taxis hang out, and most dive shops are based.

Aside from the beach, the main attraction in Placencia is the world-renowned **main-street sidewalk**, cited in the *Guinness Book of World Records* as "the world's most narrow street." It is 24 inches wide in spots and runs north-south through the sand for over a mile. Homes, hotels, Guatemalan goods shops, craft makers,

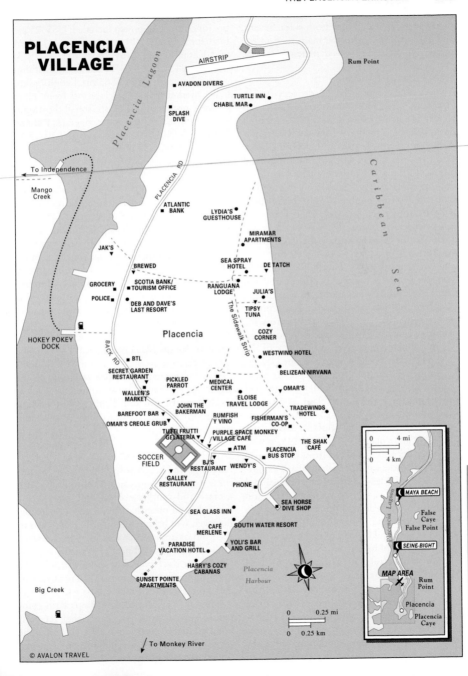

PLACENCIA VILLAGE

Placencia Lagoon

AIRSTRIP

Rum Point

AVADON DIVERS

TURTLE INN
CHABIL MAR

SPLASH DIVE

To Independence

Mango Creek

PLACENCIA RD

Caribbean Sea

ATLANTIC BANK

LYDIA'S GUESTHOUSE

MIRAMAR APARTMENTS

JAK'S

BREWED

SEA SPRAY HOTEL

DE TATCH

GROCERY

SCOTIA BANK/ TOURISM OFFICE

RANGUANA LODGE

JULIA'S

POLICE

DEB AND DAVE'S LAST RESORT

TIPSY TUNA

The Sidewalk Strip

Placencia

COZY CORNER

HOKEY POKEY DOCK

BACK RD

BTL

WESTWIND HOTEL

BELIZEAN NIRVANA

SECRET GARDEN RESTAURANT

PICKLED PARROT

MEDICAL CENTER

OMAR'S

WALLEN'S MARKET

ELOISE TRAVEL LODGE

JOHN THE BAKERMAN

TRADEWINDS HOTEL

BAREFOOT BAR

RUMFISH Y VINO

FISHERMAN'S CO-OP

OMAR'S CREOLE GRUB

TUTTI FRUTTI GELATERIA

PURPLE SPACE MONKEY VILLAGE CAFÉ

THE SHAK CAFÉ

ATM

PLACENCIA BUS STOP

SOCCER FIELD

BJ'S RESTAURANT

WENDY'S

GALLEY RESTAURANT

PHONE

SEA GLASS INN

SEA HORSE DIVE SHOP

CAFÉ MERLENE

SOUTH WATER RESORT

PARADISE VACATION HOTEL

YOLI'S BAR AND GRILL

HARRY'S COZY CABANAS

Placencia Harbour

SUNSET POINTE APARTMENTS

Big Creek

To Monkey River

0   0.25 mi

0   0.25 km

MAYA BEACH

0   4 mi

0   4 km

False Caye
False Point

SEINE BIGHT

MAP AREA

Rum Point

Placencia

Placencia Caye

© AVALON TRAVEL

SOUTHERN COAST

and tour guide offices line both sides. Several side paths connect it to the main road in the village. No bikes are allowed; pedestrians only.

Sports and Recreation

There's no shortage of guide services in Placencia, where most tour operators offer service to all nearby destinations: Cockscomb Basin Wildlife Sanctuary, Monkey River, snorkeling and fishing trips with lunch on a beautiful caye, the Mayan ruins of Lubaantun and Nim Li Punit, and a variety of paddling tours. For any of these trips, also refer to the dive shops and fishing guides listed in this chapter.

Many tour operators have their offices in shacks clustered in the village or by the main dock area in town, just past the gas station; most are subcontracted by the hotels that offer tours to their guests. If you're going it on your own, ask around and know that prices are often based on a minimum number of passengers, usually four. Prices vary little, but it's definitely worth comparing. Monkey River day trips, for example, range US$60-75 pp, depending on whether lunch is included and the size of the boat. Half-day snorkel trips are about US$35-75 pp, depending on group size. Most tours require that you sign up the day before; reef tours typically leave around 9am, and inland tours around 7am.

I highly recommend **Splash Dive** (tel. 501/523-3080 or cell 501/610-0235, www. splashbelize.com) for inland trips, snorkel and dive tours to the cayes, or whale shark experiences. Their guides and drivers are professional and very friendly, and no request is ever too much for owner Patty Ramirez, who loves to meet travelers and is absolutely top-notch—she goes above and beyond to make sure you're taken care of and happy.

Nite Wind (tel. 501/503-3487 or cell 501/660-6333, doylegardiner@yahoo.com) is reliable for tours, as is **Seahorse Dive Shop** (tel. 501/523-3166, www.belizescuba.com). Locally owned **Ocean Motion** (tel. 501/523-3363, www.oceanmotionplacencia.com) gets great reviews and offers snorkeling and fishing tours to Ranguana and Silk Cayes (US$70

pp, lunch and equipment included; US$325 per boat for fishing 11-19 miles offshore). Hubert and Karen Young's **Joy Tours** (tel. 501/523-3325 or cell 501/601-0273, www.belizewithjoy. com, Monkey River US$63 pp, Laughingbird Caye snorkel US$75 pp) is across from Tim's Chinese restaurant. Clint, the son of the proprietress of Lydia's Guesthouse, operates **Pelican Tours** (tel. 501/634-8476 or 501/630-2795, lydias@btl.net); he'll take you to the reef or Monkey River (US$65 pp).

BEACHES

Placencia Village offers a long uninterrupted stretch of thick golden sand, good for walks, jogs, and dips. The beach is public, so you can feel free to spread your towel anywhere, as long as it's unoccupied by a resort's lounge chairs. The water isn't perfect Caribbean turquoise-clear, but it's clear enough and refreshing. Popular stretches are just across from Tipsy Tuna, ideal for grabbing lunch, some sun, and even some beach volleyball.

The prettiest beaches I have seen on the peninsula are in the Maya Beach area. You can pick any of the restaurants in that area—Robert's Grove, for instance—to lunch and swim off the beach for the day. A great unpretentious spot to chill for the day with a cocktail is the Maya Breeze Inn's beach bar; just bring a towel and your own snacks.

DIVING AND SNORKELING

Although the beach is usually fine for swimming and lounging, you won't see much with a mask and snorkel except sand, sea grass, a few fish, and other bathers. A short boat ride, however, will bring you to the barrier reef and the kind of underwater viewing you can write home about. Snorkel gear is available for rent (US$5 per day) everywhere, and trips to the cayes and reefs cost around US$50 per half-day, depending on the distance.

There are a handful dive shops with comparable prices, and you can either let your hotel arrange everything or do it yourself. The three well-known ones include, for starters, **Splash Dive Center** (tel. 501/523-3080 or cell

© LEBAWIT GIRMA

view of the Placencia Village beach from Belizean Nirvana hotel

501/610-0235, www.splashbelize.com, 2-tank dive US$120, snorkeling US$90 pp, lunch included) with two locations: an appointment and tour booking office across from Scotiabank (while they await completion of the new marina and Fishermen's Coop, after which they plan to return to their original location) and a top-notch Dive Center on the north end, across from Chabil Mar. The Dive Center is where Splash's fleet of six boats, including a brand-new 46-foot Newton, are docked, and from where trips depart. Splash has the most professional operation I've seen in Belize, from the way they handle their gear to the attention they pay to their customers, first-timers or experienced. They take care of everything, from pickups to fittings to food. Owner Patty Ramirez—named a Sea Hero in 2012 by *Scuba Diving* magazine for her dive center's contributions to community building and marine environmental awareness—left a banking career 13 years ago to pursue her passion. Along with her partner, Ralph, they're a classic example of a passion turned into a success story. Splash

also offers inland tours across Stann Creek and Belize.

Avadon Divers (tel. 501/503-3377, U.S. tel. 888/509-5617, www.avadondiversbelize.com) is another safe operation run by a brother-and-sister team with many years of experience. Call or check with your hotel for a trip schedule. **Seahorse Dive Shop** (near the town dock, tel. 501/523-3166, www.belizescuba.com, whale shark dive US$185 pp, 2-tank local reef dive US$110 pp), is highly recommended for whale shark tours. Farther north from the village, you'll find a couple of other serious dive operations linked to their respective resorts, with professional shops at Robert's Grove Beach Resort and Turtle Inn.

FISHING

Placencia has always been a fishing town for its sustenance, but with the advent of tourism, it has gained a worldwide reputation for sportfishing. Deepwater possibilities include wahoo, sailfish, marlin, kingfish, and dolphin fish; fly-fishing can hook you a grand

SOUTHERN COAST

slam—bonefish, tarpon, permit, and snook (all catch-and-release). Fortunately, serious angling means serious local guides, several of whom (like the Godfrey brothers, Earl and Kurt) have been featured on ESPN and in multiple fishing magazines. Hire Earl at **Trip'N Travel Southern Guides Fly Fishing and Saltwater Adventures** (Placencia Office Supply Bldg., tel. 501/523-3205, lgodfrey@btl. net). Most tour operators listed in this chapter offer fishing trips, and a few specialize in them, like **Kingfisher's Tarpon Caye Lodge** (tel. 501/523-3323, www.tarponcayelodge. com, 3- or 4-night all-inclusive fishing trip US$2,160 pp), boasting decades of experience. Charlie Leslie Sr., owner and head guide, has a stellar reputation and will take you to a variety of spots, from inshore places that include nearby flats to Tarpon Caye and the remote Ycacos area. Also ask about their island cabanas for rent. Check www.placencia.com for more options.

KAYAKING AND PADDLEBOARDING

An unforgettable and underrated way to explore the near-shore cayes, mangroves, creeks, and rivers is by paddle. Plastic open kayaks are available to guests at most resorts, and many tour operators and dive shops have some for rent as well. Located behind the peninsula, the Placencia Lagoon is home to birds, saltwater crocodiles, manatees, and mangroves. While it's easily explored solo by kayak, I recommend going with a guide if you're not an experienced kayaker, in case of a surprise croc encounter. **Avadon Divers** (tel. 501/503-3377, U.S. tel. 888/509-5617, www.avadondiversbelize.com) offers guided trips (US$100 pp, half day) and rentals for self-guided exploration (US$45-60 single and double kayaks).

Stand-up paddleboarding classes are available with the energetic Tony from **BelizeFit** (tel. 501/631-7427, tony@belizefit.com, hours vary, call ahead, private lessons US$25 per hour, board rental US$12.50 per hour). Tony offers morning beach workouts (US$10) and intro lessons. There's also an on-site gym. When I stopped by one morning, he had a group of eight folks tossing exercise balls on the beach—fun stuff!

BOATING AND SAILING

Opportunities abound for day trips, sunset cruises, snorkel voyages, and sail charters, all ideal for floating around the gorgeous southern cayes. Expensive, high-end **The Moorings** (tel. 501/523-3351, U.S. tel. 800/535-7289, www.moorings.com, US$500-1,700, minimum 3-day rental) has a dock for multiple catamaran adventures on their beautiful 40- to 46-foot cats, based on the lagoon side north of the airstrip and just across from Laru Beya Resort. Bring your own crew or charter one with a crew and all the bells and whistles for a weeklong sail. **Belize Sailing Charters** (tel. 501/523-3138, www.belize-sailing-charters. com) has bareboat and crewed yacht charters. Just across from town, **Placencia Yacht Club** (tel. 501/523-3500 or 501/653-0569, http://placenciayachtclub.com) is on Placencia Caye, featuring the Tranquilo Restaurant and Bar. The über-exclusive membership-based **Tradewinds Cruise Club** has headquarters here, in case you were wondering, on the lagoon side across from Sunset Pointe Condominiums. They'll pick you up from across the lagoon if you wave. Their 50-feet luxury cats will have you gawking.

MASSAGE AND BODYWORK

Sign up for a massage or other treatment at **The Secret Garden Massage and Day Spa** (behind Wallen's, tel. 501/523-3420 or cell 501/624-6096, www.secretgardenplacencia.com), where a one-hour massage costs US$50 and a special four-hands treatment costs a bit more. If you need relief from the sun and barefooting on the beach, try the sunburn treatment and foot massage for US$50. **Robert's Grove Beach Resort Spa** (just south of Seine Bight, tel. 501/523-3565), north of town, offers a full range of treatments—for premium prices, of course. **The Turtle Inn** (1 mile north of the village, tel. 501/523-3244 or 501/523-3150, www. turtleinn.com) also has pampering services, as does the **Siripohn's Thai Massage** (across from Barefoot Bar, tel. 501/620-8718, 10am-6pm

Mon.-Sat., massage US$75 per hour) right on the front street in Placencia Village, run by experienced Thais who offer seaweed treatments and papaya body polish. Also on the main drag, check into the affordable **Serenity Day Spa** (tel. 501/523-3513 or cell 501/669-7113, zel-mac96@yahoo.com, massage US$50 per hour), a small one-massage-bed cabin run by Belizean certified masseuse Zelma. It's right on the strip, but she gets rave reviews for her "magic hands."

If you're up for a workout, check out **BelizeFit** (tel. 501/631-7427, tony@belizefit.com, hours vary, call first) right off the sidewalk between Miramar and De Tatch Restaurant. Tony offers Beach Boot Camp, Thai stretch classes, and more.

Entertainment and Events
NIGHTLIFE

Placencia's bars, restaurants, and resorts do a decent job of coordination, so special events like beach barbecues, horseshoe tournaments, karaoke, and live music are offered through the entire week—especially during the high season. Your best bet is to check the *Placencia Breeze* (www.placenciabreeze.com) newspaper and look for current schedules, because bars and parties come and go with the wind.

The **Barefoot Bar** (tel. 501/523-3515, 11am-midnight daily) is the only constantly wildly popular venue in the high season. Flip-flop clad revelers choose from hundreds of froofy cocktails and bar food; there's live music (Fri.-Sun.) and happy hour (5pm-6pm daily) as well as never-ending theme parties. Another party constant is the beachfront **Tipsy Tuna** (next to Sea Spray Hotel, tel. 501/523-3089, tipsytuna@hotmail.com, 11:30am-midnight daily), with Garífuna drumming on Wednesday nights and a general all-day-long party vibe.

Another happening and locally popular bar and restaurant a bit farther down the harbor is **Yoli's,** with barbecue and ring toss starting at 3pm on Sunday. Stop by the **Pickled Parrot** (between the sidewalk and the main road, just off the soccer field, tel. 501/636-7068, 11:30am-9:30pm daily), where you can have a Belizean panty ripper via Jell-O shot or a three-rum Parrot Piss cocktail; maybe you'll have enough of those to graduate to their so-called secret VIP section. Partiers finish the weekend nights at the local **D'Eclipse Night Club** (follow the sign just after the airstrip, 10pm-4am daily), where a DJ plays the latest tunes from reggae to dancehall, *punta,* and more. Stay vigilant; there has been the occasional incident here, but it's otherwise generally safe year-round; make sure you have a ride there and back.

FESTIVALS AND EVENTS

The biggest party of the year happens the third week of June, during **Lobsterfest.** The whole south end of town closes down for lobster-catching tournaments, costumes, and dances, and there are food booths everywhere. **Easter weekend** is popular as well, as Placencia is a destination for many Belizeans as well as foreign visitors; they typically book their rooms months in advance, so be prepared for the crowds. Look for a Halloween celebration, complete with a parade and trick-or-treating for kids and adults alike. Another annual gig, the **Mistletoe Ball,** wanders to a different hotel before Christmas every year and doubles as a fund-raiser for the local Belize Tourism Industry Association chapter. **New Year's Eve** consists of one big outdoor party out on the soccer field, with all-inclusive drinks, hats, and more for just US$2.50 pp. The local humane society organizes various fund-raising events as well; keep an eye out.

Shopping

Despite plenty of gift stores featuring Guatemalan crafts and clothes, there are a couple of talented Belizean artists and wood-carvers worth checking out and supporting. Stop by the father-and-son-operated shop **A Piece of Belize Wood Carvings** (sidewalk shortcut across from Omar's, tel. 501/621-1595 or 501/628-1279, apieceofbelize01@yahoo.com, 9am-6pm daily, US$15-50, prices vary according to the item). Bob and Tyrone Lockwood make beautiful pieces using rosewood and ziricote wood, found only in Belize, including bowls, bracelets, and home decor pieces, even customized carved doors. Feel free to bargain with them. Just steps away, still on the sidewalk, is **Made in Belize** (tel. 501/205-5511 or cell 501/627-5125, 9am-5pm daily), where Leo has a shack filled with all sorts of creative carvings, including pieces made out of driftwood, mahogany, and ziricote.

Strike A Pose (main road, Placencia Village, 9am-7pm Tues.-Fri., 10am-6pm Sat., strikeapose.placencia@gmail.com) has a random selection of trendy clothes imported from Los Angeles, including plus-size options and evening dresses, in case you need a new outfit for a hot date.

Accommodations

All of Placencia's budget lodgings are found on or within shouting distance of the sidewalk, and most of the high-end resorts are strung along the beach north of town. Remember, these are high-season double occupancy prices; expect significant discounts and negotiable rates between May and November.

UNDER US$25

Right on the sidewalk, **Omar's** (tel. 501/634-4350, US$13 shared bath, US$22.50 private bath) is a wooden flophouse. If the office is closed, head to Omar's Creole Grub to inquire. Near the Anglican school, **Eloise Travel Lodge** (tel. 501/523-3299, US$20-25) has four guest rooms with private or shared baths and a communal kitchen. There is no reception office; ask for Miss Sonia Leslie.

A better budget bet is ◖ **Lydia's Guesthouse** (tel. 501/523-3117, lydias@btl.net, US$25), toward the north end of the sidewalk. Lydia's is a longtime favorite among backpackers. The eight clean, private guest rooms with a shared tile-floor bath also share a sociable two-story porch, a communal kitchen, fans, hammocks, and a 30-second walk to the beach. Miss Lydia will make you breakfast if you make arrangements the day before; she also makes fresh Creole bread and guava jam.

If you're out of options, stop by **BJ's Restaurant** (the building on the corner of the soccer field, up the stairs, US$20-30) and ask Miss Betty about her two budget guest rooms—they're basic and nothing more than a place to crash but cheap, one with a double bed, fans, and a shared bath; the second with three single beds and a private bath, ideal for backpacking friends.

US$25-50

As you enter Placencia, there is a gate by the Placencia Bazaar gift shop; ◖ **Deb & Dave's Last Resort** (tel. 501/523-3207 or 501/600-6044, US$25) consists of four small, clean guest rooms surrounding a tidy sand courtyard and tropical garden favored by hummingbirds. The common screened-in porch space is excellent for meeting your neighbors and telling war stories from the day's paddling and snorkeling trips; there are clean shared baths for all, free Wi-Fi, and a coffeemaker.

Claiming to be the "first established hotel on the Placencia Peninsula" (since 1964), the **Sea Spray Hotel** (Placencia sidewalk, tel. 501/523-3148, www.seasprayhotel.com, US$25-65) is a decent choice, although staff friendliness can be hit or miss. It's 30 feet from the ocean and has 20 guest rooms with private baths, refrigerators, hot and cold water, and coffeepots. There are economy guest rooms and nicer units closer to the water, where guests can relax in hammocks and chairs under palm trees. **De Tatch** seafood restaurant, on the premises, is popular for breakfast and serves up lunch and dinner.

US$50-100

A good deal right on the beach is **Julia's** (tel. 501/503-3478, www.juliascabanas.com, US$65-70), with simple stand-alone cabanas complete with double beds, mini fridges, wireless Internet, porches, and hammocks. The decor is a bit of a hodgepodge, but the price is right.

Well located within the village, right off the sidewalk, is **Sea View Suites Hotel** (beside Purple Space Monkey Village Restaurant, tel. 501/523-3777, www.seaviewplacencia.com, US$75), which gets rave reviews and has nine immaculately clean tile-floor guest rooms with a beach ambiance, double or king beds, coffee-makers, microwaves, beach towels, and cable TV.

At the extreme southern end of Placencia Village, look for the brightly painted **Tradewinds Hotel** (tel. 501/523-3122, trdewndpla@btl.net, US$75-95), on five acres near the sea, offering nine cabanas with spacious guest rooms, fans, refrigerators, coffeepots, and private yards just feet from the ocean. It's a bit dated but the interior is clean.

The **Cozy Corner Hotel** (tel. 501/523-3280 or 501/523-3540, cozycorner@btl.net, US$50-70) has 10 decent guest rooms with private baths and basic amenities, right behind the Cozy Corner bar-restaurant on the beach, with a nice breezy second-story porch; some guest rooms have air-conditioning. Next door, the Tipsy Tuna plays loud music at night.

The newly renovated **Sea Glass Inn** (formerly Dianni's Guest House, tel. 501/523-3098, www.seaglassinnbelize.com, US$79) is a lovely new addition to the village, with six immaculate guest rooms with twin or double beds, air-conditioning, coffeemakers, fridges, ceiling fans, and verandas looking onto a nice quiet stretch of sand with a dock, even if it's not quite a typical beach. Walk-ins are welcome, and the inn is well located, just a few steps from the sidewalk strip and the action in the village.

(Paradise Vacation Hotel (Placencia sidewalk, tel. 501/523-3179 or U.S. tel. 904/564-9400, www.belize123.com, US$89-159) has 12 air-conditioned guest rooms, each beautifully appointed, and an on-site seaside restaurant and bar, a spa, and a gift shop. Ask about Room 12 if you want to live it up a little. There is complimentary use of bikes and kayaks as well as a rooftop hot tub with views of the Maya Mountains. **Harry's Cozy Cabanas** (Placencia sidewalk, tel. 501/523-3234, www.cozycabanas.com, US$30) has three simple cabanas with screened porches.

Westwind Hotel (tel. 501/523-3255, www.westwindhotel.com, US$80-150) has 10 guest rooms with views, light tile floors, sunny decks, private baths, and fans (air-conditioning is optional and costs a little extra if you turn it on);

there's also wireless Internet access. The family unit goes for US$150. The hotel has a friendly vibe and a nice beach to relax on, although it's a little close to the pounding music at Tipsy Tuna. The **Ranguana Lodge** (tel. 501/523-3112, www.ranguanabelize.com, US$88-94) has five private cabanas: three air-conditioned beach cabins and two cabins set back with garden views. All are spacious and have nice wood floors, walls, and ceilings.

US$100-150

Captain Jak's (Placencia Village, tel. 501/523-3481, www.captainjaksbelize.com, US$90-120) is a quaint lagoon-side resort set in a tropical garden, with cabanas, two-story cottages, and a spacious villa (US$300). Each unit has a full kitchen, hot and cold water, and plenty of space to relax.

Easy Living Apartments (tel. 501/523-3481, www.easyliving.bz, from US$135, US$810 per week) offers four slightly dated, carpeted, but fully furnished two- and three-bedroom air-conditioned units; they are ideally located off the sidewalk. **(Miramar Apartments** (toward the north end of the sidewalk, tel. 501/523-3658, www.miramarbelize.com, US$125-235) is a favorite of mine; the hot pink building, opposite Lydia's Guesthouse and next to De Tatch, has studio (my favorite, on the first floor facing the beach), one-bedroom, and three-bedroom units. Each has a king bed, a full kitchen, air-conditioning, and cable TV. The three-bedroom unit has hardwood flooring, beautiful decorations, original artwork, and a large sea-view balcony. It's a great place for a family getaway or solo traveler.

OVER US$150

Belizean Nirvana (tel. 501/523-3331, www.belizeannirvana.com, US$150-275) is one of the newer additions to the village and lives up to its boutique-hotel status. It's right in the heart of the action, with five one- and two-bedroom suites adorned with Belizean artwork, full kitchenettes, bathrobes, balconies with direct views of the beach and the sea, air-conditioning, and continental breakfast delivered to your suite at your chosen hour of the morning. Amenities are plentiful, including use of bicycles, wireless Internet, a rooftop grill (don't miss the incredible view from up there), with hammocks and a kitchen area, local cell phones you can top up during your stay, and a magic-Jack for calls overseas. The hotel can also book Tropic Air flights for you, or pick you up from Belize City at additional cost.

At **Chabil Mar** (tel. 501/523-3606, www.chabilmarvillas.com, US$375-525), the privately owned luxury villas have richly decorated interiors and are furnished with all the modern conveniences one could ask for. On the beach less than a mile north of Placencia Village, the exclusive Café Mar provides butler service so you can dine where you please: at poolside (there are two), on the pier or a private veranda, or in the comfort of your villa. It's a popular spot for small weddings.

One of the few truly upscale options that's actually in Placencia Village, **Sunset Pointe Apartments** (Placencia Lagoon, tel. 501/664-4740, U.S. tel. 904/471-3599, www.sunset-pointebelize.com, US$250-275) offers luxury two-bedroom condos for short- or long-term rental, often advertised online. They're back on the lagoon side, but they all have raised roof decks with a breeze. It's only a 10-minute walk to the beach from here, and there are many accessible restaurants and shops.

Turtle Inn (tel. 501/523-3244 or 501/523-3150, www.turtleinn.com) is one of the nation's premier luxe destinations, one of U.S. film producer Francis Ford Coppola's two Belizean properties. It is about a mile north of Placencia Village. Prices start at US$375 per night for the Garden View Cottages and go up to US$1,850 per night for the master two-bedroom pavilion house with a private entrance, a pool, and a dining pavilion. Even if you're not staying here, swing by to treat yourself to a fine meal with beautifully framed views of the ocean. Turtle Inn has seven luxury villas and 18 cottages on offer. The guest rooms are designed along Indonesian and Belizean lines, with lots of natural materials and airy space. The high thatched ceilings absorb the heat, so there are fans only, no air-conditioning; but there are music players for your iPod as well as fancy shell phones. There are two swimming pools, the über-mellow Laughing Fish Bar on the beach, and one of the peninsula's premier restaurants, the Mare Restaurant. There's also an on-site spa, dive shop, and more dining options; Auntie Luba's Belizean eatery and the Gauguin Grill are open for dinner 6pm-9pm daily.

Food

Placencia has a small number of restaurants, but there's enough variety to keep you stuffed during your visit: seafood cooked in coconut milk and local herbs, Creole stews and fry chicken, sandwiches, burritos, burgers, French, Italian, and adequate vegetarian options nearly everywhere you go.

BAKERIES AND CAFÉS

John the Bakerman (7am-close daily) makes great breads, cinnamon buns, and coffee bread, available all day; he also sells his brother's meat pies. Look for his sign on the sidewalk and get it fresh out of the oven around 5pm.

You can get your latte or cappuccino fix at the small **Brewed Awakenings** (main road, Placencia Village, tel. 501/668-1715, 6:30am-5pm Mon.-Sat.), serving up daily fresh roasted Belizean coffee from a small shack with little seating but plenty of street action. There are a dozen of flavor options, from Kahlua to Nutty Irishman, to blend in your coffee, as well as iced cappuccino and other fancy coffee concoctions.

In Placencia Village Square, (**Tutti Frutti Gelatería** (tel. 501/620-9916, tizi.lory@virgilio.it, 9am-9pm daily) serves up some of the best homemade gelato you'll have outside of Italy; it's made fresh daily with local fruits and traditional flavors. The fruit sorbets are dairy-free, and espresso drinks and iced coffees are served.

Up the road, just across from the town dock, look for **The Shak Beach Café** (tel. 501/622-1686, 7am-7pm daily), which has 21 smoothie flavors, all made with fresh fruit, along with a healthy vegetarian menu, a view of the water from their dockside tables, and good breakfasts of banana pancakes or omelets with coffee or tea (US$5-6).

BELIZEAN AND INTERNATIONAL

Omar's Creole Grub (tel. 501/634-4350, 7am-2:30pm and 6pm-9pm Sun.-Thurs., 6pm-9pm Sat.) will take care of you all day, with a lobster omelet, handmade tortillas, and guava jelly (US$9) to start the day off, then a burrito for lunch (US$4), and Creole-style barracuda steak (from US$7), pork chops, conch steak, or lobster for dinner. Chef Omar Jr. won the 2009 Lobsterfest Cook-Off with his stuffed lobster. Come for the seafood, and stay for the conversation with the vivacious Omar and family, whose children all work at the restaurant. No alcohol is served.

Walk slowly as you pass Omar's, because you might just miss a faded white screen door, where **Miss Myrtle** (main road, Placencia Village, 6am-3pm Mon.-Fri.) serves up Belizean breakfasts and delicious home-cooked boxed lunches. The mystery door is right next to the Strike A Pose clothing boutique. The coconut rice and beans are some of the moistest and most delicious I have tried.

Dawn's Grill n'Go (tel. 501/602-9302, grillngo@yahoo.com, 7am-3pm and 5:30pm-9pm Mon.-Sat., US$10-15) has finger lickin' good fried chicken—served on Friday—and a cozy spot on the main road where Miss Dawn loves to serve up her creative specials, whether local favorites or international dishes, including pastas, seafood, fajitas and lobster burgers. There's nothing "fast" tasting about the food here. Be sure to sample her decadent banana bread pudding with One Barrel rum sauce—yum!

BJ's Belizean Bellyfull (on the corner of the soccer field, 7am-7pm Mon.-Sat., 7am-4pm Sun., US$2.50-10), "where good food and God's people meet," has an upstairs outdoor porch and cheap fare: sandwiches from US$2.50, a buffet lunch, seafood and stir-fry dinners for US$10. Next door, **C Wendy's Restaurant and Bar** (tel. 501/523-3335, 7am-9:30pm daily, US$3-23) offers varied, consistently tasty Creole and international dishes at reasonable prices, the best outdoor people-watching veranda in the village, plus a glassed-in, air-conditioned seating area and a full bar. This is a great cool place to come to for Creole and Mexican cooking (they have the best breakfast stuffed fry jacks, by the way), burgers (US$3-7.50), burritos (US$4.50-8), and fancier steaks and seafood items (US$13-23). There's no hit or miss at Wendy's no matter what you order.

The long-standing **Galley Restaurant** (behind the soccer field, tel. 501/523-3133, 11am-2:30pm and 5:30pm-9pm Mon.-Sat., US$4-30) is popular among the locals for offering some of the cheapest local eats but also for their freshly made seaweed punch that Belizeans say "give yuh strong back"; draw your own conclusions. The thick crust pizzas are also a hit among residents.

The Cozy Corner (Placencia sidewalk, tel. 501/523-3280, cozycorner@btl.net, 7am-10pm Tues.-Sun., US$8-13) has a relaxed open-air atmosphere and is one of the nicer beach bars. For breakfast in Belize you can never go wrong with eggs, beans, and fry jacks; they also have a lobster burger, fish dinners, and good bar food.

FINE DINING

The revamped **C Secret Garden Restaurant** (main road, Placencia Village, tel. 501/634-9789, thesecretgardenrestaurant@live.com, 5pm-11pm Mon.-Sat., US$14-17) is a breath of fresh air, offering up tasty Caribbean and Latin and Asian-fusion dishes, including delicious pasta, seafood gumbo, chicken Maya, and Argentinian steak, among others. There's a full bar and a wonderful ambiance, with a garden patio or indoor seating. Don't miss the signature stacked ceviche or their Belizean lime tart, when available. The place fills up quickly, so be sure to make reservations.

Rumfish y Vino Wine and Gastro Bar (main road, Placencia Village, tel. 501/523-3293, www.rumfishyvino.com, 2pm-midnight daily, US$7-15) opened in 2008; the

SOUTHERN COAST

Solomons bought the place while honeymooning. Pamela, a wine specialist, imports Italian and Californian wine, and John works his magic in the kitchen. The menu features a mix of international comfort food, from fish-and-chips to pastas, short ribs, and more.

Most of the resorts north of town have fine restaurants to brag about. Grab a fistful of dollars and a taxi and bon appétit. At The Turtle Inn's **Mare Restaurant** (main road, 1 mile north of the village, tel. 501/523-3244 or 501/523-3150, www.turtleinn.com, 9am-10pm, US$15-35), the chef prepares meals with greens from his own on-site organic herb garden, as well as those grown in their upland sister resort's extensive organic vegetable garden. In fact, this is the best place to come for a fresh green salad in Placencia—as well as seafood, pasta, and oven-baked gourmet pizza.

The **Seaside Restaurant** (tel. 501/523-3565, 7am-9pm daily, US$12-28) at Robert's Grove Beach Resort serves mouthwatering seafood and imported U.S. steaks. Don't forget **Habanero Mexican Café and Bar** (tel. 501/523-3565, 3pm-9pm daily Oct.-May, US$9-15) for excellent Mexican food, just south of Seine Bight and across from Robert's Grove. A few miles farther north, **Maya Beach Hotel Bistro** (tel. 501/533-8040, 7am-9pm Tues.-Sun., US$14-28) has Placencians raving and unanimously declaring that the food and experience is well worth the US$15 taxi trip from town (or US$1 on the afternoon bus). The options here are unique—try the four sampler platters—and owner Ellen Lee can help you pair your menu choice with the right wine.

GROCERIES
Wallen's Market (8:30am-noon and 1:30pm-5:30pm Mon.-Sat.) is on the main road, close to the soccer field, and sells groceries, dry goods, and sundries. **Everyday Supermarket** (7am-9pm daily) is in the center of town.

Information and Services
TOURIST INFORMATION
The **Placencia Tourism Center** website (www.placencia.com) is one of the most organized and useful in the country. Upon arrival in town, head straight to the **Tourism Office** (back of the Scotiabank Bldg., 2nd Fl., tel. 501/523-4045, placencia@btl.net, 9am-5pm Mon.-Fri.) in Placencia Village Square. After reading the various postings on the wall, pick up a copy of the latest *Placencia Breeze* (www.placenciabreeze.com), a monthly rag with many helpful schedules and listings, including happy hours and house rentals. The tourism office also sells books, maps, music CDs, and postcards, and it has a mail drop; the office will not recommend one business over another.

The **BTL office** (8am-5pm Mon.-Fri.) is located at the bottom of the big red-and-white antenna.

BANKS
Belize Bank (8am-3pm Mon.-Thurs., 8am-4:30pm Fri.) is located by the marina and has a 24-hour ATM. **Atlantic Bank** (8am-3pm Mon.-Thurs., 8am-4:30pm Fri.) has an ATM in town, across the road from Wendy's. **Scotiabank** (8am-2:30pm Mon.-Thurs., 8am-3:30pm Fri., 9am-11:30am Sat.) has an ATM just north of the BTL office.

HEALTH AND EMERGENCIES
The **Placencia Medical Center** (tel. 501/523-3326, 8:30am-4:30pm Mon.-Fri.) is located behind the school. For after-hour emergencies, **Dr. Alexis Caballero** (tel. 501/523-4038) makes house calls, should you have a severe shellfish reaction. The village of Independence, a short boat ride away, has the nearest 24-hour clinic to Placencia. If a medevac to Belize City is not possible, this is where a patient will be taken in an emergency. There is a **private clinic** (tel. 501/601-2769) on Water Side Street and a public hospital providing health care to the poor. There is a **pharmacy** (above Wallen's Market, on the main road, close to the soccer field, tel. 501/523-3346).

For **police,** contact the Placencia police station (tel. 501/503-3142), the Seine Bight station (tel. 501/503-3148), or the Tourism Police (tel. 501/503-3181).

MEDIA AND COMMUNICATIONS
Placencia Office Supply (tel. 501/523-3205, fax 888/329-6302, plaofficesupply@gmail.com, 8am-5pm Mon.-Sat., closes at lunchtime), tucked off the main road in the town center, has a copy machine, Internet access, and can send faxes; they will let you plug into their Ethernet or use their wireless Internet (US$4 per hour).

Getting There
There are a number of ways to travel the 100-plus miles between Placencia Village and Belize City. The tip of the long peninsula is not as isolated as it used to be, and various options exist for continuing on to points south and west, including Guatemala and Honduras.

BY AIR
At last check, there were more than 20 daily flights in and out of Placencia's precarious little airstrip, to and from various destinations throughout Belize. Planes generally hop from either of Belize City's two airports to Dangriga, Placencia, and Punta Gorda (in that order, usually landing at all three), then turn around for the reverse trip north. Ask about service to Belmopan if you are headed to Cayo. For current schedules and fares, check directly with the two airlines: **Maya Island Air** (tel. 501/223-1140, U.S. tel. 800/225-6732, www.mayaislandair.com) or **Tropic Air** (tel. 501/226-2012, U.S. tel. 800/422-3435, www.tropicair.com). There is sometimes air service between nearby Savannah Airport (near Independence Village) and San Pedro Sula in Honduras; three flights a week cost about US$160.

BY CAR
The 21-mile excuse for a road from Placencia Village to where the peninsula hits the mainland was a rutted, dusty nightmare for decades. Then, in July 2008, the highest officials in the land gathered at Robert's Grove Beach Resort and signed the papers to begin the paving project that was completed in 2010. And the people rejoiced. It's now about a three- or

four-hour drive from Belize City. From Belize City, most people drive via the Hummingbird and Southern Highways. About half an hour after turning south before Dangriga, look for a left turn to Riverside, where you'll begin the peninsula road.

The **gas station** (6am-7pm daily) is located by the M&M hardware store in the center of the village.

BY BUS
Placencia Village is served by three daily bus departures and arrivals (in high season, anyway; service is spotty the rest of the year). Buses come and go from the center of the village, right next to the M&M Hardware Store, and current schedules are available at the Placencia Tourism Office and inside the Placencia Breeze. Buses to Dangriga (Ritchie's Bus Service) depart at 5:45am, 7am, 12:45pm, and 2:30pm Monday-Saturday, and 7am, 12:45pm, and 2:30pm Sunday. There's also a 6:15am express bus to Belize City (air-conditioned, US$13 pp). Otherwise, you'll need to change in Dangriga to reach Belize City. You can change again in Belmopan for a westbound Cayo bus. Cost is about US$5 or less for each leg of the journey. The more common—and quickest—bus route is via the boat to Mango Creek and Independence Village.

BY BOAT
For those traveling to points south, like Punta Gorda or Guatemala, or for those who want to avoid the Placencia Road, a boat-and-bus combo will get you back to the mainland and on your way. **Hokey Pokey Water Taxi** (tel. 501/523-2376, 501/601-0271, or 501/601-8897) provides regular service between the gas station dock behind M&M Hardware in the center of the village and the dilapidated landing at Mango Creek, charging US$5 one-way for the 15-minute trip through bird-filled mangrove lagoons. Boats leave Placencia at 6:45am, 10am, 12:30pm, 2:30pm, 4pm, and 5pm daily, and 6pm Monday-Saturday; the same boat turns around for the reverse trip: 6:30am,

SOUTHERN COAST

7:30am, 8am, 10am, 11am, noon, 2:30pm, 4:30pm, and 5:30pm. Hokey Pokey is a reliable family-run operation, proudly steered by captains Pole, Lito, and Caral.

Bus connections to all points are coordinated with the 10am and 4pm boats from Placencia, so the traveler need only worry about stepping onto the correct bus when the boat lands in Independence after the quick taxi shuttle (US$0.50) to the bus depot by Rosa's Restaurant (5:30am-3pm Mon.-Sun.). The last bus to Punta Gorda leaves at 8pm, sometimes later, and the last ride to Dangriga and Belize City is at 5:30pm. The earliest northbound bus from Punta Gorda arrives around 7am, and the James express arrives at 9am.

TO HONDURAS AND GUATEMALA

The ship to **Puerto Cortés** (tel. 501/202-4506 or 501/603-7787, Honduras tel. 504/665-1200) leaves at 9am every Friday, returning at 2pm Monday afternoon. The trip costs US$60 and takes roughly four hours, stopping in Big Creek, Belize, for immigration purposes, and carrying a maximum of 50 passengers. Buy tickets at the Placencia Tourism Office. Every now and then (sometimes as often as a couple of times a week), a boatload of passengers arrives in Placencia from Livingston, Guatemala, and seeks passengers to take with them back to Livingston (with an immigration stop in Punta Gorda). Inquire at Caribbean Tours and Travels.

Getting Around

Placencia Village itself is small enough to walk, and if you're commuting on the sidewalk, walking is your only option (riding a bike on the sidewalk can earn you a US$50 fine). Speaking of two-wheeled options, there are plenty of bicycle rentals in town. If bicycling north on the road, know that Seine Bight is five miles from Placencia and Maya Beach another 2.5 miles. The cheapest way (besides walking) to get up and down the peninsula is to hop on a bus as it travels to or from Dangriga.

TAXIS

There used to be a free shuttle service up and down the peninsula, but no longer. In the meantime, there are at least a dozen green-plated taxis hanging around the gas stations and the airstrip. Rides from town to the airstrip cost US$6 for one or two people, to the Seine Bight area one-way US$12, to Maya Beach US$15. Ask around the gas station and tourist office, and look for posted rate lists to know what you should be paying. The more trusted and long-standing taxi services include **Radiance Ritchie** (tel. 501/523-3321), and **Traveling Gecko** (tel. 501/523-4078). My own preferred driver is Noel of **Noel Taxi Service** (tel. 501/600-6047 or 501/632-0980); he works late in the night, ideal for solo female travelers.

CAR RENTAL

Rent a car for do-it-yourself land tours to the Jaguar or Mayflower nature reserves, or for trips to the ruins near Punta Gorda. Otherwise you'll pay US$50-100 pp to join a tour group. **Barefoot Rentals** (tel. 501/523-3066 or cell 501/629-9602, www.barefootservicesbelize.com) has a selection of cars (US$65-85 per day), golf carts (US$32-49 per day), and scooters (US$9 per hour). **Captain Jak's** (tel. 501/622-7104, www.captainjaks.com), right in the center of the village, rents golf carts.

MONKEY RIVER

An easy 35-minute boat ride from Placencia brings you to the mouth of the Monkey River and the village of the same name. Founded in 1891, Monkey River village was once a thriving town of several thousand loggers, *chicleros*, banana farmers, and anglers; that was then. Now, the very sleepy village of 30 families (about 150 people) makes its way with fishing and, you guessed it, tourism, though the latter has been slow as of late. Many villagers are trained and licensed tour guides who work with hotels in Placencia to provide unique wildlife-viewing experiences.

Ninety percent of the structures you see have been rebuilt since Hurricane Iris destroyed

© LEBAWIT GIRMA

Monkey River

the town in 2001. The village is accessible by boat—most often through the mangroves from Placencia—but there is also an 11-mile road from the Southern Highway that ends across the river from the village.

If you're on a tour from Placencia, after negotiating the mangrove maze your guide will take you into the river's mouth and dock up in town for a restroom break and a chance to place your lunch order for later in the day. Then you'll be off upstream, all eyes peeled for animals. You'll beach up at the trailhead to explore a piece of **Payne's Creek National Park,** a 31,000-acre reserve that is surrounded by even more protected area. You'll hike through the dense brush, now a regenerating broadleaf forest that will take decades to reach its pre-Iris glory. Then it's back down the river for lunch and a stroll through the village. Most head back to their guest rooms in Placencia, but you may wish to consider staying a night or two, either to experience the village life or to get some serious fishing time in.

Accommodations and Food

The options in Monkey River are casual inns, best appreciated by those who enjoy isolation and primitive surroundings. Most offer a set menu with a different entrée served each day. Reservations are required for meals, but all of these small cafés will serve drop-ins something, such as a burger or a beer.

Near the breezy part of town by the mini basketball court, **Alice's Restaurant** (tel. 501/543-3079, noon-3pm, US$6) offers meals served in a large dining room with a view of the sea; renting one of her airy wood guest rooms in a neighboring building costs US$23, with a fan and a shared bath with hot and cold water. **Sunset Inn** (tel. 501/720-2028, www.monkeyriverfishing.com, US$50) is a two-story green structure with eight musty guest rooms with private baths, fans, and hot and cold water. Decent meals can be had for about US$8. Monkey River native and owner Clive Garbutt knows the area inside out, and can easily guide fishing and snorkel tours. The **Black Coral Gift Shop, Bar, and Restaurant** (US$5-15) is located one street back from the riverfront and offers simple fare, local crafts, and Internet access. The family that runs this hotel has an acclaimed guide service too, especially for sportfishing trips.

All hotels and resorts offer sea and land tours and trips. Local guides and fishers are experts. Sorry, there's no dive shop yet, but bring your snorkeling gear. Overnight caye trips are available, as are river camping trips: you're dropped off at the Bladen bridge and canoe down the river, stopping at night to camp.

Islands near Placencia

GLADDEN SPIT AND SILK CAYE MARINE RESERVE

Belize's famous seasonal whale shark site is the protected **Gladden Spit and Silk Caye Marine Reserve** (tel. 501/523-3377, www.seabelize. org), 26 miles from the coast of Placencia. Gladden Spit, known as "the elbow" of the Silk Cayes Marine Reserve, is where whale sharks congregate once a month March-June to feed off spawning fish. Divers have the unique opportunity to swim alongside these giant, gentle creatures. For such a memorable experience,

contact **Splash Dive Center** (tel. 501/523-3080 or cell 501/610-0235, www.splashbelize.com).

Also part of the reserve are the **Silk Cayes,** tiny plots of land said to be the most-photographed islands of Belize. What the Silk Cayes lack in size they make up for in diving and snorkeling bliss, with rich marinelife that includes stingrays, barracuda, and lobsters. Ask Splash Dive Center about the snorkel site just off Silk Cayes, where anglers regularly clean their catch and dozens of magnificent loggerhead turtles gather to feed every day, themselves vying for the scraps of fish.

© LEBAWIT GIRMA

Laughingbird Caye National Park makes a great island getaway for the day.

HATCHET CAYE

The latest hit among couples and honeymooners, this 7.1-acre private resort (18 miles offshore from Placencia Village, tel. 501/523-3337 or 501/533-4446, www.hatchetcaye.com, US$250-300) offers eight casitas with all the amenities, outdoor decks, and an on-site dive shop with complimentary sports gear—from kayaks to Hobie Cats, paddleboards, and fishing gear. There's also a small beachfront swimming pool, bar, and restaurant. It has a bit more of an upscale vibe, and it gets rave reviews from vacationing lovebirds.

◖ LAUGHINGBIRD CAYE NATIONAL PARK

Located close to the Silk Cayes and managed by the nonprofit **Southern Environmental Association** (SEA Belize, office near Placencia town dock, tel. 501/523-3377, www.seabelize. org), Laughingbird Caye National Park is an important protected area encompassing over 10,000 acres. With swaying palms, small beautiful beaches, an absence of biting bugs, shallow sandy swimming areas, and interesting snorkeling and diving, it's a popular day trip from Placencia.

This particular kind of caye is referred to as a *faro;* the arms on each end make a kind of enclosure around a lagoon area on the leeward side. In this way, the island acts much like a mini atoll. That's good news for those wishing to **dive** the eastern side of the island. You'll find a lot of elkhorn coral and fish life. Grunts, damselfish, parrot fish, houndfish, bonefish, and even rays and nurse sharks are to be found here.

This site was designated in December 1991. The reserve is visited regularly, mostly by researchers and travelers brought out by tour operators from Placencia for picnics, snorkeling, and diving. Private yachts and sea kayaks also use the site regularly, and some mooring buoys have been installed to prevent anchor damage to the surrounding reef. There is one **trail** through the center of the caye.

SEA Belize also manages the Sapodilla Cayes, Placencia Lagoon, and Gladden Spit and Silk Cayes Marine Reserve, a famous whale shark site. Both the Silk Cayes and Laughingbird Caye can be enjoyed in one day's trip.

PUNTA GORDA AND THE TOLEDO DISTRICT

The Toledo District is "God's country," according to 15-year adventure tour guide veteran and Punta Gorda resident Bruno Kuppinger. Because it's the farthest in distance from Belize City, few pick "PG"—as Belizeans affectionately call this area—over the more conveniently reached Cayo. But just an hour and a half on a regional flight from Belize City will land visitors in the real

© LEBAWIT GIRMA

HIGHLIGHTS

LOOK FOR **⟨** TO FIND RECOMMENDED SIGHTS, ACTIVITIES, DINING, AND LODGING.

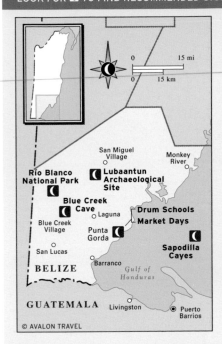

© AVALON TRAVEL

⟨ Drum Schools: Two renowned drum mas-

ters teach how to play the Garífuna drums or the West African *djembe* drum, keeping Punta Gorda's African diaspora culture alive (page 261).

⟨ Market Days: Punta Gorda comes alive on market days, with eateries, shopping, music, and vendors and goods from all the district's villages (page 267).

⟨ Sapodilla Cayes: This distant yet alluring cluster of cayes offers rarely visited dive sites with abundant marinelife, powdery white sand beaches—and utter seclusion (page 277).

⟨ Lubaantun Archaeological Site: The ancestors of today's Maya used this ceremonial center, which—along with nearby Nim Li Punit and Uxbenka—boasts stunning views, thick forests, and several long-standing legends (page 283).

⟨ Río Blanco National Park: In addition to waterfalls, this beautiful national park offers diverse flora and fauna plus the possibility of jaguar sightings. Bring your camera (page 286).

⟨ Blue Creek Cave: Swim up to 600 yards inside this stunning cave—the source of the Río Blanco—located near the village of Blue Creek (page 287).

backcountry of Belize, where they'll find all that is authentically Belizean in one place: virgin rainforests, waterfalls, five Maya archeological sites, proximity to pristine cayes for snorkeling and sportfishing, and a population considered the most diverse in the country. The Creole, the East Indians, the Garífuna, and the Maya all coexist here in a world where most home cooking is still done on a fire hearth and deer dances of the past are performed in the present.

The Toledo District has the lowest per capita income in Belize, yet it is also the most expensive in which to live. More than 10,000 Q'eqchi' and Mopan Maya are subsistence farmers in the Toledo countryside. This is chocolate country—home to organic cacao farms that supply all four of Belize's quality chocolate producers.

While tourism isn't yet booming, more restaurants are sprouting, jungle lodges continue to thrive while new ones appear, the cacao trail is growing, and cultural celebrations, PG's strength, are numerous—the annual Chocolate Festival and the Battle of the Drums are two of the country's most popular events, often selling out most accommodations in the district. Rapid improvements to the Southern Highway and San Antonio Road, giving easier access to sights and villages, and daily air service to and

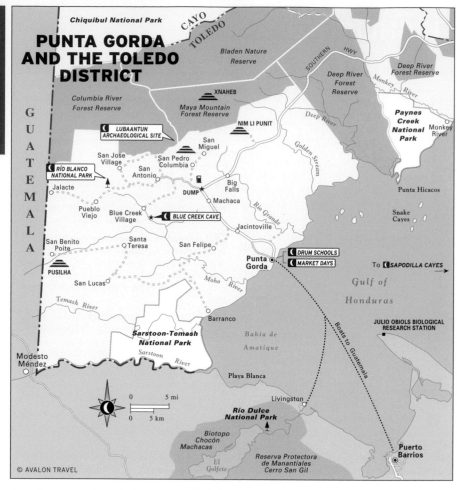

from Punta Gorda are helping to put Toledo on the map. There's never-ending hope that visitors will realize this is the most untouched part of Belize.

PLANNING YOUR TIME

To best explore the Toledo District, you'll need to set aside at least 4-5 days or more. Spend a full day exploring **Punta Gorda,** the urban heart of the deep south. Take a walk along **The Waterfront,** sign up for a lesson at one of the **Drum Schools,** and definitely time your visit to coincide with one of Punta Gorda's **Market Days.**

Make a day-trip to **Port of Honduras Marine Reserve and Snake Cayes,** where you can snorkel, dive, or simply soak in the views from the observation tower. Or save your relaxation for a two-day adventure to **Sapodilla Cayes,** for snorkeling and diving amid shipwrecks before lazing on the prettiest of beaches.

Continue your excursion into the Toledo District with a visit to the upcountry village of San Pedro Columbia and tour nearby

Lubaantun Archaeological Site, a notable Maya ruin. **Río Blanco National Park** lies east toward the Guatemalan border and offers a spectacular waterfall, hiking trail, caves, and plenty of stunning scenery, or see where the Río Blanco begins at stunning **Blue Creek Cave.**

Punta Gorda and Vicinity

Toledo District's county seat and biggest town, PG is simultaneously the lazy end of the road and an exciting jumping-off point to upland villages, offshore cayes, Guatemala, or Honduras. Punta Gorda's 5,000 or so inhabitants live their daily lives getting by from hurricane to hurricane.

Punta Gorda is a simple port, with no real beach but plenty of swimming spots, and its crooked streets are framed by many old dilapidated wooden buildings. The majority of inhabitants in town are of Garífuna and East Indian descent, although there are representatives of most of the country's ethnic groups. Fishing was the main support of the local people for centuries; today many anglers work for a nearby high-tech shrimp farm. Local farmers grow rice, mangoes, bananas, sugarcane, and beans—mainly for themselves and the local market. Fair trade-certified and organic cacao beans are an important export as well, used to make chocolate by the Green & Black's company in England.

ORIENTATION

Punta Gorda is a casual village with few street names. Arriving from the north, you'll cross a bridge over Joe Taylor Creek, and then be greeted by the towering Sea Front Inn, with the Caribbean on your left. After the road splits at the UNO gas station, it forms North Park Street (a diagonal street one block long) on the right and Front Street on the left. Following Front Street will take you through town, past the boat taxi pier, the immigration office, the market, and several eating establishments; continue all the way south to Nature's Way Guest House at the bottom of Church Street, followed by Blue Belize Guest House. The municipal dock and town plaza, just a couple of blocks in from the sea, form the town center.

If you arrive by bus or at the town dock from Guatemala, prepare to be greeted by a few local hustlers; feel free to shake them off by firmly refusing their services.

SIGHTS
The Waterfront

Even though there is no real lounging beach or developed waterfront, people go swimming and sunning off the dock just north of Joe Taylor Creek. The waterfront is rocky but quiet and tranquil, with small waves lapping the shoreline, and a walk along its length, especially at sunrise, should be a top priority of your visit.

Central Park

The **town park,** on a small triangle of soil roughly in the center of town, has an appropriately sleepy air to it, though plenty of activity swirls around it. At the north end is a raised stage dedicated to the "Pioneers of Belizean Independence." In the center of the park is a dry fountain, along with a few green cement benches, and a giant clock tower on the south end. On market days, this is an especially pleasant spot to take a break, enjoy the blue sky, and watch the activities of the villagers who have come in to sell their produce.

◖ Drum Schools

PG's diverse population provides a chance to learn drumming from two African-rooted cultures: Garífuna and Creole. For Garífuna drumming, Raymond "Ray" McDonald of the **Warasa Drum School** (New Rd., tel. 501/632-7701, www.warasadrumschool.com, 4:30pm-8pm Mon.-Fri., 9am-8pm Sat.-Sun., US$12.50 per hour drum lesson, US$25 per hour drum

PUNTA GORDA

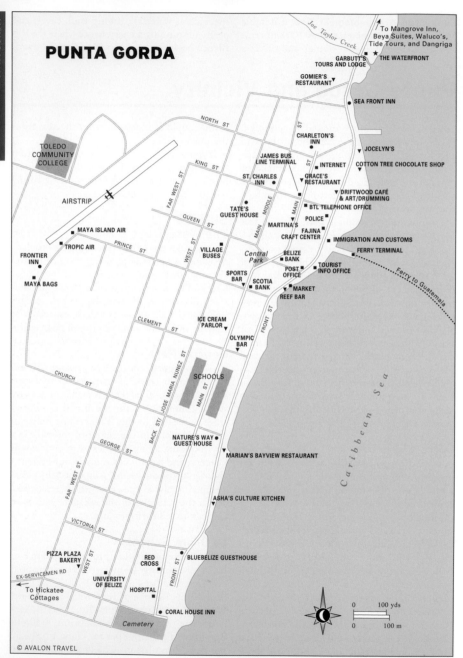

PUNTA GORDA

TOLEDO COMMUNITY COLLEGE

AIRSTRIP

NORTH ST

KING ST

FAR WEST ST

QUEEN ST

PRINCE ST

WEST ST

CLEMENT ST

CHURCH ST

JOSE MARIA NUNEZ ST

BACK ST

GEORGE ST

FAR WEST ST

VICTORIA ST

WEST ST

FRONT ST

MAIN ST

EX-SERVICEMEN RD

← To Hickatee Cottages

MAYA ISLAND AIR

TROPIC AIR

FRONTIER INN

MAYA BAGS

TATE'S GUEST HOUSE

VILLAGE BUSES

SPORTS BAR

SCOTIA BANK

ICE CREAM PARLOR

OLYMPIC BAR

SCHOOLS

NATURE'S WAY GUEST HOUSE

PIZZA PLAZA BAKERY

RED CROSS

UNIVERSITY OF BELIZE

HOSPITAL

CORAL HOUSE INN

Cemetery

Joe Taylor Creek

To Mangrove Inn, Beya Suites, Waluco's, Tide Tours, and Dangriga ↑

GARBUTT'S TOURS AND LODGE   ★ **THE WATERFRONT**

GOMIER'S RESTAURANT ▼

ST

SEA FRONT INN

CHARLETON'S INN

JAMES BUS LINE TERMINAL

ST. CHARLES INN

MAIN ST

MIDDLE ST

JOCELYN'S ▼

INTERNET   **COTTON TREE CHOCOLATE SHOP**

GRACE'S RESTAURANT

▼ **DRIFTWOOD CAFÉ & ART/DRUMMING**

BTL TELEPHONE OFFICE

POLICE

MARTINA'S

FAJINA CRAFT CENTER

IMMIGRATION AND CUSTOMS

FERRY TERMINAL

Central Park

BELIZE BANK

POST OFFICE

TOURIST INFO OFFICE

MARKET

REEF BAR

Ferry to Guatemala

Caribbean Sea

MARIAN'S BAYVIEW RESTAURANT ▼

ASHA'S CULTURE KITCHEN ▼

BLUEBELIZE GUESTHOUSE

0   100 yds
0   100 m

© AVALON TRAVEL

© LEBAWIT GIRMA

Central Park is a great place to watch all the activity in town.

making) is one of Belize's top drummers and a local star in Punta Gorda for his undeniable skills. He offers an introductory class on Garífuna drumming; learn about the various rhythms, how to produce the correct sound, and then start jamming. Private lessons start at US$10 per hour. Ray also teaches drum making (ask to see his very own custom collection) and drumming at various lodges in town, particularly at Hickatee Cottages. The school's location in a Garífuna Reserve area on the edge of town is currently being upgraded with a large new thatched hut.

Continue your drumming tour of Belize's south with the **Maroon Creole Drum School** (currently at Driftwood Café & Art, 9 Front St., tel. 501/632-7841 or 501/668-7733, methos_drums@hotmail.com, 7am-4pm daily, US$10 per hour), run by renowned Belizean musician and drum master Emmeth Young, previously located in San Pedro Colombia and now in his new home in Punta Gorda town. Emmeth is a talented man whose drumming and efforts to preserve Belizean culture have

been featured on the Travel Channel, among other media. Originally from the Creole village of Gales Point, Emmeth's *sambai* rhythms, which he learned as early as age eight, can be traced half a millennium back to the Ibo people of West Africa. Ask Emmeth about his "Drums not guns" initiative.

SPORTS AND RECREATION
Caving

With the largest number of Mayan villages in Belize, it's not surprising that Punta Gorda offers some of the country's most off-the-beaten-path caving and hiking sites. **Toledo Cave and Adventure Tours** (tel. 501/604-2124, belizegate@gmail.com or ibtm@gmx.net, www.travelbelize.de, US$95-115) is your best bet for trips to some of Belize's lesser-known attractions, including Yok Balum Cave, Tiger Cave, Gibnut Cave, and Oke'bal Ha. Owner Bruno Kuppinger, long-time resident of Punta Gorda, is an adventure junkie who loves to get deep in the bush. He also runs Sun Creek Lodge and offers

© LEBAWIT GIRMA

Drum master Emmeth Young teaches at his Maroon Creole Drum School.

countrywide tours and group pickups from Belize City.

For some cave tubing fun, folks rave about **Big Falls Adventures** (Southern Hwy., Big Falls, tel. 501/634-6979 or 501/631-3497, www.bigfallsextremeadventures.com, 8am-4pm daily, US$48-60, lunch US$10 extra), offering tubing along the Rio Grande river, followed by a dip in a local hot spring before getting back down into the river (I opted for the zip line across Big Falls).

Fishing

The waterways around Punta Gorda offer anglers the rare chance to bag a grand slam (permit, tarpon, bonefish, and snook). Fly-fishing is generally possible between November and May, in shallow areas around the cayes, mangroves, and river mouths. Reel fishing is possible throughout the year, up the rivers or in the ocean; cast for snappers, groupers, jacks, barracuda, mackerels, or king fish. Most guides help you bring your fish back and find someone

to cook it up for you. Fishing trips can run upward of US$400-500 for four people.

Garbutt's Marine and Fishing Lodge (tel. 501/604-3548), next to Joe Taylor Creek, at the entrance to Punta Gorda, is a top-notch operation run by the Garbutt brothers, a local duo who grew up exploring these waters. They offer one of the most reliable ways to get out to the cayes and go fly-fishing, diving, or snorkeling. Fishing charter packages for groups include on-site seafront cabin lodging (7 nights US$2,865 pp, all-inclusive). They are dive masters and offer PADI classes and certification as well as self-guided (US$5 per hour) or with a local guide (half-day US$12.50) kayak rentals.

TIDE Tours (1 Mile San Antonio Rd., tel. 501/722-2274, www.tidetours.org, 7:30am-4:30pm Mon.-Fri., reduced hours Sat.) offers snorkeling (US$145 pp for 2 people) and fishing trips to the Snake Cayes or Sapodilla Cayes. TIDE Tours is the customer service branch of the Toledo Institute for Development and Environment (TIDE), Belize's only "ridges to reef" NGO. TIDE does much of the guide training in the area, helping to teach people sustainable, often tourism-related, skills. TIDE staff promote tours to protected areas and give presentations on their work in the Port Honduras Marine Reserve, in Paynes Creek National Park, and on the Private Lands Initiative. They also do tours to archaeological sites, caves, and other inland attractions. Revenue generated from TIDE Tours is used for education and outreach efforts.

BlueBelize Tours (tel. 501/722-2678, www.bluebelize.com) is owned and run by Dan Castellanos, a local fisherman, guide, and PADI dive master who specializes in fishing (US$325 for 2 people) and snorkeling tours (US$250 for two). He has led National Geographic and BBC film crews around the area.

Kayaking

TIDE Tours (41 Front St., tel. 501/722-2129, www.tidetours.org, 7:30am-4:30pm Mon.-Fri., reduced hours Sat.) offers numerous inland and

RANGER FOR A DAY WITH YA'AXCHÉ

Zip up your boots and play ranger for a day along the rivers and trails of the Golden Stream Corridor Preserve. Thanks to the **Ya'axché Conservation Trust** (pronounced "ya-chay," 22 Alejandro Vernon St., tel. 501/722-0108, www.yaaxche.org), you can now experience a day in the life of a rainforest ranger in the deep south of Belize.

Established in 1997, the Ya'axché Conservation Trust works to maintain and manage the health of Belize's forests, rivers, and reefs in and around the "Maya Golden Landscape" of southern Belize, an area which includes the Golden Stream Corridor Preserve and the 100,000-acre Bladen Nature Reserve. To date, Ya'axché has some of the best-trained rangers in the country. In 2012, the organization's then-executive director, Lisel Alamilla, now Belize's Minister of Forestry, Fisheries and Sustainable Development, was awarded the prestigious Whitley Fund for Nature for her leadership in conservation work at Ya'axché.

The day starts at the Golden Stream Field Center, located off the Southern Highway and easily accessible by bus. Sign up to join the day's patrol and hike alongside rangers, learning to detect illegal activities—like hunting—by logging bird and mammal species along the riverside trail. Other tasks include tracking jaguar and tapir tracks, learning to spot various birds, and, weather permitting, cooling off in the Golden Stream River.

While there's no set fee for this unique Ranger for a Day experience, a donation of US$30-45 is suggested. All contributions go toward the rangers' salaries—giving back to the community at large and helping sustain a fantastic organization.

---

sea trips, including river kayaking (US$90 pp for 2 people). Kayak rentals (US$2.50 per hour) are also available. Many guesthouses also include complimentary kayak use. In town, you can explore Joe Taylor Creek, and if you're staying inland, the riverside lodges are ideal to launch your canoe.

ENTERTAINMENT AND EVENTS
Nightlife

There are a handful of small bars scattered around town, some with pool tables, all with lots of booze. The nightlife in Punta Gorda is a bit scattered, and there's no one best hot spot. You pretty much have to hop from one spot to another to find the crowd, or ask around. The most consistent place you'll find is on week nights at **Reef Bar** (Front St., tel. 501/622-9783, 5pm-midnight Mon.-Tues., noon-midnight Wed.-Sat., 6pm-midnight Sun., US$3-5), where you can enjoy a drink on a top deck overlooking the waterfront. There's dancing and live drumming, mostly as it gets closer to the weekend. The **Olympic Bar** (Clement St.) is

also good spot to get a drink after dinner before taking it up a notch.

Waluco's Bar & Grill (Mile 1, San Antonio Rd., tel. 501/630-3672 or 501/664-7186, 7am-2pm and 5pm-10pm Mon.-Thurs., 7am-midnight Fri.-Sat., US$3.50-10), the name of which means "son of the soil" in Garífuna, is right across from the sea, a short walk north of town, although at night a taxi or bicycle is best. It's sometimes a happening spot, with live music and drumming on Friday and Sunday as well as during festival times. You'll find plenty of karaoke and some pool tables at **Seaside Heights** (tel. 501/722-2450, 10:30am-3pm and 5pm-midnight Mon.-Wed. and Thurs.-Sun.), just a block away from Waluco's. A little outside of town, you'll find a few more bars and nightclubs, open only on random weekends (9pm-2am), including **Roots Rock Reggae** and **Embassy** on the Southern Highway just outside of town.

Festivals and Events

Toledo's biggest event is the annual **Chocolate Festival** (Front St., www.chocolatefestivalofbelize.com, 3rd weekend in May) at the park in

TOLEDO'S CHOCOLATE TRAIL

The cacao tree (*Theobroma cacao*, "food of the gods") has gained renewed importance in the culture and economy of Mayans in southern Belize. Thousands of years ago, Mayan kings and priests worshipped the cacao (or *kakaw*) bean, using it as currency and drinking it in a sacred, spicy beverage. A revival of southern Belize's cacao industry has since led to choco-tourism. A few area lodges and families have found ways to connect ancient cacao farming with the modern craze for high-quality fair-trade food and products.

Today, farmers sell their cacao crop to the **Toledo Cacao Growers Association** (TCGA, one block north of the town park on Main St., Punta Gorda, tel. 501/722-2992, www.tcgabelize.com), a nonprofit coalition of small farms that sells the beans to acclaimed chocolatier Green & Black's, a United Kingdom-based company specializing in fair-trade and organic-certified chocolate bars. Some beans remain in Belize, used by a few Mayan families and small-batch chocolate makers to produce chocolate for the domestic market.

Sustainable Harvest International (SHI, tel. 501/722-2010, U.S. tel. 207/669-8254, www.sustainableharvest.org) is a nonprofit organization working to alleviate poverty and deforestation throughout Central America. The organization works with more than 100 cacao-growing families, helping them develop multistory forest plots that mimic the natural forest; this provides a diversity of food and marketable produce for the families, plus a home for threatened plants and animals. Coffee, plantains, and other shade-loving crops are planted alongside the cacao trees, under a hardwood canopy. Sustainable Harvest Belize estimates that for every acre converted to multistory cacao forest, five acres are saved from destructive slash-and-burn practices. The organization offers sustainable chocolate tours and other voluntourism opportunities at work sites in southern Belize. Accommodations range from rustic homestays to the stilted cabins of Cotton Tree Lodge, where SHI maintains a demo garden.

Punta Gorda Town. It's a weekend-long tribute to Belizean chocolate and the organic cacao farmers of the Toledo District. From a Wine and Chocolate Evening to open-air concerts with traditional Mayan and Garífuna music and chocolate tastings, Cacao for Kids storytelling and games, chocolate-flavored cocktails, and an all-day food and crafts fair on Front Street, there are events from Friday evening through Sunday to entertain both children and adults who come from all over Belize. Be sure to reserve accommodations ahead of time, and bring plenty of small change—there's no telling how much chocolate or art you'll be tempted to take home. The best part is that all the funds from the festival go to support community projects.

The **Deer Dance Festival** takes place over a week in August in the village of San Antonio. There are Mayan arts, crafts, music, and food showcased, but the highlight is the costume performance of the deer dance, an ancient ritual that reenacts the hunting of a deer, from chase to capture, acted out to traditional Mayan harps and violins. This is one of the most off-the-beaten-path cultural events you could attend.

One of the largest Garífuna cultural events in the country, the **Battle of Drums** (50 Main St., bissystems@btl.net, www.battleofthedrums.org) takes place in Punta Gorda, usually the weekend preceding November 19, Garífuna Settlement Day. While there are weekend-long events celebrating Garífuna culture through concerts and food fetes, the main event takes place on Saturday night, when drumming teams from all of Belize's Garífuna towns and villages, and from neighboring Honduras and Guatemala, compete for the winning title of best Garífuna drumming team. It's a spectacular display of music and dance and culture. Hotel rooms book up almost half a year in advance, so be prepared, and check the local papers for ticket prices, event times, and location details. You can also contact Beya Suites (tel. 501/722-2188 or 501/722-2956), the chief organizers of this event, for more information.

Mayan culture is celebrated in all its glory on **Maya Day** (Tumul K'in Center of Learning, Blue Creek, Mar.) in the village of Blue Creek. Folks descend from all over Belize to attend this event, which includes traditional dancing and performances, tortilla baking competitions, firewood splitting contests, plenty of *caldo* tastings, and other Mayan-inspired recreation. Get a copy of the latest *Toledo Howler* from the BTIA Tourist Office (Main St., tel. 501/722-2531) or pick up a local newspaper for details.

SHOPPING

Located next door to the airstrip, at **Maya Bags** (tel. 501/722-2175, www.mayabags.org, 9am-5pm Mon.-Fri.) craft workshop, about 90 women from eight Mayan villages participate in this craft and export venture. The women make hand-woven bags (US$50-140), embroidered yoga mats (US$43), beach bags, *jipijapa* purses, and other unique products. The bags are absolutely gorgeous, especially the clutches. If you have time, you can order a custom embroidered design; the craftsmanship is so good that the bags were featured in *Vogue* magazine in 2010 and sold in Barneys for several years. They also make home decorating items, from vases to throw pillows.

Tienda La Indita Maya (24 Main Middle St., 9am-5pm) carries handmade jewelry, wooden bowls, pottery, and other handicrafts. The store lies just north of Central Park, at the end opposite the clock tower. Also check the **Fajina Women's Group Craft Center** on Front Street near the ferry pier (7am-11am Mon.-Sat.). It's a small co-op for quality Mayan crafts run by the Q'eqchi' and Mopan women. You'll find *jipijapa* baskets, *cuxtales,* slate carvings, calabash carvings, jewelry, textiles, and embroidered clothes—when they're open, that is. If

the door is closed, ask upstairs at the restaurant to get it opened up.

You can find Creole drums at the **Driftwood Café & Art** (9 Front St., tel. 501/632-7841, 7am-4pm daily), made by locally renowned Creole drummer Emmeth Young, as well as other African-inspired crafts, clothing, and souvenirs.

For beautiful furniture pieces, made solely from Toledo District woods, mahogany to gorilla, stop by the showroom at **Belize Wood Works** (Front St., across from Reef's Bar, tel. 501/604-2124 or 501/665-6778, www.belize-woodworks.com, 8am-noon Mon., Wed., and Fri., 8am-4pm Sat., US$100-800), where you'll see sample dressers, chairs, and hand-carved Mayan doors. Exports are available to Canada and the United States. There are plenty of other shops along the market in town, though most of the wares are likely from neighboring Guatemala.

If you're a chocolate lover, don't miss the **Cotton Tree Chocolate Shop** (2 Front St., just south of the UNO Station, tel. 501/621-8772, www.cottontreechocolate.com, 10am-5pm). They make milk, white, and dark chocolates; in addition to free chocolate samples, tours are available by appointment. A small gift shop sells chocolates, cocoa mix, cocoa butter, whole vanilla beans, and handmade chocolate soap by Dawn and Jo's Soap Company, which looks good enough to eat.

◀ Market Days

Although there are four weekly market days, Wednesday and Saturday are the biggest. Monday and Friday are smaller but still interesting. Many Maya vendors sell wild coriander, yellow or white corn, chili peppers of various hues, cassava, tamales wrapped in banana leaves, star fruit, mangoes, and much more. Many of the women and children bring handmade crafts as well. Laughing children help their parents. If you're inclined to snap a photo, ask permission first—and perhaps offer to buy something. Folks here are the most sensitive to photos that I've encountered in Belize. If you're refused, smile and put your lens cap back on.

ACCOMMODATIONS
Under US$25
Punta Gorda's few hotels and guesthouses occupy the blocks of Front Street near the main dock as well as a couple farther back; a good rule of thumb is not to book a room that is accessed via a smoky bar and pool hall (for example, at the Mira Mar). Quieter options are only a few blocks or a few minutes off the waterfront and an easy walk or bike ride away.

You're apt to run into all sorts of interesting travelers from around the world at **Nature's Way Guest House** (65 Front St., tel. 501/702-2119, natureswayguesthouse@hotmail.com, US$19-24), which really is more akin to a hostel. Set at the back of a lush well-kept garden are six small, very basic guest rooms with bunk beds, fan-cooled and all sharing baths. There are also three basic guest rooms with private baths and showers, although they are not much different in decor. Nature's Way serves a good breakfast, and you'll have access to all the activities in the area. The place is run by Chet Schmidt and his Belizean wife. Chet is an American expat and Vietnam veteran who has been here for over four decades; he also spent 13 years teaching in the surrounding villages. He can help arrange kayak trips, rainforest treks, camping, exploration of uninhabited cayes, visits to archaeology sites, and Maya and Garífuna guesthouse stays with award-winning TEA.

Located on a quiet street toward the very back of the town center is the **Circle Inn** (117 West St., tel. 501/722-2726), a Garífuna-owned guesthouse, run by Aurora "Rhoda" Coe, who does a good job of making sure her seven basic guest rooms are clean and fresh; four are shared with double or single beds (US$13-18) and three have double beds and private baths (US$20). It's a decent place to rest your head if everything else is booked in town, and about a 15-minute walk to the town center.

US$25-50
St. Charles Inn (23 King St., tel. 501/722-2149, stcharlespg@btl.net, US$32.50 or US$43.50 with a/c) is centrally located, with a dozen guest rooms and a shady veranda that allows you to observe village life below. The well-kept guest rooms include springy mattresses, private baths, fans, and small TVs.

As you leave the airport, you'll see the **Frontier Inn** (3 Airport St., tel. 501/722-2450, frontierinn@btl.net, US$35), a white two-story cement building. Twelve good value, immaculate tile-floored guest rooms have TVs, wireless Internet, private baths, hot water, colorful bedspreads and walls; there's even a standby generator. The place is owned by a local airplane pilot. It's a short two-minute bike ride from here to the center of town.

Tate's Guest House (34 Jose Maria Nunez St., tel. 501/722-0147, tatesguesthouse@yahoo.com, US$19-45) is a comfortable home with five double guest rooms in a quiet neighborhood setting. Ask for rooms 4 or 5; they are spacious, with ceiling fans, TVs, sunrooms, louvered windows, and tile floors, and each has an additional entrance through the backyard. Internet access is available.

Charlton's Inn (9 Main St., a block from Uno gas station, tel. 501/722-2197, www.charltonsinn.com, US$44) is close to everything in town, and James buses stop across the street. The 27 guest rooms are well kept, with hot and cold water, private baths, TV, air-conditioning, wireless Internet, and fans; there are also nine furnished apartments available with monthly rates.

US$50-150
Occupying a breezy, ocean-looking rise next to the hospital, **Coral House Inn** (151 Main St., tel. 501/722-2878, www.coralhouseinn.net, US$90-100) is an excellent seafront bed-and-breakfast with a small pool and bar and a quiet yard. It was opened after the owners drove to Belize from Idaho in their VW Microbus. The four guest rooms are pleasantly decorated with soft colors, local artwork, and comfortable beds; continental breakfast, use of bicycles, and wireless Internet are free for guests. This is where one of Belize's recent former prime ministers used to stay when in Punta Gorda. Ask about the nearby Seaglass Cottage, a little one-bedroom, one-bath,

small-kitchen option, pitched on a bluff above the ocean (US$125).

One mile outside Punta Gorda, up Ex-Servicemen Road, **Hickatee Cottages** (tel. 501/662-4475, www.hickatee.com, US$80-120) is a wonderful option on the edge of the rainforest. Your expatriate British hosts are knowledgeable about local flora and fauna, passionate about their "lifestyle business," and strive to run a green hotel and involve the local community as much as possible. After you've settled into your well-appointed wooden cottage (private bath, hardwood furniture, ceiling fans, and veranda) or the garden suite (more space, furnishings, and a kitchenette), take a walk through the beautiful grounds and nature trail, followed by a dip in the plunge pool. Hickatee Cottages is very popular with birders and naturalists; guests wander on a rainforest trail, participate in howler monkey research, watch orchid bees at work while having a cup of Toledo organic coffee, and observe the wild creatures of the night on the bug board. Bicycles are available to get to and from town. Ask about visiting the on-site farm, fruit trees, nursery, and orchid collection (40 native species at last count); rates also include a free visit to **Fallen Stones Butterfly Farm** (Wednesday afternoon, advance reservations required, maximum four people—an incredible opportunity). Also on-site, **Charlie's Bar** offers home-cooked healthy meals (breakfast and lunch about US$8, dinner US$17.50). Hickatee sometimes offers cultural nights, including weekly drumming lessons with Ray McDonald, a local Garífuna musician.

◖ **BlueBelize Guest House** (tel. 501/722-2678, www.bluebelize.com, US$75-135 plus tax) is owned by renowned marine biologist Rachel Graham and managed by a lovely couple, Kate and Adam. The five cozy furnished suites—including one for honeymooners—are large enough to feel like apartments and are tastefully decorated, with one or two bedrooms, en suite baths, kitchenettes or full kitchens, hot and cold water, ceiling fans, lovely seating areas, and wireless Internet. The guest rooms open onto verandas or patios literally a stone's throw from the water's edge. Use of bikes is complimentary, as is continental breakfast, served on your veranda or in your suite. BlueBelize is very popular with visiting doctors, scientists, and volunteers, as well as travelers escaping cold dark winters up north.

You can't miss the **Sea Front Inn** (4 Front St., tel. 501/722-2300, www.seafrontinn.com, US$119, includes continental breakfast) as you enter town: It comprises two towering stone buildings across the street from the sea. The 14 guest rooms and three apartments are also available for monthly rentals. Guests find comfortable, spacious guest rooms, no two alike, with TVs, fans, air-conditioning, private baths, and handmade furniture built with hardwoods. The third floor is the kitchen, dining room, and common area, overlooking the ocean.

Also on the waterfront, just before the bridge taking you into town, the Garífuna-owned and tourism board award-winning **Beya Suites** (tel. 501/722-2188 or 501/722-2956, www.beyasuites.com, US$75-175) looks like a giant pink-and-white wedding cake. Inside you'll find cheery staff to show you to one of the comfortable, air-conditioned, tile-floored guest rooms with large baths and a sinus-clearing floral scent. There's a rooftop, a restaurant (breakfast only), a bar, a conference area, and fast Internet. Ask about apartments and weekly rates. Owner Darius Avila is the founder of the popular Battle of the Drums, an annual Garífuna cultural event held in Punta Gorda every November.

Over $150

The area's sole rainforest-luxe property is **Belcampo Belize** (tel. 501/722-0050, www.belcampoinc.com/bz, US$470), located atop a forested perch high above the Río Grande and a gorgeous expanse of rainforest, five miles north of PG. This is a unique spot targeting a unique market. Belcampo's property encompasses 12,000 acres of rainforest and organic citrus, coffee, and cacao farms, including 4.5 miles of riverfront (reached by a rainforest elevator!) and Nicholas Caye, a pristine island in the Sapodilla Cayes. The sea is a 20-minute boat ride down the river, where you'll head for your sportfishing and snorkeling tours. Amenities include a pool, a farm-to-fork restaurant, kayaks and mountain bikes, a breakaway sitting room and veranda, and a spa as well as a screened rainforest veranda in your canopy-level tree house suite (there are 12); you may see a brightly colored toucan from your shower window or get a wakeup call from a howler monkey.

FOOD

Punta Gorda offers mainly cheap local eats, with the added benefit of fresh seafood and a few excellent vegetarian options. Many restaurants are closed on Sunday and for a few hours between meals. The town has several good bakeries, and fruit and veggies are cheap and abundant on **Market Days** (Mon., Wed., Fri.-Sat.). Some of the best breakfast and lunch joints in the market building are also only open these days; look closely just behind the market stands, along the wall, and you'll see hungry souls chowing down on Central American treats and coffee for dirt cheap. Notice which has the most crowds and place your order. Ask at any corner store for a sampling of the local Mennonite yogurt and bread and be sure to try a seaweed shake, which you can buy fresh and cold at Johnson's Hardware Store, across from the market. Keep an eye out for **Ms. Adriana,** who is one of the few Garífuna women at the market, commuting all the way from the village of Barranco; she sells cassava cake, kola nuts, and other interesting items on the sidewalk across from the market.

Barbecue

Don't miss Belizean barbecue chicken on Saturday, a tradition in much of Belize. The best in town is at **Kay's Barbecue Spot** (Queen St., near Jose Maria Nunez St., close to the Central Park, 8am-3pm Mon., Wed., and Fri.-Sat.). You'll see her grill steaming up the block while she fills the stream of orders. The chicken comes with generous sides of rice and beans and a large fresh tortilla, all for US$3. Get here early, as she can run out by 2pm.

Belizean

There are some great fast-food places surrounding Central Park. **Grace's Restaurant** (Main St., tel. 501/702-2414, 6:30am-10:30pm daily) is a long-standing joint with typical Belizean fare like stew chicken (US$4), tasty conch soup (US$9), and eggs and beans with fry jacks. It gets traffic all day long, especially at breakfast, and there's a ton of seating space. Close to Charlton's Inn, **El Café** (6am-2pm and 6pm-10pm Mon.-Sat., 7am-2pm Sun., US$4-10) has cheap diner-style Belizean food all day long.

Waluco's Bar & Grill (Mile 1, San Antonio Rd., tel. 501/630-3672 or 501/664-7186, 7am-2pm and 5pm-10pm Mon.-Thurs., 7am-midnight Fri.-Sun., US$3.50-10) serves up daily local lunch specials, including stew chicken and fry fish, with the usual sides of rice and beans, *callaloo,* or coleslaw. The dinner menu is more varied, with pastas, burgers, and barbecue. There may be music to go along with your meal if you come on a Friday or Sunday night.

Just next door to the Hibiscus Cafe is **Seaside Heights** (tel. 501/722-2450, 10:30am-3pm and 5pm-midnight Mon.-Wed., 10:30am-midnight Thurs.-Sun., US$4-10), serving Belizean, Central American, and East Indian options. Entrées range from burritos to *tarkari,* and there's a full bar and a huge top-deck seating area overlooking the waterfront. Add to that a pool table and plenty of karaoke nights.

℃ Martina's Kitchen (Main St., tel. 501/623-3330, 7am-3pm Mon.-Fri., US$3) is where the best johnnycakes are baked. They serve good ol' Belizean breakfast and lunch plates; orders are taken from a small window, and there's decent seating space. You'll get a basket of four johnnycakes with your eggs and coffee. Locals flock in and out with their takeout bags.

℃ Jocelyn's Cuisine & Catering (Front St., tel. 501/661-9267, 6am-9pm daily, US$2.50-4) is a cozy little seaside shack across from the UNO gas station with a lot of charm, serving delicious plates of local breakfast—freshly made johnnycakes, fry jacks, and even waffles—and a lunch of jerk chicken or Belizean stews and seafood. There's seating under the

VILLAGE HOMESTAYS

For the culturally curious traveler, the unique guesthouse and homestay programs in the Toledo District offer a threefold attraction: 1. firsthand observation of daily rural life in southern Belize; 2. a chance to interact with one of several proud distinct cultures while participating in a world-renowned model of ecotourism; and 3. a unique way to go deep into the lush natural world of the forests, rivers, caves, and waterfalls of southwestern Belize.

Simple guesthouse and family home networks in participating villages offer a range of conditions and privacy, but most are simple, primitive, and appreciated most by those with an open mind. Activities include tours of the villages and surrounding natural attractions. For nighttime entertainment, traditional dancing, singing, and music can usually be arranged; otherwise it's just stargazing and conversation.

These are poor villages, and the local brand of ecotourism provides an alternative to subsistence farming that entails slashing and burning the rainforest. Additionally, the community-controlled infrastructure helps ensure a more equitable distribution of tourism dollars than most tour operations (members rotate duties of guiding, preparing meals, and organizing activities).

Guests usually pay about US$11 for three meals. Breakfast in Maya villages is generally eggs, homemade tortillas, and coffee or a cacao drink. All meals are indigenous fare, and lunch is the largest meal of the day; it is often chicken *caldo* (a soup cooked with Mayan herbs) or occasionally a local meat dish like iguana ("bush chicken") or gibnut (paca, a large rodent). Fresh tortillas round out the meal. Supper is the lightest meal of the day and generally includes "ground" food (a root vegetable such as potatoes) that the guide and visitors might harvest along the rainforest trail. The *comal* (tortilla grill) is always hot, and if you're invited, try your hand at making tortillas.

Families are located in the villages of Aguacate and San Jose:

- Contact Louis Cucul at the **Aguacate Belize Homestay Program** (Aguacate, tel. 501/633-9954, cucullouis@hotmail.com, www.aguacatebelize.com/homestay-program, US$9 per night, meals US$3.50 per meal, registration fee US$5).

- Contact Justino Pec at the **San Jose Homestay Program** (San Jose, tel. 501/722-0109 or cell 501/668-7378, peck.justino@gmail.com).

The **Toledo Ecotourism Association** (TEA) is the umbrella organization for the guesthouse program, which is cooperatively managed and includes village representatives in the respective towns. At last count, there were six participating villages. For the Toledo Ecotourism Association program, a registration fee, one night's lodging, and three meals run US$28 pp per night. Other activities, like storytelling, crafts lessons, and village tours are available for US$3.50 per hour. Prices are standardized throughout the participating villages. Other activities, such as paddling trips, forest and cave tours (US$14 pp), and music and dance sessions cost more, but are still extremely reasonably priced—especially with a group. If visiting during the rainy season, be advised that trails and caves may be inaccessible.

Interested participants should contact organizer Chet Schmidt at **Nature's Way** (tel. 501/702-2119, www.teabelize.org) to arrange visits and pay the registration fee (US$5). Guests will be briefed about the program and told how to reach the village (the villages are available on a rotating basis). One full day may be sufficient, as the villages are quite small; if you would like to explore the surrounding landscape, plan an extra day.

tree on picnic tables, with a lovely breeze from the water.

The **Snack Shack** (near BTL parking lot, tel. 501/702-0020, 7am-3pm Mon.-Fri., 7am-1pm Sat.) is an expat favorite for breakfast, especially its giant US$3 egg burritos, a "gringo breakfast" option, fruit shakes, pancakes, and bagels. For lunch, there's a "build your own" tortilla option (US$5), with flavored tortillas of your choice. It's walking distance from the Immigration station and good for a snack before you leave.

Chinese

A few Chinese restaurants offer reliable chop suey; some expats call **Hang Cheon** (Main St., tel. 501/722-2064, 10am-2pm and 5pm-midnight daily, US$3-10) the best Chinese in town.

Creole

◖ Olympic Grill (Main St., tel. 501/702-0078, 7am-2pm and 5pm-10pm Mon.-Sat., US$4-9) is a local favorite, serving up Creole cuisine, including stews, pig tail, and fry fish. Perched over the water, steps from BlueBelize is **Asha's Culture Kitchen** (80 Front St., tel. 501/632-8025, 4pm-10pm Fri.-Wed., US$5-13), a wooden casita with quite possibly the best outdoor deck and dinner setting in town. Asha's serves Creole seafood dishes made to order as well as curries and other entrées. A bright chalkboard menu with blue checks lists they day's availability, served up with two sides in generous portions (the garlic mashed potatoes are good). There is occasional live drumming here.

A couple of restaurants have opened their doors on the highway out of Punta Gorda. Look for Miss Aida's **Hibiscus Café** (Wild Cone St., tel. 501/632-7859, 9am-9pm daily, US$9-13), serving up authentic Creole cuisine—including boil-up, seafood curries, and local pastries and juices—served under a tastefully decorated *palapa,* or the front and back garden, filled with hammocks and more seating options. Miss Aida cooks with spices from

© LEBAWIT GIRMA

Asha's Culture Kitchen has lovely views for dinner.

her garden and makes her own wines. I toured her cooking quarters and I can tell you, it looks like a museum, or rather, your grandmother's kitchen, filled with dozens of jars on shelves, juices, ice cream, and all sorts of goodies.

East Indian

An easy place to recommend for lunch or dinner is **Marian's Bayview Restaurant** (76 Front St., tel. 501/722-0129, 11am-2pm and 6pm-10pm Mon.-Sat., noon-2pm and 7pm-9pm Sun., US$5), located on a rooftop over the water on the south edge of Punta Gorda, across from Nature's Way. Marian's serves East Indian cuisine, seafood, or a good ol' plate of rice and beans from her buffet—all with a view of Guatemala and Honduras across the sea.

Ital and Vegetarian

The best Ital restaurant is [**Gomier's Restaurant** (5 Alejandro Vernon St., tel. 501/722-2929, 11am-2pm and 5pm-10pm Mon.-Sat., US$3-9), set in a small, humble space at the north entrance to town across from the Punta Gorda welcome sign. Expect a healthy haven of whole grains, homemade tofu, and lots of "good for you" options with a delicious veggie, vegan, and seafood menu. The tiny restaurant offers tasty and creative daily specials, such as barbecued tofu served with baked beans, bread, and coleslaw, plus a veggie grain casserole served with a salad (about US$5), a bulging soysage burger (US$3), delicious conch soup (in season), and tofu pizza. There's also fresh local fruit juices (try the golden plum), soy milk, and soy ice cream. Ask Gomier about his vegan cooking classes.

Mayan

If you don't have the time to visit the Mayan villages, be sure to stop by **Fajina Restaurant** (Front St., tel. 501/666-6141 or 501/666-6144, fajina.craft.center@gmail.com, 7am-8:30pm daily, US$3.50) for traditional Maya fare, typically a delicious bowl of *caldo,* served with seven corn tortillas. The small casual eatery is run by the same women's group that operates the craft shop downstairs. Occasionally you'll find *callaloo,* boiled plantains, or cohune cabbage on the daily menu.

Mexican

Palma's Tortilla Factory (Main St., 7am-1pm Mon.-Sat.) makes fresh tortillas every day and sells them for US$2.50 per pound; they also make tacos (3 for US$0.50), *panades, tamales,* and the like.

Seafood

The **Reef Bar** (Front St., tel. 501/622-9783, 5pm-midnight Mon.-Tues., noon-midnight Wed.-Sat., 6pm-midnight Sun., US$3-5) is a convivial rooftop affair on the water's edge, above the market, with the best view in town. The friendly Garífuna women in the kitchen and bar serve good seafood options, including conch and lobster in season, along with other local dishes. There's drumming and dancing on Friday night, and Garífuna *hudut* on the weekend, as well as Belizean boil-up, both of which you should sample while in Belize. Saturday is barbecue day, and the grills steam away while reggae music plays over the waterfront.

Casual Dining

As you follow the highway north out of Punta Gorda, look for a driveway and sign on your left just as the road is about to turn away from the sea. Here you'll find [**Mangrove Inn and Restaurant** (tel. 501/623-0497, 5pm-10pm daily, US$6-10), a family affair (although you no longer have to walk through your hosts' living room) with a charming dining balcony, complete with a bar, cozy lighting, and African decor. The cook, Iconie, has worked in fancy resorts across Belize but prefers working at home. Expect savory fish dishes, pot pies, pasta, fresh salads, and rolls.

Tucked at the back of town, the **Pizza Plaza Bakery** (121 West St., tel. 501/702-2676, 11am-9pm daily), on the south end of town, one street behind the university, occasionally has baked goods, including brownies, cookies, bagels, Creole bread, and honey whole-wheat oatmeal bread. Miss Norma also makes grilled

PUNTA GORDA

sandwiches or pizza for lunch, although you'd better call and check first.

Groceries

Check at one of the two **Supaul's** stores for local yogurt. Sophia Supaul's store on Alejandro Vernon Street (known locally as Green Supaul's, 10am-7pm daily) carries imported cheeses (French brie in PG!) and Mary's Yogurt (a must-try, in many flavors, including coconut), local jams and honey, a decent wine selection, couscous, white chocolate, vegetables, and fruits.

INFORMATION AND SERVICES
Tourist Information

Look for the **Toledo Tourism Information Center** (Front St., tel. 501/722-2531, btiatoledo@btl.net, 8:30am-4:30pm Mon.-Fri., 8:30am-noon Sat.), not far from the Town Dock and run by the Belize Tourism Industry Association. This is a concerted effort by local businesses to provide excellent and organized information to visitors; they'll recommend accommodations, tour companies, transportation, and more. You can pick up a print or PDF copy of *The Toledo Howler* (www.belizenews. com/howler), a local magazine published by the BTIA, for upcoming events and updated transportation schedules, often including a recent map of the area.

For information on the **Toledo Ecotourism Association** (TEA), and how you can you sign up to stay in one of the six village guesthouses or visit the villages, contact **Chet Schmidt at Nature's Way** (tel. 501/702-2119, www.teabelize.org). Near the municipal dock, you'll find the **Immigration Office** (tel. 501/722-2247, 8am-close daily), for departures to and arrivals from Guatemala and Honduras. The departure tax is US$15 if you spent up to 24 hours in Belize, plus the US$4 PACT fee if you've been here longer.

Banks

The **Belize Bank** (tel. 501/722-2326, 8am-3pm Mon.-Thurs., 8am-4:30pm Fri.) is right across from the town square and has an ATM. Continue one block south for **Scotiabank** (8am-2:30pm Mon.-Thurs., 8am-4pm Fri., 9am-11:30am Sat.), which has a 24-hour international ATM. Grace's Restaurant (Main St., tel. 501/702-2414, 6:30am-10:30pm daily) is also a licensed **Casa de Cambio** and can change dollars, Guatemalan quetzales, or traveler's checks. You may also find a freelance moneychanger hanging around the dock at boat time.

Media and Communications

Opposite the immigration office are a couple of government buildings, including the **post office.** There are two Internet places just north of the park on Main Street, both with nice airconditioning and decent machines: **Dreamlight Computer Center** (Main St. and North St., tel. 501/702-0113 or 501/607-0033, dreamlightpg@yahoo.com, 6:30am-8:30pm Mon.-Sat., 9am-1pm Sun., first hour US$1.50 per hour, US$2 per hour thereafter) and **V-Comp Technologies** (29 Main St., tel. 501/722-0093 or 501/601-0342, 8am-8:30pm daily, US$1.50 per hour), a nice operation with printing, copying, scanning, and even DVDs for sale.

Health and Emergencies

Punta Gorda has a **police department** (tel. 501/722-2022), a **fire department** (tel. 501/722-2032), and a **hospital** (tel. 501/722-2026 or 501/722-2161) for emergencies. **NJV's Pharmacy** (Front St., tel. 501/722-2177, 8am-1pm and 4pm-8pm Mon.-Sat.) is a well-stocked drugstore, with everything from a pharmacy to books and office supplies.

GETTING THERE

If you're coming to the area by bus, plan on nearly a full day of travel on either end of your trip south (at least 5-6 hours from Belize City). Consider taking the quick flight from Belize City, Placencia, or Dangriga to Punta Gorda.

By Air

Daily southbound flights from Belize City to Dangriga continue to Placencia and then to

Punta Gorda. This is the quickest and most comfortable way to get to PG. For the return trip, **Tropic Air** (tel. 501/226-2012, U.S. tel. 800/422-3435, www.tropicair.com) and **Maya Island Air** (tel. 501/223-1140, U.S. tel. 800/225-6732, www.mayaislandair.com) each offer five flights to Placencia, Dangriga, and Belize City between 6:30am and 4pm daily. Tropic is usually more reliable and frequent in southern Belize.

By Car and Bus

Punta Gorda is just under 200 miles from Belize City, a long haul by bus, even with the newly surfaced Southern Highway speeding things up. Count on 3-4 hours by car, 5-6 hours by express bus, or seven hours on a non-express bus. **James Bus Lines** (tel. 501/722-2049) has a centrally located terminal in Punta Gorda, at King and Main Streets, and runs up to 10 buses daily between Punta Gorda and Belize City, departing 3:50am-3:50pm Sunday-Friday, with one express at 6am. The first departure from Belize City is a 5:30am express, and then service continues until 3:45pm; the only other express is this last bus of the day. The fare is US$11 one-way. The James Bus makes a loop through PG before heading out of town. A few other bus lines make the trip, but much less regularly.

Remember that you can get off in Independence and take a boat to Placencia, or you can get off at any other point, like Cockscomb Maya Centre (Cockscomb Basin Wildlife Sanctuary) or Dangriga.

GETTING AROUND

Ask your hotel if they provide free use of a bicycle, or rent one at **Gomier's Restaurant** (5 Alejandro Vernon St., tel. 501/722-2929, 11am-2pm and 5pm-10pm Mon.-Sat.), near the entrance to Punta Gorda (US$10 per day). It's a great way to navigate the town, which can sometimes be a tad spread out on foot.

Bus

Every day has a different schedule, but buses go to the Maya villages on Monday, Wednesday, Friday, and Saturday, generally around 11am, departing from Jose Maria Nunez Street (between Prince and Queen Street). From here it's possible to get to **Golden Stream, Silver Creek, San Pedro, San Miguel, Aguacate, Blue Creek, San Antonio,** and other villages. Some buses drop you off at the entrance road, leaving a walk of a mile or two. It's possible to make it a day trip and return later in the afternoon. Check the Toledo Tourism Information Center on Main Street for updated village bus schedules, or grab a copy of the latest *Toledo Howler* newspaper in town.

Taxi

Punta Gorda's taxis will take you anywhere within city limits for about US$3-4; look for their green license plates. It's US$10 to drive the six miles to Belcampo and US$12.50 to Jacintoville and the Tranquility Lodge. Or you can call on **Jonathan Supaul** (tel. 501/669-4823 or 501/628-0460, 5am-10pm daily). Also try **Castro's Taxi** (tel. 501/602-3632).

Car Rental

The folks at **Sun Creek Lodge** (tel. 501/604-2124 or 501/665-6778, ibtm@gmx.net) will deliver a rental car anywhere in Punta Gorda (if you're not staying with them); the cost is US$75 per day with a three-day minimum, or US$480 per week for a 4WD vehicle. They can also deliver to Belize City for a two-week minimum rental. Fill your gas tank at the **UNO Station** (Front St.), right across from the ocean; they accept traveler's checks and credit cards.

Tours

Toledo offers more cultural tours than any other district, thanks to its diverse population that includes East Indians, Maya, Garinagu, Creoles, and more. You can spend the morning in a Mayan community, and the afternoon at a seaside Garífuna fishing village a couple of hours later, and observe two entirely different worlds and lifestyles.

The most unique immersion experience in Toledo is to sign up for a Mayan village homestay. You can arrange this with the

Toledo Ecotourism Association (TEA) program—contact Chet Schmidt at Nature's Way (tel. 501/702-2119, teabelize.org); with the **Aguacate Belize Homestay Program** (tel. 501/633-9954, www.aguacatebelize.com/homestay-program, US$9pp per night, meals US$3.50pp per meal, US$5 registration fee); or with the village of **San Jose** (contact Justino Pec, tel. 501/722-0109).

Otherwise, if you're short on time but want a taste of Mayan life, an excellent option is to go on **Eladio Pop's Cacao Trail** in San Pedro Colombia. Eladio is a one-of a-kind individual, full of enthusiasm and knowledge of organic farming. He will walk you through his cacao orchards and land, showing you the cacao process from bean to chocolate. You'll end up at his home, where you'll get to watch cacao roasting and grind some yourself before tasting a delicious cup of hot chocolate the way the Maya used to have it. Tours are arranged through local operators, including **Toledo Cave and Adventure Tours** (tel. 501/604-2124, belizegate@gmail.com or ibtm@gmx.net, www.travelbelize.de, US$90 pp).

TIDE Tours (41 Front St., tel. 501/722-2129, www.tidetours.org, 7:30am-4:30pm Mon.-Fri., reduced hours Sat.), the tour operating arm of PG's leading NGO, specializes in cultural visits, including half a day in **Barranco,** a traditional Garífuna village, where you'll get to tour, sample Garífuna food, visit the museum and the sacred ceremonial temple (US$95pp for 2 people) or a craft lesson in the village of San Miguel, coupled with a visit to Lubaantun (US$65pp for 2 people). TIDE offers several tour combos.

If you're feeling even more adventurous, visit the **Forest Home Village,** four miles in on the San Antonio Road, for a peek into the large East Indian population of Toledo and to sample East Indian specialties. The East Indians have been in Belize since the 1860s. Ask for Gabriel Pate, chairperson of the Indian community.

Islands near Punta Gorda

The Toledo District is the gateway to the least visited of Belize's Caribbean islands—the Snake Cayes and the Sapodilla Cayes. For those who have the time to venture this far south, the snorkeling and dive sites are beyond rewarding, and with fewer boats (if any at all), you're likely to be one of the few out in the water. Just be sure not to attempt the journey in rough weather—unless you want to feel as if you came out of a washing machine.

Closest to Punta Gorda, a mere 45-minute boat ride away, are the Snake Cayes, part of the Port Honduras Marine Reserve, ideal for snorkeling, diving, and swimming. The area's islands, from Port Honduras to the Sapodilla Cayes, are not one bit about luxury—it's about adventure and experiencing nature at its best, with simple accommodations, including cabins or camping options at Lime Caye, and basic rooms on Hunting Caye. You might not even use your room, it's that pretty outside. Try to stay at least two days in the Sapodilla Cayes area if you're heading that far. The Snake Cayes are an easy day trip from Punta Gorda.

PORT OF HONDURAS MARINE RESERVE

The limits of the **Port of Honduras Marine Reserve** (park fee US$5) begin just three miles outside Punta Gorda, stretching as far as 160 square miles and encompassing mangrove forests and 138 mangrove cayes, some of which are home to a frigate and booby bird colony on Booby Cay, plenty of fresh water from five rivers that flow into the reserve, including the Rio Grande, and in the distance, the seven-hill range with its peaks towering over the reserve. The Snake Cayes and a few other gorgeous islands are accessible for snorkeling and sportfishing—you'll likely notice private yachts on your way across the reserve, as top anglers head here for the best fly-fishing in the area.

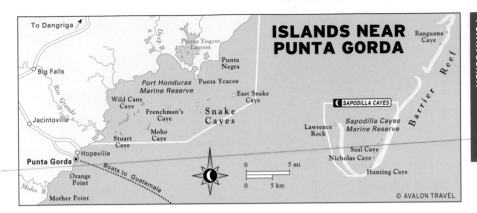

The Port Honduras Marine Reserve is co-managed and funded by the nonprofit **Toledo Institute for Development and Environment** (TIDE, tel. 501/722-2274, info@tidebelize.org), based in Punta Gorda. Their marine conservation efforts in the area are significant, the most notable of which has been the protection of, and increase in, the number of West Indian manatees. Seven years after gaining protected status, the reserve now boasts the second-largest population of these gentle sea cows. The park rangers play an important part in monitoring illegal fishing activity and removing gill nets, as well as protecting Middle Snake Caye, a no-entry caye used for monitoring mangroves and marinelife research.

Abalon Caye

Your first stop will be at **Abalon Caye,** located in the center of the reserve. Abalon Caye is home to the ranger station and six full-time rangers. Whatever you do, don't miss climbing up the 60-foot-tall ranger station's **observation tower,** used to spot vessel activity. A steep, narrow wooden staircase leads to views of the reserve. The 180-degree panorama includes the Snakes Cayes as well as neighboring Guatemala and even the Cockscomb range.

Snake Cayes

After Abalon Caye, head over to the **Snake Cayes,** the main area of the reserve, used for recreation purposes only—swimming, snorkeling, diving and sportfishing. **West Snake Caye** (also called lagoon snake caye) has the largest beach and the best snorkeling, and it's popular for beach barbecues. There's a lighthouse at **East Snake Caye.**

☾ SAPODILLA CAYES

One of the seven wonders of the Belize Barrier Reef Reserve System (declared a World Heritage Site in 1996), the **Sapodilla Cayes** are as remote as it gets. Few people make it out here from the mainland; most visitors venture over from neighboring Honduras and Guatemala. Located 35 miles or 2.5 hours by boat from the shores of Punta Gorda, it's quite the trek (don't even attempt it on a cloudy, choppy day), but the snorkeling and diving, the beaches at Lime and Hunting Cayes, and the overall stunning landscape make it worth the extra leg journeying here.

The reserve covers 80 square miles and is comanaged by the Fisheries Department and the **Southern Environmental Association** (SEA, tel. 501/523-3377, www.seabelize.org). Contact the office to find out about volunteering or possible tourism-related projects on these stunning islands.

Diving and Snorkeling

The Shipwreck is right off Lime Caye, a 10-15-feet deep dive site where you'll spot abundant marinelife—blue tangs, white grunts, angelfish, butterfly fish, lionfish, schoolmasters, and

© LEBAWIT GIRMA

The Sapodilla Cayes have some of the prettiest beaches.

vibrant coral—surrounding a massive sunken ship. There are also colorful schools of fish and amazing visibility, even in cloudy weather. The waters around **Ragged Caye** are also a good snorkeling spot. **Lime Caye Wall** is best for divers, with plenty of big fish such as groupers, snappers, and moray eels.

Reef Conservation International

If you're looking for a vacation that combines conservation education and recreation, Reef Conservation International (ReefCI, tel. 501/702-0229 or 501/629-4266, www. reefci.com, divers US$1,195 per week, nondivers US$895 per week, all inclusive) offers weekly and monthly dive trips to stay on Tom Owens Caye, a small one-acre private island in the Sapodilla Cayes with incredible snorkeling. The boat leaves Punta Gorda on Monday morning and returns on Friday afternoon. Reef Conservation offers scuba certification courses and help with research projects, always in small groups. It's worth stressing that not only will you be diving in the Sapodilla

Cayes, but you'll most likely be the only dive boat in the water (nondivers are also welcome). ReefCI offers various packages; there's often a discount for walk-in travelers and last-minute bookings. In addition to diving, ReefCI customers have the opportunity to get involved in a number of projects, such as helping with the removal of the invasive lionfish and other preservation projects in the Sapodilla Cayes Marine Reserve. They also have the unique opportunity to get involved with the survey work, learn about the environment, and identify fish, coral, and invertebrates—and to combine this with recreational dives and other activities.

Accommodations and Food

You can stay overnight at **Lime Caye** (tel. 501/722-0070 or cell 501/604-3548, garbutts-marine@yahoo.com, 2-day package US$345, 4-day package US$700, includes cabin, food, snorkeling, transportation, and park fee), a 3.5-acre island with a protected turtle nesting beach (June 1-Oct. 31). Owned by the

Garbutt family, Lime Caye has one of the prettiest beaches in the area. Stays range from two to six days and are in one of five rustic cabins or a bunkhouse with four rooms. The stand-alone cabins at the back of the island have stunning porch views of the reef. You can also camp (US$10). **Sanny's Kitchen** serves daily meals and classic cocktails.

Minutes from Lime Caye is **Hunting Caye,** where the University of Belize has rooms for rent; you can also pitch a tent. Hunting Caye feels more spread out than Lime Caye, but it's as laid-back and has an equally lovely beach.

GETTING THERE

You'll find it more affordable to get to the Snake Cayes or the Sapodilla Cayes for a day trip when there's a group of at least four people heading out. Check your dates with **TIDE** (tel. 501/722-2274, info@tidebelize.org) or with Dennis Garbutt of **Garbutt's Marine** (tel. 501/722-0070 or cell 501/604-3548), both excellent transfer options; they can keep you posted on availability and tour dates. If you're staying on Lime Caye, the Garbutts will arrange for your transportation to and from the resort.

Mayan Upcountry Villages and Archaeological Sites

The wild, unique, and stunning southwestern chunk of Belize is referred to as "upcountry" or simply "the villages." The Toledo District settlements to the west of Punta Gorda are home to Q'eqchi' or Mopan Maya, whose descendants fled to Belize to escape oppression and forced labor in their native Guatemala. Anthropologists now believe that the Mopan were probably the original inhabitants of Belize, but that they were forcibly removed by the Spanish in the late 17th century. The Q'eqchi' were close neighbors with the Mopan and the Manche Ch'ol, a Mayan group completely exterminated by the Spanish. The older folks continue to maintain longtime traditional farming methods, culture, and dress. Modern machinery is sparse—they use simple digging sticks and machetes to till the soil, and water is hand-carried to the fields during dry spells. It's not an easy life.

On the outskirts of each town, the dwellings are relatively primitive; they often have open doorways covered by a hanging cloth, hammocks, and dirt floors, and animals may wander throughout. People use primitive latrines or just take a walk into the rainforest. They bathe in the nearest creek or river, a routine that becomes a source of fun as much as cleanliness.

Within the towns, past the thatched homes on each side of the road, it becomes apparent that the effects of modern conveniences are only beginning to arrive. When a family can finally afford electricity, the first things that appear are a couple of lights and a refrigerator—the latter allows the family to earn a few dollars by selling chilled soft drinks and such. After that, it's a television set; you can see folks sitting in open doorways, their faces lit by the light inside.

SAN FELIPE AND JACINTOVILLE

Closest to Punta Gorda, Jacintoville is located just seven miles out of town, traveling along the Southern Highway. From there, a side road heading south leads to the village of San Felipe. (This same road will also eventually get you to Barranco.)

Cyrila Cho (tel. 501/742-4050 or cell 501/660-2840, www.cyrilaschocolate.org) and her family in the village of San Felipe offer a five-hour chocolate tour beginning with a visit to an organic cacao farm and continuing with lunch in Cyrila's home. She and her daughter then lead a chocolate-making session.

Tucked away on the San Felipe Road,

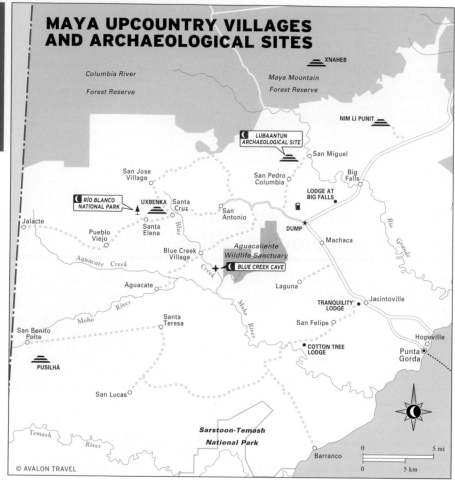

MAYA UPCOUNTRY VILLAGES AND ARCHAEOLOGICAL SITES

about eight miles outside Punta Gorda, **☾ Tranquility Lodge** (tel. 501/677-9921, www.tranquility-lodge.com, US$110-135) offers four well-appointed guest rooms popular with avid bird-watchers and orchid lovers; both have plenty to explore right here on Tranquility's 20 lush acres (only five of which are developed at the lodge area). There were 75 species of orchids at last count—both planted and volunteers—and more than 200 identified species of birds. Rates include breakfast; guest rooms have clean tile floors, private baths,

air-conditioning, and fans. When there are no other guests, it's like having your own private lodge. Upstairs from the guest rooms is a beautiful screened-in (but very open) dining room, where you'll enjoy gourmet dinners (US$15-25). All rates are negotiable in the off-season. There's direct access to an excellent swimming hole on the Jacinto River, as well as a number of walking trails.

Cotton Tree Lodge (tel. 501/670-0557, U.S. tel. 212/529-8622, www.cottontreelodge. com, US$179-219, US$419 pp all-inclusive)

THE UNSPOILED SOUTH: TOLEDO'S CONSERVATION TRAIL

Belize has the highest percentage of forest cover in Central America and the largest barrier reef system in the western hemisphere. These rich natural resources have survived relatively intact, primarily due to Belize having the lowest population density in the Central American region. This enviable status, however, is at risk, particularly in the south, where the country's most pristine environment—in the lush Toledo District—is faced with rapid population growth and immigration, combined with increasing deforestation and illegal fishing along marine and terrestrial borders.

Nonetheless, the Toledo District has managed to fight back and continues to rise as an example in protecting its fragile ecosystems. Over the past twenty years, conservation efforts in the heavily forested and biodiverse district have strengthened. As early as the 1990s, commercial interest from Malaysian logging was met with fierce resistance from local indigenous activists. The bulldozing of Toledo's forests had damaged drinking water supplies, leading to opposition from downstream communities. The late Mayan leader Julian Cho organized and led resistance to unsustainable logging on traditional Mayan land. The Government of Belize responded by cancelling these companies' licenses.

More recent conservation successes are owed to the implementation and use of a comanagement program, created by the Belizean government, whereby areas designated officially "protected"—such as the 100,000-acre no-public-access Bladen Nature Reserve—are monitored by nongovernmental organizations and residents of communities close to these protected areas, all working together and sharing in the financial burden of accomplishing the gigantic task. This comanagement system promotes both sustainable development and conservation, helping the local communities who depend on the health and sustainability of these resources.

Today, hope lies in the recent appointment of one of Toledo's own residents and award-winning conservationist Lisel Alamilla as the new Minister of Forestry, Fisheries and Sustainable Development. Of note is Alamilla's 2012 moratorium on the logging of rosewood from Toledo's forests. A few busts of illegal harvesting have since been made, including in January 2013, when up to 700 pieces of the precious wood intended for export were discovered adjacent to Tambran Village. The export-quality logs were seized and set ablaze by the Minister herself, in the presence of the media, to send a clear message to the perpetrators. The remaining logs were handed to local communities for traditional house building.

Toledo has unique tropical forests and pristine coral reefs that provide livelihoods to the most culturally diverse population in Belize. If the protection of its resources continues in this vein, this district can be a globally recognized example of sustainable development.

(Contributed by Lee McLoughlin, manager of the Protected Areas Management Program at Ya'axché Conservation Trust.)

is 12 miles up the Moho River from PG and is accessed either by boat or via the road to Barranco. Its 16 stilted thatched-roof cabins along the river's edge are connected by a raised plank walkway; ask about the deep-rainforest tree house. The lodge is one of several in the area trying to take "green" to new levels; Cotton Tree conducts voluntourism projects with Sustainable Harvest International, has developed a unique septic system using banana plants, and raises 50 percent of the food it serves in its own organic garden. Available activities include the cacao trail, treks to Blue Creek Cave, mountain hikes, river and village trips, visits to ruins, and the like, plus hands-on classes in subjects like chocolate making and Garífuna drumming. Sportfishing and fly-fishing trips are available as well. There is one honeymoon suite with a jetted tub and one cabin with wheelchair access.

LAGUNA

Laguna is a small Q'eqchi' Mayan village of around 250 people living against a backdrop of limestone karst hills. The village is home to howler monkeys and many types of parrots, which can be seen flying over the village daily. Laguna is also home to a loosely organized women's crafts group that produces *cuxtales* (pronounced "CUSH-ta-les," traditional woven Mayan bags), table mats, beading, baskets, embroidery, beaded necklaces, and earrings. There is a long, muddy farmers road that leads to the confluence of Blue Creek and the Moho River; this two- to three-hour hike is very beautiful but is only recommended in the dry season (Mar.-May). There's also a super-cool cave about a 20-minute hike away; it's really best to have a licensed guide with you.

Laguna is the oldest member of the **TEA** guesthouse program (tel. 501/702-2119, www.teabelize.org), and there is a guesthouse with a nice veranda; beds are equipped with mosquito nets. A TEA guesthouse stay includes all meals and the opportunity to interact and cook or farm with local Q'eqchi' indigenous people. Local tours, craft demonstrations, and cultural performances are available at an additional cost.

To get to the village, take the Laguna bus directly to the village, or take any bus that can drop you at the Laguna junction (10 miles from Punta Gorda). It is only about three miles to the village from the highway.

BIG FALLS

Hugging a lush bend of the Río Grande as it sweeps near the roadside village of Big Falls, **The Lodge at Big Falls** (tel. 501/732-4444 or 501/610-0126, www.thelodgeatbigfalls.com, US$160-265) is an elegant and quiet retreat in a peaceful, well-maintained, green clearing. The nine cabanas are ideal for a nature-loving couple looking for a comfortable base from which to explore the surrounding country or just to laze in the pool and listen to the forest sounds. Special rates are offered for multiple nights and for families; it's a 20-minute drive to the town of Punta Gorda, and many day trips are

available, as the Lodge at Big Falls is centrally located in the Toledo District.

Sun Creek Lodge (tel. 501/604-2124 or cell 501/665-6778, www.suncreeklodge.com, US$40-100) offers four octagonal cabanas with central posts and thatched roofs. Some have shared rainforest showers and toilets, a few have private baths, and the spacious Sun Creek Suite is for families or groups. Sun Creek is popular with European backpackers in that comfy-yet-primitive way. The on-site tour company **Toledo Cave & Adventure Tours** will take you wherever you want to go in the area, with active hikes being their forte—including trips and expeditions unavailable anywhere else. Car rental is available. Sun Creek Lodge is at Mile 14 on the Southern Highway, about two miles from "Dump," near the Shell gas station. Owner Bruno Kuppinger, long time PG resident and adventure tour guide, will pick you up from the Punta Gorda airstrip, or arrange pickup from Belize City for large groups.

If you're driving through the area, make time for lunch (or any other meal) at **Coleman's Café** in Big Falls (tel. 501/630-4432 or 501/630-4069, 11am-4pm and 6pm-9pm daily, buffet US$7.50), located just off the highway, on the entrance road to Rice Mill. This is home-cooked Belizean food at its finest, and the restaurant is run by a friendly and accommodating family. Creole dishes, cohune cabbage, and East Indian curries are among the offerings. They even have free changing restrooms for those who need to get dry from their tours and grab a cold one.

NIM LI PUNIT ARCHAEOLOGICAL SITE

Near the village of Indian Creek, **Nim Li Punit** (Mile 75, Southern Hwy., 501/665-5126, 8am-5pm daily, US$5) is atop a hill with expansive views of the surrounding forests and mountains. The site saw preliminary excavations in 1970 that documented a 30-foot-tall carved stela (stone monument), the tallest ever found in Belize—and among the tallest in the Mayan world. A total of about 25 stelae have been found on the site, most dated AD 700-800.

Although looters damaged the site, excavations by archaeologist Richard Leventhal in 1986 and by the Belize Institute of Archaeology (IOA) in the late 1990s and early 2000s uncovered several new stelae and some notable tombs. The stelae and artifacts are displayed in the very nice visitors center built by the IOA.

Nim Li Punit is located 25 miles north of Punta Gorda Town; it's about 0.5 miles west of the highway, along a narrow road marked by a small sign.

☾ LUBAANTUN ARCHAEOLOGICAL SITE

Located on a ridge between two creeks, **Lubaantun** ("Place of the Fallen Stones") consists of five layers of construction and is unique compared to other sites due to the absence of engraved stelae. The site was first reported in 1875 by American Civil War refugees from the southern United States and was first studied in 1915. It is believed that as many as 20,000 people lived in this former trading center.

Lubaantun was built and occupied during the Late Classic Period (AD 730-890). Eleven major structures are grouped around five main plazas—in total the site has 18 plazas and three ball courts. The tallest structure rises 50 feet above the plaza, and from it you can see the Caribbean Sea, 20 miles distant. Lubaantun's disparate architecture is completely different from Mayan construction in other parts of Latin America.

Most of the structures are terraced, and you'll notice that some corners are rounded—an uncommon feature throughout the Mundo Maya. Lubaantun has been studied and surveyed several times by Thomas Gann and, more recently, in 1970 by Norman Hammond. Distinctive clay whistle figurines (similar to those found in Mexico's Isla Jaina) illustrate lifestyles and occupations of the era. Other artifacts include the mysterious crystal skull, obsidian blades, grinding stones (much like those still used today to grind corn), beads, shells, turquoise, and shards of pottery. From all of this, archaeologists have determined that the city flourished until the 8th century AD. It was a farming community that traded with the highland areas of today's Guatemala, and the people worked the sea and maybe the cayes just offshore.

To reach Lubaantun from Punta Gorda, drive 1.5 miles west past the gas station to the Southern Highway, then take a right. Two miles farther, you'll come to the village of San Pedro. From here, go left around the church to the concrete bridge. Cross and drive almost one mile—the road is passable during the dry season.

THE SKULL OF DOOM: MYSTERY SOLVED

In 1924, Anna Mitchell-Hedges, the daughter of explorer F. A. Mitchell-Hedges, allegedly found a perfectly formed quartz crystal skull at the Lubaantun archaeological site on her 17th birthday. The object has been the subject of much mystery and controversy over the years. Was it made by the Maya to conjure death? Atlanteans? Aliens? Did Mitchell-Hedges plant it for the pleasure of his daughter? Is the whole story a hoax?

The world got its answer in 2007 when the Smithsonian Institute put the Mitchell-Hedges skull under a scanning electron microscope. Researcher Jane MacLaren Walsh concluded, "This object was carved and polished using modern, high-speed, diamond-coated, rotary cutting and polishing tools of minute dimensions. This technology is certainly not pre-Columbian. I believe it is decidedly 20th century."

The skull currently resides in North America with the widower of Anna Mitchell-Hedges. Despite the Smithsonian's findings, some still warned of dire consequences if the skull is not returned to Lubaantun by December 21, 2012, but that also proved untrue.

SAN PEDRO COLUMBIA

San Pedro is one of the biggest of the villages and is home to well-known Mayan musicians as well as Eladio Pop's Cacao Trail. A small Catholic church in town has an equally small cemetery; it sits on a hilltop surrounded by a few thatched dwellings.

Eladio Pop's Cacao Trail is a fantastic experience. Eladio is a one-of-a-kind Maya who will take you all over his farm and show you how the Maya once made chocolate, from the cacao tree all the way to his home, where his wife will roast, grind, and make hot chocolate the old fashioned way. Contact **Toledo Cave and Adventure Tours** (cell 501/665-6778) to arrange a trip to Eladio's.

Two miles upriver from San Pedro Columbia you'll find **Maya Mountain Research Farm** (MMRF, tel. 501/630-4386, www.mmrfbz. org), a registered NGO and working demonstration farm situated on 70 acres. Maya Mountain promotes sustainable agriculture, renewable energy, appropriate technology, and food security using permaculture principles and applied biodiversity. The farm also operates on solar power and offers a number of courses. The property has more than 500 species of plants (including lots of cacao), and the staff are working to establish an ethnobotanical garden of useful plants with their Q'eqchi' Maya names and uses. Accommodations are simple rustic affairs, with solar lighting and Internet access.

From the turnoff for Punta Gorda at Mile 86 on the Southern Highway, take the road north. At about Mile 1½, there is a turnoff on the right that heads for San Pedro Columbia and other villages. The **Chun Bus** makes the run from Punta Gorda to nearby San Antonio (11:30am Mon.-Sat., about US$4 round-trip), but doesn't stop in San Pedro Columbia; instead you will have to leave the bus at the road and trek in several miles.

SAN MIGUEL

This friendly Q'eqchi' Mayan village has a village guesthouse, a nearby river, thatched

village of San Pedro Columbia

© LEBAWIT GIRMA

houses, and people in traditional dress carrying dishes and clothes (in buckets on their heads) from the swiftly flowing river. San Miguel is also experiencing intense change with recent access to electricity, water, better roads, and increased educational opportunities. During times when the villagers are harvesting coffee, you can witness the process of picking, shelling, drying, and grinding organic coffee. Tours of the village, cave, and milpa are also available. All activities are US$3.50 per hour. The Mayan site of Lubaantun, famous for the discovery of the Crystal Skull and unique architectural features, is about three miles from San Miguel. You can either walk to the site or charter a vehicle (US$7.50). The village does not have a restaurant, but meals are cooked and served at local homes (breakfast or dinner US$3.25, lunch US$4).

San Miguel is home to one guesthouse, run by **Vicente Martin** (tel. 501/602-6240, martinack@live.com, dorm bed US$10) and his family, who live across the street from the accommodations. The guesthouse is a traditional thatched structure comprising a bedroom, which may be shared among multiple travelers (although it is likely you will be the only one there); a main living area with a desk, a chair, and a hammock; and a covered outdoor veranda with hammocks. They also provide electricity, linens, and mosquito nets, and a shower and toilet are on the premises. The family offers cooking lessons where you can learn to make corn tortillas (*xoroc li cua* in Q'eqchi'), along with *caldo* and other traditional dishes. They also offer handicraft lessons on calabash carving and traditional embroidery.

San Miguel buses leave Punta Gorda three times a day Monday-Saturday. You can catch the village bus on Jose Maria Nunez Street. The first bus leaves at 11:30am and is marked "Silver Creek." The bus has a 30-minute layover in Silver Creek before heading on to San Miguel. The other buses are also marked "Silver Creek" and leave the park at 4pm and 4:30pm. The bus ride is about 1.5 hours. Buses leave San Miguel for Punta Gorda at 6am, 12:30pm, and 1pm Monday-Saturday.

SAN ANTONIO

The village of San Antonio is famous for its exquisite traditional Q'eqchi' embroidery. However, the younger generation is being whisked right along into 21st-century Belizean society, so who knows how much longer it will survive. Contact **Toledo Cave and Adventure Tours** (tel. 501/604-2124, belizegate@gmail.com or ibtm@gmx.net, www.travelbelize.de, US$95-115) for a guided trip to Blue Creek Cave (bring a swimsuit) and advice about the area. This is also great bird-watching country.

Accommodations

Along a paved portion of San Antonio Road, two Mayan statues greet you at the entrance of **The Farm Inn** (Santa Cruz Rd., tel. 501/732-4781 or 501/604-4918, www.thefarminnbelize.com, US$90-160, includes a full farm breakfast), the latest addition to Toledo's unique "jungle lodge" offerings. This remote solar-powered riverside guesthouse is tucked amid 52 acres of land, most of which is being farmed. It is home to 3,000 cacao trees, and guests are welcome to stroll through the cacao plantation. The main guesthouse, closest to the river, is a home transformed into several guest rooms for a cozy green getaway. The deck views of the surrounding canopy are stunning. There are also two garden side cabanas, and a 26- by 26-foot swimming pool is forthcoming. Camping is available (US$10); the inn can provide tents. Owners Petro and Pieter Steunenberg moved to Belize from South Africa, hence the on-site outdoor restaurant serving a mix of Belizean and African cuisine. There are nature trails, including one leading to the river below, complimentary use of kayaks, and a bird-watching tower. Tours can also be arranged. The lodge is conveniently located within a 10-minute drive in either direction of two beautiful parks and waterfalls: the San Antonio Falls and my favorite, Río Blanco National Park.

Getting There

To reach San Antonio, after leaving San Pedro, return to the main road and make a right turn. Soon you'll be in San Antonio, just down the road. From San Antonio the road is passable as far as Aguacate (another Q'eqchi' village). Uxbenka is west of San Antonio near the village of Santa Cruz and is easy to get to via the trucks that haul supplies a couple of times a week. Known only by locals until 1984, Uxbenka is where seven carved stelae were found, including one dating from the Early Classic Period.

The **Chun Bus** makes the run from Punta Gorda to San Antonio (11:30am Mon.-Sat., about US$4 round-trip). Note that this bus doesn't stop in San Pedro Columbia; instead you have to leave the bus at the road and trek in several miles. Catch the Chun Bus at Jose Maria Nunez Street in Punta Gorda to ensure getting a seat. Remember: No buses run on Sunday.

UXBENKA ARCHAEOLOGICAL SITE

Difficult to access and largely unexcavated (actually, some recent excavations were covered back up to protect them), the small site of Uxbenka was discovered in 1984 and has more than 20 stelae. The site is perched on a ridge overlooking the traditional Mayan village of Santa Cruz and provides a grand view of the foothills and valleys of the Maya Mountains. Here you'll see hillsides lined with cut stones. This construction method is unique to the Toledo District. Uxbenka ("Old Place") was named by the people of nearby Santa Cruz.

Uxbenka is located just outside Santa Cruz, about three miles west of San Antonio village. The most convenient way to see the site is with a rental car. Contact the **Uxbenka Kini'chahau Association** (UKKA, tel. 501/628-9535, ask for Jose Mes) for more information.

◖ RÍO BLANCO NATIONAL PARK

Established in 1994 and comanaged by the **Río Blanco Mayan Association** (the people of Santa Cruz, who volunteer their time as the park wardens, and chairperson Jose Mes) and by the government, Río Blanco National Park is a favorite, providing stunning scenery and natural beauty for the visitor and an alternative income for members of neighboring villages. The park is 105 acres and encompasses a spectacular waterfall that is 20 feet high and ranges from a raging 100 feet wide during the rainy season to about 10 feet during the dry season. Locals say the turquoise pool under the waterfall is bottomless (one claims to have dived 60 feet and never touched bottom, though another says he touched it at 20 feet). The adventurous can jump off the surrounding rocks and fall 20 feet into crystal-clear water. There are also several pools to the back of the falls, plenty of space for a picnic, and two miles of nature trails, which include the cave where the Río Blanco river enters the mountain and a suspended cable bridge over the river.

Río Blanco National Park (tel. 501/628-9535, US$5) is a community-based effort, and 10 percent of all entrance fees go back into the surrounding villages, home to indigenous Maya. On-site, visit the **Craft & Snack Shop** (run by the Río Blanco Women's Association) for things like baskets, jewelry, embroidery, plus the only cold beverages in the area. There is a picnic area under the visitors center.

Getting There

Río Blanco National Park is about 30 miles west of Punta Gorda, between the villages of Santa Cruz and Santa Elena on the road to Jalacte. From Punta Gorda Town, the park is a smooth one-hour drive or an easy hop off the bus. It's also an easy two-minute hike from the Visitors Center (at park entrance) along a clear rainforest trail to reach the waterfall.

Two small bus companies serve the village of Jalacte, leaving from Jose Maria Nunez Street in Punta Gorda at 11:30am (Chun Bus, Mon.-Sat.), and 4pm (Bol Bus, Mon., Wed., and Fri.-Sat.); they return from the village on the same days at 3pm. Double-check the latest copy of the *Toledo Howler* to ensure the schedule hasn't changed, as it so frequently does around these parts.

BLUE CREEK VILLAGE
◖ Blue Creek Cave
This village of some 275 Q'eqchi' and Mopan Maya was first settled in 1925. It is also called Ho'keb Ha, "the place where the water comes out," describing the spot where the Río Blanco emerges from the side of a mountain and becomes Blue Creek, home to an extensive cave system. You'll need a guide who's familiar with these caves; ask at Punta Gorda or at one of the nearby Mayan villages. Many of these folks know the nearby caves well. You can swim up to 600 yards into the cave; it's pretty stunning, with a small waterfall in the cave. Bring a flashlight and a swimsuit.

To get here, Kan's bus leaves Punta Gorda at 11:30am Monday-Saturday; Teck's bus leaves at noon on Monday, Wednesday, Friday, and Saturday.

Tumul K'in Center of Learning
Located in the village of Blue Creek, the Tumul K'in Center of Learning (tel. 501/608-1070, www.tumulkinbelize.org) was established in 2002 to help preserve Mayan heritage, traditions, and practices. Most impressive is the center's Residential Academic Program. This Mayan high school of sorts takes in teenagers age 13-16 for a four-year stint. In addition to regular academic classes, such as math and science, the students learn Q'eqchi and Mopan, arts and crafts (pottery, sewing, basketry, and marimba playing), and specialize in one of four areas: agricultural science and production, agro-processing, eco-cultural tourism, and sustainable use of natural resources.

The center runs its own farm and sells various products to help sustain the school, including jams, honey, and bottled water. There are also cultural tours and ecotours for visitors. You can visit several Mayan villages in a day, learn to dance to the marimba, or have a "Maya for a Day" experience, where you get to immerse yourself in a day in the life of a Mayan family—making tortillas, helping with household chores, and bathing in the river. Plenty of nature and adventure tours are also offered in the

area. Maya Day, one of Toledo's biggest events, is organized by the center.

Accommodations
International Zoological Expeditions (IZE, tel. 501/532-2404, U.S. tel. 508/655-1461, info@izebelize.com, www.ize2belize.com) has a lodge at the Blue Creek Rainforest Station that can host cottage guests at the rustic site. Guests must hike 0.3 miles up into the rainforest along a trail that borders Blue Creek to reach the group of simple cabins with bunk beds, screens, lights, and electric fans. One cabin has a queen bed. Baths are in the main lodge, where meals are served. The rate of US$115 pp per night covers lodging, three meals, and two daily activities of your choice (for example, guided hikes into the rainforest and a cave).

PUSILHÁ ARCHAEOLOGICAL SITE
Along the Moho River is a forgotten city, today mostly covered by corn and rainforest. Since its discovery in 1927, Pusilhá has received little attention due the remoteness of the ruins. Early investigations by the British Museum Expedition revealed stelae, extraordinary ceramics, eccentric flints, and the remains of a stone bridge. In 2001, shortly after a dirt-track road connected the village to the rest of Belize, the Pusilhá Archaeology Project resumed investigations under the direction of Dr. Geoffrey Braswell. Recent analyses of ceramics suggest that Pusilhá was an important regional trading center.

A community-driven project, **Kehil Ha Jungle Lodge** (tel. 501/632-7855, www.ke-hilha.com) provides accommodations for researchers, students, and adventurous travelers. Ask around the village for opportunities to explore the ruins, local caves, waterfalls, and the surrounding rainforest. Pusilhá is near San Benito Poite village, a few miles from the Guatemalan border. Contact licensed tour guide **Manuel Cucul** (tel. 501/534-8659) or head there with **TIDE Tours** (41 Front St., tel. 501/722-2129, www.tidetours.org,

ANDY PALACIO: GARÍFUNA AND BELIZEAN LEGEND

Barranco's pride and joy is Andy Palacio, whose pictures are still plastered around the village—clipped from old magazines, at the bar, inside homes, at the local museum, and on the village bulletin board. The talented artist, popular singer, and Garífuna activist was born in Barranco and was buried in his home village far too soon; the star suffered a heart attack at the age of 47, and his death left behind a grieving nation.

Palacio's legacy is undisputed—anxious to preserve the Garífuna culture and language, he used music as his medium. The Afro-influenced rhythms of *punta* and *paranda* are accompanied by moving lyrics that carry socially conscious messages: "Our ancestors fought to remain Garífuna / Why must we be the ones to lose our culture?"

His last album, *Wátina*, was recorded with the Garífuna Collective, a group of Garífuna musicians from Belize, Honduras, and Guatemala. *Wátina* won worldwide acclaim and awards and put Garífuna music back in vogue, especially with the younger generation. (If you can, grab or download a copy; I still listen to it regularly).

A year before his death, Andy Palacio was awarded the prestigious WOMEX and named UNESCO Artist for Peace. You can visit both his childhood home and his grave in Barranco.

7:30am-4:30pm Mon.-Fri., US$95 pp for 2 people).

BARRANCO

Barranco is an isolated, authentic Garífuna village, where activities include fishing along the river as well as traveling by dugout canoe up the river into the Sarstoon-Temash National Park to see howler monkeys, hickatees (river turtles), and iguanas. Many of Barranco's 600 inhabitants have traveled far from their village to become some of Belize's most renowned musicians, painters, and researchers; many have earned advanced degrees in their fields, giving Barranco one of the highest per capita PhD percentages in Central America.

Go on a tour of the village with **Alvin,** a local resident and tour guide who will share Garífuna culture and history along the way. Visit a traditional Garífuna thatched-roof home—including the home of famous Garífuna artist Andy Palacio—and view the inside of the impressive *dügü,* or Garífuna temple, used for family reunions. Sample a Garífuna lunch of fried fish stewed in coconut broth, and visit the Barranco House of Culture for more on this fascinating Afro-Caribbean culture. Return for a refreshing glass of *hiu* (a spicy drink made of cassava and sweet potato) at the local bar and an evening of drumming.

You can get to Barranco by bus from the park in Punta Gorda, by boat from the Punta Gorda dock, or with your tour operator. **TIDE Tours** (41 Front St., tel. 501/722-2129, www.tidetours.org, 7:30am-4:30pm Mon.-Fri.) is your best bet for a trip to Barranco. If you can, arrange to return by boat—it's a lot faster and more pleasant than the 2.5-hour bumpy ride back to Punta Gorda.

NORTHERN BELIZE

Northern Belize is home to the largest mestizo population (descendants of the Yucatán Maya and the Spanish) in the country. Tourism is slowly emerging in these parts, but often only as a stop on the way to nearby sights. Agriculture remains the region's main economic base. A closer look into this little-visited part of Belize reveals more history and nature than meets the

HIGHLIGHTS

LOOK FOR (TO FIND RECOMMENDED SIGHTS, ACTIVITIES, DINING, AND LODGING.

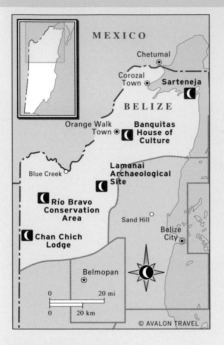

(**Banquitas House of Culture:** Located in Orange Walk Town, this exhibition hall features displays on history, industry, and culture (page 291).

(**Lamanai Archaeological Site:** Lamanai is one of the top attractions in all of Belize, and the most popular site in the region. A network of trails leads you through a partially excavated city on the shore of beautiful New River Lagoon, with its abundant birdlife and other wildlife (page 299).

(**Río Bravo Conservation Area:** Participate in a variety of research projects at Programme for Belize's field stations, deep in Belize's northwestern wilds (page 303).

(**Chan Chich Lodge:** Staying at this lodge at the Gallon Jug Estate means experiencing nature at its best, with thousands of rainforest and farmland acres. You may spot one of five species of Belize's big cats on your morning walk (page 304).

(**Sarteneja:** This remote village of fishers and boat builders is the perfect off-the-beaten-path destination for curious travelers (page 314).

eye. The Orange Walk and Corozal Districts are home to protected areas filled with rainforest and wildlife, including populations of jaguars, pumas, ocelots, jaguarundis, and even regionally endemic birds such as the ocellated turkey.

The Orange Walk District includes the archeological site of Lamanai and its impressive rainforest trails, the Río Bravo Conservation Area (a large private nature reserve), and the majestic New River, Belize's largest body of fresh water—28 miles long with abundant birds and wildlife. Morelet's crocodiles and Mesoamerican river turtles, locally known as hickatee turtles, inhabit these waters,

along with numerous fish, wading birds, and waterfowl.

Orange Walk Town is the area's hub, a small commercial and farming center. Orange Walk's annual summer fiesta and a full-blown Carnival on Independence Day lure most of the country up north to partake in Latin-flavored celebrations.

Corozal, a peaceful bayside town, is an hour's bus ride north from Orange Walk. Enjoy taking a stroll or bicycle ride along the seawall, picnicking at one of the many seaside parks, or taking a dip by "Miami Beach." Nearby, you can explore two of the country's oldest Mayan archeological sites—Cerros and Santa

Rita. The authentic fishing village of Sarteneja lies across Corozal Bay and is well worth the trip for its turquoise waters and beach shoreline. South of Sarteneja, the extensive coastal lagoons of Shipstern are largely undeveloped and are home to manatees, dolphins, and flocks of native and migratory birds.

PLANNING YOUR TIME

Both **Orange Walk** and **Corozal** towns are small enough to be explored in a couple of hours each. There are also day trips from both towns to Chetumal (Mexico), Lamanai, and Cerro Maya (commonly known as "Cerros") archaeological sites. To really dig into the north, plan on at least a night or two at the **Lamanai Outpost Lodge** or in Indian Church Village; situated close to the ruins, this is the best, fullest way to experience **Lamanai Archaeological Site** and the surrounding rainforest. Add an extra of couple of days to venture to the **Río Bravo Conservation Area** or plan a stay at **Chan Chich Lodge** and explore Gallon Jug Estate, one of the vastest and lushest rainforest areas in the country.

Some travelers link Corozal into a loop that includes Ambergris Caye, using the boat service between Corozal and San Pedro. This offers a chance to stop off at **Sarteneja,** a fishing village with a beautiful sandy shoreline and the home of Belize's wooden sailboat tradition.

Orange Walk Town

Located 66 miles north of Belize City and 30 miles south of Corozal, Orange Walk is one of the larger communities in Belize. Its 16,700 inhabitants work in local industry and agriculture. If you're passing through, stop and look around. The town has three banks, a few hotels, and a choice of small casual eateries. Roads leading from Orange Walk access 20 villages and a handful of lesser-known small archaeological sites.

Outside of town, you'll find historic sites that include **Indian Church Village;** a 16th-century Spanish mission; and the ruins of Belize's original sugar mill, a 19th-century structure built by British colonialists. Heading west and then southwest, you'll find **Blue Creek,** a Mennonite development where Belize's first hydroelectric plant was built. This is also your gateway to New River Lagoon and the Lamanai ruins.

SIGHTS
◖ Banquitas House of Culture
Situated along the banks of the New River, Banquitas Plaza (Main St., tel. 501/322-0517, banquitashoc@nichbelize.org, 9am-6pm Mon.-Fri., free) is an exhibition hall that presents a broad exhibit about Orange Walk-area history, culture, and industry, along with the work of local artisans. The hall also hosts special traveling exhibits on Mayan and African archaeology and the modern culture of Central America. The plaza comes alive on Friday and Saturday nights, when young Orange Walk couples stroll the river walk enjoying the cool evening together. The nearby amphitheater hosts monthly cultural activities.

SPORTS AND RECREATION
Beaches
About 20 minutes south of Orange Walk Town, on the old Northern Highway, you can join the locals and indulge in the white sandy beaches and shady coconut trees of **Honey Camp Lagoon,** which is as nice as any on the cayes. It's mostly a locals' picnic spot; you'll find some basic food services and tons of people during Semana Santa (Easter week).

Birding and Wildlife-Watching
Trips up and down the **New River** and around the New River Lagoon are adventures for the entire family, with a chance to see Morelet's crocodiles and iguanas sunning on the bank. By day you'll see the sights of verdant rainforest and wildlife along the river. Most people

combine a river trip with a visit to the ruins of Lamanai.

Your Orange Walk hotel or a local guide company can arrange a trip up the lagoon. Night safaris can be especially exciting, offering a chance to see the habits of animals that come out to play only after the sun sets; you'll need the help of a good guide and a spotlight.

ENTERTAINMENT AND EVENTS

Orange Walk's main summertime event, **Fiestarama** (July) is held at the main football stadium in Orange Walk Town. Families and friends indulge in games, amusement park rides, mestizo foods, rum tastings, and live concerts well into the night. The highlight for me was witnessing the town's talented and lively marching bands, performing along Queen Victoria Avenue to promote the start of the event on Saturday afternoon, and later at the stadium. The weekend usually ends with a live concert. While the fun officially begins at 3pm, the crowds don't arrive until 8pm.

The most colorful time of the year in Orange Walk is during the **Orange Walk Carnival** (Sept. 21), with a full-blown Latin and mestizo-inspired carnival sponsored by the local rum companies. The parade takes place all along the Northern Highway, starting in the heart of the town, close to the D'Victoria Hotel. It's well worth the two-hour drive north from Belize City to watch the extravagant parade, with young marching bands and women in beautiful traditional mestizo outfits, and to indulge in some of the best street food in the country.

ACCOMMODATIONS

Orange Walk has a combination of well-equipped business-oriented hotels and a few old budget standards.

Under US$25

Akihito Hotel (22 Queen Victoria Ave., tel. 501/302-0185, akihitolee@yahoo.com) charges US$22.50 for standard rooms, more for air-conditioning; most guest rooms have shared baths (US$15-18). Dorm beds go for US$7.50-9

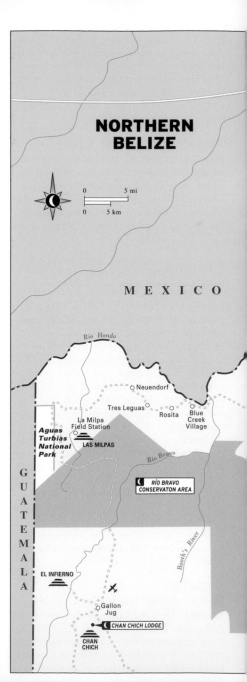

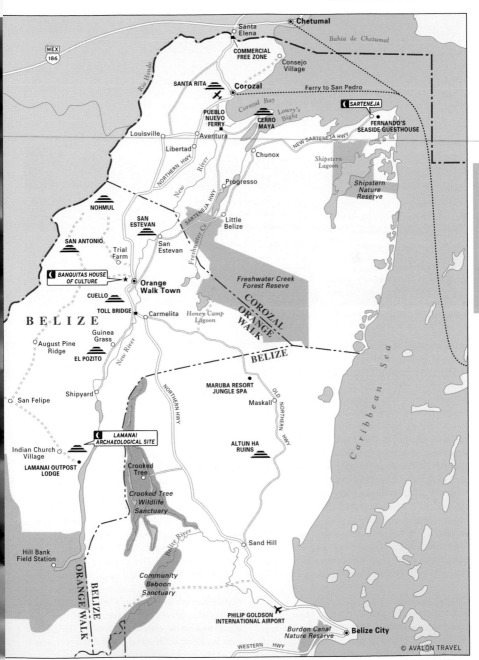

© AVALON TRAVEL

© LEBAWIT GIRMA

Abundant in birds and wildlife, New River is one of Belize's most beautiful rivers.

pp. The hotel tax is included in all room rates. Run by the Lees, this is a good sleep for the dollar, and centrally located. It's clean, with cool tiled interiors, and offers just about every basic amenity the traveler needs: laundry service, credit card phone calls, high-speed wireless Internet, and cable TV. There's a decent upstairs common area as well. The Lees are an excellent source of information about the Orange Walk area, including which restaurants are good and which bars to avoid.

Lucia's Guesthouse (68 San Antonio Rd., tel. 501/322-2244, www.hosteltrail.com/hostels/luciasguesthouse, US$15-20) is a basic traveler's rest house; guest rooms with private baths are US$20. Air-conditioning is available. Coming from Belize City, hang a left at the fire station downtown and continue 0.5 miles.

US$25-50

Named after the patron saint of travelers, the family-run **Hotel St. Christopher's** (Main St., tel. 501/302-1064 or 501/322-2420, stchristophershotel@btl.net) is popular with large groups; it has 22 colorful, traditional Spanish-feeling guest rooms with tiled floors and private baths for US$39 with fan, US$54.50 with air-conditioning. Amenities include wireless Internet, laundry service, private parking, and complimentary coffee in the lobby. A conference room, which seats 70, is available for meetings or catered meals. Located on the riverfront, the hotel has plenty of space for recreation: kayak and paddle rentals, a volleyball court, picnic tables, and greenery to attract birds and other wildlife. A few of the guest rooms have shared balconies with a view of the river.

You'll find good value at **Hotel de la Fuente** (14 Main St., tel. 501/322-2290, www.hoteldelafuente.com, US$35-85), where 22 varied guest rooms offer a range of amenities, including fully equipped apartments and free wireless Internet (which may or may not work, depending on your room's location); it's great for business travelers. All guest rooms are non-smoking and have air-conditioning. An entirely new building with 10 additional guest rooms is set at the back, away from the street.

One street up, **◖ Orchid Palm Inn** (22 Queen Victoria Ave., tel. 501/322-0719, fax 501/322-3947, www.orchidpalminn.com, US$35-64) offers similar amenities, including a nice lobby, air-conditioning, and wireless Internet, with more of a boutique hotel feel. The deluxe rooms are immaculate and cozy, with coffeemakers, fridges, and cable TV. All these hotels are centrally located.

◖ Lamanai Riverside Retreat (tel. 501/302-3955, lamanairiverside@hotmail.com, US$40) is a small family-run business located on the New River. It has three basic guest rooms with fans (air-conditioning is also available), cable TV, and private baths. The Pelayos can take care of all your needs with a nice open-air riverside bar and restaurant on-site and a variety of tour offerings. This place is unique in Orange Walk. Grab a drink, take a seat just a few steps from the river, and watch the occasional crocodile gliding by.

FOOD

◖ Central Park Restaurant (New Market, near the village bus terminal, a.k.a. "Fort Cairns") is actually a collection of six restaurants styled after the old-school open market located next door. They serve everything a hungry traveler could want: burgers, tacos, empanadas, pizza, hot dogs, bacon and eggs breakfasts, rice and beans for lunch, sweet cakes, waffles, and the usual assortment of beverages, all for a couple of bucks.

Lamanai Riverside Retreat (Lamanai Alley, tel. 501/302-3955, lamanairiverside@hotmail.com, US$5-15) is open daily for breakfast, lunch, and dinner. It's a nice setting to relax after a long day of traveling and sightseeing. Their mid-range dinner menu includes burgers, fajitas, burritos, and seafood dishes; fresh fruit juices and a full bar are also available. Karaoke nights (Fri., sometimes Sun.) attract a local crowd, and occasionally there is live music.

An exciting addition to Orange Walk Town's limited dining scene is **Paniscea Restaurant** (Banquitas Plaza, Main St., tel. 501/62-1273 or 501/623-7200, gstables@gmail.com, 3pm-3am Wed.-Mon., US$10-20), open only for dinner and offering international dishes, including chicken cordon bleu, rib eye steak, pastas, and seafood options. Service is friendly and fast, and the setting is nice, overlooking the New River on one side and a garden courtyard on the other. And hooray for a Sunday option besides street-side tacos or greasy Chinese. Happy hour specials go on all day on Saturday, and there's an occasional late DJ night.

◖ Nahil Mayab (corner of Guadalupe St. and Santa Ana St., tel. 501/322-0831, www.nahilmayab.com, 10am-3pm Mon., 10am-10pm Tues.-Thurs., 10am-11:30pm Fri.-Sat., US$5-15) is still the local Belizean favorite, or all-around favorite, offering the best dining atmosphere in Orange Walk; the outdoor patio is set in a beautiful tropical garden, and the air-conditioned restaurant has an attractive Mayan theme. The food is excellent; the menu includes Mayan and mestizo specialties (the tacos *arracheras* are popular), including seafood, steaks, and pastas, with happy hour 5:30pm-7pm daily. They also have a new kids menu with finger foods and sandwiches. Nahil Mayab means "House of the Maya."

A few steps below Nahil Mayab is a more casual affair, **Juanita's Restaurant** (tel. 501/302-2677, 6am-3pm and 6pm-9:30pm Mon.-Sat., US$3-5) serving rice and beans and all the other Creole dishes in a classic Belizean atmosphere.

Panificadora La Popular (6:30am-8pm Mon.-Sat., 7:30am-12:30pm and 3pm-6pm Sun.) is regarded as the best bakery in town, and quite possibly in the country. There is a huge selection of breads and pastries. Get pizza by the slice starting at 3pm, or have a whole pizza ready in 15 minutes (tel. 501/322-3229 to place an order). **Escalante Bakery and Café** (8 Cinderella St., 2:30pm-8pm Mon.-Sat.) serves espresso drinks and freshly baked goods, including sweet breads, cinnamon rolls, muffins, and brownies.

Orange Walk may have the highest per capita number of Chinese restaurants in all of Central America, but be warned, the food is greasy and sometimes unclean or dated (food

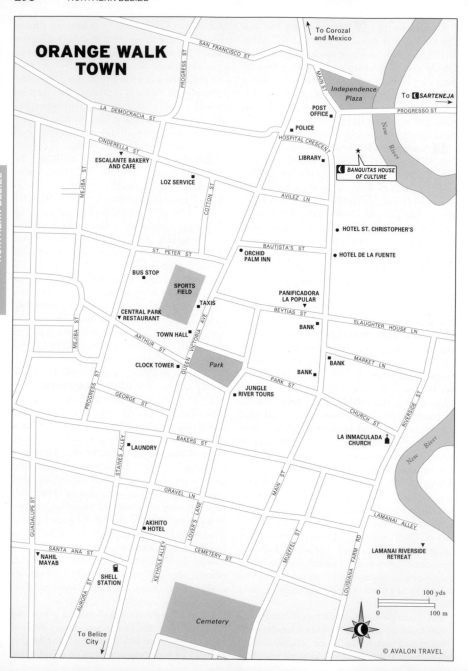

ORANGE WALK TOWN

To Corozal and Mexico

Independence Plaza

To SARTENEJA

SAN FRANCISCO ST

PROGRESS ST

LA DEMOCRACIA ST

MAIN ST

PROGRESSO ST

New River

POST OFFICE

POLICE

HOSPITAL CRESCENT

CINDERELLA ST

LIBRARY

BANQUITAS HOUSE OF CULTURE

ESCALANTE BAKERY AND CAFE

MEJIBA ST

LOZ SERVICE

COTTON ST

AVILEZ LN

HOTEL ST. CHRISTOPHER'S

ST. PETER ST

BAUTISTA'S ST

HOTEL DE LA FUENTE

ORCHID PALM INN

BUS STOP

SPORTS FIELD

PANIFICADORA LA POPULAR

CENTRAL PARK RESTAURANT

TAXIS

BEYTIAS ST

SLAUGHTER HOUSE LN

BANK

MEJIBA ST

ARTHUR ST

TOWN HALL

QUEEN VICTORIA AVE

BANK

MARKET LN

CLOCK TOWER

Park

BANK

RIVERSIDE ST

PROGRESS ST

GEORGE ST

PARK ST

JUNGLE RIVER TOURS

CHURCH ST

New River

BAKERS ST

LA INMACULADA CHURCH

STAINES ALLEY

LAUNDRY

GRAVEL LN

MAIN ST

GUADALUPE ST

LOVER'S LANE

AKIHITO HOTEL

LAMANAI ALLEY

SANTA ANA ST

NAHIL MAYAB

KEYHOLE ALLEY

CEMETERY ST

MUFFEL ST

LOUISIANA FARM RD

LAMANAI RIVERSIDE RETREAT

AURORA ST

SHELL STATION

0   100 yds
0   100 m

Cemetery

To Belize City

© AVALON TRAVEL

CHIMOLE TO TAMALITOS: MESTIZO EATS

Northern Belize has a reputation for serving the best mestizo food in the country, a mix of Spanish and Mayan cuisine. Mestizo food is most often sold from a shack or eatery window on the roadside, and also happens to be some of the cheapest and tastiest food around—the "three for a dolla" tacos are filling enough to send any budget traveler away happy. But there's a lot more to sample. Most of these mestizo dishes have corn as their common ingredient.

- **Chimole,** or "black dinner" as the locals call it, is a dark-colored and seasoned chicken soup, cooked with onions, tomatoes, potatoes, squash, black *recado* (a Belizean curry paste), and boiled eggs. Freshly made tortillas accompany this meal.

- **Escabeche** is a white-colored onion soup, served with a handful of tortillas. It's said to be excellent for a hangover. Other ingredients include garlic, white vinegar, cinnamon, and jalapeño peppers. Some also serve it with a slice of roasted chicken on the side.

- **Garnaches** are my favorite—small deep-fried corn tortillas topped with refried beans, grated cheese, chopped onions and peppers, thinly sliced tomatoes, and cilantro soaked in lime juice. These crispy treats are seriously addictive.

- **Tamalitos** are a Belizean take on the Mexican style-tamale, made with Mayan masa corn flour and wrapped in plantain or banana leaves.

poisoning victim, here). But if you're desperate, there's the established **Lee's Chinese Restaurant** (San Antonio Rd., near the fire station, 9am-midnight, US$3-12).

For a cold treat, head to the local favorite, **IceBreak** (5 Park St., tel. 501/322-0602, 8am-7:30pm Mon.-Thurs., 8am-10pm Fri.-Sat., 5pm-10pm Sun.). The outdoor veranda is ideal for people-watching.

Orange Walk's fanciest meals are found outside of town at **El Establo** (tel. 501/322-0094, http://aguallos.com/elestablo, 11am-9pm Tues.-Sat., 11am-5pm Sun., US$5-20), serving Belizean food as well as bar snacks. Ask any taxi driver to take you there.

INFORMATION AND SERVICES

Orange Walk Town is the commercial center of the district, so there are many small shops selling all kinds of merchandise, including agricultural supplies, local cookware (such as a cast-iron *comal* or a tortilla press, both heavy but useful souvenirs), and many used American-clothing shops. There are three major **banks** on Main Street and basic services for travelers, including laundry and cheap food. For an Internet café, try **FarWorld Tech** (65 Cinderella St., tel. 501/322-0716, 8am-6pm Mon.-Fri., 9am-1pm Sat., US$2 per hour).

GETTING THERE AND AROUND

During the cane harvest, the one-lane highway is a parade of trucks stacked high with sugarcane and waiting in long lines at the side of the road to get into the Tower Hill sugar mill. Night drivers beware: The trucks aren't new and often have no lights.

By Bus

There is no main bus station, but the buses traveling between Corozal and Belize City all stop to idle next to **Fort Cairns** (the site is supposedly temporary, but nobody knows where the bus station is moving to) for a few minutes before lumbering on—they pass about every hour until 6pm. Buses passing through town after 6pm usually briefly stop by Town Hall. The last bus to Belize City passes around 6:45pm, and service to Corozal continues hourly until about 9pm. Some of the buses are express, but it's hard to tell which ones, unless they are the comfy, air-conditioned charter

NORTHERN BELIZE

buses. Sunday service is about every two hours. Buses to Indian Church village (near Lamanai) leave only on Friday, returning Monday. There are hourly buses to San Felipe to the west and Sarteneja to the east. Buses to Sarteneja can be found across the street from Banquitas House of Culture by the Zeta Ice Factory.

By Boat

Traveling by boat is a pleasant way to get anywhere, especially up the New River to Lamanai. Enjoy nature's best along the shore of the river and the labyrinthine passageways through the wetlands. You never know what you'll see next—long-legged birds, orchids in tall trees, hummingbirds, crocs—it's like a treasure hunt. Bring your binoculars. Ask anywhere for directions to the boat dock. Some boat operators depart from the New Hill Toll Bridge south of town.

By Taxi

There are a few taxi stands (tel. 501/322-2050 or 501/322-2560) located on Queen Victoria Avenue, next to the sports field and across from the park. **Elido Vasquez** (tel. 501/651-1718) is a reliable and wonderful taxi driver. Fares around the central part of Orange Walk Town run US$2.50, US$7.50 to the toll bridge, and US$10 to the airstrip.

CUELLO RUINS

Located on the property of a Caribbean rum warehouse are the minor ruins of Cuello (4 miles west of Orange Walk on Yo Creek). Check in at the gate office (tel. 501/322-2141,

8:30am-4:30pm daily), then investigate these relatively undisturbed ruins, consisting of a large plaza with seven structures in a long horizontal mound. There are three temples; see if you can find the uncovered ones. These structures (as at Cahal Pech) have a different look than most Mayan sites. They are covered with a layer of white stucco, as they were in the days of the Maya.

The ruins of Cuello were studied in the 1970s by a Cambridge University archaeology team led by Norman Hammond. A small ceremonial center, a proto-Classic temple, has been excavated. Lying directly in front is a large excavation trench, partially backfilled, where the archaeologists gathered the historical information that revolutionized previous concepts of the antiquity of the ancient Maya. Artifacts indicate that the Maya traded with people hundreds of miles away. Among the archaeologists' out-of-the-ordinary findings were bits of wood that proved, after carbon testing, that Cuello had been occupied as early as 2600 BC, much earlier than ever believed. Archaeologists now find, however, that these tests may have been incorrect, and the site's age is in dispute.

Also found was an unusual style of pottery—apparently in some burials, clay urns were placed over the heads of the deceased. It's also speculated that it was here, over a long period, that the primitive strain of corn seen in early years was refined and developed into the higher-producing plant of the Classic Period. Continuous occupation for approximately 4,000 years was surmised, with repeated layers of structures all the way into the Classic Period.

Lamanai

Set on the edge of a forested broad lagoon are the temples of Lamanai. One of the largest and longest-inhabited ceremonial centers in Belize, Lamanai is believed to have served as an imperial port city encompassing ball courts, pyramids, and several more exotic Mayan features. Hundreds of buildings have been identified in the two-square-mile area. Archaeologist David Pendergast headed a team from the Royal Ontario Museum that, after finding a number of children's bones buried under a stela, presumed that human sacrifice was a part of the residents' religion. Large masks that depict a ruler wearing a crocodile headdress were found in several locations, hence the name Lamanai ("Submerged Crocodile"). The Institute of Archaeology has done a great deal of work at this site, and the main temples are impressive even to those not well versed in Mayan history.

The High Temple can be climbed to yield a 360-degree view of the surrounding rainforest and lagoon.

With the advent of midday cruise ship tours, the site boasts a dock, a visitors center, craft shops, and a museum. Lamanai is also a popular site for day-trippers from Ambergris Caye and can be quite crowded in the middle of the day, especially during the week. For a more solitary experience, go early in the morning or late in the afternoon, as cruise ship crowds arrive at noon and disappear in less than two hours.

◖ LAMANAI ARCHAEOLOGICAL SITE

The Lamanai Archaeological Site (8am-5pm daily, US$10 pp) comprises four large temples, a residential complex, and a reproduction stela of a Mayan elite, Lord Smoking Shell.

© LEBAWIT GIRMA

temple at Lamanai

Excavations reveal continuous occupation and a high standard of living into the Post-Classic Period, unlike at other ancient Mayan sites in the region. Lamanai is believed to have been occupied from 1500 BC to the 19th century—Spanish occupation is also apparent, with the remains of two Christian churches and a sugar mill that was built by British colonialists.

The landscape at most of Lamanai is forest, and trees and thick vines grow from the tops of buildings. The only sounds are birdcalls and howler monkey voices echoing off the stone temples. These are some of the notable sites:

Two significant tombs were found at the **Mask Temple** (structure N9-56), built around AD 450. There are also two Early Classic stone masks; the second mask on the temple was exposed in late 2010.

At 100 feet high, the **High Temple** (structure N10-43) is the tallest securely dated Pre-Classic structure in the Mayan world. Among many findings were a dish containing the skeleton of a bird and Pre-Classic vessels dating to 100 BC. The view above the canopy is marvelous, and on a clear day you can see the hills of Quintana Roo in Mexico.

The game played in **Ball Court** held great ritual significance for the Maya, although because of the small size of Lamanai's court, some think it was just symbolic. In 1980, archaeologists raised the huge stone disc marking the center of the court and found lidded vessels on top of a puddle of mercury; miniature vessels inside contained small jade and shell objects.

The **Royal Complex** was the residence of up to two dozen elite Lamanai citizens; you can see their beds, doorways, and the like. It was excavated in 2005.

Dating to the 6th century AD, the **Jaguar Temple** (structure N10-9) had structural modifications in the 8th and 13th centuries. Jade jewelry and a jade mask were discovered here, as was an animal motif dish. Based on the animal remains and other evidence, archaeologists now believe that this was the site of an enormous party and feast to celebrate the end of a drought in AD 950.

In 1983 archaeologists began an investigation of **Stela Temple** (structure N10-27), where they discovered a large stone monument, designated Stela 9. The elaborately carved stela depicts Lord Smoking Shell in ceremonial dress. Hieroglyphic text on Stela 9, while incomplete, indicates that this monument was erected to commemorate the accession of Smoking Shell, the Lord of Lamanai. Further excavations near the base of the monument revealed a cache of human remains and artifacts, believed to be associated with a dedication ritual. Today, a replica stands at the stela temple; the original can be viewed in the museum at Lamanai.

Birding and Wildlife-Watching

The trip to the site, up the New River Lagoon, is its own safari; once you're at the ruins, you'll see numbered trees that correspond to an informational pamphlet available from the caretakers at the entrance of Lamanai Reserve.

Birders, look around the **Mask Temple** and **High Temple** for Montezuma oropendolas and their drooping nests. Black vultures are often spotted slowly gliding over the entire area. A woodpecker with a distinct double-tap rhythm and a red cap is the male pale-billed woodpecker.

Near the High Temple, small flocks of collared aracaris, related to the larger toucan, forage the canopy for fruits and insects. The black-headed trogon is more spectacular than its name implies, with a yellow chest, a black-and-white tail, and an iridescent blue-green back. Although it looks as if the northern jacana is walking on water, it's the delicate floating vegetation that holds the long-toed bird above the water as it searches along the water's edge for edible delicacies. Other fauna spotted by those who live here are jaguarundis, agoutis, armadillos, Central American river turtles, and roaring howler monkeys.

Getting There

All regional tour operators in Orange Walk, Corozal, and Belize City offer water tours to Lamanai. It is the most impressive way to approach the site, and a time-saver as well, compared to going by land. Bob the crocodile and

NORTHERN BELIZE

a group of spider monkeys have become regular tour stops, as they are accustomed to feeding routines. (Some boats invite spider monkeys on board to eat bananas, which should be discouraged; they can become aggressive toward people and cause serious injury.) Ask about night safaris, bird-watching tours, and sunrise trips up and down the New River.

Most hotels can arrange tours with licensed guides. Tours include the entrance fee, drinks, and usually a catered lunch as part of the deal; prices range US$40-70 pp. **Jungle River Tours** (20 Lovers Lane, tel. 501/670-3035 or 501/629-3069, US$40 pp for a group of 4) is the oldest operating guide service, with a reputation for giving the best boat tours of Lamanai. Jungle River boats leave from a landing near the historic La Inmaculada Catholic Church. **Errol Cadle Eco Tours** (tel. 501/610-1753, errolcadle1@yahoo.com, US$50 pp for up to 10 people, includes lunch) is a top-notch guide service and will cater to travelers who want a less frenetic pace when it comes to their boat trips; meals and drinks are provided. You can also try the reputable **Lamanai River Tours** (14 Main St., tel. 501/302-1600, www.hoteldelafuente.com, US$50 pp for 4 people, private tour US$230 for 3 people).

Most visitors use one of the tour companies based in Orange Walk or the transfer services of their accommodations, but it is possible to do it yourself as well. A two-person boat transfer from Orange Walk should cost about US$125, less if you can get in with a bigger group. You can drive the San Felipe road in about 1.5 hours, depending on road conditions.

INDIAN CHURCH VILLAGE

The ruins of Lamanai huddle to one side of New River Lagoon and sprawl westward through the forest and under the village of Indian Church, which was relocated by the government from one part of the site to another in 1992. It is reachable by boat from Orange Walk or by road from San Felipe.

Contribute directly to the local economy by shopping at the **Indian Church Village Artisans Center,** a community-based organization founded in 2000 with the assistance of professional archaeologists, artisans, and architects working at the nearby Lamanai site. The center provides workspace, tools, material, craft training, English classes, and a computer center to interested villagers. The center has a small shop at the Lamanai site, or you can check out the artisans' wares at their workshop in the village. Artisans produce silver and bronze jewelry, hand-sewn purses, bags, embroidered pillowcases, slate carvings, and fired clay statues. Most of the artwork emulates artifacts found at the Lamanai site, including silver pendants of the Lord Smoking Shell stela. Stop by the village workshop yourself or ask your guide to take you by the shop at the Lamanai site.

Accommodations

The Indian Church villagers have been hosting groups of foreign archaeologists, anthropologists, and biologists (and the odd gringo volunteer) for decades. In addition to the places listed, there are a few informal homestay options available. Find out the latest developments in the village's foray into tourism by calling the community phone (tel. 501/309-1015), or just wander into town and see what you find. Note that Indian Church is off the electricity and telephone grid, and solar panels and gasoline generators provide power. All budget options provide meals and cultural activities and can hook you up with local guides for the ruins and wildlife tours.

Olivia and David Gonzalez (tel. 501/668-8593 or 501/667-3232, from US$20-40 pp) have moved up from rustic wooden guest rooms connected to their home to a row of modern cement guest rooms with private baths and basic amenities, including a few hours of electricity each evening. **Doña Blanca's Guest House** (tel. 501/665-0044, US$40 with 3 meals, US$25 room only) has 15 guest rooms with private baths, solar power, and hot and cold showers. Also available are very basic cabanas, ideal for the backpacker, with private baths (US$8). Call ahead to give them time to prepare your room.

About 0.5 miles up the bank of the

lagoon from the Lamanai archaeological site, **Lamanai Outpost Lodge** (tel. 501/672-2000, U.S. tel. 888/733-7864, www.lamanai.com) is one of Belize's premier rainforest retreats. Lamanai Outpost offers a low-key, escape-to-nature kind of setting, perfect for the bird-watcher, Mayaphile, naturalist, or traveler who wants to get away from the tourist trail for a while. The area is rich in animal life, including close to 400 species of birds as well as crocodiles, margays, jaguarundis, anteaters, tayras, arboreal porcupines, and the fishing bulldog bat.

From the moment the staff greet you at the dock, you know you're in capable, welcoming hands. The lodge boasts 17 elegantly rustic thatched-roof, rough-hewn wood cabanas detailed with converted brass oil lamps and other amenities that contribute to an old-fashioned feel (although a couple of guest rooms add plasma-screen TVs, air-conditioning, and wireless Internet access to the old-timey mix). Outside, lush, landscaped grounds of orchids, ceiba trees, and palmettos provide cooling shade as you walk the gravel paths. Below the resort's lodge and dining room (which are the only parts of the complex visible from the river) lies the shore of the lagoon, where you'll find a dock, a swimming area, canoes, boats of various types, and an assortment of deck chairs. The dock is particularly peaceful at sunset. Activities keep you busy from pre-dawn hikes and canoe trips to nighttime "spotlight cruises." All-inclusive packages start at US$676; there's a two-night minimum stay, and rates include transfer to and from Belize City, meals, and two guided adventure activities per night booked. See the website for summer specials and individual pricing options.

The owners of Lamanai Outpost are involved in several scientific research projects that also allow nature-study opportunities for guests. Study topics include local bats, archaeology, howler monkeys, Morelet's crocodiles, and ornithology. Guests with some group programs can participate in the work.

Food

In Indian Church village, you'll find cheap local food at the **Grupo de Mujeres Las Orquidias Restaurant** (about US$5 per meal). This is a communal effort of nine women from nine families who are adept at dealing with both groups and individuals.

Getting There

You can take the village bus to Indian Church, which leaves Orange Walk at 5pm-6pm on Friday and Monday. The same buses depart Indian Church at 5am-5:30am on the same days, so you'll have to make a weekend out of it—or more. On the opposite end of the time, comfort, and price spectrum, you can charter a 15-minute flight from Belize City to Lamanai Outpost Lodge's airstrip with one of Belize's private charter services.

Blue Creek and the Río Bravo

As the road meanders west from Orange Walk and Cuello, numerous small villages dot the border region. Occasionally you see a soft-drink sign attached to a building, but there's not much in the way of facilities between Orange Walk and Blue Creek. Heading west from San Felipe, you soon find flat, open farmland, with Mennonite accoutrements, dominating the landscape. Low, open paddy fields provide great bird-watching opportunities as well as placid scenery. In the foothills of the Maya highlands is Blue Creek village. Climbing up into the foothills you can see the flatlands of the Río Hondo and New River drainages to the east. The small village to the right is La Union, on the other side of the Mexican border. This part of Northern Belize is much hillier and has an increasingly wild feel to it.

BLUE CREEK VILLAGE

In the village of Blue Creek, **The Hillside Bed & Breakfast** (about 30 miles west of Orange Walk, tel. 501/323-0155, bchillsideb_b@ yahoo.com, US$50) is an incredibly unique and peaceful place to stay. Guests experience Belizean Mennonite hospitality and life on a working farm. (As far as I know, this is the only lodging offered in a Mennonite community in Belize.) Guest rooms feature all the basic amenities, including air-conditioning, and rates include breakfast in the kitchen. Companies visiting the area have occasionally booked the entire place for a few months at a time, so call first before heading there.

At the top of the hill are the Linda Vista Credit Union and a **gas station**-general store. Fill up the tank if you're driving on to Río Bravo or Chan Chich, as this is the last gas station until you come back this way.

◖ RÍO BRAVO CONSERVATION AREA

At the dramatic boundary of the Programme for Belize Río Bravo Conservation Area (RBCMA), the cleared pastureland runs into a wall of rainforest. There is a gate at the border, and if you aren't expected, the guard won't let you pass. Once inside the gate, you've entered the Río Bravo Conservation Area.

Programme for Belize (1 Eyre St., Belize City, tel. 501/227-5616 or 501/227-1020, www. pfbelize.org) is a Belizean nonprofit organization, established in 1988, to promote the conservation of the natural heritage of Belize and wise use of its natural resources, centering on the Río Bravo Conservation and Management Area (RBCMA), a 260,000-acre chunk of Belize where Programme for Belize demonstrates the practical application of its principles (the land was originally slated for clearing). The RBCMA represents approximately 4 percent of Belize's total land area and is home to a rich sample of biodiversity, which includes 392 species of birds, 200 species of trees, 70 species of mammals, 30 species of freshwater fish, and 27 species of conservation concern.

Within the conservation area, the research station is housed in a cluster of small thatched-roof buildings. Programme for Belize is dedicated to scientific research, agricultural experimentation, and protecting indigenous wildlife and the area's Mayan archaeological sites—all this while creating self-sufficiency through development of ecotourism and sustainable rainforest agriculture, such as chicle production. A scientific study continues to determine the best management plan for the reserve and its forests.

Ongoing projects include archaeological research at the La Milpa Maya Site and other sites on the RBCMA in conjunction with Boston University and the University of Texas; timber and pine savanna research programs aimed at identifying the most optimal approach to sustainable timber extraction; a carbon sequestration pilot program, the first of seven globally approved projects to start on-the-ground research on how forest conservation could combat global warming; ecological research and monitoring of migratory and resident avifauna, such as the yellow-headed parrot; a freshwater management program, which looks at the New River Lagoon, its tributaries, and the New River; and the biological connectivity program, which looks at the RBCMA and the critical links it forms with other protected areas in northern Belize.

La Milpa Field Station

Programme for Belize's La Milpa Field Station lies nestled deep in the forests of northwestern Belize. This station is only three miles from the third-largest archaeological site in the country, the La Milpa archaeological site, which is just one of at least 60 archaeological sites found on the Río Bravo. Hiking nature trails, rainforest trekking, and birding are the order of the day at La Milpa. Spend a day in the nearby mestizo and Mennonite villages for a taste of Belizean culture or tour breathtaking and majestic ancient Mayan sites. Birders can compile a list of more than 150 species during a three-day trip to La Milpa.

For **accommodations,** guests can choose between charmingly rustic thatched-roof cabanas

(US$50-55 pp) with private baths or a comfortable and tastefully decorated dormitory (US$41 pp) featuring state-of-the-art "green" technology with shared baths. The La Milpa venue has meeting facilities, telephones, and dining facilities and is family oriented, with 24-hour electricity and hot and cold water. All-inclusive packages start at US$180 pp, which includes accommodations, three buffet-style meals, and two guided tours on the property. Contact Programme for Belize for details.

Hill Bank Field Station

Located on the banks of the New River Lagoon, the Hill Bank Field Station serves as a research base for sustainable forest management and specialized tourism, which incorporates research activities into the visitors' forest experience. Hill Bank, an important site in Belize's colonial history, served as a center of intensive timber extraction for more than 150 years, commencing in the 17th century. The Hill Bank experience brings to life the architecture and artifacts of colonial land use, such as the quaint wooden buildings of logging camps, antique steam engines, and railroad tracks.

Explore the wilds of Hill Bank by canoeing, crocodile spotting, hiking nature trails, birding, and rainforest trekking. The scenic boat ride, replete with wildlife sightings along the New River Lagoon, is a great experience in itself. For **accommodations,** guests stay in Hill Bank's Caza Balanza, which features 100 percent solar power, no-flush composting toilets, and a rainwater collection system, with shared baths (US$41 pp). Or choose a charming double cabana with private baths (US$50-55 pp) and verandas overlooking the New River Lagoon. Contact Programme for Belize for details.

CHAN CHICH RUINS

As recently as 1986, the only way in to the Mayan site of Chan Chich (Kaxil Uinich) was with a machete in hand and a canoe to cross the swiftly flowing rivers. Most people making the trip were either loggers, pot farmers, or grave robbers. Then, in the northwestern corner

of Belize in Orange Walk District, near the Guatemalan border, an old overgrown logging road, originally blazed by the Belize Estate and Produce Company for logging, was reopened, and consequently the site of Chan Chich was rediscovered.

When found, three of the temples showed obvious signs of looting, with vertical slit trenches just as the looters had left them. No one will ever know what valuable artifacts were removed and sold to private collectors. The large main temple on the upper plaza had been violated to the heart of what appears to be one or more burial chambers. A painted frieze runs around the low ceiling. Today, the only temple inhabitants greeting outsiders are armies of small bats and spider monkeys.

The ruins provide opportunity for discovery and exploration, and the population and diversity of wildlife here are probably greater than anywhere else in Belize. The nine miles of hiking trails wind through the verdant rainforest and provide ample opportunities to see wildlife, including big cats.

This is not a public archaeological site, and the ruins are unexcavated. Chan Chich Lodge looks after the site.

Gallon Jug Village and Estate

Originally the hub of the British Belize Estate and Produce Company's mahogany logging operation, this land was purchased by Barry Bowen. **Gallon Jug Village and Estate** (tel. 501/227-7031, www.gallonjug.com) is now a diverse and privately owned working farm, ranch, and community, with an airstrip, a post office, a coffee-roasting facility, and a school. The scientific research conducted here, led by Bruce and Carolyn Miller, has focused on jaguars and neotropical bats.

◖ Chan Chich Lodge

It's safe to say that there's no other lodge in Belize like **Chan Chich** (Gallon Jug Estate, U.S. tel. 800/343-8009 or tel. 501/223-4419, US$320 includes breakfast), the country's very first rainforest eco-lodge. This elegant yet unpretentious retreat is surrounded on all sides by unexcavated pyramids and the second largest tropical forest in the Americas. The landscaped grounds, subtly lit pool and jetted tub, and sunset views from the tops of the mounds complement the spacious cabanas, which rest inside an actual Maya plaza and feature modern amenities like water coolers, refrigerators, huge tiled baths, and natural insulation and ventilation. Though decried by some archaeologists when it was built in 1988, the presence of Chan Chich Lodge serves as a deterrent to temple looters and marijuana traffickers, both of which used to thrive in northern Belize.

Guests spend their days birding (more than 80 percent of visitors are avid birders from North America), exploring the ruins and hiking trails, canoeing at the nearby Laguna Verde, or horseback riding from the Gallon Jug stables. Birding opportunities include seeing trogons, ocellated turkeys, toucans, and hundreds of other birds. All five species of Belizean cat, including jaguars, pumas, and jaguarundis, live in the surrounding forest and are spotted regularly on the property. If you're one of the lucky ones, you might get to write your sighting on the lodge's daily log board. Tours of the coffee plantation and experimental farm at Gallon Jug provide the opportunity to learn all the steps in the coffee-making process as well other sustainable agricultural initiatives taking place here. And the day doesn't end at the peaceful dining veranda, where the best steak in the country is served, among other Belizean cuisine options. If you're not signed up for the night safari, then you can finish off at the Looter's Trench Bar. Ask about a nighttime canoe ride along Laguna Seca to spot crocodiles and absorb the sheer magnitude of life in the rainforest at night. Chan Chich is 130 miles from Belize City, an all-day drive from the international airport or a (much easier) 30-minute charter flight to Gallon Jug. In addition to accommodations, add about US$70 per day for meals, plus tours, guides, and taxes.

NORTHERN BELIZE

© LEBAWIT GIRMA

Belize's first-ever jungle lodge, Chan Chich is still its most unique, with a stunning rainforest and wildlife.

NORTHERN BELIZE

Corozal and Vicinity

Corozal Town's 9,000 or so inhabitants casually get by while the bay washes against the seawall running the length of town. While English is the official language, Spanish is just as common, since many residents are descendants of early-day Mayan and mestizo refugees from neighboring Mexico. Historically, Corozal was the scene of attacks by the Maya during the Caste War. What remains of Fort Barlee can be found in the center of town (west of Central Park).

The town was almost entirely wiped out during Hurricane Janet in 1955 and has since been rebuilt. As you stroll the quiet streets, you'll find a library, a museum, the town hall, government administrative offices, a Catholic church, two secondary schools, five elementary schools, one gas station, a government hospital, a clinic, a few small hotels, a couple of bars, and several restaurants. There's not a whole lot of activity here, unless you happen to be in town during the Mexican-style "Spanish" fiestas of Christmas, Carnival, and Columbus Day; there are also a few local events in mid-September and a monthly art festival. Nevertheless, Corozal has a special aura; you'll see families, lovers, and friends along the Bay's various parks, running, playing, watching the sunset, or frolicking in the water.

SIGHTS

There are no major attractions per se for visitors in Corozal, just a couple of historical sights, but it's an unassuming base for fishing trips, nature watching, and tours of a few nearby ruins and waterways. Some trips include day trips to the Shipstern Wildlife Nature Reserve, Sarteneja village, and the Maya sites of Cerros and Santa Rita. Visitors enter Corozal from the north (from Mexico), from the south on the Northern Highway, or from Ambergris Caye to the east by boat or plane. Getting oriented to Corozal is easy, since it's laid out on a grid system with avenues running north and south (parallel to the seawall) and streets running east and west. Corozal's two primary avenues are 4th and 5th, which run the length of town. The majority of restaurants and stores of interest to travelers are on, or are adjacent to, these streets. Wander through the town square, stroll the waterfront and the Market Square in town, and strike up a conversation with the locals or expats who've come to love the laid-back lifestyle. Many of the seaside parks, especially the one called Miami Beach, are popular hangouts on the weekend and holidays.

Corozal Town Mural

In the **Town Hall** (across Central Park, 8am-4:30pm Mon.-Fri.) you'll find a dramatic historical mural painted by Manuel Villamour. The bright painting depicts the history of Corozal, including the drama of the downtrodden Maya, the explosive revolt called the Caste War, and the inequities of colonial rule. It's well worth stopping in for a look.

Corozal House of Culture

The country's newest **House of Culture** (tel. 501/422-0071, 8am-5pm Mon.-Fri.) opened in February 2012 in a refurbished historical building that was once a municipal market, built in 1886. It is slowly being stocked with historical displays on Corozal's past and biographies on Corozaleños of note. Stop in to view the current month's exhibit, such as a fascinating look into the lives of indentured East Indians brought to Corozal in the 19th century to work the sugar plantations.

East Indian Museum

Dubbed "Window to the Past" by its founder and curator Lydia Ramcharan Pollard, the **East Indian Museum** (129 South End, tel. 501/402-3314, 9am-11:30am and 2pm-4:30pm Mon.-Fri., 9am-11:30am Sat.) is the first museum in the Caribbean—and the only one in Belize—dedicated to East Indian history, heritage, and

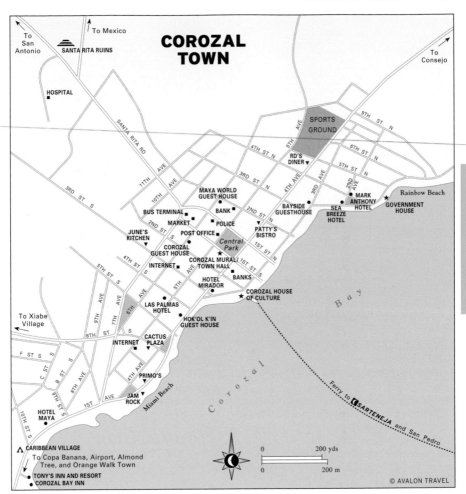

culture. The museum was established in 2001, and its collections, gathered by Pollard through various means, include cooking utensils, musical instruments, and more. It is located on the Northern Highway, where Corozal town meets Ranchito village.

SPORTS AND RECREATION

Corozal has beautiful, well-maintained stretches of green all along its seaside—**Mothers' Park, Children's Park,** and **Miami Beach Park.** Some parks include playgrounds, while others step into the bay, where children splash around or lovers cuddle up on concrete platforms, gazing at the sky. Spending a stolen morning hour at the park or sunset with friends is a favorite local activity. For fishing or boat activity while in Corozal, your best bet is **Our Island Tours and Charters** (tel. 501/633-9372 or 501/633-0081, ourislandtours@yahoo.com, full day of fishing US$400 for 4 people), offering boat rides to nearby Cerros, across the bay, for some Mayan history, or across the New River or Rio Hondo for fishing.

© LEBAWIT GIRMA

Corozal is a small town that hugs the bay.

ENTERTAINMENT AND EVENTS

For bars, try **Machie's Pool Hall** (2nd St. N. near 4th Ave. N.) for billiards and dominoes tournaments. At Miami Beach on the south end of town are two popular open-air bars: swing by **Jam Rock** (1st Ave. S.) while the bartender mixes a *michelada,* or have a cold drink and *botanas* at **Primo's Casita Bar,** across the street. The most popular event in town is **Art in the Park,** a monthly arts and crafts festival held on the second or third weekend in Central Park. More than 30 local artists—from painters to wood-carvers—showcase the best of Corozal's talent. You can snag unique local crafts and gifts here, and enjoy mestizo food and live music.

SHOPPING

Corozal has lots of little shops, grocery stores, bookstores, and a few gift shops. You'll find locally made jewelry, pottery, woodcarvings, clothing, textiles, and a host of other mementos here and there, but the place is not overrun with gift shops yet. **White Sapphire** (7th Ave., south of the UNO station, 10am-6pm) has a large selection of local crafts and jewelry. Gifts, books, postcards, and other supplies can be obtained at **A&R** (4th Ave., 9am-5pm), near Patty's Bistro.

ACCOMMODATIONS
Under US$25

Maya World Guest House (tel. 501/666-3577 or 501/627-2511, byronchuster@gmail.com, US$22.50-30) has clean rooms surrounding a well-kept, cheery garden, and cheery owners. It features a massive communal kitchen, cozy common areas, and a top-floor veranda with plenty of chairs and hammocks. The central location and conveniences such as bike rental and laundry service attract backpackers. **Caribbean Village RV Park and Campground** (tel. 501/422-2725, menziestours@btl.net) offers full RV hookups (US$20) and camping (US$5 pp).

Sea Breeze Hotel (tel. 501/422-3051 or 501/605-9341, gwyn_lawrence@yahoo.com,

ARCHAEOLOGICAL SITES NEAR COROZAL

The nearby ruins of Cerros and Santa Rita are not as immediately awe-inspiring as, say, Lamanai or Caracol, but they are still interesting and easy to visit.

CERRO MAYA

Commonly referred to as "Cerros," the Cerro Maya ("Maya Hill") archaeological site lords over both sea and jungle on a peninsula across from Corozal called Lawry's Bite. Cerros was an important coastal trading center during the Late Pre-Classic Period (350 BC–AD 250) and was occupied as late as 1300 AD. Magnificent frescoes and stone heads were uncovered by archaeologist David Friedel, signifying that elite rule was firmly fixed by the end of the Pre-Classic Period. The tallest of Cerros's temples rises to 70 feet, and because of the rise in the sea level, the one-time stone residences of the elite Maya are partially flooded.

It would appear that Cerros not only provisioned oceangoing canoes, but also was in an ideal location to control ancient trade routes that traced the Río Hondo and New River from the Yucatán to Petén and the Usumacinta basin. A plaster-lined canal for the sturdy, oversized ocean canoes was constructed around Cerros. Archaeologists have determined that extensive fishing and farming on raised fields took place, probably to outfit the traders. But always the question remains: Why did progress suddenly stop?

Be prepared for vicious mosquitoes at Cerros, especially if there's no breeze. You can reach the site by boat in minutes—hire one at **Tony's Inn** in Corozal or check with a travel agent. If you travel during the dry season (Jan.-Apr.), you can get to Cerros by car; it takes up to 45 minutes, and you'll have to employ the hand-cranked Pueblo Nuevo Ferry. Admission to the ruins is US$10 per person.

Guests at **Cerros Beach Resort** (tel. 501/623-9763 or 501/623-9530, www.cerrosbeachresort.com, US$40-60) can bike to the ruins; keep an eye out for jaguarundis, gray foxes, and coatimundis along the way. Cerros Beach Resort is a quiet, off-the-grid location with four screened-in thatch cabanas with private bathrooms and hot water.

SANTA RITA

This site, one mile northeast of Corozal, was still a populated community of Maya when the Spanish arrived. The largest Santa Rita structure was explored at the turn of the 20th century by Thomas Gann. Sculptured friezes and stucco murals were found along with a burial site that indicates flourishing occupation in the Early Classic Period (about AD 300), as well as during the Late Post-Classic Period (AD 1350-1530). Two significant burials were found from distant periods in the history of Santa Rita: one from AD 300 was a female and the other was a king from a period 200 years later.

In 1985, archaeologists Diane and Arlen Chase discovered a tomb with a skeleton covered in jade and mica ornaments. It has been excavated and somewhat reconstructed under the Chases' jurisdiction; only one structure is accessible to the public. Post-Classic murals, mostly destroyed over the years, combined Maya and Mexican styles that depict the ecumenical flavor of the period. Some believe that Santa Rita was part of a series of coastal lookouts. Santa Rita is probably more appealing to archaeology buffs than to the average tourist.

www.theseabreezehotel.com, US$20-35) offers the best budget accommodations in Corozal. guest rooms have cable TV, fans (air-conditioning for additional cost), hot water, and wireless Internet. The seaside location of this hotel offers a cooling breeze in the evening. Call ahead or email, as this place has only seven guest rooms and gets busy. The second-floor bar (for guests only) is a great place to meet other travelers and is a quick walk from the main thoroughfares. Bikes are available for guests to explore the town by day. Enjoy a freshly brewed cup of coffee in the morning and breakfast on request.

US$25-50

Just two blocks south of the town center, and

right across from the water, the ◖Hok'ol K'in Guest House (89 4th Ave., tel. 501/422-3329, maya@btl.net, www.corozal.net, US$21-65) was begun by a former Peace Corps volunteer with the intention of supporting local Mayan community endeavors. In Yucatec Maya, Hok'ol K'in means "Coming of the Rising Sun," a sight you'll see from your window if you're up early enough—follow your sun salutations with an excellent breakfast (and real coffee!) on the patio downstairs. Hok'ol K'in's 10 immaculate guest rooms have private baths, verandas, cable TV, and fans; free wireless Internet is available. Ask about available trips and homestays (or visits) with local families; the staff are very helpful in arranging things to do. This is one of the few lodgings in Belize equipped to handle a wheelchair (one room only, so be sure to specify if it's needed). There's a bar, and the restaurant (7am-7pm daily) serves a variety of good meals.

The Copper Horse Inn (2nd Ave. N. at 4th St. N., tel. 501/671-4663, brent.bell55@hotmail.com, www.copperhorseinn.com, US$30), overlooking Corozal Bay, has seven guest rooms with cable TV, hot and cold water, and queen beds; air-conditioning is available for additional cost. The on-site bar and restaurant has some of the best food in town. CJ's Lodge (2nd St., off Northern Hwy., tel. 501/621-1799 or 501/623-0212, cjshotel@gmail.com, US$25) is an affordable option geared toward both long- and short-term stays, with friendly owners. Guest rooms are comfortably furnished and have wireless Internet, hot and cold water, air-conditioning, and cable TV. A communal kitchen is on-site as well as a swimming pool and a tranquil garden area. The on-site restaurant serves only breakfast, on weekends.

Hotel Mirador (tel. 501/422-0189, www.mirador.bz, US$35-75) is a 24-room lodging across from the main dock and seawall; the rooftop boasts the best views in town. The guest rooms are spotless, with private baths and hot and cold water, and the hallways are cavernous. There's cable TV and wireless Internet, plus you'll get lots of friendly help from your hosts, Jose and Lydia Gongora. Deluxe guest

rooms with air-conditioning start at US$50. The bay-facing guest rooms have wonderful light and views. On the road leading into town from the south, the Hotel Maya and Apartments (South End, tel. 501/422-2082 or 501/422-2874, www.hotelmaya.net, US$35-50) offers 20 guest rooms with air-conditioning, TV, and private baths; the restaurant serves breakfast only. Furnished two-bedroom apartments with air-conditioning start at US$400 per month.

Las Palmas Hotel (formerly Nestor's, but completely rebuilt, tel. 501/422-0196, www.laspalmashotelbelize.com, US$45-75) is in the heart of town, with 27 full-service guest rooms that include air-conditioning, private baths, hot and cold water, mini fridges and microwaves, wireless Internet, gated parking, 24-hour security, and a backup generator. Bayside Guest House (31 3rd Ave., tel. 501/625-7824, US$45) has four guest rooms with hot and cold water, ceiling fans, cable TV, Internet, and air-conditioning for an additional cost. Continental breakfast is included. The terrace bar and restaurant is open to guests for an evening meal or drink.

US$50-100

Three seaside options are on the south end of town, clustered together on what is locally known as "Gringo Lane." At Tony's Inn and Beach Resort (tel. 501/422-2055 or 501/422-3555, tonys@btl.net, from US$85), "beach" may be stretching it a bit, and the 24 guest rooms are set up more like a Motel 6 than a resort. Still, the large guest rooms have air-conditioning, private baths, and hot and cold water. The Y-Not Bar and Grill is in a nice setting on the water, and the hotel has its own marina and runs a variety of local trips.

Right next door to Tony's Inn, you'll find the Corozal Bay Inn (tel. 501/422-2691, www.corozalbay.biz, US$20-75), a couples-oriented cluster of 10 cute thatched-roof cabanas set around 396 truckloads of sand imported from Belize's Pine Mountain Ridge; the inn offers a swimming pool, a lively bar, and guest rooms with air-conditioning, big-screen TVs, large private baths, and fridges. There are complimentary bikes too. A bit more to the south, in a very quiet, out-of-the-way spot, the **Copa Banana** (409 Bay Shore Dr., tel. 501/422-0284, www.copabanana.bz, US$55) has lovely tropical-decor guest rooms and suites open to the sea breeze (but also air-conditioned) has a shared living room and kitchen area and lots of space, plus free use of bikes, coffee, tea, and juices.

At **Almond Tree Hotel Resort** (425 Bayshore Dr., tel. 501/628-9224, www.almondtreeresort.com, US$85-149), in a quiet location down the road from Tony's Inn, each of the six guest rooms has its own elegant decor and comfortable beds; larger units are equipped with a kitchenette and a living room. The view from the upstairs wraparound veranda is wonderful. Downstairs is a bar and restaurant where breakfast is available on request and cold Belikin is on tap. Outside, you can relax poolside, walled by a tropical garden, or talk to the owner, Lynn, about arranging an activity that suits your interests: fishing by dory, a trip to the cayes, or inland tours.

Serenity Sands Bed and Breakfast (3 miles north of Corozal and 1 mile off of Consejo Rd., tel. 501/669-2394, www.serenitysands.com, US$85-105) has four tastefully decorated upper-level guest rooms with queen or twin beds, air-conditioning, and private balconies over Corozal Bay. The two-bedroom guesthouse (US$125) can accommodate a family of six. The hotel is off the grid and uses organic products as often as possible. There's complimentary Internet access and a well-stocked library.

FOOD

The town market has a selection of cheap eats and is your best bet early in the morning if you have to eat and run to catch a bus just up the street.

Belizean

For Belizean options, head to **RD's Diner** (4th Ave., tel. 501/422-3796, 8am-10pm daily, US$5-9), by the sports ground, which serves Belizean and American food, including seafood

and pasta, and daily rice and beans options. **Patty's Bistro** (2nd St. N., tel. 501/402-0174, 7am-9pm daily, US$5-9) is a nice little option for Belizean lunches and dinners. The conch soup has a unique hint of coconut, as does the curry shrimp entrée (US$7.50). There are fajitas and chicken dishes for less, and the burgers are excellent. Meals are served in an air-conditioned dining room.

If hamburgers or pasta are your fancy, head to **Copper Horse Restaurant** (Copper Horse Inn, 2nd Ave. N. at 4th St. N., tel. 501/671-4663, 11am-9pm daily, US$5-12). The Belizean food is on par with Patty's and their ceviche is fantastic; the view is of the sea. Try the home-cooked daily specials at **June's Kitchen** (3rd St. S., tel. 501/422-2559, www.corozal.com/junes, breakfast and lunch daily, dinner by reservation only, US$4), where you're basically eating in Miss June's living room or on her porch. The breakfast plates are famous and huge, or stick to rice and beans with stewed chicken.

Corozo Blues (Northern Hwy., tel. 501/422-0090, www.corozoblues.com, 10am-midnight daily, US$10-18), found just before the turn off to Tony's Inn, is a new addition with a lovely setting and average food. But if you're looking to relax by the water in cozy cushioned seats or in your own gazebo set in a lush garden, it may be worthwhile. Serving international food and one local dish, dining options include wood-fired brick-oven pizzas, burgers, salads, and steaks.

Indian and Chinese

There are plenty of Chinese options, but the favorite is **Wood House Bistrot** (1st Ave., noon-9pm Tues.-Sat., US$5-10), next to Primo's in Miami Beach. Wood House is a step up from the dingy fast food Chinese stops; the spicy wontons and consistently fresh seafood make this place stand out. A close runner-up is the **Romantic Bar and Restaurant** (3rd St. S., 10am-midnight, US$3-10), on the ground floor of the Mirador Hotel. Their diverse menu features daily specials such as curry masala gibnut, cow-foot soup, and lasagna.

Across from the immigration office is **Venky's** (5th Ave., tel. 501/402-0536, hours vary), a take-out place for curries and other East Indian foods.

Mexican and Yucatecan

For solid, super-cheap Mexican snacks and meals, **Cactus Plaza** (6th St. S, tel. 501/422-0394, 6pm-close Fri.-Sun.) has a very popular street-side café; drinks, beers, and juices are served all night (till the club inside closes, anyway). This is also the center of the nightlife on weekends. The **Purple Toucan Restaurant Bar and Grill** (4th Ave., tel. 501/622-9200, 11am-3:30pm and 6pm-11pm Mon.-Sat., US$2-5), beside Atlantic Bank, features *cochinita pibil, poc chuc,* and other Yucatecan specialties. There's ample seating.

Groceries

D's Superstore (College Rd., 9am-10pm) is the largest grocery in town. **Family Supermarket** (near Fort Barlee, 8am-midnight) is another option that is more centrally located.

INFORMATION AND SERVICES

Corozal's main web portal (www.corozal.com) is a fount of information for travelers. Corozal also has several ATMs and branches of **Belize Bank, Scotiabank,** and **Atlantic Bank** (8am-2pm Mon.-Thurs., 8:30am-4:30pm Fri.). For emergencies, contact the **fire department** (tel. 501/422-2105), **police** (tel. 501/422-2022), or the **hospital** (tel. 501/422-2076). For Internet access, try the **Hotel Mirador** (across from the main dock and seawall, tel. 501/422-0189, www.mirador.bz) or **M.E. Computer Systems** (3rd St. S., 9am-9pm Mon.-Sat.). You can also find a couple of desktops at **Stellar Link** (39A 4th Ave., tel. 501/402-2043, 9am-5pm Mon.-Fri., 9am-1pm Sat.). There are a few other Internet places around the central park.

GETTING THERE AND AROUND
By Air

There are five inexpensive daily flights on each airline between Corozal and San Pedro. Contact **Tropic Air** (tel. 501/226-2012, U.S. tel. 800/422-3435, www.tropicair.com) or **Maya Island Air** (tel. 501/223-1140, U.S. tel. 800/225-6732, mayair@btl.net, www.mayaislandair.com) for schedules.

By Bus

Buses are in disarray, so check the schedule at Corozal's Northern Transport Bus Station before departure. Northbound buses from Belize City alternate final destinations between Corozal and Chetumal, taking three hours to Corozal (US$6) and leaving Belize City frequently 5:30am-7:30pm daily. Southbound buses from Corozal leave regularly between 3:45am and 7pm daily, all of them originating 15 minutes or so earlier in Santa Elena. If you have connections to make in Chetumal, be aware that, unlike Belize, Mexico uses daylight saving time.

By Boat

The *Thunderbolt* (tel. 501/631-3400 or 501/422-0026, thunderbolttravels@yahoo.com, US$22.50 pp) departs for San Pedro at 7am daily. Special promotions are often run during peak holiday times, so call ahead. From San Pedro, the boat leaves the Westside dock at 3pm daily; the trip takes about two hours and stops in Sarteneja are possible on request.

By Taxi

There are a few taxi stands in town: **Los Toucanes Taxi Union** (tel. 501/402-2070) is by the market, a few steps away from the bus station; **Corozal Central Park Taxi Union** (tel. 501/422-2035) is by the central park. You can get around town for US$2.50, to the airstrip for US$5, to the border for US$10, or to Chetumal and Cerros for US$30—all convenient ways to go if you have a few people to split the costs. You can also contact **Belize VIP Service** (tel. 501/422-2725, www.belizevipautorental.com) for car rentals as well as transfers.

Tours

One of the best independent guides around is

© LEBAWIT GIRMA

The *Thunderbolt* has daily service between Corozal and Ambergris Caye.

Vital Nature and Mayan Tours (tel. 501/602-8975, www.cavetubing.bz), also known as Vitalino Reyes, whose years of experience qualify him to teach and certify many of Corozal's other guides. Vital runs tours to local ruins, the caves at Jaguar Paw, the Belize Zoo, night safaris, or anywhere else you want to go. **Belize VIP Transfer Services** (tel. 501/422-2725, www.belizetransfers.com) is your best bet for charter transportation, with brand-new vehicles that are great for groups. Belize VIP specializes in local tours (including a day tour of Corozal and Cerros), trips to Lamanai, Chetumal transfers (and other Mexican attractions), and Tikal or Flores trips to Guatemala. **George & Esther Moralez Travel Service** (tel. 501/422-2485, www.gettransfers.com) offers transfer services and tours. They will also help you with hotel and local flight bookings (dial 00 before the phone number when calling from Mexico to Belize). **Hok'ol K'in Guest House** (89 4th Ave., tel. 501/422-3329, maya@btl.net, www.corozal.net) handles all such trips as well, especially to local villages.

CONSEJO VILLAGE

Nine miles north of Corozal, the tiny fishing village of Consejo is home to a beach hideaway, an upscale hotel, a nine-hole golf course, and a retirement community of some 400 North Americans called **Consejo Shores** (www.consejoshores.com).

Rent one of three bayside units at **Smuggler's Den** (2 miles northwest of Consejo, tel. 501/600-9723, http://smugglersdenbelize.tripod.com, US$40-65), which are nicely furnished and have hot and cold water; they are quite a bargain if you're looking for isolation. Two units have private baths and kitchenettes, but the unit without a kitchen is cheaper. Discounts are sometimes available on request. Smuggler's is locally famous for its Sunday afternoon roast beef dinners; reserve in advance.

Right in Consejo, **Casablanca by the Sea** (tel. 501/423-1018, U.S. tel. 781/235-1024, www.casablanca-bythesea.com, US$75-150) is an intimate hotel with lovely grounds and views of the Bay of Consejo. Casablanca has eight stately guest rooms with queen beds, private baths, air-conditioning, hot and cold water, and TVs. The bar and dining room offer excellent seafood dishes as well as other meals, all enjoyed while watching the lights of Chetumal across the bay. There are also rooftop stargazing, volleyball, and top-notch conference and group facilities.

The **Millennium Restaurant** (Wed.-Mon., US$2-10), in the heart of Consejo village, is a friendly watering hole and eatery serving up daily specials at great prices.

SHIPSTERN NATURE RESERVE

In Corozal District, Shipstern is in the northeastern corner of the Belize coast. Thirty-two square miles of moist forest, savanna, and wetlands have been set aside to preserve as-yet-unspoiled habitats of well-known insect, bird, and mammal species associated with the tropics. The reserve is home to about 300 species of birds, 70 species of reptiles and amphibians, and more than 270 species of butterflies (they began the production of live butterfly pupae through intensive breeding). The reserve also encompasses the shallow **Shipstern Lagoon,** dotted with mangrove islands, which creates wonderful habitat for many wading birds.

The International Tropical Conservation Foundation has been extremely generous in supporting Shipstern. As at most reserves, the objective is to manage and protect habitats and wildlife, as well as to develop an education program that entails teaching the local community and introducing children to the concept of wildlife conservation in their area. Shipstern, however, goes a step farther by conducting an investigation of how tropical countries such as Belize can develop self-supporting conservation areas through the controlled, intensive production of natural commodities found within such wildlife settlements. Developing facilities for the scientific study of the reserve area and its wildlife is part of this important program.

Visitors Center

Start at the **visitors center** (3 miles outside of Sarteneja, tours 9am-noon and 1pm-3pm daily except Christmas, New Year's Day, and Easter, US$5). The admission fee includes a guided tour of the visitors center, butterfly garden, botanical trail, and observation tower. The forest is alive with nature's critters and fascinating flora, and the guides' discerning eyes spot things that most often miss. Before starting your 20- to 30-minute walk, pick up a book with detailed descriptions of the trail and the trees at the visitors center. The lovely **Botanical Trail** starts at the parking lot by the visitors center and meanders through the forest. Visitors have the opportunity to see three types of hardwood forests with 100 species of trees, many of which are labeled with their Latin and Yucatec Maya names.

Getting There

It is easiest to take a boat from Corozal or to hire a local tour guide to arrange travel. From Corozal and Orange Walk, figure a little more than an hour to drive here. The road takes you through **San Estevan** and then to **Progresso.** Turn right just before entering Progresso to **Little Belize** (a Mennonite community). Continue on to **Chunox. Sarteneja** is three miles beyond Shipstern. Don't forget a long-sleeved shirt, pants, mosquito repellent, binoculars, and a camera for your exploration of the reserve.

Sarteneja Adventure Tours (tel. 501/633-0067, www.sartenejatours.com) provides standard tours and overnight camping trips, with opportunities to explore Shipstern's trails by day or night and visit local caves, Maya ruins, and nesting bird colonies. While accommodations are available by special request, visitors are encouraged to stay overnight in Sarteneja village.

SARTENEJA

From the Mayan "Tzaten-a-ha" ("give me the water"), **Sarteneja** was named after the 13 Mayan wells found in the area, carved into limestone bedrock and providing potable water. In addition to being a picturesque fishing village, Sarteneja is the only place on mainland Belize where you can watch the sun set over the water. The spot was first settled by the Maya as an important trading area. It is thought to have been occupied from 600 BC to AD 1200, and period gold, copper, and shells continue to turn up in the area. Mexican refugees from the Yucatán Caste Wars settled here in the mid-19th century, again attracted by the availability of drinking water. The village took a pounding from Hurricane Janet in 1955 but rebounded and became known for its boat builders and free-diving lobster and conch fishers.

Today, 80 percent of Sarteneja's households remain reliant on the resources of the Belize Reef. Tourism is creeping in, and Sarteneja offers one of the more off-the-beaten-path experiences in the country. Located on Corozal Bay, it is a well-kept secret in Belize, and few travelers have heard about its breathtaking sunsets, sportfishing, turquoise swimming waters, and importance as a protected area for manatees and bird-nesting colonies in the Corozal Bay Wildlife Sanctuary. This is slowly changing, as more travelers now stop here on their way to the northern cayes. Bring your swimwear—the water is beautiful and a stop here feels like an island getaway.

Wooden Boats

Sarteneja is known for the annual **Easter Regatta,** during which newly painted sailboats of the artisan fishing fleet, crewed by local anglers, race against each other in a tradition that has continued since 1950. The regatta, on Easter weekend, includes live music, food, and fun, local "catch the greasy pig" games. Master boat builders Juan Guerrero and Jacobo Verde handcraft traditional wooden vessels at their workshops in Sarteneja—the wooden boat building tradition is unique in Belize and also in all of Central America. During fishing season, these boats dock in Belize City by the Swing Bridge. If you're interested in culture and boats, ask around for the **Mitzi-Ba Wooden Boat Building** workshop to see master builder Juan Guerrero at work. If you're lucky, you'll witness one being designed from scratch.

NORTHERN BELIZE

© LEBAWIT GIRMA

Sarteneja is just 30 minutes from Corozal and the hub of Belize's fishing boats.

Sports and Recreation

Sarteneja's location is ideal for fishing, kayaking, sailing, or exploring the nearby reserves. You can rent kayaks from the **Tour Guide Association** office (Front St., tel. 501/621-8336 or 501/633-0067, www.sartenejatours.com, US$5 per hour double kayak, up to 5 hours maximum), or hop on their Manatee Day tour to go manatee spotting (US$20 pp). The **beach** on the long, pretty coastline offers swimming and relaxing. The farther east you go, the prettier and more isolated the swimming areas get. Rent a bicycle from **Brisis Bike Rental** if your guesthouse doesn't provide one. Other options include hiking in the Shipstern Nature Reserve, exploring the Bacalar Chico Marine Reserve on the northern tip of Ambergris Caye, or fishing along Corozal Bay (US$30 pp for 2 people) with Ritchie Cruz of **Ritchie's Place** (Front St., tel. 501/668-1531).

With access to nearby Mayan sites and ties to the barrier reef at Bacalar Chico, Sarteneja has a lot to offer the adventurous traveler in search of the real Belize. The community is aware of its resources, and groups have joined forces to form the **Sarteneja Alliance for Conservation and Development** (N. Front St., sacdsarteneja@gmail.com), which comanages Corozal Bay Wildlife Sanctuary. Local anglers, now trained as guides, offer a number of guided tours, both marine and inland.

Sarteneja is also the location of the **Manatee Rehabilitation Centre,** run by Wildtracks, a local NGO that takes in and rehabilitates orphan manatee calves as part of a national program to protect this threatened species. The center is only open to visitors by special arrangement. To visit the Rehabilitation Centre, contact the **Sarteneja Tour Guide Association** (www.sartenejatours.com, tel. 501/621-8336 or 501/633-0067). Their office is located on the seafront; take a left from the arrival dock. They can also help visitors find licensed local tour guides.

Accommodations

Most accommodations, eateries, and bars can be found along Front Street, abutting the sea and dock.

Experience local culture through the **Sarteneja Homestay Program** (tel. 501/634-8032, 501/661-8395, or 501/664-5490, sartenejahomestay@gmail.com, US$25 pp, includes meals). There are 13 participating families in the program, providing a unique village opportunity. Stay for a night or a week in a safe, comfortable, private room with shared indoor toilet. Enjoy three home-cooked meals, learn how to make tortillas, and practice your Spanish. The program gets rave reviews; don't hesitate to call a day ahead or ask on short notice.

Fernando's Seaside Guesthouse (tel. 501/423-2085, www.cybercayecaulker.com/sarteneja.html, US$40-50 plus tax) was the first to open its doors in Sarteneja. It has upgraded its guest rooms, offering private baths, air-conditioning, cable TV, wireless Internet, and a nice veranda with hammocks and a waterfront view (a discount is available without air-conditioning). Like most men in Sarteneja, the owner, Fernando Alamilla, was once a full-time fisherman who used to sail and fish for up to 10 days at a time. His son, Fernando Jr., is a friendly and gregarious man who helps run the guesthouse and who can help arrange tours, transportation (including Tropic Air flights to the cayes), or pick you up from Chetumal for a fee.

Backpackers Paradise (tel. 501/423-2016, http://bluegreenbelize.org) is outside of Sarteneja, about a 15-minute brisk walk from the arrival dock. Accommodations at this funky, laid-back, rustic, and friendly hangout range from camping (US$3.50 pp) to guest rooms with shared baths and a few private cabanas (US$12.50-40). **Nathalie's Restaurant** (8am-2pm and 6pm-8pm daily), also on-site, serves up wonderful and affordable dishes, including crepes made by the Vietnamese-French proprietress. Free wireless Internet is available, bicycles (US$10) and horses (US$35) can be rented for the day, and guided day trips are available as well. Guests can use the communal kitchen to prepare meals (Sarteneja has a few grocery shops and *tortillerias*) and can relax in the shared screened reading room peppered with hammocks. If you choose, ask to be picked up from the dock by Nathalie in her horse and buggy.

Food
Ritchie's Place (Front St., tel. 501/668-1531, 6am-10pm daily, US$2-5) has a good selection of fresh dishes, prepared by Ritchie's wife and featuring fish empanadas and other mestizo delicacies. Owner Ritchie Cruz will also arrange fishing trips. **Liz's Fast Food** (tel. 501/665-5998 or 501/668-4478, 6:30am-2pm and 6:30pm-10pm daily) is found two streets back from the seafront. This place is the local favorite, serving tasty, cheap, and traditional food in a friendly snack-stall setting. Expect three-for-US$1 Belizean tacos, empanadas, and *garnaches* as well as rice and beans. The homemade *horchata* (a rice-based drink) is worth trying. Off Front Street, **Yadi's Pizza** (tel. 501/650-6480, 2pm-10pm Mon.-Sat., US$3-5) serves up pizzas, quesadillas, burritos, and a variety of flavorful bites in a cute diner-type setting.

Information and Services
You can get online at **Backpackers Paradise** for US$2.50 per hour. Laundry service is also available (US$5 per load). Be forewarned: There are no ATM machines or banks in Sarteneja, only a local credit union for Belizeans, so bring enough cash to last your stay.

Getting There and Around
Sarteneja has been linked to the rest of Belize by land for less than 40 years—roads are rugged and dusty and, during rainy season, often flooded and rutted. The road from Corozal to Sarteneja was recently upgraded through a European Union-funded project; although the road remains unpaved, it was a significant improvement. Still, expect a few rough spots after a heavy rain.

BY BOAT
Most visitors get to Sarteneja by boat from Corozal or San Pedro. *Thunderbolt* water

taxi (tel. 501/422-0026 or cell 501/610-4475; Captain's cell 501/631-3400, www.ambergriscaye.com/thunderbolt), a well-run and locally owned operation, will stop in Sarteneja on its once-daily Corozal-San Pedro run. They depart Corozal at 7am, arriving in Sarteneja 40 minutes later before heading on to San Pedro. The San Pedro-Corozal boat (about 90 minutes) departs at 3pm from San Pedro, stopping at Sarteneja at approximately 4:30pm. Note that Sarteneja is an on-request-only stop on the way back, so let the captain and crew know as you board if you're heading to Sarteneja only on a day trip from Corozal, to be sure to get picked up in Sarteneja on the 4:30pm return boat (Corozal-Sarteneja US$12.50 one-way, US$25 round-trip, San Pedro-Sarteneja US$22.50, US$42.50 round-trip). The *Thunderbolt* runs every day of the year except Christmas Day and Good Friday.

BY AIR
Tropic Air has two flights a day that will stop at Sarteneja's tiny airstrip on request. Flights leave San Pedro at 7am and 4:45pm, arriving in Sarteneja 10 minutes later, as part of the San Pedro-Corozal schedule. Flights will stop later in the day if there is more than one passenger requesting to be dropped off or picked up in Sarteneja.

BY BUS
The bus from Belize City is often full of returning anglers and is the most exciting way to get here. The distinctive light-blue Sarteneja buses leave Belize City from a riverside lot next to the Supreme Court Building. Four buses make the three-hour ride (US$5 one-way), the first at noon and the last at 5pm Monday-Saturday. All buses stop just before the bridge at the Zeta Ice Factory in Orange Walk to pick up more passengers. Buses depart Sarteneja for Belize City (via Orange Walk) between 4 and 6:30am. There is a direct bus from Chetumal, via Corozal and Orange Walk, which runs every day (including Sunday), leaving Chetumal at midday or 1pm (depending on whether or not Mexico is on daylight saving time). It departs

for Corozal and Chetumal at 6am every morning. Buses from Corozal are intermittent, so it's best to check with the Corozal bus station first. There is also local traffic going to Sarteneja from Orange Walk via San Estevan.

BY CAR

From Corozal, head south and turn left at the sign for Tony's Inn. Follow this road, veering right until you come to a stone wall; then go left. Follow this road until you reach the first ferry across the New River, an experience in itself and free of charge. Sometimes there are lineups on Friday and Monday, so

anticipate a bit of a wait. After crossing, continue on the unsurfaced road until you reach a T junction. Turn left toward Copper Bank, Cerros, and the ferry to Chunox. On entering Copper Bank, keep driving until you see the signs for Donna's Place (an excellent eatery) and the Cerros ruins. If you're not stopping to eat or visit the ruins, turn left at the ruins sign and proceed until you see the sign for the ferry crossing. After crossing, continue until you reach another T junction. Turn left for Sarteneja, or right for Chunox and the grinding drive through Little Belize back to Orange Walk.

Chetumal, Mexico

An exciting dose of culture shock is an easy 15 miles from Corozal. Chetumal, capital of the Mexican state of Quintana Roo, is a relatively modern, midsize city of more than 200,000—nearly as many people as in the entire country of Belize! If you don't come for the culture (wonderful museums, a few parks, a zoo, and a delicious seafront), then you must be here to shop in the new American-style mall or see a first-run film in Chet's brand-new air-conditioned Cineplex, located in the Plaza de las Americas mall.

Chetumal can be visited as a day trip from Corozal or used as a base from which to visit the many Yucatecan archaeological sites—including Tulum, just up the coast. It's also a gateway to Mexico's well-known Caribbean resort areas: Cancún, Cozumel, Playa del Carmen, and Akumal. Chetumal presents the businesslike atmosphere of a growing metropolis without the bikini-clad tourist crowds of the north. A 10-minute walk takes you to the waterfront from the marketplace and most of the hotels. Modern, sculpted monuments stand along a breezy promenade that skirts the broad crescent of the bay. Explore the backstreets, where worn, wooden buildings still have a Central American-Caribbean look. The largest building in town—white, three stories, close to the

waterfront—houses most of the government offices. Wide tree-lined avenues and sidewalks front dozens of small variety shops.

SIGHTS

Do not miss the **Museo de la Cultura Maya** (9am-7pm Tues.-Thurs. and Sun., 9am-8pm Fri.-Sat., US$5), located at the new market; it is an impressive and creative experience by any standard. The **Museo Municipal** is excellent as well, with a great deal of contemporary Mexican art.

On Avenida Heroes, five miles north of the city, is **Calderitas Bay,** a breezy area for picnicking, dining, camping, and RVing. Tiny **Isla Tamalcas,** 1.5 miles off the shore of Calderitas, is the home of the primitive capybara, the largest of all rodents. Twenty-one miles north of Chetumal on Highway 307 is **Cenote Azul,** a circular cenote over 200 feet deep and 600 feet across and filled with brilliant blue water. This is a spectacular place to stop for a swim, lunch at the outdoor restaurant, or just to have a cold drink.

ACCOMMODATIONS AND FOOD

Chetumal has quite a few hotels in all price categories (including a Holiday Inn near the

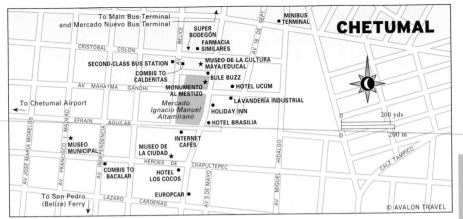

new market), as well as many fine cafés specializing in fresh seafood. A favorite budget hotel in Chetumal is the vibrantly decorated **Hotel Ucum** (www.hotelucumchetumal.com, US$20), with parking, a pool, and hot showers included. **Hotel Brasilia** (US$18) is another option. Both are visible from Avenida Heroes, the main street, which is home to most of the city's other hotels and the Museo Mundo Maya. If your bus from Cancún or Playa del Carmen arrives late at night, **Hotel Santa Teresa** (US$42) is conveniently located one block from the ADO bus terminal.

GETTING THERE AND AROUND

Corozal-based **Belize VIP Transfer Services** (tel. 501/422-2725, www.belizetransfers.com) and **George & Esther Moralez Travel Service** (tel. 501/422-2485, www.gettransfers.com) will arrange Chetumal transfers (and other Mexican attractions) and trips to local ruins. Also check with the **Hok'ol K'in Guest House** (tel. 501/422-3329, maya@btl.net, www.corozal.net) in Corozal.

By Bus

Buses from Belize City to Corozal and Chetumal travel throughout the day all the way through the border (you'll need to get off twice to pass through immigration controls and pay a US$19 exit fee) to the Nuevo Mercado Lazaro Cardenas in Chetumal. A local Chetumal bus from Corozal costs US$1.25; a taxi to the border costs US$10. If it's running, the express bus to Chetumal from Belize City takes about four hours and costs US$11. Also check with the various kiosks and travel agents in and near the Water Taxi Terminal by the Swing Bridge in Belize City for direct bus service to Chetumal.

If you're traveling by bus from Belize, you will pass the main ADO bus terminal on Avenue Insurgentes; ask the driver to stop at the Pemex gas station on the corner of Insurgentes and Heroes Avenues. Bus travel is a versatile and inexpensive way to travel the Quintana Roo coast—there are frequent trips to Playa del Carmen and Cancún, and a new fleet of luxury express buses is a treat after Belize's school bus system. Chetumal is part of the loop between Campeche, Cancún, and Mérida. Fares and schedules change regularly; currently the fare to Cancún is about US$30. It's about a 22-hour bus ride from Chetumal to Mexico City.

By Boat

Chetumal can also be reached by water taxi on the **San Pedro Belize Express** (tel. 501/226-3535, www.belizewatertaxi.com, US$37.50 one-way), which departs for Chetumal at 7:30am (or 7am from Caye Caulker) and returns at 3pm. **San Pedro Water Jets Express** (tel. 501/226-2194, www.sanpedrowatertaxi.

NORTHERN BELIZE

com, US$40 one-way) leaves San Pedro at 8am and returns from Chetumal at 3pm.

By Car

A good paved road connects Chetumal with Mérida, Campeche, Villahermosa, and Francisco Escarcega. Highway 307 links all of Quintana Roo's coastal cities. Expect little traffic, and you'll find that gas stations are well spaced if you top off at each one. Car rentals are scarce in Chetumal; go to the Hotel Los Cocos for Avis. Chetumal is an economical place to rent a car (if one is available), since the tax is only 6 percent. If you're driving, watch out for "No Left Turn" signs in Chetumal.

BACKGROUND

The Land

GEOGRAPHY

Belize lies on the northeast coast of Central America, above the corner where the Honduran coast takes off to the east. Belize's 8,866 square miles of territory are bordered on the north by Mexico, on the west and south by Guatemala, and on the east by the Caribbean Sea and the Belize Barrier Reef. From the northern Río Hondo border with Mexico to the southern border with Guatemala, Belize's mainland measures 180 miles long, and it is 68 miles across at its widest point. Offshore, Belize has more than 200 cayes, or islands. Both the coastal region and the northern half of the mainland are flat, but the land rises in the south and west to over 3,000 feet above sea level. The Maya Mountains and Cockscomb range from the country's backbone and include Belize's highest point, **Doyle's Delight** (3,688 feet). Mangrove swamps cover much of the humid coastal plain.

In the west, the Cayo District contains the **Mountain Pine Ridge Reserve.** At one time a magnificent Caribbean pine forest, it has, over the decades, been reduced by lumber removal, fires, and the pine bark beetle. Despite vast beetle damage, the upper regions of Mountain Pine Ridge still provide spectacular scenery, with sections of thick forest surrounding the

Macal River as it tumbles over huge granite boulders (except where the river was dammed at Chalillo). **Thousand Foot Falls** plunges 1,600 feet to the valley below and is the highest waterfall in Central America. The **Río Frío** cave system offers massive stalactites and stalagmites to the avid spelunker. The diverse landscape includes limestone-fringed granite boulders.

Over thousands of years, what was once a sea in the northern half of Belize has become a combination of scrub vegetation and rich tropical hardwood forest. Near the Mexican border, much of the land has been cleared, and it's here that the majority of sugar crops are raised, along with family plots of corn and beans. Most of the northern coast is swampy, with a variety of grasses and mangroves that attract waterfowl and wading birds. Rainfall in the north averages 60 inches annually, though it's generally dry November-May.

Cayes and Atolls

More than 200 cayes (pronounced "keys" and derived from the Spanish *cayo* for "key" or "islet") dot the blue waters off Belize's eastern coast. They range in size from barren patches that are submerged at high tide to the largest two, Ambergris Caye—25 miles long and nearly 4.5 miles across at its widest point—and Caye Caulker, five miles long. Some cayes are inhabited by people, others only by wildlife. The majority are lush patches of mangrove that challenge the geographer's definition of what makes an island (that's why you'll never see a precise figure of how many there are).

Most of the cayes lie within the protection of the 180-mile-long Belize Barrier Reef, which parallels the mainland. Without the protection of the reef—in essence a breakwater—the islands would be washed away. Within the reef, the sea is relatively calm and shallow.

Beyond the reef are three of the Caribbean's four atolls: **Glover's Reef, Turneffe Islands,** and **Lighthouse Reef.** An atoll is a ring-shaped coral island surrounding a lagoon, always beautiful, and almost exclusively found

Caye Caulker

© LEBAWIT GIRMA

in the South Pacific. The three types of cayes are **wet cayes,** which are submerged part of the time and can support only mangrove swamps; **bare coral outcroppings** that are equally uninhabitable; and **sandy islands** with littoral forest, which is the most endangered habitat in Belize due to development pressure. The more inhabited cayes lie in the northern part of the reef and include Caye Caulker, Ambergris Caye, St. George's Caye, and Caye Chapel.

Reefs

The polyps of reef-building corals deposit calcium carbonate around themselves to form a cup-like skeleton or corallite. As these small creatures continue to reproduce and die, their sturdy skeletons accumulate. Over eons, broken bits of coral, animal waste, and granules of soil contribute to the strong foundation for a reef that will slowly rise toward the surface. In a healthy environment, it can grow 1-2 inches a year.

Reefs are divided into three types: atoll, fringing, and barrier. An **atoll** can be formed around the crater of a submerged volcano. The polyps begin building their colonies on the round edge of the crater, forming a circular coral island with a lagoon in the center. Thousands of atolls occupy the world's tropical waters. Only four are in the Caribbean Sea; three of those are in Belize's waters.

A **fringing reef** is coral living on a shallow shelf that extends outward from shore into the sea. A **barrier reef** runs parallel to the coast, with water separating it from the land. Sometimes it's actually a series of reefs with channels of water in between. This is the case with some of the larger barrier reefs in the Pacific and Indian Oceans.

The Belize Barrier Reef is part of the greater Mesoamerican Barrier Reef, which extends from Mexico's Isla Mujeres to the Bay Islands of Honduras. The Belizean portion of the reef begins at Bacalar Chico in the north and ends with the Sapodilla Cayes in the south. At 180 miles long, it is the longest reef in the western and northern hemispheres.

CORAL

Coral is a unique limestone formation that grows in innumerable shapes, such as delicate lace, trees with reaching branches, pleated mushrooms, stovepipes, petaled flowers, fans, domes, heads of cabbage, and stalks of broccoli. Corals are formed by millions of tiny carnivorous polyps that feed on minute organisms and live in large colonies of individual species. Coral polyps have cylinder-shaped bodies, generally less than half an inch long. One end is attached to a hard surface (the bottom of the sea, the rim of a submerged volcano, or the reef itself). The mouth at the other end is encircled with tiny tentacles that capture the polyp's minute prey with a deadly sting. At night, coral reefs really come to life as polyps emerge to feed. Related to the jellyfish and sea anemone, polyps need sunlight and clear saltwater not colder than 70°F to survive. Symbiotic algal cells, called zooxanthellae, live within coral tissues and provide the polyps with much of their energy requirements and coloration.

Estuaries

The marshy areas and bays at the mouths of rivers where salt water and fresh water mix are called estuaries. Here, nutrients from inland are carried out to sea by currents and tides to nourish reefs, sea grass beds, and the open ocean. Many plants and animals feed, live, or mate in these waters. Conchs, crabs, shrimp, and other shellfish thrive here, and several types of jellyfish and other invertebrates call this home. Seabirds, shorebirds, and waterfowl of all types frequent estuaries to feed, nest, and mate. Crocodiles, dolphins, and manatees are regular visitors. Rays, sharks, and tarpon hunt and mate here. During the wet season, the estuaries of Belize pump a tremendous amount of nutrients into the sea.

Mangroves

The doctor on Christopher Columbus's ship reported in 1494 that mangroves in the Caribbean were "so thick that a rabbit could scarcely walk through." Mangroves live on the edge between land and sea, forming dense

BELIZE CORAL WATCH

Belize's world-class reefs are impacted by overfishing, coastal development, sewage, sedimentation, coral bleaching, and inappropriate or uninformed marine tourism practices. Linda Searle, Belize Coral Watch Program Coordinator and founder of ECOMAR, says that when you touch coral, you are destroying the thin layer of living tissue that keeps the coral healthy. It's like when people get a cut on their skin, she explains; the area becomes more susceptible to invasion by bacteria and disease. When a "cut" on a coral does not heal, this space can become invaded by a disease that can spread to the rest of the coral head, killing the entire colony. Divers and snorkelers can be strong and effective advocates for coral reef conservation. Experienced divers know the best way to enjoy a reef is to slow down, relax, and watch, leaving the reefs undisturbed. Follow these guidelines developed by the **Coral Reef Alliance** (CORAL, www.coral.org) to be a coral-friendly diver.

PREPARE FOR YOUR DIVE TRIP

- Give diver orientations and briefings.
- Hold buoyancy-control workshops.
- Actively support local marine protected areas.
- Use available moorings (anchors and chains destroy fragile corals and sea grass beds).
- Use available wastewater pump-out facilities.
- Make sure garbage is well stowed, especially light plastic items.
- Take away everything brought on board, such as packaging and used batteries.

IN THE WATER

- Never touch corals; even slight contact can harm them, and some corals can sting or cut you.
- Carefully select points of entry and exit to avoid walking on corals.
- Make sure all of your equipment is well secured.
- Make sure you are neutrally buoyant at all times.
- Maintain a comfortable distance from the reef, so that you're certain to avoid contact.
- Learn to swim without using your arms.
- Move slowly and deliberately in the water
- Practice good finning and body control to avoid accidental contact with the reef or stirring up the sediment.
- Know where your fins are at all times, and don't kick up sand.
- Stay off the bottom, and never stand or rest on corals.
- Avoid using gloves and kneepads in coral environments.
- Become a Belize Coral Watch Volunteer nothing living or dead out of the water, except recent garbage.
- Do not chase, harass, or try to ride marinelife.
- Do not touch or handle marinelife except under expert guidance and following established guidelines.
- Never feed marinelife.
- Use photographic and video equipment only if you are an advanced diver or snorkeler; cameras are cumbersome and affect a diver's buoyancy and mobility.

REMEMBER, LOOK BUT DON'T TOUCH.

As a Belize Coral Watch Volunteer, you'll learn how to identify coral species, coral reef ecology, coral disease, and coral bleaching. After attending a training session, you will be equipped with the knowledge needed to help identify resilient reefs in Belize. Divers and snorkelers are asked to monitor sites and submit reports online. Look for a dive or snorkel center or resort that participates in "Adopt a Reef" with ECOMAR, and help them complete surveys. For more information on becoming a Coral Watch Volunteer, contact **ECOMAR** (www.ecomarbelize.org).

mangroves on the Old Belize River

thickets that act as a protective border against the forces of wind and waves. Four species grow along many low-lying coastal areas on the mainland and along island lagoons and fringes. Of these, the red mangrove and the black mangrove are most prolific. Red mangroves in excess of 30 feet tall are found in tidal areas, inland lagoons, and river mouths, but always close to the sea. Their signature is arching prop roots, which provide critical habitat and nursery grounds for many reef fish. The black mangrove grows to almost double that height. Its roots are slender upright projectiles that grow to about 12 inches, protruding all around the mother tree. Both types of roots provide air to the tree.

MANGROVE SUCCESSION

Red mangroves (*Rhizophora mangle*) specialize in creating land—the seedpods fall into the water and take root on the sandy bottom of a shallow shoal. The roots, which can survive in seawater, then collect sediments from the water and the tree's own dropping leaves to create soil. Once the red mangrove forest has created land, it makes way for the next mangrove in the succession process. The black mangrove (*Avicennia germinans*) can actually out-compete the red mangrove at this stage, because of its ability to live in anoxic soil (without oxygen). In this way, the red mangrove appears to do itself in by creating an anoxic environment. But while the black mangrove is taking over the upland of the community, the red mangrove continues to dominate the perimeter, as it continuously creates more land from the sea. One way to identify a black mangrove forest is by the thousands of dense pneumataphores (tiny air roots) covering the ground under the trees.

Soon, burrowing organisms such as insects and crabs begin to inhabit the floor of the black mangrove forest, and the first ground covers, *Salicornia* and saltwort (*Batis maritima*) take hold—thereby aerating the soil and enabling the third and fourth mangrove species in succession to move in: the white mangrove (*Laguncularia racemosa*) and the gray mangrove

(*Conocarpus erectus*), also known locally as buttonwood.

DESALINIZERS

Each of the three primary mangrove species lives in a very salty environment, and each has its own special way of eliminating salt. The red mangrove concentrates the salt taken up with seawater into individual leaves, which turn bright yellow and fall into the prop roots, thereby adding organic matter to the system. The black mangrove eliminates salt from the underside of each leaf. If you pick a black mangrove leaf and lick the back, it will taste very salty. The white mangrove eliminates salt through two tiny salt pores located on the petiole (the stem that connects the leaf to the branch). If you sleep in a hammock under a white mangrove tree, you will feel drops of salty water as the tree "cries" on you. The buttonwood also has tiny salt pores on each petiole.

IMPORTANCE OF MANGROVES

Mangrove islands and coastal forests play an essential role in protecting Belize's coastline from destruction during natural events such as hurricanes and tropical storms. Along with the sea grass beds, they also protect the Belize Barrier Reef by filtering sediment from river runoff before it reaches and smothers the delicate coral polyps. However, dense mangrove forests are also home to mosquitoes and biting flies. The mud and peat beneath mangrove thickets is often malodorous with decaying plant matter and hydrogen sulfide-producing bacteria. Many developers would like nothing better than to eliminate mangroves and replace them with sandy beaches surrounded by seawalls. But such modification to the coastline causes accelerated erosion and destruction of seaside properties, especially during severe storms.

Birds of many species use the mangrove branches for roosting and nesting sites, including swallows, redstarts, warblers, grackles, herons, egrets, ospreys, kingfishers, pelicans, and roseate spoonbills. Along the seaside edge of red mangrove forests, prop roots extend into the water, creating tangled thickets unparalleled

as nurseries of the sea. Juveniles of commercial species, such as snapper, hogfish, and lobster, find a safe haven here. The flats around mangrove islands are famous for recreational fisheries such as bonefish and tarpon.

The three-dimensional labyrinth created by expanding red mangroves, sea grass beds, and bogues (channels of seawater flowing through the mangroves) provides the home and nursery habitat for nurse sharks, American crocodiles, dolphins, and manatees.

Snorkeling among the red mangrove prop roots is a unique experience where you can witness the abundant marinelife that grow on prop roots and live between the roots. It is within the algae, plants, corals, and sponges that grow on the roots that juvenile spiny lobsters and sea horses can be found.

Destruction of mangroves is illegal in most of Belize; cutting and removal of mangroves requires a special permit and mitigation.

Sea Grass

Standing along the coast of Belize and looking seaward, many visitors are surprised to see something dark in the shallow water just offshore. They expect the sandy bottom typical of many Caribbean islands. However, it is this "dark stuff" that eventually will make their day's snorkeling, fishing, or dining experience more enjoyable. What they are noticing is sea grass, another of the ocean's great nurseries.

Sea grasses are plants with elongated ribbon-like leaves. Just like the land plants they evolved from, sea grasses flower and have extensive root systems. They live in sandy areas around estuaries, mangroves, reefs, and open coastal waters. Turtle grass has broader, tape-like leaves and is common down to about 60 feet. Manatee grass, found to depths of around 40 feet, has thinner, more cylindrical leaves. Both cover large areas of seafloor and intermix in some areas, harboring an amazing variety of marine plants and animals. Barnacles, conchs, crabs, and many other shellfish proliferate in the fields of sea grass. Anemones, seahorses, sponges, and starfish live here. Grunts, filefish, flounder, jacks, rays, and wrasses feed here. Sea turtles and manatees often graze in these lush marine pastures.

These beds and flats are being threatened in some areas by unscrupulous developers who are dredging sand for cement and landfill material (especially on Ambergris Caye).

CLIMATE

The climate in Belize is subtropical, with a mean annual temperature of 79°F, so you can expect a variance between 50°F and 95°F. The dry season generally lasts from December-ish through May, and the wet season June through November, although it has been known to rain sporadically all the way into February.

Rainfall varies widely between the north and south of Belize. Corozal in the north receives 40-60 inches a year, while Punta Gorda averages 160-190 inches, with an average humidity of 85 percent. Occasionally during the winter, "Joe North" (a.k.a. cold fronts) sweeps down from North America across the Gulf of Mexico, bringing rainfall, strong winds, and cooling temperatures. Usually lasting only a couple of days, they often interrupt fishing and influence the activity of lobsters and other fish. Fishers invariably report increases in their catches several days before a norther.

The "mauger" season, when the air is still and the sea is calm, generally comes in August; it can last for a week or more. All activity halts while locals stay indoors as much as possible to avoid the onslaught of mosquitoes and other insects.

Hurricanes

Since record keeping began in 1787, scores of hurricanes have made landfall in Belize. In an unnamed storm in 1931, 2,000 people were killed and almost all of Belize City was destroyed. The water rose nine feet in some areas, even onto Belize City's Swing Bridge. Though forewarned by Pan American Airlines that the hurricane was heading their way, most of the townsfolk were unconcerned, believing that their protective reef would keep massive waves away from their shores. They were wrong.

The next devastation came with Hurricane

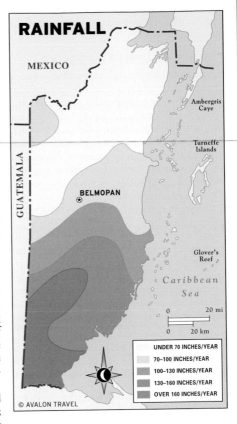

Hattie in 1961. Winds reached a velocity of 150 mph, with gusts of 200 mph; 262 people drowned. It was after Hurricane Hattie that the capital of the country was moved from Belize City (just 18 inches above sea level) to Belmopan. Then, in 1978, Hurricane Greta took a heavy toll in dollar damage, although no lives were lost. More recent serious hurricanes affecting Belize include Mitch in 1998, Keith in 2000, Iris in 2001, and Dean in 2007. There have also been a number of less serious "northers." In the summer of 2008, Tropical Storm Arthur caused severe flooding throughout the country, and major bridges were washed out. In 2010 Hurricane Richard did an unexpected two-step into the Cayo District, destroying the Belize Zoo and a swath of forest canopy in the center of the country.

ENVIRONMENTAL ISSUES

Because of the country's impressive network of protected areas and relatively low population density, the widespread deforestation that occurs in other parts of Central America is not nearly as big a problem in Belize. However, Belize faces its own set of challenges. Perhaps the biggest problem is improper disposal of solid and liquid wastes, both municipal and industrial, particularly agro-wastes from the shrimp and citrus industries.

Mining of aggregates from rivers and streams has negative impacts on local watersheds and the coastal zones into which they empty, where sedimentation can be destructive to reef and other marine systems. Unchecked, unplanned development, especially in sensitive areas like barrier beaches, mangroves, islands, and riverbanks, where changes to the landscape often have wide and unanticipated effects, is another problem.

Energy—or lack thereof—is a major issue for Belize, which historically has had to buy expensive power from neighboring Mexico. The controversial construction of the Chalillo Dam on the upper Macal River brought all of Belize's energy and environmental issues to the forefront (the saga of Chalillo is told in *The Last Flight of the Scarlet Macaw* by Bruce Barcott).

The discovery of oil in 2005 near Spanish Lookout fueled a market of foreign prospectors hoping to tap into new petroleum resources. Oil exploration concessions have been granted for most of Belize's land and marine areas—including, recently, to US Capital Energy Limited to drill in the Toledo District on ancestral Mayan lands—which has caused much concern among environmental groups.

Meanwhile, the Belize Barrier Reef Reserve System was added to the List of World Heritage Sites in Danger in 2009 due to concerns over mangrove cutting and excessive development—and efforts to begin offshore oil drilling.

Flora and Fauna

Belize's position at the biological crossroads between North and South America has given it an astonishingly broad assortment of wildlife. Belize's wide-ranging geography and habitat have also been a primary factor in the diversity and complexity of its ecosystems and their denizens.

FLORA

Belize is a Garden of Eden. Four thousand species of native flowering plants include 250 species of orchids and approximately 700 species of trees. Most of the country's forests have been logged off and on for more than 300 years (2,000 years, if you count the widespread deforestation during the time of the ancient Maya). The areas closest to the rivers and coast were the hardest hit because boats could be docked and logs easily loaded to be taken farther out to sea to the large ships used to haul the precious timber.

Forests

Flying over the countryside gives you a view of the patchwork landscape of cleared areas and secondary growth. Belize consists of four distinct forest communities: **pine-oak, mixed broadleaf, cohune palm,** and **riverine** forests. Pine-oak forests are found in sandy dry soils. In the same areas, large numbers of mango, cashew, and coconut palm trees are grown near homes and villages. The mixed broadleaf forest is a transition area between the sandy pine soils and the clay soils found along the river. Often the mixed broadleaf forest is broken up here and there and doesn't reach great height; it's species-rich but not as diverse as the cohune forest. The cohune forest area is characterized by the cohune palm, which is found in fertile clay soil where a moderate amount of rain falls throughout the year. The cohune nut was an important part of the Mayan diet.

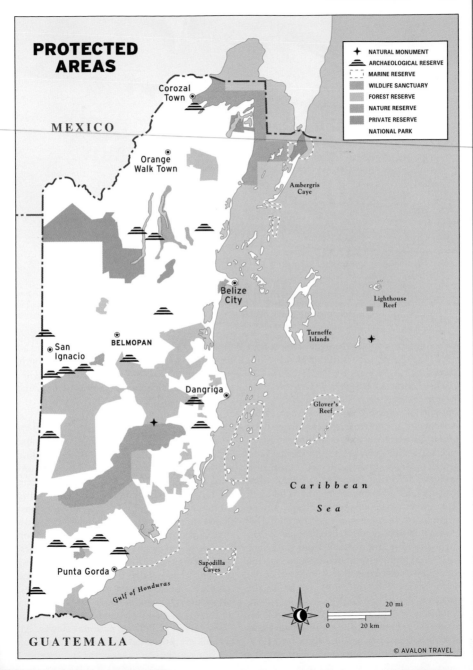

PROTECTED AREAS

Legend:
- ✦ NATURAL MONUMENT
- ▲ ARCHAEOLOGICAL RESERVE
- ☐ MARINE RESERVE
- WILDLIFE SANCTUARY
- FOREST RESERVE
- NATURE RESERVE
- PRIVATE RESERVE
- NATIONAL PARK

MEXICO

Corozal Town

Orange Walk Town

Ambergris Caye

Belize City

Lighthouse Reef

Turneffe Islands

San Ignacio

BELMOPAN

Dangriga

Glover's Reef

Caribbean Sea

Punta Gorda

Sapodilla Cayes

Gulf of Honduras

GUATEMALA

0   20 mi
0   20 km

© AVALON TRAVEL

© LEBAWIT GIRMA

The national flower of Belize is the black orchid.

Archaeologists say that where they see a cohune forest, they know they'll find evidence of the Maya.

The cohune forest gives way to the riverine forest along river shorelines, where vast amounts of water are found year-round from excessive rain and from the flooding rivers. About 50-60 tree varieties and hundreds of species of vines, epiphytes, and shrubs grow here. Logwood, mahogany, cedar, and pine are difficult to find along the easily accessible rivers because of extensive logging. The forest is in different stages of growth and age. To find virgin forest, it's necessary to go high into the mountains that divide Belize. Because of the rugged terrain and distance from the rivers, these areas were left almost untouched. Even today, few roads exist. If left undisturbed for many, many years, the forest will eventually regenerate itself.

Among the plantlife of Belize, look for **mangroves, bamboo,** and **swamp cypresses** as well as ferns, bromeliads, vines, and flowers creeping from tree to tree, creating dense growth. On the topmost limbs, orchids and air ferns reach for the sun. As you go farther south, you'll find the classic tropical rainforest, including tall mahoganies, *campeche, sapote,* and ceiba, thick with vines.

Orchids

In remote areas of Belize, one of the more exotic blooms, the orchid, is often found on the highest limbs of tall trees. Of all the orchid species reported in Belize, 20 percent are terrestrial (growing in the ground) and 80 percent are epiphytic (attached to a host plant—in this case trees—and deriving moisture and nutrients from the air and rain). Both types grow in many sizes and shapes: tiny buttons, spanning the length of a long branch; large-petaled blossoms with ruffled edges; or intense, tiger-striped miniatures. The lovely flowers come in a wide variety of colors, some subtle, some brilliant. The black orchid is Belize's national flower. All orchids are protected by strict laws, so look but don't pick.

KEEPING WILDLIFE WILD

You are guaranteed to see wildlife in Belize, whether in the wild or in captivity. However, in Belize some poached birds and wildlife are often sold on the international market, while others end up in Belizean homes or in businesses who want to add "color" to attract tourists. **Belize Bird Rescue** (www.belize-birdrescue.com), a nonprofit organization, reports that 65 percent of all wild-caught captive birds die before they reach sale. Of those that make it, most are sold to people who have no idea how to raise a baby bird.

This is particularly a big a deal for the yellow-headed Amazon parrot (*Amazona oratrix*), a gorgeous species under serious threat of extinction in the world. Its numbers have plummeted from 70,000 to 7,000 in the last two decades. Human encroachment on their habitat fuels nest-robbing for the illegal pet trade.

In order to discourage the illegal trade in parrots and other animals:

· **Don't** have your photograph taken with captive indigenous wildlife. By encouraging the keepers of the wildlife, more will be taken from the wild.

· **Don't** patronize establishments with captive wildlife on display unless they are government sanctioned as a breeding or educational facility such as a zoo. There is no educational value to a single monkey or bird in a restaurant.

· **Don't** believe anyone who tells you that they "rescued" an orphan animal or bird, unless they are licensed rescue facility. The vast majority of these animals were captured from the wild or bought from dealers. If people really want to rescue a bird or animal, they will turn them over to a proper rescue or rehab facility.

· **Don't** buy goods made from animal hides, skins, teeth or claws, or exoskeletons such as bugs and corals. Some leather goods are okay but exotic ones (crocodile, snake, etc.) normally are not. Jewelry made from jaguar teeth has also appeared on the streets being offered to tourists. Buying them contributes to the decline of the remaining jaguar population. In Belize it is also prohibited to sell any products made out of sea turtles.

· **Do** contact the Belize Forest Department (tel. 501/822-2079, www.forestdepartment.gov.bz) if you observe any conditions where endangered terrestrial animals are being held in captivity or offered for sale. If you observe the sale of turtle meat or jewelry, report the location and date immediately to the Belize Fisheries Department (tel. 501/224-4552, www.agriculture.gov.bz/fisheries_dept.html).

FAUNA

A walk through the jungle brings you close to myriad animal and bird species, many of which are critically endangered in other Central American countries—and the world. Bring your binoculars and a camera, and be vewy, vewy quiet.

Birds

If you're a serious birder, you know all about Belize. Scores of species can be seen while sitting on the deck of your jungle lodge: big and small, rare and common, resident and migratory—and with local guides aplenty to help find them in all the vegetation. The **keelbilled toucan** is the national bird of Belize and is often seen perched on a bare limb in the early morning.

Cats

Seven species of felines are found in North America, five of them in Belize. For years, rich adventurers came to Belize on safari to hunt the jaguar for its beautiful skin. Likewise, hunting margay, puma, ocelots, and jaguarundis was a popular sport in the rainforest. Today, hunting endangered cats (and other species) in Belize is illegal, and there are many protected areas to help protect their wide-ranging habitats.

The **jaguar** is heavy-chested with sturdy muscled forelegs, a relatively short tail, and small rounded ears. Its tawny coat is uniformly spotted and the spots form rosettes: large circles with smaller spots in the center. The jaguar's belly is white with black spots. The male can weigh 145-255 pounds, females 125-165 pounds. Largest of the cats in Central America and the third-largest cat in the world, the jaguar is about the same size as a leopard. It is nocturnal, spending most daylight hours snoozing in the sun. The male marks an area of about 65 square miles and spends its nights stalking deer, peccaries, agoutis, tapirs, monkeys, and birds. If hunting is poor and times are tough, the jaguar will go into rivers and scoop fish with its large paws. The river is also a favorite spot for the jaguar to hunt the large tapir when it comes to drink. Females begin breeding at about three years old and generally produce twin cubs.

The smallest of the Belizean cats is the **margay,** weighing in at about 11 pounds and marked by a velvety coat with exotic designs in yellow and black and a tail that's half the length of its body. The bright eye-shine indicates it has exceptional night vision. A shy animal, it is seldom seen in open country, preferring the protection of the dense forest. The "tiger cat," as it is called by locals, hunts mainly in the trees, satisfied with birds, monkeys, and insects as well as lizards and figs.

Larger and not nearly as catlike as the margay, the black or brown **jaguarundi** has a small flattened head, rounded ears, short legs, and a long tail. It hunts by day for birds and small mammals in the rainforests of Central America. The **ocelot** has a striped and spotted coat and an average weight of about 35 pounds. A good climber, the cat hunts in trees as well as on the ground. Its prey include birds, monkeys, snakes, rabbits, young deer, and fish. Ocelots usually have litters of two kittens but can have as many as four. The **puma** is also known as the cougar or mountain lion. The adult male measures about six feet in length and weighs up to 198 pounds. It thrives in any environment that supports deer, porcupines, or rabbits. The puma hunts day or night.

Primates

In Creole, the **black howler monkey** (*Alouatta caraya*) is referred to as a "baboon" (in Spanish, *saraguate*), though it is not closely related to the African species with that name. Because the howler prefers low-lying tropical rainforests (under 1,000 feet of elevation), Belize is a perfect habitat. The monkeys are commonly found near the riverine forests, especially on the Belize River and its major branches. The adult howler monkey is entirely black and weighs 15-25 pounds. Its most distinctive trait is a roar that can be heard up to a mile away. A bone in the throat acts as an amplifier; the cry sounds much like that of a jaguar. The howler's unforgettable bark is said by some to be used to warn other monkey troops away from its territory. Locals, on the other hand, say the howlers roar when it's about to rain, to greet the sun, to say good night, or when they're feeding. The **Community Baboon Sanctuary** is the best place to see howler monkeys in the wild in Belize, though they are very common in the forests around many jungle lodges throughout the country.

Spider monkeys (*Ateles geoffroyi*) are smaller than black howlers and live in troops of a dozen or more, feeding on leaves, fruits, and flowers high in the jungle canopy. Slender limbs and elongated prehensile tails assist them as they climb and swing from tree to tree. Though not as numerous in Belize as howler monkeys because of disease and habitat loss, they remain an important part of the country's natural legacy.

Rodents

A relative of the rabbit, the **agouti** or "Indian rabbit" has coarse gray-brown fur and a hopping gait. It is most often encountered scampering along a forest trail or clearing. Not the brightest of creatures, it makes up for this lack of wit with typical rodent libido and fecundity. Though it inhabits the same areas as the paca, these two seldom meet, as the agouti minds its business during the day and the paca prefers nighttime pursuits. The agouti is less delectable than the paca. Nonetheless, it is taken by animal and human hunters and is a staple food of jaguars.

The **paca,** or **gibnut,** is a quick, brownish rodent about the size of a small dog, with white spots along its back. Nocturnal by habit and highly prized as a food item by many Belizeans, the gibnut is more apt to be seen by the visitor on an occasional restaurant menu than in the wild.

A member of the raccoon family, the **coatimundi**—or "quash"—has a long, ringed tail, a masked face, and a lengthy snout. Sharp claws aid the coati in climbing trees and digging up insects and other small prey. Omnivorous, the quash also relishes rainforest fruits. Usually seen in small troops of females and young, coatis have an amusing, jaunty appearance as they cross a jungle path, tails at attention.

Tapirs

The national animal of Belize, the **Baird's tapir** (*Tapirus bairdii*) is found from the southern part of Mexico through northern Colombia. It is stout-bodied (91-136 pounds), with short legs, a short tail, small eyes, and rounded ears. Its nose and upper lip extend into a short but very mobile proboscis. Totally herbivorous, tapirs usually live near streams or rivers in the forest. They bathe daily and also use the water as an escape when hunted either by humans or by their prime predator, the jaguar. Shy, nonaggressive animals, they are nocturnal with a definite home range, wearing a path between the jungle and their feeding area.

Reptiles
IGUANAS

Found all over Central America, lizards of the family *Iguanidae* include various large plant-eaters, in many sizes and typically dark in color with slight variations. The young iguana is bright emerald green. The common lizard grows to three feet long and has a blunt head and long flat tail. Bands of black and gray circle its body, and a serrated column reaches down the middle of its back, almost to its tail. During mating season, it's common to see brilliant orange males on sunny branches near the river. This reptile is not aggressive, but if cornered it will bite and use its tail in self-defense.

Though hawks prey on young iguanas and their eggs, humans still remain its most dangerous predator. It is not unusual to see locals along dirt paths carrying sturdy specimens by the tail to put in the cook pot. Iguana stew is believed to cure or relieve various human ailments, such as impotence. Another reason for their popularity at the market is their delicate white flesh, which tastes so much like chicken that locals refer to iguana meat as "bamboo chicken."

CROCODILES

Though they're often referred to as alligators, Belize has only crocodiles, the **American** (*Crocodylus acutus,* up to 20 feet) and the **Morelet's** (*Crocodylus moreletii,* up to 8 feet). Crocodiles have a well-earned bad reputation in Africa, Australia, and New Guinea for feeding on humans, especially the larger saltwater varieties. Their American cousins are fussier about their cuisine, preferring fish, dogs, and other small mammals to people. But when humans feed crocs, either intentionally or by tossing food waste into the water, the animals can acquire a taste for pets, making them extremely dangerous. When apex predators become fearless of people, they are more prone to attack, especially small children. The territories of both croc species overlap in estuaries and brackish coastal waters. They are most abundant in the rivers, swamps, and lagoons of Belize City and Orange Walk Districts. Able to filter excess salt from its system, only the American crocodile ventures to the more distant cayes, including Turneffe Islands. Endangered throughout their ranges, both crocs are protected by international law and should not be disturbed. Often seen floating near the edges of lagoons or canals during midday, they are best observed at night with the help of a flashlight. When caught in the beam, their eyes glow red (LED flashlights make white eye-shine).

SNAKES

Of the 59 species of snakes that have been identified in Belize, at least nine are venomous, notably the infamous **fer-de-lance** (locally called a "Tommy Goff"), the most poisonous snake in Central America, and the coral snake.

Marinelife

Belize is world-famous for the diversity of its rich underwater wildlife, primarily due to its unique geology, the barrier reef lagoon system, and a government that actively works to protect marine habitat. There is also a great deal of marine research in Belize, often with opportunities for visitors to get involved. While all the standard Caribbean species are found in Belizean waters, there are a few animals in particular worth noting.

MANATEES

These "gentle giants of the sea" are large and bulky—weighing 600-1,200 pounds. Manatees belong to the taxonomic order Sirenia, a group of four species that represents the only herbivorous marine mammals living today. There are three species of manatees: the **Amazonian** manatee (*Trichechus inunguis*), the **West African** manatee (*Trichechus senegalensis*), and the **West Indian** manatee (*Trichechus manatus*). The two subspecies of the West Indian manatee are the Florida manatee (*T. m. latirostris*) and the Antillean manatee (*T. m. manatus*). Belize has long been considered the last stronghold for West Indian manatees in Central America and the Caribbean. West Indian manatees are also found year-round in Florida and are sparsely distributed throughout Central America and the Caribbean; they live as far south as Brazil. The **Antillean** subspecies (which excludes the Florida animals) is red-listed by the World Conservation Union (IUCN) as endangered, in continuing decline, with severely fragmented populations.

With a relatively short coastline extending from the Gulf of Honduras in the south to Chetumal Bay in the north, Belize reports the greatest density of Antillean manatees in the Caribbean region, perhaps because of the extensive sea grass, mangrove, coastal, and riverine habitat within the Belize Barrier Reef Lagoon system, or perhaps because manatees have been protected by local laws since the 1930s and are currently listed as endangered under the Wildlife Protection Act of 1981.

Belize has designated several wildlife sanctuaries and protected areas for the benefit of manatees and other marinelife, including Swallow Caye Wildlife Sanctuary, Southern Lagoon Wildlife Sanctuary, Corozal Bay Wildlife Sanctuary, Bacalar Chico National Park and Marine Reserve, South Water Caye Marine Reserve, Burden Canal (part of the Belize River system), and Port Honduras Marine Reserve. Many foreign researchers, including Caryn Self-Sullivan, PhD, and James A. "Buddy" Powell, PhD, as well as Belizean biologists, including manatee researcher Nicole Auil of EcoHealth Alliance and Jamal Galves, and manatee tour guide and advocate Lionel "Chocolate" Heredia of Caye Caulker, who was instrumental in the creation of Swallow Caye Wildlife Sanctuary, have dedicated years of work to a country-wide research program, aerial surveys, and the stranding network through Coastal Zone Management Institute (www.coastalzonebelize.org). Orphaned manatees in Belize are cared for by Wildtracks in Sarteneja, where volunteer positions are often available. For more information about manatees, visit www.sirenian.org.

SHARKS AND RAYS

There are at least 42 species of sharks and rays in the waters of Belize. Most people get a good close glimpse of nurse sharks and southern stingrays on their trip to Hol Chan, and divers occasionally spot other species as well, such as the Caribbean reef shark or the great hammerhead, especially on trips to the farther atolls, particularly Lighthouse Reef. (The only recorded shark attacks in Belizean waters were due to sheer stupidity: a spear fisherman who refused to give up a fish to a curious shark, and a tour guide who pulled a nurse shark by the tail and wouldn't let go.) To learn more about

© LEBAWIT GIRMA

a manatee in the north channel of the Belize Barrier Reef during the summer mating season

sharks in Belize and how you can help them, check out www.belizesharks.org.

Although Belize is home to many species of sharks, the biggest and most notable is the **whale shark** (*Rhincodon typus*). Like all sharks it has a cartilaginous skeleton and visible gill slits, yet it feeds on zooplankton like a whale. It is the largest fish in the sea (up to 66 feet in length and weighing over 15 tons). Whale sharks bear live young (up to 300 have been found in one female), are believed to be long-lived—living more than 60 years—and may require up to 30 years to mature. According to biologist Rachel Graham, PhD, who has been studying whale sharks since 1998, Belize hosts the only known aggregation of whale sharks that feeds on the eggs of large schools of reproducing snappers. Although this must occur elsewhere in the world, to date Belize is the only known site where it has been observed.

History

Early recorded comments following Columbus's fourth voyage to the New World led the Spaniards to hastily conclude that the swampy shoreline of what is now Belize was unfit for human habitation. Someone should have told that to the Maya, who had been enjoying the area for quite some time. The pre-Columbian history of Belize is closely associated with that of its nearby neighbors: Mexico, Guatemala, and Honduras. The Maya were the first people to inhabit the land. They planted milpas (cornfields), built ceremonial centers, and established villages with large numbers of people throughout the region.

ANCIENT CIVILIZATION

Around 1000 BC, the Olmec culture, believed to be the earliest in the area and the predecessors to the Maya, began to spread throughout Mesoamerica. Large-scale ceremonial centers grew along Gulf Coast lands, and much of Mesoamerica was influenced by the Olmec religion of worshipping jaguar-like gods. The Olmec also developed the New World's first calendar and an early system of writing.

The Classic Period

The Classic Period, beginning about AD 250, is now hailed as the peak of cultural development among the Maya. For the next 600 years, until AD 900, the Maya made phenomenal progress in the development of artistic, architectural, and astronomical skills. They constructed impressive buildings during this period and wrote codices (folded bark books) filled with hieroglyphic symbols that detailed complicated mathematical calculations of days, months, and years. Only the priests and the privileged held this knowledge and continued to learn and develop it until, for some unexplained reason, the growth suddenly halted. A new militaristic society was born, built around a blend of ceremonialism, civic and social organization, and conquest.

Maya Society Collapses

All evidence points to an abrupt work stoppage. After about AD 900, no buildings were constructed and no stelae, which carefully detailed names and dates to inform future generations of their roots, were erected. What happened to the priests and nobles, the guardians of religion, science, and the arts, who conducted their ritual ceremonies and studies in the large stone pyramids? Why were the centers abandoned? What happened to the knowledge of the intelligentsia? Theories abound. Some speculate about a social revolution—the people were tired of subservience and were no longer willing to farm the land to provide food, clothing, and support for the priests and nobles. Other theories include population pressure on local resources, that there just wasn't enough land to provide food and necessities for the large population. Others believe drought, famine, or epidemics were responsible.

Whatever happened, it's clear that the special knowledge concerning astronomy, hieroglyphics, and architecture was not passed on to Mayan descendants. Why did the masses disperse, leaving once-sacred stone cities unused and ignored?

COLONIALISM

In 1530, the conquistador Francisco de Montejo y Álvarez attacked the Nachankan and Belize Maya, but his attempt to conquer them failed. This introduction of Spanish influence did not have the impact on Belize that it did in the northern part of the Caribbean coast until the Caste War.

Hernán Cortés

After Columbus's arrival in the New World, other adventurers traveling the same seas soon found the Yucatán Peninsula. Thirty-four-year-old Cortés sailed from Cuba in 1519 against the will of the Spanish governor. With 11 ships, 120 sailors, and 550 soldiers, he set out to

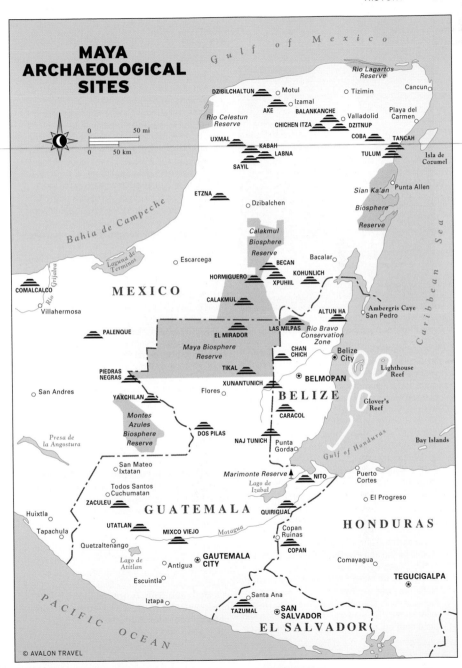

MAYA ARCHAEOLOGICAL SITES

Gulf of Mexico

Rio Lagartos Reserve

DZIBILCHALTUN   ○ Motul   ○ Tizimin   Cancun

○ Izamal

AKE   BALANKANCHE

Rio Celestun Reserve   CHICHEN ITZA   ○ Valladolid   Playa del Carmen

DZITNUP

UXMAL   KABAH   COBA   TANCAH

0   50 mi   SAYIL   LABNA   TULUM   Isla de Cozumel

0   50 km

ETZNA   Sian Ka'an

○ Dzibalchen   Biosphere

Bahia de Campeche   Reserve

Laguna de Terminos   Calakmul Biosphere Reserve   ○ Bacalar

○ Escarcega   BECAN   KOHUNLICH

COMALCALCO   HORMIGUERO   XPUHIIL

Villahermosa   CALAKMUL   ALTUN HA   Ambergris Caye

San Pedro

MEXICO   LAS MILPAS   Rio Bravo Conservation Zone

PALENQUE   EL MIRADOR   CHAN CHICH   ● Belize City   Lighthouse Reef

PIEDRAS NEGRAS   Maya Biosphere Reserve   TIKAL   XUNANTUNICH   ★ BELMOPAN

○ Flores   BELIZE   Glover's Reef

○ San Andres   YAXCHILAN   CARACOL   Bay Islands

Montes Azules Biosphere Reserve   DOS PILAS   NAJ TUNICH   Punta Gorda

Presa de la Angostura   San Mateo Ixtatan   Marimonte Reserve   NITO   ○ Puerto Cortes

Todos Santos Cuchumatan   Lago de Izabal   ○ El Progreso

Huixtla   ZACULEU   GUATEMALA   QUIRIGUAL

UTATLAN   HONDURAS

Tapachula   MIXCO VIEJO   Motagua   Copan Ruinas

○ Quetzaltenango   COPAN   ○ Comayagua

Lago de Atitlan   ○ Antigua   ★ GAUTEMALA CITY   TEGUCIGALPA ★

○ Escuintla   ○ Santa Ana

○ Iztapa   TAZUMAL   ★ SAN SALVADOR

PACIFIC OCEAN   EL SALVADOR

Caribbean Sea

Rio Grijalva

Rio

© AVALON TRAVEL

CAVE ARCHAEOLOGY AND THE MAYA

The Maya used caves for religious and ceremonial purposes.

Large populations of Maya were concentrated in the limestone foothills, where water supplies and clay deposits were plentiful. Caves were a source of fresh water, especially during dry periods. Clay pots of grain were safely stored for long periods of time in the cool air and, thousands of years later, can be seen today. Looting of caves has been a problem for decades, and as a result, all caves in Belize are considered archaeological sites.

The Maya used caves for utilitarian as well as religious and ceremonial purposes. The ancient Maya believed that upon entering a cave, one entered the underworld, or Xibalba, the place of beginnings and of fright. They believed there were nine layers of the underworld, and as much as death and disease and rot were represented by the underworld, so was the beginning of life. Caves were a source of water—a source of life—for the Maya. Water that dripped from stalactites was used as holy water for ceremonial purposes. The underworld was also an area where souls had hopes of defeating death and becoming ancestors. As a result, rituals, ceremonies, and even sacrifices were performed in caves, evidenced today by many pots, shards, implements, and burial sites.

Caves were important burial chambers for the ancient Maya, and more than 200 skeletons have been found in more than 20 caves. One chamber in Caves Branch was the final earthly resting spot for 25 individuals. Many of these burial chambers are found deep in the caves, leading to speculation that death came by sacrificing the living, as opposed to carrying in the dead. Some burial sites show possible evidence of commoners being sacrificed to accompany the journey of an elite who had died—but who really knows?

The first written accounts related to cave archaeology began in the late 1800s. A British medical officer by the name of Thomas Gann wrote of his extensive exploration of caves throughout the country. In the late 1920s, he was also part of the first formal study of some ruins and caves in the Toledo District, and his papers provide insight no one else can give to modern-day archaeologists.

Little else was done until 1955, when the Institute of Archaeology was created by the government of Belize. Starting in 1957, excavations were organized throughout the years under various archaeologists. Excavations in the 1970s led to many important archaeological discoveries, including pots, vessels, and altars. In the 1980s, a series of expeditions was undertaken to survey the Chiquibul cave system. Other finds during this period include a burial chamber and one cave with over 60 complete vessels and other ceremonial implements.

Today, projects are underway in many caves around the country. The Institute of Archaeology does not have a museum—yet. They've been talking about one for years. In the meantime, you may have to get a little wet and dirty to go visit some of these artifacts yourself. Start by calling up a cave tour guide in Cayo, like **Belizean Sun Tours** (tel. 501/823-2781 or cell 501/665-2808, www.belizeansun.com) or **Pacz Tours** (tel. 501/604-6921 or 501/824-0536, www.pacztours.net).

search for slaves, a lucrative business with or without the approval of the government. His search began on the Yucatán coast and eventually encompassed most of Mexico. However, he hadn't counted on the resistance and cunning of the Maya. The fighting was destined to continue for many years—a time of bloodshed and death for many of his men and for the Maya. Anthropologists and historians estimate that as many as 90 percent of Maya were killed by diseases such as smallpox after the arrival of the Spaniards.

Roman Catholicism

Over the years, the majority of the Maya were baptized into the Roman Catholic faith. Most priests did their best to educate the people, teach them to read and write, and protect them from the growing number of Spanish settlers who used them as slaves. The Maya practiced Catholicism in their own manner, combining their ancient beliefs, handed down throughout the centuries, with Christian doctrine. These mystic yet Christian ceremonies are still performed in baptisms, courtship, marriages, illness, farming, house building, and fiestas.

Pirates and the Baymen

While all of Mesoamerica dealt with the problems of economic colonialism, the Yucatán Peninsula had an additional problem: harassment by vicious pirates who made life in the coastal areas unstable. In other parts of the Yucatán Peninsula, the passive indigenous people were ground down, their lands taken away, and their numbers greatly reduced by the European settlers' epidemics and mistreatment.

British buccaneers sailed the coast, attacking the Spanish fleet at every opportunity. These ships were known to carry unimaginable riches of gold and silver from the New World back to the king of Spain. The Belizean coast became a convenient place for pirates to hole up during bad weather or for a good drinking bout. And although no one planned it as a permanent layover, by 1650 the coast had the beginnings of a British pirate lair and settlement. As pirating slacked off on the high seas, British buccaneers

discovered they could use their ships to carry logwood back to a ready market in England (logwood is a low-growing tree that provided rich dyes for Europe's growing textile industry until artificial dyes were developed). These early settlers were nicknamed the Baymen.

For 300 years the Baymen of Belize cut the logwood, and then, when the demand for logwood ceased, they starting cutting down mahogany trees from the vast forests. For three centuries the local economy depended on exported logs and imported food.

Agreement with Spain

In the meantime, the Spanish desperately tried to maintain control of this vast New World across the ocean. But it was a difficult task, and brutal conflicts continually flared between the Spanish and either the British inhabitants or the Maya. The British Baymen were continually run out but always returned. Treaties were signed and then rescinded. The British meanwhile made inroads into the country, importing Africans into slavery (beginning in the 1720s) to cut and move the trees.

Politically, Belize (or, more to the point, its timber) was up for grabs, and a series of treaties did little to calm the Ping-Pong effect between the British and the Spanish over the years. One such agreement, the Treaty of Paris, did little to control the Baymen—or the Spanish.

In 1763, Spain "officially" agreed to let the British cut logwood. The decree allowed roads (along the then-designated frontiers) to be built in the future, though definite boundaries were to be agreed on later. For nearly 150 years the only "roads" built were narrow tracks to the rivers; the rivers became Belize's major highways. Boats were common transportation along the coast, and somehow road building was postponed, leaving boundaries vaguely defined and people on both sides of the border unsure. This was the important bit of history that later encouraged the Spanish-influenced Guatemalans to believe that Belize had failed to carry out the 1763 agreement by building roads, which meant the land reverted back to Spain. Even after Spain vacated Guatemala, Guatemalans tried throughout the 20th century to claim its right to Belizean territory.

The Battle of St. George's Caye

The Baymen held on with only limited rights to the area until the final skirmish on St. George, a small caye just off Belize City. The Baymen, with the help of an armed sloop and three companies of a West Indian regiment, won the battle of St. George's Caye on September 10, 1798, ending the Spanish claim to Belize once and for all. After that battle, the British Crown ruled Belize until independence was gained in 1981.

Land Rights

In 1807 slavery was *officially* abolished in Belize by England. This was not agreeable to the powerful British landowners, and in many quarters it continued to flourish. Changes were then made to accommodate the will of the powerful. The local government no longer "gave" land to settlers as it had for years (British law now permitted the formerly enslaved and other "coloureds" to hold title). The easiest way to keep them from possessing land was to charge for it—essentially barring the majority in the country from landownership. So, in essence, slavery continued.

Caste War

It was inevitable that the Maya would eventually revolt in a furious attack. This bloody uprising in the Yucatán Peninsula in the 1840s was called the Caste War. Although the Maya were farmers and for the most part not soldiers, in this savage war they took revenge on European men, women, and children by rape and murder. When the winds of war reversed and the Maya were on the losing side, the vengeance wreaked on them was merciless. Some settlers immediately killed any Maya on sight, regardless of that person's beliefs. Some Maya were taken prisoner and sold to Cuba as slaves; others left their villages and hid in the rainforest, in some cases for decades. Between 1846 and 1850, the population of the Yucatán Peninsula was reduced from 500,000 to 300,000. Guerrilla warfare ensued, with the escaped Maya making repeated sneak attacks on the European settlers. Quintana Roo, adjacent to Belize along the Caribbean coast, was considered a dangerous no-man's-land for more than 100 years until, in 1974, with the promise of tourism, the territory was admitted to the United Mexican States. The "war" didn't really end on the peninsula until the Chan Santa Cruz people finally made peace with the Mexican federal government in 1935, more than 400 years after it had begun.

Restored Mayan Pride

Many of the Maya who escaped slaughter during the Caste War fled to the isolated rainforests of Quintana Roo and Belize. The Maya revived the religion of the "talking cross," a pre-Columbian oracle representing gods of the four cardinal directions. This was a religious-political fusion. Three determined survivors of the Caste War—a priest, a master spy, and a ventriloquist—all wise leaders, knew their people's desperate need for divine leadership.

HISTORY IN A NUTSHELL

The peaceful country of Belize is a sovereign democratic state of Central America located on the Caribbean. The government is patterned on the system of parliamentary democracy and experiences no more political turmoil than any other similar government, such as that of Great Britain or the United States.

IMPORTANT DATES

- 1798: Battle of St. George's Caye
- 1862: Became a British colony
- 1954: Attained universal adult suffrage
- 1964: Began self-government
- 1973: Name of the territory changed from British Honduras to Belize
- 1981: Attained full independence

As a result of their leadership and advice from the talking cross, the shattered people came together in large numbers and began to organize. The community guarded the location of the cross, and its advice made the Maya strong once again.

They called themselves Chan Santa Cruz ("People of the Little Holy Cross"). As their confidence developed, so did the growth and power of their communities. Living very close to the Belize (then British Honduras) border, they found they had something their neighbors wanted. The Chan Santa Cruz Maya began selling timber to the British and in return received arms, giving the Maya even more power. Between 1847 and 1850, in the years of strife during the Caste War in neighboring Yucatán, thousands of Mayan, mestizo, and Mexican refugees who were fleeing the Spaniards entered Belize. The Yucatecans introduced the Latin culture, the Roman Catholic religion, and agriculture. This was the beginning of the Mexican tradition in northern Belize, locally referred to as "Spanish tradition." The food is typically Mexican, with tortillas, black beans, tamales, squash, and plantains. For many years, these mestizos kept to themselves and were independent of Belize City.

They settled mostly in the northern sections of the country, which is apparent by the Spanish names of the cities: Corozal, San Estevan, San Pedro, and Punta Consejo. By 1857 the immigrants were growing enough sugar to supply Belize, with enough left over to export the surplus (along with rum) to Britain. After their success proved to the tree barons that sugarcane could be lucrative, the big landowners became involved. Even in today's world of low-priced sugar, the industry is still important to Belize's economy.

INDEPENDENCE

In 1862 the territory of British Honduras was officially created, even though it had been ruled by the British crown since 1798. The average Belizean had few rights and a very low living standard. Political unrest grew in a stifled atmosphere. Even when a contingent of Belizean soldiers traveled to Europe to fight for the British in World War I, the black men were scorned. But when these men returned from abroad, the pot of change began to boil. Over the next 50 years the country struggled through power plays, another world war, and economic crises, but always the seed was there—the desire to be independent. The colonial system had been falling apart around the world, and when India gained its freedom in 1947, the pattern was set. Many small undeveloped countries began to gain independence and started to rely on their own ingenuity to build an economy that would benefit their people.

Even though Belize was self-governing by 1964, it was still dominated by outside influences until September 1981, when it gained its independence from the British crown. In September 1981 the Belizean flag was raised for the first time—the birth of a new country. Belize joined the United Nations, the Commonwealth of Nations, and the Non-Aligned Movement. The infant country's first parliamentary elections were held in 1984. You can see that original Belizean flag at the George Price Centre in Belmopan.

Government and Economy

GOVERNMENT

The **Government of Belize** (www.belize.gov.bz), or "GOB," as you'll see it referred to in the newspapers, is directed by an elected prime minister. The bicameral legislature, or National Assembly, comprises an appointed senate and an elected house of representatives. Belize has two main political parties, PUP (People's United Party) and UDP (United Democratic Party). As in most democracies, the political rhetoric can get very animated, but political-based violence is unheard of.

The current prime minister, Dean Barrow of the UDP, took the post from longtime PUP front man Said Musa in 2008. Barrow's party had been gaining ground in recent years, especially as PUP rulers became increasingly implicated in various corruption scandals. The country's constitution, judicial code, and other legal documents are explained and can be downloaded from the **Ministry of the Attorney General** (www.belizelaw.org).

WHAT'S IN A NAME?

No one knows for sure where the name Belize originated or what it means. The country was called Belize long before the British took the country over and renamed it British Honduras. In 1973 the locals changed it back to the original Belize as a first step on the road to independence. There are several well-known theories about its meaning. Some say it's a corruption of the name Wallis (wahl-EEZ), from the pirate (Peter Wallace) who roamed the high seas centuries ago and visited Belize. Others suggest that it's a distortion of the Mayan word *belix*, which means "muddy river." Still others say it could be a further distortion of the Maya word *belikin*, the modern name of the local beer.

ECONOMY

The economy of Belize was traditionally based on the export of logwood, mahogany, and chicle (the base for chewing gum, from the chicle tree). Today, tourism, agriculture, fisheries, aquaculture (shrimp farming), and small manufactured goods give the country an important economic boost, but it is still dependent on imported goods to get by. The main exports are sugar, citrus, bananas, lobster, and timber. Overall, domestic industry is severely constrained by relatively high labor and energy costs, a very small domestic market, and the "brain drain" of Belize's most qualified managers, health professionals, and academics to the United States and Europe.

In general, and despite books by PUP economists declaring that all is well, Belize's economy is a mess, and the GOB has been on the verge of bankruptcy for years. In 2004, the government was rocked by a scandal over the use of millions of dollars of pension funds to pay the foreign debts of bankrupt companies controlled by government insiders. This led to the collapse of the overextended Development Finance Corporation (DFC), the effects of which are still being felt and evaluated today.

Thanks to tax concessions given to foreign investors, Belize has attracted new manufacturing industries, including plywood, veneer, matches, beer, rum, soft drinks, furniture, boat building, and battery assembly.

TOURISM

Belize is now a common destination for North American and European travelers. Tourism is one of the most critical economies in the country, responsible for about one in seven jobs and 22 percent of the country's GDP. The **Belize Tourism Board** (tel. 501/227-2420, www.travelbelize.org) has gotten the word "Belize" buzzing on the lips of millions of potential visitors who, only a few years ago, had never even heard of the tiny country. Today, roughly 250,000

GEORGE PRICE

George Price was Belize's first prime minister on independence in 1981, then served the position again 1989-1993. Born in 1919, Price entered politics in 1944 and never looked back. He did not step down from the leadership of the People's United Party, which he founded in 1950, until 1996 when he retired in Belize City. Price also served as the mayor of Belize City several times. He was the most respected and loved individual in Belize, and you'd be hard-pressed to find anyone who didn't admire him. George Price died on September 19, 2011, just two days shy of the country's 30th anniversary of independence. Belize held its very first state funeral that year, which I had the privilege of attending, and I witnessed the most spectacular display of love and unity all across the country. Belizeans were lined up for hours in the hot sun along the highways and streets of Belize City and Belmopan, waving flags, banners, and personal thank-you messages to their national hero. The **George Price Centre for Peace and Development** (www.gpcbelize.com) in Belmopan is a must-see to learn more about Price's central role in Belizean history.

overnight visitors come to Belize each year; the majority (about 150,000) are from the United States.

In 2011 there were 716 registered hotels providing jobs to nearly 5,000 Belizeans, and that's not counting restaurant employees, guides, transportation services, etc. Tourism has encouraged the preservation of vast tracts of forests and reefs; it has helped the Institute of Archaeology enhance and develop Belize's archaeological sites as destinations, making possible astounding excavations and discoveries at the Caracol, Xunantunich, Lamanai, Altun Ha, and Cahal Pech ruins.

Of course, tourism can be a double-edged sword, and Belize's founding father, George Price, warned against it; Price said tourism would make Belizeans indentured servants to rich foreigners.

Cruise Ships

The image of numerous hulking cruise ships on the watery eastern horizon of Belize City is striking. The arrival of the cruise industry to Belize's shores in the 1990s was both much hailed and a highly contentious event. It happened quickly, and Belize soon recorded the highest growth in cruise ship arrivals in the entire Caribbean region: Annual cruise visitor arrivals grew from 14,183 in 1998 to a peak of more than 851,000 in 2004. The year 2010 saw 767,000 cruise visits, according to the Belize Tourism Board, with a slight 3.7 percent drop in 2012.

The Belize Tourism Board officially promotes visits by cruise ships. There are approximately 2,000 people in Belize City who rely on cruise ships for their livelihoods, most of whom work in Tourism Village shops and restaurants. The Board acknowledges the need to balance cruise ship tourism with overnight tourism, making sure that one does not take over the other.

In Belize City, cruise ship arrival days are boom days for taxi drivers, tour operators, and shopkeepers. But critics say that's not enough. Stewart Krohn, an esteemed Belizean journalist, writes that inviting cruise ship tourism is the equivalent of selling Belize cheaply. In one editorial, he wrote, "Tourism, at its heart, is a cultural encounter. Long, relaxed, unhurried stays by visitors who have time to meet, interact with, and understand Belizeans and Belize not only means more money in our pockets for beds, food, drinks, and tours; it produces the kind of relationships that small countries in a highly competitive world find increasingly necessary." Such meaningful encounters are impossible with hurried busloads of day-trippers, he argues. "Cruise tourism at best produces a few pennies for a few people; at worst a negative impression born of an impersonal encounter."

Other critics cite the impact on Belize's tiny, fragile infrastructure—damage to roads by cruise bus traffic, maxed-out septic systems, trash on the trails and in the caves. Passengers don't spend much onshore, and few of their dollars trickle very far from the pockets of those who own Tourism Village.

One thing is certain: Bring up cruise tourism at a Belizean barbecue, and you'll hear some fiery opinions (especially if you mention the expansion of cruise ships into Placencia and southern Belize). Despite resistance from Placencians, including many small business owners, the go-ahead was given, and it's a done deal. A brand new pier is currently under construction in Placencia Village. Many fear this upcoming cruise ship tourism will destroy the responsible tourism Placencia has worked so hard to build, as well as the natural resources surrounding the area.

People and Culture

The extraordinary diversity of Belize's tiny population (about 320,000) allows Belizeans to be doubly proud of their heritage—once for their family's background (Maya, Creole, Garífuna, Mennonite, etc.) and again for their country. The mestizo (mixed Spanish and indigenous descent) population has risen to about 50 percent of the country's total, with Creoles making up about 25 percent, Maya 10-12 percent, Garífuna 6 percent, and others 9 percent (in the 2000 census). Here's a bit of background about Belize's diverse demography, but keep in mind that every one of these groups continues to mingle with the others, at least to some extent, ensuring continuing creolization.

CREOLES

Creoles are a mix of two distinctive ethnic backgrounds: African and European, and they use the local English-Creole dialect. Many Creoles are also descended from other groups of immigrants. The center of Creole territory and culture is Belize City. Half of Belize's ethnic Creoles live here, and they make up more than three-quarters of the city's population. Rural Creoles live along the highway between Belmopan and San Ignacio, in isolated clusters in northern Belize District, and in a few coastal spots to the south—Gales Point, Mullins River, Mango Creek, Placencia, and Monkey River.

Cheap labor was needed to do the grueling timber work in thick, tall rainforests. The British failed to force it on the maverick Maya, so they brought Africans whom they enslaved, indentured laborers from India, and Caribs from distant Caribbean islands, as was common in the early 16th and 17th centuries. "Creolization" started when the first waves of British and Scottish began to intermingle with these imported enslaved and servants.

MESTIZOS

Also referred to as "Ladinos" or just "Spanish," mestizos make up the quickest-growing demographic group in Belize and encompass all Spanish-speaking Belizeans, descended from some mix of Maya and Europeans. These immigrants to Belize hail from the nearby countries of Guatemala, El Salvador, Honduras, and Mexico. Once the predominant population (after immigration from the Yucatecan Caste War), mestizos are now the second-most-populous ethnic group of Belize. They occupy the old "Mexican-mestizo corridor" that runs along New River between Corozal and Orange Walk. In west-central Belize—Benque Viejo and San Ignacio—indigenous people from Guatemala have recently joined the earlier Spanish-speaking immigrants from Yucatán.

THE MAYA

Small villages of Maya—Mopan, Yucatec, and Q'eqchi'—still practicing some form of their ancient culture dot the landscape and comprise

KEEPING THE "ECO" IN TOURISM

The word *ecotourism* was created in the 1980s with the best of intentions—ostensibly, to describe anything having to do with environmentally sound and culturally sustainable tourism. It was the "business" of preventing tourism from spoiling the environment and using tourism as an economic alternative to spoiling the environment for some other reason.

The success of the concept—and its marketing value—led to a worldwide surge in the usage of that prefix we know so well, even if its actual practice may sometimes fall short of original intentions. Indeed, *eco* has been used and abused all over the world, and Belize is no exception. Some word-savvy tourism marketers have tried to freshen things up by using "alternative" or "adventure" tourism; when trying to describe an operation that practices the original definition of ecotourism, better terms are "sustainable," "responsible," "ethical," or even "fair-trade" tourism.

Belize is generally acknowledged as one of the world's most successful models of ecotourism. In 2009 Belize hosted the **Third Annual World Conference for Responsible Tourism,** featuring experts from around the world speaking on local economic development through tourism, the impact of mass tourism on local communities, and climate change.

The **Belize Audubon Society** (BAS, www.belizeaudubon.org) is the main organization concerned with keeping the "eco" in tourism—and in keeping pressure on the government of Belize to do the same.

roughly 10-12 percent of Belize's population. After the Europeans arrived and settled in Belize, many of the Maya moved away from the coast to escape hostile Spanish and British intruders who arrived by ship to search for slaves. Many Mayan communities continue to live much as their ancestors did and are still the most politically marginalized people in Belize, although certain villages are becoming increasingly empowered and developed, thanks in part to tourism (although some would argue at a cultural cost). Most modern Maya practice some form of Christian religion integrated with ancient beliefs. But ancient Mayan ceremonies are still quietly practiced in secluded pockets of the country, especially in southern Belize.

THE GARÍFUNA

The, Garífuna people, in plural Garinagu, came to exist on the Lesser Antillean island of San Vicente, which in the 1700s had become a refuge for escaped slaves from the sugar plantations of the Caribbean and Jamaica. These displaced Africans were accepted by the native Carib islanders, with whom they freely intermingled. The new island community members vehemently denied their African origins and proclaimed themselves Native Americans. As the French and English began to settle the island, the Garífuna (as they had become known) established a worldwide reputation as expert canoe navigators and fierce warriors, resisting European control. The English finally got the upper hand in the conflict after tricking and killing the Garífuna leader, and in 1797 they forcefully evacuated the population from San Vicente to the Honduran Bay Island of Roatan. From there, a large proportion of the Garífuna migrated to mainland Central America, all along the Mosquito Coast.

On November 19, 1823, so the story goes, the first Garífuna boats landed on the beaches of what is now Dangriga, one of the chief cultural capitals of the Garinagu. They landed in Belize under the leadership of Alejo Beni, and a small Garífuna settlement grew in Stann Creek, where they fished and farmed. They began bringing fresh produce to Belize City but were not welcome to stay for more than 48 hours without getting a special permit—the Baymen wanted the produce but feared that these free blacks would help the enslaved escape, causing a loss of the Baymen's tight control.

The Garífuna language is a mixture of Amerindian, African, Arawak, and Carib,

© LEBAWIT GIRMA

a *jankanu* dancer in Dangriga

dating from the 1700s. The Garinagu continued to practice what was still familiar from their ancient West African traditions—cooking with a mortar and pestle, dancing, and especially music, which consisted of complex rhythms with a call-and-response pattern that was an important part of their social and religious celebrations. An eminent person in the village is still the drum maker, who continues the old traditions, along with making other instruments used in these singing and dancing ceremonies that often last all night.

There are a number of old dances and drum rhythms still used for a variety of occasions, especially around Christmas and New Year's. If you are visiting Dangriga, Hopkins, Seine Bight, Punta Gorda, or Barranco during these times (or on Settlement Day, November 19), expect to see, and possibly partake in, some drumming. Feel free to taste the typical foods and drinks. If you consume too much "local dynamite" (rum and coconut milk) or bitters, have a cup of strong chicory coffee, said by Garinagu "to mek we not have goma" (prevent a hangover).

EAST INDIANS

From 1844 to 1917, under British colonialism, 41,600 East Indians were brought to British colonies in the Caribbean as indentured workers. They agreed to work for a given length of time for one "master." Then they could either return to India or stay on and work freely. Unfortunately, the time spent in Belize was not as lucrative as they were led to believe it would be. In some cases, they owed so much money to the company store (where they received half their wages in trade and not nearly enough to live on) that they were forced to "reenlist" for a longer period. Most of them worked on sugar plantations in the Toledo and Corozal Districts, and many of the East Indian men were assigned to work as local police in Belize City. In a town aptly named Calcutta, south of Corozal Town, many of the population today are descendants of the original indentured East Indians. Forest Home near Punta Gorda also has a large settlement. About 47 percent of the ethnic group lives in these two locations. The East Indians usually have large families and live on small farms with orchards adjacent to their homes. A few trade in pigs and dry goods in mom-and-pop businesses. Descendants of earlier East Indian immigrants speak Creole and Spanish. A few communities of Hindi-speaking East Indian merchants live in Belize City, Belmopan, and Orange Walk.

MENNONITES

Making up more than 3 percent of the population of Belize, German-speaking Mennonites are the most recent group to enter Belize on a large scale. This group of Protestant settlers from the Swiss Alps wandered over the years to northern Germany, southern Russia, Pennsylvania, and Canada in the early 1800s, and to northern Mexico after World War I. The quiet, staid Mennonites and their isolated agrarian lifestyle conflicted with local governments in these countries, leading to a more nomadic existence.

Most of Belize's Mennonites first migrated from Mexico between 1958 and 1962.

THE GULISI PRIMARY SCHOOL

The Garinagu in Belize have been struggling to keep their culture alive, particularly with the younger generation. English and Creole dominate the language scene, and with a diverse population, as well as a young population influenced by mainstream American pop culture and media, a significant number of Garífuna youth are not learning their native tongue, which isn't taught in most schools.

Enter the Gulisi Primary School. Established in 2007 and located adjacent to the Gulisi Garífuna Museum in Dangriga, it's unique in its genre: In addition to a regular primary school academic curriculum, it has a mandatory trilingual system which requires students to take Garífuna language classes, along with English, the main language of instruction, and Spanish. The goal is to keep Garífuna children rooted in their culture and thus preserve their heritage, but not at the expense of a good education.

Teachers are required to speak fluent Garífuna (government-assisted funding covers their salaries), and the 185 students wear Garífuna-colored uniforms. The school accepts children up to the 8th grade, including those from other cultures who are willing to learn Garífuna alongside everyone else. So successful is the school that it now faces overcrowding. Occasionally, classes are held in part of the museum next door.

For more information, contact Mrs. Phyllis Cayetano (pcayetano@gmail.com), the school's founder and general manager.

A few came from Peace River in Canada. In contrast to other areas where they lived, the Mennonites bought large blocks of land (about 148,000 acres) and began to farm. Shipyard (in Orange Walk District) was settled by a conservative wing; Spanish Lookout (in Cayo District) and Blue Creek (in Orange Walk District) were settled by more progressive members. In hopes of averting future problems with the government, Mennonites made agreements with Belize officials that guarantee them freedom to practice their religion, use their language in locally controlled schools, organize their own financial institutions, and be exempt from military service.

Over the 30-plus years that Mennonites have been in Belize, they have slowly merged into Belizean activities. Although they practice complete separation of church and state (and do not vote), their innovations in agricultural production and marketing have advanced the entire country. Mennonite farmers are probably the most productive in Belize; they commonly pool their resources to make large purchases such as equipment, machinery (in those communities that use machinery), and supplies. Their fine dairy industry is the best in the country, and they supply the domestic market with eggs, poultry, fresh milk, cheese, and vegetables.

LANGUAGE

More than eight languages are commonly spoken in Belize. English is the official language, although Belizean Creole (or "Kriol") serves as the main spoken tongue among and between groups. There are an increasing number of Spanish speakers in Belize, as Central American immigrants continue to arrive. Spanish is the primary language of many native Belizean families, especially among descendants of Yucatecan immigrants who inhabit the Northern Cayes, Orange Walk, and Corozal Districts. As a tourist, there are only a few areas of Belize, mainly rural outposts in northern and western Belize, where knowing Spanish is essential to communicate. The Garinagu speak Garífuna, and the various Mennonite communities speak different dialects of Old German. Then there are Mopan, Yucatec, and Q'eqchi' Maya tongues. Still other immigrant groups, like Chinese and Lebanese, also often speak their own languages amongst themselves.

The Arts

Belize has a fairly rich arts scene for such a small country. Several painters and visual artists from Belize have made a name for themselves internationally. Start your research by looking up the work of Gilvano Swasey, Pen Cayetano, Michael Gordon, Benjamin Nicholas, Carolyn Carr, Chris Emmanuel, and Yasser Musa, to name only a few. The government ministry responsible for the arts is the **National Institute for Culture and History** (NICH, www.nichbelize.org), which comprises four organizations: The Institute of Creative Arts (in Belize City), Museum of Belize and Houses of Culture (locations in Belize City, Orange Walk, Benque Viejo del Carmen, and San Ignacio), the Institute of Archaeology (in Belmopan), and the Institute for Social and Cultural Research (in Belmopan).

ARTS AND CRAFTS

You'll have a selection of Belizean and Guatemalan crafts to choose from when visiting any archaeological site, as vendors typically set up rows of stalls with similar gifts, crafts, textiles, and basketwork. You'll also see slate carvings, a recently resurrected skill of the Maya. Among the leading slate carvers are **the Garcia Sisters, Lesley Glaspie,** and the **Magana family.** Their work can be found in several Cayo shops as well as elsewhere in the country (especially Aurora's shop near the entrance to Cockscomb). The Garcia sisters helped revive the slate craze, and their quality has always been high. **Mennonite furniture pieces** like hardwood chairs and small tables make possible take-home items. Orange Gifts (in Cayo) has the best selection of crafts for sale in the country.

MUSIC

The music of Belize is heavily influenced by the syncopated beats of Africa as they combine with modern sounds from throughout Latin America, the Caribbean, and North America. The most popular Belizean music is *punta,* a fusion of traditional Garífuna rhythms and modern electric instruments. The "Ambassador of Punta Rock" was Andy Palacio, a prolific musician from the southern village of Barranco, who died in 2008 and was honored as a national hero. While Andy Palacio revived interest in paranda and punta, the creator of the punta rock genre was actually Pen Cayetano, another renowned Garífuna musician, artist, and advocate. The newer form of *punta* is characterized by driving, repetitive dance rhythms and has its acoustic roots in a type of music called *paranda.* A recent PBS special described *paranda* as "nostalgic ballads coupling acoustic guitar with Latin melodies and raw, gritty vocals … which can feature traditional Garífuna percussion like wood blocks, turtle shells, forks, bottles, and nails." A few of the original *paranda* masters, like Paul Nabor in Punta Gorda, can still be found in their hometowns throughout Belize. Several excellent compilation albums of Belizean and Honduran *punta* and *paranda* music are available from Stonetree Records.

Brukdown (or "Bruckdong") began in the timber camps of the 1800s, when the workers, isolated from civilization for months at a time, would let off steam by drinking a

SUNDAY: A DAY OF REST

Belize is serious about its Sundays. Expect businesses in most parts of the country (even restaurants and cafés) to close on Sunday. The streets are empty as well, giving a ghost-town feel to places like downtown Belize City. Usually, the only stores and eateries open are Chinese shops and maybe a few taco stands on the street.

full bottle of rum and then beating on the empty bottle—or the jawbone of an ass, a coconut shell, or a wooden block—anything that made a sound. Add to that a harmonica, guitar, and banjo, and you've got the unique sound of *brukdown*. This is a traditional Creole rhythm kept alive by the legendary Mr. Peters and his **Boom and Chime** band until Mr. Peters passed away in 2010 at the age of 79. Over the last five years, dub-poetry has emerged as an important format for musical expression in Belize. The most popular artist of this is **Leroy "The Grandmaster" Young,** whose album *Just Like That* is a wonderful listening experience and has been acclaimed by numerous international reviewers.

In the southern part of Belize, you'll likely hear the strains of ancient Mayan melodies played on homemade wooden instruments, including Q'eqchi' harps, violins, and guitars. In Cayo District in the west, listen for the resonant sounds of marimbas and wooden xylophones—from the Latin influence across the Guatemala border. In the Corozal and Orange Walk Districts in the north, Mexican *ranchera* and *romantica* music is extremely popular. Of course reggae is popular throughout the country, especially on the islands (Bob Marley is king in Belize).

Stonetree Records (www.stonetreerecords.com) has the most complete catalogue of truly Belizean music, covering a wide range of musical genres and styles. This author's favorites include *Wátina,* a soulful album featuring traditional *paranda* music by the renowned, deceased Andy Palacio and the Garífuna Collective, and *Belize City Boil-Up,* a funky collection of remastered vintage Belizean soul tracks from the 1950s, 1960s, and 1970s, featuring The Lord Rhaburn Combo, Jesus Acosta and the Professionals, The Web, Harmonettes, Nadia Cattouse, and Soul Creations.

In addition to recording and marketing dozens of albums, Stonetree, based in the town of Benque Viejo in Cayo, western Belize, is also very active in encouraging new Belizean musicians to experiment and develop their individual sounds. Buy albums online, or pick up a couple of CDs at any gift shop or music store during your visit.

FESTIVALS AND EVENTS

When a public holiday falls on Sunday, it is celebrated on the following Monday. If you plan to visit during holiday time, make advance hotel reservations—especially if you plan to spend time in Dangriga during Settlement Day on November 19 (the area has limited accommodations). Note: On Sunday and a few holidays (Easter and Christmas), most businesses close for the day, and some close the day after Christmas (Boxing Day); on Good Friday most buses do not run. Check ahead of time.

National Heroes and Benefactors Day

On March 9, this holiday is celebrated with various activities, mostly water sports. English sportsman Baron Henry Edward Ernest Victor Bliss, who remembered Belize with a generous legacy when he died, designated a day of sailing and fishing in his will. A formal ceremony is held at his tomb below the lighthouse in the Belize Harbor, where he died on his boat. Fishing and sailing regattas begin after the ceremony.

Easter

Easter weekend in Belize is big: there are concerts, parties, and plenty of dancing and libation flowing all weekend from Belize City to the Northern Cayes and the South Coast. But the most unique, cultural celebration in the country takes place in the devoutly Catholic historic western town of Benque Viejo del Carmen. The town celebrates Semana Santa (Holy Week) with events starting on Palm Sunday and ending on Good Friday with a re-enactment of the Passion of Christ (crucifixion). The weeklong events include *alfombras,* a 12-year tradition of creating colorful sawdust carpets on the streets in town to mark the route of the Santo Entierro procession, which represents carrying the body of the crucified Christ to the tomb.

Maya Dances

If you're traveling in the latter part of September in San Antonio Village in the Toledo District, you have a good chance of seeing the **deer dance** performed by the Q'eqchi' Maya villagers. Dancing and celebrating begins around the middle of August, but the biggest celebration begins with a *novena,* nine days before the feast day of San Luis.

Actually, this festival was only recently revived. The costumes were burned in an accidental fire some years back at a time when (coincidentally) the locals had begun to lose interest in the ancient traditions. Thanks to the formation of the **Toledo Maya Cultural Council,** the Maya once again are realizing the importance of recapturing their past. Some dances are now performed during an annual Cacao Festival in Toledo District during the last weekend in May.

San Pedro Day

If you're wandering around Belize near June 26-29, hop a boat or plane to San Pedro and join the locals in a festival they have celebrated for decades, **El Día de San Pedro,** in honor of the town's namesake, Saint Peter. This is good fun; hotel reservations are suggested. **Carnaval,** one week before Lent, is another popular holiday on the island. The locals walk in a procession through the streets to the church, celebrating the last hurrah (for devout Catholics) before Easter. There are lots of good dance competitions.

St. George's Caye Day

On September 10, 1798, at St. George's Caye off the coast of Belize, British buccaneers fought and defeated the Spaniards over the territory of Belize. The tradition of celebrating this victory is still carried on each year, followed by a weeklong calendar of events from religious services to carnivals. During this week, Belize City feels like a carnival with parties everywhere. On the morning of September 10, the whole city parades through the streets and enjoys local cooking, spirits, and music with an upbeat atmosphere that continues well into the

© LEBAWIT GIRMA

The month of September is the most festive time in Belize.

beginning of Independence Day on September 21.

The city also celebrates its very own **Belize Carnival,** usually held in mid-September, following St. George's Caye Day, and consisting of a full-blown Caribbean-style costume parade and dancing in the streets and along Central American Boulevard, with hundreds of themed floats blasting soca or *punta* music.

National Independence Day

On September 21, 1981, Belize gained independence from Great Britain. Each year, Belizeans celebrate with carnivals on the main streets of downtown Belize City and in all the district towns, as well as on the main cayes of Ambergris and Caye Caulker. Like giant county fairs, they include displays of local arts, crafts, and cultural activities, while happy Belizeans dance to a variety of exotic *punta,* soca, and reggae rhythms. Again, don't miss the chance to sample local dishes from every ethnic group in the country. With this holiday back-to-back with the celebration of the Battle of St. George's Caye and Belize Carnival, Belize enjoys two weeks of riotous, cacophonous partying, known nationwide as the **September Celebrations.**

Garífuna Settlement Day

On November 19, Belize recognizes the 1823 arrival and settlement of the first Garífuna people in the southern districts of Belize. Belizeans from all over the country gather in Dangriga, Hopkins, Punta Gorda, and Belize City to celebrate with the Garinagu. The day begins with the **reenactment** of the arrival of the settlers and continues with all-night dancing to the local Garífuna drums and live *punta* bands. Traditional food—and copious amounts of rum, beer, and bitters—is available at street stands and local cafés. November 19 in Dangriga is one of the most unique and memorable celebrations I've experienced in Belize, and anywhere in the Caribbean, for that matter.

Christmas and New Year's

Christmas is celebrated around the country, shops stay open late pre-Christmas Day, and there is a surge in visitors until just after Christmas, with hotels booked weeks ahead. Belizeans celebrate the eve, day of, and day after Christmas (Boxing Day). Prepare for two full days when stores are closed and everyone is home with family. New Year's is more festive, with various options for parties, concerts, and indoor parties across the country. San Pedro, Caye Caulker, and Placencia Village are known to have the liveliest New Year's bashes. In Belize City, the Radisson Fort George often puts on a New Year's Eve Gala with live music, food, and drinks.

ESSENTIALS

Getting There

BY AIR

To Belizeans in 1927, flying was a far-fetched idea when American hero Charles Lindbergh paid a dramatic visit to the small Caribbean nation as part of his ongoing effort to promote and develop commercial aviation. At the time Lindbergh had just completed his famous non-stop flight across the Atlantic. On his visit to Belize, the Barracks Green in Belize City served as his runway, and the sound of his well-known aircraft, *The Spirit of St. Louis,* attracted hundreds of curious spectators.

Today, dozens of daily international flights fly in and out of the country, served by a growing number of major carriers. In general, airfares to Belize range from expensive to exorbitant, although rates occasionally dip throughout the year.

Most travelers to Belize arrive at **Philip Goldson International Airport** (BZE, 501/225-2045, www.pgiabelize.com), 10 miles west of Belize City, located outside the community of Ladyville. The airport is named after Philip Stanley Wilberforce Goldson (1923-2001), a respected newspaper editor, activist, and politician. The midsize airport offers gift shops, currency exchange, and two restaurants; Internet access is available in the Sun Garden

Restaurant upstairs from the American terminal. Check out the "waving deck" upstairs by the other bar-restaurant for exciting farewell and hello energy. The airport's ongoing runway and apron expansion is hoping to attract new carriers from farther away, particularly from Europe.

When it's time to leave, don't forget to carry enough U.S. dollars for your US$36 departure fee (if it's not already included in your ticket).

Airport Transportation

After clearing customs, you'll be besieged by taxi drivers offering rides into town for a fixed US$25; split the cost with fellow travelers if you can. If you are not being picked up by a resort or tour company and you choose to rent a car, look for the 11 rental car offices, all together on the same little strip, across the parking lot from the arrival area.

Connections within Belize

If you're continuing to the cayes, you can fly directly to Caye Caulker or San Pedro via the domestic airlines **Tropic Air** (tel. 501/226-2012, U.S. tel. 800/422-3435, www.tropicair.com) or **Maya Island Air** (tel. 501/223-1140 or 501/223-1362, www.mayaislandair.com). You can also take a taxi into town and get on a boat for about half the price and just a few hours longer. If it's your first time in Belize, flying is worth it, with gorgeous aerial views of the water, surrounding cayes, and Barrier Reef.

From Mexico

Because airfares to Belize are so high, a few travelers choose to fly into the Mexican state of Quintana Roo on the Yucatán Peninsula, especially to Cancún, where discounted airfares are common. By bus from Mexico is a cinch; many daily buses travel from the main terminal in Chetumal all the way to Belize City and back. You'll have to get out to wait in various customs and immigration lines, and it's a longer journey, but just follow the crowd and you'll be fine. There are also several Mexican bus lines that run daily between Chetumal, Belize City, Cayo (Benque), and Guatemala. Belize's **Tropic Air** (tel. 501/226-2012, U.S. tel. 800/422-3435, www.tropicair.com) now offers direct service (Mon.-Fri., US$155 each way) between Cancún and Belize City's international airport.

BY BOAT

Boats travel to Punta Gorda back and forth daily from Puerto Barrios, Guatemala. There are two boat services to Puerto Cortés, Honduras (one leaves from Placencia, the other from Dangriga). Vessels traveling to the area must have permission from the Belizean Embassy in Washington DC.

By Bus from Mexico

After passing through customs at the airport, you will find service desks for shuttle transportation and the ADO bus ticket agent. You want to go Playa del Carmen, an hour south, where you will make a connection to Chetumal. It costs about US$23 for a shared shuttle to Playa del Carmen; private shuttle service is US$70-80, depending on group size. Visit the airport's website (www.cancun-airport.com) to search for rates and reserve shuttle transportation. The airport personnel are very helpful in directing you where you need to go and ensuring you have transportation from the airport; shuttle vans are immediately outside, and buses are located to the right.

A bus to Playa del Carmen (about US$10) is the most economical route. Riviera buses are comfortable and air-conditioned; if you're the type of person who packs a sweater for your tropical vacation, it may be useful. After arriving at the station, a few blocks from an amazing beach, you have two options: continue immediately to Chetumal near the Belize border, or overnight in Playa del Carmen. Playa del Carmen has two bus stations: Terminal Alterna on Calle 20 and Terminal Turística (a.k.a. Terminal Riviera, 5th Ave. and Ave. Juárez); you can buy tickets for any destination at either station, so always double-check where your bus departs from when you buy a ticket.

If you continue directly to Chetumal, check the bus schedule; you may need to take a taxi (US$2.50) to Terminal Turística. Buses to

Chetumal (US$13.50-20) depart every hour until 5:15pm; the trip takes 5-6 hours and has a few stops in between if you need to grab a snack or use the restroom. Chances are you'll arrive in Chetumal later in the evening, and public transportation options to Belize may not be available.

If you'd rather linger in Playa Del Carmen, you won't be sorry; find a hotel, head to the beach, or stroll along 5th Avenue. You can book a morning bus to Chetumal, and most likely, it will be departing from Terminal Turística.

The main ADO bus terminal in Chetumal is not too far from the Neuvo Mercado, where local buses to Belize depart. Outside the station you can find a taxi or continue walking across the plaza to Avenue Insurgentes. Continue left toward the Pemex gas station on the corner and turn right onto Avenue Heroes. Continue two blocks to Calle Segundo Circuito Periférico and turn left. You'll see the repainted school buses waiting at Nuevo Mercado Lazara Cardenas, in a parking lot on the right side of the street.

BY CAR
From the United States

The road from Brownsville, Texas, to the border of Belize is just under 1,400 miles. If you don't stop to smell the cacti, you can make the drive in three days, especially now that there is a toll-road bypass around Veracruz and the Tuxtla mountains. The all-weather roads are paved, and the shortest route through Mexico is by way of Tampico, Veracruz, Villahermosa, Escárcega, and Chetumal. There is often construction on Mexican Highways 180 and 186. Lodging is available throughout the drive, although it is most concentrated in the cities and on the Costa Esmeralda, a beautiful strip of mostly deserted beach near Nautla (prices start at around US$20 for a very simple double). If attempting this trip, be sure you have a valid credit card, Mexican liability insurance, a passport, and a driver's license—all original documents and one set of photocopies.

One very important detail when entering Mexico from the United States is to request a *doble entrada* on your passport to avoid steep fees. This should only cost about US$10, if it's available. Returning to Mexico from Belize, you'll pay a US$19 pp Belizean exit tax.

From Mexico

It is possible to rent a car in Cancún and continue south on a Belizean adventure, but it'll cost you both money and patience. Still, with the money you save with the cheaper airfare into Cancún, the mobility may be worth it. Cancún is 229 miles from the border at Santa Elena, roughly 4.5 hours in a car on Highway 307. Corporate international rental companies will not let you take their vehicles across the border, so you'll have to find a more accommodating Mexican company, like **J. L. Vegas,** with one office near the airport and another in the Crystal Hotel. Next, you'll need to "make the papers," as the car guy will surely remind you. Another company that says they'll let you drive into Belize is **Caribbean Rent A Car** (U.S. tel. 866/577-1342, Mexico tel. 800/212-0750, www.cancunrentacar.com).

The most crucial part of driving into Belize from Mexico is having a letter of permission from the car's owner; customs will scrutinize this document. Next, to avoid being turned back at the border, be sure to get the vehicle sprayed with insecticide (US$5) from one of the roadside sprayers near the border—it's tough to pick them out, but look for a little white shack past the bridge after leaving Mexico and keep your receipt for when you reach customs and immigration. After passing through Mexican immigration (have your passport stamped and hand in your tourist card), you will cross a bridge welcoming you to Belize. On the right hand side, you will see two unsigned buildings where you must purchase insurance. The tire fumigation is near the fork in the road before the free zone. You will likely be greeted when you first pull over by men offering to help you through the stations, but their services are unnecessary. Still, it can be wise to befriend these touts, as many of them are related to the officers at the border. Give a small tip and ask them to clean your windows while you are getting insurance at the Atlantic house (you must have insurance before you enter immigration).

Although in Mexico proof of registration suffices as proof of ownership, in Belize you may be asked to show a title. You will not need a Temporary Vehicle Importation permit if entering for one month or less; for more time, you may need to post a bond on your vehicle (in greenbacks, to be refunded in Belizean dollars later).

Getting Around

BY AIR

It is very reasonable and common to get around the country in puddle-jumper planes. Some Belizean airstrips are paved and somewhat official looking (Belize City and San Pedro, for example); the rest are more like short abandoned roadways or strips of mowed grass, but they work just fine. Because such small planes are used, you not only watch the pilot handling the craft, you may also get to sit next to him or her if the flight is full (which is easy in a 12-seater). Best of all, flying low and slow in these aircraft allows you to get a panoramic view of the Belize Barrier Reef, cayes, coast, and rainforest (keep your camera handy).

Two airlines offer regularly scheduled flights to all districts in Belize, from both the international and municipal airports: **Tropic Air** (tel. 501/226-2012, U.S. tel. 800/422-3435, reservations@tropicair.com, www.tropicair.com) and **Maya Island Air** (tel. 501/223-1140, mayair@btl.net, www.mayaislandair.com). Daily flights are available from Belize City to Caye Caulker, San Pedro, Dangriga, Placencia, Punta Gorda, and a handful of other tiny strips around the country. Brand-new routes include flights linking San Pedro to the Cayo District. The Maya Island Air and Tropic Air flights usually combine several destinations in one route, so if you're traveling to PG, you may have to land and take off in Dangriga and Placencia first. Ditto for Caulker and San Pedro, the two of which are linked together. There are also regular flights to Flores, Guatemala, and you can fly between Corozal and San Pedro. If your scheduled flight is full, another will taxi up shortly and off you go.

Several charter flight companies will arrange trips to remote lodges like Lighthouse Reef Resort, Blancaneaux Lodge in the Mountain Pine Ridge, and Gallon Jug airstrip near Chan Chich. **Javier's Flying Service** (municipal airport, tel. 501/824-0460 or cell 501/610-0446, www.javiersflyingservice.com) is one such charter, offering local and international flights, air ambulance, and day tours.

By Helicopter

Charter a chopper for a transfer, adventure tour, filming or photography assignment, aerial property survey, search and rescue mission, or medevac with **Astrum Helicopters** (Mile 3½, Western Highway, near Belize City, tel. 501/222-5100, www.astrumhelicopters.com); expect to pay around US$1,000 per hour (US$250 pp for most sightseeing tours). Astrum is a modern, professional outfit with new aircraft and a very skilled father-son pilot team.

BY BUS

Save money, meet Belizeans, and see the countryside in an unrushed trip between towns. The motley fleet of buses that serves the entire country ranges from your typical run-down recycled yellow school bus to plush, air-conditioned luxury affairs. Belize buses are relatively reliable, on time, and less chaotic than the chicken-bus experience in other parts of Central America and Mexico. Even so, buses make many extra stops, including a requisite break in Belmopan for anywhere from 5 to 30 minutes for all buses traveling between Belize City and points west and south; it's a good restroom and taco break.

Your best up-to-date resource for all Belize

© LEBAWIT GIRMA

Buses in Belize cover the entire country and fares are cheap.

bus schedules and information is www.belize-bus.wordpress.com, an independent website that pays impressive attention to travel details. Another website with bus schedules is www.guidetobelize.info. Travel time from Belize City to Corozal or San Ignacio is about two hours, to Dangriga 2-3 hours, and to Punta Gorda 5-6 hours. Fares average US$2-4 to most destinations, US$7-12 for the longer routes.

In Belize City, nearly all buses still begin and end at the **Novelo's Terminal** (tel. 501/207-4924, 501/207-3929, or 501/227-7146; it's still called that even though the company no longer exists), located on West Collett Canal Street in Belize City. Reach it by walking west on King Street, across Collett Canal, and into the terminal—definitely use a taxi when departing or arriving at night. Another walking route from the downtown area and water taxi is to go west along Orange Street, a busy shopping area, cross over the canal, then turn left and continue a short distance to the terminal.

James Bus runs the most reliable daily Punta Gorda service, using the block in front of

the Shell station on Vernon Street (two blocks north of the Novelo's) as its terminal.

There are at least a dozen booths to buy a ticket on the various international express bus services **to Guatemala and Mexico.** All are located inside or in front of the Caye Caulker Water Taxi Terminal and Swing Bridge. Boat-bus connections are convenient and easy to make, but it all happens in the middle of one of Belize's busiest intersections.

BY CAR

Driving Belize's handful of highways gives you the most independence when traveling throughout the country, but it is also the most expensive. Rental fees were running US$75-125 per day and gasoline was approaching US$6 per gallon at press time. You'll also have to be adept at avoiding careless drivers and obstacles like pedestrians, farm animals, cyclists, iguanas, and the occasional moped-riding cruise ship passengers.

In some areas, like the Mountain Pine Ridge and other hinterlands, there is no public transportation, and a sturdy rental car is a good way to go if you're into traveling on your own schedule.

Rental Cars

One of the first things you'll see on walking out of the arrival lounge at the international airport is a strip of about a dozen car rental offices offering small, midsize, and 4WD vehicles. Vans and passenger cars are also available, some with air-conditioning. Insurance is mandatory but (like taxes) not always included in the quoted rates. If you know exactly when you want the car, it's helpful and often cheaper to make reservations. Note the hour you pick up the car and try to return it before that time: A few minutes over could cost you another full day's rental fee. Also take the vehicle inspection seriously to make sure you don't get charged for someone else's dings. And don't forget to fill the tank up before giving it back.

Crystal Auto Rental (Goldson International Airport; and Mile 5, Northern Hwy., tel. 501/223-1600, www.crystal-belize.com) has the largest, newest, most reliable fleet of cars in Belize. It is also the only company that will allow you to drive across the border into Guatemala or Mexico, but you won't be insured. **Jabiru Auto Rental** (tel. 501/224-4680, www.jabiruautorental.bz) is also reliable and has low Internet rates. **Budget Rent a Car** (tel. 501/223-2435, www.budget-belize.com) offers new cars that are well maintained. You'll find a few other international brands with local Belizean branches, including **Avis.**

If you plan on traveling in the Cayo region, it's cheaper to use one of the San Ignacio-based car rental options. Start with **Cayo Rentals** (at the UNO station at the top of the hill, 81 Benque Viejo Rd., tel. 501/824-2222, cayo-rentals@btl.net); US$75 per 24 hours *includes* taxes and insurance. Also in Cayo, **Matus Car Rentals** (18 Benque Viejo Rd., tel. 501/824-2005, www.matuscarrental.com) is another option with a handful of sturdy cars, and there is a Land Rover rental place in Central Farm, just east of San Ignacio, if you really planning on going off-road.

TRAVEL SPECIALISTS AND TOUR COMPANIES
Belize Travel Specialists

More than travel agents, not quite tour operators, Belize country specialists are small, independent operations that work directly with their clients to arrange all kinds of niche, group, and solo travel within Belize. There is usually no charge for their services, so you really can't go wrong by letting them handle some of the planning and booking.

Belize Trips (tel. 501/610-1923, U.S. tel. 561/210-7015, www.belize-trips.com) helps you arrange active itineraries, weddings, and honeymoons and can book you at the best mid- to upscale accommodations in the country. Owner Katie Valk finds out exactly what kind of experience her clients want and then, through her vast network of friends and colleagues across the country, makes that experience happen. Katie is a self-described "music business refugee from New York City" who has lived full time in Belize for 20-odd years, and you'll often find her swinging a machete through the bush or paddling her kayak as she seeks out and test-drives every adventure she promotes.

Barb's Belize (U.S. tel. 888/321-2272, www.barbsbelize.com) is another small operation that offers custom itineraries for any budget, from backpacker to decadent. Barb's specializes in unique interests such as traditional herbal medicine, jungle survival, and extreme adventure expeditions. She charges US$50 for her planning services and advice, which she credits to your invoice if you book through her.

Adventure Travel

Dangriga- and Vancouver-based **Island Expeditions** (U.S. tel. 800/667-1630, www.islandexpeditions.com) has been leading exciting sea kayaking, rafting, ruins, nature, and snorkeling adventures in Belize since 1987. It's a very experienced and professional outfit, and they have stunning island camps in Glover's Reef and Lighthouse Reef Atolls with canvas-wall platform tents. They also offer popular

DRIVING TIPS

© LEBAWIT GIRMA

Speed bumps in Belize are called "sleeping policemen."

- Drive defensively! Expect everyone out there to make sudden passes and unexpected turns—it's your job to stay out of their way.

- Valid U.S. or other foreign driver's licenses and international driving permits are accepted in Belize for a period of three months after entering the country.

- Try not to drive at night if you can avoid it. Besides the additional hazards of night driving in general, some Belizean drivers overuse their high beams, and many vehicles have no taillights.

- Watch out for unmarked speed bumps. No matter how slow you drive, on some you may bottom out.

- Driving rules are U.S.-style with one very strange exception: Sometimes a vehicle making a left-hand turn is expected to pull over to the right, let traffic behind pass, and then execute the turn.

- Tires frequently pop, so make sure you have a good spare to get you to the nearest used-tire dealer. New tires may be hard to come by, but Belizeans are geniuses with a patch kit. A decent used spare can be had for around US$30, a patch job about US$5.

- If you plan on traveling during the rainy season or without a 4WD vehicle, make sure you are prepared in the event you get stuck in the mud.

- In general, road conditions may dictate where you can and cannot go, and it is always best to ask around town if you plan to go off the beaten path. Watch out for speed bumps, even on the highways.

- If you're going to the cayes and leaving a vehicle on the mainland, be sure to seek out a secure pay parking lot in your city of departure, especially if it's Belize City (the municipal airport is probably the best choice).

- Expect police checkpoints anywhere around the country: They'll check your seat belt, car papers, and driver's license, and, courtesy of the U.S. Drug Enforcement Agency, dogs will sniff the vehicle for any drugs.

lodge-to-lodge sea kayaking trips and inland river adventures, and can help you outfit your own kayak expedition.

Slickrock Adventures (U.S. tel. 800/390-5715, www.slickrock.com), based on their primitively plush camp on a private island in Glover's Reef Atoll, offers paddling trips of various lengths and specializes in sea kayaking, windsurfing, and inland activities like mountain biking.

With decades of experience as a premier land operator in Belize, **International Expeditions** (U.S. tel. 800/633-4734, belize@ietravel.com, www.ietravel.com) has a full-time office in Belize City. They offer group and independent nature travel in sturdy, comfortable vehicles and are staffed by travel and airline specialists, naturalists, and an archaeologist. Trips run 7-14 days with two- and three-day add-ons available.

You'll also find an interesting menu of tours offered by **Intrepid Travel** (tel. 800/970-7299, http://intrepidtravel.com), an Australian company that runs trips around the world and has a dozen trips that include Belize, some Maya-themed.

Tour Operators

For those interested in letting someone else do the driving (and planning, booking, etc.), various tour operators are reliable. In Belize City, Sarita and Lascelle Tillet of **S & L Travel and Tours** (91 N. Front St., tel. 501/227-7593 or 501/227-5145, www.sltravelbelize.com) operate as a husband-wife team. They drive late-model air-conditioned sedans or vans and travel throughout the country, with airport pickup available. The Tillets have designed several great special-interest vacations and will custom-design to your interests, whether they be the Mayan archaeological zones (including Tikal), the cayes, or the caves and the countryside.

InnerQuest Adventures (U.S. tel. 800/990-4376, www.innerquest.com) has over 14 years of experience leading wildlife-viewing trips with local guides around the country. They've been featured in dozens of magazines. Minnesota-based **Magnum Belize Tours** (U.S. tel. 800/447-2931, www.magnumbelize.com) is one of the biggest, longest-standing tour operators, with an extensive network of resorts across the country; the staff is very experienced and can customize every aspect of your trip.

Sea & Explore (U.S. tel. 800/345-9786, www.seaexplore.com) is run by owners Sue and Tony Castillo, native Belizeans who take pleasure and pride in sharing their country with visitors by means of customized trips. They know every out-of-the-way destination and make every effort to match clients with the right areas of the country to suit their interests. Susan worked with the Belize Tourism Board before coming to the United States.

Mary Dell Lucas of **Far Horizons Archaeological and Cultural Trips** (U.S. tel. 800/552-4575 or 415/482-8400, www.farhorizons.com) is known throughout the Maya world for her excellent archaeological knowledge and insight. Her company provides trips into the most fascinating Mayan sites, regardless of location. Although Mary is an archaeologist herself, she often brings specialists along with her groups.

Also check **Jaguar Adventures Tours and Travel** (4 Fort St., tel. 501/223-6025, www.jaguarbelize.com), located in Belize City and offering night walks at the Belize Zoo, cave tubing trips, visits to Mayan ruins, snorkeling the reef, and diving the atolls, to name a few adventures.

Belize Travel Representatives (U.S. tel. 800/451-8017, www.belizetravelrepresentatives.com) specializes in tour packages to the

DISTANCES FROM BELIZE CITY

Belmopan	55 miles
Benque Viejo	81 miles
Corozal Town	96 miles
Dangriga	105 miles
Orange Walk Town	58 miles
Punta Gorda	210 miles
San Ignacio	72 miles

cayes, Placencia, and most of the mainland resorts and lodges. They also have some of the most extensive archaeologically themed tours in Belize. Contact **The Mayan Traveler** (www. themayantraveler.com, U.S. tel. 888/843-6292 or 281/367-3386); they can satisfy even the most serious temple junkie, going to some of the most spectacular sites in the region.

Accommodations and Food

HOTELS AND HOMESTAYS

Of the 716 licensed hotels in Belize, the vast majority are very small boutiques. Large foreign-owned hotel chains are rare in Belize, although the very first Four Seasons is soon to come on Caye Chapel.

The Belize Hotel Association (BHA, 13 Cork St., Belize City, tel. 501/223-0669, www. belizehotels.org) is a nonprofit industry organization of some of the country's most respected resorts and lodges. They work with the Belize Tourism Board and handle much of the global marketing for Belize; they also have a helpful listing of accommodations on their website.

Budget accommodations are ample in Belize, with nightly rates under US$25. In Belize, US$10-15 is the bottom line for low-cost lodging. Guesthouses and budget hotels sometimes offer a shared dormitory or bunkroom, often with shared baths and cold water.

Some villages around the country try to emulate the guesthouse and homestay networks available in the southern Toledo villages. Such options are usually primitive accommodations, often lacking electricity, running water, and flush toilets.

Hotel Rates

Exact hotel rates are an elusive thing in Belize; seasonal pricing fluctuations are compounded by various hotel taxes and service charges, sometimes as much as 25-30 percent above the quoted rate. Using a credit card can add another 3-5 percent. Universal standards for presenting prices are absent in Belize's hotel industry. Always make sure the rate you are quoted is actually the same amount you will be asked to pay.

High season is loosely considered to be mid-December through the end of April and is marked by a rise in both the number of visitors and the price of most accommodations. Some places kick their rates up even higher during Christmas, New Year's, and Easter, calling these "holiday" or "peak" rates. A minority of hotels keep their rates the same year-round, but it's rarely that simple.

Great deals are abundant in the **low season** (May-Nov.), when room rates plummet across the board, and walk-in specials can save you as much as 50 percent off normal winter (high-season) rates.

FOOD

Throughout this book (and throughout Belize), you will find references to "Belizean" food, often preceded by words like "simple" and "cheap." It should be noted that the very idea of a national cuisine is as new as every other part of Belizean identity. Since the times of the Baymen, Belize has been an import economy, surviving mostly on canned meats like "bully beef" and imported grains and packaged goods. With independence, however, came renewed national pride, and with the arrival of travelers seeking "local" food, the word "Belizean" was increasingly applied to the varied diet of so many cultures. Anthropologist Richard Wilk wrote about the process in his book, *Home Cooking in the Global Village: Caribbean Food from Buccaneers to Ecotourists.*

The common denominator of Belizean food is **rice and beans,** a starchy staple pronounced as one word with a heavy accent on the first syllable: *"RICE-'n'-beans!"* Belizeans speak of the dish with pride, as if they invented the combination, and you can expect a massive mound of it with most midday meals. Actually, Belizean

PRIVATE ISLAND DREAMS

Who's ever dreamed of starring in their own episode of *Lost*? If you've got the money, you've got exclusive access to a handful of Belize's cayes.

- **French Louie Caye** (tel. 501/523-3636, www.frenchlouiecayebelize.com, 3-night package US$1,150): The caye is about eight miles east of Placencia Village, with its own beach, coral reef, fishing dock, a two-bedroom cabin, and a spacious lodge. The on-site caretaker cooks "catch and eat" meals and can take you on a night snorkel tour.

- **Hatchet Caye** (tel. 501/533-4446, www.hatchetcaye.com/belize-private-island-rental, US$250-300): Located 17 miles east of Placencia, the island accommodates 26 guests for weddings, group retreats, and more. There's a beautiful beach, a swimming pool, and a restaurant on-site, plus a full-service dive shop.

- **Lime Caye** (tel. 501/722-0070 or cell 501/604-3548, garbuttsmarine@yahoo.com, US$10 camping): This island is the site of turtle nesting (Nov. 1-May 31) and offers basic seafront huts and a pretty beach.

- **Ranguana Caye** (U.S. tel. 800/565-9757, tel. 501/523-3565, www.robertsgrove.com/belize-private-islands, US$566, 3-night package US$1,035): A semiprivate island two acres in size, 0.5 miles from the reef, and 18 miles (90 minutes by boat) from the Placencia Peninsula, with three rustic cabanas, private baths, and a housekeeper.

- **Reef Conservation International** (tel. 501/702-0229 or 501/629-4266, www.reefci.com, divers US$1,195 per week, nondivers US$895 per week, all inclusive): Located off the coast from Punta Gorda is Tom Owens Caye, a small one-acre private island in the Sapodilla Cayes with incredible snorkeling. Packages include weekly and monthly dive trips as well as marine conservation work.

- **Robert's Caye** (U.S. tel. 800/565-9757, tel. 501/523-3565, www.robertsgrove.com/belize-private-islands, US$490): A one-acre semiprivate island 10 miles from the Placencia coast, with four thatched-roof cabanas and access to a small bar and restaurant.

- **Tarpon Caye Lodge** (tel. 501/523-3323, www.tarponcayelodge.com, US$140, 4-night all-inclusive fishing package US$2,160): Located a 30-minute boat ride from the Placencia Peninsula, this island caters to people looking to simply relax on a private Caribbean island, with fly-fishing, spin-fishing, and deep-sea fishing from the private lodge.

rice and beans *is* closer to the Caribbean version than the Latin: They use red beans, black pepper, and grated coconut, instead of the black beans and cilantro common in neighboring Latin countries. The rest of your plate will be occupied by something like **stew beef, fry chicken,** or a piece of fish, plus a small mound of either potato or cabbage salad. Be sure to take advantage of so much fresh fruit: oranges, watermelon, star fruit, soursop, mangoes, and papaya, to name a few.

For breakfast, you should try some **fry jacks** (fluffy fried-dough crescents) or **johnnycakes** (flattened biscuits) with your eggs, beans, and bacon.

One of the cheapest and quickest meal options, found nearly everywhere in Belize, is Mexican "fast-food" snacks, especially **taco stands,** which are everywhere you look, serving as many as five or six soft-shell chicken tacos for US$1. Also widely available are **salbutes,** a kind of hot, soggy taco dripping in oil; **panades,** little meat pies; and **garnaches,** which are crispy tortillas under a small mound of tomato, cabbage, cheese, and hot sauce.

Speaking of hot sauce, you'll definitely want to try to take home **Marie Sharp's** famous habanero sauces, jams, and other creative products. Marie Sharp is an independent Belizean success story, and many travelers visit her factory and store just outside Dangriga. (Her products are available on every single restaurant table and in every gift shop in the country.) Her sauce is good on pretty much everything.

You must try some fry jacks with eggs for breakfast.

© LEBAWIT GIRMA

Then, of course, there's the international cuisine, in the form of many excellent foreign-themed restaurants. San Pedro and Placencia, in particular, have burgeoning fine-dining scenes.

Many restaurants in Belize have flexible hours of operation, and often close for a few hours between lunch and dinner. The omnipresent Chinese restaurants provide authentic Chinese cuisine of varying quality. Most Chinese places sell cheap "fry chicken" take-out and are often your only meal options on Sunday and holidays.

Seafood

One of the favorite Belize specialties is fresh fish, especially along the coast and on the islands, but even inland Belize is never more than 60 miles from the ocean. There's lobster, shrimp, red snapper, sea bass, halibut, barracuda, conch, and lots more prepared in a variety of ways.

Conch has been a staple in the diet of the Mayan and Central American communities along the Caribbean coast for centuries. There are conch fritters, conch steak, and conch stew; it's also often used in ceviche—uncooked seafood marinated in lime juice with onions, peppers, tomatoes, and a host of spices. In another favorite, conch is pounded, dipped in egg and cracker crumbs, and sautéed quickly (like abalone steak in California) with a squirt of fresh lime. Caution: If it's cooked too long, it becomes tough and rubbery. Conch fritters are minced pieces of conch mixed into a flour batter and fried—delicious. On many boat trips, the crew will catch a fish and some conch and prepare them for lunch, either as ceviche, cooked over an open beach fire, or in a "boil-up," seasoned with onions, peppers, and *achiote,* a fragrant red spice grown locally since the time of the early Maya.

DRINKS
Beer

Perhaps the most important legacy left by nearly three centuries of British imperialism is a national affinity for dark beer. Nowhere else

RESPONSIBLE SEAFOOD

Many ocean waters are overfished, due in large part to increasing demand from tourists. These helpful tips will ensure you eat seafood responsibly.

- Don't order seafood out of season. The once-prolific lobster (season closed Feb. 15-June 15) is becoming scarce in Belizean waters, and conch (season closed July 1-Sept. 30) is not nearly as easy to find as it once was. Most reputable restaurateurs follow the law and don't buy undersize or out-of-season seafood; however, a few have no scruples.

- Small snappers are great fish to eat. Not only are they delicious, but they are one of the most sustainably caught fish in Belize (often caught locally with a hook and line).

- When dining out, don't patronize any restaurant offering shark fin soup or *panades* made with shark meat. Not only are sharks critical to a functional marine ecosystem, but the meat is high in methyl mercury, so it's bad for you too.

- Avoid any restaurant that displays endangered reef fish, like the Nassau grouper or goliath grouper, in tanks as meal choices. In fact, stay away from grouper in general, especially goliath grouper (*Epinephelus itajara*, locally known as jewfish), a critically endangered species that is also high in methyl mercury.

- Lastly, don't buy marine curios such as shark teeth or jaws, starfish, or coral.

in Central America will you find ale as hearty and dark as you do in any bar, restaurant, or corner store in Belize, where beer is often advertised separately from stout, a good sign indeed for those who prefer more bite and body to their brew.

At the top of the heap are the slender, undersize 280-milliliter (9.5-ounce) bottles of **Guinness Foreign Extra Stout,** known affectionately by Belizeans as "short, dark, and lovelies." Yes, Guinness—brewed in Belize under license from behind the famous St. James's Gate in Dublin, Ireland, and packing a pleasant 7.5 percent punch of alcohol. No, this is not the same sweet nectar you'll find flowing from your favorite Irish pub's draft handle at home, but c'mon, you're in Central America. Enjoy.

Asking for a "beer" will get you a basic **Belikin,** which, when served cold, is no better or worse than any other regional draft. Brewed in Belize since 1971 by Bowen & Bowen Limited, it's the only beer in the Caribbean and Central America that uses a high percentage of malt, very close to Germany's 100 percent. **Belikin Stout** weighs in with a slightly larger 342-milliliter (11.5-ounce) bottle and distinguishable from a regular beer bottle by its blue bottle cap. Stouts run 6.5 percent alcohol and

are a bit less bitter than Guinness, but still a delicious, meaty meal that goes down much quicker than its caloric equivalent of a loaf of bread. **Belikin Premium** (4.8 percent alcohol) boasts a well-balanced body and is brewed with four different types of foreign hops; demand often exceeds supply in many establishments, so order early.

Lastly, the tiny green bottles belong to **Lighthouse Lager,** a healthy alternative to the heavies, but packing a lot less bang for the buck with only 4.2 percent alcohol and several ounces less beer (often for the same price).

All beer is brewed and distributed by the same company, Bowen and Bowen, in Ladyville, just north of Belize City; they also have the soft-drink market cornered. Most Belizeans vigorously wipe the open bottle mouths with the napkin that comes wrapped around the top—you'd be smart to do the same. Beers in Belize cost US$1.50-3 a bottle, depending on where you are.

Rum

Of all the national rums, **One Barrel** stands proudly above the rest. Smooth enough to enjoy on the rocks (add a bit of Coca-Cola for coloring if you need to), One Barrel has a sweet,

Belikin Beer is the "beer of Belize."

butterscotchy aftertaste and costs about US$8 for a one-liter bottle, or US$3 per shot (or rum drink). The cheaper option is **Caribbean Rum,** which is fine if you're mixing it with punch, cola, or better yet, coconut water in the coconut. Everything else is standard white-rum gut rot.

The **Panty Ripper** is Belize's national cocktail—a perfect blend of coconut rum and a splash of pineapple juice. Don't underestimate it as a girly drink; a couple of well-made panty rippas can get you well tipsy.

Bitters

Bitters are made by soaking herbs like *palo del hombre* (man-root) and jackass bitters in 80-proof white rum or gin. They are available under the counter of many a bar and corner store, a liquid baby-maker known in Garífuna as *gífit.* Bitters are a cure-all used to treat everything from the common cold to cancer, sometimes taken as a daily shot to keep your system clean.

Belizean Garífuna expats used to bring bitters back to the United States by the gallon.

The most famous bitters maker in the country was Doctor Mac (also known as "Big Mac"), a formidable man who used to make a "fertility" version of bitters for women, with the bottles labeled either "boy" or "gal." The latest bitters-making wonder is "Kid B," a spry 76-year-old from Silk Grass Village, who spent 36 years as a welterweight prize fighter in Chicago. Find him at **Kid B's Cool Spot** (in Silk Grass, north of the Hopkins turnoff), just off the Southern Highway.

In addition to curing what ails you, however, bitters can get you quite wasted. Be careful with any usage—both for your liver's sake and because some say the ingredients carry trace amounts of arsenic. Talk about a hangover.

Nonalcoholic Beverages

There are wonderful natural fruit drinks to be had throughout Belize. Take advantage of fresh lime, papaya, watermelon, orange, and other healthy juices during your travels—they are usually made with purified water, at least in most tourist destinations.

© LEBAWIT GIRMA

Tips for Travelers

VISAS AND OFFICIALDOM
Passports

U.S. citizens must have a passport valid for the duration of their visit to Belize; U.S. citizens, British Commonwealth subjects, and citizens of Belgium, Denmark, Finland, Greece, Iceland, Italy, Liechtenstein, Luxembourg, Mexico, Spain, Switzerland, Tunisia, Turkey, and Uruguay do not need a visa. They are automatically granted a 30-day tourist pass and technically must have onward or return air tickets and proof of sufficient money (though I've never heard of anyone checking this). Visitors for purposes other than tourism, or who want to stay longer than 30 days, need to visit an immigration office of the Government of Belize.

If you are planning on staying more than 30 days, you can ask for a new stamp at any immigration office in the country—there's one in every district, including in San Pedro, Belize City and Dangriga—or you can cross the border and return, but this technique is no guarantee of readmission, particularly if you're gone only for a few days. The fee to extend for a month is US$25.

Make a photocopy of the pages in your passport that have your photo and information. When you get the passport stamped at the airport, it's a good idea to make a photocopy of that page as well, and store the copies somewhere other than with your passport. This will facilitate things if your passport ever gets lost or stolen. Also consider taking a small address book, credit cards, a travel insurance policy, and an international phone card for calling home. A separate passport pouch can be used for documents, but make sure it's waterproof so it won't get soggy when you sweat.

Foreign Embassies

Only a handful of countries have embassies in Belize. The **United States Embassy** (Floral Park Rd., Belmopan, tel. 501/822-4011, fax 501/822-4012, embbelize@state.gov, http:// belize.usembassy.gov) is open for U.S. citizen services 8am-noon and 1pm-5pm Monday-Friday in its brand-new US$50 million fortified building. The after-hours emergency number for American citizens is 501/610-5030. For inquiries pertaining to American citizens, email ACSBelize@state.gov.

U.S. citizens are strongly encouraged by the **State Department** (www.travel.state.gov) to register their trip online, no matter how short, so that the local embassy has emergency contact information on file.

The **British High Commission** (Embassy Square, P.O. Box 91, Belmopan, tel. 501/822-2146, brithicom@btl.net, www.ukinbelize.fco.gov.uk/en) is open 8am-noon and 1pm-4pm Monday-Thursday and 8am-2pm Friday. El Salvador and India also have embassies in Belmopan.

Countries with embassies in Belize City include China, Cuba, Mexico, Colombia, Holland, Sweden, and Taiwan.

CONDUCT AND CUSTOMS

Cameras can be a help or hindrance when trying to get to know the locals. When traveling in the backcountry, you'll run into folks who don't want their pictures taken. Keep your camera put away until the right moment. *Always* ask permission first, and if someone doesn't want his or her picture taken, accept the refusal with a gracious smile and move on. Especially sensitive to this are Mennonites and Maya, who often specifically request that you not take their photos. Many Internet cafés have readers for your digital camera card, so you can make backups as you go. To be safe, travel with extra cards, readers, and cables.

WHAT TO TAKE

Pack for hot weather (80-95°F, both humid and dry), as well as the occasional cool front (60-80°F). At least one pair of pants and a light shell jacket are recommended, as rainy season can

EMBASSIES AND CONSULATES OF BELIZE

For the most recent update on Belize's diplomatic corps abroad, check the Ministry of Foreign Affairs website (www.mfa.gov.bz).

BELGIUM

Embassy of Belize and Mission of Belize to the European Communities
Blvd. Brand Whitlock 136
1200 Brussels, Belgium
tel. 32/2-732-6204
fax 32/2-732-6246
embelize@skynet.be

CANADA

Belize does not have an embassy or an ambassador in Canada, only honorary consuls:

Bob Dhillon
Honorary Consul of Belize
305 10th Ave. SE
Calgary, AB T2G 0W2
tel. 403/215-6072, 403/560-6520,
or 403/215-6063
bdhillon@mainst.biz

David W. Smiling
Honorary Consul of Belize
Vancouver, BC
belize@smilingassociates.com
tel. 604/306-7645

COSTA RICA

Consulate of Belize
Apartado Postal 11 121-1000
Calle 36, Aves. 7 and 9
San José, Costa Rica
tel. 506/2223-1037 or 506/2223-6654
fax 506/2233-6587
jgamboa@gamboaydengo.com

FRANCE

Permanent Delegation of Belize to UNESCO
1 rue Miollis, Office M. 345-346
Paris 75015, France
tel. 33/1-45-68-32-11
fax 33/1-47-20-18-74
dl.belize@unesco-delegations.org

GUATEMALA

Embassy of Belize
5 Ave. 5-55, Zona 14
Edificio Euro Plaza, Torre 2, Oficina 1502
Ciudad de Guatemala
tel. 502/2367-3883 or 502/2367-3885
fax 502/2367-3884
embelguat@yahoo.com
www.embajadadebelize.org

HONDURAS

Embassy of Belize
Hoteles de Honduras

---

push all the way into February, and it's guaranteed to be damp June through November. Long sleeves are helpful for avoiding mosquito bites and sunburn. Cayo and the Mountain Pine Ridge can drop to sweater weather in any part of the wet season and even in December. Bring a small first-aid kit, a flashlight or headlamp, and waterproof plastic bags for protection during rain or boat travel.

OPPORTUNITIES FOR STUDY AND EMPLOYMENT

There are many opportunities for voluntourists to get their feet wet in the world of international development and resource conservation work throughout Belize. Some regional chapters listed throughout this book offer local volunteer opportunities or ways to help the community. For those interested in spending some time lending a hand, sharing their expertise, or supporting community efforts, there's plenty to choose from. Some of these programs cost money and some don't; be sure you know exactly what you're getting into when you sign up. Also, be clear on what kind of work your position will entail, as well as your host organization's expectations and Belizean legal requirements. Speaking of

R/do Hotel Honduras Maya
Tegucigalpa, Honduras
tel. 504/238-4614
fax 504/238-4617
consuladobelice@yahoo.com

MEXICO
Consulate of Belize
Ave. Nader 34
Cancún, Quintana Roo, Mexico
tel. 52/555-520-1274 or 52/555-520-1346
fax 52/555-520-6089
embelize@prodigy.net.mx
nel.bel@prodigy.net.mx

Embassy of Belize
215 Calle Bernardo de Galvez
Col. Lomas de Chapultepec
Mexico, DF 11000
tel. 52/5-520-1274
embelize@prodigy.net.mx

UNITED KINGDOM
Belize High Commission
45 Crawford Place, 3rd Fl.
London, W1H 4LP, United Kingdom
tel. 44/20-7723-3603
fax 44/20-7723-9637
bzhc-lon@btconnect.com
www.belizehighcommission.com

UNITED STATES
Consulate General
Korean Trade Center Park Mile Plaza
4801 Wilshire Blvd., Suite 250
Los Angeles, CA 90010
tel. 323/634-9900
belizeconsulate@sbcglobal.net

Debbie M. Schell
Honorary Consul of Belize
780 Lee St., Suite 109
Des Plaines, IL 60016
tel. 847/759-9833
dschell@bzconsulchicago.org

Embassy of Belize
2535 Massachusetts Ave. NW
Washington, DC 20008
tel. 202/332-9636
belize@oas.org
www.embassyofbelize.org

Permanent Mission of Belize
to the United Nations
675 3rd Ave., Suite 1911
New York, NY 10017
tel. 212/593-0999
fax 212/593-0932
blzun@belizemission.com
www.un.int/belize

which, Belizean immigration officially requires long-term volunteers to apply for special visas, a process that takes months and is not cheap. Some NGOs get around this (for short-term assignments, anyway) by calling their volunteers "interns."

The **Belize Audubon Society** (BAS, tel. 501/223-5004, 12 Fort St., Belize City, www.belizeaudubon.org) accepts qualified volunteers and interns for a variety of land and marine projects, with a three-month minimum (less for marine projects). Past skilled BAS volunteers have worked in community education; helped create trail signs, brochures, and management

guidelines for protected areas and wardens; and analyzed the effectiveness of BAS gift shops. **Habitat for Humanity Belize** (tel. 501/223-2929), a world leader in providing low-income housing, operates in Belize City and beyond and accepts qualified volunteers and church groups to help erect home projects.

The **Belize Botanic Gardens** (tel. 501/824-3101, www.belizebotanic.org) sponsors a program where volunteers pay US$550 for room and board while working on various garden projects.

The **Cornerstone Foundation** (tel. 501/824-2373, www.cornerstonefoundationbelize.org)

is a humanitarian NGO, based in the Cayo District, whose volunteer opportunities include HIV/AIDS education and awareness, special education, adult literacy, working with youth or women, and teaching business skills.

Trekforce Belize (8 St. Mark St., Belize City, tel. 501/223-1442, www.trekforce.org. uk) offers challenging conservation, community, and research trips from two weeks to five months, including "jungle survival," Spanish school in Guatemala, and a teaching assignment in a rural Belizean school.

Aspiring organic farmers will want to check up on the few Belize listings for the **World Wide Opportunities on Organic Farms** (www. wwoof.org) network, which at last check had five independent host opportunities in Belize. You can often work on the farm in exchange for room and board, but conditions vary from site to site.

Sustainable Harvest International's **Smaller World Program** (U.S. tel. 207/669-8254, shi@ sustainableharvest.org, www.sustainablehar-vest.org) has an office in Punta Gorda, where they coordinate sustainable agriculture projects with 100 area farmers. SHI offers service trips for groups, staying in rustic homestays or the relatively upscale Cotton Tree Lodge. Typical service trips for volunteers are 10 days long and include side trips to natural and cultural sites. Some projects they've done include organic gardens, multistory cacao and coffee plots, composting latrines, organic fertilizers and pesticides, bio-digesters, and wood-conserving stoves. In Belize, the trips include sustainable chocolate tours and family voluntourism trips.

Field Research and Educational Travel

Belize shines in this category. There are many opportunities to learn, teach, and volunteer at the **Belize Zoo and Tropical Education Center** (tel. 501/220-8004, www.belizezoo.org). The **Oceanic Society** (U.S. tel. 800/326-7491, www.oceanic-society.org), a nonprofit conservation organization, maintains a field station in the Turneffe Islands Atoll and invites curious travelers to participate in educational marine

ecotourism activities, such as snorkel and kayak programs to learn about coral reef ecology and whale shark research projects (about US$2,000 includes everything for eight-day trips). The family program includes interaction with Belizean and American researchers.

Get involved with **ACES/American Crocodile Education Sanctuary** (tel. 501/666-3871 or 501/631-6366, acesnpo@hughes.net, www.americancrocodilesanctuary.org), a non-profit conservation organization licensed by the Belize Forest Department to protect Belize's critical habitats and protected species, especially crocodilians, through scientific research and education. Anyone wishing to learn, observe, or help biologist Cherie Chenot-Rose collect data and conduct research is welcome, including students; 100 percent of their donations and proceeds go to croc care, croc rescues, research, and education.

Volunteer opportunities are also available at **Wildtracks** (tel. 501/650-6578, www.wildtracksbelize.org), which hosts both Belize's Manatee Rehabilitation Centre and Primate Rehabilitation Centre, in partnership with the Belize Forest Department. Volunteer placements are normally for one month or more, and volunteers need to apply in advance through Global Nomadic or Global Vision International.

The St. George's Caye Research Station & Field School was founded in 2009 by **ECOMAR** (17 Princess Margaret Dr. LF, P.O. Box 1234, Belize City, tel. 501/223-3022, www.ecomar-belize.org), which hosts archaeology students and also high school and university professors interested in bringing their students to study marine ecosystems in the area. Other groups stay on St. George's Caye to participate in the Coral Watch Program and learn how to identify coral bleaching.

Want to be a behavioral ecologist or marine mammal biologist? Join **Caryn Self-Sullivan, PhD** (U.S. tel. 540/287-8207, www.sirenian.org, caryns@sirenian.org), and her research team for two intense weeks of total immersion in the world of animal behavior, ecology, and conservation of Antillean manatees, bottlenose dolphins, coral reefs, mangrove forests, and sea grass beds in Belize. Earn up to four credit hours during this total immersion field course where you will live, work, and study from a marine science field station on a pristine private island off the coast of Belize, the Spanish Bay Conservation & Research Center at Hugh Parkey's Belize Adventure Lodge (www.belizeadventurelodge.com). The course is generally held in May of each year.

In Toledo District, the **Belize Foundation for Research and Environmental Education** (BFREE, tel. 501/671-1299, www.bfreebz.org) offers student programs from one week to a whole semester, with lots of activities and cultural immersion programs available. BFREE has spearheaded amphibian research and monitoring in the Maya Mountains as a participant in the Maya Forest Anuran Monitoring Project, among other things. Also, the **Belize Rainforest Institute** (tel. 501/824-2164, www.mayamountain.com) provides weeklong courses and workshops on such topics as rainforest ecology, butterflies, cultures of Belize, and ecotourism. There is also a huge array of research and educational programs at **Monkey Bay Wildlife Sanctuary** (tel. 501/820-3032, www.monkeybaybelize.org), which specializes in groups and classes.

Look up the summer workshops and other educational trips offered by **International Zoological Expeditions** (U.S. tel. 800/548-5843, www.ize2belize.com); they've got bases and considerable experience in South Water Caye and the Toledo District.

Programme for Belize (1 Eyre St., Belize City, tel. 501/227-5616, www.pfbelize.org) is the group that manages the 260,000-acre Río Bravo Conservation Area and has a full menu of ecology and rainforest workshops.

Two miles upriver from the village of San Pedro Columbia, in southern Belize, the **Maya Mountain Research Farm** (www.mmrfbz.org) is a registered NGO and working demonstration farm that promotes sustainable agriculture, appropriate technology, and food security using permacultural principles and applied biodiversity, and it offers hands-on coursework in all of the above.

Maya Study and Archaeological Field Work

For Mayaphiles and archaeology students, the **Belize Valley Archaeology Reconnaissance Project** (BVAR, www.bvar.org, bvararchaeology@gmail.com) conducts research and offers field schools at several sites in western Belize. Expect BVAR and other organizations to be offering a host of opportunities throughout 2012, at which academics, researchers, archaeologists, and other professionals from around the world will present the teachings of the Maya.

U.S. Peace Corps

The Peace Corps (www.peacecorps.gov) is a U.S. government program created by John F. Kennedy in 1961 whose original goal was to improve the image of the United States in the Third World by sending volunteers deep into the countryside of developing countries. Fifty years later, some 8,000 volunteers are serving in more than 70 countries around the world. Accepted participants serve a two-year tour preceded by three months of intensive language and cultural training in the host country; they receive a bare-bones living allowance and earn a nominal "readjustment allowance" at the completion of their service.

The first group of Peace Corps volunteers arrived in Belize in 1962. Since that time, more than 1,700 volunteers have worked in Belize in a variety of projects. Currently, there are about 70 volunteers providing assistance in education, youth development, rural community development, environmental education, and HIV/AIDS prevention. Pre-service training is conducted in rural Creole and mestizo villages and includes Spanish, Q'eqchi', and Garífuna language classes, depending on where the volunteer is being sent. Volunteers are placed throughout the country's six districts to work with government agencies and NGOs.

Galen University

Galen University (tel. 501/824-3226, www.galen.edu.bz), based in the Cayo District, offers a Semester Study Abroad program (tuition, room, board, transportation, and field-trip fees US$10,065) of 15 credit hours, accredited through the University of Indianapolis. Students get to immerse in Belizean life and engage in community service, field trips, and regular classes of their choice, taught by local and international faculty members. Summer Abroad courses are also available from June through July, with options such as animal science, land-ocean interface, protected areas practicum, and forensic anthropology.

ACCESS FOR TRAVELERS WITH DISABILITIES

There are probably about as many wheelchair ramps in all of Belize as there are traffic lights (three); disabled travelers will generally be treated with respect, but expect logistics to be challenging in places. **Experience Belize Tours** (tel. 501/601-9890, U.S. tel. 205/383-2921, www.experiencebelizetours.com) offers wheelchair-accessible tours for seniors, slow walkers, and disabled travelers. **Hok'ol K'in Guest House** in Corozal (tel. 501/422-3329, www.corozal.net) has nice wheelchair-accessible suites and facilities. There is also a "Belize disabled travel holiday" listed on ResponsibleTravel.com.

TRAVELING WITH CHILDREN

Children love Belize, and Belizeans love children: It's very much a family-oriented society. While a select few romantic resorts do not allow children, most do. Any place offering a special "family package" is a place to start your research. Always check in advance and tell the staff the ages of your children. You'll find most resorts are quite experienced at dealing with all ages.

For babies, be prepared with your own travel kit, but don't stress it too much if you forget something. There is a modern selection of jarred food, diapers, bottles, formula, and the like at Brodie's supermarkets in Belize City. If you're short on jars, or if baby wants more than breast milk, you'll find enough fresh fruit and fish to keep your baby growing the whole time you're in Belize. A few resorts can provide a crib

in your room if you want one, but make sure you verify this in advance; otherwise bring your own fold-up contraption, which can be great for the beach too, especially since you can easily drape a mosquito net over the top.

Once in Belize, a visit to the zoo is a must. There are a few kid-friendly cave trips, and, of course, scrambling on the pyramids at any of the archaeological sites is heaven for young explorers. Just be extra careful about covering them up with loose, long clothing against the sun and mosquitoes, and make sure they stay hydrated while they rage through the rainforest. Also, during the rainy season, it's best to steer clear of river activities like cave tubing, since rivers can be unpredictable when they swell with rain.

WOMEN TRAVELING ALONE

For the independent woman, Belize is a great place for group or solo travel. Its size makes it easy to get around, English is spoken everywhere, and if you so desire, you won't be lacking for a temporary travel partner in any part of the country. You'll meet many fellow travelers at the small inexpensive inns and guesthouses. Belizeans are used to seeing all combinations of travelers; solo women are no exception.

That said, sexual harassment of females traveling alone or in small groups can be a problem, although most incidents are limited to no more than a few catcalls. Just keep on walking; I've found that usually, some minor acknowledgment that you have heard them will shut harassers up more quickly than totally ignoring them. If they persist and follow to talk to you, tell them you're "on a mission," i.e., rushing to your next stop; don't feel obligated to stop and respond. Although violent sexual assault is not a common occurrence, it does occur (like anywhere in the world). Several American travelers were the victims of sexual assaults in recent years. At least one of these rapes occurred after the victim accepted a ride from a new acquaintance, while another occurred during an armed robbery at an isolated resort. Never give the name of your hotel or your room number to someone you don't know.

GETTIN' HITCHED AND HONEYMOONIN'

Belize's reputation for romance is growing, and an increasing number of resorts cater to exotic weddings and honeymoon packages, including ceremonies conducted underwater, atop Mayan pyramids, or in caves. (Actually, I don't think anyone's been married in a cave yet, but someone's bound to do it.) Most couples, however, are quite content with a barefoot beach ceremony.

For a US$50 marriage license, the couple must arrive in Belize three business days before submitting marriage paperwork to the Registrar General's office on the fourth business day. A rush job costs US$250 and allows you to obtain your marriage license before arriving in Belize, in which case you can get married on your first day in country, if you so wish. For this service, you'll need a travel agent or wedding planner to act on your behalf in Belize.

The **Registrar General of Belize** (tel. 501/227-2053, www.belizelaw.org) handles marriage licenses. You'll need to show proof of citizenship (i.e., a valid passport), proof that you're over 18, and, where applicable, a certified copy of a divorce certificate or death decree to annul a previous marriage. Forms can be obtained at two locations: the General Registry, Supreme Court Building, Belize City, and the Solicitor General's Office, East Block Building, Belmopan. No blood test is required.

A few select Belize wedding specialists can help you facilitate the paperwork, find ministers, and handle your party's flowers, accommodations, receptions, and everything else. Contact **Iraida Gonzales** (www.belizeweddings.com) in San Pedro, **Lee Nyhus** (www.secretgardenplacencia.com) in Placencia, and **Katie Valk** (www.belize-trips.com), who provides services anywhere in the country.

Wearing revealing clothes *will* attract lots of gawking attention, possibly more than you want. Most of the small towns and villages are safe even at night, with the exception of Belize City—don't walk anywhere there at night, even with friends.

A few international tour companies specialize in trips for independent, active women. For "uncommon advice for the independent woman traveler," pick up a copy of Thalia Zepatos's *A Journey of One's Own* (Eighth Mountain Press), a highly acclaimed women's travel resource.

SENIOR TRAVELERS

Active seniors enjoy Belize. Some like the tranquility of the cayes, others the bird-watching in the Maya ruins. Many come to learn about the jungle and its creatures or about archaeology. **Road Scholar** (formerly Elderhostel, U.S. tel. 800/454-5768, www.roadscholar.org) has a number of tours to Belize, including dolphin and reef ecology projects.

GAY AND LESBIAN TRAVELERS

Although there are plenty of out-and-about gay Belizean men (in Kriol, "batty-men"), particularly in San Pedro, there is no established community or any gay clubs, per se. The foreign gay travelers we've seen were totally accepted by both their fellow lodge guests and Belizean hosts. Still, the act of "sodomy" (between men) is officially illegal in Belize, so a bit of discretion is advised.

Health and Safety

For up-to-date health recommendations and advice, consult the Belize "Mexico and Central America" page of the **U.S. Centers for Disease Control and Prevention** (CDC, wwnc.cdc.gov/travel/regions/central-america.htm) or call their International Travelers Hotline (877/394-8747). Another excellent resource is the Belize page of **www.mdtravelhealth.com.** You can also call the Belizean embassy in your country for up-to-date information about outbreaks or other health problems.

STAYING HEALTHY

Ultimately, your health is dependent on the choices you make, and chief among these is what you decide to put in your mouth. Expect your digestive system to take some time getting accustomed to the new food and microorganisms in the Belizean diet. During this time (and after), use common sense: wash your hands with soap often; alcohol-based hand sanitizers are less effective at removing germs from your hands. Eat food that is well cooked and still hot when served. Be wary of uncooked foods, including shellfish and salads. Most importantly, be aware of flies, the single worst transmitter of food-borne illnesses. Prevent flies from landing on your food, glass, or table setting. You'll notice Belizeans are meticulous about this, and you should be too. If you have to leave the table, cover your food with a napkin or have someone else wave a hand over it slowly.

Drinking the Water

Even though most municipal water systems are well treated and probably safe, there is not much reason to take the chance, especially when purified bottled water is so widely available and relatively cheap. Canned and bottled drinks, including beer, are usually safe, but should never be used as a substitute for water when trying to stay hydrated, especially during a bout of traveler's diarrhea or when out in the sun.

If you plan on staying awhile in a rural area of Belize, check out camping catalogs for water filters that remove chemical as well as biological contamination. Alternatively, six drops of liquid iodine (or three of bleach) will kill everything that needs to be killed in a liter of water—good in a pinch (or on a backcountry camping trip), but not something you'll find yourself practicing on a daily basis. Also, bringing any water to a full boil is 100 percent effective in killing bacteria.

Oral Rehydration Salts

Probably the single most effective preventative and curative medicine you can carry is packets of powdered salt and sugar, which, when mixed with a liter of water (drink in small sips), is the best immediate treatment for dehydration due to diarrhea, sun exposure, fever, infection, or hangover. Particularly in the case of diarrhea, rehydration salts are essential to your recovery. They replace the salts and minerals your body has lost due to liquid evacuation (be it from sweating, vomiting, or urinating), and they're essential to your body's most basic cellular transfer functions. Whether or not you like the taste (odds are you won't), consuming enough rehydration packets and water is very often the difference between being just a little sick and feeling really, really awful.

Sports drinks like Gatorade are super-concentrated mixtures and should be diluted with water to make the most of the active ingredients. If you don't, you'll pee out the majority of the electrolytes. Rehydration packets are available from any drugstore or health clinic. They can also be improvised, according to the following recipe: mix a half teaspoon of salt, a half teaspoon baking soda, and four tablespoons of sugar in one quart of boiled or carbonated water. Drink a full glass of the stuff after each time you use the bathroom. Add a few drops of lemon juice to make it more palatable.

Sun Exposure

Belize is located a scant 13-18 degrees of latitude from the equator, so the sun's rays strike the earth's surface at a more direct angle than in northern countries. The result is that you will burn faster and sweat up to twice as much as you are used to. Did we mention that you should drink lots of water?

Ideally, do like the majority of the locals do, and stay out of the sun between 10am and 2pm. It's a great time to take a nap anyway. Use sunscreen of at least SPF 30, and wear a hat and pants. Should you overdo it in the sun, make sure to drink lots of fluids—that means water, not beer (or at least water and beer). Treat sunburns with aloe gel, or better yet, find a fresh aloe plant to break open and rub over your skin.

DISEASES AND COMMON AILMENTS

There is moderate incidence of hepatitis B in Belize. Avoid contact with bodily fluids or bodily waste. Get vaccinated if you anticipate close contact with nature or plan to reside in Central America for an extended period of time. Get a rabies vaccination if you intend to spend a long time in Belize. Should you be bitten by an infected dog, rodent, or bat, immediately cleanse the wound with lots of soap, and get prompt medical attention.

Tuberculosis is spread by sneezing or coughing, and the infected person may not know he or she is a carrier. If you are planning to spend more than four weeks in Belize (or plan on spending time in the Belize jail), consider having a tuberculin skin test performed before and after visiting. Tuberculosis is a serious and possibly fatal disease but can be treated with several medications. No cases of cholera have been reported in Belize since 2000.

Ciguatera

This is a toxin occasionally found in large reef fish. It is not a common circumstance, but it is possible for groupers, snappers, and barracuda to carry this toxin. If, after eating these fish, you experience diarrhea, nausea, numbness, or heart arrhythmia, see a doctor immediately. The toxin is found in certain algae on reefs in all the tropical areas of the world. Fish do nibble on the coral, and if they happen to find this algae, over a period of time the toxin accumulates in their systems. The longer they live and the larger they get, the more probable it is they will carry the toxin, which is not destroyed when cooked.

Dengue Fever

Dengue, or "bone-breaking fever," is a flulike, mosquito-carried illness that will put a stop to your fun in Central America like a baseball bat to the head. Dengue's occurrence is extremely low in Belize, but a few dozen cases are still reported each year. There is no vaccine, but dengue's effects can be successfully minimized with plenty of rest, acetaminophen (for the fever and aches), and as much water and hydration salts as you can manage. Dengue itself is undetectable in a blood test, but a low platelet count indicates its presence. If you believe you have dengue, you should get a blood test as soon as possible, to make sure it's not the hemorrhagic variety, which can be fatal if untreated.

Diarrhea and Dysentery

Generally, simple cases of diarrhea in the absence of other symptoms are nothing more serious than "traveler's diarrhea." If you do get a good case, your best bet is to let it pass naturally. Diarrhea is your body's way of flushing out the bad stuff, so constipating medicines like Imodium A-D are not recommended, as they keep the bacteria (or whatever is causing your intestinal distress) within your system. Save the Imodium (or any other liquid glue) for emergency situations like long bus rides or a hot date. Most importantly, drink lots of water! Not replacing the fluids and electrolytes you are losing will make you feel much worse than you need to. If the diarrhea persists for more than 48 hours, is bloody, or is accompanied by a fever, see a health professional immediately. That said, know that all bodies react differently to the changes in diet, schedule, and stress that go along with traveling, and many visitors to Belize stay entirely regular and solid throughout their trips.

Pay attention to your symptoms: Diarrhea can also be a sign of amoebic (parasitic) or bacillary (bacterial) dysentery, both caused by some form of fecal-oral contamination. Often accompanied by nausea, vomiting, and a mild fever, dysentery is easily confused with other diseases, so don't try to self-diagnose. Stool-sample examinations are cheap, can be performed at most clinics and hospitals, and are your first step to getting better. Bacillary dysentery is treatable with antibiotics; amoebic dysentery is treated with one of a variety of drugs that kill off all the flora in your intestinal tract. Of these, Flagyl is the best known, but other non-FDA-approved treatments like tinidazole are commonly available, cheap, and effective. Do not drink alcohol with these drugs, and eat something like yogurt or acidophilus pills to repopulate your tummy.

Malaria

By all official accounts, malaria is present in Belize, although you'll be hard-pressed to find anybody—Belizean or expat—who has actually experienced or even heard of a case of it. Still, many travelers choose to take a weekly prophylaxis of chloroquine or its equivalent. The CDC specifically recommends travelers to Belize use brand-name Aralen pills (500 mg for adults), although you should ask your doctor for the latest drug on the market. A small percentage of people have negative reactions to chloroquine, including nightmares, rashes, or hair loss. Alternative treatments are available, but the best method of all is to not get bitten by mosquitoes, which transmit the disease.

BITES AND STINGS

Thousands of people dive in Belize's Caribbean and hike its forests every day of the year without incident. The information on possible bites and stings is only to let you know what's out there, not to scare you into remaining in your resort. Know what you're getting into and be sure your guide does as well, and then get into it.

Botfly

Also known as *torsalo,* screw-worm, or *Dermatobia hominis,* this insect looks like the common household fly. The big difference is that the botfly deposits its eggs on mosquitoes, which then implant them in an unsuspecting warm-blooded host. Burrowing quickly under the skin, the maggot sets up housekeeping. To breathe, it sticks a tiny tube through the skin, and there it stays until one of two things happen: you kill it, or it graduates and leaves home (to witness this, Google "botfly removal" and get ready for an eyeful).

A botfly bite starts out looking like a mosquito bite, but if the bite gets red and tender instead of healing, get it checked out. Though uncomfortable and distasteful, it's not a serious health problem if it doesn't get infected. A tiny glob of petroleum jelly or tobacco over the air hole often works to draw out or suffocate the creature; just make sure you squeeze all of it out.

Mosquitoes and Sand Flies

Mosquitoes are most active during the rainy season (June-Nov.) and in areas with stagnant water, like marshes, puddles, and rice fields. They are more common in the lower, flatter regions of Belize than they are in the hills, though even in the highlands, old tires, cans, and roadside puddles can provide the habitat necessary to produce swarms of mosquitoes. The mosquito that carries malaria is active during the evening and at night, while the dengue fever courier is active during the day, from dawn to dusk. They are both relatively simple to combat, and ensuring you don't get bitten is the best prophylaxis for preventing the diseases.

First and foremost, limit the amount of skin you expose—long sleeves, pants, and socks will do more to prevent bites than the strongest chemical repellent. Choose accommodations with good screens, and if this is not possible, use a fan to blow airborne insects away from your body as you sleep. Avoid being outside or unprotected in the hour before sunset, when mosquito activity is heaviest, and use a mosquito net tucked underneath your mattress when you sleep. Consider purchasing a light-weight backpackers' net, either freestanding or to hang from the ceiling, before you come south—mosquito nets are more expensive in Belize than at home. Some accommodations provide nets; others are truly free of biting bugs and don't need them. If you know where you're staying, ask before you arrive whether you'll need a net. Once in Belize, you can purchase mosquito coils, which burn slowly, releasing a mosquito-repelling smoke; they're cheap and convenient, but try to place them so you're not breathing the toxic smoke yourself.

Sand flies don't carry any diseases that we know about, but, man, do they *suck!* Actually, these tiny midges, or no-see-ums, bite. Hard. They breed in wet, sandy areas and are only fought by the wind (or a well-screened room). Don't scratch those bites! If you do, you'll not only have massive red bumps on your skin, it will itch for days, even in the middle of the night, and you risk infection. For prevention, any thick oil is usually enough of a barrier—most people like baby oil or hempseed oil, and some swear that a hint of lavender scent in the oil keeps sand flies away too.

Scorpions, Spiders, and Snakes

Scorpions are common in Belize, especially in dark corners, at beaches, and in piles of wood. Belizean scorpions look nasty—black and big—but their stings are no more harmful than that of a bee and are described by some as what a cigarette burn feels like. Your lips and tongue may feel a little numb, but the venom is nothing compared to that of their smaller, translucent cousins in Mexico. Needless to say, to people who are prone to anaphylactic shock, it can be a more serious or life-threatening experience. Everyone has heard that when in a rainforest, never put on your shoes without checking the insides—good advice—and always give your clothes a good visual going-over and a vigorous shake before putting them on. Scorpions occasionally drop out of thatched ceilings.

Don't worry; despite the prevalence of all kinds of arachnids, including big, hairy tarantulas, spiders do not aggressively seek out people to bite and do way more good than harm by eating things like Chagas bugs. If you'd rather the spiders didn't share your personal space, shake out your bedclothes before going to sleep and check your shoes before putting your feet in them.

Of the 59 species of snakes that have been identified in Belize, at least nine are venomous, most notably the fer-de-lance (locally called a "Tommy Goff"), considered the most dangerous snake in Central America, and the coral snake. The chances of the average visitor being bitten are slim. Reportedly, most snake-bite victims are children. However, if you plan on extensive jungle exploration, check with your doctor before you leave home. Antivenin is available, doesn't require refrigeration, and keeps indefinitely. It's also wise to be prepared for an allergic reaction to the antivenin—bring an antihistamine and epinephrine. The most important thing to remember if bitten: *Don't panic and don't run.* Physical exertion and panic cause the venom to travel through your body much faster. Lie down and stay calm; have someone carry you to a doctor. Do not cut the wound, use a tourniquet, or ingest alcoholic beverages.

Marine Hazards

Anemones and sea urchins live in Belize waters. Some can be dangerous if touched or stepped on. The long-spined black sea urchin can inflict great pain, and its poison can cause an uncomfortable infection. Don't think that you're safe in a wetsuit, booties, and gloves. The spines easily slip through the rubber, and the urchin is encountered at all depths. If you should run into one of the spines, remove it quickly and carefully, disinfect the wound, and apply antibiotic cream. If you have difficulty removing the spine, or if it breaks, see a doctor—pronto! Local remedies include urinating on the wound if nothing else is available.

Tiny brown gel-encased globules called *pica-pica* produce a horrible rash; look for clouds of these guys around any coral patch before getting in. Avoid the bottom side of a moon jellyfish, as well as the Portuguese man-of-war (usually only in March). Sea wasps are tiny four-tentacled menaces that deliver a sting. In addition, many varieties of fire coral will make you wish you hadn't. Cuts from coral, even if just a scratch, will often become infected. If you should get a deep cut, or if bits of coral are left in the wound, see a doctor.

MEDICAL CARE

Although there are hospitals and health clinics in most urban areas and towns, care is extremely limited compared with more developed countries. Serious injuries or illness may require evacuation to another country, and you should consider picking up cheap travel insurance that covers such a need—otherwise, you're looking at US$12,000 just for the medevac transportation.

Many Belizean doctors and hospitals require immediate cash payment for health services, sometimes prior to providing treatment. Uninsured travelers or travelers whose insurance does not provide coverage in Belize may face extreme difficulties if serious medical treatment is needed. **International Medical Group** (www.imglobal.com) is one reliable provider that offers short-term insurance specifically for overseas travelers and expats for very reasonable rates.

Belize Medical Associates (5791 St. Thomas St., tel. 501/223-0302, 501/223-0302, bzmedasso@btl.net, www.belizemedical.com) is the only private hospital in Belize City. They provide 24-hour assistance and a wide range of specialties. Look under "Hospitals" in the BTL yellow pages for an updated listing of other options. In Santa Elena, **La Loma Luz Hospital** (tel. 501/824-2087 or 501/804-2985, www.lalomaluz.org) offers primary care as well as 24-hour emergency services and is one of the best private hospitals in the country.

First-Aid Kit

At the very minimum, consider the following items for your first-aid kit: rehydration salts, sterile bandages or gauze, moleskin for blister prevention, antiseptic cream, strong sunblock (SPF 30), aloe gel, some kind of general antibiotic for intestinal trouble, acetaminophen (Tylenol) for pain and fevers, eye drops (for dust), and antifungal cream (clotrimazole).

Medications and Prescriptions

Many medications are available in pharmacies in Belize. Definitely plan on the conservative side: Bring adequate supplies of all your prescribed medications in their original containers, clearly labeled and in date; in addition, carry a signed, dated letter from your physician describing all medical conditions and listing your medications, including their generic names. If carrying syringes or needles, carry a physician's letter documenting their medical necessity. Pack all medications in your carry-on bag and, if possible, put a duplicate supply in the checked luggage. If you wear glasses or contacts, bring an extra pair. If you have significant allergies or chronic medical problems, wear a medical alert bracelet.

Female travelers taking contraceptives should know the generic name for the drug they use. Condoms are cheap and easy to find. Any corner pharmacy will have them, even in small towns of just a few thousand people.

CRIME

Most of the crime in Belize (besides drug possession and trafficking) is petty theft and burglary, although gang-related violence in Belize City is a worsening problem. It's best not to wear expensive jewelry when traveling. And don't carry large amounts of money, your passport, or your plane tickets if not necessary; if you must carry these things, wear a money belt under your clothes. Most hotels have safe-deposit boxes. Don't flaunt cameras and video equipment or leave them in sight in cars when sightseeing, especially in some parts of Belize City. This is a poor country and petty theft is its number-one crime.

It is not wise to wander around alone on foot late at night in Belize City or anywhere. Go out with others if possible, and take a taxi. Most Belizeans are friendly, decent people; however, as in every community, there are a small percentage of unscrupulous thieves who will steal anything given the opportunity. To many Belizeans, foreigners come off as "rich," whether they are or not. Local hustlers are quite creative when it comes to conning you out of some cash. Keep your wits about you, pull out of conversations that appear headed in that direction, don't give out your hotel name or room number or mention them where they can be overheard by strangers. If you're a woman riding a bike at night, don't put your purse in the basket in plain sight or hide your cash and valuables on your person.

In emergencies, dial **911** or **90** for police assistance. The number for fire and ambulance is also 90.

Police

If you are the victim of a crime while overseas, in addition to reporting it to local police, contact your embassy or consulate as soon as possible. The embassy or consulate staff can assist you in finding appropriate medical care, contacting family members or friends, and will explain how funds can be transferred to you. Although the investigation and prosecution of the crime is solely the responsibility of local authorities, consular officers can help you to understand the local criminal justice process and to find an attorney if needed. Belize police detectives and tourism police respond quickly and take these matters—even near misses—seriously.

Belizean police can hold somebody for 48 hours with no charges (one U.S. embassy warden called prison conditions in Belize "medieval," though this situation is improving). Some police officers have been arrested for rape and routinely beat and torture detainees (usually Belizeans). On the whole, though, most officers are good folks, making the best of a poorly paid job with very few resources. Don't try to bribe them if you're in trouble—you'll only contribute to a more corrupt system that does not need any encouragement.

Drugs

Belize's modern history began with law-breaking pirates hiding out among the hundreds of cayes, lagoons, and uninhabited coastlines of the territory. The same natural features have made Belize a fueling stopover for Colombian cocaine traffickers. The drug runners' practice of paying off their Belizean helpers with product (in addition to sums of cash) has created a national market for cocaine and crack with devastating effects, especially in Orange Walk Town and numerous coastal communities.

The U.S. Drug Enforcement Agency (DEA) is active in Belize—as it is throughout Central America—to battle the flow of cocaine and other illegal drugs; the agency provides boat patrols, overflights, drug war technology and herbicides, and sniffing dogs at roadside checkpoints.

Cannabis sativa grows naturally in the soils and climate of Belize, although the country is no longer the major producer it once was. In the early 1980s, the DEA put an end to that with chemical-spraying programs, seizing and destroying 800 tons of marijuana in one year. Today, small-scale production continues, primarily for the domestic market. Some argue that the job vacuum created by marijuana suppression led directly to Belize's role in the trafficking of cocaine and the subsequent entrance of crack into Belizean communities.

Foreign travelers will most likely be offered pot (locally known as "ta-boom-boom") at some point during a visit. Legally, marijuana prohibition is alive and well in Belize, despite widespread use throughout the population. The policy allows harsh penalties for possession of even tiny quantities for both nationals and visitors alike.

Prostitution

Although illegal in Belize, prostitution is alive and well at a handful of brothels throughout the country (usually on the highways outside major towns). Prostitutes are rarely Belizean and are often indentured sex slaves unwittingly recruited from Honduras, Guatemala, or El Salvador with false promises of legitimate employment.

Information and Services

MONEY

The currency unit is the Belize dollar (BZD), which has been steady at BZD$2 to US$1 for some years. While prices are given in U.S. dollars in this book, travelers should be prepared to pay in Belizean currency on the street, aboard boats, in cafés, and at other smaller establishments. Everyone else accepts U.S. dollars.

When you buy or sell currency at a bank, be sure to retain proof of sale. The following places are authorized to buy or sell foreign currency: Atlantic Bank Ltd., Scotiabank, Barclays Bank, Belize Bank of Commerce and Industry, and Belize Global Travel Services Ltd. All are close together near the plaza in Belize City and in other cities. Most banks are open until 1pm Monday-Friday and until 11am Saturday. You can also change money, sometimes at a rate a bit better than 2:1, at Casas de Cambio. But because Casas de Cambio must charge the official rate, many people still go to the black market, which gives a better rate.

At the Mexico-Belize border, you'll be approached by money changers (and you can bet they don't represent the banks). Many travelers buy just enough Belizean dollars to get themselves into the city and to the banks. Depending on your mode of transportation and destination, these money changers can be helpful. Strictly speaking, though, this is illegal—so suit yourself. The exchange rate is the same, but you'll have no receipt of sale. If selling a large quantity of Belizean dollars back to the bank, you might be asked for that proof.

Banks

Many banks are only open until 1pm or 2pm Monday-Thursday (staying open a bit later on Friday) and are often closed for lunch. Banks are always closed Saturday afternoon and Sunday. Automated teller machines (ATMs) are available in nearly all major Belizean towns, but they may operate on different card networks (Plus, Cirrus, etc.). You may have to try a few to get your card to work; it's best to check before traveling. They're also often out of cash, particularly close to the weekends or major holidays.

Costs

Make no mistake: Belize vies with Costa Rica for being the most expensive country in Central America, and backpackers entering Belize from Mexico, Guatemala, and Honduras can expect some serious sticker shock after crossing the border. This was true even before the advent of tourism because of the import-reliant economy and whatever other invisible market hands guide such things. Shoestring travelers squeaking by on US$25-50 pp per day in Belize are most likely stone sober and eating street tacos three times a day; they are not paying for tours or taxis, and they are surely not diving in the Blue Hole. They can still have a grand old time, though, camped out in the bush (or in a US$10 room), doing lots of self-guided hiking, paddling, and cultural exploring. It's possible to travel on this little—but it depends on your comfort zone and definition of a good time.

If you've only got a seven-day vacation, you won't have to stretch your dollars over as many weeks or months as Jimmie Backpacker and his dog, Dreddie, and can thus spend more on lodging and activities. Figure at least US$100 pp per day if you want to pay for day trips and don't want to share a bath; serious divers or anglers should add a bit more. Weeklong packages at many dive and jungle resorts run US$1,000-1,600 and go up from there.

There are usually low-budget, decent quality exceptions to the rule across Belize, and I've tried to point all of those out in each region. In general, though, prices are high and getting higher. Many mid- and upscale accommodations have raised their rates by as much as 20 percent—and not all have increased the quality of their service to match. Alcohol is always a good indicator: A bottle of One Barrel Rum is peaking at US$12 in most stores; a six-pack of Belikin beer can go for US$10.

Be prepared for some additional taxes and service charges on your bill, which sometimes are and sometimes are not included in quoted rates:

- General sales tax (GST): 10 percent
- Hotel tax: 9 percent
- Service charge (often placed on bill): 10-15 percent
- Airport departure tax: US$20

If you use your credit card, it will cost you a little more at most businesses, sometimes an extra 3-5 percent of the bill.

Tipping

Most restaurants and hotels include a 10-15 percent service charge on the bill; if they don't, you should pay this amount yourself. It is not customary to tip taxi drivers unless they help you with your luggage. Always tip your tour guide 10-15 percent if he or she has made your trip an enjoyable one.

MEDIA AND COMMUNICATIONS
Mail

Posting a letter or postcard is easy and cheap, costing well under US$1, and the stamps are gorgeous. If you visit the outlying cities or cayes, bring your mail to Belize City to post—it's more apt to get to its destination quickly. Post offices are located in the center of (or nearby) all villages and cities in Belize, although they usually don't look too post-officey from the outside. You can receive mail in any town without getting a P.O. box—just have the mail addressed to your name, care of "General Delivery," followed by the town, district, and "Belize."

FedEx, DHL, and other international couriers are widely available, and the Mailboxes, Etc. in Belize City (on Front St., just up from the Water Taxi Terminal) can take care of most of

© LEBAWIT GIRMA

It's cheap and easy to mail postcards; there's a local post office in every district.

your mailing and package needs. Sending mail within Belize, you can use either the post office system or hand your package to a bus driver or go through the bus station office.

Cell Phones

Some car rental companies offer a free cell phone; always ask. If not, they'll rent you one. Otherwise, **DigiCell** (www.digicell.bz) offers prepaid temporary service to travelers. Get it at BTL's Airport Service Center, or bring your own GSM 1900 MHz handset and purchase a SIM pack from any DigiCell distributor nationwide. There are several local cellular services, both analog and digital, and coverage along roadways and in major towns is decent but still improving. You'll need your passport or ID with you when visiting a BTL store to purchase a SIM card—by law all cell numbers must now be registered.

Smart Phones (Mile 2½, Northern Hwy., Belize City, tel. 501/678-1010, www.smart-bz. com) is more user-friendly and cheaper than BTL and the rest, offering roaming service on your CDMA 800 MHz phone from home (including Verizon and Sprint). Activation fee is US$20, then you use prepaid cards available throughout the country.

International Calls

To call out of Belize, find a phone with international direct dialing service, then dial the international access code **00,** followed by your country code, and then the city or area code and the number. The country code for Canada and the United States is 1, Britain is 44, and Australia is 61. BTL's telephone directory has a complete listing of country codes. An (often cheaper) alternative is to dial 10-10-199 instead of 00, followed by the country code, etc. Although they are not toll-free from Belize, 800 numbers are dialed as they are written, preceded by the 00.

Belize's country code is **501.** To receive a call in Belize from the United States, for example, tell the caller to dial 011 to tap into the international network, followed by 501 and your seven digit number. To call collect to Belize from other countries, dial the MCI operator at 800/265-5328.

Public Telephones

Buy a prepaid phone card from **Belize Telecommunications Limited** (BTL, www. btl.net) and punch in the card's numbers every time you borrow a phone or use a pay phone. All towns also have a local BTL office, usually identified by a giant red and white radio tower somewhere very nearby; they can place calls anywhere in the country or the world for you and will assign you to a semiprivate booth after they've dialed the number. They can also connect you to your homeland phone carrier. Note: According to one BTL employee, credit-card calls made through hotel phones are expensive because the touch-tone "international operator" charges US$16 per minute.

VoIP Services

Skype and VoIP (voice over Internet protocol) are finally available in Belize, unrestricted and—believe it or not—only a recent development. Free VoIP services (like Skype) offer dirt-cheap rates on international calls and are getting better to use by the day. Prior to April 2013, BTL blocked full and open access to VoIP-based services and applications. You can now use Skype freely wherever you get free WiFi access, and save on international calls.

Internet Access

Web access is widely available throughout the country and is improving all the time. Crappy dial-up connections are now the exception rather than the norm, and broadband (DSL, cable, and satellite) is springing up everywhere. If you're in town for a while, many Internet businesses have monthly memberships that include unlimited access. You are welcome to sign up for a BTL account if you don't have your own ISP (Internet service provider), but that may lead to more headaches then you need, and there are many other options.

Wireless Internet (Wi-Fi) access is increasingly available in Belize's accommodations, bars, and restaurants. I won't go so far as to tell you to *expect* wireless access yet, but if it's a concern of yours, definitely inquire whether your hotel has it or not. Most of these connections are free—with the exception of BTL Hotspots, which are US$16 per 24-hour period (plus tax!), and it's your only option at a handful of upscale hotels, including the Radisson and the Inn at Robert's Grove.

Newspapers and Magazines

Four weekly, highly politicized Belizean newspapers come out on Friday, with occasional midweek editions, and you'll find many a Belizean conducting the weekly ritual of reading his favorite over a cup of instant coffee, and then going to happy hour to yap away about the latest scandal. *Amandala* and the *Reporter* seem to be the most objective and respected of these rags. The other two are *The Belize Times* and *The Guardian*. There are also publications in San Pedro and Placencia.

The Image Factory in Belize City is a good place for books and periodicals, and there are only a couple of other bookshops in the country. In most hotel gift shops, you'll find at least a few colorful Belizean history and picture books put out by Cubola Productions, a local publisher specializing in all things Belize, including maps, atlases, short stories, novels, and poems written by Belizeans. Cubola's publications give great insight into the country.

You will not find the *International Herald Tribune* on every newsstand like in other destinations. In fact, you probably won't find it at all. Check with the Radisson Hotel or Fort Street Guest House in Belize City, where you can sometimes find the *Miami Herald,* a relatively recent *Newsweek,* or if you're lucky, the *New York Times* or the *Times* of London. **Brodie's** (Albert St.) and **The Book Center** (North Front St.) also carry American magazines.

MAPS AND TOURIST INFORMATION
Maps
The most readily available and up-to-date map of Belize is published by International Travel Maps, whose 1:250,000 map of Belize makes a useful addition to any guidebook (or wall). The best, biggest country map to hang on your wall at home, or in your classroom (it's way too big to use as a travel guide) is a physical-political 1:265,000 scale, distributed by Cubola Productions and available at Angelus Press in Belize City for US$40. All of Belize's most heavily touristed areas create updated town maps, found most often at visitor information booths and car (or golf cart) rental places.

The **Government of Belize Land Department** in Belmopan has detailed topographic maps for the entire country—spendy at US$40 per quad, but vital if you're doing any serious backcountry travel. The British Army and United Kingdom Ordinance Survey have created a number of map series of various scales, but tracking them down will be a challenge.

Tourist Information
The **Belize Tourism Board** (BTB, 64 Regent St., tel. 501/227-2420, U.S. tel. 800/624-0686, info@travelbelize.org, www.travelbelize.org) has a central office in Belize City, near the Mopan Hotel. The **Belize Tourism Industry Association** (10 N. Park St., tel. 501/227-1144, www.btia.org) can also answer many of your questions and give you lodging suggestions. **The Belize Hotel Association** (BHA, 13 Cork St., Belize City, tel. 501/223-0669, www.belizehotels.org) is a nonprofit industry organization of some of the country's most respected resorts and lodges. The BHA can help you decide where to stay.

USEFUL NUMBERS

- Police, fire, ambulance: 90 or 911
- Directory assistance: 113 or 115
- To report crimes: 0/800-922-8477
- To report child abuse: 0/800-776-8328
- Operator assistance: 114 or 115
- Date, time, and temperature: 121

You'll find more information at the **Embassy of Belize** in the United States (2535 Massachusetts Ave. NW, Washington, DC 20008, U.S. tel. 202/332-9636, www.embassyofbelize.org) and also the **Caribbean Tourism Association** (80 Broad St., Suite 3302, New York, NY 10004, U.S. tel. 212/635-9530, www.onecaribbean.org).

WEIGHTS AND MEASURES

The local time is Greenwich mean time minus six hours year-round, the same as U.S. central standard time; Belize does not use daylight saving time. Electricity is the U.S. standard 110 volts, 60 cycles, and uses U.S. two-prong plugs. Most distances are measured in inches, feet, yards, and miles, although there is some limited use of the metric system.

Time

As in many other Central American and Caribbean cultures, the Belizean clock is not as rigidly precise as it is in other parts of the world. "Nine o'clock am" is not necessarily a moment in time that occurs once a morning, as it is a general guideline that could extend an hour or two in either direction (usually later). Creoles say, "Time longa den da roop, mon" ("time is longer than the rope"), which means the same as the Spanish *Hay mas tiempo que vida* ("there is more time than there is life")—both of which boil down to the unofficial motto of Caye Caulker: "Go slow!"

A great deal of patience is required of the traveler who wishes to adapt to this looser concept of time. Buses generally leave when they are scheduled, but may stop for frustratingly long breaks during the journey. Don't use Belize Time as an excuse to be late for your tour bus pickup, and don't get angry when your taxi driver stops to briefly chat and laugh with a friend.

RESOURCES

Phrasebook

KRIOL

I was once told that you're only a true Belizean if you speak Kriol. It's the first thing you'll hear when you arrive in Belize—the accent, the intonation, and the sentences that chop away at articles and verbs. Creole or Kriol is the lingua franca here. Like most patois tongues in the Caribbean, it has its roots in the days of slavery, when the workers in mahogany camps were exposed to English and mixed it with their own West African dialects, hence the choppy grammar and the borrowed English words. Over time, efforts were made to ensure that Kriol was properly studied, written, and recorded as a language, thanks to the National Kriol Council, created in 1995 to promote all aspects of the Creole culture. Keeping this language going has been their goal, as a way of instilling a sense of identity and cultural pride in its people. It's now spoken and understood by almost all Belizeans, even non-Creoles, and knowing a couple of phrases is a great way to immerse and break the ice.

Basic Phrases

Gud maanin! Good morning!
Weh di gaan an? What's up?
Aarite. All right.
Cho! What on earth!
Weh yuh naym? What's your name?
Yuh da Belize? Are you from Belize?
Weh gaan ahn gyal? What's up, girl?
Da weh time? What time is it?
Mi naym da ... My name is ...
Si yoo lata. See you later.

Ah tayad/mi tayad. I'm tired.
Weh/weh-paat ... Where is ... ?
Evryting gud/aarite. Everything's fine.
Haul your rass! Get the hell out of here!
Fu Chroo? Really? (Is that right?)
Gud night. Good evening.
Mi love Bileez! I love Belize!

Sayings

Wahnti wahnti kyah geti an geti geti nuh wahnti. You always want what you can't have.
Dah no so, dah naily so. Where there's smoke, there's fire.
Wait bruk down bridge. Don't make me wait too long.
Sleep wit' yo' own eye. Only rely on what you know, not what others tell you.
One one craboo fill barrel. Every little bit counts (craboo is a Belizean fruit).
Ah wah know who seh Kriol noh gat no kulcha? Who said the Creole don't have any culture? (A phrase coined by renown Belizean Creole artist and performer, Leela Vernon).

GARÍFUNA

A mix of Arawak, Carib, traces of West African dialects, French, and Spanish, the Garífuna language is being spoken less and less by the younger generation, and isn't taught in Belize's school system. But it's hard to believe that this is a dying tongue after spending time in the south, and hearing Garinagu addressing each other in their language every day. When I took the bus from Hopkins to Dangriga, and even walking around the village and town, there was no Creole and no English exchanged, just Garífuna. If you're feeling brave, you too can practice and use these phrases to break the ice.

Basic Phrases

Mabuiga! Welcome!
Buiti binafi. Good morning.
Buiti rabounweyu. Good afternoon.
Buiti guñoun. Good night.
Ida bian? How are you?
Magadientina. I'm fine.
Seremein. Thank you.
Ka biri? What is your name?
… niri bai My name is ….
Uwati megeiti. You are welcome.
Ka fidu ínwirúbei? What's up?

Q'EQCHI MAYAN

Most of southern Belize's people of indigenous descent speak Q'eqchi' Maya—though some communities speak the Mopan language instead, which is more closely related to Yucatec Maya or Itzá Maya.

In Belize, you may see the word Q'eqchi' spelled different ways. "Kekchi" is how Protestant missionaries labeled the Maya of southern Belize, and British colonial officials wrote "Ketchi." Today, in neighboring Guatemala, the indigenous leaders of the Guatemalan Academy of Maya Languages (ALMG) have developed a standard Maya transliteration that the Q'eqchi' leaders in Belize have begun to use as well.

Making even a small attempt to speak and learn the language of your Mayan hosts will deepen your experience. Never mind the laughs your funny accent will attract—your noble attempts are an amusing novelty, and no one means any harm. Persist, and you will be rewarded in ways you would never have expected—indeed, learning another language in such an immersive setting is one of the most humbling and empowering experiences a traveler can have.

Should you want to learn more than the few words presented here, track down the grammar book and cassette tapes by Q'eqchi' linguist

Rigoberto Baq, available in Guatemala City at the Academia de Lenguas Mayas (www.almg. org.gt) or at their regional offices in Coban, Alta Verapaz (in the municipal palace), or Poptán, Petén.

Greetings

All Q'eqchi' words are stressed on the last syllable. One of the first things you will probably be asked is, *"B'ar xat chalk chaq?"* (bar shaht chalk chok), to which you can respond, *"Xin chalk chaq sa'* New York" (sheen chalk chok sah New York, or wherever you are from).

In Q'eqchi', there are no words for "good morning," "good afternoon," or "good evening." You simply use the standard greeting, *"Ma sa sa' laa ch'ool"* (mah sah sah lah ch'ohl), literally, "Is there happiness in your heart?" (In Q'eqchi', however, you wouldn't use a question mark because the "Ma" indicates a question.) A proper response would be *"Sa in ch'ool"* (sah een ch'ohl), "Yes, my heart is happy."

Although it is falling out of custom with the younger generation, if you are speaking with an older woman or man, she or he would be delighted to be greeted with the terms of respect for the elderly: *Nachin* (nah cheen) for an elder woman, and *Wachin* (kwah cheen) for an elder man.

If you decide to go swimming in one of Toledo's beautiful rivers, you might want to ask first *Ma wan li ahin sa' li nima* (mah kwan lee aheen sa le neemah), which means "Are there crocodiles in the river?"

"Ani laa kab'a?" (anee lah kabah) means "What's your name?" You can respond: *Ix [woman's name] in kab'a"* (eesh … een kabah) or *Laj [man's name] in kab'a"* (lahj … een kabah).

Basic Phrases

Chan xaawil? (chan shaa kwil) What's up?
Jo xaqa'in (hoe shakaeen) Not much, just fine.
B'an usilal (ban ooseelal) Please.
B'antiox (ban teeosh) or T'ho-kre (ta HOH cree) Thank you.
Us (oos) Good.
Yib' i ru (yeeb ee rue) Bad, ugly.

Hehe **(eheh)** Yes.
Ink'a **(eenk'ah)** No.
K'aru? **(kaieeroo)** What?
B'ar? **(bar)** Where?
Joq'e? **(hoekay)** When?
Jarub?' **(hahrueb)** How many?
Jonimal tzaq? **(hoeneemahl ssahq)** How much does it cost?
Chaawil aawib **(chah kwil aakweeb)** Take care of yourself (a good way to say good-bye).
Jowan chik **(hoek wan cheek)** See you later.
wi chik **(kwee cheek)** again
wa **(kwah)** tortilla
kenq **(kenk)** beans
molb' **(mohlb)** eggs
kaxlan wa **(kashlan kwah)** bread
tib' **(cheeb)** meat
tzilan **(sseeelan)** chicken
kuy **(kue-ee)** pork, pig

kar **(car)** fish
chin **(cheen)** orange
kakaw **(cacao)** chocolate
ha' **(hah)** water
woqxinb'il ha' **(kwohk sheen bill hah)** boiled water
cape **(kahpay)** coffee
sulul **(suelul)** mud
ab' **(ahb)** hammock
chaat **(chaht)** bed
nima' **(neemah)** river
kokal **(kohkahl)** children
chaab'il **(chahbill)** good
kaw **(kauw)** hard
najt **(nahjt)** far
nach **(nahch)** close

Special thanks to Clark University anthropologist Liza Grandia, PhD, who spent four years among the Maya.

Suggested Reading

Start with Belizean writers, particularly the novels of Zee Edgell, and then continue with the catalog of **Cubola Productions** (www. cubola.com), a publishing company whose Belizean writers series includes six anthologies of short stories, poetry, drama, folk tales, and works by women writers. Cubola also publishes sociology, anthropology, and education texts; seek them out at any bookstore or gift shop in Belize, or order a few titles before your trip. **Angelus Press** is the other main publisher of Belizean writers. There is a large Angelus Press store in Belize City, as well as in other districts. You'll also want to read a book—or six—by **Emory King;** King arrived in Belize in 1953 when his yacht crashed on the reef at English Caye and has been talking and writing about his adopted country ever since.

ARCHAEOLOGY AND MAYA CULTURE

Berman, Joshua. *Moon Maya 2012: A Guide to Celebrations in Mexico, Guatemala, Belize & Honduras.* Berkeley, CA: Avalon Travel, 2011. This book is a 100-page guide that covers how to witness a solstice sunrise from atop a Mayan temple, visit an archaeological dig, stay with a family in a traditional Mayan village, or experience multicountry Mayan tours.

Carrasco, David. *Religions of Mesoamerica: Cosmovision and Ceremonial Centers.* San Francisco: Waveland Press, 1998. Carrasco details the dynamics of two important cultures—the Aztec and the Maya—and discusses the impact of the Spanish conquest and the continuity of native traditions.

Coe, Michael D. *The Maya,* 8th ed. New York: Thames and Hudson, 2011. This updated classic, which has been in print for nearly 50 years, attempts to understand the "most intellectually sophisticated and aesthetically refined pre-Columbian culture." The new edition has information on new discoveries, including the polychrome murals of Calakmul and evidence of pre-Classic sophistication. Coe, an archaeologist, anthropologist, epigrapher, and author, is a forefather of Mayan studies. This book is mandatory reading for both amateur Mayanists and pros.

De Landa, Friar Diego. *Yucatán: Before and After the Conquest.* New York: Dover Publications, 1978 (translation of original manuscript written in 1566). The same man who provided some of the best, most lasting descriptions of ancient Maya also singlehandedly destroyed the most Maya artifacts and writings of anyone in history.

González, Gaspar Pedro. *13 B'aktun: Mayan Visions of 2012 and Beyond.* Berkeley, CA: North Atlantic Books, 2010. González is a Q'anjobal Mayan novelist, philosopher, and scholar from Guatemala. This book, translated to English by Dr. Robert Sitler, is unlike any other you'll read on the subject. It is written as a deep, lyrical dialogue—not just about 2012, but about all of creation, blending "past and present thought into a persuasive plan for moving into the new era."

Jenkins, John Major. *The 2012 Story: The Myths, Fallacies, and Truth Behind the Most Intriguing Date in History.* New York: Jeremy P. Tarcher, 2009. Jenkins is one of the most prolific, passionate 2012-ologists out there. *2012 Story* is his most all-encompassing book yet, covering the entire story—from the ancients' forward-reaching stone inscriptions to the modern-day 2012 meme and a summary of his and others' work on the subject.

Sitler, Robert. *The Living Maya: Ancient Wisdom in the Era of 2012.* Berkeley, CA: North Atlantic Books, 2010. This book begins with the Yucatec Maya greeting *"Bix a bel?"* which means, "How is your road?" And that's right where the author puts us—on the road in the Guatemalan highlands and southern Mexico. Robert Sitler is a professor at Stetson University in DeLand, Florida. In *The Living Maya,*

he draws lessons from his four decades studying Maya culture and traveling in the Mundo Maya. The most important messages we can take from the Maya, he writes, are: "Cherish our babies, connect with our communities, revere the natural world that sustains us, seek the wisdom of humanity's elders, and immerse ourselves in direct experience of this divine world."

Stephens, John L. *Incidents of Travel in Central America, Chiapas and Yucatán.* New York: Dover Publications, 1969 (originally New York: Harper & Bros., 1841). In this classic 19th-century travelogue, Stephens's writing is wonderfully pompous, amusing, and incredibly astute—with historical and archaeological observations that still stand today. If you can, find a copy with the original set of illustrations by Stephens's expedition partner.

FICTION

Edgell, Zee. *Beka Lamb.* Portsmouth, NH: Heinemann, 1982. The first internationally recognized Belizean novel, this story of a girl named Beka who is growing up with her country is required reading for all Belizean high schoolers and offers an excellent view of Belizean family life, history, and politics.

Lukowiak, Ken. *Marijuana Time.* London: Orion, 2000. Follow the author's experiences on a six-month "hardship posting" to Belize in 1983 with the British military: "The long days are palliated by a constant and increasingly compulsive supply of drugs and japes, until he starts using his position in the army post-room to send improbably large bundles of the stuff home—to his army flat in Aldershot."

Miller, Carlos Ledson. *Belize: A Novel.* Bloomington, IN: Xlibris, 1999. This history-laden piece of fiction offers an impressively thorough snapshot of Belize over the last 40 years.

Westlake, Donald. *High Adventure.* New York: Mysterious Press, 1986. Another marijuana-smuggling action thriller: "You are in the jungles of Belize. You pick your way carefully along the overgrown trail until you come to the clearing. There, above you, rest the ruins of a Mayan pyramid. Is that a stone whistle at your feet? An idol of the bat-god? Riches surround you and Kirby Galway will be more than happy to smuggle your finds to the United States in a bale of marijuana. Aren't you glad you met Kirby?"

HEALTH

Arvigo, Rosita. *Sastun: One Woman's Apprenticeship with a Maya Healer and Their Efforts to Save the Vani.* San Francisco: Harper, 1995. One of the better-known books about Belize, which tells the story of the American-born author's training with 87-year-old Elijio Panti, the best-known Mayan medicine man in Central America. It takes place in the remote, roadless expanse of the Cayo District in western Belize.

Bezruchka, Stephen. *The Pocket Doctor: A Passport to Healthy Travel.* Seattle: Mountaineers Books, 1999.

Schroeder, Dirk. *Staying Healthy in Asia, Africa, and Latin America.* Emeryville, CA: Avalon Travel, 2000. An excellent resource that fits in your pocket for easy reference.

Werner, David. *Where There Is No Doctor.* Berkeley, CA: Hesperian Foundation, 1992. A standard in the field.

HISTORY

Shoman, Assad. *13 Chapters of a History of Belize.* Belize City: Angelus Press, 1994. A no-nonsense history of Belize from a Belizean perspective.

Sutherland, Anne. *The Making of Belize: Globalization in the Margins.* London: Bergin & Garvey, 1998. This book deserves to be read by any visitor to Belize, whether arriving as a tourist or as a volunteer with one of the many

international conservation organizations now operating there.

Wilk, Richard. *Home Cooking in the Global Village: Caribbean Food from Buccaneers to Ecotourists.* New York: Palgrave Macmillan, 2006. Using food to describe Belize's longtime struggle within "the great paradox of globalization," Wilk raises questions like "How can you stay local and relish your own home cooking, while tasting the delights of the global marketplace?" Includes menus, recipes, and "bad colonial poetry."

NATURE AND FIELD GUIDES

As Belize is one of the most exhaustively studied tropical countries in the world, there are innumerable references that span every conceivable niche of flora, fauna, and geology. They come in massive coffee-table sizes with color plates as well as in pocket-size field guides: *Tarantulas of Belize, Hummingbirds of Belize, Orchids of Belize,* and so on. Following are a few titles that make up the tip of the iceberg for this category.

Arvigo, Rosita, and Michael Balick (foreword by Mickey Hart). *Rainforest Remedies: 100 Healing Herbs of Belize.* Twin Lakes, WI: Lotus Press, 1998.

Beletsky, Les. *Belize and Northern Guatemala: The Ecotravellers' Wildlife Guide.* San Diego, CA: Academic Press, 1999. One of the best reasonably sized general nature guides to the area, with abundant color plates for all types of fauna.

Chalif, Edward L., and Roger Tory Peterson. *Peterson Field Guide to Mexican Birds.* New York: Houghton Mifflin Harcourt, 1999. This is one of the best birder bibles for this region.

Dunn, Jon L., and Jonathan Alderfer. *National Geographic Field Guide to the Birds of North America.* Washington, DC: National Geographic, 2006. A gorgeous field guide worth lugging into the jungle.

Jones, H. Lee, and Dana Gardner, illustrator. *Birds of Belize*. Austin, TX: University of Texas Press, 2003. This is the long-awaited, much-acclaimed bible of Belize birding (say *that* three times fast); it's a big book (445 pages, 56 color plates, 28 figures, 234 maps), prompting some birders I met to cut out all the plates and travel with those only.

Sayers, Brendan, and Brett Adams. *Guide to the Orchids of Belize*. Benque Viejo del Carmen, Belize: Cubola Productions, 2009. This is an excellent field guide to the many orchids found throughout Belize.

Stevens, Katie. *Jungle Walk: Birds and Beasts of Belize, Central America*. Belize City: Angelus Press, 1991. Order through International Expeditions, tel. 800/633-4734.

PHOTOGRAPHY

Jovaisa, Marius. *Heavenly Belize*. Lithuania: Unseen Pictures, 2009 (www.heavenlybelize.com). This is a magnificent coffee-table tome of aerial photography. The Lithuanian author is an ultralight aircraft pilot who wanted to share the extraordinary vistas he had discovered. If you don't pick it up in Belize, download the iPad version from iTunes, with more multimedia features than just the book.

TRAVEL AND MEMOIR

Barcott, Bruce. *The Last Flight of the Scarlet Macaw: One Woman's Fight to Save the World's Most Beautiful Bird*. New York: Random House, 2008. Fantastic nonfiction narrative about the Chalillo Dam in western Belize, a highly contentious construction project on the upper Macal River in Cayo. The author skillfully lays out the story and characters around the dam business, while providing a sweeping panoramic snapshot of a unique country as it makes its debut in the new global economy.

Bolland, O. Nigel. *Belize: A New Nation in Central America*. Boulder, CO: Westview, 1986. This book is one of many sociopolitical analyses by this prolific author.

Duffy, Rosaleen. *A Trip Too Far: Ecotourism, Politics and Exploitation*. Sterling, VA: Earthscan, 2002. A critical look at the impacts of ecotourism, using Belize as a case study.

Fry, Joan. *How to Cook a Tapir: A Memoir of Belize*. Lincoln, NE: University of Nebraska Press, 2009. The story of a young teacher's year abroad, living among the Maya in southern Belize in 1962. The author offers an intimate glimpse at Mayan village life in this heartfelt, oftentimes funny story of how she "painstakingly baked and boiled her way up the food chain" to gain acceptance among her neighbors and students.

Pattullo, Polly. *Last Resorts: The Cost of Tourism in the Caribbean,* 2nd edition. London: Latin America Bureau, 2005. Pattullo provides an interesting breakdown of how the Caribbean tourism industry is structured, as well as a hard-hitting commentary on who benefits and how, providing numerous examples from Belize.

Rabinowitz, Alan. *Jaguar: One Man's Struggle to Establish the World's First Jaguar Preserve*. Washington, DC: Island Press/Shearwater Books, 2000 (originally 1986). If you've only got time to read one book on Belize, I recommend this excellent eco-memoir. In addition to telling the true story of his jaguar work in Belize, Rabinowitz gives an alluring glance at Belize's wild postindependence, pre-tourism phase.

Suggested Films

There are many excellent short films on Belize, on both the natural world and cultural issues. Look up Richard and Carol Foster's *Path of the Rain Gods* and Channel 5's *The Sea of Belize* and *The Land of Belize*. Then tune in to www.trphoto.blip.tv, which has some gorgeous educational shorts on Belize; these would be excellent for families to watch together before or after their trip to Belize.

Curse of The Xtabai, by Make-Belize Films (www.makebelizefilms.com). If you're into drama and fiction, check out U.S. producer Matthiew Klinck's first feature film. The story revolves around an evil spirit, Xtabai, unleashed onto the population of a Mayan village after an oil company blows open a sealed Mayan cave in San Antonio. What ensues is an attempt to save the villagers from an epidemic of deadly fevers, through sacred tasks as dictated by a Mayan elder.

Punta Soul, produced and directed by Nyasha Laing (www.parandamedia.com). This 2008 documentary film by a Belizean tells the story of Garífuna music as it evolved with the Garífuna people's journey from the Caribbean islands to Central America. Laing addresses how the rhythms continue to influence the cultural revival of the ethnic communities in Belize. Buy the DVD at the Image Factory in Belize City.

Three Kings of Belize, by Katia Paradis. This 2007 film is a beautiful, poignant tribute to Belizean musicians Paul Nabor, Wilfred Peters, and Florencio Mess, who represent Garífuna, Creole, and Mayan music traditions, respectively. Though their music is internationally recognized, they live humble lives in Belizean villages. The film moves at the slow, relaxed pace of Belize itself. To find a copy, go to the Image Factory in Belize City or contact Stonetree Records (www.stonetreerecords.com).

Internet Resources

Belize Search
www.belizesearch.com
The premier search engine for all things Belize, with access to 250,000 Belizean Web pages and documents (and growing).

Ambergris Caye
www.ambergriscaye.com
The official site of Ambergris Caye, with links to the whole country and a hugely popular user forum (10,000 unique visits a day).

Belize Audubon Society
www.belizeaudubon.org
Belize Audubon manages a number of national parks and protected areas throughout the country and is the place to go for basic info on

visiting them. It also has background information on birding and checklists.

The Belize Forums
www.belizeforum.com/belize
This is one of the more popular forums, inhabited by many prolific and colorful Belizophiles.

Belize Tourism Board
www.travelbelize.org
The official BTB website is quite helpful for anyone planning a trip, and it's filled with gorgeous photography as well.

Best of Cayo
www.bestofcayo.com
Constantly updated reviews of Cayo businesses

and activities. These are also the folks behind the "Official San Ignacio & Santa Elena Town Cayo Transactor" page on Facebook.com.

Caye Caulker Vacation
www.cayecaulkervacation.com
The official site of the Belize Tourism Industry Association's Caye Caulker chapter is filled with information on where to stay, and how to best spend your time on the island with the best sunsets in Belize, just a 20-minute boat ride from San Pedro.

Centers for Disease Control and Prevention
www.cdc.gov
Check here for the latest health recommendations for travelers by the U.S. government.

Destination Belize
www.destinationbelize.com
The online version of the print magazine, *Destination Belize,* provides a summary on each main tourist destination in the country, and a shortlist of things to do and see.

Government of Belize
www.belize.gov.bz
The official page of the GOB, an informative portal to the country.

Naturalight
www.belizenet.com
This is the main portal to the vast Naturalight network, which hosts a variety of sites and forums.

Planeta
www.planeta.com
This is one of the premier ecotourism sites around; look up the Belize page for all kinds of wikis, current events, and interesting articles.

San Pedro Sun
www.sanpedrosun.com
Belizean news and links from this island newspaper, in addition to the latest Ambergris scoop.

Transitions Abroad
www.transitionsabroad.com
Information on working, studying, and volunteering abroad, including updated listings of available positions.

United States Embassy in Belize
www.belize.usembassy.gov
Official site of the U.S. Embassy in Belize.

Index

List of Maps

www.moon.com

DESTINATIONS | EXPLORE | MAPS | BOOKS

MOON.COM is ready to help plan your next trip! Filled with fresh trip ideas and strategies, interviews, informative travel tips, and a printable map library, Moon.com is all you need to get out and explore the world—or even places in your own backyard. While at Moon.com, sign up for our monthly email newsletter for updates on new guidebook releases, giveaway alerts, and expert advice from our on-the-go Moon authors. When you travel with Moon, expect an experience that is uncommon and truly unique.

KEEP UP WITH MOON: f 🐦 ⓟ

MAP SYMBOLS

══════ Expressway		Highlight	✈ Airport		Golf Course
───── Primary Road	○	City/Town	✈ Airfield	🅿	Parking Area
───── Secondary Road	◉	State Capital	▲ Mountain		Archaeological Site
═ ═ ═ Unpaved Road	◉	National Capital	✦ Unique Natural Feature		Church
─ ─ ─ Trail	★	Point of Interest			Gas Station
·········· Ferry	•	Accommodation	Waterfall		Dive Site
─■─■─ Railroad	▼	Restaurant/Bar	▲ Park		Mangrove
─── Pedestrian Walkway	■	Other Location	🅣 Trailhead		Reef
▭▭▭ Stairs	Λ	Campground	Lighthouse		Swamp

CONVERSION TABLES

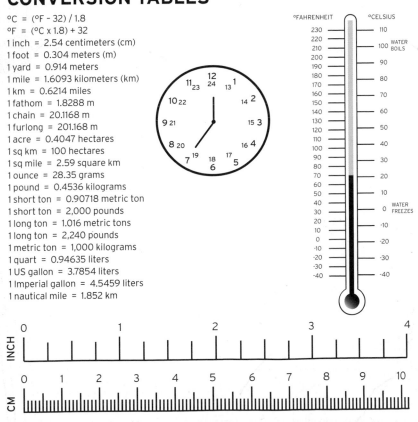

°C = (°F – 32) / 1.8
°F = (°C x 1.8) + 32
1 inch = 2.54 centimeters (cm)
1 foot = 0.304 meters (m)
1 yard = 0.914 meters
1 mile = 1.6093 kilometers (km)
1 km = 0.6214 miles
1 fathom = 1.8288 m
1 chain = 20.1168 m
1 furlong = 201.168 m
1 acre = 0.4047 hectares
1 sq km = 100 hectares
1 sq mile = 2.59 square km
1 ounce = 28.35 grams
1 pound = 0.4536 kilograms
1 short ton = 0.90718 metric ton
1 short ton = 2,000 pounds
1 long ton = 1.016 metric tons
1 long ton = 2,240 pounds
1 metric ton = 1,000 kilograms
1 quart = 0.94635 liters
1 US gallon = 3.7854 liters
1 Imperial gallon = 4.5459 liters
1 nautical mile = 1.852 km

°FAHRENHEIT | °CELSIUS

WATER BOILS (100°C / 210°F)
WATER FREEZES (0°C / 30°F)

MOON BELIZE

Avalon Travel
a member of the Perseus Books Group
1700 Fourth Street
Berkeley, CA 94710, USA
www.moon.com

Editor: Sabrina Young
Series Manager: Kathryn Ettinger
Copy Editor: Christopher Church
Production and Graphics Coordinator: Darren Alessi
Cover Designer: Darren Alessi
Map Editor: Kat Bennett
Cartographers: Kat Bennett, Stephanie Poulain
Indexer: Greg Jewett

ISBN-13: 978-1-61238-638-6
ISSN: 1533-9130

Printing History
1st Edition – 1991
10th Edition – December 2013
5 4 3 2 1

Front cover photo: © Lebawit Lily Girma
Title page and photos on pages 1-24
© Lebawit Lily Girma

Printed in China by RR Donnelley

KEEPING CURRENT

If you have a favorite gem you'd like to see included in the next edition, or see anything
that needs updating, clarification, or correction, please drop us a line. Send your comments via email to feedback@moon.com, or use the address above.